T0189605

Lecture Notes in Computer Science 13903

Formal Methods

Subline of Lecture Notes in Computer Science

More information about this series at https://link.springer.com/bookseries/558

Kristin Yvonne Rozier ·
Swarat Chaudhuri
Editors

NASA Formal Methods

15th International Symposium, NFM 2023
Houston, TX, USA, May 16–18, 2023
Proceedings

Editors
Kristin Yvonne Rozier
Iowa State University
Ames, IA, USA

Swarat Chaudhuri
University of Texas at Austin
Austin, TX, USA

ISSN 0302-9743 ISSN 1611-3349 (electronic)
Lecture Notes in Computer Science
ISBN 978-3-031-33169-5 ISBN 978-3-031-33170-1 (eBook)
https://doi.org/10.1007/978-3-031-33170-1

This Springer imprint is published by the registered company Springer Nature Switzerland AG
The registered company address is: Gewerbestrasse 11, 6330 Cham, Switzerland

Preface

This publication contains the proceedings of the 15th NASA Formal Methods Symposium (NFM 2023), which was held May 16–18 2023 at the University of Houston-Clear Lake in Houston, Texas, USA.

The widespread use and increasing complexity of mission-critical and safety-critical systems at NASA and in the aerospace industry require advanced techniques that address these systems' specification, design, verification, validation, and certification requirements. The NASA Formal Methods Symposium (NFM) is a forum to foster collaboration between theoreticians and practitioners from NASA, academia, and industry. NFM's goals are to identify challenges and to provide solutions for achieving assurance for such critical systems.

New developments and emerging applications like autonomous software for uncrewed deep space human habitats, caretaker robotics, Unmanned Aerial Systems (UAS), UAS Traffic Management (UTM), and the need for system-wide fault detection, diagnosis, and prognostics provide new challenges for system specification, development, and verification approaches. The focus of these symposiums is on formal techniques and other approaches for software assurance, including their theory, current capabilities and limitations, as well as their potential application to aerospace, robotics, and other NASA-relevant safety-critical systems during all stages of the software life-cycle.

The NASA Formal Methods Symposium is an annual event organized by the NASA Formal Methods (NFM) Steering Committee, comprised of researchers spanning several NASA centers. NFM 2023 was hosted by the University of Houston-Clear Lake (UHCL). It was organized by a collaboration between UHCL, University of Texas at Austin, Iowa State University, and NASA-Johnson Space Center in Houston, Texas.

NFM was created to highlight the state of the art in formal methods, both in theory and in practice. The series is a spin-off of the original Langley Formal Methods Workshop (LFM). LFM was held six times in 1990, 1992, 1995, 1997, 2000, and 2008 near NASA Langley in Virginia, USA. The 2008 reprisal of LFM led to the expansion to a NASA-wide conference. In 2009 the first NASA Formal Methods Symposium was organized at NASA Ames Research Center in Moffett Field, CA. In 2010, the Symposium was organized by NASA Langley Research Center and NASA Goddard Space Flight Center, and held at NASA Headquarters in Washington, D.C. The third NFM symposium was organized by the Laboratory for Reliable Software at the NASA Jet Propulsion Laboratory/California Institute of Technology, and held in Pasadena, CA in 2011. NFM returned to NASA Langley Research Center in 2012 in nearby Norfolk, Virginia. NASA Ames Research Center organized and hosted NFM 2013, the fifth Symposium in the series. NFM 2014 was organized via a collaboration between NASA Goddard Space Flight Center, NASA Johnson Space Center, and NASA Ames Research Center, and held at JSC. NASA JPL hosted the seventh NFM in 2015 in

Pasadena, CA. In 2016, the eighth NFM Symposium visited the University of Minnesota, hosted by a collaboration between academia and NASA. 2017 brought the ninth NFM back to NASA Ames Research Center. NASA Langley hosted NFM's 10th anniversary edition in 2018. NFM 2019 was organized by a collaboration between Rice University, NASA JSC, and Iowa State University. In the years 2020 and 2021, NFM was held virtually, organized by NASA Ames and NASA Langley respectively. NFM returned in hybrid (online and in-person) format in 2022, where it was held at Caltech and organized by a collaboration between Caltech, University of Southern California, JPL, and NASA.

NFM 2023 encouraged submissions on cross-cutting approaches that bring together formal methods and techniques from other domains such as machine learning, control theory, robotics, probabilistic reasoning, and quantum computing among others. The topics covered by the Symposium include but are not limited to: formal verification, including theorem proving, model checking, and static analysis; advances in automated theorem proving including SAT and SMT solving; use of formal methods in software and system testing; run-time verification; techniques and algorithms for scaling formal methods, such as abstraction and symbolic methods, compositional techniques, as well as parallel and/or distributed techniques; code generation from formally verified models; safety cases and system safety; formal approaches to fault tolerance; theoretical advances and empirical evaluations of formal methods techniques for safety-critical systems, including hybrid and embedded systems; formal methods in systems engineering and model-based development; correct-by-design controller synthesis; formal assurance methods to handle adaptive systems.

Two lengths of papers were considered: regular papers describing fully developed work and complete results, and two categories of short papers: (a) tool papers describing novel, publicly-available tools; (b) case studies detailing complete applications of formal methods to real systems with publicly-available artifacts, or substantial work-in-progress describing results from designing a new technique for a new application, with appropriate available artifacts. Artifacts enabling reproducibility of the paper's major contributions were strongly encouraged and considered in PC evaluations. Artifacts may appear in online appendices; websites with additional artifacts, e.g., for reproducibility or additional correctness proofs, were encouraged.

The Symposium received 75 submissions: 63 regular papers, and 12 short papers (9 tool papers and 3 case studies) in total. Out of these, a total of 29 papers, 26 regular papers and 3 short papers, were accepted, giving an overall acceptance rate of 38% (a 41% rate for regular papers and a 25% rate for short papers). All submissions went through a rigorous reviewing process, where each paper was read by at least three (and on average 3.9) reviewers. Submitting authors listed affiliations from 21 countries; NFM 2023 received the most submissions from institutions in the United States (109), Germany (32), the United Kingdom (12), France (11), Japan (10), Denmark (9), Israel (9), Spain (8), Austria (7), and the Netherlands (7).

In addition to the refereed papers, the symposium featured three invited talks. Representing NASA JSC, Dr. Julia Badger delivered a keynote talk on "Formal Guarantees for Autonomous Operation of Human Spacecraft." Professor Sanjit A. Seshia from UC Berkeley gave a keynote talk on "Design Automation for Verified

AI-Based Autonomy." Professor Ken McMillan from UT Austin delivered a keynote talk on "Proof-Based Heuristics for Quantified Invariant Synthesis."

The organizers are grateful to the authors for submitting their work to NFM 2023 and to the invited speakers for sharing their insights. NFM 2023 would not have been possible without the collaboration of the Steering Committee, Program Committee, our many external reviewers, and the support of the NASA Formal Methods community. We are also grateful to our collaborators at University of Houston-Clear Lake's College of Science and Engineering, including for financial support and local organization. The NFM 2023 website can be found at https://conf.researchr.org/home/nfm-2023.

March 2023

Kristin Yvonne Rozier
Swarat Chaudhuri

Organization

Program Committee

Julia Badger	NASA, USA
Stanley Bak	Stony Brook University, USA
Suguman Bansal	Georgia Institute of Technology, USA
Dirk Beyer	LMU Munich, Germany
Nikolaj Bjørner	Microsoft, USA
Sylvie Boldo	Inria and Université Paris-Saclay, France
Georgiana Caltais	University of Twente, The Netherlands
Swarat Chaudhuri	UT Austin, USA
Darren Cofer	Rockwell Collins, USA
Jim Dabney	University of Houston-Clear Lake, USA
Jennifer Davis	Collins Aerospace, USA
Ewen Denney	NASA, USA
Catherine Dubois	ENSIIE-Samovar, France
Rohit Dureja	IBM Corporation, USA
Alexandre Duret-Lutz	EPITA's Research Lab (LRE), France
Bruno Dutertre	Amazon Web Services, USA
Aaron Dutle	NASA, USA
Souradeep Dutta	University of Pennsylvania, USA
Rüdiger Ehlers	Clausthal University of Technology, Germany
Chuchu Fan	MIT, USA
Marie Farrell	University of Manchester, UK
Bernd Finkbeiner	CISPA Helmholtz Center for Information Security, Germany
Alwyn Goodloe	NASA, USA
Arie Gurfinkel	University of Waterloo, Canada
Klaus Havelund	Jet Propulsion Laboratory, USA
Constance Heitmeyer	Naval Research Laboratory, Washington, DC, USA
Marijn Heule	Carnegie Mellon University, USA
Kerianne Hobbs	Air Force Research Laboratory, USA
Bardh Hoxha	Toyota Research Institute North America, USA
Susmit Jha	SRI International, USA
Rajeev Joshi	AWS, USA
Panagiotis Manolios	Northeastern University, USA
Anastasia Mavridou	SGT Inc. / NASA Ames Research Center, USA
Stefan Mitsch	Carnegie Mellon University, USA
Cesar Munoz	Amazon, USA
Natasha Neogi	NASA-Langley, USA
Corina Pasareanu	CMU, NASA, KBR, USA

Ivan Perez	KBR / NASA Ames Research Center, USA
Zvonimir Rakamaric	Amazon Web Services (AWS), USA
Giles Reger	Amazon Web Services, USA and University of Manchester, UK
Kristin Yvonne Rozier	Iowa State University, USA
Johann Schumann	NASA, USA
Cristina Seceleanu	Mälardalen University, Sweden
Yasser Shoukry	University of California, Irvine, USA
Laura Titolo	National Institute of Aerospace, USA
Oksana Tkachuk	Amazon Web Services, USA
Aaron Tomb	Amazon Web Services, USA
Stefano Tonetta	FBK-irst, Italy
Nestan Tsiskaridze	Stanford University, USA
Caterina Urban	Inria, France
Cristian-Ioan Vasile	Lehigh University, USA
Virginie Wiels	ONERA/DTIS, France
Huan Xu	University of Maryland, USA
Huafeng Yu	Boeing Research & Technology, USA

Additional Reviewers

Backeman, Peter
Baier, Daniel
Bazille, Hugo
Bombardelli, Alberto
Bärenz, Manuel
Cai, Feiyang
Campion, Marco
Chen, Yongchao
Clement, Francois
Conrad, Esther
Feliu Gabaldon, Marco Antonio
Ferlez, James
Garg, Kunal
Gerhold, Marcus
Gorostiaga, Felipe
Goyal, Srajan
Gu, Rong
Guedri, Wissal
Hahn, Ernst Moritz
Herencia-Zapana, Heber
Herranz, Ángel
Kabra, Aditi
Kamburjan, Eduard
Kamdoum Deameni, Loich
Kauffman, Sean
Khalimov, Ayrat
Kochdumper, Niklas
Kremer, Gereon
Kumar, Ankit
Laurent, Jonathan
Le, Thi Thieu Hoa
Liu, Cong
Luo, Ertai
Mangal, Ravi
Mata, Andrew
Meng, Yue
Minopoli, Stefano
Noetzli, Andres
Ozdemir, Alex
Reynolds, Conor
Sheikhi, Sanaz
Siber, Julian
Slagel, Joseph
Slagel, Tanner
Spiessl, Martin
Stan, Daniel
Tahat, Amer
Tan, Yong Kiam

Vedrine, Franck
Wachowitz, Henrik
Walter, Andrew
Wendler, Philipp
White, Lauren
Winter, Stefan
Yu, Mingxin
Zhang, Songyuan
Zhao, Yibo
Ziat, Ghiles

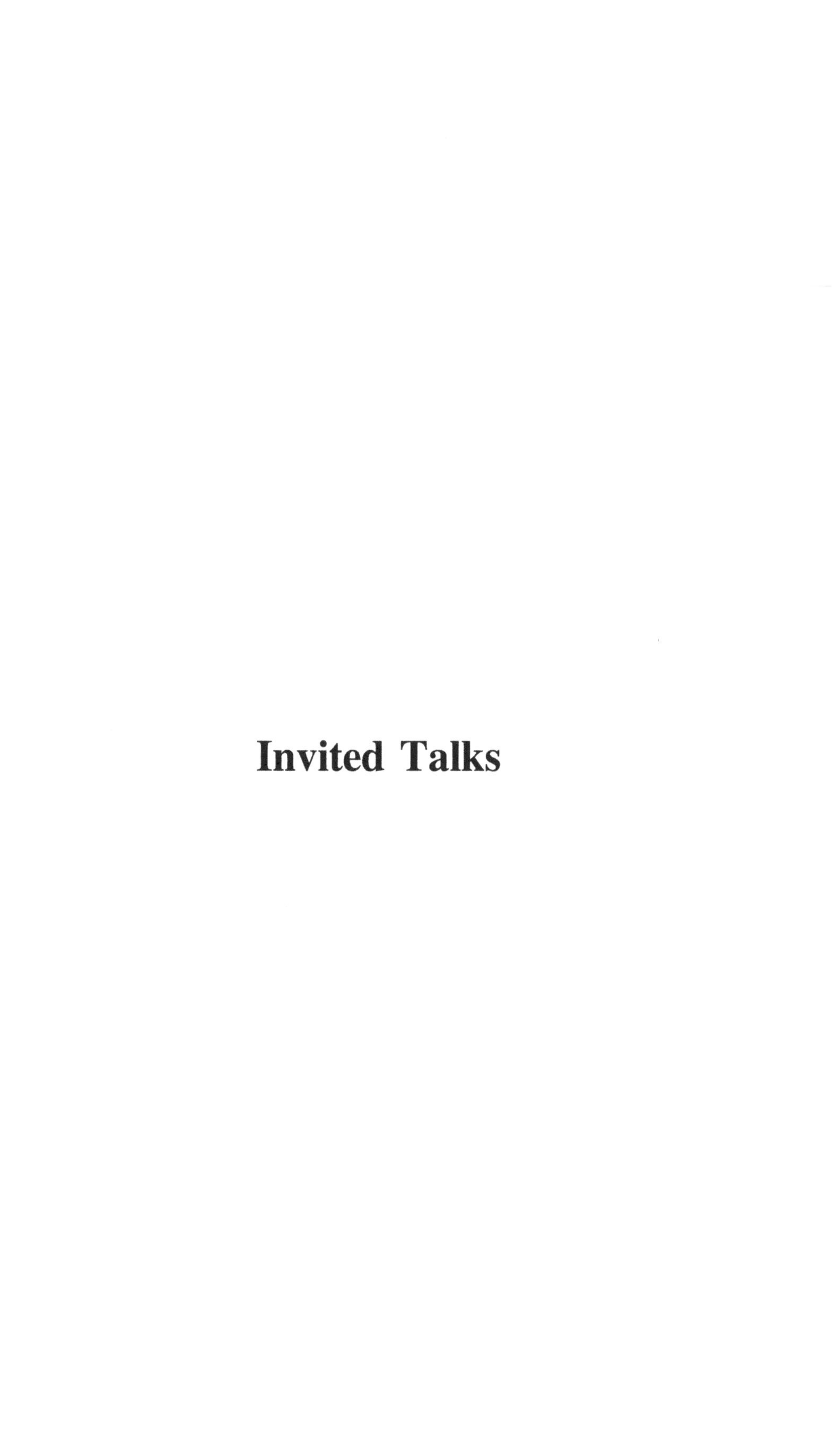

Invited Talks

Design Automation for Verified AI-Based Autonomy

Sanjit A. Seshia

EECS Department, University of California, Berkeley
sseshia@eecs.berkeley.edu

Abstract. Cyber-physical systems (CPS) integrate computation with physical processes. The past decade has seen tremendous growth in autonomous and semi-autonomous CPS, including autonomous vehicles and robotics, enabled by innovations in artificial intelligence (AI) and machine learning. However, the wider deployment of AI-based autonomy is being held back by the limitations of current technology with respect to safety, reliability, security, and robustness.

Verified artificial intelligence (AI) is the goal of designing AI-based systems that have strong, ideally provable, assurances of correctness with respect to formally specified requirements [3]. This talk will review the challenges to achieving Verified AI, and the initial progress the community has made towards this goal. Building on this progress, there is a need to develop a new generation of design automation techniques, rooted in formal methods, to enable and support the routine development of high assurance AI-based autonomy. I will describe our work on the design and verification of AI-based autonomy in CPS, implemented in the open-source Scenic [2] and VerifAI [1] toolkits. The use of these tools will be demonstrated on industrial case studies involving deep learning-based autonomy in ground and air vehicles. Our vision is to facilitate the computer-aided design of provably safe and robust AI-based autonomy in a manner similar to that enabled today by tools for the design automation of reliable integrated circuits.

References

1. Dreossi, T., et al.: VerifAI: a toolkit for the formal design and analysis of artificial intelligencebased systems. In: Proceedings Computer Aided Verification (CAV) (2019)
2. Fremont, D.J., et al.: Scenic: a language for scenario specification and data generation. Mach. Learn. J. (2022). https://doi.org/10.1007/s10994-021-06120-5
3. Seshia, S.A., Sadigh, D., Sastry, S.S.: Toward verified artificial intelligence. Commun. ACM **65**(7), 46–55 (2022)

Formal Guarantees for Autonomous Operation of Human Spacecraft

Abstract. As NASA embraces the Artemis Program goal of a sustained human presence on the Moon, the consideration of technologies needed for Martian exploration remains at the forefront. One significant technology gap is the ability to autonomously control complex, safety-critical, integrated spacecraft systems across the operational range of the vehicle and mission. The Gateway lunar space station has focused on autonomous spacecraft control as a major operational goal with the addition of a new software distributed hierarchical control architecture. The Vehicle Systems Manager (VSM) sits atop this control architecture and provides autonomous control for mission, fault, and resource management at the vehicle level. This novel functionality depends strongly on correct behavior at every level of the architecture, and verification of this new system will require special consideration. The Autonomous Systems Management Architecture (ASMA) uses formally specified assume-guarantee contracts between the distributed and hierarchical control system components to assess proper behavior of the overall system. This talk will discuss the design, architecture, and plans for formal methods analysis of the Gateway ASMA and VSM.

Proof-Based Heuristics for Quantified Invariant Synthesis

Kenneth L. McMillan

The University of Texas at Austin, USA
kenmcm@cs.utexas.edu

Abstract. The problem of generating inductive invariants for parameterized or infinite-state systems has attracted continuous interest over the last several decades. The fact that the invariants require quantifiers presents challenges both in heuristically synthesizing them and in verifying them. Many approaches attempt to transform the synthesis problem in an incomplete way to finding finite-state or quantifier-free invariants, or attempt to generalize from proofs of finite instances in some way. Other methods go at the problem more directly, using some form of inductive synthesis (i.e., synthesis from examples). We will discuss some recent progress in this area and consider whether proof-based heuristics might also have a role to play in the problem synthesizing quantified invariants.

Contents

Verification of LSTM Neural Networks with Non-linear Activation Functions

Farzaneh Moradkhani(✉), Connor Fibich, and Martin Fränzle

Carl von Ossietzky Universität, 26111 Oldenburg, Germany
{farzaneh.moradkhani,connor.fibich,martin.fraenzle}@uol.de

Abstract. Recurrent neural networks are increasingly employed in safety-critical applications, such as control in cyber-physical systems, and therefore their verification is crucial for guaranteeing reliability and correctness. We present a novel approach for verifying the dynamic behavior of *Long short-term memory networks* (LSTMs), a popular type of *recurrent neural network* (RNN). Our approach employs the *satisfiability modulo theories* (SMT) solver iSAT solving complex Boolean combinations of linear and non-linear constraint formulas (including transcendental functions), and it therefore is able to verify safety properties of these networks.

Keywords: Formal verification · Recurrent neural networks · LSTM · SMT solving · iSAT

1 Introduction

Intelligent systems employing artificial neural networks (ANNs) have become widespread. ANNs have in particular gained popularity as a useful computational paradigm for classification, clustering, and pattern recognition, thereby mechanizing potentially safety-critical decisions in cyber-physical systems.

A key obstacle in the deployment of neural networks to critical infrastructures and systems is the lacking comprehensibility and predictability of their computational mechanisms, calling for formal verification of their function. Such verification, however, is complicated both by the sheer size of ANNs, often comprising millions of artificial neurons, and the underlying computational paradigm of massively parallel analog data flow devoid of any focusing control flow. Due to size and non-linearity, neural network verification is difficult especially for their state-based variants like recurrent neural networks, as nowadays widely used in speech recognition, natural language processing, sequential data processing, and prediction of trajectories and maneuvers on autonomous cars [18]. Many deep neural networks, such as convolutional neural networks (CNN), are feed-forward networks, meaning that form analog combinational circuits where the

This work is supported by the German Research Foundation DFG through the Research Training Group "SCARE: System Correctness under Adverse Conditions" (DFG-GRK 1765/2) and project grant FR 2715/5-1.

K. Y. Rozier and S. Chaudhuri (Eds.): NFM 2023, LNCS 13903, pp. 1–15, 2023.
https://doi.org/10.1007/978-3-031-33170-1_1

signal moves only in one direction from the input layer through a sequence of hidden layers to the output layer, and they do not maintain state in that they store previous data or computation results. *Recurrent neural networks* (RNNs) in contrast have a feedback layer through which the network output, along with the next input, is fed back to the network. An RNN can thus remember previous state information and exploit this memory to process subsequent inputs. These types of neural networks are particularly useful for processing series or sequential data, in which processing can maintain an internal state or memory to store information related to previous input.

Although some studies have been conducted so far to formally and machanically verify feed-forward neural networks [9,13,15,16], verifying recurrent neural networks is a relatively young research area. Akintunde et al. [7] realize formal verification by unraveling RNNs into FFNNs and compiling the resulting verification problem into a Mixed-Integer linear program (MILP). Jacoby et al. [12] proposed a method for the formal verification for systems composed of a stateful agent implemented by an RNN interacting with an environment. Their method relies on the application of inductive invariants for the reduction of RNN verification to FFNN verification. These techniques remained currently confined to piecewise linear, ReLU-Type neural networks. More general and flexible classes of RNN, including LSTMs and generative adversarial networks (GAN), however contain layers that feature nonlinear transfer functions such as sigmoid and tanh. Therefore, Mohammadinejad et al. [14] proposed a differential verification method for verifying RNN with nonlinear activation functions, where their verification goal is to certify the approximate equivalence of two structurally similar neural network functions, rather than verifying behavioral invariants.

In this paper, aiming at RNN verification against a formal safety specification, we investigate an automatic RNN verification strategy based on expanding the core of the SMT solver iSAT [10] to handle networks with nonlinear activation functions like sigmoid and tanh. iSAT is well-suited for this task, as it (1.) was designed specifically for dealing with complex Boolean combinations of non-linear arithmetic facts involving transcendental functions, and (2.) has mechanisms for *bounded model checking* (BMC) [8] built in.

The rest of the paper is organized as follows. We start in Sect. 2 with some background on LSTM. Our verification approach is described in Sect. 3, and we demonstrate it on case studies of automatic braking and collision detection between satellites and orbiting objects in Sect. 4. We conclude with Sect. 5.

2 Background

Recurrent neural networks are a type of neural networks that is particularly useful for processing series or sequential data by being able to maintain an internal state or memory to store information related to previous input. This feature is especially important in various applications related to discovering structures

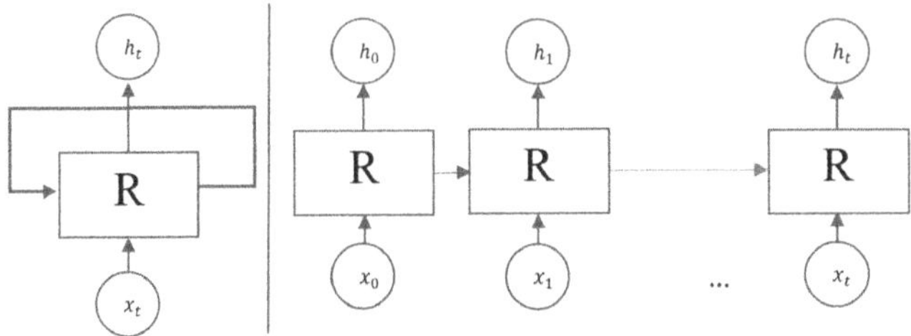

Fig. 1. Recurrent neural network element (left). The behavior at any time point is given by the unfolding of its time-discrete feedback behavior (right).

in series or consecutive data, such as time series, speech, text, financial data, audio, video, and so on. On such data structures, the recursive neural network can provide computational power that feedforward networks cannot due to their inability to maintain, retrieve, and process non-local information. As an example, a feedforward network can only learn bounded-range addition while being inapt to do arbitrary length addition; an RNN in contrast could learn to pursue digitwise addition of unlimited length (yet not unbounded multiplication).

Figure 1 shows a recursive network cell. It first takes x_0 from the input sequence and then delivers h_0 as the output, which together with the next input x_1 is fed to the next time step. Therefore, h_0 and x_1 are the basis of the network computation in the next time-step, which otherwise is stateless. This computation scheme carries on recursively such that state h_{t-1} along with input x_t the basis of the computation in step t.

LSTM Networks [11] are an improved version of such basic recurrent neural networks that actively controls when to remember past data via a fixed memory structure [11,20]. The problem of gradients vanishing during the training of recurrent neural networks is addressed hereby. LSTMs are suitable for classifying, processing, and predicting time series in the presence of time delays of unknown duration. The network is trained using back-propagation.

A crucial difference between an LSTM and a basic RNN is that LSTMs comprise so-called gates, which actively regulate the flow of information between memory and computational units. This permits active control of the lifetime of stored information and overcomes basic RNN's difficulties in remembering properties overarching long sequences and in storing information for long periods. Therefore, LSTM networks are a special type of recursive neural networks that have the ability to learn long-term dependencies.

2.1 LSTM Architecture

Figure 2 shows the structure of an LSTM cell. It uses a series of 'gates', which control how the information in a sequence of data comes into, is stored in, and leaves the memory part of the network. Though some variants exist, there typically are three gates in an LSTM cell: a forget gate, an input gate, and an output gate, and these gates can be thought of as filters for information flow.

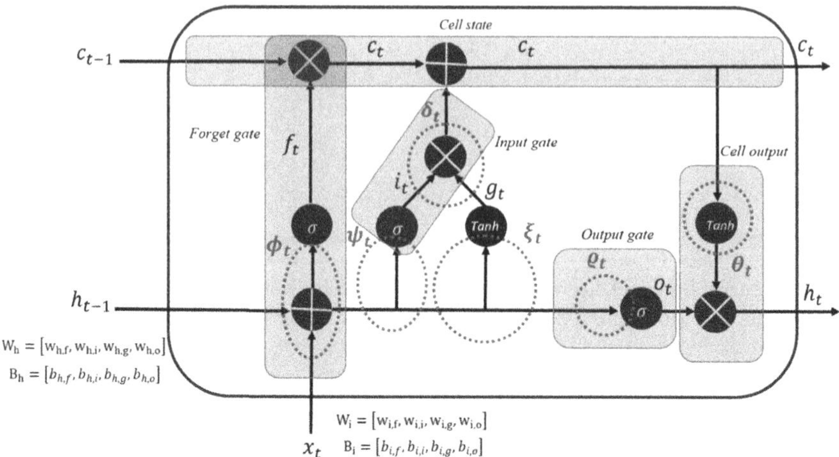

Fig. 2. LSTM structure. The auxiliary variables represented by ψ_t, ϕ_t, ζ_t, δ_t, ϱ_t and θ_t with dashed circles are only required for the iSAT encoding. [20].

The **input gate** is built to update the value (and thus the information) stored in the cell state c_t. A weighted sum of the input information of the new step x_t and the stored state information from the previous step h_{t-1} enters this gate and passes through the sigmoid function to decide whether state information in c_{t-1} is stored (gate value close to 1) or nulled out (gate value close to 0).

$$i_t = \sigma(w_{h,i}h_{t-1} + w_{i,i}x_t + b_{h,i} + b_{i,i}) \tag{1}$$

The **cell state** is the horizontal line going through the top of the Fig. 2. The input information of the new step x_t, along with the hidden state information of the previous step h_{t-1}, enters a tanh function to normalize their values into the range -1 to 1. Finally, the output of the sigmoid function and tanh are multiplied together so that they decide with which weight the data should be passed to the cell state. The characteristic equations of its dynamic behavior, as shown in (2) and (3).

$$g_t = \tanh(w_{h,g}h_{t-1} + w_{i,g}x_t + b_{h,g} + b_{i,g}) \tag{2}$$

$$c_t = i_t \odot g_t + f_t \odot c_{t-1} \tag{3}$$

The **forget gate** can be said to decide whether to store or to forget state information. The input information of the new step x_t, together with the hidden state information of the previous step h_{t-1}, enters this gate and passes through the sigmoid function. The sigmoid function looks at the previous state h_{t-1} and the input x_t, and for each number in the c_{t-1} cell state, returns a number between 0 (delete this) and 1 (hold this) as output. Intermediate values are possible;

the closer the output is to zero, the smaller is its impact of previous stored information on the next stored value. The characteristic equation is:

$$f_t = \sigma(w_{h,f}h_{t-1} + w_{i,f}x_t + b_{h,f} + b_{i,f}) \tag{4}$$

The **output gate** prepares the state information to be stored. First, the input information of the new step is entered along with the hidden state information of the previous step of a sigmoid function. The updated cell state value is entered into the tanh function. The output of these two functions is multiplied together to decide what information the hidden state will take with it to the next step. Finally, the new cell state and the new hidden state are moved to the next time step.

$$o_t = \sigma(w_{h,o}h_{t-1} + w_{i,o}x_t + b_{h,o} + b_{i,o}) \tag{5}$$

The **cell output** is the output of the cell to its vicinity as well as to the state feedback for the next time step. It is defined as:

$$h_t = y_t = o_t \odot \tanh(c_t) \tag{6}$$

3 Approach to LSTM Verification

The main focus of our research is to investigate automatic functional verification of LSTMs with the help of the SMT solver iSAT [10]. The core of iSAT is based on a tight integration of recent CDCL-style SAT solving techniques with interval constraint propagation (ICP), which is one of the subtopics of the area of constraint programming and is an incomplete procedure to efficiently reduce the domain of a set of variables concerning the conjunction of constraints, thereby enclosing the set of possible solutions to the constraints. iSAT can be used for determining the satisfiability of formulas containing arbitrary Boolean combinations of linear and non-linear (including transcendental functions) constraints. With its bounded model checking layer, iSAT is able to falsify safety invariants and related properties for systems containing non-linear dynamics. Therefore, we suggest iSAT as a verification tool to solve safety queries for neural networks containing activation functions beyond those encountered in the piecewise linear ReLU networks, especially for sigmoid and tanh activation functions as present in LSTMs. The mathematical operators in iSAT are shown in Table 1. By reduction to these, it is possible to encode nonlinear activation functions that comprise transcendental arithmetic. For instance, the sigmoid and tanh functions can be reduced to equation systems containing the exponential function e^x [16]. Consider x_{i-1} being the input and $\theta_{i,j}$ the output of a sigmoid activation function in the jth node in the ith layer. Then the following Eq. (8) is the characteristic Eq. (7) of this node. using standard algebraic transformations to eliminate division, this can be translated into iSAT syntax as Eq. (8).

$$\theta_{i,j} = \sigma_{sigma}(x_{i-1}) = \frac{1}{1 + e^{x_{i-1}}} \tag{7}$$

Table 1. Arithmetic operation in iSAT [5].

Operator	Args	Meaning
ite	3	If-then-else
exp, exp2, exp10	1	Exponential function regarding bases e, 2, 10
Log, log2, log10	1	Logarithmic function regarding bases e, 2,10
sin	1	Sine(unit: radian)
cos	1	Cosine(unit: radian)
abs	1	absolute value
min	2	minimum
max	2	maximum
pow	2	nth power, (2nd argument) has to be an integer, $n \geq 0$
nrt	2	nth root, (2nd argument) has to be an integer, $n \geq 1$

$$\theta_{i,j} * (1 + exp(x_{i-1})) = 1 \tag{8}$$

With its bounded model checking layer unravelling symbolic transition relations, iSAT can falsify invariant safety properties for systems containing non-linear dynamics. To encode such symbolic transition systems, variables in iSAT may occur in primed x' or unprimed x form [5]. A primed variable x' reflects the value of the variable x at the next step. For instance, we will use h' and c' to model LSTM memory. The characteristic equations, translated to iSAT syntax, here represent computation of next state values h_t and c_t based on inputs and current cell state c_{t-1} and hidden state h_{t-1}.

There are three implementations of the iSAT algorithm, staring from the first implementation named HySAT [10]. New operators specifically targeting non-linear neural networks by natively dealing with sigmoid and tanh have recently been introduced to the input language of the second version, now known as iSAT. To more clearly distinguish between the iSAT algorithm and the second implementation of iSAT, in the following we refer to this version as iSAT2. The most recent iSAT version is named iSAT3 [17] and is commercially available. While HySAT and iSAT2 both operate directly on simple bounds, iSAT3 takes a step back towards a slightly more lazy approach and explicitly maps each simple bound to a abstracting Boolean literal again.

3.1 Encoding LSTMs into iSAT

In order to obtain the recurrent neural network to be verified, we train a neural network containing LSTMs nodes. As usual, this training factually alternates between training and testing phases until the network is empirically found to be well-behaved. We then proceed to verification by first extracting all parametric features that have been adjusted, i.e. learned, during the training . This means we have to export all weights W and biases B for every gate in the LSTM that have been determined during the training by the optimization procedure of back-propagation.

Assume a layer in the LSTM ν that has n inputs forming an input vector $X = [x_0, x_1, x_2, ..., x_n]$ ranging over $x_i \in [L_x, U_x] \subset \mathbb{R}$, where L_i and U_i are the lower bound and upper bound, resp. These inputs can be the outputs from another neural network layer like a fully connected layer, or inputs to the overall network. The neural network layer then receives input sequences, where $x_{i,t}$ is i-th input at time-step t. Similarly, the layer features outputs y_i with an output interval $y_i \in [L_y, U_y] \subset \mathbb{R}$. As the LSTM is a stateful network, there also are states $H = [h_0, h_1, h_2, ..., h_{t-1}, h_t]$ and $C = [c_0, c_1, c_2, ..., c_{t-1}, c_t]$ in some layers, representing hidden and cell state as inputs from the previous and current time-step. $O = [o_1, o_2, o_3, ..., o_t]$ is the output of the last layer and thus of the whole LSTM.

In our subsequent discussion of an LSTM network, all units are pooled to a vector: g is the vector of cell input, i is the vector of input gates, f is the vector of forgetting gate, c is the vector of memory cell states, o is the vector of output gates, and y is the vector of cell outputs. Weight and bias values, unlike input and output values, are constants entering the verification phase and are known prior to the verification by extraction from the trained LSTM. W is the overall weight vector. For an LSTM cell, the weights $W_i = [w_{i,f}, w_{i,i}, w_{i,g}, w_{i,o}]$ and $W_h = [w_{h,g}, w_{h,i}, w_{h,f}, w_{h,o}]$ correspond to the weights of the connections between inputs and cell input, input gate, forget gate, and output gate. The vectors $B = [b_g, b_i, b_f, b_o]$ are the bias vectors of cell inputs, input gates, forget gates, and output gates, respectively. The LSTM also generates the signals c_t and h_t providing the state output to the next time step, specializing the respective mechanism from an RNN. We consider variable μ to count time steps across the recursive network evaluation process.

We encode the dynamic behaviour of the LSTM as a symbolic transition system, employing the primed-variable notation of iSAT to encode as h' and c' the next-state values of LSTM cell states c_{t+1} and hidden state h_{t+1} .

The following Eqs. (9)–(23) illustrate translation of an LSTM node, where $\mu = t$ to iSAT. In that respect, for example, the Eq. (10) is a direct translation of Eq. (1). The $\odot$ between the two variables here refers to the elementwise multiplication of two input vectors with k elements. All variables occurring in the formula to be solved have to be declared in iSAT. Types supported by iSAT are bounded intervals of reals, of computational floats, or of integers, as well as Boolean. For simplicity let denote ψ_t, ϕ_t, ζ_t, δ_t and ϱ_t the auxiliary variables of input, forget, cell, output gates and cell output respectively, as shown in Fig. 2.

Translation of input gate

$$\psi_t = w_{h,i}h' + w_{i,i}x_t + b_{h,i} + b_{i,i} \tag{9}$$

$$i_t = \sigma(\psi_t) \text{ translates to } i_t * (1 + exp10(\psi_t)) = 1 \tag{10}$$

Translation of forget gate

$$\phi_t = w_{h,f}h' + w_{i,f}x_t + b_{h,f} + b_{i,f} \tag{11}$$

$$f_t = \sigma(\phi_t) \text{ translates to } f_t * (1 + exp10(f_t)) = 1 \tag{12}$$

Translation of cell gate

$$\zeta_t = w_{h,g}h' + w_{i,g}x_t + b_{h,g} + b_{i,g} \tag{13}$$

$$g_t = \tanh(\zeta_t) \text{ translates to } g_t * (exp10(\zeta_t) + exp10(-\zeta_t)) = (\zeta_t) - exp10(-\zeta_t)) * 1 \tag{14}$$

$$c_t = i_t \odot g_t + f_t \odot c' \tag{15}$$

$$\delta_{i,t} = i_{1,t} * g_{1,t} + i_{2,t} * g_{2,t} + ... + i_{k,t} * g_{k,t} \tag{16}$$

$$\delta_{j,t} = f_{1,t} * c'_1 + f_{2,t} * c'_2 + ... + f_{k,t} * c'_k \tag{17}$$

$$c_t = \delta_{i,t} + \delta_{j,t} \tag{18}$$

Output gate

$$\varrho_t = w_{h,o}h' + w_{i,o}x_t + b_{h,o} + b_{i,o} \tag{19}$$

$$o_t = \sigma(\varrho_t) \text{ translates to } o_t * (1 + exp10(\varrho_t)) = 1 \tag{20}$$

Translation of cell output

$$y_t = o_t \odot \tanh(c_t) \tag{21}$$

$$\theta_t = \tanh(c_t) \text{ translates to } \theta_t * (exp10(c_t) + exp10(-c_t)) = (c_t) - exp10(-c_t)) * 1 \tag{22}$$

$$y_t = o_{1,t} * \theta_{1,t} + o_{2,t} * \theta_{2,t} + ... + o_{k,t} * \theta_{k,t} \tag{23}$$

The above translation scheme provide a compositional translation of an LSTM into a symbolic transition system of size linear in the size of the LSTM.

4 Case Study

In order to evaluate our translation and verification method, the suggested technique was tested on two different LSTM networks. First, a network trained on a data set of recorded traffic from the NGSIM project [3] and second satellite collision avoidance released by the European Space Agency (ESA) [2].

Table 2. NGSIM database [3].

Vehicle_ID	Frame_ID	Local_X	Local_Y	Length	Width	Vel	Acc	Lane_ID	Leading
288	1570	50.366	267.751	14	6.5	18.74	9.79	4	292
288	1757	51.159	314.237	14	6.5	0	−1.78	4	292
288	1948	24.405	699.007	14.5	7.4	51.31	11.25	1	291
288	1911	52.399	313.651	14	6.5	0.04	0	4	292
289	2086	19.455	2154.879	15.5	5.9	2	50	−5.33	300
289	903	41.523	1045.145	17	8.4	5	2.89	3	291

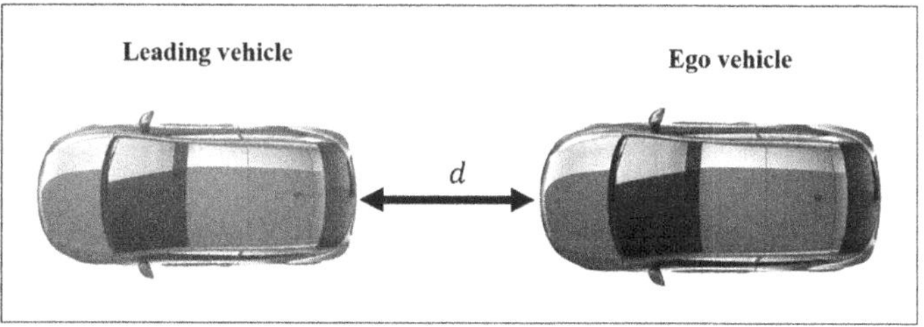

Fig. 3. Visualization of the distance between cars.

4.1 NGSIM

The data set comprises information about the positions, speeds, accelerations, and lanes used by cars traveling on US Highway 101 between 7:50 am and 8:35 a.m. The study area is 640 m long and consists of five lanes. Table 2 illustrates a snippet of this data set. The data covers several vehicles, each identified by a unique number. As this identifier is recorded in the Vehicle_ID column, individual cars can be tracked over an extended duration of time by filtering for the rows featuring the respective identifier, providing a time series for the movements of Vehicle_ID. A classifier network predicting near collisions can thus be trained on these data. As the data set represents time series of state snapshots and as the dynamics has to be recovered from correlating these snapshots, we decided to train an LSTM for this classification task (Fig. 3).

Our proof obligation, to be discharged by iSAT, then was to check whether the trained network correctly detects near collisions.

The safe distance between two vehicles is defined by the Vienna Convention as a "sufficient distance [...] to avoid a collision if the vehicle in front should suddenly slow down or stop" [1]. As a result, a safe distance between the ego vehicle and the leading vehicle must always be maintained, and this distance has to be large enough for safely avoiding collision even when an emergency deceleration happens up front.

Two cars with a distance of d from each other may collide if the car in front, the $vehicle_{leading}$, suddenly slows down or stops. Therefore, the distance from $vehicle_{ego}$ to $vehicle_{leading}$ must always be maintained large enough to accommodate sudden maximal deceleration. A corresponding distance requirement can easily be computed from the laws of Newtonian mechanics, physical parameters of the cars, and reaction times as follows, such that a close-form safety specification can be established as basis of the formal verification follow.

The future position of a vehicle for a point in time $t \geq 0$ is according to the laws of accelerated movement:

$$x(t) = x_0 + vt + \frac{1}{2}at^2 \tag{24}$$

If the position of the vehicle at t_0 is $x_0 \in \mathbb{R}$ then the ego vehicle collides with the leading vehicle iff their positions are equal for some future $t \geq 0$. A collision thus can happen if

$$\exists\, t \geq 0 : x_{ego(t)} = x_{leading(t)}, 0 \leq t \leq t_{max} \tag{25}$$

is true.

Then based on (24) and (25) we have a potential for an unavoidable collision iff the following constraint system (31) is satisfiable

$$v_{ego}t + \frac{1}{2}at^2 = x + v_{leading}t + \frac{1}{2}at^2 \wedge 0 \leq t \leq \frac{v_{ego}}{a}\ , \tag{26}$$

where a is the maximum deceleration (which for simplicity is assumed to be the same for both cars; generalizations, also such involving reaction times, are easy to obtain). We derive Eq. (27) specifying a physically justified braking demand by removing the identical summand $\frac{1}{2}at^2$ occurs on both sides and simplifying Eq. (26):

$$state_{brake} \iff 0 \leq xa \leq v_{ego} * (v_{ego} - v_{leading}) \tag{27}$$

Here, a is the maximum deceleration of the ego vehicle respectively. The ego vehicle could intrude into the leading vehicle's safety envelope or even collide with that if the right-hand side of the implication in Eq. (27) becomes true. This right-hand side predicate thus constitutes a specification of braking demand, as needed to maintain safe distance.

Equation (27) consequently provides the formal specification for the braking advisories, both used for labelling training cases in supervised learning and for the verification. Note that such verification still is necessary even if the very same predicate was used as a label in supervised learning, as a neural network will neither generate a loss (i.e., error rate) of 0 across all training points nor is it predictable how it will generalize between training points.

To train a neural network for giving emergency braking advisories, the experiments were performed on the following computer configuration: Intel(R) Core(TM) i7-4600U CPU @ 2.10GHz, 64 GB Memory, and Ubuntu OS. We created a classification model with 50 LSTM nodes with 4 time steps and 3 fully connected layers. The safe and unsafe labels were being assigned during the training by Eq. (27). This provided a supervised learning problem based on

Table 3. The result of verifying the case study.

Target	p_{ego}	v_{ego}	$p_{leading}$	$v_{leading}$	$P_{time-second}$	State
$state_{brake}$ and $!state_{nn\_brake}$	148	22	155	1	120.02	candidate solution
$!state_{brake}$ and $state_{nn\_brake}$	-	-	-	-	200.41	Unsatisfiable

the features frame_ID, lane_ID, velocity, acceleration of, and positions of ego and leading vehicles extracted from 1,048,576 recorded of NGSIM database which was divided into train and test datasets. The training resulted in ca. 98% accuracy across the test dataset. The trained LSTM network was subsequently translated into iSAT constraint format [5,10] according to the translation rules exposed in Sect. 3 and in [16]. The iSAT constraint formula, thus reflecting the behavior of the full LSTM, is called Φ subsequently.

The LSTM network features two float-valued outputs γ_{unsafe} and γ_{safe} and classifies the situation based on which of these two evidences appears stronger: Whenever the outputs satisfy $\gamma_{unsafe} > \gamma_{safe}$ then the network detects a critical condition, i.e., generated a braking advisory. Verification amounts to showing that the LSTM outputs, as defined by the LSTM structure and weights or, equivalently, its logical encoding ϕ, always agree to the output required by Eq. (27). The output of the LSTM can be recovered from its logical encoding ϕ as

$$state_{nn\_brake} \iff \phi \wedge (\gamma_{safe} < \gamma_{unsafe}) \tag{28}$$

Functional verification of the LSTM now amounts to showing that the Eqs. (27) and (28) are consistent in so far that the LSTM can never, i.e. under no input sequence, reach a state where its output $state_{nn\_brake}$ defined according to constraint system (28) is different from the expected label $state_{brake}$ due to Eq. (27).

Conditions when, according to the requirement defined in formula (27), an emergency braking maneuver is required, yet the neural networks based on condition (28) fails to offer an emergency braking advisory are of particular interest: In this case study, we aim to see whether the neural network may ever fail to provide the necessary braking advice, i.e. whether (28) can provide a no-braking advisory when (27) determines emergency braking necessary. By providing the following verification target (29), iSAT2 can be asked to check for satisfiability of this condition (and provides a satisfying assignment, i.e. a counterexample to safety of the LSTM, if such exists).

$$\texttt{Target} :state_{brake} \wedge \neg state_{nn\_brake} \tag{29}$$

iSAT, when asked to solve the conjoined system (27) $\wedge$ (28) with the reachability target (29), returns a candidate solution as a result: when the position of ego vehicle is at 148 m with a speed of 22 m/s and at the same time the leading vehicle is at 155 m with a speed of 1 m/s, then obviously emergency braking would be overdue, but the trained LSTM provides a wrong generalization from its training points here, reporting $\neg state_{nn\_brake}$. This obviously is a highly critical problem. For the opposite, less critical problem of the LSTM providing a braking advisory where it should not (i.e., the verification target being

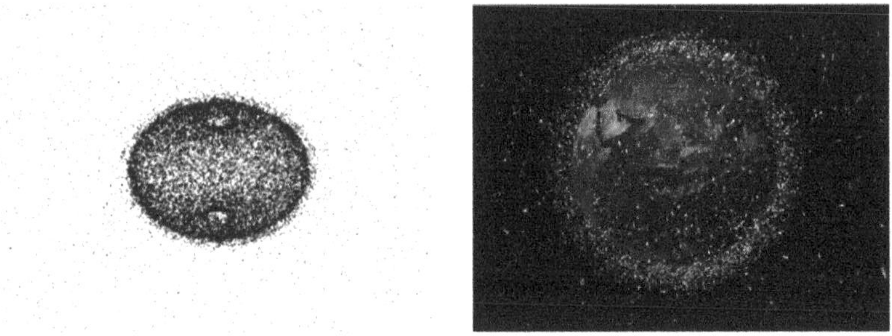

Fig. 4. Visualization of the density of objects orbiting the low Earth orbit [4,6].

`Target` :$\neg state_{brake} \wedge state_{nn\_brake}$), iSAT did not find any satisfying instance, showing that this cannot happen (Table 3).

4.2 Satellite Collision Detection

We investigate the scalability of our proposed method in the second case study, which provides information about satellites and objects orbiting in space. A typical *low Earth orbit* (LEO) satellite nowadays sends out hundreds of hazard alerts each week for close encounters with other space objects such as satellites or space debris. According to estimates made by the *European Space Agency* (ESA) in January 2019, more than 34,000 objects that are larger than 10 cm orbit our planet, of which 22,300 are monitored, and their locations are reported in a shared database around the world [2]. Figure 4 shows how the spatial density of objects in LEO orbits is represented.

Preventing spacecraft collisions has become crucial to satellite operations. Various operators are informed by elaborate and frequently updated calculations of the collision risk between orbiting objects, and can then devise risk reduction strategies. When a probable near approach with any object is identified, the collected data is put together in a *Conjunction Data Message* (CDM). Each CDM carries a variety of information regarding the approach, including the *time of closest approach* (TCA), the satellite's name, the type of prospective collider item, the relative position between the chaser and target, etc. It also includes a self-reported risk that was calculated utilizing various CDM elements. Generally, for each potential near approach, 3 CDMs are recorded daily over the duration of one week. Therefore, for each event, there is a time series of CDMs.

The ESA provided a significant compiled dataset comprising data regarding close approach events in the form of conjunction data messages (CDMs) from 2015 to 2019. This dataset was used in the Spacecraft Collision Avoidance Challenge, a machine-learning competition where teams had to create models to forecast the likelihood of an orbiting object colliding with another [19]. An event is deemed to be of high risk when its last recorded risk is greater than -6, and of low risk when it is less than or equal to -6 (the possible ranges for these values are -30 (lowest risk) to 0 (maximum risk)).

Table 4. Memory usage and time solving of iSAT2 and iSAT3 on satellite collision detection dataset.

Nodes	*variabels*	*iSAT2*			*iSAT3*		
		State	*Memory*	*Time(second)*	*State*	*Memory*	*Time(second)*
Sg_{20}	12,768	UNSAT	1.14	1.160	UNSAT	1.14	0.227
Sg_{40}	42,001	UNSAT	1.14	3.152	UNSAT	1.14	0.847
Sg_{60}	88,130	UNSAT	1.14	6.891	UNSAT	1.14	1.963
Sg_{80}	151,054	UNSAT	1.14	11.835	UNSAT	1.14	5.734
Sg_{100}	230,782	UNSAT	1.13	18.412	UNSAT	1.14	6.162
Sg_{120}	327,308	UNSAT	1.14	26.327	UNSAT	1.14	9.933
Sg_{140}	440,628	UNSAT	990.70	35.544	UNSAT	1.14	12.128
Sg_{160}	570,736	UNSAT	1,562.94	47.017	UNSAT	1.14	15.97
Sg_{180}	717,645	UNSAT	1,562.94	59.463	UNSAT	1.14	21.107
S_{200}	881,349	UNSAT	1,562.94	73.186	UNSAT	8,111.68	54.483
Sg_{400}	3,441,142	UNSAT	1,823.22	290.076	TIMEOUT		
Sg_{600}	7,676,411	UNSAT	1,823.22	669.826	TIMEOUT		
Sg_{800}	9,691,159	UNSAT	283,417.80	1,271.90	ML		
Sg_{1000}	15,085,373	UNSAT	299,361.27	1,993.22	ML		
Th_{20}	12,732	UNSAT	1.14	0.846	UNSAT	1.1367	0.235
Th_{40}	42,122	UNSAT	1.14	3.163	UNSAT	1.14	0.885
Th_{60}	88,311	UNSAT	1.14	6.258	UNSAT	1.14	2.166
Th_{80}	151,298	UNSAT	1.14	12.254	UNSAT	1.14	4.586
Th_{100}	231,088	UNSAT	1.13	22.246	UNSAT	1.14	7.295
Th_{120}	327,672	UNSAT	1.14	24.761	TIMEOUT		
Th_{140}	441,050	UNSAT	990.70	32.305	TIMEOUT		
Th_{160}	571,218	UNSAT	1,562.94	1,102.19	TIMEOUT		
Th_{180}	718,208	TIMEOUT			TIMEOUT		

In a formal verification using our LSTM encoding technique, we could employ

$$\texttt{Target}: \ \gamma_0 > -6 \tag{30}$$

with the output γ_0 being the characteristic output of the trained neural network, to reflect a dangerous condition, and check satisfiability of (30). The verification processes were run on Oldenburg University's high performance computing cluster CARL using a node equipped with two Intel Xeon E5-2650 v4 12C CPUs at 2.2GHz and each process being limited to 300 GB of RAM and 24 h processing time limitation. We selected seven out of 103 features like the team which achieved the final score in the competition [19]. In order to test scalability, our trained models consist of varying numbers of LSTM nodes in two layers, with the last three CDM serving as a time step.

To compare the scalability of LSTM verification using iSAT2 and iSAT3, we measured the performance of each solver with respect to the *Solver time* and also *Memory usage* to evaluate the trained LSTM networks with two different activation functions, tanh and sigmoid. Solver time refers to the CPU time in seconds which each solver used during the verification process to determine satisfiability. Memory usage was retrieved from the cluster's workload management system SLURM for each verification process and is reported in megabyte. The provided values are a slight overestimation since the workload management system can only measure how much memory is allocated to the process and does not provide any information about the memory actually used during the verification process. Table 4 shows the performance comparison between iSAT2 and its successor iSAT3. Sg and Th represent the total number of LSTM nodes in every trained network with sigmoid and tanh activation function, respectively.

TIMEOUT and ML denote that the solving process was aborted due to exceeding the time or memory limit, respectively. The findings seem to indicate that iSAT2, employing an embedding of Boolean reasoning into real-valued intervals and interval constraint propagation and thus saving a SAT-modulo-theory style Boolean abstraction of (arithmetic) theory constraints by means of Boolean trigger variables for theory atoms, on LSTM verification benchmarks for larger instances outperforms its commercially successful successor iSAT3, which employs Boolean literal abstraction of theory atoms. This is an issue requiring further investigation, as it may prompt ideas on the development of dedicated solvers for LSTM verification. LSTM verification problems are by their very nature characterized by extremely large numbers of variables spanning a vast search space for constraint solving, like in example Sg_{1000} with around 15 millions of real-valued variables, and Boolean literal abstraction for theory-related facts seems to become detrimental here.

5 Conclusion

Recent breakthroughs in autonomous and robotic systems, in which neural networks are incorporated in parts of the design, render formal verification of the resulting systems both necessary and extremely difficult. This research proposes a new approach to verify LSTMs, a general class of recurrent neural networks. The SMT solver iSAT, which solves large Boolean combinations of linear and non-linear constraint formulae (including transcendental functions, thus especially covering the sigmoidal and tanh-shaped transfer functions occurring in LSTMs) and has built-in functionality for bounded model checking by unraveling a symbolic transition relation, is exploited for checking safety of recurrent neural networks with non-linear activation functions. First experiments show this approach feasible for non-trivial recurrent neural networks of LSTM type, but also indicate the need for specialized solver structures overcoming the overhead induced by the Boolean trigger literal abstraction usually used in SAT-modulo-theory based constraint solving.

References

1. Economic commission for Europe, inland transport committee, "vienna convention on road traffic". http://www.unece.org/fileadmin/DAM/trans/conventn/crt1968e.pdf
2. European space agency, "collision detection dataset". https://www.kelvins.esa.int

3. Federal highway administration research and technology, "US highway 101 dataset". https://www.fhwa.dot.gov/publications/research/operations/07030
4. space track. www.space-track.org
5. iSAT Quick Start Guide. AVACS H1/2 iSAT Developer Team (2010)
6. Agency, E.S.: Space debris by the numbers. https://www.esa.int
7. Akintunde, M.E., Kevorchian, A., Lomuscio, A., Pirovano, E.: Verification of RNN-based neural agent-environment systems. In: The Thirty-Third AAAI Conference on Artificial Intelligence, AAAI 2019, The Thirty-First Innovative Applications of Artificial Intelligence Conference, IAAI 2019, The Ninth AAAI Symposium on Educational Advances in Artificial Intelligence, EAAI 2019, Honolulu, Hawaii, USA, 27 January - 1 February 2019, pp. 6006–6013. AAAI Press (2019). https://doi.org/10.1609/aaai.v33i01.33016006
8. Biere, A., Cimatti, A., Clarke, E., Zhu, Y.: Symbolic model checking without BDDs. In: Cleaveland, W.R. (ed.) TACAS 1999. LNCS, vol. 1579, pp. 193–207. Springer, Heidelberg (1999). https://doi.org/10.1007/3-540-49059-0_14
9. Ehlers, R.: Formal verification of piece-wise linear feed-forward neural networks. In: D'Souza, D., Narayan Kumar, K. (eds.) ATVA 2017. LNCS, vol. 10482, pp. 269–286. Springer, Cham (2017). https://doi.org/10.1007/978-3-319-68167-2_19
10. Fränzle, M., Herde, C., Teige, T., Ratschan, S., Schubert, T.: Efficient solving of large non-linear arithmetic constraint systems with complex Boolean structure. J. Satisf. Boolean Model. Comput. **1**(3–4), 209–236 (2007). https://doi.org/10.3233/sat190012
11. Hochreiter, S., Schmidhuber, J.: Long short-term memory. Neural Comput. **9**(8), 1735–1780 (1997). https://doi.org/10.1162/neco.1997.9.8.1735
12. Jacoby, Y., Barrett, C., Katz, G.: Verifying recurrent neural networks using invariant inference. In: Hung, D.V., Sokolsky, O. (eds.) ATVA 2020. LNCS, vol. 12302, pp. 57–74. Springer, Cham (2020). https://doi.org/10.1007/978-3-030-59152-6_3
13. Katz, G., Barrett, C., Dill, D.L., Julian, K., Kochenderfer, M.J.: Reluplex: an efficient SMT solver for verifying deep neural networks. In: Majumdar, R., Kunčak, V. (eds.) CAV 2017. LNCS, vol. 10426, pp. 97–117. Springer, Cham (2017). https://doi.org/10.1007/978-3-319-63387-9_5
14. Mohammadinejad, S., Paulsen, B., Deshmukh, J.V., Wang, C.: DiffRNN: differential verification of recurrent neural networks. In: Dima, C., Shirmohammadi, M. (eds.) FORMATS 2021. LNCS, vol. 12860, pp. 117–134. Springer, Cham (2021). https://doi.org/10.1007/978-3-030-85037-1_8
15. Pulina, L., Tacchella, A.: Never: a tool for artificial neural networks verification. Ann. Math. Artif. Intell. **62**, 403–425 (2011)
16. Rizaldi, A., Immler, F.: A formally verified checker of the safe distance traffic rules for autonomous vehicles. Arch. Formal Proofs 2020 (2020). https://www.isa-afp.org/entries/Safe_Distance.html
17. Scheibler, K.: isat3 manual. isat3 0.04-20170301 (2017)
18. Sighencea, B.I., Stanciu, R.I., Caleanu, C.: A review of deep learning-based methods for pedestrian trajectory prediction. Sensors **21**(22), 7543 (2021). https://doi.org/10.3390/s21227543
19. Uriot, T., et al.: Spacecraft collision avoidance challenge: design and results of a machine learning competition. Astrodynamics **6**(2), 121–140 (2022)
20. Yu, Y., Si, X., Hu, C., Zhang, J.: A review of recurrent neural networks: LSTM cells and network architectures. Neural Comput. **31**(7), 1235–1270 (2019). https://doi.org/10.1162/neco_a_01199

Open- and Closed-Loop Neural Network Verification Using Polynomial Zonotopes

Niklas Kochdumper[1(✉)], Christian Schilling[2], Matthias Althoff[3], and Stanley Bak[1]

[1] Stony Brook University, Stony Brook, NY, USA
{niklas.kochdumper,stanley.bak}@stonybrook.edu
[2] Aalborg University, Aalborg, Denmark
christianms@cs.aau.dk
[3] Technical University of Munich, Garching, Germany
althoff@tum.de

Abstract. We present a novel approach to efficiently compute tight non-convex enclosures of the image through neural networks with ReLU, sigmoid, or hyperbolic tangent activation functions. In particular, we abstract the input-output relation of each neuron by a polynomial approximation, which is evaluated in a set-based manner using polynomial zonotopes. While our approach can also can be beneficial for open-loop neural network verification, our main application is reachability analysis of neural network controlled systems, where polynomial zonotopes are able to capture the non-convexity caused by the neural network as well as the system dynamics. This results in a superior performance compared to other methods, as we demonstrate on various benchmarks.

Keywords: Neural network verification · Neural network controlled systems · Reachability analysis · Polynomial zonotopes · Formal verification

1 Introduction

While previously artificial intelligence was mainly used for soft applications such as movie recommendations [9], facial recognition [23], or chess computers [11], it is now also increasingly applied in safety-critical applications, such as autonomous driving [32], human-robot collaboration [27], or power system control [5]. In contrast to soft applications, where failures usually only have minor consequences, failures in safety-critical applications in the worst case result in loss of human lives. Consequently, in order to prevent those failures, there is an urgent need for efficient methods that can verify that the neural networks used for artificial intelligence function correctly. Verification problems involving neural networks can be grouped into two main categories:

- **Open-loop verification:** Here the task is to check if the output of the neural network for a given input set satisfies certain properties. With this setup one can for example prove that a neural network used for image classification is robust against a certain amount of noise on the image.

K. Y. Rozier and S. Chaudhuri (Eds.): NFM 2023, LNCS 13903, pp. 16–36, 2023.
https://doi.org/10.1007/978-3-031-33170-1_2

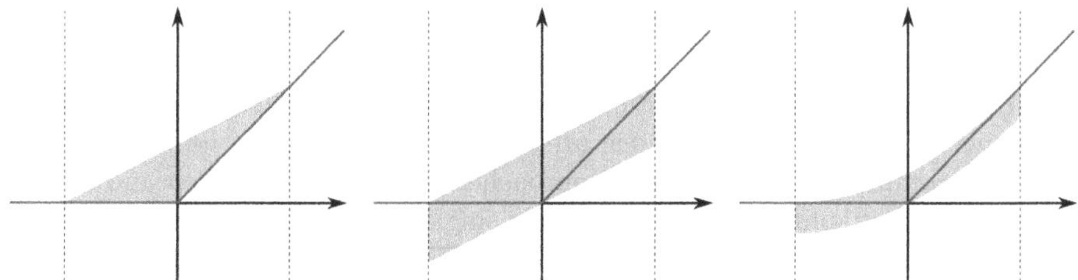

Fig. 1. Triangle relaxation (left), zonotope abstraction (middle), and polynomial zonotope abstraction (right) of the ReLU activation function.

- **Closed-loop verification:** In this case the neural network is used as a controller for a dynamical system, e.g., to steer the system to a given goal set while avoiding unsafe regions. The safety of the controlled system can be verified using reachability analysis.

For both of the above verification problems, the most challenging step is to compute a tight enclosure of the image through the neural network for a given input set. Due to the high expressiveness of neural networks, their images usually have complex shapes, so that convex enclosures are often too conservative for verification. In this work, we show how to overcome this limitation with our novel approach for computing tight non-convex enclosures of images through neural networks using polynomial zonotopes.

1.1 State of the Art

We first summarize the state of the art for open-loop neural network verification followed by reachability analysis for neural network controlled systems. Many different set representations have been proposed for computing enclosures of the image through a neural network, including intervals [43], polytopes [38], zonotopes [34], star sets [40], and Taylor models [21]. For neural networks with ReLU activation functions, it is possible to compute the exact image. This can be either achieved by recursively partitioning the input set into piecewise affine regions [42], or by propagating the initial set through the network using polytopes [38,48] or star sets [40], where the set is split at all neurons that are both active or inactive. In either case the exact image is in the worst case given as a union of 2^v convex sets, with v being the number of neurons in the network. To avoid this high computational complexity for exact image computation, most approaches compute a tight enclosure instead using an abstraction of the neural network. For ReLU activation functions one commonly used abstraction is the triangle relaxation [15] (see Fig. 1), which can be conveniently integrated into set propagation using star sets [40]. Another possibility is to abstract the input-output relation by a zonotope (see Fig. 1), which is possible for ReLU, sigmoid, and hyperbolic tangent activation functions [34]. One can also apply Taylor model arithmetic [26] to compute the image through networks with sigmoid and hyperbolic tangent activation [21], which corresponds to an abstraction of the input-output relation by a Taylor series expansion. In order to better capture dependencies between different neurons, some approaches also abstract the input-output relation of multiple neurons at once [28,36].

While computation of the exact image is infeasible for large networks, the enclosures obtained by abstractions are often too conservative for verification. To obtain complete verifiers, many approaches therefore use branch and bound strategies [7] that split the input set and/or single neurons until the specification can either be proven or a counterexample is found. For computational reasons branch and bound strategies are usually combined with approaches that are able to compute rough interval bounds for the neural network output very fast. Those bounds can for example be obtained using symbolic intervals [43] that store linear constraints on the variables in addition to the interval bounds to preserve dependencies. The DeepPoly approach [35] uses a similar concept, but applies a back-substitution scheme to obtain tighter bounds. With the FastLin method [45] linear bounds for the overall network can be computed from linear bounds for the single neurons. The CROWN approach [49] extends this concept to linear bounds with different slopes as well as quadratic bounds. Several additional improvements for the CROWN approach have been proposed, including slope optimization using gradient descent [47] and efficient ReLU splitting [44]. Instead of explicitly computing the image, many approaches also aim to verify the specification directly using SMT solvers [22,30], mixed-integer linear programming [8,37], semidefinite programming [31], and convex optimization [24].

For reachability analysis of neural network controlled systems one has to compute the set of control inputs in each control cycle, which is the image of the current reachable set through the neural network controller. Early approaches compute the image for ReLU networks exactly using polytopes [46] or star sets [39]. Since in this case the number of coexisting sets grows rapidly over time, these approaches have to unite sets using convex hulls [46] or interval enclosures [39], which often results in large over-approximations. If template polyhedra are used as a set representation, reachability analysis for neural network controlled systems with discrete-time plants reduces to the task of computing the maximum output along the template directions [12], which can be done efficiently. Neural network controllers with sigmoid and hyperbolic tangent activation functions can be converted to an equivalent hybrid automaton [20], which can be combined with the dynamics of the plant using the automaton product. However, since each neuron is represented by an additional state, the resulting hybrid automaton is very high-dimensional, which makes reachability analysis challenging. Some approaches approximate the overall network with a polynomial function [14,18] using polynomial regression based on samples [14] and Bernstein polynomials [18]. Yet another class of methods [10,21,33,41] employs abstractions of the input-output relation for the neurons to compute the set of control inputs using intervals [10], star sets [41], Taylor models [21], and a combination of zonotopes and Taylor models [33]. Common tools for reachability analysis of neural network controlled systems are JuliaReach [6], NNV [41], POLAR [19], ReachNN* [16], RINO [17], Sherlock [13], Verisig [20], and Verisig 2.0 [21], where JuliaReach uses zonotopes for neural network abstraction [33], NVV supports multiple set representations, ReachNN* applies the Bernstein polynomial method [18], POLAR approximates single neurons by Bernstein polynomials [19], RINO computes interval inner- and outer-approximations [17], Sherlock uses the polynomial regression approach [14], Verisig performs the conversion to a hybrid automaton [20], and Verisig 2.0 uses the Taylor model based neural network abstraction method [21].

1.2 Overview

In this work, we present a novel approach for computing tight non-convex enclosures of images through neural networks with ReLU, sigmoid, or hyperbolic tangent activation functions. The high-level idea is to approximate the input-output relation of each neuron by a polynomial function, which results in the abstraction visualized in Fig. 1. Since polynomial zonotopes are closed under polynomial maps, the image through this function can be computed exactly, yielding a tight enclosure of the image through the overall neural network. The remainder of this paper is structured as follows: After introducing some preliminaries in Sect. 2, we present our approach for computing tight enclosures of images through neural networks in Sect. 3. Next, we show how to utilize this result for reachability analysis of neural network controlled systems in Sect. 4. Afterwards, in Sect. 5, we introduce some special operations on polynomial zonotopes that we require for image and reachable set computation, before we finally demonstrate the performance of our approach on numerical examples in Sect. 6.

1.3 Notation

Sets are denoted by calligraphic letters, matrices by uppercase letters, and vectors by lowercase letters. Given a vector $b \in \mathbb{R}^n$, $b_{(i)}$ refers to the i-th entry. Given a matrix $A \in \mathbb{R}^{o \times n}$, $A_{(i,\cdot)}$ represents the i-th matrix row, $A_{(\cdot,j)}$ the j-th column, and $A_{(i,j)}$ the j-th entry of matrix row i. The concatenation of two matrices C and D is denoted by $[C\ D]$, and $I_n \in \mathbb{R}^{n \times n}$ is the identity matrix. The symbols $\mathbf{0}$ and $\mathbf{1}$ represent matrices of zeros and ones of proper dimension, the empty matrix is denoted by $[\ ]$, and $\operatorname{diag}(a)$ returns a diagonal matrix with $a \in \mathbb{R}^n$ on the diagonal. Given a function $f(x)$ defined as $f: \mathbb{R} \to \mathbb{R}$, $f'(x)$ and $f''(x)$ denote the first and second derivative with respect to x. The left multiplication of a matrix $A \in \mathbb{R}^{o \times n}$ with a set $\mathcal{S} \subset \mathbb{R}^n$ is defined as $A\mathcal{S} := \{A\, s \mid s \in \mathcal{S}\}$, the Minkowski addition of two sets $\mathcal{S}_1 \subset \mathbb{R}^n$ and $\mathcal{S}_2 \subset \mathbb{R}^n$ is defined as $\mathcal{S}_1 \oplus \mathcal{S}_2 := \{s_1 + s_2 \mid s_1 \in \mathcal{S}_1, s_2 \in \mathcal{S}_2\}$, and the Cartesian product of two sets $\mathcal{S}_1 \subset \mathbb{R}^n$ and $\mathcal{S}_2 \subset \mathbb{R}^o$ is defined as $\mathcal{S}_1 \times \mathcal{S}_2 := \big\{[s_1^T\ s_2^T]^T \mid s_1 \in \mathcal{S}_1, s_2 \in \mathcal{S}_2\big\}$. We further introduce an n-dimensional interval as $\mathcal{I} := [l, u]$, $\forall i\ l_{(i)} \leq u_{(i)}$, $l, u \in \mathbb{R}^n$.

2 Preliminaries

Let us first introduce some preliminaries required throughout the paper. While the concepts presented in this work can equally be applied to more complex network architectures, we focus on feed-forward neural networks for simplicity:

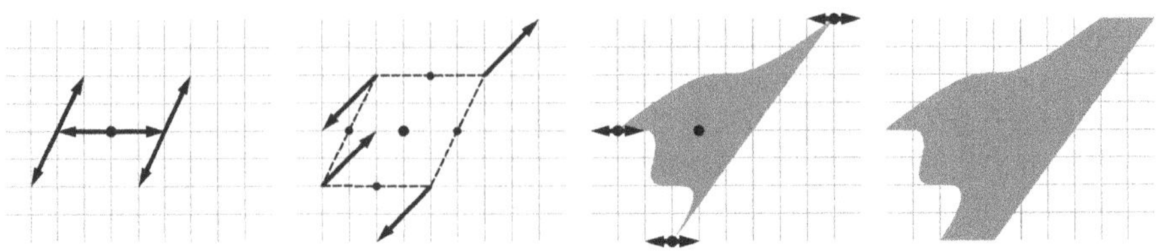

Fig. 2. Step-by-step construction of the polynomial zonotope from Example 1.

Definition 1. *(Feed-forward neural network) A feed-forward neural network with κ hidden layers consists of weight matrices $W_i \in \mathbb{R}^{v_i \times v_{i-1}}$ and bias vectors $b_i \in \mathbb{R}^{v_i}$ with $i \in \{1, \dots, \kappa+1\}$ and v_i denoting the number of neurons in layer i. The output $y \in \mathbb{R}^{v_{\kappa+1}}$ of the neural network for the input $x \in \mathbb{R}^{v_0}$ is*

$$y := y_{\kappa+1} \;\; \text{with} \;\; y_0 = x, \;\; y_{i(j)} = \mu\Bigg(\sum_{k=1}^{v_{i-1}} W_{i(j,k)}\, y_{i-1(k)} + b_{i(j)} \Bigg), \; i = 1, \dots, \kappa+1,$$

where $\mu : \mathbb{R} \to \mathbb{R}$ is the activation function.

In this paper we consider ReLU activations $\mu(x) = \max(0, x)$, sigmoid activations $\mu(x) = \sigma(x) = 1/(1+e^{-x})$, and hyperbolic tangent activations $\mu(x) = \tanh(x) = (e^x - e^{-x})/(e^x + e^{-x})$. Moreover, neural networks often do not apply activation functions on the output neurons, which corresponds to using the identity map $\mu(x) = x$ for the last layer. The image $\mathcal{Y}$ through a neural network is defined as the set of outputs for a given set of inputs $\mathcal{X}_0$, which is according to Def. 1 given as

$$\mathcal{Y} = \Bigg\{ y_{\kappa+1} \;\Bigg|\; y_0 \in \mathcal{X}_0, \; \forall i \in \{1, \dots, \kappa+1\} : \; y_{i(j)} = \mu\Bigg(\sum_{k=1}^{v_{i-1}} W_{i(j,k)}\, y_{i-1(k)} + b_{i(j)} \Bigg) \Bigg\}.$$

We present a novel approach for tightly enclosing the image through a neural network by a polynomial zonotope [2], where we use the sparse representation of polynomial zonotopes [25][1]:

Definition 2. *(Polynomial zonotope) Given a constant offset $c \in \mathbb{R}^n$, a generator matrix of dependent generators $G \in \mathbb{R}^{n \times h}$, a generator matrix of independent generators $G_I \in \mathbb{R}^{n \times q}$, and an exponent matrix $E \in \mathbb{N}_0^{p \times h}$, a polynomial zonotope $\mathcal{PZ} \subset \mathbb{R}^n$ is defined as*

$$\mathcal{PZ} := \Bigg\{ c + \sum_{i=1}^{h} \Bigg(\prod_{k=1}^{p} \alpha_k^{E_{(k,i)}} \Bigg) G_{(\cdot,i)} + \sum_{j=1}^{q} \beta_j G_{I(\cdot,j)} \;\Bigg|\; \alpha_k, \beta_j \in [-1, 1] \Bigg\}.$$

The scalars α_k are called dependent factors since a change in their value affects multiplication with multiple generators. Analogously, the scalars β_j are called independent factors because they only affect the multiplication with one generator. For a concise notation we use the shorthand $\mathcal{PZ} = \langle c, G, G_I, E \rangle_{PZ}$.

[1] In contrast to [25, Def. 1], we explicitly do not integrate the constant offset c in G. Moreover, we omit the identifier vector used in [25] for simplicity.

Let us demonstrate polynomial zonotopes by an example:

Example 1. The polynomial zonotope

$$\mathcal{PZ} = \left\langle \begin{bmatrix} 4 \\ 4 \end{bmatrix}, \begin{bmatrix} 2 & 1 & 2 \\ 0 & 2 & 2 \end{bmatrix}, \begin{bmatrix} 1 \\ 0 \end{bmatrix}, \begin{bmatrix} 1 & 0 & 3 \\ 0 & 1 & 1 \end{bmatrix} \right\rangle_{PZ}$$

defines the set

$$\mathcal{PZ} = \left\{ \begin{bmatrix} 4 \\ 4 \end{bmatrix} + \begin{bmatrix} 2 \\ 0 \end{bmatrix} \alpha_1 + \begin{bmatrix} 1 \\ 2 \end{bmatrix} \alpha_2 + \begin{bmatrix} 2 \\ 2 \end{bmatrix} \alpha_1^3 \alpha_2 + \begin{bmatrix} 1 \\ 0 \end{bmatrix} \beta_1 \;\middle|\; \alpha_1, \alpha_2, \beta_1 \in [-1, 1] \right\}.$$

The construction of this polynomial zonotope is visualized in Fig. 2.

3 Image Enclosure

We now present our novel approach for computing tight non-convex enclosures of images through neural networks. The general concept is to approximate the input-output relation of each neuron by a polynomial function, the image through which can be computed exactly since polynomial zonotopes are closed under polynomial maps. For simplicity, we focus on quadratic approximations here, but the extension to polynomials of higher degree is straightforward.

The overall procedure for computing the image is summarized in Algorithm 1, where the computation proceeds layer by layer. For each neuron in the current layer i we first calculate the corresponding input set in Line 5. Next, in Line 6, we compute a lower and an upper bound for the input to the neuron. Using these bounds we then calculate a quadratic approximation for the neuron's input-output relation in Line 7. This approximation is evaluated in a set-based manner in Line 8. The resulting polynomial zonotope $\langle c_q, G_q, G_{I,q}, E_q \rangle_{PZ}$ forms the j-th dimension of the set $\mathcal{PZ}$ representing the output of the whole layer (see Line 9 and Line 12). To obtain a formally correct enclosure, we have to account for the error made by the approximation. We therefore compute the difference between the activation function and the quadratic approximation in Line 10 and add the result to the output set in Line 12. By repeating this procedure for all layers, we finally obtain a tight enclosure of the image through the neural network. A demonstrating example for Algorithm 1 is shown in Fig. 3.

For ReLU activations the quadratic approximation only needs to be calculated if $l < 0 \wedge u > 0$ since we can use the exact input-output relations $g(x) = x$ and $g(x) = 0$ if $l \geq 0$ or $u \leq 0$ holds. Due to the evaluation of the quadratic map defined by $g(x)$, the representation size of the polynomial zonotope $\mathcal{PZ}$ increases in each layer. For deep neural networks it is therefore advisable to repeatedly reduce the representation size after each layer using order reduction [25, Prop. 16]. Moreover, one can also apply the `compact` operation described in [25, Prop. 2] after each layer to remove potential redundancies from $\mathcal{PZ}$. Next, we explain the approximation of the input-output relation as well as the computation of the approximation error in detail.

Algorithm 1. Enclosure of the image through a neural network

Require: Neural network with weight matrices W_i and bias vectors b_i, initial set $\mathcal{X}_0$.
Ensure: Tight enclosure $\mathcal{PZ} \supseteq \mathcal{Y}$ of the image $\mathcal{Y}$.

1: $\mathcal{PZ} \leftarrow \mathcal{X}_0$
2: **for** $i \leftarrow 1$ to $\kappa + 1$ **do** (loop over all layers)
3: $\quad c \leftarrow \mathbf{0},\ G \leftarrow \mathbf{0},\ G_I \leftarrow \mathbf{0},\ \underline{d} \leftarrow \mathbf{0},\ \overline{d} \leftarrow \mathbf{0}$
4: $\quad$ **for** $j \leftarrow 1$ to v_i **do** (loop over all neurons in the layer)
5: $\quad\quad \mathcal{PZ}_j \leftarrow W_{i(j,\cdot)} \mathcal{PZ} \oplus b_{i(j)}$ (map with weight matrix and bias using (5))
6: $\quad\quad l, u \leftarrow$ lower and upper bound for $\mathcal{PZ}_j$ according to Prop. 1
7: $\quad\quad g(x) = a_1\, x^2 + a_2\, x + a_3 \leftarrow$ quad. approx. on $[l, u]$ according to Sect. 3.1
8: $\quad\quad \langle c_q, G_q, G_{I,q}, E_q \rangle_{PZ} \leftarrow$ image of $\mathcal{PZ}_j$ through $g(x)$ according to Prop. 2
9: $\quad\quad c_{(j)} \leftarrow c_q,\ G_{(j,\cdot)} \leftarrow G_q,\ G_{I(j,\cdot)} \leftarrow G_{I,q},\ E \leftarrow E_q$ (add to output set)
10: $\quad\quad \underline{d}_{(j)}, \overline{d}_{(j)} \leftarrow$ difference between $g(x)$ and activation function acc. to Sect. 3.2
11: $\quad$ **end for**
12: $\quad \mathcal{PZ} \leftarrow \langle c, G, G_I, E \rangle_{PZ} \oplus [\underline{d}, \overline{d}]$ (add approximation error using (6))
13: **end for**

3.1 Activation Function Approximation

The centerpiece of our algorithm for computing the image of a neural network is the approximation of the input-output relation defined by the activation function $\mu(x)$ with a quadratic expression $g(x) = a_1\, x^2 + a_2\, x + a_3$ (see Line 7 of Algorithm 1). In this section we present multiple possibilities to obtain good approximations.

Polynomial Regression

For polynomial regression we uniformly select N samples x_i from the interval $[l, u]$ and then determine the polynomial coefficients a_1, a_2, a_3 by minimizing the average squared distance between the activation function and the quadratic approximation:

$$\min_{a_1, a_2, a_3} \frac{1}{N} \sum_{i=1}^{N} \left(\mu(x_i) - a_1\, x_i^2 - a_2\, x_i - a_3 \right)^2. \tag{1}$$

It is well known that the optimal solution to (1) is

$$\begin{bmatrix} a_1 \\ a_2 \\ a_3 \end{bmatrix} = A^{\dagger} b \ \text{ with } \ A = \begin{bmatrix} x_1^2 & x_1 & 1 \\ \vdots & \vdots & \vdots \\ x_N^2 & x_N & 1 \end{bmatrix}, \quad b = \begin{bmatrix} \mu(x_1) \\ \vdots \\ \mu(x_N) \end{bmatrix},$$

where $A^{\dagger} = (A^T A)^{-1} A^T$ is the Moore-Penrose inverse of matrix A. For the numerical experiments in this paper we use $N = 10$ samples.

Closed-Form Expression

For ReLU activations a closed-form expression for a quadratic approximation can be obtained by enforcing the conditions $g(l) = 0$, $g'(l) = 0$, and $g(u) = u$. The solution to the corresponding equation system $a_1\, l^2 + a_2\, l + a_3 = 0$, $2a_1 l + a_2 = 0$, $a_1\, u^2 + a_2\, u + a_3 = u$ is

$$a_1 = \frac{u}{(u-l)^2}, \quad a_2 = \frac{-2lu}{(u-l)^2}, \quad a_3 = \frac{u^2(2l-u)}{(u-l)^2} + u,$$

which results in the enclosure visualized in Fig. 1. This closed-form expression is very precise if the interval $[l, u]$ is close to being symmetric with respect to the origin ($|l| \approx |u|$), but becomes less accurate if one bound is significantly larger than the other ($|u| \gg |l|$ or $|l| \gg |u|$).

Taylor Series Expansion

For sigmoid and hyperbolic tangent activation functions a quadratic fit can be obtained using a second-order Taylor series expansion of the activation function $\mu(x)$ at the expansion point $x^* = 0.5(l + u)$:

$$\begin{aligned}&\mu(x) \approx \mu(x^*) + \mu'(x^*)(x - x^*) + 0.5\,\mu''(x^*)(x - x^*)^2 = \\ &\underbrace{0.5\,\mu''(x^*)}_{a_1}\,x^2 + \big(\underbrace{\mu'(x^*) - \mu''(x^*)\,x^*}_{a_2}\big)x + \underbrace{\mu(x^*) - \mu'(x^*)x^* + 0.5\,\mu''(x^*)\,x^{*2}}_{a_3},\end{aligned}$$

where the derivatives for sigmoid activations are $\mu'(x) = \sigma(x)(1 - \sigma(x))$ and $\mu''(x) = \sigma(x)(1 - \sigma(x))(1 - 2\sigma(x))$, and the derivatives for hyperbolic tangent activations are $\mu'(x) = 1 - \tanh(x)^2$ and $\mu''(x) = -2\tanh(x)(1 - \tanh(x)^2)$. The Taylor series expansion method is identical to the concept used in [21].

Linear Approximation

Since a linear function represents a special case of a quadratic function, Algorithm 1 can also be used in combination with linear approximations. Such approximations are provided by the zonotope abstraction in [34]. Since closed-form expressions for the bounds $\underline{d}$ and $\overline{d}$ of the approximation error are already specified in [34], we can omit the error bound computation described in Sect. 3.2 in this case. For ReLU activations we obtain according to [34, Theorem 3.1]

$$a_1 = 0, \quad a_2 = \frac{u}{u-l}, \quad a_3 = \frac{-u\,l}{2(u-l)}, \quad \underline{d} = \frac{-u\,l}{2(u-l)}, \quad \overline{d} = \frac{u\,l}{2(u-l)},$$

which results in the zonotope enclosure visualized in Fig. 1. For sigmoid and hyperbolic tangent activations we obtain according to [34, Theorem 3.2]

$$\begin{aligned}&a_1 = 0, \quad a_2 = \min(\mu'(l), \mu'(u)), \quad a_3 = 0.5(\mu(u) + \mu(l) - a_2(u + l)), \\ &\underline{d} = 0.5(\mu(u) - \mu(l) - a_2(u - l)), \quad \overline{d} = -0.5(\mu(u) - \mu(l) - a_2(u - l)),\end{aligned}$$

where the derivatives of the sigmoid function and the hyperbolic tangent are specified in the paragraph above.

We observed from experiments that for ReLU activations the closed-form expression usually results in a tighter enclosure of the image than polynomial regression. For sigmoid and hyperbolic tangent activations, on the other hand,

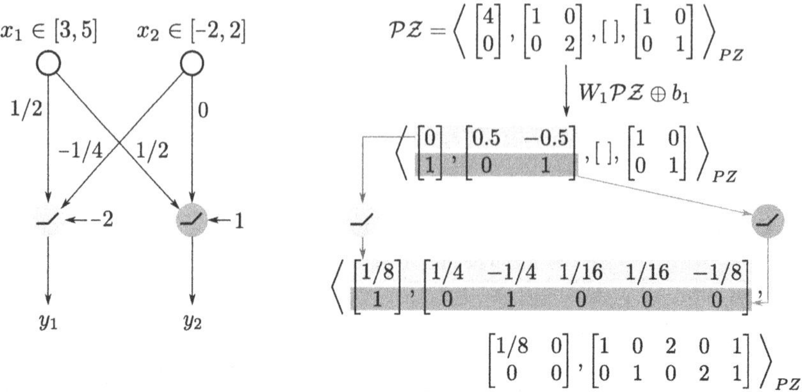

Fig. 3. Exemplary neural network with ReLU activations (left) and the corresponding image enclosure computed with polynomial zonotopes (right), where we use the approximation $g(x) = 0.25\,x^2 + 0.5\,x + 0.25$ for the red neuron and the approximation $g(x) = x$ for the blue neuron. (Color figure online)

polynomial regression usually performs better than the Taylor series expansion. It is also possible to combine multiple of the methods described above by executing them in parallel and selecting the one that results in the smallest approximation error $[\underline{d}, \overline{d}]$. Since the linear approximation does not increase the number of generators, it represents an alternative to order reduction when dealing with deep neural networks. Here, the development of a method to decide automatically for which layers to use a linear and for which a quadratic approximation is a promising direction for future research.

3.2 Bounding the Approximation Error

To obtain a sound enclosure we need to compute the difference between the activation function $\mu(x)$ and the quadratic approximation $g(x) = a_1\,x^2 + a_2\,x + a_3$ from Sec. 3.1 on the interval $[l, u]$. In particular, this corresponds to determining

$$\underline{d} = \min_{x \in [l,u]} \underbrace{\mu(x) - a_1\,x^2 - a_2\,x - a_3}_{d(x)} \quad \text{and} \quad \overline{d} = \max_{x \in [l,u]} \underbrace{\mu(x) - a_1\,x^2 - a_2\,x - a_3}_{d(x)}.$$

Depending on the type of activation function, we use different methods for this.

Rectified Linear Unit (ReLU)

For ReLU activation functions we split the interval $[l, u]$ into the two intervals $[l, 0]$ and $[0, u]$ on which the activation function is constant and linear, respectively. On the interval $[l, 0]$ we have $d(x) = -a_1\,x^2 - a_2\,x - a_3$, and on the interval $[0, u]$ we have $d(x) = -a_1\,x^2 + (1 - a_2)\,x - a_3$. In both cases $d(x)$ is a quadratic function whose maximum and minimum values are either located on the interval boundary or at the point x^* where the derivative of $d(x)$ is equal to zero. The lower bound on $[l, 0]$ is therefore given as $\underline{d} = \min(d(l), d(x^*), d(0))$ if $x^* \in [l, 0]$ and $\underline{d} = \min(d(l), d(0))$ if $x^* \notin [l, 0]$, where $x^* = -0.5\, a_2/a_1$. The upper bound as well as the bounds for $[0, u]$ are computed in a similar manner. Finally, the overall bounds are obtained by taking the minimum and maximum of the bounds for the intervals $[l, 0]$ and $[0, u]$.

Sigmoid and Hyperbolic Tangent

Here our high-level idea is to sample the function $d(x)$ at points x_i with distance Δx distributed uniformly over the interval $[l, u]$. From rough bounds for the derivative $d'(x)$ we can then deduce how much the function value between two sample points changes at most, which yields tight bounds $\overline{d}_b \geq \overline{d}$ and $\underline{d}_b \leq \underline{d}$. In particular, we want to choose the sampling rate Δx such that the bounds $\overline{d}_b, \underline{d}_b$ comply to a user-defined precision $\delta > 0$:

$$\overline{d} + \delta \geq \overline{d}_b \geq \overline{d} \quad \text{and} \quad \underline{d} - \delta \leq \underline{d}_b \leq \underline{d}. \tag{2}$$

We observe that for both, sigmoid and hyperbolic tangent, the derivative is globally bounded by $\mu'(x) \in [0, \overline{\mu}]$, where $\overline{\mu} = 0.25$ for the sigmoid and $\overline{\mu} = 1$ for the hyperbolic tangent. In addition, it holds that the derivative of the quadratic approximation $g(x) = a_1\, x^2 + a_2\, x + a_3$ is bounded by $g'(x) \in [\underline{g}, \overline{g}]$ on the interval $[l, u]$, where $\underline{g} = \min(2a_1 l + a_2, 2a_1 u + a_2)$ and $\overline{g} = \max(2a_1 l + a_2, 2a_1 u + a_2)$. As a consequence, the derivative of the difference $d(x) = \mu(x) - g(x)$ is bounded by $d'(x) \in [-\overline{g}, \overline{\mu} - \underline{g}]$. The value of $d(x)$ can therefore at most change by $\pm \Delta d$ between two samples x_i and x_{i+1}, where $\Delta d = \Delta x \max(|-\overline{g}|, |\overline{\mu} - \underline{g}|)$. To satisfy (2) we require $\Delta d \leq \delta$, so that we have to choose the sampling rate as $\Delta x \leq \delta / \max(|-\overline{g}|, |\overline{\mu} - \underline{g}|)$. Finally, the bounds are computed by taking the maximum and minimum of all samples: $\overline{d}_b = \max_i d(x_i) + \delta$ and $\underline{d}_b = \min_i d(x_i) - \delta$. For our experiments we use a precision of $\delta = 0.001$.

4 Neural Network Controlled Systems

Reachable sets for neural network controlled systems can be computed efficiently by combining our novel image enclosure approach for neural networks with a reachability algorithm for nonlinear systems. We consider general nonlinear systems

$$\dot{x}(t) = f\big(x(t), u_c(x(t), t), w(t)\big), \tag{3}$$

where $x \in \mathbb{R}^n$ is the system state, $u_c : \mathbb{R}^n \times \mathbb{R} \to \mathbb{R}^m$ is a control law, $w(t) \in \mathcal{W} \subset \mathbb{R}^r$ is a vector of uncertain disturbances, and $f : \mathbb{R}^n \times \mathbb{R}^m \times \mathbb{R}^r \to \mathbb{R}^n$ is a Lipschitz continuous function. For neural network controlled systems the control law $u_c(x(t), t)$ is given by a neural network. Since neural network controllers are usually realized as digital controllers, we consider the sampled-data case where the control input is only updated at discrete times $t_0, t_0 + \Delta t, t_0 + 2\Delta t, \dots, t_F$ and kept constant in between. Here, t_0 is the initial time, t_F is the final time, and Δt is the sampling rate. Without loss of generality, we assume from now on that $t_0 = 0$ and t_F is a multiple of Δt. The reachable set is defined as follows:

Algorithm 2. Reachable set for a neural network controlled system

Require: Nonlinear system $\dot{x}(t) = f(x(t), u_c(x(t),t), w(t))$, neural network controller $u_c(x(t),t)$, initial set $\mathcal{X}_0$, disturbance set $\mathcal{W}$, final time t_F, sampling rate Δt.
Ensure: Tight enclosure $\mathcal{R} \supseteq \mathcal{R}([0,t_F])$ of the reachable set $\mathcal{R}([0,t_F])$.

1: $t_0 \leftarrow 0$, $\mathcal{R}(t_0) \leftarrow \mathcal{X}_0$
2: **for** $i \leftarrow 0$ to $t_F/\Delta t - 1$ **do** (loop over all control cycles)
3: $\mathcal{Y} \leftarrow$ image of $\mathcal{R}(t_i)$ through the neural network controller using Algorithm 1
4: $\widehat{\mathcal{R}}(t_i) \leftarrow \mathcal{R}(t_i) \times \mathcal{Y}$ (combine reachable set and input set using (7))
5: $t_{i+1} \leftarrow t_i + \Delta t$, $\tau_i \leftarrow [t_i, t_{i+1}]$ (update time)
6: $\widehat{\mathcal{R}}(t_{i+1}), \widehat{\mathcal{R}}(\tau_i) \leftarrow$ reachable set for extended system in (4) starting from $\widehat{\mathcal{R}}(t_i)$
7: $\mathcal{R}(t_{i+1}) \leftarrow [I_n \ \mathbf{0}]\, \widehat{\mathcal{R}}(t_{i+1})$, $\mathcal{R}(\tau_i) \leftarrow [I_n \ \mathbf{0}]\, \widehat{\mathcal{R}}(\tau_i)$ (projection using (5))
8: **end for**
9: $\mathcal{R} \leftarrow \bigcup_{i=0}^{t_F/\Delta t - 1} \mathcal{R}(\tau_i)$ (reachable set for the whole time horizon)

Definition 3. *(Reachable set) Let $\xi(t, x_0, u_c(\cdot), w(\cdot))$ denote the solution to* (3) *for initial state $x_0 = x(0)$, control law $u_c(\cdot)$, and the disturbance trajectory $w(\cdot)$. The reachable set for an initial set $\mathcal{X}_0 \subset \mathbb{R}^n$ and a disturbance set $\mathcal{W} \subset \mathbb{R}^r$ is*

$$\mathcal{R}(t) := \big\{ \xi(t, x_0, u_c(\cdot), w(\cdot)) \;\big|\; x_0 \in \mathcal{X}_0, \forall t^* \in [0,t] : \; w(t^*) \in \mathcal{W} \big\}.$$

Since the exact reachable set cannot be computed for general nonlinear systems, we compute a tight enclosure instead. We exploit that the control input is piecewise constant, so that the reachable set for each control cycle can be computed using the extended system

$$\begin{bmatrix} \dot{x}(t) \\ \dot{u}(t) \end{bmatrix} = \begin{bmatrix} f(x(t), u(t), w(t)) \\ \mathbf{0} \end{bmatrix} \tag{4}$$

together with the initial set $\mathcal{X}_0 \times \mathcal{Y}$, where $\mathcal{Y}$ is the image of $\mathcal{X}_0$ through the neural network controller. The overall algorithm is specified in Algorithm 2. Its high-level concept is to loop over all control cycles, where in each cycle we first compute the image of the current reachable set through the neural network controller in Line 3. Next, the image is combined with the reachable set using the Cartesian product in Line 4. This yields the initial set for the extended system in (4), for which we compute the reachable set $\widehat{\mathcal{R}}(t_{i+1})$ at time t_{i+1} as well as the reachable set $\widehat{\mathcal{R}}(\tau_i)$ for the time interval τ_i in Line 6. While it is possible to use arbitrary reachability algorithms for nonlinear systems, we apply the conservative polynomialization algorithm [2] since it performs especially well in combination with polynomial zonotopes. Finally, in Line 7, we project the reachable set back to the original system dimensions.

5 Operations on Polynomial Zonotopes

Algorithm 1 and Algorithm 2 both require some special operations on polynomial zonotopes, the implementation of which we present now. Given a polynomial zonotope $\mathcal{PZ} = \langle c, G, G_I, E\rangle_{PZ} \subset \mathbb{R}^n$, a matrix $A \in \mathbb{R}^{o\times n}$, a vector $b \in \mathbb{R}^o$, and an interval $\mathcal{I} = [l, u] \subset \mathbb{R}^n$, the affine map and the Minkowski sum with an interval are given as

$$A\,\mathcal{PZ} \oplus b = \langle Ac + b, AG, AG_I, E\rangle_{PZ} \tag{5}$$

$$\mathcal{PZ} \oplus \mathcal{I} = \langle c + 0.5(u + l), G, [G_I \; 0.5\,\mathrm{diag}(u - l)], E\rangle_{PZ}, \tag{6}$$

which follows directly from [25, Prop. 8], [25, Prop. 9], and [1, Prop. 2.1]. For the Cartesian product used in Line 4 of Algorithm 2 we can exploit the special structure of the sets to calculate the Cartesian product of two polynomial zonotopes $\mathcal{PZ}_1 = \langle c_1, G_1, G_{I,1}, E_1\rangle_{PZ} \subset \mathbb{R}^n$ and $\mathcal{PZ}_2 = \langle c_2, [G_2\; \widehat{G}_2], [G_{I,2}\; \widehat{G}_{I,2}], [E_1\; E_2]\rangle_{PZ} \subset \mathbb{R}^o$ as

$$\mathcal{PZ}_1 \times \mathcal{PZ}_2 = \left\langle \begin{bmatrix} c_1 \\ c_2 \end{bmatrix}, \begin{bmatrix} G_1 & \mathbf{0} \\ G_2 & \widehat{G}_2 \end{bmatrix}, \begin{bmatrix} G_{I,1} & \mathbf{0} \\ G_{I,2} & \widehat{G}_{I,2} \end{bmatrix}, [E_1\; E_2] \right\rangle_{PZ}. \tag{7}$$

In contrast to [25, Prop. 11], this implementation of the Cartesian product explicitly preserves dependencies between the two sets, which is possible since both polynomial zonotopes have identical dependent factors. Computing the exact bounds of a polynomial zonotope in Line 6 of Algorithm 1 would be computationally infeasible, especially since this has to be done for each neuron in the network. We therefore compute a tight enclosure of the bounds instead, which can be done very efficiently:

Proposition 1. *(Interval enclosure) Given a polynomial zonotope* $\mathcal{PZ} = \langle c, G, G_I, E\rangle_{PZ} \subset \mathbb{R}^n$*, an enclosing interval can be computed as*

$$\mathcal{I} = [c + g_1 - g_2 - g_3 - g_4, c + g_1 + g_2 + g_3 + g_4] \supseteq \mathcal{PZ}$$

with

$$g_1 = 0.5 \sum_{i\in\mathcal{H}} G_{(\cdot,i)},\; g_2 = 0.5 \sum_{i\in\mathcal{H}} |G_{(\cdot,i)}|,\; g_3 = \sum_{i\in\mathcal{K}} |G_{(\cdot,i)}|,\; g_4 = \sum_{i=1}^{q} |G_{I(\cdot,i)}|$$

$$\mathcal{H} = \left\{ i \;\middle|\; \prod_{j=1}^{p} \big(1 - E_{(j,i)} \bmod 2\big) = 1 \right\},\quad \mathcal{K} = \{1, \dots, h\} \setminus \mathcal{H},$$

where $x \bmod y$*,* $x, y \in \mathbb{N}_0$ *is the modulo operation and* $\setminus$ *denotes the set difference.*

Proof 1. We first enclose the polynomial zonotope by a zonotope $\mathcal{Z} \supseteq \mathcal{PZ}$ according to [25, Prop. 5], and then compute an interval enclosure $\mathcal{I} \supseteq \mathcal{Z}$ of this zonotope according to [1, Prop. 2.2]. □

The core operation for Algorithm 1 is the computation of the image through a quadratic function. While it is possible to obtain the exact image by introducing new dependent factors, we compute a tight enclosure for computational reasons:

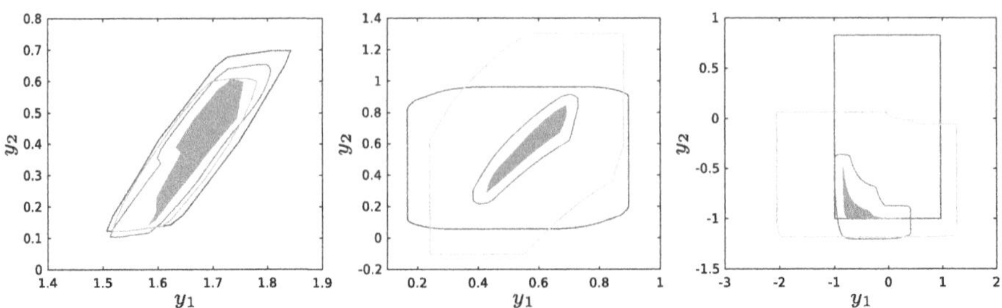

Fig. 4. Image enclosures computed with zonotopes (red), star sets (green), Taylor models (purple), and polynomial zonotopes (blue) for randomly generated neural networks with ReLU activations (left), sigmoid activations (middle), and hyperbolic tangent activations (right). The exact image is shown in gray. (Color figure online)

Proposition 2. *(Image quadratic function) Given a polynomial zonotope $\mathcal{PZ} = \langle c, G, G_I, E \rangle_{PZ} \subset \mathbb{R}$ and a quadratic function $g(x) = a_1 x^2 + a_2 x + a_3$ with $a_1, a_2, a_3, x \in \mathbb{R}$, the image of $\mathcal{PZ}$ through $g(x)$ can be tightly enclosed by*

$$\{g(x) \mid x \in \mathcal{PZ}\} \subseteq \langle c_q, G_q, G_{I,q}, E_q \rangle_{PZ}$$

with

$$\begin{aligned} c_q &= a_1 c^2 + a_2 c + a_3 + 0.5\, a_1 \sum_{i=1}^{q} G_{I(\cdot,i)}^2, \quad G_q = \big[(2a_1 c + a_2) G \;\; a_1 \widehat{G}\big], \\ E_q &= \big[E \;\; \widehat{E}\big], \quad G_{I,q} = \big[(2a_1 c + a_2) G_I \;\; 2a_1 \overline{G} \;\; a_1 \check{G}\big], \end{aligned} \tag{8}$$

where

$$\begin{aligned} &\widehat{G} = \big[G^2 \;\; 2\widehat{G}_1 \;\; \ldots \;\; 2\widehat{G}_{h-1}\big], \quad \widehat{E} = \big[2E \;\; \widehat{E}_1 \;\; \ldots \;\; \widehat{E}_{h-1}\big], \\ &\widehat{G}_i = \big[G_{(i)} G_{(i+1)} \;\; \ldots \;\; G_{(i)} G_{(h)}\big], \quad i = 1, \ldots, h-1, \\ &\widehat{E}_i = \big[E_{(\cdot,i)} + E_{(\cdot,i+1)} \;\; \ldots \;\; E_{(\cdot,i)} + E_{(\cdot,h)}\big], \quad i = 1, \ldots, h-1, \\ &\overline{G} = \big[G_{(1)} G_I \;\; \ldots \;\; G_{(h)} G_I\big], \quad \check{G} = \big[0.5\, G_I^2 \;\; 2\check{G}_1 \;\; \ldots \;\; 2\check{G}_{q-1}\big], \\ &\check{G}_i = \big[G_{I(i)} G_{I(i+1)} \;\; \ldots \;\; G_{I(i)} G_{I(q)}\big], \quad i = 1, \ldots, q-1, \end{aligned} \tag{9}$$

and the squares in G^2 as well as G_I^2 are interpreted elementwise.

Proof 2. The proof is provided in Appendix A.

6 Numerical Examples

We now demonstrate the performance of our approach for image computation, open-loop neural network verification, and reachability analysis of neural network controlled systems. If not stated otherwise, computations are carried out in

MATLAB on a 2.9GHz quad-core i7 processor with 32GB memory. We integrated our implementation into CORA [3] and published a repeatability package[2].

Image Enclosure

First, we demonstrate how our approach captures the non-convexity of the image through a neural network. For visualization purposes we use the deliberately simple example of randomly generated neural networks with two inputs, two outputs, and one hidden layer consisting of 50 neurons. The initial set is $\mathcal{X}_0 = [-1, 1] \times [-1, 1]$. We compare our polynomial-zonotope-based approach with the zonotope abstraction in [34], the star set approach in [40] using the triangle relaxation, and the Taylor model abstraction in [21]. While our approach and the zonotope abstraction are applicable to all types of activation functions, the star set approach is restricted to ReLU activations and the Taylor model abstraction is limited to sigmoid and hyperbolic tangent activations. The resulting image enclosures are visualized in Fig. 4. While using zonotopes or star sets only yields a convex over-approximation, polynomial zonotopes are able to capture the non-convexity of the image and therefore provide a tighter enclosure. While Taylor models also capture the non-convexity of the image to some extent they are less precise than polynomial zonotopes, which can be explained as follows: 1) The zonotopic remainder of polynomial zonotopes prevents the rapid remainder growth observed for Taylor models, and 2) the quadratic approximation obtained with polynomial regression used for polynomial zonotopes is usually more precise than the Taylor series expansion used for Taylor models.

Open-Loop Neural Network Verification

For open-loop neural network verification the task is to verify that the image of the neural network satisfies certain specifications that are typically given by linear inequality constraints. We examine the ACAS Xu benchmark from the 2021 and 2022 VNN competition [4,29] originally proposed in [22, Sec. 5], which features neural networks that provide turn advisories for an aircraft to avoid collisions. All networks consist of 6 hidden layers with 50 ReLU neurons per layer. For a fair comparison we performed the evaluation on the same machine that was used for the VNN competition. To compute the image through the neural networks with polynomial zonotopes, we apply a quadratic approximation obtained by polynomial regression for the first two layers, and a linear approximation in the remaining layers. Moreover, we recursively split the initial set to obtain a complete verifier. The comparison with the other tools that participated in the VNN competition shown in Table 1 demonstrates that for some verification problems polynomial zonotopes are about as fast as the best tool in the competition.

Neural Network Controlled Systems

The main application of our approach is reachability analysis of neural network controlled systems, for which we now compare the performance to other state-of-the-art tools. For a fair comparison we focus on published results for which the

[2] https://codeocean.com/capsule/8237552/tree/v1.

Table 1. Computation times[a] in seconds for different verification tools on a small but representative excerpt of network-specification combinations of the ACAS Xu benchmark. The symbol - indicates that the tool failed to verify the specification.

Net.	Spec.	Cgdtest	CROWN	Debona	ERAN	Marabou	MN-BaB	nnenum	nnv	NV.jl	oval	RPM	venus2	VeriNet	Poly. zono.
1.9	1	0.37	1.37	111	3.91	0.66	48.7	0.41	-	1.44	0.71	-	0.53	0.55	**0.31**
2.3	4	-	0.95	1.78	1.91	0.57	12.2	**0.06**	-	-	0.97	-	0.46	0.17	0.16
3.5	3	0.41	0.37	1.15	1.85	0.61	6.17	**0.05**	-	-	0.58	34.1	0.42	0.25	0.32
4.5	4	-	0.35	0.20	1.82	0.61	5.57	**0.08**	0.24	-	0.48	-	0.42	0.21	0.16
5.6	3	0.38	0.63	2.27	1.82	0.66	6.51	**0.08**	-	-	0.52	40.6	0.48	0.37	0.43

[a] Times taken from https://github.com/stanleybak/vnncomp2021_results and https://github.com/ChristopherBrix/vnncomp2022_results.

Table 2. Computation times[b] in seconds for reachability analysis of neural network controlled systems considering different tools and benchmarks. The dimension, the number of hidden layers, and the number of neurons in each layer is specified in parenthesis for each benchmark, where $a = 100$, $b = 5$ for ReLU activation functions, and $a = 20$, $b = 3$ otherwise. The symbol - indicates that the tool failed to verify the specification.

	ReLU			sigmoid					hyp. tangent				
	Sherlock	JuliaReach	Poly. zono.	Verisig	Verisig 2.0	ReachNN*	POLAR	Poly. zono.	Verisig	Verisig 2.0	ReachNN*	POLAR	Poly. zono.
B1 $(2,2,20)$				-	49	69	23	**2**	-	48	-	25	**8**
B2 $(2,2,20)$				12	8	32	10	**1**	-	-	-	**3**	-
B3 $(2,2,20)$				98	47	130	37	**3**	98	43	128	38	**3**
B4 $(3,2,20)$				24	12	20	4	**1**	23	11	20	4	**1**
B5 $(3,3,100)$				196	1063	31	25	**2**	-	168	-	31	**2**
TORA $(4,3,a)$	30	2040	**13**	136	83	13402		**1**	134	70	2524		**1**
ACC $(6,b,20)$	4	**1**	2						-	1512	-	312	**2**
Unicycle $(3,1,500)$	526	93	**3**										
Airplane $(12,3,100)$	-	29	**7**										
Sin. Pend. $(2,2,25)$	1	1	**1**										

[b] Computation times taken from [33, Table 1] for Sherlock and JuliaReach, from [21, Table 2] for Verisig, Verisig 2.0, and ReachNN*, and from [19, Tab. 1] for POLAR.

authors of the tools tuned the algorithm settings by themselves. In particular, we examine the benchmarks from [33] featuring ReLU neural network controllers, and the benchmarks from [21] containing sigmoid and hyperbolic tangent neural network controllers. The goal for all benchmarks is to verify that the system reaches a goal set or avoids an unsafe region. As the computation times shown in Table 2 demonstrate, our polynomial-zonotope-based approach is for all but two benchmarks significantly faster than all other state-of-the-art tools, mainly since it avoids all major bottlenecks observed for the other tools: The polynomial approximations of the overall network used by Sherlock and ReachNN* are often imprecise, JuliaReach loses dependencies when enclosing Taylor models by zonotopes, Verisig is quite slow since the nonlinear system used to represent the neural network is high-dimensional, and Verisig 2.0 and POLAR suffer from the rapid remainder growth observed for Taylor models.

7 Conclusion

We introduced a novel approach for computing tight non-convex enclosures of images through neural networks with ReLU, sigmoid, and hyperbolic tangent activation functions. Since we represent sets with polynomial zonotopes, all required calculations can be realized using simple matrix operations only, which makes our algorithm very efficient. While our proposed approach can also be applied to open-loop neural network verification, its main application is reachability analysis of neural network controlled systems. There, polynomial zonotopes enable the preservation of dependencies between the reachable set and the set of control inputs, which results in very tight enclosures of the reachable set. As we demonstrated on various numerical examples, our polynomial-zonotope-based approach consequently outperforms all other state-of-the-art methods for reachability analysis of neural network controlled systems.

Acknowledgements. We gratefully acknowledge the financial support from the project justITSELF funded by the European Research Council (ERC) under grant agreement No 817629, from DIREC - Digital Research Centre Denmark, and from the Villum Investigator Grant S4OS. In addition, this material is based upon work supported by the Air Force Office of Scientific Research and the Office of Naval Research under award numbers FA9550-19-1-0288, FA9550-21-1-0121, FA9550-23-1-0066 and N00014-22-1-2156. Any opinions, findings, and conclusions or recommendations expressed in this material are those of the authors and do not necessarily reflect the views of the United States Air Force or the United States Navy.

Appendix A

We now provide the proof for Prop. 2. According to Def. 2, the one-dimensional polynomial zonotope $\mathcal{PZ} = \langle c, G, G_I, E \rangle_{PZ}$ is defined as

$$\begin{aligned}\mathcal{PZ} &= \Big\{ c + \underbrace{\sum_{i=1}^{h} \Big(\prod_{k=1}^{p} \alpha_k^{E_{(k,i)}} \Big) G_{(i)}}_{d(\alpha)} + \underbrace{\sum_{j=1}^{q} \beta_j G_{I(j)}}_{z(\beta)} \;\Big|\; \alpha_k, \beta_j \in [-1,1] \Big\} \\ &= \big\{ c + d(\alpha) + z(\beta) \;\big|\; \alpha, \beta \in [-\mathbf{1}, \mathbf{1}] \big\},\end{aligned} \quad (10)$$

where $\alpha = [\alpha_1 \ \dots \ \alpha_p]^T$ and $\beta = [\beta_1 \ \dots \ \beta_q]^T$. To compute the image through the quadratic function $g(x)$ we require the expressions $d(\alpha)^2$, $d(\alpha)z(\beta)$, and $z(\beta)^2$, which we derive first. For $d(\alpha)^2$ we obtain

$$\begin{aligned} d(\alpha)^2 &= \Big(\sum_{i=1}^{h} \Big(\prod_{k=1}^{p} \alpha_k^{E_{(k,i)}} \Big) G_{(i)} \Big) \Big(\sum_{j=1}^{h} \Big(\prod_{k=1}^{p} \alpha_k^{E_{(k,j)}} \Big) G_{(j)} \Big) \\ &= \sum_{i=1}^{h} \sum_{j=1}^{h} \Big(\prod_{k=1}^{p} \alpha_k^{E_{(k,i)}+E_{(k,j)}} \Big) G_{(i)} G_{(j)} \\ &= \sum_{i=1}^{h} \Big(\prod_{k=1}^{p} \alpha_k^{2E_{(k,i)}} \Big) G_{(i)}^2 + \sum_{i=1}^{h-1} \sum_{j=i+1}^{h} \Big(\prod_{k=1}^{p} \underbrace{\alpha_k^{E_{(k,i)}+E_{(k,j)}}}_{\alpha_k^{\widehat{E}_{i(k,j)}}} \Big) 2 \underbrace{G_{(i)} G_{(j)}}_{\widehat{G}_{i(j)}} \\ &\overset{(9)}{=} \sum_{i=1}^{h(h+1)/2} \Big(\prod_{k=1}^{p} \alpha_k^{\widehat{E}_{(k,i)}} \Big) \widehat{G}_{(i)}, \end{aligned} \tag{11}$$

for $d(\alpha)z(\beta)$ we obtain

$$\begin{aligned} d(\alpha)z(\beta) &= \Big(\sum_{i=1}^{h} \Big(\prod_{k=1}^{p} \alpha_k^{E_{(k,i)}} \Big) G_{(i)} \Big) \Big(\sum_{j=1}^{q} \beta_j G_{I(j)} \Big) \\ &= \sum_{i=1}^{h} \sum_{j=1}^{q} \underbrace{\Big(\beta_j \prod_{k=1}^{p} \alpha_k^{E_{(k,i)}} \Big)}_{\beta_{q+(i-1)h+j}} G_{(i)} G_{I(j)} \overset{(9)}{=} \sum_{i=1}^{hq} \beta_{q+i} \overline{G}_{(i)}, \end{aligned} \tag{12}$$

and for $z(\beta)^2$ we obtain

$$\begin{aligned} z(\beta)^2 &= \Big(\sum_{i=1}^{q} \beta_i G_{I(i)} \Big) \Big(\sum_{j=1}^{q} \beta_j G_{I(j)} \Big) = \sum_{i=1}^{q} \sum_{j=1}^{q} \beta_i \beta_j \, G_{I(i)} G_{I(j)} \\ &= \sum_{i=1}^{q} \beta_i^2 G_{I(i)}^2 + \sum_{i=1}^{q-1} \sum_{j=i+1}^{q} \beta_i \beta_j \, 2 \, G_{I(i)} G_{I(j)} \\ &= 0.5 \sum_{i=1}^{q} G_{I(i)}^2 + \sum_{i=1}^{q} \underbrace{(2\beta_i^2 - 1)}_{\beta_{(h+1)q+i}} 0.5 \, G_{I(i)}^2 + \sum_{i=1}^{q-1} \sum_{j=i+1}^{q} \underbrace{\beta_i \beta_j}_{\beta_{a(i,j)}} \; 2 \; \underbrace{G_{I(i)} G_{I(j)}}_{\check{G}_{i(j)}} \\ &\overset{(9)}{=} 0.5 \sum_{i=1}^{q} G_{I(i)}^2 + \sum_{i=1}^{q(q+1)/2} \beta_{(h+1)q+i} \, \check{G}_{(i)}, \end{aligned} \tag{13}$$

where the function $a(i,j)$ maps indices i, j to a new index:

$$a(i,j) = (h+2)q + j - i + \sum_{k=1}^{i-1} q - k.$$

In (12) and (13), we substituted the expressions $\beta_j \prod_{k=1}^{p} \alpha_k^{E_{(k,i)}}$, $2\beta_i^2 - 1$, and $\beta_i \beta_j$ containing polynomial terms of the independent factors β by new independent factors, which results in an enclosure due to the loss of dependency. The substitution is possible since

$$\beta_j \prod_{k=1}^{p} \alpha_k^{E_{(k,i)}} \in [-1,1], \quad 2\beta_i^2 - 1 \in [-1,1], \quad \text{and} \quad \beta_i \beta_j \in [-1,1].$$

Finally, we obtain for the image

$$\begin{aligned}
&\{g(x) \mid x \in \mathcal{PZ}\} = \{a_1 x^2 + a_2 x + a_3 \mid x \in \mathcal{PZ}\} \\
&\overset{(10)}{=} \{a_1(c + d(\alpha) + z(\beta))^2 + a_2(c + d(\alpha) + z(\beta)) + a_3 \mid \alpha, \beta \in [\mathbf{-1}, \mathbf{1}]\} \\
&= \{a_1 c^2 + a_2 c + a_3 + (2a_1 c + a_2) d(\alpha) + a_1 d(\alpha)^2 \\
&\quad + (2a_1 c + a_2) z(\beta) + 2a_1 d(\alpha) z(\beta) + a_1 z(\beta)^2 \mid \alpha, \beta \in [\mathbf{-1}, \mathbf{1}]\} \\
&\overset{(11),(12),(13)}{\subseteq} \Big\langle a_1 c^2 + a_2 c + a_3 + 0.5\, a_1 \sum_{i=1}^{q} G_I^2, \big[(2a_1 c + a_2) G \;\; a_1 \widehat{G}\big], \\
&\qquad \big[(2a_1 c + a_2) G_I \;\; 2a_1 \overline{G} \;\; a_1 \check{G}\big], \big[E \;\; \widehat{E}\big] \Big\rangle_{PZ} \overset{(8)}{=} \langle c_q, G_q, G_{I,q}, E_q \rangle_{PZ},
\end{aligned}$$

which concludes the proof.

References

1. Althoff, M.: Reachability analysis and its application to the safety assessment of autonomous cars. Ph.D. thesis, Technical University of Munich (2010)
2. Althoff, M.: Reachability analysis of nonlinear systems using conservative polynomialization and non-convex sets. In: Proceedings of the International Conference on Hybrid Systems: Computation and Control, pp. 173–182 (2013)
3. Althoff, M.: An introduction to CORA 2015. In: Proceedings of the International Workshop on Applied Verification for Continuous and Hybrid Systems, pp. 120–151 (2015)
4. Bak, S., Liu, C., Johnson, T.: The second international verification of neural networks competition (VNN-COMP 2021): Summary and results. arXiv:2109.00498 (2021)
5. Beaufays, F., Abdel-Magid, Y., Widrow, B.: Application of neural networks to load-frequency control in power systems. Neural Netw. **7**(1), 183–194 (1994)
6. Bogomolov, S., et al.: JuliaReach: a toolbox for set-based reachability. In: Proceedings of the International Conference on Hybrid Systems: Computation and Control, pp. 39–44 (2019)
7. Bunel, R., et al.: Branch and bound for piecewise linear neural network verification. J. Mach. Learn. Res. **21**(42) (2020)
8. Cheng, C.H., Nührenberg, G., Ruess, H.: Maximum resilience of artificial neural networks. In: Proceedings of the International Symposium on Automated Technology for Verification and Analysis, pp. 251–268 (2017)

9. Christakou, C., Vrettos, S., Stafylopatis, A.: A hybrid movie recommender system based on neural networks. Int. J. Artif. Intell. Tools **16**(5), 771–792 (2007)
10. Clavière, A., et al.: Safety verification of neural network controlled systems. In: Proceedings of the International Conference on Dependable Systems and Networks, pp. 47–54 (2021)
11. David, O.E., Netanyahu, N.S., Wolf, L.: DeepChess: end-to-end deep neural network for automatic learning in chess. In: Proceedings of the International Conference on Artificial Neural Networks, pp. 88–96 (2016)
12. Dutta, S., et al.: Learning and verification of feedback control systems using feedforward neural networks. In: Proceedings of the International Conference on Analysis and Design of Hybrid Systems, pp. 151–156 (2018)
13. Dutta, S., et al.: Sherlock-a tool for verification of neural network feedback systems. In: Proceedings of the International Conference on Hybrid Systems: Computation and Control, pp. 262–263 (2019)
14. Dutta, S., Chen, X., Sankaranarayanan, S.: Reachability analysis for neural feedback systems using regressive polynomial rule inference. In: Proceedings of the International Conference on Hybrid Systems: Computation and Control, pp. 157–168 (2019)
15. Ehlers, R.: Formal verification of piece-wise linear feed-forward neural networks. In: Proceedings of the International Symposium on Automated Technology for Verification and Analysis, pp. 269–286 (2017)
16. Fan, J., Huang, et al.: ReachNN*: a tool for reachability analysis of neural-network controlled systems. In: Proceedings of the International Symposium on Automated Technology for Verification and Analysis, pp. 537–542 (2020)
17. Goubault, E., Putot, S.: RINO: robust inner and outer approximated reachability of neural networks controlled systems. In: Proceedings of the International Conference on Computer Aided Verification, pp. 511–523 (2022)
18. Huang, C., et al.: ReachNN: reachability analysis of neural-network controlled systems. Trans. Embed. Comput. Syst. **18**(5s) (2019)
19. Huang, C., et al.: POLAR: A polynomial arithmetic framework for verifying neural-network controlled systems. In: Proceedings of the International Symposium on Automated Technology for Verification and Analysis, pp. 414–430 (2022)
20. Ivanov, R., et al.: Verisig: verifying safety properties of hybrid systems with neural network controllers. In: Proceedings of the International Conference on Hybrid Systems: Computation and Control, pp. 169–178 (2019)
21. Ivanov, R., et al.: Verisig 2.0: verification of neural network controllers using Taylor model preconditioning. In: Proceedings of the International Conference on Computer Aided Verification, pp. 249–262 (2021)
22. Katz, G., et al.: Reluplex: an efficient SMT solver for verifying deep neural networks. In: Proceedings of the International Conference on Computer Aided Verification, pp. 97–117 (2017)
23. Khan, S., et al.: Facial recognition using convolutional neural networks and implementation on smart glasses. In: Proceedings of the International Conference on Information Science and Communication Technology (2019). Article 19
24. Khedr, H., Ferlez, J., Shoukry, Y.: PEREGRiNN: penalized-relaxation greedy neural network verifier. In: Proceedings of the International Conference on Computer Aided Verification, pp. 287–300 (2021)
25. Kochdumper, N., Althoff, M.: Sparse polynomial zonotopes: a novel set representation for reachability analysis. Trans. Autom. Control **66**(9), 4043–4058 (2021)
26. Makino, K., Berz, M.: Taylor models and other validated functional inclusion methods. Int. J. Pure and Appl. Math. **4**(4), 379–456 (2003)

27. Mukherjee, D., et al.: A survey of robot learning strategies for human-robot collaboration in industrial settings. Robot. Comput.-Integr. Manuf. **73** (2022)
28. Müller, M.N., et al.: PRIMA: precise and general neural network certification via multi-neuron convex relaxations. Proceedings on Programming Languages 1 (2022). Article 43
29. Müller, M.N., et al.: The third international verification of neural networks competition (VNN-COMP 2022): summary and results. arXiv preprint arXiv:2212.10376 (2022)
30. Pulina, L., Tacchella, A.: Challenging SMT solvers to verify neural networks. AI Commun. **25**(2), 117–135 (2012)
31. Raghunathan, A., Steinhardt, J., Liang, P.: Semidefinite relaxations for certifying robustness to adversarial examples. In: Proceedings of the International Conference on Neural Information Processing Systems, pp. 10900–10910 (2018)
32. Riedmiller, M., Montemerlo, M., Dahlkamp, H.: Learning to drive a real car in 20 minutes. In: Proceedings of the International Conference on Frontiers in the Convergence of Bioscience and Information Technologies, pp. 645–650 (2007)
33. Schilling, C., Forets, M., Guadalupe, S.: Verification of neural-network control systems by integrating Taylor models and zonotopes. In: Proceedings of the AAAI Conference on Artificial Intelligence, pp. 8169–8177 (2022)
34. Singh, G., et al.: Fast and effective robustness certification. In: Proceedings of the International Conference on Advances in Neural Information Processing Systems (2018)
35. Singh, G., et al.: An abstract domain for certifying neural networks. Proce. Prog. Lang. **3** (2019). Article 41
36. Singh, G., et al.: Beyond the single neuron convex barrier for neural network certification. In: Proceedings of the International Conference on Advances in Neural Information Processing Systems (2019)
37. Tjeng, V., Xiao, K.Y., Tedrake, R.: Evaluating robustness of neural networks with mixed integer programming. In: Proceedings of the International Conference on Learning Representations (2019)
38. Tran, H.D., et al.: Parallelizable reachability analysis algorithms for feed-forward neural networks. In: Proceedings of the International Conference on Formal Methods in Software Engineering, pp. 51–60 (2019)
39. Tran, H.D., et al.: Safety verification of cyber-physical systems with reinforcement learning control. Trans. Embedded Comput. Syst. 18(5s) (2019). Article 105
40. Tran, H.D., et al.: Star-based reachability analysis of deep neural networks. In: Proceedings of the International Symposium on Formal Methods, pp. 670–686 (2019)
41. Tran, H.D., et al.: NNV: The neural network verification tool for deep neural networks and learning-enabled cyber-physical systems. In: Proc. of the Int. Conf. on Computer Aided Verification. pp. 3–17 (2020)
42. Vincent, J.A., Schwager, M.: reachable polyhedral marching (RPM): a safety verification algorithm for robotic systems with deep neural network components. In: Proceedings of the International Conference on Robotics and Automation, pp. 9029–9035 (2021)
43. Wang, S., et al.: Formal security analysis of neural networks using symbolic intervals. In: Proceedings of the USENIX Security Symposium, pp. 1599–1614 (2018)
44. Wang, S., et al.: Beta-CROWN: efficient bound propagation with per-neuron split constraints for neural network robustness verification. In: Proceedings of the International Conference on Neural Information Processing Systems (2021)

45. Weng, L., et al.: Towards fast computation of certified robustness for ReLU networks. In: Proceedings of the International Conference on Machine Learning, pp. 5276–5285 (2018)
46. Xiang, W., et al.: Reachable set estimation and safety verification for piecewise linear systems with neural network controllers. In: Proceedings of the American Control Conference, pp. 1574–1579 (2018)
47. Xu, K., et al.: Fast and complete: enabling complete neural network verification with rapid and massively parallel incomplete verifiers. In: Proceedings of the International Conference on Learning Representations (2021)
48. Yang, X., et al.: Reachability analysis of deep ReLU neural networks using facet-vertex incidence. In: Proceedings of the International Conference on Hybrid Systems: Computation and Control (2021). Article 18
49. Zhang, H., et al.: Efficient neural network robustness certification with general activation functions. In: Proceedings of the International Conference on Neural Information Processing Systems, pp. 4944–4953 (2018)

Verifying Attention Robustness of Deep Neural Networks Against Semantic Perturbations

Satoshi Munakata[1(✉)], Caterina Urban[2], Haruki Yokoyama[1], Koji Yamamoto[1], and Kazuki Munakata[1]

[1] Fujitsu, Kanagawa, Japan
munakata.satosi@jp.fujitsu.com
[2] Inria & ENS | PSL & CNRS, Paris, France

Abstract. It is known that deep neural networks (DNNs) classify an input image by paying particular attention to certain specific pixels; a graphical representation of the magnitude of attention to each pixel is called a *saliency-map*. Saliency-maps are used to check the validity of the classification decision basis, e.g., it is not a valid basis for classification if a DNN pays more attention to the background rather than the subject of an image. Semantic perturbations can significantly change the saliency-map. In this work, we propose the first verification method for *attention robustness*, i.e., the local robustness of the changes in the saliency-map against combinations of semantic perturbations. Specifically, our method determines the range of the perturbation parameters (e.g., the brightness change) that maintains the difference between the actual saliency-map change and the expected saliency-map change below a given threshold value. Our method is based on activation region traversals, focusing on the outermost robust boundary for scalability on larger DNNs. We empirically evaluate the effectiveness and performance of our method on DNNs trained on popular image classification datasets.

1 Introduction

Classification Robustness. Deep neural networks (DNN) are now dominant solutions in computer vision, notably for image classification [20]. However, quality assurance is essential when DNNs are used in safety-critical systems [2]. From an assurance point of view, one key property that has been extensively studied is the robustness of the classification against input perturbations [16]. In particular, a long line of work has focused on robustness to adversarial input perturbations [35]. However, DNNs have been shown to also be vulnerable to input perturbations likely to naturally occur in practice, such as small brightness changes, translations, rotations, and other spacial transformations [7,8,11,19,40]. In this paper we focus on such *semantic perturbations*. A number of approaches have been proposed to determine the range of perturbation parameters (e.g., the amount of brightness change and translation) that do not change the classification [3,23]. However, we argue that classification robustness is not a sufficient quality assurance criterion in safety-critical scenarios.

K. Y. Rozier and S. Chaudhuri (Eds.): NFM 2023, LNCS 13903, pp. 37–61, 2023.
https://doi.org/10.1007/978-3-031-33170-1_3

Classification Validity. It is known that DNNs classify an input image by paying particular attention to certain specific pixels in the image; a graphical representation of the magnitude of attention to each pixel, like a heatmap, is called *saliency-map* [28,34]. A saliency-map can be obtained from the gradients of DNN outputs with respect to an input image, and it is used to check the validity of the classification decision basis. For instance, if a DNN classifies the subject type by paying attention to a background rather than the subject to be classified in an input image (as in the case of "Husky vs. Wolf [26]"), it is not a valid basis for classification. We believe that such low validity classification should not be accepted in safety-critical situations, even if the classification labels are correct. Semantic perturbations can significantly change the saliency-maps [12,13,24]. However, existing robustness verification methods only target changes in the classification labels and not the saliency-maps.

Our Approach: Verifying Attention Robustness. In this work, we propose the first verification method for *attention robustness*[1], i.e., the local robustness of the changes in the saliency-map against combinations of semantic perturbations. Specifically, our method determines the range of the perturbation parameters (e.g., the brightness change) that maintains the difference between (a) the actual saliency-map change and (b) the expected saliency-map change below a given threshold value. Regarding the latter (b), brightness change keeps the saliency-map unchanged, whereas translation moves one along with the image. Although the concept of such difference is the same as *saliency-map consistency* used in semi-supervised learning [12,13], for the sake of verification, it is necessary to calculate the minimum and maximum values of the difference within each perturbation parameter sub-space. Therefore, we specialize in the gradient-based saliency-maps for the image classification DNNs [28] and focus on the fact that DNN output is linear with respect to DNN input within an activation region [14]. That is, the actual saliency-map calculated from the gradient only is constant within each region; thus, we can compute the range of the difference by sampling a single point within each region if the saliency-map is expected to keep, while by convex optimization if the saliency map is expected to move. Our method is based on traversing activation regions on a DNN with layers for classification and semantic perturbations; it is also possible to traverse (i.e., verify) all activation regions in a small DNN or traverse only activation regions near the outermost robust boundary in a larger DNN. Experimental results demonstrate that our method can show the extent to which DNNs can classify with the same basis regardless of semantic perturbations and report on performance and performance factors of activation region traversals.

Contributions. Our main contributions are:

- We formulate the problem of attention robustness verification; we then propose a method for verifying attention robustness for the first time. Using our

[1] In this paper, the term "attention" refers to the focus of certain specific pixels in the image, and not to the "attention mechanism" used in transformer models [39].

method, it is also possible to traverse and verify all activation regions or only ones near the outermost decision boundary.
- We implement our method in a python tool and evaluate it on DNNs trained with popular datasets; we then show the specific performance and factors of verifying attention robustness. In the context of traversal verification methods, we use the largest DNNs for performance evaluation.

2 Overview

Situation. Suppose a situation where we have to evaluate the weaknesses of a DNN for image classification against combinations of semantic perturbations caused by differences in shooting conditions, such as lighting and subject position. For example, as shown in Fig. 1, the original label of the handwritten text image is *"0"*; however, the DNN often misclassifies it as the other labels, with changes in brightness, patch, and translations. Therefore, we want to know in advance the ranges of semantic perturbation parameters that are likely to cause such misclassification as a weakness of the DNN for each typical image. However, classification robustness is not sufficient for capturing such weaknesses in the following cases.

Case 1. Even if the brightness changes so much that the image is not visible to humans, the classification label of the perturbed image may happen to match the original label. Then vast ranges of the perturbation parameters are evaluated as robust for classification; however, such overestimated ranges are naturally invalid and unsafe. For instance, Fig. 2 shows the changes in MNIST image "8" and the actual saliency-map when the brightness is gradually changed; although the classification seems robust because the labels of each image are the same, the collapsed saliency-maps indicate that the DNN does not pay proper attention to text "8" in each image. Therefore, our approach uses the metric *attention inconsistency*, which quantifies the degree of collapse of a saliency-map, to further evaluate the range of the perturbation parameter as satisfying the property *attention robustness*; i.e., the DNN is paying proper attention as well as the original image. Attention inconsistency is a kind of distance (cf. Fig. 4) between an actual saliency-map (second row) and an expected one (third row); e.g., the saliency-map of *DNN-1* for translation perturbation (column (T)) is expected to follow image translation; however, if it is not, then attention inconsistency is high. In addition, Fig. 2 shows an example of determining that attention robustness is satisfied if each attention inconsistency value (third row) is less than or equal to threshold value δ.

Case 2. The classification label often changes by combining semantic perturbations, such as brightness change and patch, even for the perturbation parameter ranges that each perturbation alone could be robust. It is important to understand what combinations are weak for the DNN; however, it is difficult to verify all combinations as there are many semantic perturbations assumed in an operational environment. In our observations, a perturbation that significantly

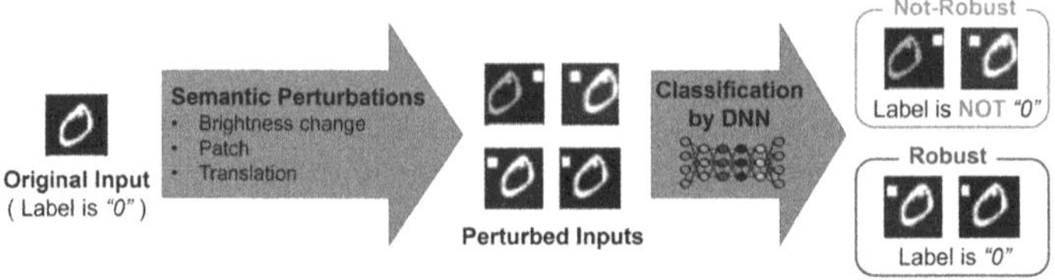

Fig. 1. Misclassifications caused by combinations of semantic perturbations.

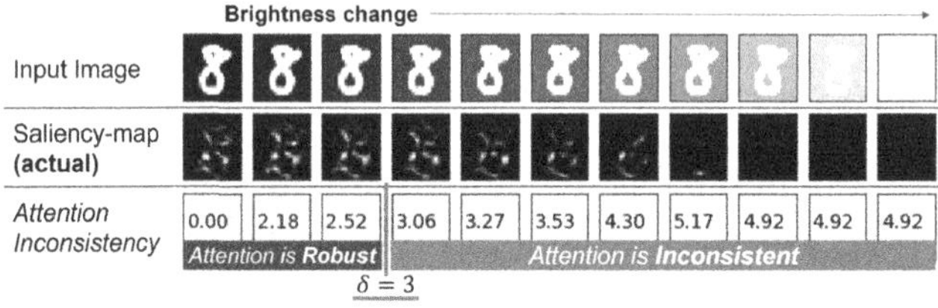

Fig. 2. Perturbation-induced changes in images (first row), saliency-maps (second row) and the metric quantified the degree of collapse of each saliency-map (third row); where δ denotes the threshold to judge a saliency-map is valid or not.

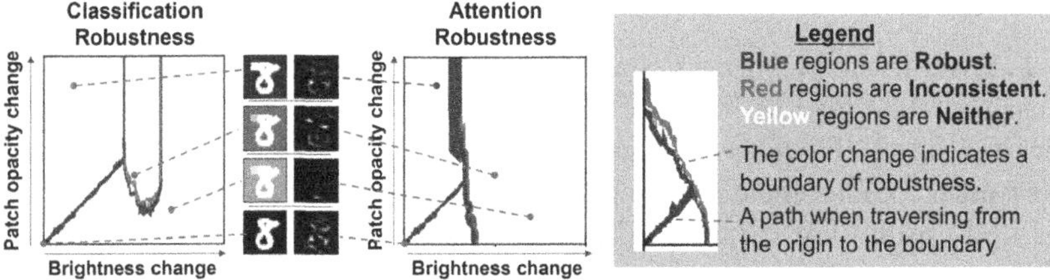

Fig. 3. The outermost boundaries of classification robustness (left) and attention robustness (right); the origin at the bottom-left corresponds to the input image without perturbation, and each plotted point denotes the perturbed input image (middle). The shapes of the boundaries indicate the existence of regions that the DNN successfully classifies without sufficient evidence.

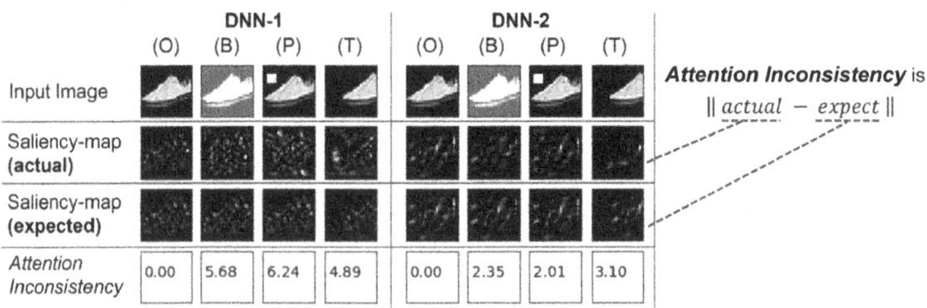

Fig. 4. Differences in changes in saliency-maps for two DNNs. Each saliency-map of DNN-1 above is more collapsed than DNN-2's: where columns (O), (B), (P), and (T) denote original (i.e., without perturbations), brightness change, patch, and translation, respectively.

collapses the saliency-map is more likely to cause misclassification when combined with another perturbation because another perturbation can change the intensity of pixels to which the DNN should not pay attention. Therefore, to understand the weakness of combining perturbations, our approach visualizes the *outermost boundary* at which the sufficiency of robustness switches on the perturbation parameter space. For instance, Fig. 3 shows connected regions that contain the outermost boundary for classification robustness (left side) or attention robustness (right side). The classification boundary indicates that the DNN can misclassify the image with a thin patch and middle brightness. In contrast, the attention boundary further indicates that the brightness change can collapse the saliency-map more than patching, so we can see that any combinations with the brightness change pose a greater risk. Even when the same perturbations are given, the values of attention inconsistency for different DNNs are usually different (cf. Fig. 4); thus, it is better to evaluate what semantic perturbation poses a greater risk for each DNN.

3 Problem Formulation

Our method targets feed-forward ReLU-activated neural networks (ReLU-FNNs) for image classification. A ReLU-FNN *image classifier* is a function $f\colon X \to Y$ mapping an N^f-dimensional (pixels $\times$ color-depth) image $x \in X \subseteq \mathbb{R}^{N^f}$ to a classification label $argmax_{j \in Y} f_j(x)$ in the K^f-class label space $Y = \{1, \ldots, K^f\}$, where $f_j : X \to \mathbb{R}$ is the confidence function for the j-th class. ReLU-FNNs include fully-connected neural networks and convolutional neural networks (CNNs).

The ReLU activation function occurs in between the linear maps performed by the ReLU-FNN layers and applies the function $max(0, x_{l,n})$ to each neuron $x_{l,n}$ in a layer $l \in L^f$ (where L^f is the number of layers of ReLU-FNN f). When $x_{l,n} > 0$, we say that $x_{l,n}$ is *active*; otherwise, we say that $x_{l,n}$ is *inactive*. We write $ap^f(x)$ for the *activation pattern* of an image x given as input to a ReLU-FNN f, i.e., the sequence of neuron activation statuses in f when x is taken as input. We write AP^f for the entire set of activation patterns of a ReLU-FNN f.

Given an activation pattern $p \in AP^f$, we write $ar^f(p)$ for the corresponding *activation region*, i.e., the subset of the input space containing all images that share the same activation pattern: $x \in ar^f(p) \Leftrightarrow ap^f(x) = p$. Note that, neuron activation statuses in an activation pattern p yield half-space constraints in the input space [14,18]. Thus, an activation region $ar^f(p)$ can equivalently be represented as a convex polytope described by the conjunction of the half-space constraints resulting from the activation pattern p.

Classification Robustness. A *semantic perturbation* is a function $g : \Theta \times X \to X$ applying a perturbation with N^g parameters $\theta \in \Theta \subseteq \mathbb{R}^{N^g}$ to an image $x \in X$ to yield a perturbed image $g(\theta, x) \stackrel{\text{def}}{=} g_{N^g}(\theta_{N^g}, \cdot) \circ \cdots \circ g_1(\theta_1, x) = g_{N^g}(\theta_{N^g}, \ldots g_1(\theta_1, x), \ldots) \in X$, where $g_i : \mathbb{R} \times X \to X$ performs the i-th atomic semantic perturbation with parameter θ_i (with $g_i(0, x) = x$ for any image $x \in X$). For instance, a brightness decrease perturbation g_b is a(n atomic) semantic perturbation function with a single brightness adjustment parameter $\beta \geq 0$: $g_b(\beta, x) \stackrel{\text{def}}{=} ReLU(x - \mathbf{1}\beta)$.

Definition 1 (Classification Robustness). *A perturbation region $\eta \subset \Theta$ satisfies* classification robustness*—written $CR(x;\eta)$—if and only if the classification label $f(g(\theta, x))$ is the same as $f(x)$ when the perturbation parameter θ is within η: $CR(x;\eta) \stackrel{\text{def}}{=} \forall\theta \in \eta.\ f(x) = f(g(\theta, x))$.*

Vice versa, we define *misclassification robustness* when $f(g(\theta, x))$ is always different from $f(x)$ when θ is within η: $MR(x;\eta) \stackrel{\text{def}}{=} \forall\theta \in \eta.\ f(x) \neq f(g(\theta, x))$.

The *classification robustness verification problem* $Prob^{CR} \stackrel{\text{def}}{=} (f, g, x0, \Theta)$ consists in enumerating, for a given input image $x0$, the perturbation parameter regions $\eta^{CR}, \eta^{MR} \subset \Theta$ respectively satisfying $CR(x0;\eta^{CR})$ and $MR(x0;\eta^{MR})$.

Attention Robustness. We generalize the definition of saliency-map from [28] to that of an *attention-map*, which is a function $map_j : X \to X$ from an image $x \in X$ to the heatmap image $m_j \in X$ plotting the magnitude of the contribution to the j-th class confidence $f_j(x)$ for each pixel of x. Specifically, $map_j(x) \stackrel{\text{def}}{=} filter\left(\frac{\partial f_j(x)}{\partial x_1}, \ldots, \frac{\partial f_j(x)}{\partial x_{Nf}}\right)$, where $filter(\cdot)$ is an arbitrary image processing function (such as normalization and smoothing) and, following [28,36], the magnitude of the contribution of each pixel $x_1, \ldots, x_{N^f}$ is given by the gradient with respect to the j-th class confidence. When $filter(x) \stackrel{\text{def}}{=} |x|$, our definition of map_j matches that of saliency-map in [28]. Note that, within an activation region $ar^f(p)$, f_j is linear [14] and thus the gradient $\frac{\partial f_j(x)}{\partial x_i}$ is a constant value.

We expect attention-maps to change consistently with respect to a semantic image perturbation. For instance, for a brightness change perturbation, we expect the attention-map to remain the same. Instead, for a translation perturbation, we expect the attention-map to be subject to the same translation. In the following, we write $\tilde{g}(\cdot)$ for the attention-map perturbation corresponding to a given semantic perturbation $g(\cdot)$. We define *attention inconsistency* as the difference between the actual and expected attention-map after a semantic perturbation: $ai(x;\theta) \stackrel{\text{def}}{=} \sum_{j \in Y} dist\Big(map_j(g(\theta, x)), \tilde{g}\big(\theta, map_j(x)\big)\Big)$, where $dist\colon X \times X \to \mathbb{R}$ is an arbitrary distance function such as Lp-norm ($||x - x'||_p$). Note that, when $dist(\cdot)$ is L2-norm, our definition of attention inconsistency coincides with the definition of saliency-map consistency given by [12].

Definition 2 (Attention Robustness). *A perturbation region $\eta \subset \Theta$ satisfies* attention robustness*—written $AR(x;\eta,\delta)$—if and only if the attention inconsistency is always less than or equal to δ when the perturbation parameter θ is within η: $AR(x;\eta,\delta) \stackrel{\text{def}}{=} \forall\theta \in \eta.\ ai(x;\theta) \leq \delta$.*

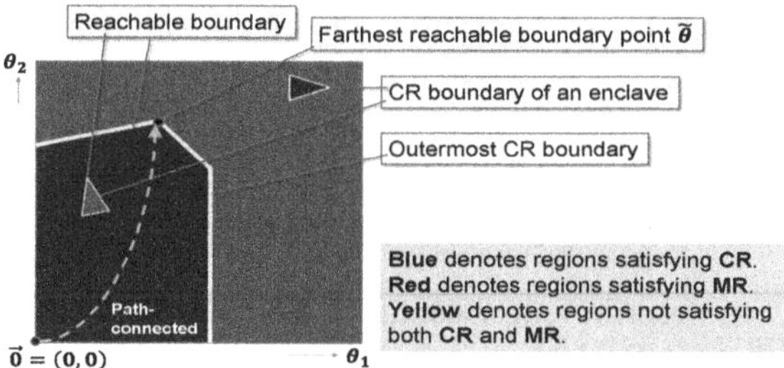

Fig. 5. Illustration of outermost CR boundary on a 2-dimensional perturbation parameter space. The origin **0** is the original image without perturbation.

When the attention inconsistency is always greater than δ, we have *inconsistency robustness*: $IR(x;\eta,\delta) \stackrel{\text{def}}{=} \forall\theta \in \eta.\ ai(x;\theta) > \delta$.

The *attention robustness verification problem* $Prob^{AR} \stackrel{\text{def}}{=} (f, g, x0, \Theta, \delta)$ consists in enumerating, for a given input image $x0$, the perturbation parameter regions $\eta^{AR}, \eta^{IR} \subset \Theta$ respectively satisfying $AR(x0;\eta^{AR},\delta)$ and $IR(x0;\eta^{IR},\delta)$.

Outermost Boundary Verification. In practice, to represent the trend of the weakness of a ReLU-FNN image classifier to a semantic perturbation, we argue that it is not necessary to enumerate all perturbation parameter regions within a perturbation parameter space Θ. Instead, we search the *outermost CR/AR boundary*, that is, the perturbation parameter regions η that lay on the CR/AR boundary farthest away from the original image.

An illustration of the outermost CR boundary is given in Fig. 5. More formally, we define the outermost CR boundary as follows:

Definition 3 (Outermost CR Boundary). *The outermost CR boundary of a classification robustness verification problem, $ob^{CR}(Prob^{CR})$, is a set of perturbation parameter regions $HS \subset \mathcal{P}(\Theta)$ such that:*

1. *for all perturbation regions $\eta \in HS$, there exists a path connected-space from the original image $x0$ (i.e., $\mathbf{0} \in \Theta$) to η that consists of regions satisfying CR (written $Reachable(\eta; x0)$);*
2. *all perturbation regions $\eta \in HS$ lay on the classification boundary, i.e., $\exists\theta,\theta' \in \eta.\ f(g(\theta, x0)) = f(x0) \wedge f(g(\theta', x0)) \neq f(x0)$;*
3. *there exists a region $\eta \in HS$ that contains the farthest reachable perturbation parameter point $\tilde{\theta}$ from the original image, i.e., $\tilde{\theta} = max_{\theta\in\Theta}||\theta||_2$ such that $Reachable(\{\theta\}; x0)$.*

The definition of the outermost AR boundary is analogous. Note that not all perturbation regions inside the outermost CR/AR boundary satisfy the CR/AR property (cf. the enclaves in Fig. 5).

The *outermost CR boundary verification problem* and *outermost AR boundary verification problem* $Prob_{ob}^{CR} = (f, g, x0, \Theta)$ and $Prob_{ob}^{AR} = (f, g, x0, \Theta, \delta)$

consist in enumerating, for a given input image $x0$, the perturbation parameter regions η_{ob}^{CR} and η_{ob}^{AR}) that belong to the outermost CR and AR boundary $ob^{CR}(Prob^{CR})$ and $ob^{AR}(Prob^{AR})$.

4 Geometric Boundary Search (*GBS*)

In the following, we describe our Geometric Boundary Search (*GBS*) method for solving $Prob_{ob}^{CR}$, and $Prob_{ob}^{AR}$ shown in Algorithm 1 and 2. In Appendix H.8, we describe a baseline Breadth-First Search (*BFS*) method for solving $Prob^{CR}$, and $Prob^{AR}$ (enumerating all perturbation parameter regions).

4.1 Encoding Semantic Perturbations

After some variables initialization (cf. Line 1 in Algorithm 1), the semantic perturbation g is encoded into a ReLU-FNN $g^{x0} : \Theta \rightarrow X$ (cf. Line 2).

In this paper, we focus on combinations of atomic perturbations such as brightness change (B), patch placement (P), and translation (T). Nonetheless, our method is applicable to any semantic perturbation as long as it can be represented or approximated with sufficient accuracy.

For the encoding, we follow [23] and represent (combinations of) semantic perturbations as a piecewise linear function by using affine transformations and ReLUs. For instance, a brightness decrease perturbation $g_b(\beta, x0) \stackrel{\text{def}}{=} ReLU(x0-\mathbf{1}\beta)$ (cf. Sect. 3) can be encoded as a ReLU-FNN as follows:

$$g_b(\beta, x0) \xrightarrow{\text{encode}} \begin{bmatrix} 1\,0\dots0 \\ 0\,1\dots0 \\ \dots \\ 0\,0\dots1 \end{bmatrix} ReLU\left(\begin{bmatrix} -1\,1\,0\dots0 \\ -1\,0\,1\dots0 \\ \dots \\ -1\,0\,0\dots1 \end{bmatrix} \begin{bmatrix} \beta \\ x0_1 \\ \dots \\ x0_{Nf} \end{bmatrix}\right) + \mathbf{0}$$

which we can combine with the given ReLU-FNN f to obtain the compound ReLU-FNN $f \circ g_b^{x0}$ to verify. The full encoding for all considered (brightness, patch, translation) perturbations is shown in Appendix H.5.

4.2 Traversing Activation Regions

GBS then performs a traversal of activation regions of the compound ReLU-FNN $f \circ g^{x0}$ near the outermost CR/AR boundary for $Prob_{ob}^{CR}/Prob_{ob}^{AR}$. Specifically, it initializes a queue Q with the activation pattern $ap^{f \circ g^{x0}}(\mathbf{0})$ of the original input image $x0$ with no semantic perturbation, i.e., $\theta = \mathbf{0}$ (cf. Line 3 in Algorithm 1, we explain the other queue initialization parameters shortly). Given a queue element $q \in Q$, the functions $p(q)$, $isFollowing(q)$, and $lineDistance(q)$ respectively return the 1st, 2nd, and 3rd element of q.

Then, for each activation pattern p in Q (cf. Line 6), *GBS* reconstructs the corresponding perturbation parameter region η (subroutine *constructActivationRegion*, Line 7) as the convex polytope resulting from p (cf. Sect. 3 and η in Fig. 6(1a)).

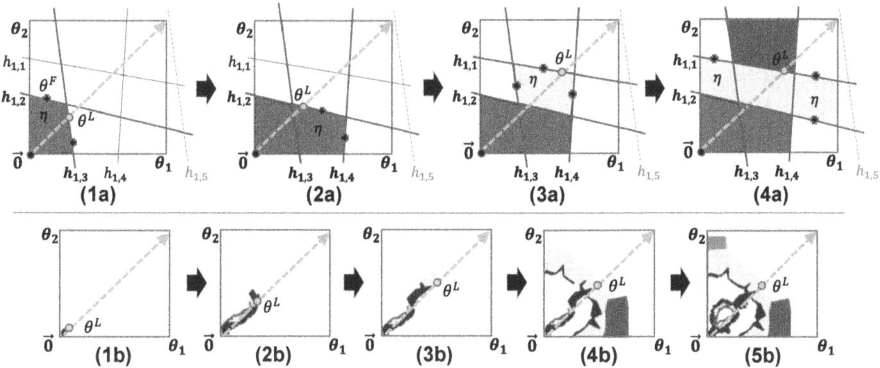

Fig. 6. A running example of *GBS*. The upper row shows the basic traversing flow, while the lower row shows the flow of avoiding enclaves. $h_{l,n}$ denotes a half-space corresponding to neuron activity $p_{l,n}$.

Next, for each neuron $x_{l,n}$ in $f \circ g^{x0}$ (cf. Line 11), it checks whether its activation status cannot flip within the perturbation parameter space Θ, i.e., the resulting half-space would have no feasible points within Θ (subroutine *isStable*, Line 12, cf. half-space $h_{1,5}$ in Fig. 6(1a)). Otherwise, a new activation pattern p' is constructed by flipping the activation status of $x_{l,n}$ (subroutine *flipped*, Line 13) and added to a local queue Q' (cf. Line 9, and 23, 25) if p' has not been observed already (cf. Line 14) and it is feasible (subroutine *calcInteriorPointOnFace*, Lines 15–16, cf. point θ^F and half-space $h_{1,2}$ in Fig. 6(1a)).

The perturbation parameter region η is then simplified to $\tilde{\eta}$ (subroutine *simplified*, Line 2 in Algorithm 2; e.g., reducing the half-spaces used to represent η to just $h_{1,2}$ and $h_{1,3}$ in Fig. 6(1a)). $\tilde{\eta}$ is used to efficiently calculate the range of attention inconsistency within η (subroutine *calcRange*, Line 3 in Algorithm 2, cf. Sect. 4.4), and then attention/inconsistency robustness can be verified based on the range (Line 5 and 8 in Algorithm 2). Furthermore, classification/misclassification robustness can be verified in the same way if subroutine *calcRange* returns the range of confidence $f_{f(x0)}(g^{x0}(\theta)) - f_j(g^{x0}(\theta))$ within $\tilde{\eta}$ (cf. Sect. 4.4) and $\delta = 0 \wedge w^\delta = 0$. At last, the local queue Q' is pushed onto Q (cf. Line 29 in Algorithm 1).

To avoid getting stuck around enclaves inside the outermost CR/AR boundary (cf. Fig. 5) during the traversal of activation regions, *GBS* switches status when needed between "searching for a decision boundary" and "following a found decision boundary". The initial status is set to "searching for a decision boundary", i.e., $\neg isFollowing$ when initializing the queue Q (cf. Line 3). The switch to $isFollowing$ happens when region η is on the boundary (i.e., $lo \leq \delta \leq up$) or near the boundary (i.e., $\delta - w^\delta \leq lo \leq \delta + w^\delta$, cf. Line 15 in Algorithm 2 and Fig. 6(3a,1b,3b)), where w^δ is a hyperparameter to determine whether the region is close to the boundary or not. The hyperparameter w^δ should be greater than 0 to verify attention/inconsistency robustness because attention inconsis-

Algorithm 1. $gbs(f, g, x0, \Theta; \delta, w) \rightarrow (H^{CR}, H^{MR}, H^{CB}, H^{AR}, H^{IR}, H^{AB})$

Input: $f, g, x0, \Theta, \delta$
Output: $H^{CR}, H^{MR}, H^{CB}, H^{AR}, H^{IR}, H^{AB} \subset \mathcal{P}(\Theta)$
1: $H^{CR}, H^{MR}, H^{CB}, H^{AR}, H^{IR}, H^{AB} \leftarrow \{\}, \{\}, \{\}, \{\}, \{\}, \{\}$
2: $g^{x0} \leftarrow g(\cdot, x0)$ *// partially applying $x0$ to g; i.e, $g^{x0}(\theta) = g(\theta, x0)$.*
3: $Q \subset AP^{f \circ g^{x0}} \times \mathbb{B} \times \mathbb{R} \leftarrow \{(ap^{f \circ g^{x0}}(\mathbf{0}), \bot, 0)\}$ *// queue for boundary search.*
4: $OBS \subset AP^{f \circ g^{x0}} \leftarrow \{\}$ *// observed activation patterns.*
5: **while** $\#|Q| > 0$ *// loop for geometrical-boundary search.* **do**
6: $q \leftarrow popMaxLineDistance(Q)$; $p \leftarrow p(q)$; $OBS \leftarrow OBS \cup \{p\}$
7: $\eta \leftarrow constructActivationRegion(f \circ g^{x0}, p)$
8: $FS \subset \mathbb{Z} \times \mathbb{Z} \leftarrow \{\}$ *// (l, n) means the n-th neuron in l-th layer is a face of η*
9: $Q' \subset AP^{f \circ g^{x0}} \times \mathbb{B} \times \mathbb{R} \leftarrow \{\}$ *// local queue for an iteration.*
10: *// Push each activation region connected to η.*
11: **for** $l = 1$ **to** #layers of $f \circ g^{x0}$; $n = 1$ **to** #neurons of the l-th layer **do**
12: continue **if** $isStable(p, l, n, \Theta)$ *// skip if activation of $x_{l,n}$ cannot flip in Θ.*
13: $p' \leftarrow flipped(p, l, n)$ *// flip activation status for neuron $x_{l,n}$.*
14: continue **if** $p' \in OBS$ **else** $OBS \leftarrow OBS \cup \{p'\}$ *// skip if p' was observed.*
15: $\theta^F \leftarrow calcInteriorPointOnFace(\eta, l, n)$
16: continue **if** $\theta^F = null$ *// skip if p' is infeasible.*
17: $FS \leftarrow FS \cup \{(l, n)\}$ *// (l,n) is a face of η.*
18: $\theta^L \leftarrow calcInteriorPointOnLine(\eta, l, n)$
19: **if** $isFollowing(q) \wedge \theta^L \neq null \wedge ||\theta^L||_2 > lineDistance(q)$ **then**
20: $q \leftarrow (p, \bot, lineDistance(q))$ *// Re-found the line in boundary-following.*
21: **end if**
22: **if** $\neg isFollowing(q) \wedge \theta^L \neq null$ **then**
23: $Q' \leftarrow Q' \cup \{(p', \bot, ||\theta^L||_2)\}$ *// continue line-search.*
24: **else**
25: $Q' \leftarrow Q' \cup \{(p', isFollowing(q), lineDistance(q))\}$ *// continue current.*
26: **end if**
27: **end for**
28: ***(... Verify*** η***...)*** *// See Algorithm 2 for AR/IR (analogous for CR/MR)*
29: $Q \leftarrow Q \cup Q'$ *// Push*
30: **end while**

tency changes discretely for ReLU-FNNs (cf. Sect. 4.3). *GBS* can revert back to searching for a decision boundary if, when following a found boundary, it finds a reachable perturbation parameter region that is farther from $\mathbf{0}$ (cf. Lines 19–20 in Algorithm 1 and Fig. 6(2b)).

4.3 Calculating Attention Inconsistency

Gradients within an Activation Region. Let $p \in AP^{f \circ g^{x0}}$ be an activation pattern of the compound ReLU-FNN $f \circ g^{x0}$. The gradient $\frac{\partial f_j(g^{x0}(\theta))}{\partial \theta_s}$ is constant within $ar^{f \circ g^{x0}}(p)$ (cf. Sect. 3). We write $g_i^{x0}(\theta)$ for the i-th pixel x_i of a perturbed image in $\{g^{x0}(\theta) \mid \theta \in ar^{f \circ g^{x0}}(p)\} \subset X$. The gradient $\frac{\partial g_i^{x0}}{\partial \theta} = \frac{\partial x_i}{\partial \theta}$ is also a

Algorithm 2. (Expanding from Algorithm 1 for $AR(x0;\eta,\delta)/IR(x0;\eta,\delta)$)

$(\ldots$ ***Verify*** $\eta\ldots)$
$\tilde{\eta} \leftarrow$ *simplified*(η, FS) // *limit the constraints on* η *to* FS.
$(lo, up) \leftarrow$ *calcRange*$(x0;\tilde{\eta})$ // *the range ([lower and upper) of ai within* $\tilde{\eta}$.
nearBoundary $\leftarrow (lo \leq \delta \leq up) \vee (\delta - w^{\delta} \leq lo \leq \delta + w^{\delta}) \vee (\delta - w^{\delta} \leq up \leq \delta + w^{\delta})$
if $lo \leq up \leq \delta$ /* *satisfying AR* */ **then**
    $H^{AR} \leftarrow H^{AR} \cup \{\tilde{\eta}\}$
    $Q' \leftarrow \{\}$ **if** *isFollowing*$(q) \wedge \neg$*nearBoundary* // *no traversing connected regions.*
else if $\delta < lo \leq up$ /* *satisfying IR* */ **then**
    $H^{IR} \leftarrow H^{IR} \cup \{\tilde{\eta}\}$
    $Q' \leftarrow \{\}$ **if** $\neg$*nearBoundary* // *no traversing connected regions.*
else
    $H^{AB} \leftarrow H^{AB} \cup \{\tilde{\eta}\}$
end if
if $\neg$*isFollowing*$(q) \wedge$ *nearBoundary* **then**
    $(\ldots$***Update*** Q' ***such that*** $\forall q' \in Q.$ *isFollowing*$(q')\ldots)$ // *switch to boundary-following.*
end if

constant value. By the chain rule, we have $\frac{\partial f_j(x)}{\partial x_i} = \frac{\partial f_j(g^{x0}(\theta))/\partial \theta_s}{\partial x_i/\partial \theta_s}$. Thus $\frac{\partial f_j(x)}{\partial x_i}$ is also constant. This fact is formalized by the following lemma:

Lemma 1. $\frac{\partial f_j(x)}{\partial x_i} = C \quad (x \in \{g^{x0}(\theta) \mid \theta \in ar^{f\circ g^{x0}}(p)\})$

(cf. the small example in Appendix H.7). Therefore, the gradient $\frac{\partial f_j(x)}{\partial x_i}$ can be computed as the weights of the j-th class output for ReLU-FNN f about activation pattern $ap^f(\dot{x})$; where, $\dot{x} = g^{x0}(\dot{\theta})$ and $\dot{\theta}$ is an arbitrary sample within $ar^{f\circ g^{x0}}(p)$ (cf. Appendix H.1). For the perturbed gradient $\tilde{g}(\theta, \frac{\partial f_j(x)}{\partial x_i})$, let $\tilde{g}(\theta)$ be the ReLU-FNN $g^{\frac{\partial f_j(x)}{\partial x_i}}(\theta')$. Thus, the same consideration as above applies.

Attention Inconsistency (AI). We assume both $filter(\cdot)$ and $dist(\cdot)$ are convex downward functions for calculating the maximum/minimum value by convex optimization. Specifically, $filter(\cdot)$ is one of the identity function (I), the absolute function (A), and the 3×3 mean filter (M). $dist(\cdot)$ is one of the L_1-norm (L_1) and the L_2-norm (L_2): where, w is the width of image $x \in X$.

4.4 Verifying CR/MR and AR/IR

Our method leverages the fact that the gradient of a ReLU-FNN output with respect to the input is constant within an activation region (cf. Sect. 3); thus, CR/MR can be resolved by linear programming, and AR/IR can be resolved by just only one sampling if the saliency-map is expected to keep or convex optimization if the saliency-map is expected to move.

Verifying CR/MR. When $x0$ is fixed, each activation region of the ReLU-FNN $f(g(\theta, x0)) : \Theta \rightarrow Y$ is a region in the perturbation parameter space Θ.

Table 1. ReLU-FNNs used in our experiments. Networks with name prefix "M-" ("F-") is trained on MNIST (Fashion-MNIST). In column Layers, "FC' denotes fully connected layers while "Conv" denotes convolutional layers.

Name	#Neurons	Layers	Name	#Neurons	Layers
M-FNN-100	100	FC×2	F-FNN-100	100	FC×2
M-FNN-200	200	FC×4	F-FNN-200	200	FC×4
M-FNN-400	400	FC×8	F-FNN-400	400	FC×8
M-FNN-800	800	FC×16	F-FNN-800	800	FC×16
M-CNN-S	2,028	Conv×2,FC×1	F-CNN-S	2,028	Conv×2,FC×1
M-CNN-M	14,824	Conv×2,FC×1	F-CNN-M	14,824	Conv×2,FC×1

Within an activation region $\eta \subset \Theta$ of the ReLU-FNN $f(g(\theta, x0))$, $CR(f, g, x0, \eta)$ is satisfied if and only if the ReLU-FNN output corresponding to the label of the original image $x0$ cannot be less than the ReLU-FNN outputs of all other labels, i.e., $min_{j \in Y \setminus \{f(x0)\}, \theta \in \eta} f_{f(x0)}(x) - f_j(g(\theta, x0)) > 0 \Leftrightarrow CR(f, g, x0, \eta)$ Each DNN output $f_j(g(\theta, x0))$ is linear within η, and thus, the left-hand side of the above equation can be determined *soundly* and *completely* by using an LP solver (Eq. 3(c) in Appendix H.1). Similarly, $MR(f, g, x0, \eta)$ is satisfied if and only if the ReLU-FNN output corresponding to the label of the original image $x0$ cannot be greater than the ReLU-FNN outputs of any other labels.

Verifying AR/IR. Within an activation region $\eta \subset \Theta$ of the ReLU-FNN $f(g(\theta, x0))$, $AR(f, g, x0, \eta, \delta)$ is satisfied if and only if the following equation holds: $max_{\theta \in \eta} ai(\theta, x0) \leq \delta \Leftrightarrow AR(f, g, x0, \eta, \delta)$ If $filter(\cdot)$ and $dist(\cdot)$ are both convex downward functions (CDFs), as the sum of CDFs is also a CDF, the left-hand side of the above equation can be determined by comparing the values at both ends. On the other hand, $IR(f, g, x0, \eta, \delta)$ is satisfied if and only if the following equation holds: $min_{\theta \in \eta} ai(\theta, x0) > \delta \Leftrightarrow IR(f, g, x0, \eta, \delta)$ The left-hand side of the above equation can be determined by using a convex optimizer. Note that if the saliency-map is expected to keep against perturbations, the above optimization is unnecessary because $ai(\theta \in eta, x0)$ is constant.

Thus, it is straightforward to conclude that our GBS method is sound and complete for verifying CR/MR and AR/IR over the explored activation regions:

Theorem 1. *Our GBS method shown in Algorithm 1 and 2 is sound and conditionally complete for solving* $Prob_{ob}^{CR}$, *and* $Prob_{ob}^{AR}$.

- *If the outermost CR/AR boundary truly exists in* Θ *and the boundary bisects* Θ *into two parts, one with the origin* $\mathbf{0}$ *and the other with its diagonal point (cf. Fig. 5), then our GBS method always explores the boundary.*
- *Otherwise, our GBS method does not always find CR/AR boundaries (including enclaves) that should be considered the outermost CR/AR boundary.*

5 Experimental Evaluation

Our *GBS* method is implemented as an open-source Python tool. It is available at https://zenodo.org/record/6544905. We evaluated *GBS* on ReLU-FNNs trained on the MNIST [6] and Fashion-MNIST [41] datasets. Table 1 shows the different sizes and architectures used in our evaluation. During each experiment, we inserted semantic perturbation layers (cf. Sect. 4.1) with a total of 1,568 neurons in front of each ReLU-FNN. All experiments were performed on virtual computational resource "rt_C.small" (with CPU 4 Threads and Memory 30 GiB) of physical compute node "V" (with *2 CPU; Intel Xeon Gold 6148 Processor 2.4 GHz 20 Cores (40 Threads)*, and *12 Memory; 32 GiB DDR4 2666 MHz MHz RDIMM (ECC)*) in the *AI Bridging Cloud Infrastructure (ABCI)* [1].

In our evaluation, we considered three variants of GBS: *gbs-CR*, which searches the CR boundary, *gbs-AR*, which searches the AR boundary, and *gbs-CRAR*, which searches the boundary of the regions satisfying both CR and AR. For *gbs-AR* and *gbs-CRAR* we used the definitions $filter(x) \stackrel{\text{def}}{=} x$, $dist(x, x') \stackrel{\text{def}}{=} ||x - x'||_2$, $\delta \stackrel{\text{def}}{=} 3.0$, and $w^\delta = 0.2$ (for *gbs-CR* we used $\delta = 0$ and $w^\delta = 0$, cf. Sect. 4.2).

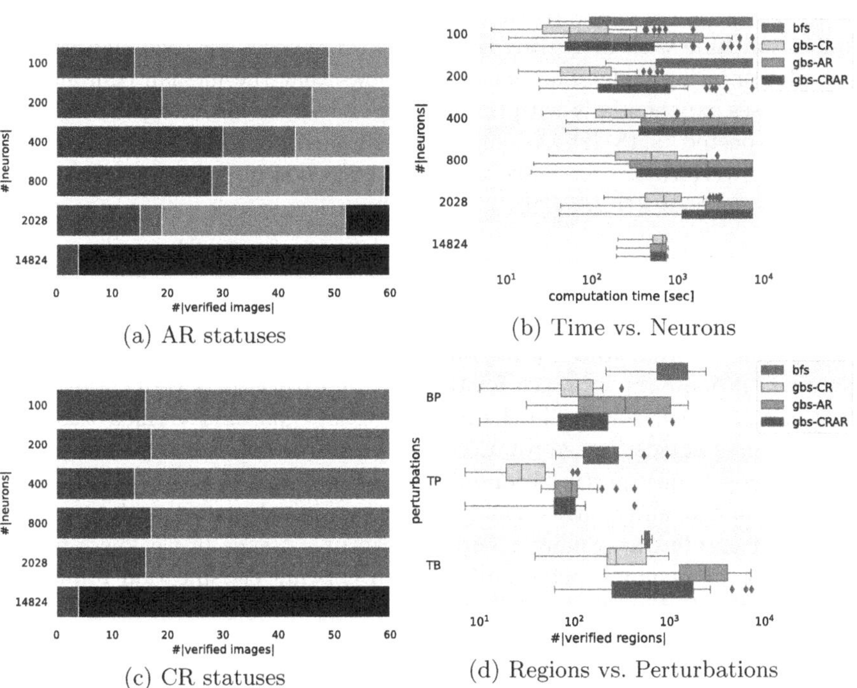

(a) AR statuses

(b) Time vs. Neurons

(c) CR statuses

(d) Regions vs. Perturbations

Fig. 7. Experimental Results. (Color figure online)

Figure 7a and 7b show the breakdown of the verification result for *gbs-AR* and *gbs-CR* over 10 images (not used for training) from each dataset considering three combinations of semantic perturbations (brightness+patch (BP), translation+patch (TP), translation+brightness (TB)). The blue, red, gray, and black bars denote robust (i.e., all explored activation regions were verified to be robust), not-robust (i.e., all activation regions on the outermost CR/AR boundary were explored and at least one of them was found to violate robustness), timed out, and out-of-memory, respectively. We used a time out of two hours for each robustness verification. The figures show that *gbs-AR* timed out at a higher rate for smaller size DNNs than *gbs-CR*. This is due to the fact that *gbs-AR* verified robustness for more images and generally explored more activation regions than *gbs-CR* as also shown in Fig. 7d, which compares the number of verified (explored) activation regions for each combination of perturbations. Looking further into this difference, it turns out that the choice of the hyperparameter $w^\theta = 0.2$ also caused *gbs-AR* to explore the AR boundary more extensively than necessary. It remains for future work to study how to choose a good value for w^θ to narrow this search. Overall, however, Fig. 7d shows that *GBS* (which searches the outermost CR/AR boundary) reduces as intended the number of explored activation regions with respect to the baseline *BFS* (which enumerates all perturbation parameter regions). This, in turn, directly affects the performance of the algorithms as demonstrated in Fig. 7c, which shows the trend of increasing computation time with increasing the number of neurons for each algorithm as a box plot on a log scale. The figure also shows that the median computation time increases exponentially with the number of neurons for all algorithms. This result is expected [9,18,42] and suggests that incorporating abstractions and approximate verification methods [25,30,43] is needed in order to scale to very large DNNs such as *VGG16* [29].

6 Related Work

Robustness Verification. To the best of our knowledge, we are the first to formulate and propose an approach for the attention robustness verification problem (see, e.g., recent surveys in the area [2,16,38]). [30] first verified classification robustness against image rotation, and [3] verified classification robustness against other semantic perturbations such as image translation, scaling, shearing, brightness change, and contrast change. However, in this paper, we have argued that attention robustness more accurately captures trends in weakness for the combinations of semantic perturbations than existing classification robustness in some cases (cf. Sect. 2). In addition, approximate verification methods such as *DeepPoly* [30] fail to verify near the boundary [32] while our GBS method enables verification near the boundary by exploratory and exact verification.

[23] proposed that any Lp-norm-based verification tools can be used to verify the classification robustness against semantic perturbations by inserting special DNN layers that induce semantic perturbations in the front of DNN layers for classification. In order to transform the verification problem on the inherently

high-dimensional input image space X into one on the low-dimensional perturbation parameter space Θ, we adopted their idea, i.e., inserting DNN layers for semantic perturbations ($\Theta \to X$) in front of DNN layers for classification ($X \to Y$). However, it is our original idea to calculate the value range of the gradient for DNN output $(\partial f_j(g(\theta, x_i))/\partial x_i)$ within an activation region on the perturbation parameter space (cf. Sects. 4.3–4.4).

Traversing Activation Regions. Since [18] first proposed the method to traverse activation regions, several improvements and extensions have been proposed [9,21]. All of them use all breadth-first searches with a priority queue to compute the maximum safety radius or the maxima of the given objective function in fewer iterations. In contrast, our algorithm GBS uses a breadth-first search with a priority queue to reach the outermost CR/AR boundary in fewer iterations while avoiding enclaves.

[9] responded to the paper reviewer that traversing time would increase exponentially with the size of a DNN [10]. Our experiment also showed that larger DNNs increase traversing time due to the denser activation regions. The rapid increase in the number of activation regions will be one of the biggest barriers to the scalability of traversing methods, including our method. Although the upper bound theoretical estimation for the number of activation regions increases exponentially with the number of layers in a DNN [14,15] reported that actual DNNs have surprisingly few activation regions because of the myriad of infeasible activation patterns. Therefore, it will need to understand the number of activation regions of DNNs operating in the real world. To improve scalability, there are several methods of targeting only low-dimensional subspaces in the high-dimensional input space for verification [22,31,33]. We have similarly taken advantage of low-dimensionality, e.g., using low-dimensional perturbation parameters to represent high-dimensional input image pixels as mediator variables (i.e., partially applied perturbation function $g^{x0}(\theta) = x'$) to reduce the elapsed time of LP solvers, determining the stability of neuron activity from few vertices of perturbation parameter space Θ. Another possibility to improve scalability is the method of partitioning the input space and verifying each partition in a perfectly parallel fashion [37]. Our implementation has not been fully parallelized yet but it should be relatively straightforward to do as part of our future work.

Saliency-Map. Since [28] first proposed the method to obtain a saliency-map from the gradients of DNN outputs with respect to an input image, many improvements and extensions have been proposed [5,27,34]. We formulated an attention-map primarily using the saliency-map definition by [28]. However, it remains for future work to formulate attention robustness corresponding to improvements, such as gradient-smoothing [5] and line-integrals [34].

It is known that semantic perturbations can significantly change the saliency-maps [12,13,24]. [12] first claimed the saliency-map should consistently follow image translation and proposed the method to quantify saliency-map consistency. We formulated attention inconsistency ac primarily using the saliency-map consistency by [12]. While there have been works on the empirical studies of the attribution robustness [4,17], the verification of it has not been studied.

7 Conclusion and Future Work

We have presented a verification method for attention robustness based on traversing activation regions on the DNN that contains layers for semantic perturbations and layers for classification. Attention robustness is the property that the saliency-map consistency is less than a threshold value. We have provided a few cases that attention robustness more accurately captures trends in weakness for the combinations of semantic perturbations than existing classification robustness. Although the performance evaluation presented in this study is not yet on a practical scale, such as VGG16 [29], we believe that the attention robustness verification problem we have formulated opens a new door to quality assurance for DNNs. We plan to increase the number of semantic perturbation types that can be verified and improve scalability by using abstract interpretation in future work.

H Appendix

H.1 Linearity of Activation Regions

Given activation pattern $p \in AP^f$ as constant, within activation region $ar^f(p)$ each output of ReLU-FNN $f_j(x \in ar^f(p))$ is linear for x (cf. Fig. 8) because all ReLU operators have already resolved to 0 or x [14]. i.e., $f_j(x \in ar^f(p)) = A'_j x + b'_j$: where, A'_j and b'_j denote simplified weights and bias about activation pattern p and class j. That is, the gradient of each ReLU-FNN output $f_j(x)$ within activation region $ar^f(p)$ is constant, i.e., the following equation holds: where $C \in \mathbb{R}$ is a constant value.

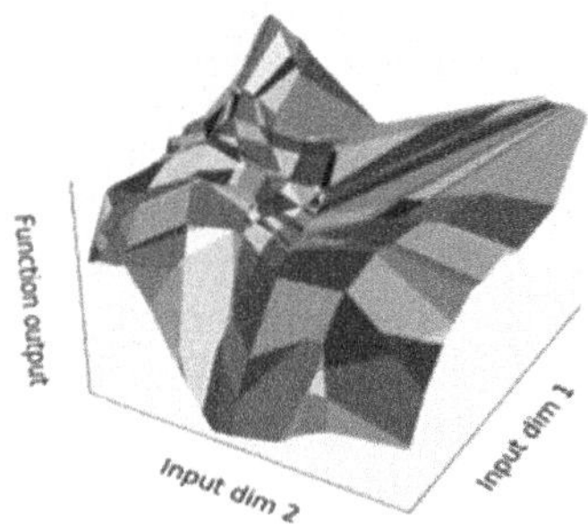

Fig. 8. An example of activation regions [14]. ReLU-FNN output is linear on each activation region, i.e., each output plane painted for each activation region is flat.

$$Feasible^f(p \in AP^f) \Rightarrow \frac{\partial f_j(x)}{\partial x_i} = C \quad (x \in ar^f(p)) \tag{1}$$

An activation region can be interpreted as the H-representation of a convex polytope on input space $\mathbb{R}^{N^f}$. Specifically, neuron activity $p_{l,n}$ and p have a one-to-one correspondence with a half-space and convex polytope defined by the intersection (conjunction) of all half-spaces, because $f_n^{(l)}(x)$ is also linear when $p \in AP^f$ is constant. Therefore, we interpret activation region $ar^f(p)$ and the following H-representation of convex polytope $HConvex^f(x;p)$ each other as needed: where, A'' and b'' denote simplified weights and bias about activation pattern p, and $A''_{l,n}x \leq b''_{l,n}$ is the half-space corresponding to the n-th neuron activity $p_{l,n}$ in the l-th layer.

$$HConvex^f(x;p) \overset{\text{def}}{=} A''x \leq b'' \equiv \bigwedge_{l,n} A''_{l,n}x \leq b''_{l,n} \tag{2}$$

H.2 Connectivity of Activation Regions

When feasible activation patterns $p, p' \in AP^f$ are in a relationship with each other that flips single neuron activity $p_{l,n} \in \{0,1\}$, they are connected regions because they share single face $HFace^f_{l,n}(x;p) \overset{\text{def}}{=} A''_{l,n}x = b''_{l,n}$ corresponding to flipped $p_{l,n}$ [18]. It is possible to flexibly traverse activation regions while ensuring connectivity by selecting a neuron activity to be flipped according to a prioritization; several traversing methods have been proposed [9,18,21]. However, there are generally rather many neuron activities that become infeasible when flipped [18]. For instance, half-spaces $h_{1,3}$ is a face of activation region η in Fig. 6(1a); thus, flipping neuron activity $p_{1,3}$, *GBS* can traverse connected region η in Fig. 6(1b). In contrast, half-space $h_{1,1}$ is not a face of activation region η in Fig. 6(1a); thus, flipping neuron activity $p_{1,1}$, the corresponded activation region is infeasible (i.e., the intersection of flipped half-spaces has no area).

H.3 Hierarchy of Activation Regions

When feasible activation patterns $p, p' \in AP^f$ are in a relationship with each other that matches all of L'^f-th upstream activation pattern $p_{\leq L'^f} \overset{\text{def}}{=} [p_{l,n} \mid 1 \leq l \leq L'^f, 1 \leq n \leq N^f_l]$ $(1 \leq L'^f \leq L^f)$, they are included parent activation region $ar^f_{\leq L'^f}(p)$ corresponding to convex polytope $HConvex^f_{\leq L'^f}(x;p) \overset{\text{def}}{=} \bigwedge_{l \leq L'^f, n} A''_{l,n}x \leq b''_{l,n}$ [21]. That is, $\forall x \in ar^f(p).\ x \in ar^f_{\leq L'^f}(p)$ and $\forall x \in \mathbb{R}^{N^f}.\ HConvex^f(x;p) \Rightarrow HConvex^f_{\leq L'^f}(x;p)$.

Similarly, we define L'^f-th downstream activation pattern as $p_{\geq L'^f} \overset{\text{def}}{=} [p_{l,n} \mid L'^f \leq l \leq L^f, 1 \leq n \leq N^f_l]$ $(1 \leq L'^f \leq L^f)$.

H.4 Linear Programming on an Activation Region

Based on the linearity of activation regions and ReLU-FNN outputs, we can use *Linear Programming (LP)* to compute **(a)** the feasibility of an activation region, **(b)** the flippability of a neuron activity, and **(c)** the minimum (maximum) of a ReLU-FNN output within an activation region. We show each LP encoding of the problems (a,b,c) in the *SciPy* LP form[2]: where, $p \in AP^f$ is a given activation pattern of ReLU-FNN f, and $p_{l,n}$ is a give neuron activity to be flipped.

$$
\begin{aligned}
&\textbf{(a)}\ \exists x \in \mathbb{R}^{N^f}.\ HConvex^f(x;p) \overset{\text{encode}}{\longrightarrow} \min_x \mathbf{0}x\ \ \textbf{s.t.},\ A''x \leq b'' \\
&\textbf{(b)}\ \exists x \in \mathbb{R}^{N^f}.\ HConvex^f(x;p) \wedge HFace^f_{l,n}(x;p) \\
&\qquad\qquad\qquad \overset{\text{encode}}{\longrightarrow} \min_x \mathbf{0}x\ \ \textbf{s.t.},\ A''x \leq b'',\ A''_{l,n}x = b''_{l,n} \\
&\textbf{(c)}\ \min_x f_j(x)\ \ \textbf{s.t.},\ HConvex^f(x;p) \overset{\text{encode}}{\longrightarrow} \left(\min_x A'_j x\ \ \textbf{s.t.},\ A''x \leq b''\right) + b'_j
\end{aligned}
\tag{3}
$$

H.5 Full Encoding Semantic Perturbations

We focus here on the perturbations of brightness change (B), patch (P), and translation (T), and then describe how to encode the combination of them into ReLU-FNN $g^{x0} : \Theta \to X$: where, $|\theta^{(l)}| = \dim \theta^{(l)}$, w is the width of image $x0$, px, py, pw, ph are the patch x-position, y-position, width, height, and tx is the amount of movement in x-axis direction. Here, perturbation parameter $\theta \in \Theta$ consists of the amount of brightness change for (B), the density of the patch for (P), and the amount of translation for (T). In contrast, perturbation parameters not included in the dimensions of Θ, such as w, px, py, pw, ph, tx, are assumed to be given as constants before verification.

$$
\begin{aligned}
g(\theta, x0) &\overset{\text{encode}}{\longrightarrow} g^{x0}(\theta) \quad \textit{// partially applying given constant } x0 \textit{ to } g. \\
g^{x0}(\theta) &= g^{(5)}(\theta \circ x0) \quad \textit{// concat } x0 \\
g^{(1)}(\mu) &= A^{(T)}\mu \quad \textit{// translate} \\
g^{(2)}(\mu) &= A^{(P)}g^{(1)}(\mu) \quad \textit{// patch} \\
g^{(3)}(\mu) &= A^{(B)}g^{(2)}(\mu) \quad \textit{// brightness change} \\
g^{(4)}(\mu) &= -ReLU(g^{(3)}(\mu)) + \mathbf{1} \quad \textit{// clip } max(0, x_i) \\
g^{(5)}(\mu) &= -ReLU(g^{(4)}(\mu)) + \mathbf{1} \quad \textit{// clip } min(1, x_i)
\end{aligned}
$$

$$
A^{(B)} = \left[a^{(B)}_{r,c}\right], A^{(P)} = \left[a^{(P)}_{r,c}\right], A^{(T)} = \left[a^{(T)}_{r,c}\right]
$$

[2] https://docs.scipy.org/doc/scipy/reference/generated/scipy.optimize.linprog.html.

Fig. 9. MNIST images used for experiments.

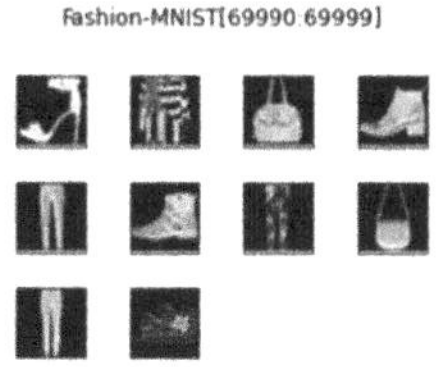

Fig. 10. Fashion-MNIST images used for experiments.

$$a^{(B)}_{r,c} = \begin{cases} 1 \; (c = 1 \wedge r \geq |\theta^{(l+1)}|) & \textit{// add } \theta^{(l)}_1 \\ 1 \; (c = r + 1) & \textit{// copy } \theta^{(l)}_{\geq 2} \textit{ and } x_i \\ 0 \; (otherwise) & \end{cases}$$

$$a^{(P)}_{r,c} = \begin{cases} 1 \; (c = 1 \wedge On(r)) & \textit{// add } \theta^{(l)}_1 \\ 1 \; (c = r + 1) & \textit{// copy } \theta^{(l)}_{\geq 2} \textit{ and } x_i \\ 0 \; (otherwise) & \end{cases}$$

$$On(r) \stackrel{\text{def}}{=} \textbf{let } i{:=}r - |\theta^{(l+1)}|.\ (px \leq \lfloor i/w \rfloor \leq px + pw) \wedge (py \leq i \bmod w \leq py + ph)$$

$$a^{(T)}_{r,c} = \begin{cases} 1 & (c = r + 1 \wedge r \leq |\theta^{(l+1)}|) & \textit{// copy } \theta^{(l)}_{\geq 2} \\ 0 & (c = 1 \wedge \neg(1 \leq t(r) \leq s(r) \leq N)) & \textit{// zero padding} \\ x0_{tgt(r)} - x0_{src(r)} & (c = 1 \wedge r \geq |\theta^{(l+1)}|) & \textit{// add } \theta^{(l)}_1 \Delta x0_i \\ 1 & (c = s(r) + |\theta^{(l)}| \wedge r > |\theta^{(l+1)}|) & \textit{// copy } x0_i \\ 0 & (otherwise) & \end{cases}$$

$$s(r) \stackrel{\text{def}}{=} \textbf{let } i{:=}r - |\theta^{(l+1)}|.\ (\lfloor i/w \rfloor + tx - 1)w + (i \bmod w)$$

$$t(r) \stackrel{\text{def}}{=} \textbf{let } i{:=}r - |\theta^{(l+1)}|.\ (\lfloor i/w \rfloor + tx - 2)w + (i \bmod w)$$

H.6 Images Used for Our Experiments

We used 10 images (i.e., Indexes 69990–69999) selected from the end of the MNIST dataset (cf. Fig. 9) and the Fashion-MNIST dataset (cf. Fig. 10), respectively. We did not use these images in the training of any ReLU-FNNs.

H.7 An Example of Lemma 1

Lemma 1 is reprinted below (Fig. 11).

$$\frac{\partial f_j(x)}{\partial x_i} = C \ \ (x \in \{g^{x0}(\theta) \mid \theta \in ar^{f \circ g}(p)\})$$

A small example of Lemma 1 (cf. Figure 11)

Let $X = [0,1]^3$, $Y = \mathbb{R}^2$, $\Theta = [0,1]^1$, $x0 \in X = (1, 0.5, 0.1)$, $g^{x0}(\theta \in \Theta) \in X = ReLU(-\theta\mathbf{1} + x0)$, and $f(x \in X) \in Y = ReLU(x_1 + x_2, x_1 + x_3)$. Because $g^{x0}(0.6) = ReLU(0.4, -0.1, -0.5)$ and $f(g^{x0}(0.6)) = ReLU(0.4, 0.4)$, $p = ap^{f \circ g}(0.6) = [1, 0, 0|1, 1] \in AP^{f \circ g}$.
Then, $p_{\geq 2} = [1, 1] = ap^f(g^{x0}(0.6)) \in AP^f$.
Here, $ar^{f \circ g}(p)$ corresponding to $HConvex^{f \circ g}(\theta; p) \equiv -\theta + 1 \geq 0 \wedge -\theta + 0.5 \leq 0 \wedge -\theta + 0.1 \leq 0 \wedge -\theta + 1 \geq 0 \wedge -\theta + 1 \geq 0 \equiv 0.5 \leq \theta \leq 1$, on the other hand, $ar^f(p_{\geq 2})$ corresponding to $HConvex^f(x; p_{\geq 2}) \equiv x_1 + x_2 \geq 0 \wedge x_1 + x_3 \geq 0$. Because $0 \leq x_1 + x_2 = x_1 + x_3 = 1 - \theta \leq 0.5$ $(\theta \in ar^{f \circ g}(p))$, $\forall \theta \in ar^{f \circ g}(p)$. $g^{x0}(\theta) \in ar^f(p_{\geq 2})$.

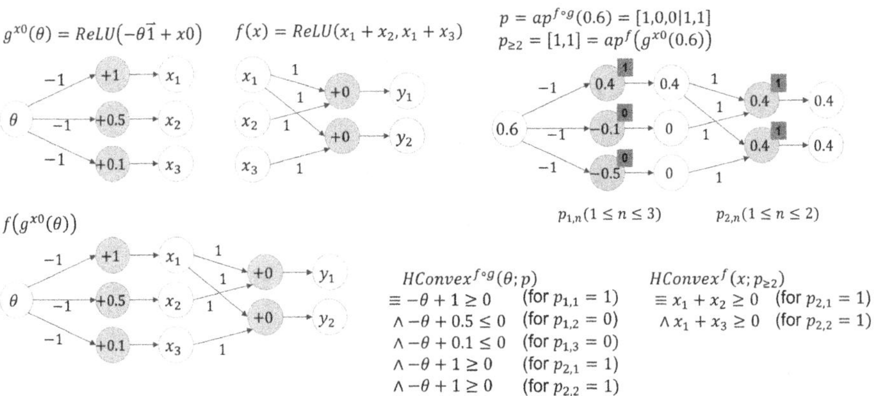

Fig. 11. An image for a small example of Lemma 1.

H.8 Algorithm BFS

Algorithm BFS traverses entire activation regions in perturbation parameter space Θ, as shown in Fig. 12.

Algorithm BFS initializes Q with $ap^{f \circ g^{x0}}(\mathbf{0})$ (Line 3). Then, for each activation pattern p in Q (Lines 5–6), it reconstructs the corresponding activation region η (subroutine constructActivationRegion, Line 8) as the H-representation of p (cf. Eq. 2). Next, for each neuron in $f \circ g^{x0}$ (Line 12), it checks whether the neuron activity $p_{l,n}$ cannot flip within the perturbation parameter space Θ,

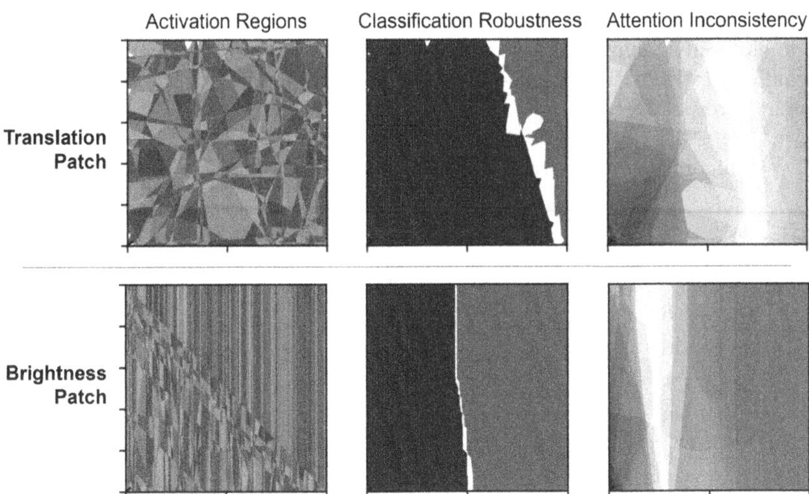

Fig. 12. Examples of *BFS* results. (Near the edges, polygons may fail to render, resulting in blank regions.)

i.e., one of the half-spaces has no feasible points within Θ (subroutine isStable, Line 13). Otherwise, a new activation pattern p' is constructed by flipping $p_{l,n}$ (subroutine flipped, Line 14) and added to the queue (Line 20) if p' is feasible (subroutine calcInteriorPointOnFace, Lines 17–18). Finally, the activation region η is simplified (Line 24) and used to verify CR (subroutine solveCR and solveVR, Lines 25–27, cf. Sect. 4.4) and VR (subroutine solveAR and solveIR, Lines 32–34, cf. Sect. 4.4).

H.9 Details of Experimental Results

Table 2 shows the breakdown of verification statuses in experimental results for each algorithm and each DNN size (cf. Sect. 5). In particular, for traversing AR boundaries, we can see the problem that the ratio of "Timeout" and "Failed (out-of-memory)" increases as the size of the DNN increases. This problem is because gbs-AR traverses more activation regions by the width of the hyperparameter w^{δ} than gbs-CR. It would be desirable in the future, for example, to traverse only the small number of activation regions near the AR boundary.

Table 2. Breakdown of verification statuses. "Robust" and "NotRobust" mean algorithm found "only robust regions" and "at least one not-robust region", respectively. "Timeout" and "Failed" mean algorithm did not finish "within 2 h" and "due to out-of-memory", respectively.

algorithm	#neurons	Robust	NotRobust	Timeout	Failed
bfs	100	13	22	25	0
bfs	200	11	15	34	0
gbs-CR	100	16	44	0	0
gbs-CR	200	17	43	0	0
gbs-CR	400	14	46	0	0
gbs-CR	800	17	43	0	0
gbs-CR	2028	16	44	0	0
gbs-CR	14824	4	0	0	56
gbs-AR	100	14	35	11	0
gbs-AR	200	19	27	14	0
gbs-AR	400	30	13	17	0
gbs-AR	800	28	3	28	1
gbs-AR	2028	15	4	33	8
gbs-AR	14824	4	0	0	56
gbs-CRAR	100	14	41	5	0
gbs-CRAR	200	19	33	8	0
gbs-CRAR	400	30	14	16	0
gbs-CRAR	800	28	6	26	0
gbs-CRAR	2028	15	8	32	5
gbs-CRAR	14824	4	0	0	56

Algorithm 3. $bfs(f, g, x0, \Theta, \delta) \rightarrow (H^{CR}, H^{MR}, H^{CB}, H^{AR}, H^{IR}, H^{AB})$

Input: $f, g, x0, \Theta, \delta$
Output: $H^{CR}, H^{MR}, H^{CB}, H^{AR}, H^{IR}, H^{AB} \subset \mathcal{P}(\Theta)$

$H^{CR}, H^{MR}, H^{CB}, H^{AR}, H^{IR}, H^{AB} \leftarrow \{\}, \{\}, \{\}, \{\}, \{\}, \{\}$
$g^{x0} \leftarrow g(\cdot, x0)$ *// partially applying $x0$ to g; i.e, $g^{x0}(\theta) = g(\theta, x0)$.*
$Q \subset AP^{f \circ g^{x0}} \leftarrow \{ap^{f \circ g^{x0}}(\mathbf{0})\}$ *// queue for breadth-first search.*
$OBS \subset AP^{f \circ g^{x0}} \leftarrow \{\}$ *// observed activation patterns.*
while $\#|Q| > 0$ *// loop for breadth-first search.* **do**
  $p \leftarrow pop(Q)$
  $OBS \leftarrow OBS \cup \{p\}$
  $\eta \leftarrow constructActivationRegion(f \circ g^{x0}, p)$

  // Push the connected activation regions of η.
  $FS \subset \mathbb{Z} \times \mathbb{Z} \leftarrow \{\}$ *// (l, n) means the n-th neuron in l-th layer is a face of η*
  for $l = 1$ to the layer size of DNN $f \circ g^{x0}$, $n = 1$ to the neuron size of the l-th layer **do**
    continue **if** $isStable(p, l, n, \Theta)$ *// skip if neuron activity $p_{l,n}$ cannot flip within Θ.*
    $p' \leftarrow flipped(p, l, n)$ *// flip neuron activity $p_{l,n}$.*
    continue **if** $p' \in OBS$ *// skip if p' has already observed.*
    $OBS \leftarrow OBS \cup \{p'\}$
    $\theta^F \leftarrow calcInteriorPointOnFace(\eta, l, n)$
    continue **if** $\theta^F = null$ *// skip if p' is infeasible.*
    $FS \leftarrow FS \cup \{(l, n)\}$
    $Q \leftarrow Q \cup \{p'\}$ *// push.*
  end for

  // Verify activation region η.
  $\tilde{\eta} \leftarrow simplified(\eta, FS)$ *// limit the constraints on η to FS.*
  if $solveCR(x0; \tilde{\eta})$ **then**
    $H^{CR} \leftarrow H^{CR} \cup \{\tilde{\eta}\}$
  else if $solveMR(x0; \tilde{\eta})$ **then**
    $H^{MR} \leftarrow H^{MR} \cup \{\tilde{\eta}\}$
  else
    $H^{CB} \leftarrow H^{CB} \cup \{\tilde{\eta}\}$
  end if
  if $solveAR(x0; \tilde{\eta})$ **then**
    $H^{AR} \leftarrow H^{AR} \cup \{\tilde{\eta}\}$
  else if $solveIR(x0; \tilde{\eta})$ **then**
    $H^{IR} \leftarrow H^{IR} \cup \{\tilde{\eta}\}$
  else
    $H^{AB} \leftarrow H^{AB} \cup \{\tilde{\eta}^{AB}\}$
  end if
end while
return $H^{CR}, H^{MR}, H^{CB}, H^{AR}, H^{IR}, H^{AB}$

References

1. AIRC, A: ABCI system overview (2022). https://docs.abci.ai/en/system-overview/
2. Ashmore, R., Calinescu, R., Paterson, C.: Assuring the machine learning lifecycle: desiderata, methods, and challenges. ACM Comput. Surv. (CSUR) **54**(5), 1–39 (2021)
3. Balunovic, M., Baader, M., Singh, G., Gehr, T., Vechev, M.: Certifying geometric robustness of neural networks. In: NeurIPS, vol. 32 (2019)
4. Chen, J., Wu, X., Rastogi, V., Liang, Y., Jha, S.: Robust attribution regularization. In: Advances in Neural Information Processing Systems, vol. 32 (2019)
5. Daniel, S., Nikhil, T., Been, K., Fernanda, V., Wattenberg, M.: Smoothgrad: removing noise by adding noise. In: ICMLVIZ. PMLR (2017)
6. Deng, L.: The MNIST database of handwritten digit images for machine learning research. IEEE Signal Process. Mag. **29**(6), 141–142 (2012)
7. Engstrom, L., Tran, B., Tsipras, D., Schmidt, L., Madry, A.: Exploring the landscape of spatial robustness. In: ICML, pp. 1802–1811. PMLR (2019)
8. Fawzi, A., Frossard, P.: Manitest: are classifiers really invariant? In: BMVC, pp. 106.1–106.13 (2015)
9. Fromherz, A., Leino, K., Fredrikson, M., Parno, B., Pasareanu, C.: Fast geometric projections for local robustness certification. In: ICLR (2021)
10. Fromherz, A., Leino, K., Fredrikson, M., Parno, B., Pasareanu, C.: Fast geometric projections for local robustness certification—openreview (2021). https://openreview.net/forum?id=zWy1uxjDdZJ
11. Gao, X., Saha, R.K., Prasad, M.R., Roychoudhury, A.: Fuzz testing based data augmentation to improve robustness of deep neural networks. In: ICSE, pp. 1147–1158. IEEE, ACM (2020)
12. Guo, H., Zheng, K., Fan, X., Yu, H., Wang, S.: Visual attention consistency under image transforms for multi-label image classification. In: CVPR, pp. 729–739. IEEE, CVF (2019)
13. Han, T., Tu, W.W., Li, Y.F.: Explanation consistency training: facilitating consistency-based semi-supervised learning with interpretability. In: AAAI, vol. 35, pp. 7639–7646. AAAI (2021)
14. Hanin, B., Rolnick, D.: Deep ReLU networks have surprisingly few activation patterns. In: NeurIPS, vol. 32 (2019)
15. Hinz, P.: An analysis of the piece-wise affine structure of ReLU feed-forward neural networks. Ph.D. thesis, ETH Zurich (2021)
16. Huang, X., et al.: A survey of safety and trustworthiness of deep neural networks: Verification, testing, adversarial attack and defence, and interpretability. Comput. Sci. Rev. **37**, 100270 (2020)
17. Jha, S.K., Ewetz, R., Velasquez, A., Ramanathan, A., Jha, S.: Shaping noise for robust attributions in neural stochastic differential equations. In: Proceedings of the AAAI Conference on Artificial Intelligence, vol. 36, pp. 9567–9574 (2022)
18. Jordan, M., Lewis, J., Dimakis, A.G.: Provable certificates for adversarial examples: fitting a ball in the union of polytopes. In: NeurIPS, vol. 32 (2019)
19. Kanbak, C., Moosavi-Dezfooli, S., Frossard, P.: Geometric robustness of deep networks: analysis and improvement. In: CVPR, pp. 4441–4449 (2018)
20. Krizhevsky, A., Sutskever, I., Hinton, G.E.: ImageNet classification with deep convolutional neural networks. In: NeurIPS, vol. 25 (2012)

21. Lim, C.H., Urtasun, R., Yumer, E.: Hierarchical verification for adversarial robustness. In: ICML, vol. 119, pp. 6072–6082. PMLR (2020)
22. Mirman, M., Hägele, A., Bielik, P., Gehr, T., Vechev, M.: Robustness certification with generative models. In: PLDI, pp. 1141–1154. ACM SIGPLAN (2021)
23. Mohapatra, J., Weng, T.W., Chen, P.Y., Liu, S., Daniel, L.: Towards verifying robustness of neural networks against a family of semantic perturbations. In: CVPR, pp. 244–252. IEEE, CVF (2020)
24. Montavon, G., Samek, W., Müller, K.R.: Methods for interpreting and understanding deep neural networks. Digit. Signal Process. **73**, 1–15 (2018)
25. Müller, M.N., Makarchuk, G., Singh, G., Püschel, M., Vechev, M.T.: PRIMA: general and precise neural network certification via scalable convex hull approximations. Proc. ACM Program. Lang. **6**(POPL), 1–33 (2022)
26. Ribeiro, M.T., Singh, S., Guestrin, C.: "Why should I trust you?" explaining the predictions of any classifier. In: KDD, pp. 1135–1144. ACM SIGKDD (2016)
27. Selvaraju, R.R., Cogswell, M., Das, A., Vedantam, R., Parikh, D., Batra, D.: Grad-CAM: visual explanations from deep networks via gradient-based localization. In: ICCV. IEEE (2017)
28. Simonyan, K., Vedaldi, A., Zisserman, A.: Deep inside convolutional networks: visualising image classification models and saliency maps. In: ICLR (2014)
29. Simonyan, K., Zisserman, A.: Very deep convolutional networks for large-scale image recognition. In: ICLR (2015)
30. Singh, G., Gehr, T., Püschel, M., Vechev, M.: An abstract domain for certifying neural networks. In: POPL, pp. 1–30. ACM New York (2019)
31. Sotoudeh, M., Thakur, A.V.: Computing linear restrictions of neural networks. In: NeurIPS, vol. 32 (2019)
32. Sotoudeh, M., Thakur, A.V.: Provable repair of deep neural networks. In: PLDI, pp. 588–603. ACM SIGPLAN (2021)
33. Sotoudeh, M., Thakur, A.V.: SyReNN: a tool for analyzing deep neural networks. In: TACAS, pp. 281–302 (2021)
34. Sundararajan, M., Taly, A., Yan, Q.: Axiomatic attribution for deep networks. In: ICML, pp. 3319–3328. PMLR (2017)
35. Szegedy, C., et al.: Intriguing properties of neural networks. In: ICLR (2014)
36. Tsipras, D., Santurkar, S., Engstrom, L., Turner, A., Madry, A.: Robustness may be at odds with accuracy. In: ICLR (2019)
37. Urban, C., Christakis, M., Wüstholz, V., Zhang, F.: Perfectly parallel fairness certification of neural networks. Proc. ACM Program. Lang. **4**(OOPSLA), 1–30 (2020)
38. Urban, C., Miné, A.: A review of formal methods applied to machine learning. CoRR abs/2104.02466 (2021). https://arxiv.org/abs/2104.02466
39. Vaswani, A., et al.: Attention is all you need. In: Advances in Neural Information Processing Systems, vol. 30 (2017)
40. Xiao, C., Zhu, J., Li, B., He, W., Liu, M., Song, D.: Spatially transformed adversarial examples. In: ICLR (2018)
41. Xiao, H., Rasul, K., Vollgraf, R.: Fashion-MNIST: a novel image dataset for benchmarking machine learning algorithms (2017). arXiv:1708.07747
42. Xu, S., Vaughan, J., Chen, J., Zhang, A., Sudjianto, A.: Traversing the local polytopes of ReLU neural networks: a unified approach for network verification. In: AdvML. AAAI (2022)
43. Yang, P., et al.: Enhancing robustness verification for deep neural networks via symbolic propagation. Formal Aspects Comput. **33**(3), 407–435 (2021)

Formalizing Piecewise Affine Activation Functions of Neural Networks in Coq

Andrei Aleksandrov(✉) and Kim Völlinger

Technische Universität Berlin, Berlin, Germany
andrei.aleksandrov@campus.tu-berlin.de, voellinger@tu-berlin.de

Abstract. Verification of neural networks relies on activation functions being *piecewise affine* (PWA)—enabling an encoding of the verification problem for theorem provers. In this paper, we present the first formalization of PWA activation functions for an *interactive* theorem prover tailored to verifying neural networks within Coq using the library Coquelicot for real analysis. As a proof-of-concept, we construct the popular PWA activation function ReLU. We integrate our formalization into a Coq model of neural networks, and devise a verified transformation from a neural network $\mathcal{N}$ to a PWA function representing $\mathcal{N}$ by composing PWA functions that we construct for each layer. This representation enables encodings for proof automation, e.g. Coq's tactic `lra` – a decision procedure for linear real arithmetic. Further, our formalization paves the way for integrating Coq in frameworks of neural network verification as a fallback prover when automated proving fails.

Keywords: Piecewise Affine Function · Neural Network · Interactive Theorem Prover · Coq · Verification

1 Introduction

The growing importance of neural networks motivates the search of verification techniques for them. Verification with *automatic* theorem provers is vastly under study, usually targeting feedforward networks with *piecewise affine* (PWA) activation functions since the verification problem can be then encoded as an SMT or MILP problem [2]. In contrast, few attempts exist on investigating *interactive* provers. Setting them up for this task though offers not only a fallback option when automated proving fails but also insight on the verification process.

That is why in this paper, we work towards this goal by presenting the first formalization of PWA activation functions for an interactive theorem prover tailored to verifying neural networks with Coq. We constructively define PWA functions using the polyhedral subdivision of a PWA function [26] since many algorithms working on polyhedra are known [27] with some tailored to reasoning about reachability properties in neural networks [31]. Motivated by verification, we restrict PWA functions by a polyhedron's constraint to be *non-strict* in order to suit linear programming [30] and by employing *finitely* many polyhedra to fit SMT/MILP solvers [12,30]. We use reals supported by the library Coquelicot

K. Y. Rozier and S. Chaudhuri (Eds.): NFM 2023, LNCS 13903, pp. 62–78, 2023.
https://doi.org/10.1007/978-3-031-33170-1_4

to enable future reasoning about gradients and matrices with COQ's standard library providing the tactic `lra` – a decision procedure for linear real arithmetic. As a proof-of-concept, we construct the activation function RELU– one of the most popular in industry [21] and formal verification [9]. Furthermore, we devise a sequential COQ model of feedforward neural networks integrating PWA activation layers. Most importantly, we present a verified transformation from a neural network $\mathcal{N}$ to a PWA function representing $\mathcal{N}$ with the main benefit being again encodings for future proof automation. To this end, we introduce two verified binary operations on PWA functions – usual function composition and an operator to construct a PWA function for each layer. In particular, we provide the following contributions with the corresponding COQ code available on GITHUB[1]:

1. a constructive formalization of PWA functions based on a polyhedral subdivision tailored to verification of neural networks (Sect. 3),
2. a construction of the popular activation function RELU (Sect. 3),
3. a sequential model for feedforward neural networks with parameterized layers, one of which for PWA layers (Sect. 4),
4. composition for PWA functions and an operator for constructing higher dimensional PWA functions out of lower dimensional ones (Sect. 4), and
5. a verified transformation from a feedforward neural network with PWA activation to a single PWA function representing the network (Sect. 4).

Related Work. A variety of work on using automatic theorem provers to verify neural networks exists with the vast majority targeting feedforward neural networks with PWA activation functions [7,9,13,16,19,20,25]. In comparison, little has been done regarding interactive theorem provers with some mechanized results from machine learning [5,23], a result on verified training in LEAN [28] and, relevant to this paper, pioneering work on verifying networks in ISABELLE [8] and in COQ [3]. Apart from [8] targeting ISABELLE instead of COQ, both network models are not generalized by entailing a formalization of PWA functions and they do not offer a model of the network as a (PWA) function – both contributions of this paper.

2 Preliminaries

We clarify notations and definitions important to this paper. We write $dom(f)$ for a function's domain, $dim(f)$ for the dimension of $dom(f)$ and $(f \circ g)(x)$ for function composition. For a matrix M, M^T is the transposed matrix. We consider block matrices. To clarify notation, consider a block matrix made out of matrices $M_1, ..., M_4$:

$$\left[\begin{array}{c|c} M_1 & M_2 \\ \hline M_3 & M_4 \end{array}\right]$$

[1] At https://github.com/verinncoq/formalizing-pwa with matrix_extensions.v (Sect. 2), piecewise_affine.v (Sect. 3.1), neuron_functions.v (Sect. 3.2), neural_networks.v (Sect. 4.1 and 4.4) and pwaf_operations.v (Sect. 4.2 and 4.3).

2.1 Piecewise Affine Topology

We give the important definitions regarding PWA functions [24,26,33]. In all following definitions, $n \in \mathbb{N}$.

Definition 1. (Linear Constraint). *For some* $c \in \mathbb{R}^n, b \in \mathbb{R}$, *a* linear constraint *is an inequality of form* $c^T x \leq b$ *for any* $x \in \mathbb{R}^n$.

Definition 2. (Polyhedron[2]). *A* polyhedron P *is the intersection of finitely many halfspaces, meaning* $P := \{x \in \mathbb{R}^n | c_1^T x \leq b_1 \wedge ... \wedge c_m^T x \leq b_m\}$ *with* $c_i \in \mathbb{R}^n, b_i \in \mathbb{R}$ *and* $i \in \{1, ..., m\}$.

We denote the constraints of P as $\mathcal{C}(P) := \{(c_1^T x \leq b_1), ..., (c_m^T x \leq b_m)\}$ for readability even though a constraint is given by c_i and b_i while x is arbitrary.

Definition 3. (Affine Function[3]). *A function* $f : \mathbb{R}^m \rightarrow \mathbb{R}^n$ *is called* affine *if there exists* $M \in \mathbb{R}^{n \times m}$ *and* $b \in \mathbb{R}^n$ *such that for all* $x \in \mathbb{R}^m$ *holds:* $f(x) = Mx + b$.

Definition 4. (Polyhedral Subdivision). *A* polyhedral subdivision *of* $S \subseteq \mathbb{R}^n$ *is a finite set of polyhedra* $\mathbf{P} := \{P_1, \ldots, P_m\}$ *such that (1)* $S = \bigcup_{i=1}^m P_i$ *and (2) for all* $P_i, P_j \in \mathbf{P}, x \in P_i \cap P_j$, *and for all* $\epsilon > 0$ *there exists* $x' \in \mathbb{R}^n$ *such that* $|x - x'| < \epsilon$, *and* $x' \notin P_i \cap P_j$.

Definition 5. (Piecewise Affine Function) *A continuous function* $f : D \subseteq \mathbb{R}^m \rightarrow \mathbb{R}^n$ *is* piecewise affine *if there is a polyhedral subdivision* $\mathbf{P} = \{P_1, \ldots, P_l\}$ *of* D *and a set of affine functions* $\{f_1, \ldots, f_l\}$ *such that for all* $x \in D$ *holds* $f(x) = f_i(x)$ *if* $x \in P_i$.

2.2 Neural Networks

Neural networks approximate functions by learning from sample points during training [10] with arbitrary precision [11,15,17]. A feedforward neural network is a directed acyclic graph with the edges having weights and the vertices (neurons) having biases and being structured in layers. Each layer first computes the weighted sum (an affine function) and then applies an activation function (non-linear, possibly pwa). In many machine learning frameworks (e.g. PyTorch), these functions are modelled as separate layers followed up by each other. Every network has an input and an output layer with optional hidden layers in between.

[2] In literature often referred to as a convex, closed polyhedron.

[3] A linear function is a special case of an affine function [32]. However, in literature, the term linear is sometimes used for both.

2.3 Interactive Theorem Prover Coq & Library Coquelicot

We use the interactive theorem prover Coq [29] providing a non-turing-complete functional programming language extractable to selected functional programming languages and a proof development system – a popular choice for formal verification of programs and formalization of mathematical foundations. Additionally, we use the real analysis library Coquelicot [6] offering derivatives, integrals, and matrices compatible with Coq's standard library.

Extensions in Coq: *Column Vectors & Block Matrices.* For this paper, we formalized column vectors and block matrices on top of Coquelicot. A column vector `colvec` is identified with matrices and equipped with a dot product `dot` on vectors and some lemmas to simplify proofs. Additionally, we formalized several notions for Coquelicot's matrix type. We provide multiplication of a matrix with a scalar `scalar_mult`, noted as `(_ * _)%scalar`, and transposition `transpose` of matrices. We provide operations on different shapes of matrices and vectors such as a right-to-left construction of block diagonal matrices `block_diag_matrix`, a specialization thereof on vectors `colvec_concat` and extensions of vectors with zeroes on the bottom `extend_colvec_at_bottom` or top `extend_colvec_on_top`, denoted as follows: $\left[\begin{array}{c|c} M_1 & 0 \\ \hline 0 & M_2 \end{array}\right]$, $\left[\begin{array}{c} \vec{v}_1 \\ \hline \vec{v}_2 \end{array}\right]$, $\left[\begin{array}{c} \vec{v} \\ \hline \vec{0} \end{array}\right]$, and $\left[\begin{array}{c} \vec{0} \\ \hline \vec{v} \end{array}\right]$. We proved lemmas relating all operations, new and existing, with each other, and overloaded the notations `*` and `+`. The extension is tightly coupled to reals, but could be generalized to `Ring` and may serve as a foundation of matrix operations on shapes as widely used in scientific computing.

3 Formalization of Piecewise Affine Functions in Coq

We formalize PWA functions tailored to neural network verification with PWA activation. As a proof-of-concept, we construct the activation function Rectified Linear Unit (ReLU) – one of the most popular activation functions in industry [21] and formal verification [9].

3.1 Inductive Definition of PWA Functions

We define a linear constraint with a dimension *dim* and parameters, vector $c \in \mathbb{R}^{dim}$ and scalar $b \in \mathbb{R}$, being satisfied for a vector $x \in \mathbb{R}^{dim}$ if $c \cdot x \leq b$:

```
Inductive LinearConstraint (dim:nat) : Type :=
| Constraint (c: colvec dim) (b: R).

Definition satisfies_lc {dim: nat} (x: colvec dim) (l: LinearConstraint dim)
: Prop := match l with | Constraint c b ⇒ (c * x)%v <= b end.
```

We define a polehydron as a finite set of linear constraints together with a predicate stating that a point lies in a polyhedron:

```
Inductive ConvexPolyhedron (dim: nat) : Type :=
| Polyhedron (constraints: list (LinearConstraint dim)).
Definition in_convex_polyhedron {dim: nat} (x: colvec dim) (p:
    ConvexPolyhedron dim) :=
match p with | Polyhedron lcs ⇒
  forall constraint, In constraint lcs → satisfies_lc x constraint end.
```

Finally, we define a PWA function as a record composed of the fields body holding the polyhedral subdivision for piecewise construction, and prop for the property that functions of intersecting polyhedra coincide in the intersection such that all "pieces" together yield indeed a *function*. We call this property *univalence* (also called right-definiteness or right-uniqueness), not to be confused with the same term used in type theory.

```
Record PWAF (in_dim out_dim: nat): Type := mkPLF {
    body: list (ConvexPolyhedron in_dim * ((matrix out_dim in_dim) * colvec
        out_dim));
    prop: pwaf_univalence body; }.
```

Piecewise Construction. We construct a PWA function f by a list of polyhedra and corresponding affine functions (P, f_P) with $f_P = (M, b)$ defining a "piece" of f by an affine function with $f_P(x) = Mx + b$ if $x \in P$. For evaluation, we search a polyhedron containing x and compute the affine function:

```
Fixpoint pwaf_eval_helper
    {in_dim out_dim: nat}
    (body: list (ConvexPolyhedron in_dim * ((matrix (T:=R) out_dim in_dim) *
        colvec out_dim)))
    (x: colvec in_dim) :=
    match body with
    | nil ⇒ None
    | body_el :: next ⇒
        match body_el with
        | (polyh, affine_f) ⇒
            match polyhedron_eval x polyh with
            | true ⇒ Some affine_f
            | false ⇒ pwaf_eval_helper next x
    end end end.
```

The presented function either outputs None in case when no such polyhedron is found (i.e. $x \notin dom(f)$) or returns body_el such that the PWA function is evaluated using M and b. The final output is computed in the wrapper function pwaf_eval not presented here. For the purpose of proving, we define a predicate in_pwaf_domain for the existence of a polyhedron for an input and a predicate is_pwaf_value for stating the function is evaluated to a certain value.

Univalence. We enforce the construction to be a function by stating univalence, i.e. all pairs of polyhedra having coinciding affine functions in their intersection, requiring a proof for each instance of type `PWAF`:

```
Definition pwaf_univalence {in_dim out_dim: nat}
  (l: list (ConvexPolyhedron in_dim *
    ((matrix out_dim in_dim) * colvec out_dim))) :=
  ForallPairs (fun e1 e2 ⇒ let p1 := fst e1 in let p2 := fst e2 in
      forall x, in_convex_polyhedron x p1 ∧ in_convex_polyhedron x p2 →
        let M1 := fst (snd e1) in let b1 := snd (snd e1) in
        let M2 := fst (snd e2) in let b2 := snd (snd e2) in
          ((M1 * x) + b1 = (M2 * x) + b2)%M) l.
```

Class of Formalized PWA Functions. Motivated by PWA activation functions in the context of neural network verification, our PWA functions are restricted by

(1) all linear constraints being *non-strict*, and
(2) being defined over a union of *finitely* many polyhedra.

Restriction (1) is motivated by linear programming usually dealing with non-strict constraints [30], and restriction (2) by MILP/SMT solvers commonly accepting finitely many variables [12,30]. Since we use that every continuous PWA function on $\mathbb{R}^n$ admits a polyhedral subdivision of the domain [26], all continuous PWA functions with a finite subdivision can be encoded.

For PWA functions not belonging to this class, consider any discontinuous PWA function since discontinuity violates restriction (1), and any periodic PWA function as excluded by restriction (2) due to having infinitely many "pieces".

Choice of Formalization. We use real numbers (instead of e.g. rationals or floats) to enable COQUELICOT's reasoning about derivatives – interesting for neural networks' gradients. COQUELICOT builds up on the reals of COQ's standard library allowing the use of COQ's tactic `lra` – a COQ-native decision procedure for linear real arithmetic. An alternative would be the library MATHCOMP-ANALYSIS[4] which, at the time of development, did not support the `lra` tactic for reals.[5] Beyond, COQUELICOT provides lemmas and tactics for derivation and integration which do not (yet) have equivalents in MATHCOMP-ANALYSIS.

Moreover, we use inductive types since they come with an induction principle and therefore ease proving. Besides that, the type `list` (e.g. used for the definition of PWA functions) enjoys extensive support in COQ. For example, `pwaf_univalence` is stated using the list predicate `ForAllPairs` and proofs intensively involve lemmas from COQ's standard library.

A constructive definition using the polyhedral subdivision is interesting since many efficient algorithms are known that work on polyhedra [27] with some being tailored to neural network verification [31]. We expect that such algorithms are

[4] https://github.com/math-comp/analysis.
[5] https://github.com/math-comp/algebra-tactics/pull/54.

implementable in an idiomatic functional style using our model. Furthermore, we anticipate that encodings for PWA functions [2] are also usable for proof automation in Coq.

3.2 Example: Rectified Linear Unit Activation Function

We construct ReLU as a PWA function defined by two "pieces" each of which being a linear function. The function is defined as:

$$\text{ReLU}(x) := \begin{cases} 0, & x < 0 \\ x, & x \geq 0 \end{cases}$$

Piecewise Construction. The intervals, $(-\infty, 0)$ and $[0, \infty)$, each correspond to a polyhedron in $\mathbb{R}$ defined by a single constraint: $P_{left} := \{x \in \mathbb{R}^1 | [1] \cdot x <= 0\}$ and $P_{right} := \{x \in \mathbb{R}^1 | [-1] \cdot x <= 0\}$.[6] We define these polyhedra as follows:[7]

```
Definition ReLU1d_polyhedra_left := Polyhedron 1 [Constraint 1 Mone 0].
Definition ReLU1d_polyhedra_right
    := Polyhedron 1 [Constraint 1 ((−1) ∗ Mone)%scalar 0].
```

ReLU's construction list contains these polyhedra each associated with a matrix and vector, in these cases $([0], [0])$ and $([1], [0])$, for the affine functions:

```
Definition ReLU1d_body: list (ConvexPolyhedron 1 ∗ (matrix (T:=R) 1 1 ∗
     colvec 1))
    := [(ReLU1d_polyhedra_left, (Mzero, null_vector 1));
        (ReLU1d_polyhedra_right, (Mone, null_vector 1))].
```

Univalence. Note that while ReLU's intervals are distinct, the according polyhedra with non-strict constraints are not. To ensure the construction to be a function, we prove univalence by proving that only $[0] \in (P_{left} \cap P_{right})$:

```
Lemma RelU1d_polyhedra_intersect_0:
    forall x, in_convex_polyhedron x ReLU1d_polyhedra_left ∧
      in_convex_polyhedron x ReLU1d_polyhedra_right → x = null_vector 1.
```

Finally, we ensure for each polyhedra pair holds $[1] \cdot [0] + [0] = [0] \cdot [0] + [0]$, and instantiate a PWAF by `Definition ReLU1dPWAF := mkPLF 1 1 ReLU1d_body ReLU1d_pwaf_univalence`.

On the Construction of PWA *Functions.* Besides ReLU being an important activation function, we chose it as an introductory example to focus on the

[6] Matrices involved are one-dimensional vectors since ReLU is one-dimensional. For technical reasons, in Coq, the spaces $\mathbb{R}$ and $\mathbb{R}^1$ differ with the latter working on one-dimensional vectors instead on scalars.

[7] `Mone` is Coquelicot's identity matrix which in this case is a one-dimensional vector.

structure of PWA functions. Nevertheless, this example is extendable to ReLU variants, e.g. PReLU by adding a parameter for the function slope to the "left" polyhedron. Other activation functions sharing its features of consisting of a few polyhedra and being one-dimensional work similarly. We can also construct a multi-dimensional function out of its one-dimensional version as we will illustrate for ReLU in Sect. 4.3. Different types of pooling [10] require more effort though due to a non-trivial polyhedra structure and inherent multi-dimensionality. This effort motivates a future shift towards tailored tactics easing the construction of PWA functions.

4 Verified Transformation of a Neural Network to a PWA Function

We present our main contribution: a formally verified transformation of a feedforward neural network with PWA activations into a single PWA function. First, we introduce a Coq model for feedforward neural networks (Sect. 4.1). We follow up with two verified binary operations on PWA functions at the heart of the transformation, *composition* (Sect. 4.2) and *concatenation* (Sect. 4.3), and finish with the verified transformation (Section 4.4).

4.1 Neural Network Model in Coq

We define a neural network *NNSequential* as a list-like structure containing layers parameterized on the type of activation, and the input's, output's and hidden layer's dimensions with dependent types preventing dimension mismatch:

```
Inductive NNSequential {input_dim output_dim: nat} :=
| NNOutput : NNSequential
| NNPlainLayer {hidden_dim: nat}:
    (colvec input_dim → colvec hidden_dim)
    → NNSequential (input_dim:=hidden_dim) (output_dim:=output_dim)
    → NNSequential
| NNPWALayer {hidden_dim: nat}:
    PWAF input_dim hidden_dim
    → NNSequential (input_dim:=hidden_dim) (output_dim:=output_dim)
    → NNSequential
| NNUnknownLayer {hidden_dim: nat}:
    NNSequential (input_dim:=hidden_dim) (output_dim:=output_dim)
    → NNSequential.
```

The network model has four layer types: `NNOutput` as the last layer propagates input values to the output; `NNPlainLayer` is a layer allowing any function in Coq defined on real vectors; `NNPWALayer` is a PWA activation layer – the primary target of our transformation; and `NNUnknownLayer` is a stub for a layer with an unknown function.

Informally speaking, the semantics of our model is as follows: for a layer `NNOutput` the identity function[8] is evaluated, for `NNPlainLayer` the passed function, for `NNPWALayer` the passed PWA function, and for `NNUnknownLayer` a failure is raised. Thus, the *NNSequential* type does not prescribe any specific functions of layers but expects them as parameters.

An Example of a Neural Network. We define specific layers for a network, in this case the PWA layers LINEAR and RELU. The LINEAR layer implements the generic affine function $f(x) = Wx + b$ computing the weighted sum. As an example, we consider a neural network with these two hidden layers.

```
Definition NNLinear {input_dim hidden_dim output_dim: nat}
  (W: matrix hidden_dim input_dim) (b: colvec hidden_dim)
  (NNnext: NNSequential (input_dim:=hidden_dim) (output_dim:=output_dim))
  := NNPWALayer (LinearPWAF W b) NNnext.

Definition NNReLU {input_dim output_dim: nat}
  (NNnext: NNSequential (input_dim:=input_dim) (output_dim:=output_dim))
  := NNPWALayer (input_dim:=input_dim) ReLU_PWAF NNnext.

Definition example_weights: matrix 2 2 := [[2.7, 0],[1, 0.01]].
Definition example_biases: colvec 2 := [[1], [0.25]].
Definition example_nn := (NNLinear example_weights example_biases
                          (NNReLU (NNOutput (output_dim:=2)))).
```

From a Trained Neural Network into the World of COQ. As illustrated, we can construct feedforward neural networks in COQ. Another option is to convert a neuronal network trained outside of COQ into an instance of the model. In [3] a python script is used for conversion from PYTORCH to their COQ model without any correctness guarantess, while in [8] an import mechanism from TENSORFLOW into ISABELLE is used, where correctness of the import has to be established for each instance of their model. We are working with a converter expecting a neural network in the ONNX format (i.e. exchange format supported by most frameworks) [4] to produce an according instance in our COQ model [14].[9] This converter is mostly written within COQ with its core functionality being verified. Note that fitting PWA activation functions have to be supplied by the COQ model.

Choice of Model. While feedforward neural networks are often modeled as directed acyclic graphs [1,18] a sequential model of layers is often employed alongside similar to our COQ model. A graph-based model is extendable to recurrent networks but is also adding complexity. In [8] the authors showed a sequential model to be superior to a graph-based model for verification in ISABELLE. Hence, we expect that the need for a sequential COQ model to stay even in the

[8] We use the customized identity function *flex_dim_copy*.

[9] A bachelor thesis supervised by one of the authors and scheduled for publication.

presence of a generic graph-based model. The introduced model is inspired by, to our knowledge, the only published neural network model in Coq [3], and generalizes it by having parameterized layers instead of being restricted to ReLU activation. Moreover, we decided for reals instead of customized floats in order to ease verification and to support Coquelicot's real analysis as a foundation for future proof automation tailored to neural networks in Coq. All efforts have been done with a verification process in mind starting from a trained network outside of Coq which is trustfully converted into an instance of the Coq model for which safety properties are semi-automatically verified – no extraction is intended.

4.2 Composition of PWA Functions

Besides composition being a general purpose binary operation closed over PWA functions [26], it is needed in our transformation to compose PWA layers. Since, for PWA functions $f : \mathbb{R}^l \to \mathbb{R}^n$ and $g : \mathbb{R}^m \to \mathbb{R}^l$, their composition $z = f \circ g$ is a PWA function, composition in Coq produces an instance of type PWAF requiring a construction and a proof of univalence:

```
Definition pwaf_compose {in_dim hidden_dim out_dim: nat}
   (f: PWAF hidden_dim out_dim) (g: PWAF in_dim hidden_dim)
   : PWAF in_dim out_dim := mkPLF in_dim out_dim
      (pwaf_compose_body f g) (pwaf_compose_univalence f g).
```

Piecewise Construction of Composition. Assume a PWA function f defined on the polyhedra set $\mathbf{P}^f = \{P^f_1, \ldots, P^f_k\}$ with affine functions given by the parameter set $\mathbf{A}^f = \{(M^f_1, b^f_1), \ldots, (M^f_k, b^f_k)\}$. Analogously, g is given by $\mathbf{P}^g$ and $\mathbf{A}^g$. For computing a composed function $z = f \circ g$ at any $x \in \mathbb{R}^m$, we need a polyhedron $P^g_j \in \mathbf{P}^g$ such that $x \in P^g_j$ to compute $g(x) = M^g_j x + b^g_j$ with $(M^g_j, b^g_j) \in \mathbf{A}^g$. Following, we need a polyhedron $P^f_i \in \mathbf{P}^f$ with $g(x) \in P^f_i$ to finally compute $z(x) = M^f_i g(x) + b^f_i$ with $(M^f_i, b^f_i) \in \mathbf{A}^f$.

We consider function composition on the level of polyhedra sets to construct z's polyhedra set $\mathbf{P}^z$. For each pair $P^f_i \in \mathbf{P}^f$, $P^g_j \in \mathbf{P}^g$, we create a polyhedron $P^z_{i,j} \in \mathbf{P}^z$ such that $x \in P^z_{i,j}$ iff $x \in P^g_j$ and $M^g_j x + b^g_j \in P^f_i$ with $(M^g_j, b^g_j) \in \mathbf{A}^g$. Consequently, $\mathcal{C}(P^g_j) \subseteq \mathcal{C}(P^z_{i,j})$ while the constraints of P^f_i have to be modified. For $(c_i \cdot x \leq b_i) \in \mathcal{C}(P^f_i)$ we have the modified constraint $((c^T_i M^g_j) \cdot x \leq b_i - c_i \cdot b^g_j) \in \mathcal{C}(P^z_{i,j})$. We construct a polyhedra set accordingly in Coq including empty polyhedra in case no qualifying pair of polyhedra exists:

```
Definition compose_polyhedra_helper
   {in_dim hidden_dim: nat}
   (M: matrix hidden_dim in_dim)
   (b1: colvec hidden_dim)
   (l_f: list (LinearConstraint hidden_dim)) :=
   map (fun c => match c with Constraint c b2 =>
```

```
    Constraint in_dim (transpose ((transpose c) * M)%M) (b2 - (c * b1)%v)
  end) l_f.

Definition compose_polyhedra {in_dim hidden_dim: nat}
  (p_g: ConvexPolyhedron in_dim)
  (M: matrix hidden_dim in_dim) (b: colvec hidden_dim)
  (p_f: ConvexPolyhedron hidden_dim) :=
  match p_g with | Polyhedron l1 ⇒
    match p_f with | Polyhedron l2 ⇒
      Polyhedron in_dim (l1 ++ compose_polyhedra_helper M b l2)
  end end.
```

Further, each $(M^z_{i,j}, b^z_{i,j}) \in \mathbf{A}^z$ is defined as $(M^f_j M^g_i, M^f_j b^g_i + b^f_j)$ as a result of usual composition of two affine functions:

```
Definition compose_affine_functions {in_dim hidden_dim out_dim: nat}
  (M_f: matrix (T:=R) out_dim hidden_dim) (b_f: colvec out_dim)
  (M_g: matrix (T:=R) hidden_dim in_dim) (b_g: colvec hidden_dim) :=
  (M_f * M_g, (M_f * b_g) + b_f)%M.
```

Univalence of Composition. Due to the level of details, the Coq proof for the composed function z satisfying univalence is omitted in this paper (see Theorem pwaf_compat_univalence).

Composition Correctness. For establishing the correctness of the composition, we proved the following theorem:

```
Theorem pwaf_compose_correct:
  forall in_dim hid_dim out_dim x f_x g_x
    (f: PWAF hid_dim out_dim) (g: PWAF in_dim hid_dim),
    in_pwaf_domain g x → is_pwaf_value g x g_x →
    in_pwaf_domain f g_x → is_pwaf_value f g_x f_x →
    let fg := pwaf_compose f g in
    in_pwaf_domain fg x ∧ is_pwaf_value fg x f_x.
```

4.3 Concatenation: Layers of Neural Networks as PWA Functions

While some neural networks come with each layer being *one* multi-dimensional function, many feature layers where each neuron is assigned the same lower dimensional function independently then applied to each neuron's input. Motivated by the transformation of a neural network into a single PWA function, we introduce a binary operation *concatenation* that constructs a single PWA function for each PWA layer of a neural network. Besides, concatenation is interesting by itself to construct a multi-dimensional PWA function. That is why, we finish on concatenation with the illustration of a multi-dimensional ReLU layer.

Concatenation of PWA functions has to yield an instance of type PWAF since being closed over PWA functions. Concatenation is defined as follows:

Definition 6 (Concatenation). *Let $f : \mathbb{R}^m \to \mathbb{R}^n$ and $g : \mathbb{R}^k \to \mathbb{R}^l$. The concatenation $\oplus$ is defined as:*

$$(f \oplus g)(\begin{bmatrix} x^f \\ \hline x^g \end{bmatrix}) := \begin{bmatrix} f(x^f) \\ \hline g(x^g) \end{bmatrix}$$

Piecewise Construction of Concatenation. Assume some $f, g, \mathbf{P}^f, \mathbf{P}^g, \mathbf{A}^f$ and $\mathbf{A}^g$ as previously used, and $z = f \oplus g$. The polyhedra set $\mathbf{P}^z$ contains the pairwise joined polyhedra of $\mathbf{P}^f$ and $\mathbf{P}^g$ but with each constraint of a polyhedron lifted to the dimension of z's domain. Consider a pair $P^f_i \in \mathbf{P}^f$ and $P^g_j \in \mathbf{P}^g$. For constraints $(c^f_i \cdot x^f \leq b^f_i) \in \mathcal{C}(P^f_i)$ and $(c^g_j \cdot x^g \leq b^g_j) \in \mathcal{C}(P^g_j)$ with $\begin{bmatrix} x^f \\ \hline x^g \end{bmatrix} \in \mathbb{R}^{dim(f)+dim(g)}$, the following higher dimensional constraints are in $\mathcal{C}(P^z_{i,j})$ with $P^z_{i,j} \in \mathbf{P}^z$: $\begin{bmatrix} c^f_i \\ \hline 0 \end{bmatrix} \cdot \begin{bmatrix} x^f \\ \hline x^g \end{bmatrix} \leq b^f_i$ and $\begin{bmatrix} 0 \\ \hline c^g_j \end{bmatrix} \cdot \begin{bmatrix} x^f \\ \hline x^g \end{bmatrix} \leq b^g_j$.

Thus, we get $\begin{bmatrix} x^f \\ \hline x^g \end{bmatrix} \in P^z_{i,j}$ iff $x^f \in P^f_i$ and $x^g \in P^g_j$.

Hence, the concatenation requires the pairwise join of all polyhedra $\mathbf{P}^f$ and $\mathbf{P}^g$ each with their constraints lifted to the higher dimension of z's domain:

```
Definition concat_polyhedra {in_dim1 in_dim2: nat}
    (p_f: ConvexPolyhedron in_dim1) (p_g: ConvexPolyhedron in_dim2):
    ConvexPolyhedron (in_dim1 + in_dim2) :=
    match p_f with | Polyhedron l1 ⇒
        match p_g with | Polyhedron l2 ⇒
            Polyhedron (in_dim1 + in_dim2)
                (extend_lincons_at_bottom l1 (in_dim1 + in_dim2) ++
                extend_lincons_on_top l2 (in_dim1 + in_dim2))
    end end.
```

The Coq code uses two functions for insertion of zeros similar to the dimension operations (see Sect. 2). The corresponding affine function of $P^z_{i,j}$ is then:

$$(M^z_{i,j}, b^z_{i,j}) := (\left[\begin{array}{c|c} M^f_i & 0 \\ \hline 0 & M^g_j \end{array}\right], \begin{bmatrix} b^f_i \\ \hline b^g_j \end{bmatrix}).$$

Univalence of Concatenation. The lengthy technical proof of concatenation being univalent is omitted in this paper (see `Theorem pwaf_concat_univalence`).

Concatenation Correctness. We proved the correctness of the concatenation:

```
Theorem pwaf_concat_correct:
    forall in_dim1 in_dim2 out_dim1 out_dim2 x1 x2 f_x1 g_x2
      (f: PWAF in_dim1 out_dim1) (g: PWAF in_dim2 out_dim2),
      in_pwaf_domain f x1 → is_pwaf_value f x1 f_x1 →
      in_pwaf_domain g x2 → is_pwaf_value g x2 g_x2 →
      let fg   := pwaf_concat f g in
```

```
    let x    := colvec_concat x1 x2 in
    let fg_x := colvec_concat f_x1 g_x2 in
    in_pwaf_domain fg x ∧ is_pwaf_value fg x fg_x.
```

The proof relies on an extensive number of lemmas connecting matrix operations to block matrices and vector reshaping.

Example: ReLU *Layer.* Using concatenation, we construct a multi-dimensional ReLU layer using one-dimensional ReLU (see Sect. 4.1). To construct a ReLU layer $\mathbb{R}^n \rightarrow \mathbb{R}^n$, we perform n concatenations of one-dimensional ReLU:

```
Fixpoint ReLU_PWAF_helper (in_dim: nat): PWAF in_dim in_dim :=
  match in_dim with
  | 0 ⇒ ZeroDimPWAF
  | S n ⇒ pwaf_concat ReLU1dPWAF (ReLU_PWAF_helper n)
  end.
```

In this listing, ZeroDimPWAF is a stub for a total function with signature $\mathbb{R}^0 \rightarrow \mathbb{R}^0$. We did prove that there is a unique $x \in \mathbb{R}^0$, which implies that there is only one function with this signature.

4.4 Transforming a Neural Network into a PWA Function

Building up on previous efforts, the transformation of a feedforward neural network with PWA activation functions into a single PWA function is straightforward. Using concatenation, we construct multi-dimensional PWA layers and then compose them to one PWA function representing the whole neural network as conceptually illustrated in Fig. 1 and implemented as follows in Coq:

```
Fixpoint transform_nn_to_pwaf {in_dim out_dim: nat}
  (nn: NNSequential (input_dim := in_dim) (output_dim := out_dim))
  : option (PWAF in_dim out_dim) :=
  match nn with
    | NNOutput ⇒ Some (OutputPWAF)
    | NNPlainLayer _ _ _ ⇒ None
    | NNUnknownLayer _ _ ⇒ None
    | NNPWALayer _ pwaf next ⇒
      match transform_nn_to_pwaf next with
      | Some next_pwaf ⇒ Some (pwaf_compose next_pwaf pwaf)
      | None ⇒ None
  end end.
```

Correctness of Transformation. For this transformation, we proved the following theorem in Coq to establish its correctness with nn_eval computing a network's output:

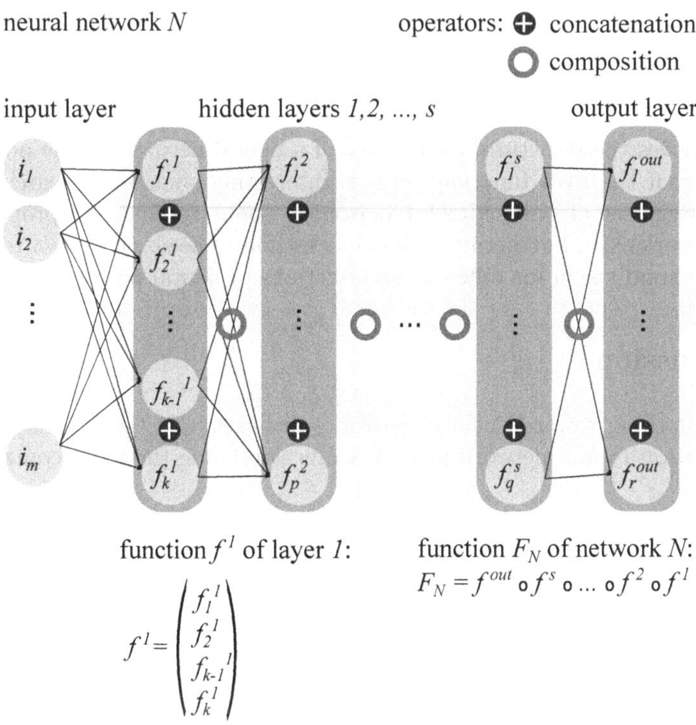

Fig. 1. Transformation of a feedforward network N with PWA activation functions into its representation as a PWA function F_N by concatenating neuron activation within each layer followed up by composing PWA layers.

```
Theorem transform_nn_to_pwaf_correct:
    forall in_dim out_dim (x: colvec in_dim) (f_x: colvec out_dim) nn
        nn_pwaf,
      Some nn_pwaf = transform_nn_to_pwaf_correct nn →
      in_pwaf_domain nn_pwaf x →
      is_pwaf_value nn_pwaf x f_x ↔ nn_eval nn x = Some f_x.
```

For a neural network $\mathcal{N}$ and its transformed PWA function $f_{\mathcal{N}}$, the theorem states that for all inputs $x \in dom(f_{\mathcal{N}})$ holds $f_{\mathcal{N}}(x) = \mathcal{N}(x)$. The proof of this theorem relies on several relatively simple properties of the composition. Note that for $dom(f_{\mathcal{N}}) = \emptyset$ the theorem trivially holds, and in fact an additional proof is required for $f_{\mathcal{N}}$'s polyhedra being a subdivision of $dom(\mathcal{N})$ (i.e. $dom(f_{\mathcal{N}}(x)) = dom(\mathcal{N}(x))$).

On the Representation of a Neural Network as a PWA *Function.* The main benefit of having a PWA function obtained from a neural network lies in the option to use simple-to-implement encodings of PWA functions for different solvers, e.g. Coq's tactic `lra` or MILP/SMT solvers [2]. Hence, this representation paves the way for proof automation when stating theorems about the input-output relation of a network in Coq. Furthermore, a representation as a PWA function moves the structural complexity of a neural network to the polyhedral subdivision of the PWA function. This is interesting since local search can be applied to the set of polyhedra for reasoning about reachability properties in neural networks [31]. Furthermore, one may estimate the size of a PWA function's polyhedral subdivision for different architectures of neural networks [22].

5 Discussion

We were working towards neural network verification in Coq with a verified transformation from a network to a PWA function being the main contribution.

Summary. We presented the first formalization of PWA activation functions for an interactive theorem prover. For our constructive formalization, we used a PWA function's polyhedral subdivision due to the numerous efficient algorithms working on polyhedra. Our class of PWA functions is on-purpose restricted to suit linear programming by using non-strict constraints and to fit SMT/MILP solvers by employing finitely many polyhedra. With ReLU, we constructed one of the most popular activation functions. We presented a verified transformation from a neural network to its representation as a PWA function enabling encodings for proof automation for theorems about the input-output relation. To this end, we devised a sequential model of neural networks, and introduced two verified binary operation on PWA functions – usual function composition together with an operator to construct a PWA function for each layer.

Future Work. Since the main benefit of having a PWA function obtained from a neural network lies in the many available encodings [9,13] targeting different solvers, we envision encodings for our network model. These encodings have to be adapted to the verification within Coq with our starting point being the tactic `lra` – a Coq-native decision procedure for linear real arithmetic. Moreover, moving the structural complexity of a neural network to the polyhedral subdivision of a PWA function, opens up on investigating algorithms working on polyhedra for proof automation with our main candidate being local search on polyhedra for reasoning about reachability properties in neural networks [31]. Further, for our model of neural networks, we intend a library of PWA activation functions with proof automation to ease construction. We also plan on a generic graph-based model for neural networks in Coq but as argued, we expect the sequential model to stay the mean of choice for feedforward networks. Additionally, since tensors are used in machine learning to incorporate complex mathematical operations, we aim to integrate a formalization of tensors tailored to neural network verification.

References

1. Aggarwal, C.C.: Neural Networks, pp. 211–251. Springer, Cham (2021)
2. Albarghouthi, A.: Introduction to neural network verification. Found. Trends Program. Lang. **7**(1–2), 1–157 (2021). https://doi.org/10.1561/2500000051
3. Bagnall, A., Stewart, G.: Certifying the true error: machine learning in coq with verified generalization guarantees. In: AAAI Conference on Artificial Intelligence (2019)
4. Bai, J., Lu, F., Zhang, K., et al.: ONNX: Open Neural Network Exchange. https://github.com/onnx/onnx (2019)
5. Bentkamp, A., Blanchette, J.C., Klakow, D.: A formal proof of the expressiveness of deep learning. J. Autom. Reas. (2019). https://doi.org/10.1007/s10817-018-9481-5
6. Boldo, S., Lelay, C., Melquiond, G.: Coquelicot: a user-friendly library of real analysis for Coq. Math. Comput. Sci. **9**(1), 41–62 (2015)
7. Botoeva, E., Kouvaros, P., Kronqvist, J., Lomuscio, A., Misener, R.: Efficient verification of ReLU-based neural networks via dependency analysis. In: Proceedings of the AAAI Conference on Artificial Intelligence, vol. 34, pp. 3291–3299 (2020). https://doi.org/10.1609/aaai.v34i04.5729
8. Brucker, A.D., Stell, A.: Verifying feedforward neural networks for classification in Isabelle/HOL. In: Proceedings of the 25th International Symposium on Formal Methods. Springer, Heidelberg (2023). https://doi.org/10.1007/978-3-031-27481-7_24
9. Bunel, R., Turkaslan, I., Torr, P.H., Kohli, P., Kumar, M.P.: A unified view of piecewise linear neural network verification. In: Proceedings of the 32nd International Conference on Neural Information Processing Systems, NIPS 2018, pp. 4795–4804. Curran Associates Inc., Red Hook (2018)
10. Calin, O.: Deep Learning Architectures: A Mathematical Approach. Springer, Heidelberg (2020). https://doi.org/10.1007/978-3-030-36721-3
11. Cybenko, G.: Approximation by superpositions of a sigmoidal function. Math. Control Signals Syst. **2**(4), 303–314 (1989)
12. De Moura, L., Bjørner, N.: Satisfiability modulo theories: introduction and applications. Commun. ACM **54**(9), 69–77 (2011)
13. Ehlers, R.: Formal verification of piece-wise linear feed-forward neural networks. In: Automated Technology for Verification and Analysis (2017)
14. Gummersbach, L.: Ein verifizierter Converter für neuronale Netze von ONNX nach Coq. Bachelor's thesis, Technische Universität Berlin (2023). to appear at Technische Universität Berlin
15. Hanin, B.: universal function approximation by deep neural nets with bounded width and ReLU activations. Mathematics **7**(10) (2019). https://doi.org/10.3390/math7100992
16. Tran, H.-D., Bak, S., Xiang, W., Johnson, T.T.: Verification of deep convolutional neural networks using imagestars. In: Lahiri, S.K., Wang, C. (eds.) CAV 2020. LNCS, vol. 12224, pp. 18–42. Springer, Cham (2020). https://doi.org/10.1007/978-3-030-53288-8_2
17. Hornik, K.: Approximation capabilities of multilayer feedforward networks. Neural Netw. **4**(2), 251–257 (1991)
18. Kruse, R., Mostaghim, S., Borgelt, C., Braune, C., Steinbrecher, M.: General Neural Networks, pp. 39–52. Springer, Cham (2022). https://doi.org/10.1007/978-1-4471-5013-8_4

19. Lin, W., et al.: Robustness verification of classification deep neural networks via linear programming, pp. 11410–11419 (2019). https://doi.org/10.1109/CVPR.2019.01168
20. Liu, C., Arnon, T., Lazarus, C., Strong, C., Barrett, C., Kochenderfer, M.J.: Algorithms for verifying deep neural networks. Found. Trends Optim. **4**(3–4), 244–404 (2021). https://doi.org/10.1561/2400000035
21. Montesinos López, O.A., Montesinos López, A., Crossa, J.: Fundamentals of artificial neural networks and deep learning. In: Multivariate Statistical Machine Learning Methods for Genomic Prediction, pp. 379–425. Springer, Cham (2022). https://doi.org/10.1007/978-3-030-89010-0_10
22. Montúfar, G., Pascanu, R., Cho, K., Bengio, Y.: On the number of linear regions of deep neural networks. In: Proceedings of the 27th International Conference on Neural Information Processing Systems, NIPS 2014, vol. 2, pp. 2924–2932. MIT Press, Cambridge (2014)
23. Murphy, C., Gray, P., Stewart, G.: Verified perceptron convergence theorem. In: Proceedings of the 1st ACM SIGPLAN International Workshop on Machine Learning and Programming Languages, MAPL 2017, pp. 43–50. Association for Computing Machinery, New York (2017). https://doi.org/10.1145/3088525.3088673
24. Rourke, C., Sanderson, B.: Introduction to Piecewise-Linear Topology. Springer, Heidelberg (1982). https://doi.org/10.1007/978-3-642-81735-9
25. Scheibler, K., Winterer, L., Wimmer, R., Becker, B.: Towards verification of artificial neural networks. In: Methoden und Beschreibungssprachen zur Modellierung und Verifikation von Schaltungen und Systemen (2015)
26. Scholtes, S.: Introduction to Piecewise Differentiable Equations. Springer, New York (2012). https://doi.org/10.1007/978-1-4614-4340-7
27. Schrijver, A.: Combinatorial Optimization: Polyhedra and Efficiency. Springer, Heidelberg (2002)
28. Selsam, D., Liang, P., Dill, D.L.: Developing bug-free machine learning systems with formal mathematics. In: Proceedings of the 34th International Conference on Machine Learning, ICML2017, vol. 70, pp. 3047–3056. JMLR.org (2017)
29. Team, T.C.D.: The Coq Proof Assistant (2022). https://doi.org/10.5281/zenodo.7313584
30. Vanderbei, R.J.: Linear Programming: Foundations and Extensions. Springer, Heidelberg (2020). https://doi.org/10.1007/978-3-030-39415-8
31. Vincent, J.A., Schwager, M.: Reachable polyhedral marching (RPM): a safety verification algorithm for robotic systems with deep neural network components. In: 2021 IEEE International Conference on Robotics and Automation (ICRA), pp. 9029–9035 (2021). https://doi.org/10.1109/ICRA48506.2021.9561956
32. Yang, X.S.: Mathematical foundations. In: Yang, X.S. (ed.) Introduction to Algorithms for Data Mining and Machine Learning, pp. 19–43. Academic Press, Cambridge (2019). https://doi.org/10.1016/B978-0-12-817216-2.00009-0
33. Ziegler, G.M.: Lectures on Polytopes. Springer, New York (1995). https://doi.org/10.1007/978-1-4613-8431-1

Verifying an Aircraft Collision Avoidance Neural Network with Marabou

Cong Liu[1(✉)], Darren Cofer[1], and Denis Osipychev[2]

[1] Collins Aerospace, Charlotte, USA
{cong.liu,darren.cofer}@collins.com
[2] Boeing, Seattle, USA
denis.osipychev@boeing.com

Abstract. In this case study, we have explored the use of a neural network model checker to analyze the safety characteristics of a neural network trained using reinforcement learning to compute collision avoidance flight plans for aircraft. We analyzed specific aircraft encounter geometries (e.g., head-on, overtake) and also examined robustness of the neural network. We verified the minimum horizontal separation property by identifying conditions where the neural network can potentially cause a transition from a safe state to an unsafe state. We show how the property verification problem is mathematically transformed and encoded as linear-constraints that can be analyzed by the Marabou model checker.

1 Introduction

Machine Learning technologies such as neural networks (NN) have been used to implement advanced functionality in complex systems, including safety-critical aircraft applications. Before such systems can be deployed outside of an experimental setting, it will be necessary to show that they can meet the verification and certification requirements of the aerospace domain.

In a typical NN, much of the complexity and design information resides in its training data rather than in the actual models or code produced in the training process. One of the key principles of avionics software certification is the use of requirements-based testing along with structural coverage metrics. These activities not only demonstrate compliance with functional requirements, but are intended to expose any unintended functionality by providing a measure of completeness. However, since it is not possible to associate particular neurons or lines of code in a NN with a specific requirement, these activities cannot provide the required level of assurance [1].

The authors wish to thank Aleksandar Zeljic for his help using Marabou. This work was funded by DARPA contract FA8750-18-C-0099. The views, opinions and/or findings expressed are those of the author and should not be interpreted as representing the official views or policies of the Department of Defense or the U.S. Government. Approved for Public Release, Distribution Unlimited.

K. Y. Rozier and S. Chaudhuri (Eds.): NFM 2023, LNCS 13903, pp. 79–85, 2023.
https://doi.org/10.1007/978-3-031-33170-1_5

Formal methods tools are being developed for NNs and may be able to address this challenge by providing a comprehensive analysis of a system over its entire input space and showing the absence of unintended behaviors. In this case study, we have used the Marabou model checker [7] to analyze a NN that was trained to compute collision avoidance flight plans for aircraft. The main contribution of the paper is to show the effectiveness of formal methods in identifying potential safety concerns in a real NN application. In fact, this NN was flight tested in a controlled experiment with two general aviation-class airplanes, but we were able to find a number of conditions which trigger unexpected (and potentially unsafe) actions [2]. Furthermore, we suggest ways in which formal analysis results can be incorporated to improve the training of future systems.

One of the unique aspects of this study is that it is focused on a NN trained using Reinforcement Learning (RL). In earlier work on the ACAS-Xu system for collision avoidance in small unmanned aircraft [5], the NN was trained using supervised learning based on a complete tabular specification of correct behavior and Reluplex [6] (a precursor of Marabou) was used to verify various safety properties. Another ACAS-Xu study [3] used formal analysis tools to show the equivalence of the NN to the tabular specification. In the current study, RL was used to compute flight plans (rather than just the avoidance maneuvers produced by ACAS-Xu), but our formal analysis exposes areas in which the training process is incomplete.

Marabou is a state-of-the-art framework for verifying deep NN. It can answer queries about NN properties by transforming each query to a satisfiability problem. Currently it only supports linear constraints for inputs and outputs. Marabou accepts three input formats: NNet, TensorFlow and ONNX. In the case study, we exported the NN model parameters from the learning environment and encoded them in the NNet format. We used the Marabou Python interface to encode the constraints and perform the verification.

The collision avoidance NN and the Marabou verification scripts are available at https://github.com/darrencofer/NFM-2023-case-study.

2 Aircraft Collision Avoidance Neural Network

We study the automated aircraft collision avoidance system described in [2]. The system's core is a NN model pre-trained on a surrogate simulation using RL. The NN model modifies the course of the controlled airplane (ownship) to provide a safe distance to another aircraft (intruder) and return to the original course when safe. The RL environment simulates various potential collision scenarios with aircraft performance similar to a Cessna 208 Caravan. The 2-D position range is $[-10{,}000, 10{,}000]$ m $\times$ $[-10{,}000, 10{,}000]$ m. The heading range is $(-180, 180]$ degree. The aircraft speed range is $[50, 70]$ mps. The required minimum separation distance (MSD) is 2,000 m. The initial and goal position are randomly generated and remain fixed during each training scenario. During the encounter, while the intruder maintains a constant direction and speed, the ownship adjusts the flight direction and speed. Not maintaining the MSD results in a penalty, while returning to the original route results in a reward.

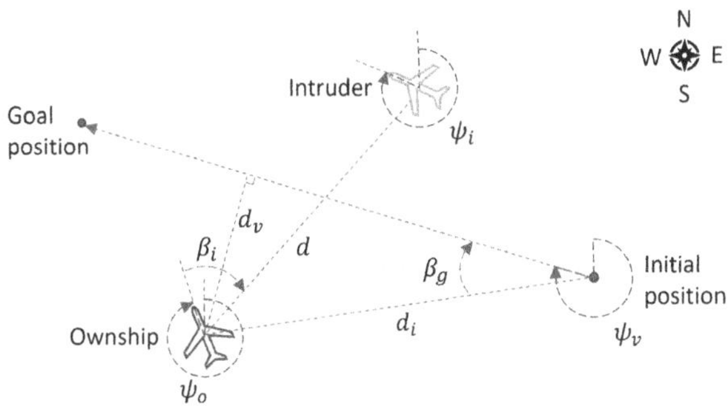

Fig. 1. System geometry for potential collision.

In the experiments, a number of policies were developed. We chose a NN that only controls the flight direction (i.e., fixed speed). It consists of 8 input nodes, 1 output node, and 2 hidden layers with 64 nodes each. All hidden nodes use rectified linear unit (ReLU) as the activation function. The output node uses tanh as the activation function. Marabou does not support tanh activation functions. So for the verification we removed the tanh activation function and mapped its outputs (e.g. value or range) back to the corresponding function input.

The NN inputs are: $\{d, d_v, d_i, v_r, \beta_i, \psi_r, \beta_g, \beta_v\}$, where d is distance from ownship to intruder, d_v is distance to vector, d_i is distance to initial position, v_r is relative speed, β_i is angle to intruder, ψ_r is relative heading, β_g is angle to goal, β_v is angle to vector. The vector is from the initial position to the goal. We define $v_r = v_i/v_o - 1$, $\psi_r = \psi_i - \psi_o$, $\beta_v = \psi_v - \psi_o$, where v_i is intruder speed, v_o is onwship speed, ψ_i is intruder heading, ψ_o is ownship heading, ψ_v is vector heading. The system geometry in shown in Fig. 1.

Note that $d_v = d_i \sin\beta_g$. This means that the NN inputs are not completely independent. We capture this dependence by encoding the relation as a constraint. Since Marabou only supports linear constraints, we set β_g as a constant in each analysis.

All NN inputs are normalized: $d, d_v, d_i \in [0, 1]$, $v_r \in [-0.3, 0.4]$, $\beta_i, \psi_r, \beta_g, \beta_v \in [-1, 1]$. The NN output range is $(-1,\ 1)$ due to the tanh function. It is linearly mapped to $(-3,\ 3)$ to compute the turn rate (ω), unit in degree per second. A positive and negative value indicates turning right and left, respectively.

3 Verifying Minimum Separation Distance

The reachability problem of a closed-loop neural network control system with non-linear dynamics is known to be undecidable [4]. Instead, we examine the condition where the ownship transitions from a safe state ($d = MSD$) to a unsafe state ($d < MSD$). This indicates that the distance function is decreasing

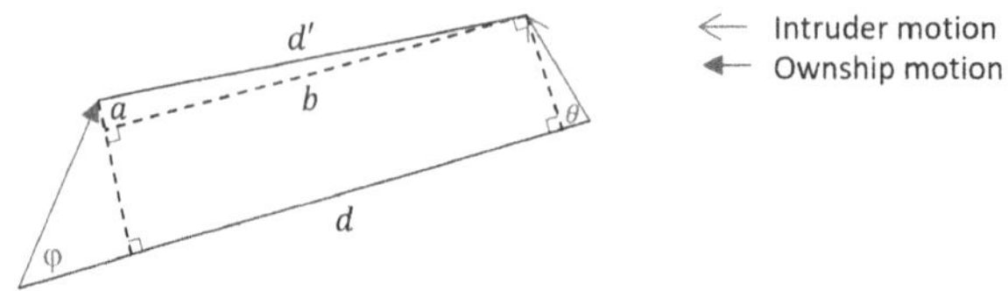

Fig. 2. Distance between ownship and intruder changes during Δt.

at the MSD boundary. We mathematically derive the derivative of the distance function and check when the neural network will generate an output action that causes the derivative to be negative at the boundary. Although the derivative function itself is non-linear due to trigonometric functions, we found that the safety conditions can be characterized by a set of linear constraints, which can be handled by Marabou. Figure 2 illustrates the derivative calculation. The filled and open arrows represent the ownship and the intruder movement during the time interval Δt, respectively, with d and d' being the distance at time t and $t + \Delta t$.

The distance d' satisfies $d'^2 = a^2 + b^2$, where:
$a = v_o \Delta t \sin \varphi - v_i \Delta t \sin \theta$,
$b = d - v_o \Delta t \cos \varphi - v_i \Delta t \cos \theta$.

Ignoring the higher order terms, we have $(d'^2 - d^2)/\Delta t = -2d(v_o \cos \varphi + v_i \cos \theta)$. Applying the chain rule $\Delta d^2/\Delta t = 2d\Delta d/\Delta t$, we have $\Delta d/\Delta t = -(v_o \cos \varphi + v_i \cos \theta)$. By definition: $\varphi = \beta_i - \omega \Delta t$, $\theta = 180 - \beta_i + \psi_r$. Letting $\alpha = \beta_i - \psi_r$, we rewrite the derivative as $\dot{d} = v_i \cos \alpha - v_o \cos \varphi$.

Assuming $v_i = v_o$, $\dot{d} < 0$ implies $\cos \alpha < \cos \varphi$. If $0 \le \alpha \le 180, 0 \le \varphi \le 180$, then it implies $\alpha > \varphi$ (i.e., $\omega \Delta t > \psi_r$). This means that at the MSD boundary, the neural network has to generate a turn angle that is less than the relative heading to prevent the distance from decreasing. Note that the turn rate ω is limited to the range $(-3, 3)$ degree per second and $\Delta t = 1$ second in simulation. This means if $\psi_r \le -3$ or $\psi_r \ge 3$, no matter what the neural network output is, the derivative will always be negative or positive, respectively. Thus, in our analysis we restrict to the scenarios where $\psi_r \in (-3, 3)$. In other words, we only look for the scenarios where the MSD violation could be avoided, but the neural network does not generate such output.

Results. For the analysis, we sampled the intruder angle between 0 and 180°, and found MSD violations for each intruder angle. The simulation used in the RL training process makes it unlikely that the critical conditions where safety is violated (e.g., MSD boundary, relative heading range) are reached very often, meaning that the NN likely has insufficient training in this region to make safe decisions.

4 Robustness Analysis

Robustness analysis helps us to understand the stability of the NN controller. In most cases, the output produced by the NN should not change dramatically in reponse to small input perturbations (such as sensor noise). We can perform a δ-local-robustness [6] to quantify the bounded-input/bounded-output stability of the NN.

To perform this analysis, we generated five arbitrary points covering a range of input conditions and NN outputs. We computed a constant δ for an input point x such that for all inputs $x' : \|x - x'\|_\infty \leq \delta$, the neural network output will not change sign (e.g., changing from turning left to right).

Table 1. Robustness analysis results.

	$\delta = 0.1$	$\delta = 0.05$	$\delta = 0.02$	$\delta = 0.01$
Point 1 (weak right turn)	SAT	SAT	SAT	UNSAT
Point 2 (strong left turn)	SAT	SAT	SAT	UNSAT
Point 3 (strong right turn)	SAT	SAT	UNSAT	UNSAT
Point 4 (strong right turn)	SAT	UNSAT	UNSAT	UNSAT
Point 5 (strong left turn)	SAT	SAT	UNSAT	UNSAT

Results. The robustness analysis results are summarized in Table 1. SAT results mean an adversarial input was found, while UNSAT results mean no such inputs exist. The results show that the neural network may be not robust. In particular at Point 2, a small input perturbation ($\delta = 0.02$) causes the ownship to change from turning strong-left to right. This may lead to unstable behavior in which the aircraft oscillates between left and right turns.

5 Specific Scenarios

We examine six encounter scenarios (system snapshots), similar to [8], where there are expected aircraft maneuvers (e.g., staying on course vs. turning left or right). We check whether the action generated by the neural network aligns with expectations. The following scenarios were considered.

Head-on. The ownship is on course and both airplanes are about to have a head-on collision. We expect the ownship shall make a turn to avoid collision.

Overtake. The ownship is on course while the intruder flies in the same direction and approaches from behind. We expect the ownship shall turn to avoid collision.

Parallel Same Direction. The ownship is on course while the intruder flies side by side in the same direction and is close. We expect the ownship shall not fly towards the intruder.

Parallel Opposite Direction. The ownship is on course while the intruder flies side by side in the opposite direction and is *dangerously* close. We expect the ownship shall not fly towards the intruder.

Table 2. Verification of mid-air encounter scenarios. All times are in seconds.

Scenario	Constraints	Result	Time
Head-on	$d = 2000$, $d_i \geq 0$, $0.4 \geq v_r \geq -0.3$, $d_v = 0$, $\beta_i \geq 0$, $\psi_r = 180$, $\beta_g = 0$, $\beta_v = 0$, $out = 0$	SAT	0.02
Overtake	$d \leq 2500$, $d_i \geq 0$, $0.4 \geq v_r \geq -0.3$, $d_v = 0$, $\beta_i \geq 0$, $\psi_r = 0$, $\beta_g = 0$, $\beta_v = 0$, $out = 0$	SAT	4.0
Parallel same direction	$d \leq 2500$, $d_i \geq 0$, $0.4 \geq v_r \geq -0.3$, $d_v = 0$, $\beta_i \geq 0$, $\psi_r = 0$, $\beta_g = 0$, $\beta_v = 0$, $out \geq 0$	UNSAT	12.3
Parallel opposite direction	$d = 2000$, $d_i \geq 0$, $0.4 \geq v_r \geq -0.3$, $d_v = 0$, $90 \geq \beta_i \geq 0$, $\psi_r = 180$, $\beta_g = 0$, $\beta_v = 0$, $out \geq 0$	SAT	0.03
Approach from right	$d = 2000$, $d_i \geq 0$, $0.4 \geq v_r \geq -0.3$, $d_v = 0$, $\beta_i \geq 0$, $\psi_r = -90$, $\beta_g = 0$, $\beta_v = 0$, $out \geq 0.1$	SAT	0.08
Far away	$d = 10000$, $d_i \geq 0$, $0.4 \geq v_r \geq -0.3$, $d_v = 0$, $\beta_g = 0$, $\beta_v = 0$, $out \leq -5$	SAT	18.7

Approach from Right. The ownship is on course while the intruder approaches the ownship from right and is *dangerously* close. We expect the ownship shall turn left.

Far Away. The ownship is on course while the intruder is far away. We expect the ownship shall stay on its course and will not make strong turns.

Results. The encoding of the scenarios and the verification results are summarized in Table 2. The NN generated outputs violating expectations in all but one of the six scenarios. Based on the analysis, we believe that the RL training method did not provide sufficient training data to cover these critical scenarios. All experiments were performed on a Linux server with Intel Xeon E5-2698 v4 CPU @ 2.20 GHz and approximately 504 GB memory.

6 Conclusion and Future Work

We analyzed an aircraft collision avoidance NN using Marabou. We verified the minimum horizontal separation property, analyzed robustness of the NN, and investigated specific interesting scenarios. The results suggest that the RL NN training approach was insufficient to guarantee safety of the system in many critical scenarios. This shows the value of formal analysis for identifying unintended behaviors that may be present in a NN.

The counterexamples generated in the verification of a property could be used to better train the NN. The counterexamples often represent hard-to-reach corner cases. We could directly use them to train the NN in a Supervised Learning environment, because usually there are well-defined expected NN outputs. We could also adjust the RL setup by directly setting these scenarios as the initial states.

It would be interesting to combine the forward reachability analysis of NN with our MSD property verification so that a simulation trace from the initial state to the violation state is generated. Also recall that at certain conditions, due to the turn rate limit, the MSD property violation is unavoidable. We could use backward reachability analysis to compute the corresponding previous system states and actions, until the NN could potentially generate an action to deviate from the collision course. These system states and desired actions could also be added to the training set.

References

1. Cofer, D.: Unintended behavior in learning-enabled systems: detecting the unknown unknowns. In: 2021 IEEE/AIAA 40th Digital Avionics Systems Conference (DASC), pp. 1–7 (2021)
2. Cofer, D., et al.: Flight test of a collision avoidance neural network with run-time assurance. In: 2022 IEEE/AIAA 41st Digital Avionics Systems Conference (DASC), pp. 1–10 (2022)
3. Damour, M., et al.: Towards certification of a reduced footprint ACAS-Xu system: a hybrid ml-based solution. In: Habli, I., Sujan, M., Bitsch, F. (eds.) Computer Safety, Reliability, and Security, pp. 34–48. Springer International Publishing, Cham (2021)
4. Huang, C., Fan, J., Chen, X., Li, W., Zhu, Q.: Polar: a polynomial arithmetic framework for verifying neural-network controlled systems. In: Bouajjani, A., Holík, L., Wu, Z. (eds.) Automated Technology for Verification and Analysis, pp. 414–430. Springer International Publishing, Cham (2022)
5. Irfan, A., et al.: Towards verification of neural networks for small unmanned aircraft collision avoidance. In: 2020 AIAA/IEEE 39th Digital Avionics Systems Conference (DASC), pp. 1–10. IEEE (2020)
6. Katz, G., Barrett, C., Dill, D.L., Julian, K., Kochenderfer, M.J.: Reluplex: an efficient SMT solver for verifying deep neural networks. In: Majumdar, R., Kunčak, V. (eds.) Computer Aided Verification, pp. 97–117. Springer International Publishing, Cham (2017)
7. Katz, G., et al.: The marabou framework for verification and analysis of deep neural networks. In: International Conference on Computer Aided Verification, pp. 443–452 (2019)
8. Manzanas Lopez, D., Johnson, T.T., Bak, S., Tran, H.D., Hobbs, K.L.: Evaluation of neural network verification methods for air-to-air collision avoidance. J. Air Transp. **31**(1), 1–17 (2023)

Strategy Synthesis in Markov Decision Processes Under Limited Sampling Access

Christel Baier[1,2], Clemens Dubslaff[1,4], Patrick Wienhöft[1,2(✉)], and Stefan J. Kiebel[1,3]

[1] Centre for Tactile Internet with Human-in-the-Loop (CeTI), Dresden, Germany
[2] Department of Computer Science, Technische Universität Dresden, Dresden, Germany
{christel.baier,patrick.wienhoeft}@tu-dresden.de
[3] Department of Psychology, Technische Universität Dresden, Dresden, Germany
stefan.kiebel@tu-dresden.de
[4] Eindhoven University of Technology, Eindhoven, The Netherlands
c.dubslaff@tue.nl

Abstract. A central task in control theory, artificial intelligence, and formal methods is to synthesize reward-maximizing strategies for agents that operate in partially unknown environments. In environments modeled by *gray-box* Markov decision processes (MDPs), the impact of the agents' actions are known in terms of successor states but not the stochastics involved. In this paper, we devise a strategy synthesis algorithm for gray-box MDPs via reinforcement learning that utilizes *interval MDPs* as internal model. To compete with limited sampling access in reinforcement learning, we incorporate two novel concepts into our algorithm, focusing on rapid and successful learning rather than on stochastic guarantees and optimality: *lower confidence bound* exploration reinforces variants of already learned practical strategies and *action scoping* reduces the learning action space to promising actions. We illustrate benefits of our algorithms by means of a prototypical implementation applied on examples from the AI and formal methods communities.

1 Introduction

Many machine learning methods take inspiration from the inner-workings of the human brain or human behavior [29]. For instance, learning based on neural networks mimics the human brain at a structural level by explicitly modeling its neurons and their activation. Taking a more high-level view, *reinforcement learning (RL)* [38] formalizes human learning behavior by reinforcing actions that are repeatedly associated with successful task solving [3]. The usual application of RL is to learn reward-optimizing strategies in environments modeled as *Markov*

The authors are supported by the DFG through the Cluster of Excellence EXC 2050/1 (CeTI, project ID 390696704, as part of Germany's Excellence Strategy) and the TRR 248 (see https://perspicuous-computing.science, project ID 389792660).

K. Y. Rozier and S. Chaudhuri (Eds.): NFM 2023, LNCS 13903, pp. 86–103, 2023.
https://doi.org/10.1007/978-3-031-33170-1_6

decision processes (MDPs) [31] where the agent has only partial knowledge and learns based on guided exploration through sample runs. Existing RL approaches prioritize stochastic guarantees and convergence to a globally optimal strategy, leading to slow learning performance and infeasibility for small sample sizes [38]. In contrast, human decision making can compete with limited sampling access, not focusing on strict optimality but on efficiency. The more urgent a task and the less time available for its solving, the more humans tend to exploit previously learned strategies – possibly sacrificing optimality but increasing the chance of finishing the task in time [32]. In the extremal case, humans rely on *habits* [43], i.e., sequences of actions that, once triggered, are executed mostly independent from reasoning about the actual task [7]. Habits avoid further costly exploration during learning by restricting the action space.

In this paper, we take inspiration from humans' ability to reason efficiently with few explorations, shaping novel RL algorithms that rapidly synthesize "good" strategies. Specifically, our learning task amounts to an agent being able to determine a strategy with high expected accumulated reward until reaching a goal, given a limited number of samples. We consider the setting where the environment is modelled as a *contracting MDP*, i.e., goal states are almost surely reached under all strategies, on which the agent has a *gray-box* view, i.e., knows the reward structures and the topology but not the exact probabilities [4]. We tackle this task of sample-bounded learning towards nearly-optimal strategies by introducing two new concepts: *lower confidence bound (LCB) sampling* and *action scoping*. Classical reward-based sampling in RL is based on upper confidence bounds (UCB) [2], balancing the *exploration-exploitation dilemma* [38]. In contrast, our LCB sampling method favors situations already shown viable during the learning process. Hence, exploration is limited when there are no good reasons for leaving well-known paths, similar to what humans do with habitual sequences of actions [43]. The second learning component is *action scoping*, restraining exploration actions when shown to be suboptimal in past samples. Scoping is parametrized to tune the degree of exploration and balance between fast strategy synthesis or increasing the chance of learning optimal strategies.

To implement our novel concepts, we provide technical contributions by presenting an RL algorithm on contracting gray-box MDPs with arbitrary rewards and various sampling methods. The learning algorithm is a sample-based approach that generates an *interval MDP (IMDP)* to approximate the environment and whose intervals are iteratively refined. While methods for analyzing IMDPs have already been considered in the literature [17,44], and IMDPs have been used in the context of RL algorithms [36], we provide a new connection of their use in PAC RL algorithms. We devise our human-inspired RL algorithms, including LCB and action scoping, by modeling knowledge of the agent as IMDP using concepts from *model-based interval estimation (MBIE)* [35] and *probably almost correct (PAC) statistical model checking (SMC)* [4]. We show that our algorithms on IMDPs are PAC for UCB and LCB sampling, i.e., the probability of a suboptimal strategy can be quantified by an arbitrarily small error tolerance. This, however, cannot be guaranteed in the case of action scoping. Towards an evaluation of LCB and action scoping, we implemented our algorithms in a prototypical tool [1]. By means of several experimental studies from the RL and formal-methods community, e.g., on multi-armed bandits [41] and RACETRACK [10], we show that LCB and action scoping foster fast strategy synthesis, providing better strategies after fewer sample runs than RL-style PAC-SMC methods. We discuss the impact of scoping parameters and related heuristics, as well as combinations of sampling strategies. In summary, our contributions are:

- A (model-based) RL algorithm for contracting gray-box MDPs with integer rewards relying on IMDP and sampling strategy refinements (see Sect. 3)
- Instances of this RL algorithm subject to lower and upper confidence bound sampling and tunable action scoping (see Sect. 4).
- A prototypical implementation of our RL algorithms and an evaluation in examples from both the RL and formal-methods communities.

Supplemental material and a reproduction package for the experiments of this paper are publicly available [1,9].

Related Work. SMC [28] for unbounded temporal properties in stochastic systems is most related to our setting, establishing algorithms also in gray-box settings [20,45]. Given a lower bound on transition probabilities, SMC algorithms have been presented for Markov chains [15], MDPs, and stochastic games [4]. Recent SMC algorithms for MDPs also include learning [4,13] but only for reachability problems. IMDPs have been investigated outside of the RL context in formal verification [14,33] for ω-regular properties, for positive rewards in contracting models [44] by an extension of the well-known value-iteration algorithm [38], and in the performance-evaluation community in the discounted setting [17]. In particular, the RL algorithms we present in this paper use an adaptation of the latter algorithm without discounting as a subroutine to successively tighten bounds on the maximal expected accumulated rewards. More recently, algorithms with convergence guarantees for reachability objectives in (interval) MDPs have been presented [6,19]. *Interval estimation* for RL has been introduced by Kaelbling [24] towards Q-learning [40] and extended to model-based approaches [42] such as MBIE [34] and the UCRL2 algorithm [23] using an error tolerance based on the L_1-norm opposed to the L_∞-norm employed in interval MDPs. In contrast, the *linearly updating intervals* [36] algorithm utilizes IMDPs but uses potentially unsafe intervals and focuses on learning on changing environments. Besides UCB sampling, the exploration-exploitation dilemma in reward-based learning has also be addressed with exploration bonuses [24,25,37,39], performing well when applied to MBIE [22,35] or in other RL methods such as E^3 [27] and R_{max} [12].

2 Preliminaries

A *distribution* over a finite set X is a function $\mu\colon X \to [0,1]$ where $\sum_{x \in X} \mu(x) = 1$. The set of distributions over X is denoted by *Dist*(X).

Markov Decision Processes (MDPs). An MDP is a tuple $\mathcal{M} = (S, A, \imath, G, R, T)$ where S, A, and $G \subseteq S$ are finite sets of states, actions, and goal states, respectively, $\imath \in S$ is an initial state, $R\colon S \to \mathbb{R}$ is a reward function, and $T\colon S \times A \rightharpoonup \mathit{Dist}(S)$ is a partial transition probability function. For state $s \in S$ and action $a \in A$ we say that a is *enabled* in s if $T(s, a)$ is defined. We assume the set $\mathit{Act}(s)$ of all enabled actions to be empty in goal states $s \in G$ and non-empty in all other states. For $(s, a, s') \in S \times A \times S$ we define $T(s, a, s') = T(s, a)(s')$ if $T(s, a)$ is defined and $T(s, a, s') = 0$ otherwise. The *successors* of s via a are denoted by $\mathit{Post}(s, a) = \{s' \mid T(s, a, s') > 0\}$. A *run* of $\mathcal{M}$ is a sequence $\pi = s_0 a_0 s_1 a_1 \ldots s_n$ where $s_0 = \imath$, $s_n \in S$, $(s_i, a_i) \in (S \backslash G) \times A$, and $s_{i+1} \in \mathit{Post}(s_i, a_i)$ for $i = 0, \ldots, n-1$. The set of all runs in $\mathcal{M}$ is denoted by $\mathit{Runs}(\mathcal{M})$. The *accumulated reward* of π is defined by $R(\pi) = \sum_{i=0}^{n-1} R(s_i)$.

An *interval MDP (IMDP)* is a tuple $\mathcal{U} = (S, A, \imath, G, R, \hat{T})$ where $S, A, \imath, G$, and R are as for MDPs, and $\hat{T}\colon S \times A \rightharpoonup \mathit{Intv}(S)$ is an *interval transition function*. Here, $\mathit{Intv}(S)$ denotes the set of interval functions $\nu\colon S \to \{[a, b] \mid 0 < a \leq b \leq 1\} \cup \{[0, 0]\}$ over S. A distribution $\mu \in \mathit{Dist}(S)$ is an *instantiation* of $\nu \in \mathit{Intv}(S)$ if $\mu(s) \in \nu(s)$ for all $s \in S$. We again say a is enabled in s if $\hat{T}(s, a)$ is defined and denote the set of enabled actions in s as $\mathit{Act}(s)$, assumed to be non-empty for all $s \in (S \setminus G)$. For each $s \in S$ and $a \in \mathit{Act}(s)$ we denote by T_s^a the set of all instantiations t_s^a of $\hat{T}(s, a)$ and define $\mathit{Post}(s, a) = \{s' \mid \underline{T}(s, a, s') > 0\}$. The MDP $\mathcal{M}$ is an *instantiation* of $\mathcal{U}$ if $T(s, a) \in T_s^a$ for all $s \in S$, $a \in A$. We denote by $[\mathcal{U}]$ the set of all instantiations of $\mathcal{U}$. Note that as all instantiations of an IMDP $\mathcal{U}$ share the same topology, the set of runs $\mathit{Runs}(\mathcal{M})$ is the same for all instantiations $\mathcal{M} \in [\mathcal{U}]$.

The semantics of the MDP $\mathcal{M}$ is given through *strategies*, i.e., mappings $\sigma\colon S \to \mathit{Dist}(A)$ where $\sigma(s)(a) = 0$ for all $a \notin \mathit{Act}(s)$. We call a run $\pi = s_0 a_0 s_1 a_1 \ldots s_n$ in $\mathcal{M}$ a *σ-run* if $\sigma(s_i)(a_i) > 0$ for all $i = 0, \ldots, n-1$. The probability of π is defined as $\Pr^\sigma(\pi) = \prod_{i=0}^{n-1} \sigma(s_i)(a_i) \cdot T(s_i, a_i, s_{i+1})$ if π is a σ-run and $\Pr^\sigma(\pi) = 0$ otherwise. The probability of some $B \subseteq \mathit{Runs}(\mathcal{M})$ w.r.t. strategy σ is defined by $\Pr^\sigma(B) = \sum_{\pi \in B} \Pr^\sigma(\pi)$. If $\Pr^\sigma(B) = 1$, then the *expected (accumulated) reward* is defined as $\mathbb{E}^\sigma(B) = \sum_{\pi \in B} \Pr^\sigma(\pi) \cdot R(\pi)$. We call $\mathcal{M}$ *contracting* [26] if $\Pr^\sigma(\Diamond G) = 1$ for all strategies σ, i.e., a goal state is almost surely reached for any strategy. The semantics of an IMDP $\mathcal{U}$ is the set of its instantiations $[\mathcal{U}]$. An IMDP $\mathcal{U}$ is *contracting* iff all MDPs in $[\mathcal{U}]$ are contracting.

Value and Quality Functions. A *value function* $V_\mathcal{M}\colon S \to \mathbb{R}$ of MDP $\mathcal{M}$ is the solution of the *Bellman equations* [11] given by $V_\mathcal{M}(s) = R(s)$ for $s \in G$ and

$$V(s) \;=\; R(s) + \max\nolimits_{a \in \mathit{Act}(s)} \sum\nolimits_{s' \in S} V_\mathcal{M}(s') \cdot T(s, a, s') \quad \text{for} \quad s \notin G.$$

The *quality* $Q_\mathcal{M}\colon S \times A \rightharpoonup \mathbb{R}$ of $\mathcal{M}$ is defined for all $s \in S$ and $a \in \mathit{Act}(s)$ by

$$Q_\mathcal{M}(s, a) \;=\; R(s) \;+ \sum\nolimits_{s' \in \mathit{Post}(s,a)} V_\mathcal{M}(s') \cdot T(s, a, s')$$

Intuitively, the quality represents the value of choosing an action a in state s continuing with a reward-maximizing strategy. For an IMDP $\mathcal{U}$, the value function differs between instantiations, leading to Bellman equations

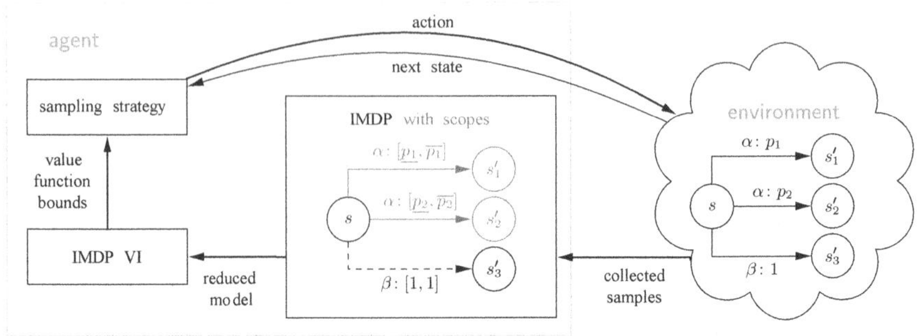

Fig. 1. Schema of reinforcement learning in gray-box MDPs. (Color figure online)

$$\underline{V}_{\mathcal{U}}(s) = \min_{\mathcal{M} \in [\mathcal{U}]} V_{\mathcal{M}}(s) \qquad \overline{V}_{\mathcal{U}}(s) = \max_{\mathcal{M} \in [\mathcal{U}]} V_{\mathcal{M}}(s)$$

for the lower and upper bounds on possible instantiations, respectively. These value functions are naturally lifted to quality functions for IMDPs. We omit subscript $\mathcal{M}$ or $\mathcal{U}$ if clear from the context. Further, we define the *pessimistically optimal strategy* $\underline{\sigma}$ for all $s \in (S \setminus G)$ as $\underline{\sigma}(s) = \arg\max_{a \in Act(s)} \underline{Q}(s, a)$ and similarly the *optimistically optimal strategy* as $\overline{\sigma}(s) = \arg\max_{a \in Act(s)} \overline{Q}(s, a)$.

3 Interval MDP Reinforcement Learning

In this section, we establish an RL algorithm for contracting gray-box MDP that generates a white-box IMDP and successively shrinks the transition probability intervals of the IMDP while updating the sampling strategy. Let $\mathcal{M} = (S, A, \imath, G, R, T)$ be a contracting MDP as above, serving as environmental model. With RL in a *gray-box* setting, the agent's objective is to determine reward-maximizing strategies knowing all components of $\mathcal{M}$ except transition probabilities T. We further make the common assumption [4,6,16] that there is a known constant p_{min} that is a lower bound on the minimal transition probability, i.e., $p_{min} \leq \min\{T(s, a, s') \mid T(s, a, s') > 0\}$.

To learn strategies in $\mathcal{M}$, samples are generated according to a *sampling strategy* determining the next action an agent performs in each state. Figure 1 shows the overall schema of the algorithm, which runs in *episodes*, i.e., batches of samples. The sampling strategy is updated after each episode by refining an internal IMDP model based on the sample runs and an IMDP value iteration.

3.1 Generating IMDPs from Sampled Gray-Box MDPs

Let $\#(s, a, s')$ denote the number of times the transition (s, a, s') occurred in samples thus far and let $\#(s, a) = \sum_{s' \in Post(s,a)} \#(s, a, s')$. The goal of each episode is to approximate $\mathcal{M}$ by an IMDP $\mathcal{U} = (S, A, \imath, G, R, \hat{T})$ that is *(1-δ)-correct*, i.e., the probability of $\mathcal{M}$ being an instantiation of $\mathcal{U}$ is at least $1-\delta$ for a given error tolerance $\delta \in \mathbb{R}$. Formally $\prod_{(s,a) \in S \times A} \mathbb{P}\big(T(s, a) \in \hat{T}(s, a)\big) \geqslant 1-\delta$ [4], where $\mathbb{P}$ refers to the probabilistic behaviour of the algorithm due to sampling

Algorithm 1: IMDP_RL($\mathcal{M}, \delta, K, N$)

Input : gray-box MDP $\mathcal{M} = (S, A, \imath, G, R, \cdot)$, error tolerance δ, $K, N \in \mathbb{N}$
Output: pessimistically and optimistically optimal strategies $\underline{\sigma}$ and $\overline{\sigma}$, value function bounds $\underline{V}$ and $\overline{V}$

forall the $(s, a) \in S \times A$ **do**
    $\sigma(s)(a) := 1/|Act(s)|$ `// initialize`
    forall the $s' \in Post(s, a)$ **do** $\hat{T}(s, a, s') := [p_{min}, 1]$
$\mathcal{U} := (S, A, \imath, G, R, \hat{T})$
forall the $k \in \{1, \ldots, K\}$ **do**
    forall the $n \in \{1, \ldots, N\}$ **do** SAMPLE($\mathcal{M}, \sigma$) `// sample runs` $\mathcal{U} :=$ UPDATE_PROB_INTERVALS($\mathcal{U}, \delta$) `// build IMDP model`
    $(\underline{V}, \overline{V}) :=$ COMPUTE_BOUNDS($\mathcal{U}, k$) `// IMDP value iteration`
    $\sigma :=$ UPDATE_STRATEGY($\mathcal{U}, \underline{V}, \overline{V}$) `// compute sampling strategy`
forall the $s \in (S \setminus G)$ **do**
    $(\underline{\sigma}(s), \overline{\sigma}(s)) := (\arg\max_{a \in Act(s)} \underline{Q}(s, a), \arg\max_{a \in Act(s)} \overline{Q}(s, a))$
return $\underline{\sigma}, \underline{V}, \overline{\sigma}, \overline{V}$

the gray-box MDP. The idea towards $(1-\delta)$-correct IMDPs is to distribute the error tolerance δ over transitions by defining a *transition error tolerance* $\eta \in \mathbb{R}$. Given a state $s \in S$, an action $s \in Act(s)$ and a successor $s' \in Post(s, a)$, we define the interval transition probability function $\hat{T}_\eta\colon S \times A \to Intv(S)$ as

$$\hat{T}_\eta(s, a, s') = \left[\tfrac{\#(s,a,s')}{\#(s,a)} - c(s, a, \eta), \tfrac{\#(s,a,s')}{\#(s,a)} + c(s, a, \eta)\right] \cap [p_{min}, 1].$$

where $c(s, a, \eta) = \sqrt{\frac{\log \eta/2}{-2\#(s,a)}}$. Hoeffding's inequality [21] then yields $T_\eta(s, a) \in \hat{T}(s, a)$ with probability at least $1-\eta$. To instantiate an environment approximation, we distribute the error tolerance δ *uniformly*, i.e., to define $\hat{T}_\eta$ and obtain $\mathcal{U}$ we set $\eta = \delta/N_t$ where N_t is the number of probabilistic transitions in $\mathcal{M}$, i.e., $N_t = |\{(s, a, s') \mid s' \in Post(s, a) \text{ and } |Post(s, a)| > 1\}|$. Note that N_t only depends on the topology of the MDP and is thus known in a gray-box setting.

Value Iteration on Environment Approximations. We rely on value iteration for IMDPs [17,44] to solve the interval Bellman equations for all possible instantiations of our environment approximation IMDP $\mathcal{U}$. Standard value iteration for IMDPs does not exhibit a stopping criterion to guarantee soundness of the results. For soundness, we extend interval value iteration [6,19] with a conservative initialization bound for the value function. For technical details of the value iteration on IMDPs we refer to the appendix.

3.2 IMDP-Based PAC Reinforcement Learning

Piecing together the parts discussed so far, we obtain an IMDP-based RL algorithm sketched in Algorithm 1 (cf. also Fig. 1), comprising K episodes with N sample runs each, updating the model and performing a value iteration (see

Line 5 and Line 6, respectively). Both K and N can be seen as parameters limiting the sampling access of the agent. The function SAMPLE in Line 6 interacts with the environment $\mathcal{M}$ and chooses either a yet not sampled action, or samples an action according to σ. A run ends when entering a goal state $s \in G$, or upon reaching a length of $|S|$. The latter is to prevent runs from acquiring a large number of samples by simply staying inside a cycle for as long as possible. In Algorithm 6, the subroutine UPDATE_PROB_INTERVALS incorporates the fresh gathered samples from the environment into the internal IMDP representation as outlined in Sect. 3.1, updating transition probability intervals. The IMDP value iteration COMPUTE_BOUNDS in Line 7 yields new upper and lower value functions bounds. The number of value iteration steps is $k \cdot |S|$, i.e., increases with each episode to guarantee that the value function is computed with arbitrary precision for a large number of episodes, also known as *bounded value iteration* [4,13]. The computed bounds are then used in UPDATE_STRATEGY in Line 8 to update the sampling strategy for the next episode. The environment approximation $\mathcal{U}$ can be achieved following several strategies according to which samples are generated [2]. A strategy that is widely used in SMC [4] or tabular RL [5,23,34,35] is *upper confidence bound (UCB)* sampling. The UCB strategy samples those actions a in state s that have highest upper bound on the quality $\overline{Q}(s,a)$, resolving the well-known exploration-exploitation dilemma in RL. This principle is also known as "optimism in the face of uncertainty" (OFU), referring to UCB allocating uncertain probability mass to the best possible outcome [2]. In our framework, standard UCB sampling will serve as the baseline approach. Lastly, we compute and return pessimistic and optimistic strategies along with their value function bounds, before returning them.

Theorem 1. *Let V^* be the solution to the Bellman equations of a given MDP $\mathcal{M}$. Then for all $\delta \in \,]0,1[$ and $K, N \in \mathbb{N}$ the value function bounds $\underline{V}$ and $\overline{V}$ returned by* IMDP_RL$(\mathcal{M}, \delta, K, N)$ *as of Algorithm 1 contain V^* with probability at least $1-\delta$, i.e., $\mathbb{P}\left(\underline{V}(s) \leqslant V^*(s) \leqslant \overline{V}(s)\right) \geqslant 1-\delta$ for all $s \in S$.*

4 Learning Under Limited Sampling Access

Previous work has shown that RL algorithms utilizing the OFU principle converge towards an optimal solution [38]. However, they are known to converge rather slowly, requiring lots of sampling data and training time. In this section, we use our IMDP-RL algorithm presented in Algorithm 1 in a setting where sampling access is limited, i.e., the parameters K and N are fixed. Then, the OFU principle might be not suitable anymore, as the strategy is learnt under an optimistic view for increasing confidence in the actions' impacts, which requires lots of samples for every action. We propose to focus on finding "good" strategies within the bounded number samples rather than on guaranteed convergence to an optimal strategy. Specifically, we present two complementary methods to reduce the action spaces during sampling: *lower confidence bound sampling* and *action scoping*. Both methods are parametrizable and thus can be adapted to the model size as well as the bound imposed on the number of samples.

4.1 Lower Confidence Bound Sampling

As new sampling strategy incorporated in Line 8 of Algorithm 1, we propose to choose an action a in a state s if it has the highest *lower bound* $\underline{Q}(s,a)$ instead of the highest *upper bound* as within UCB sampling. While then the agent still naturally chooses actions that were already sampled often with high rewards, this avoids further exploring actions with high transition uncertainty. However, such a *lower confidence bound (LCB)* sampling might result in performing exploitations only. Hence, we include an ϵ-greedy strategy [38] into LCB sampling: In each step, with probability $1-\epsilon$ the action with the highest LCB is sampled and with probability ϵ a random action is chosen. In the following, we identify LCB sampling with a degrading ϵ-greedy LCB strategy. Note that also any other exploration strategies, such as sampling with decaying ϵ or *softmax action selection* [38], can easily be integrated into LCB sampling.

While our focus of LCB sampling is on exploiting "good" actions, we can still guarantee convergence towards an optimal strategy in the long run:

Theorem 2. *Algorithm 1 with LCB sampling converges towards an optimal solution, i.e., for $K \to \infty$ both $\underline{V}$ and $\overline{V}$ converge pointwise towards V^*, and their corresponding strategies $\underline{\sigma}$ and $\overline{\sigma}$ converge towards optimal strategies.*

Similar to how UCB sampling can provide PAC guarantees [4], we can provide PAC guarantees for the value function bounds returned by Algorithm 1 as Theorem 1 guarantees that the solution is in the computed interval with high probability $1-\delta$ and Theorem 2 guarantees that the interval can become arbitrarily small converging towards the optimal solution from both sides.

4.2 Action Scoping

As another approach to compete with resource constraints, we propose to permanently remove unpromising actions from the learned IMDP model, forcing the agent to focus on a subset of enabled actions from the environment MDP. We formalize this idea by setting the *scope* of a state to the set of actions that the agent is allowed to perform in that state.

Scope Formation. As depicted in Fig. 1, scopes are introduced after each episode based on the samples of that episode. Initially, all enabled actions are within a scope. Removing an action a from the scope in s is enforced by modifying the interval transition function $\hat{T}$ of $\mathcal{U}$ to the zero interval function at (s,a), i.e., $\hat{T}(s,a,s') = [0,0]$ for all $s' \in \mathit{Post}(s,a)$. Scope formation has several notable advantages. First, removing action a from a scope in s reduces the action space $\mathit{Act}(s)$, leading to more sampling data for remaining actions as $\sigma(s)(a) = 0$ for all future episodes. Further, the removal of actions may also reduce the state space in case states are only reachable through specific actions. These positive effects of scoping come at its cost of the algorithm not necessarily converging towards an optimal strategy anymore (cf. Theorem 2). The reason is in possibly removing an optimal action due to unfortunate sampling.

Eager and Conservative Scopes. We introduce two different scoping schemes: *eager* and *conservative*. Both schemes are tunable by a parameter $h \in]0,1[$ that specifies the transition error tolerance similar as $\eta = \delta/N_t$ does in our IMDP construction (see Sect. 3.1). Intuitively, while the formal analysis by means of Line 7 in Algorithm 1 guarantees $1-\delta$ correctness, we allow for different confidence intervals depending on h when forming scopes. Here, greater h corresponds to higher tolerance and hence smaller action scopes.

To define scopes, we introduce $\mathcal{U}_h = (S, A, \imath, G, R, \hat{T}_h)$. That is, $\mathcal{U}_h$ is an IMDP with the same topology as the internal model $\mathcal{U}$, but allows an error tolerance of h in each transition. We denote the corresponding solution to the interval Bellman equations of $\mathcal{U}_h$ by $\underline{V}_h$ and $\overline{V}_h$, respectively, and the quality functions as $\underline{Q}_h$ and $\overline{Q}_h$. Additionally, the *mean quality function* $\dot{Q}$ is computed from the solution of the Bellman equations on the maximum likelihood MDP $\dot{\mathcal{M}} = (S, A, \imath, G, R, \dot{T})$ where $\dot{T}(s,a,s') = \#(s,a,s')/\#(s,a)$ are the maximum likelihood estimates of the transition probabilities.

In state s an action a is *eagerly* removed from its scope if $\dot{Q}(s,a) < \underline{V}_h(s)$, i.e., if the mean quality of a is lower than the lower bound of the (presumably) best action. The idea is that a is most likely not worth exploring if its expected value is lower than what another action provides with high probability. Likewise, an action a is *conservatively* removed from the scope of a state s if $\overline{Q}_h(s,a) < \underline{V}_h(s)$, i.e., the upper bound quality of a is lower than the lower bound of the (presumably) best action. Here the idea is similar as for eager scoping but with a more cautious estimate on the expected value from action a (observe $\overline{Q}_h(s,a) > \dot{Q}(s,a)$). Note that the parameter h is only used as an error tolerance in $\mathcal{U}_h$ in order to reduce the action scopes. The bound $\underline{V}$ and $\overline{V}$ returned in Algorithm 1 still use an error tolerance of δ/N_t per transition.

5 Implementation and Evaluation

To investigate properties of the algorithms presented, we developed a prototypical implementation in PYTHON and conducted several experimental studies, driven by the following research questions:

(RQ1) How do UCB and LCB influence the quality of synthesized strategies?
(RQ2) Does action scoping contribute to synthesize nearly optimal strategies when limiting the number of samples?

5.1 Experiment Setup

We ran our experiments on various community benchmarks from the formal-methods and RL communities. All our experiments were carried out using PYTHON 3.9 on a MacBook Air M1 machine running macOS 11.5.2. For each system variant and scoping parameter, we learn M strategies (i.e., run the algorithm M times) in $K = 50$ episodes each with batch size N as the number of state-action pairs that have a probabilistic successor distribution. Plots show results averaged over the M learned strategies. We chose an error tolerance $\delta = 0.1$, a total of $k \cdot |S|$ value iteration steps in the k-th episode, and an exploration of $\epsilon = 0.1$.

Models. For an evaluation, we focus on two models: RaceTrack and multi-armed bandits. Results for all other experiments can be found in the appendix.

In RaceTrack [8,10,18,30], an agent controls a vehicle in a two-dimensional grid where the task is to reach a goal position from some start position, not colliding with wall tiles. Figure 2 depicts two example tracks from Barto et al. [10], which we identify as "small track" (left) and "big track" (right). At each step, the movement in the last step is repeated, possibly modified by 1 tile in either direction, leading to 9 possible actions in each state. Environmental noise is modelled by changing the vehicle position by 1 in each direction with small probability. We formulate RaceTrack as RL problem by assigning goal states with one reward and all other states with zero reward. In the case that the vehicle has to cross wall tiles towards the new position, the run ends, not obtaining any reward. In RaceTrack experiments, we learn $M = 10$ strategies constrained by $N = 940$ sample runs.

The second main model is a variant of multi-armed bandits with one initial state having 100 actions, each with a biased coin toss uniformly ranging from 0.25 to 0.75 probability, gaining one reward and returning to the initial state. Here, we learn $M = 100$ strategies constrained by $N = 101$ sample runs.

5.2 Sampling Methods (RQ1)

We investigate the differences of UCB and LCB sampling within RaceTrack.

State-Space Coverage. UCB and LCB sampling differ notably in covering the state space while learning. With UCB sampling, actions with high uncertainty are more likely to be executed, lowering their upper bound and thus increasing the chance of other actions with higher uncertainty in the next sample run. Hence, UCB sampling leads to exploration of many actions and thus to a high coverage of the state space. In contrast, LCB sampling increases confidence in one particular action shown viable in past samples, leading to sample the same action sequences more often. Hence, LCB sampling is likely to cover only those states visited by one successful sampling strategy, showing low coverage of the state space. This can be also observed in our experiments. Figure 2 shows the frequency of visiting positions in the small and big example tracks, ranging from high (red) to low (white) frequencies. Both tracks already illustrate that UCB sampling provides higher state-space coverage than LCB sampling. The small track is symmetric and for each strategy striving towards a lower path, there is a corresponding equally performing strategy towards an upper path. UCB sampling treats both directions equally, while the LCB sampling method in essential learns one successful path and increases its confidence, which is further reinforced in the following samples. reached by one of the symmetric strategies.

Robustness. A further difference of the sampling methods is in dealing with less-explored situations, where UCB sampling is likely to explore new situations but LCB sampling prefers actions that increase the likelihood of returning to

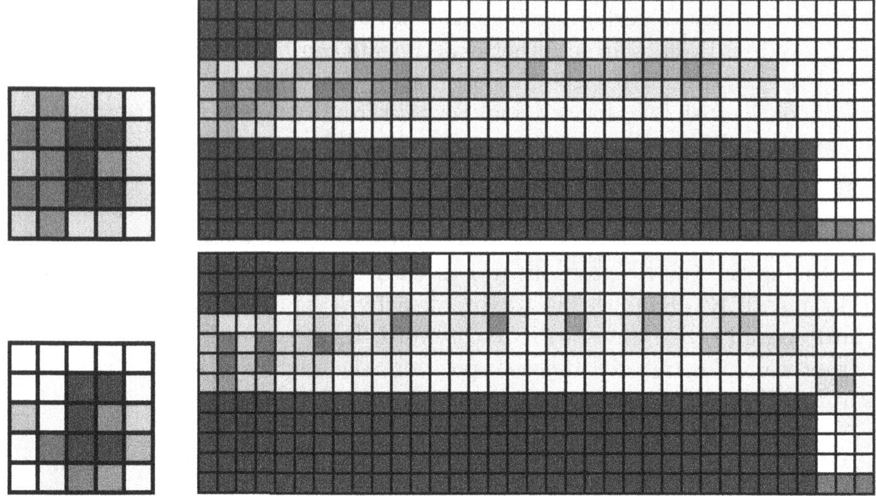

Fig. 2. RACETRACK exploration visualization of UCB sampling (top) and LCB sampling (bottom), tiles are colored by start (yellow), goal (green), wall (dark gray), and visit frequency (red-white). (Color figure online)

known states of an already learned viable strategy. This is due to those states having smaller confidence intervals and thus a greater lower bound on the value and quality functions. Figure 2 shows this effect in the frequency plot of the big track: LCB sampling leads to only few isolated positions with high visit frequencies, while UCB shows a trajectory of visited positions.

Guaranteed Bounds. The different characteristics of UCB and LCB sampling can also be observed during the learning process in the small track. In Fig. 3 on the left we show $\underline{V}$ and $\overline{V}$ after each episode. Note that these bounds apply to different strategies, i.e., the optimistically optimal strategy $\underline{\sigma}$ maximizes $\underline{V}$, while the pessimistically optimal strategy $\overline{\sigma}$ maximizes $\overline{V}$. Here, LCB provides values $\underline{V}$ more close to the optimum and, due to its exploitation strategy, gains more confidence in its learned strategy. However, unlike UCB sampling, it cannot improve on $\overline{V}$ significantly, since parts of the environment remain mostly unexplored. We plot bounds under the single fixed strategy $\underline{\sigma}$ on the right. After 50 episodes, UCB then can provide value function bounds $[0.29, 0.75]$, while LCB provides $[0.33, 0.53]$, being closer to the optimal value of 0.49.

LCB is also favourable under limited sampling access, e.g., in (mostly) symmetric environments as the small track: UCB explores the symmetry and requires at least double samples for achieving a similar confidence on the learned strategy.

Concerning **(RQ1)**, we showed that LCB sampling can provide better strategies with high confidence than UCB sampling, while UCB sampling shows better bounds when ranging over all strategies.

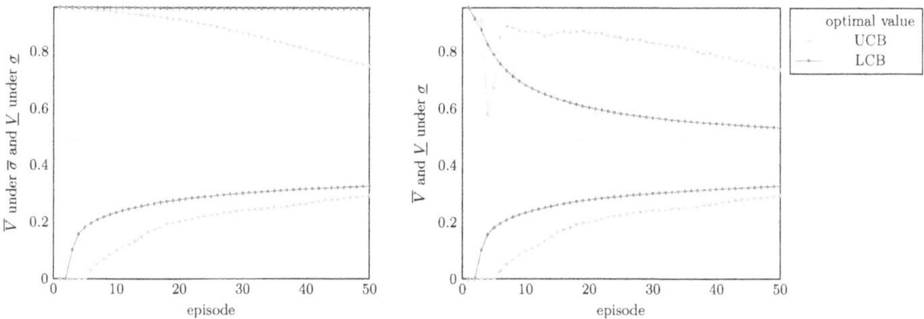

Fig. 3. Comparison of obtained bounds under all strategies (left) and under pessimistically optimal strategy $\underline{\sigma}$ (right).

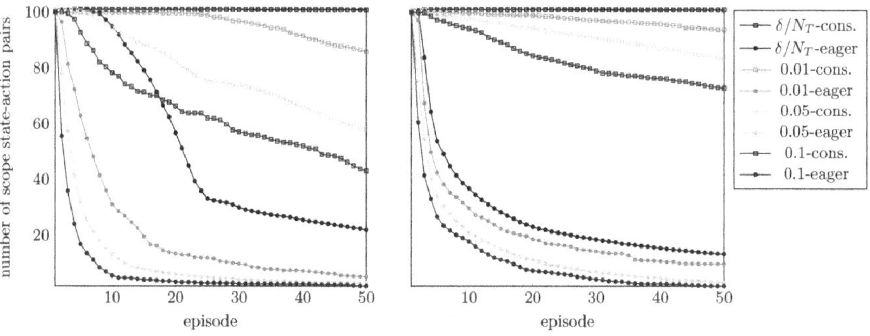

Fig. 4. Action-space reduction by action scoping (UCB left, LCB right).

5.3 Impact of Scoping (RQ2)

We now investigate the impact of action scoping and its parameter h on the multi-armed bandit experiment.

Action-Space Reduction. Figure 4 shows the number of state-action pairs in the IMDP after each episode w.r.t. UCB and LCB sampling. Here, eager and conservative action scoping is considered with various scoping parameters h. As expected, more actions are removed for greater h. Since $\dot{Q}(s,a) \leqslant \overline{Q}_h(s,a)$, eager scoping leads to more actions being removed than conservative scoping (cf. eager plots in the lower part of the figures). Observe that the choice of eager or conservative scoping has more impact than the choice of h. In terms of the sampling method we observe that for conservative scoping with UCB sampling more actions are removed from scopes than with LCB sampling. A possible explanation is that in LCB sampling, suboptimal actions do not acquire enough samples to sufficiently reduce the upper bound of their expected reward.

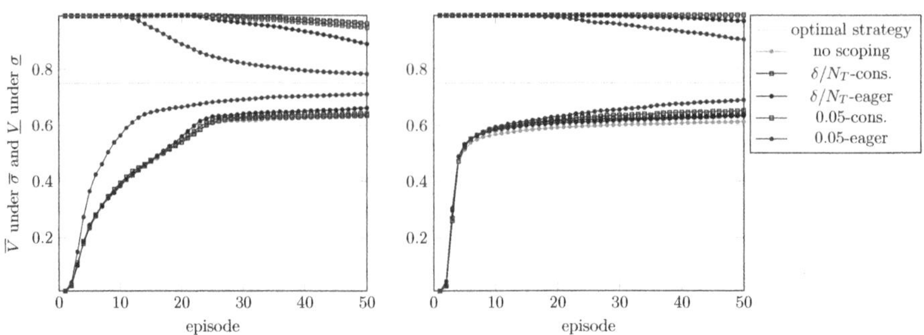

Fig. 5. Bounds of the subsystem obtained by scoping (UCB left, LCB right).

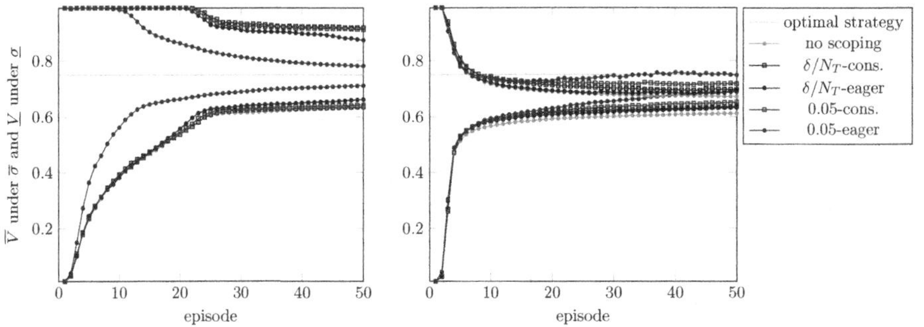

Fig. 6. Bounds for pessimistically optimal strategy (UCB left, LCB right).

Strategy Bounds. Next, we investigate the bounds obtained by the strategies returned by Algorithm 1. For brevity, we focus here on the cases $h = \delta/N_t$ and $h = 0.05$. Our results are plotted in Fig. 5 and Fig. 6 for $\underline{V}$ and $\overline{V}$ on the subsystem obtained by applying action scopes with both $\underline{\sigma}$ and $\overline{\sigma}$ and solely $\underline{\sigma}$, respectively. For UCB sampling, we observe that bounds tighten faster the more actions are removed from scopes and reduce the system size, i.e., particularly for eager scoping and for h=0.05. For LCB, scopes do not have such a drastic influence, since actions are only leaving the scope if there is an alternative action with high $\underline{V}$, in which case the latter action is sampled mostly anyway.

Sampling Strategy Quality. In Fig. 7 we plot the expected total reward of the employed sampling strategy σ in Algorithm 1 after each episode. Eager scoping tremendously improves the quality of the sampling strategy for both UCB and LCB sampling. For the UCB strategy we observe an initial monotonic increase of the online performance that eventually drops off. This is because a lot of actions cannot improve on the trivial upper bound of 1 until a lot of samples are acquired. In the first roughly 20 episodes increasingly more, mostly suboptimal, actions have their upper bound decreased, explaining the initial monotonic increase. Once all actions have and upper bound below 1, the fluctuations stem from the

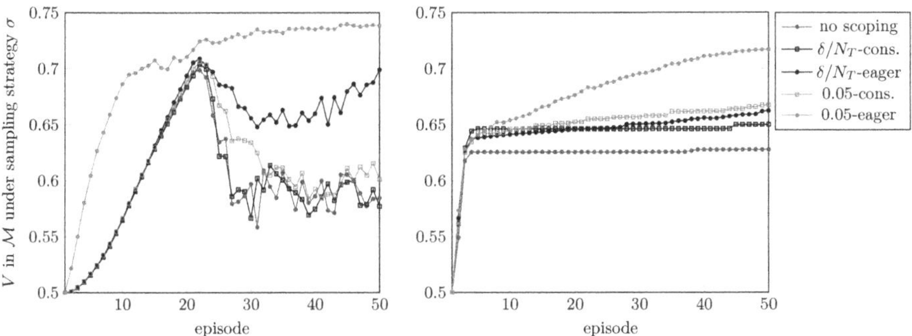

Fig. 7. Expected total reward w.r.t. sampling strategy σ (UCB left, LCB right).

fact that UCB sampling may explore a particular action takes the full N runs of an episode, even if the action is suboptimal and only has a high upper bound due to a lack of samples. Especially here, scoping helps to eliminate such actions and avoids sampling them for a full episode just to confirm the action was indeed suboptimal. For LCB sampling the better performance with scoping is due to suboptimal actions being removed and thus not eligible in the exploration step with probability ϵ.

Subsystem Bounds. With the introduction of scopes, our RL algorithm is not guaranteed to converge to optimal values. To determine whether optimal actions are removed from scopes in practice, we find the optimal strategy that only considers actions within the computed scope. Note that for the transition function we use the exact probabilities as in the environment MDP. The results are given in Table 1. Without scoping the subsystem is just the entire environment. When introducing scopes, we did not remove the optimal action via conservative scoping a single time with either sampling method, even for $h = 0.05$. Only with eager scoping we saw the optimal action being removed from the scope, but the optimal strategy in the subsystem still performs reasonably well compared to the overall optimal strategy. The fact we observe this only with eager scoping is not surprising, as removing more actions from scopes (recall Fig. 4) of course increases the chance of removing the optimal action in a state.

For **(RQ2)**, we conclude that for both UCB and LCB sampling, scoping and especially eager scoping significantly improves the quality of learned strategies after few samples, while only slightly deviating from the optimal strategy. In the UCB setting, scoping leads to further exploitation and thus better bounds.

Table 1. Values of the optimal strategy in the multi-armed bandit model.

	no	UCB-cons.		UCB-eager		LCB-cons.		LCB-eager	
	scoping	$h{=}\delta/N_t$	$h{=}0.05$	$h{=}\delta/N_t$	$h{=}0.05$	$h{=}\delta/N_t$	$h{=}0.05$	$h{=}\delta/N_t$	$h{=}0.05$
value	0.75	0.75	0.75	0.75	0.742	0.75	0.75	0.746	0.739

5.4 Further Examples

We ran our algorithms on several other environment MDPs from the RL and formal-methods communities (cf. [9]). In general, the strategy learned from LCB yields equal or higher lower bounds and tighter bounds for single strategies, while UCB sampling gives tighter bounds for the entire system. Employing action scoping generally tightens the bounds further with the eager scoping emphasizing this effect. The margins of the differences vary between the examples. In general, both LCB sampling and scoping have biggest impact on large action spaces and on models with high probability deviations such as with small error probabilities. On the flipside, we observed that LCB performs poorly when mostly or fully deterministic actions or even runs are available, as those incur little uncertainty and thus tend to have relatively large lower bounds even with few samples.

6 Concluding Remarks

We devised novel model-based RL algorithms that are inspired by efficient human reasoning under time constraints. Similar to humans tending to stick and return to known situations during strategy learning, LCB exploration favors to return to states with high confidence and proceeding with viable learned strategies. On the action level, scoping implements a reduction of the exploration space as humans do when favoring known actions without further exploration. As for humans acting under resource constraints, both ingredients have been shown to yield better strategies after few sample runs than classical RL methods, especially when choosing high scoping parameters that foster action scoping. While our methods synthesize good strategies faster, an optimal strategy might be not achievable in the limit.

We mainly discussed applications of our techniques in the setting of reinforcement learning. Nevertheless, they can well be utilized also in the formal methods domain, providing a variant for statistical model checking of MDPs, asking for the existence of a strategy to reach a goal with accumulating a certain reward.

While not the main focus of this paper, for future work it is well possible to extend our approach also to a black-box setting, i.e., without knowledge about the topology of the MDP, using similar techniques as in [4]. One advantage of using the gray-box setting is in also ensuring applicability to the instance of infinite state MDPs with finitely many actions if this MDP can be effectively explored. For this, it suffices to consider only a finite fragment of the MDP and restricting the sample lengths to a fixed bound.

References

1. https://osf.io/r24mu/?view_only=b44cec578cce44e5920f150940f68230
2. Amin, S., Gomrokchi, M., Satija, H., van Hoof, H., Precup, D.: A survey of exploration methods in reinforcement learning (2021)
3. Anderson, J.R.: Learning and Memory: An Integrated Approach, 2nd edn. Wiley, Hoboken (2000)
4. Ashok, P., Křetínský, J., Weininger, M.: PAC statistical model checking for Markov decision processes and stochastic games. In: Dillig, I., Tasiran, S. (eds.) CAV 2019. LNCS, vol. 11561, pp. 497–519. Springer, Cham (2019). https://doi.org/10.1007/978-3-030-25540-4_29
5. Auer, P., Cesa-Bianchi, N., Fischer, P.: Finite-time analysis of the multiarmed bandit problem. Mach. Learn. **47**, 235–256 (2004)
6. Baier, C., Klein, J., Leuschner, L., Parker, D., Wunderlich, S.: Ensuring the reliability of your model checker: interval iteration for Markov decision processes. In: Majumdar, R., Kunčak, V. (eds.) CAV 2017. LNCS, vol. 10426, pp. 160–180. Springer, Cham (2017). https://doi.org/10.1007/978-3-319-63387-9_8
7. Baier, C., Cuevas Rivera, D., Dubslaff, C., Kiebel, S.J.: Human-Inspired Models for Tactile Computing, chap. 8, pp. 173–200. Academic Press (2021)
8. Baier, C., Dubslaff, C., Hermanns, H., Klauck, M., Klüppelholz, S., Köhl, M.A.: Components in probabilistic systems: suitable by construction. In: Margaria, T., Steffen, B. (eds.) ISoLA 2020. LNCS, vol. 12476, pp. 240–261. Springer, Cham (2020). https://doi.org/10.1007/978-3-030-61362-4_13
9. Baier, C., Dubslaff, C., Wienhöft, P., Kiebel, S.J.: Strategy synthesis in Markov decision processes under limited sampling access. Extended Version (2023). https://arxiv.org/abs/2303.12718
10. Barto, A.G., Bradtke, S.J., Singh, S.P.: Learning to act using real-time dynamic programming. Artif. Intell. **72**(1–2), 81–138 (1995)
11. Bertsekas, D.P., Tsitsiklis, J.N.: An analysis of stochastic shortest path problems. Math. Oper. Res. **16**(3), 580–595 (1991). https://doi.org/10.1287/moor.16.3.580
12. Brafman, R.I., Tennenholtz, M.: R-max - a general polynomial time algorithm for near-optimal reinforcement learning. J. Mach. Learn. Res. **3**, 213–231 (2003). https://doi.org/10.1162/153244303765208377
13. Brázdil, T., et al.: Verification of Markov decision processes using learning algorithms. In: Cassez, F., Raskin, J.-F. (eds.) ATVA 2014. LNCS, vol. 8837, pp. 98–114. Springer, Cham (2014). https://doi.org/10.1007/978-3-319-11936-6_8
14. Chatterjee, K., Sen, K., Henzinger, T.A.: Model-checking ω-regular properties of interval Markov chains. In: Amadio, R. (ed.) FoSSaCS 2008. LNCS, vol. 4962, pp. 302–317. Springer, Heidelberg (2008). https://doi.org/10.1007/978-3-540-78499-9_22
15. Daca, P., Henzinger, T.A., Křetínský, J., Petrov, T.: Faster statistical model checking for unbounded temporal properties (2016)
16. Daca, P., Henzinger, T.A., Křetínský, J., Petrov, T.: Faster statistical model checking for unbounded temporal properties. ACM Trans. Comput. Logic **18**(2), 1–25 (2017). https://doi.org/10.1145/3060139
17. Givan, R., Leach, S., Dean, T.: Bounded-parameter Markov decision processes. Artif. Intell. **122**(1), 71–109 (2000). https://doi.org/10.1016/S0004-3702(00)00047-3
18. Gros, T.P., Hermanns, H., Hoffmann, J., Klauck, M., Steinmetz, M.: Deep statistical model checking. In: Gotsman, A., Sokolova, A. (eds.) FORTE 2020. LNCS,

vol. 12136, pp. 96–114. Springer, Cham (2020). https://doi.org/10.1007/978-3-030-50086-3_6
19. Haddad, S., Monmege, B.: Interval iteration algorithm for MDPs and IMDPs. Theoret. Comput. Sci. **735**, 111–131 (2018). https://doi.org/10.1016/j.tcs.2016.12.003
20. He, R., Jennings, P., Basu, S., Ghosh, A., Wu, H.: A bounded statistical approach for model checking of unbounded until properties, pp. 225–234 (2010)
21. Hoeffding, W.: Probability inequalities for sums of bounded random variables. J. Am. Stat. Assoc. **58**(301), 13–30 (1963)
22. Ishii, S., Yoshida, W., Yoshimoto, J.: Control of exploitation-exploration meta-parameter in reinforcement learning. Neural Netw. **15**(4), 665–687 (2002). https://doi.org/10.1016/S0893-6080(02)00056-4
23. Jaksch, T., Ortner, R., Auer, P.: Near-optimal regret bounds for reinforcement learning. J. Mach. Learn. Res. **11**(51), 1563–1600 (2010)
24. Kaelbling, L.P.: Learning in Embedded Systems. The MIT Press, Cambridge (1993). https://doi.org/10.7551/mitpress/4168.001.0001
25. Kaelbling, L.P., Littman, M.L., Moore, A.W.: Reinforcement learning: a survey. J. Artif. Int. Res. **4**(1), 237–285 (1996)
26. Kallenberg, L.: Lecture Notes Markov Decision Problems - version 2020 (2020)
27. Kearns, M., Singh, S.: Near-optimal reinforcement learning in polynomial time. Mach. Learn. **49**, 209–232 (2002). https://doi.org/10.1023/A:1017984413808
28. Legay, A., Lukina, A., Traonouez, L.M., Yang, J., Smolka, S.A., Grosu, R.: Statistical model checking. In: Steffen, B., Woeginger, G. (eds.) Computing and Software Science. LNCS, vol. 10000, pp. 478–504. Springer, Cham (2019). https://doi.org/10.1007/978-3-319-91908-9_23
29. Mitchell, T.: Machine Learning. McGraw Hill, New York (1997)
30. Pineda, L.E., Zilberstein, S.: Planning under uncertainty using reduced models: revisiting determinization. In: ICAPS (2014)
31. Puterman, M.: Markov Decision Processes: Discrete Stochastic Dynamic Programming. Wiley, Hoboken (1994)
32. Schwoebel, S., Markovic, D., Smolka, M.N., Kiebel, S.J.: Balancing control: a Bayesian interpretation of habitual and goal-directed behavior. J. Math. Psychol. **100**, 102472 (2021). https://doi.org/10.1016/j.jmp.2020.102472
33. Sen, K., Viswanathan, M., Agha, G.: Model-checking Markov chains in the presence of uncertainties. In: Hermanns, H., Palsberg, J. (eds.) TACAS 2006. LNCS, vol. 3920, pp. 394–410. Springer, Heidelberg (2006). https://doi.org/10.1007/11691372_26
34. Strehl, A., Littman, M.: An empirical evaluation of interval estimation for Markov decision processes, pp. 128–135 (2004). https://doi.org/10.1109/ICTAI.2004.28
35. Strehl, A., Littman, M.: An analysis of model-based interval estimation for Markov decision processes. J. Comput. Syst. Sci. **74**, 1309–1331 (2008). https://doi.org/10.1016/j.jcss.2007.08.009
36. Suilen, M., Simão, T., Jansen, N., Parker, D.: Robust anytime learning of Markov decision processes. In: Proceedings of NeurIPS (2022)
37. Sutton, R.S.: Dyna, an integrated architecture for learning, planning, and reacting. SIGART Bull. **2**(4), 160–163 (1991). https://doi.org/10.1145/122344.122377
38. Sutton, R.S., Barto, A.G.: Reinforcement Learning: An Introduction, 2nd edn. The MIT Press, Cambridge (2018)
39. Thrun, S.B., Möller, K.: Active exploration in dynamic environments. In: Moody, J., Hanson, S., Lippmann, R.P. (eds.) Advances in Neural Information Processing Systems, vol. 4. Morgan-Kaufmann (1992)

40. Watkins, C.J.C.H., Dayan, P.: Q-learning. Mach. Learn. **8**, 279–292 (1992). https://doi.org/10.1007/BF00992698
41. Weber, R.: On the Gittins index for multiarmed bandits. Ann. Appl. Probab. **2**(4), 1024–1033 (1992). https://doi.org/10.1214/aoap/1177005588
42. Wiering, M., Schmidhuber, J.: Efficient model-based exploration. In: Proceedings of the Sixth Intercational Conference on Simulation of Adaptive Behaviour: From Animals to Animats 6, pp. 223–228. MIT Press/Bradford Books (1998)
43. Wood, W., Rünger, D.: Psychology of habit. Annu. Rev. Psychol. **67**(1), 289–314 (2016). https://doi.org/10.1146/annurev-psych-122414-033417
44. Wu, D., Koutsoukos, X.: Reachability analysis of uncertain systems using bounded-parameter Markov decision processes. Artif. Intell. **172**(8), 945–954 (2008). https://doi.org/10.1016/j.artint.2007.12.002
45. Younes, H.L.S., Clarke, E.M., Zuliani, P.: Statistical verification of probabilistic properties with unbounded until. In: Davies, J., Silva, L., Simao, A. (eds.) SBMF 2010. LNCS, vol. 6527, pp. 144–160. Springer, Heidelberg (2011). https://doi.org/10.1007/978-3-642-19829-8_10

Learning Symbolic Timed Models from Concrete Timed Data

Simon Dierl[2], Falk Maria Howar[2], Sean Kauffman[1](✉), Martin Kristjansen[1], Kim Guldstrand Larsen[1], Florian Lorber[1], and Malte Mauritz[2]

[1] Aalborg Universitet, Aalborg, Denmark
seank@cs.aau.dk
[2] TU Dortmund University, Dortmund, Germany

Abstract. We present a technique for learning explainable timed automata from passive observations of a black-box function, such as an artificial intelligence system. Our method accepts a single, long, timed word with mixed input and output actions and learns a Mealy machine with one timer. The primary advantage of our approach is that it constructs a symbolic observation tree from a concrete timed word. This symbolic tree is then transformed into a human comprehensible automaton. We provide a prototype implementation and evaluate it by learning the controllers of two systems: a brick-sorter conveyor belt trained with reinforcement learning and a real-world derived smart traffic light controller. We compare different model generators using our symbolic observation tree as their input and achieve the best results using k-tails. In our experiments, we learn smaller and simpler automata than existing passive timed learners while maintaining accuracy.

1 Introduction

In recent years, machine learning has been integrated into more and more areas of life. However, the safety of such systems often cannot be verified due to their complexity and unknown internal structure. For such black-box systems, model learning can provide additional information. Model learning [14] typically deduces an executable representation either by monitoring the System Under Learning (SUL) (*passive learning*), or by prompting the SUL (*active learning*). Either approach produces a model consistent with the observations. These models can be used for verification methods like model checking, but often simply obtaining a graphical illustration of the internal workings of the system can provide an increase in confidence that it works as intended. The approach is especially useful for artificial intelligence (AI) systems, where a function is constructed from training data and no human-readable explanation might exist.

Active algorithms like Angluin's L* [4] have shown promising results. However, they can be difficult to apply in practice, as many systems exist that provide no way for a learner to interact with them. An example of such a system could be the controller of a smart traffic light, where the inputs are the arrival of cars in a street lane. Luckily, in the modern era of big data, many systems are monitored

K. Y. Rozier and S. Chaudhuri (Eds.): NFM 2023, LNCS 13903, pp. 104–121, 2023.
https://doi.org/10.1007/978-3-031-33170-1_7

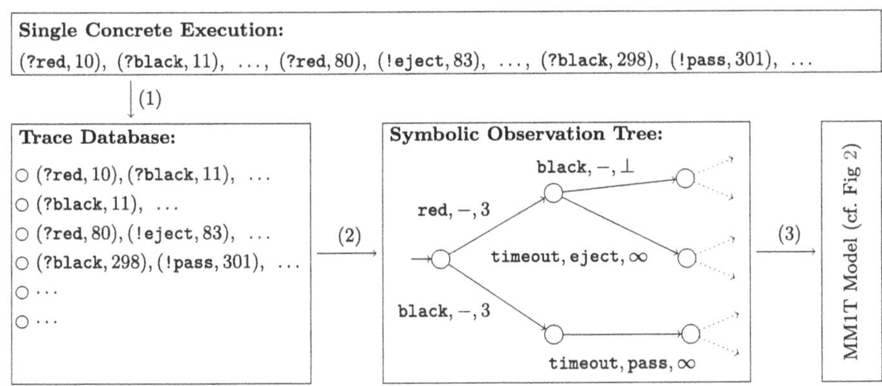

Fig. 1. Inference workflow: Find initial conditions and split into trace database (1), compute symbolic observation tree from database (2), generate MM1T (3).

throughout their deployment in the real world, producing log files that can span over months or years. Passive learning algorithms like (timed) k-tails [22,23] take large numbers of such traces, convert them into a tree-like structure, and apply state-merging techniques to collapse them into cyclic automata.

We propose the generation of a symbolic oracle, which can be used as a pre-processing step to apply both active and passive learning algorithms. Figure 1 shows our proposed workflow. The first step in creating the oracle is to instantiate a *trace database* from a *single concrete execution trace* by defining symbolic conditions on what constitutes an initial location, i.e., where the system has reset to its default configuration. This approach supports learning when only a single trace is available (e.g., a long traffic log for the controller of a specific intersection). Next, we show how to build symbolic representations of the traces. These can be exhaustively enumerated to build a *symbolic observation tree.*

By constructing a trace database and symbolic observation tree from a log of system operation, we enable both active and passive learning approaches. We demonstrate active learning using the *Mealy machine learner* by Vaandager et al. [26]. Instead of the learner interacting with the system directly, it answers *membership queries* using the symbolic observation tree. For *equivalence queries* we use random runs from the trace database for estimating the correctness of the hypothesis. Since learning algorithms designed for use with a complete oracle might ask queries that the trace database cannot answer, the inferred models will, in general, not be minimal (distinguishing states for missing information). We minimize the resulting *Mealy Machine with a Single Timer (MM1T)* via a *partial Mealy minimization* algorithm that greedily merges compatible states.

For passive learning, we directly use the symbolic tree, that, by construction, contains all the information in the database. It can be transformed into a final model by existing approaches like k-*tails* [22,23], or via *partial Mealy minimization.*

Contribution. First, we show how to turn one long trace into a trace database of short traces starting with an initial condition. We show how to identify initial conditions along the trace, based on symbolic queries, and discuss what might constitute an initial condition in a black-box system. Then, we present how to derive a symbolic observation tree from these traces, which seems to carry the right level of abstraction for human readability. Finally, we discuss and compare several post-processing methods to retrieve human-readable automata. One of these methods shows how active learning algorithms can be applied in a passive setting. We demonstrate how the readability and explainability of the produced models provide a significant advantage over previous approaches.

Case Studies. We will use a brick sorter and a smart traffic controller for an intersection as demonstrating examples. The brick sorter is inspired by [17]. It randomly receives either red or black blocks. These are scanned by a color sensor and transported along a conveyor belt for three seconds. Finally, a controller will eject red bricks, and let black bricks pass through. We use a timed automaton controller, trained using reinforcement learning with UPPAAL STRATEGO, as a basis for the experiments. The inputs to the SUL are $\{red, black\}$ and the outputs are $\{eject, pass\}$. The SUL contains an intentional bug: if two blocks arrive within three seconds, the variable storing the scanned color will be overwritten.

The traffic controller is based on the control system of a real intersection located in the city of Vejle in Denmark. The intersection is a four way crossing equipped with radar sensors that report the arrival of incoming cars, and can switch between five modes for the lights. Inputs are cars arriving at the different lanes of the streets. Outputs are the active traffic lights, e.g., $a_1 + a_2$ when the main road on both sides has a green light. We use real-word traffic data gathered over seven consecutive days, combined with outputs generated from a digital twin of the intersection. The digital twin is a model created in the tool UPPAAL according to a detailed specification of the traffic light controller.

2 Preliminaries

We denote the non-negative real number at which an action occurred as its *timestamp*. We refer to a finite set of actions, also known as an alphabet, as $\Sigma = \mathcal{I} \cup \mathcal{O}$ where $\mathcal{I}$ is the set of input actions and $\mathcal{O}$ is the set of output actions where $\mathcal{I} \cap \mathcal{O} = \varnothing$. The special actions $\top_{\mathcal{I}}$ and $\top_{\mathcal{O}}$ are used in symbolic queries and represent *any* input or output, respectively. The partial order $\sqsubseteq$ relates actions in $\mathcal{I} \cup \{\top_{\mathcal{I}}\}$ such that any pair of inputs $i_1, i_2 \in \mathcal{I}$ are incomparable when $i_1 \neq i_2$ and $\top_{\mathcal{I}}$ is an upper bound of $\mathcal{I}$ ($\forall i \in \mathcal{I}.\ i \sqsubseteq \top_{\mathcal{I}}$) and the same applies for $\mathcal{O} \cup \{\top_{\mathcal{O}}\}$. Given a finite alphabet Σ, a timed word is a pair $\rho = \langle \sigma, \tau \rangle$ where σ is a non-empty finite word over the alphabet Σ, and τ is a strictly increasing sequence of timestamps with the same length as σ. We call the set of all finite timed words $T\Sigma^*$. We also write a sequence of pairs of actions in Σ and timestamps to represent a timed word: $(\sigma_0, \tau_0), (\sigma_1, \tau_1), \ldots, (\sigma_n, \tau_n)$.

A constrained symbolic timed word is a pair $\langle \mathcal{S}, \varphi \rangle$ where $\mathcal{S}$ is a symbolic timed word and φ is a boolean combination of constraints on the symbolic timestamps of $\mathcal{S}$. The set of all symbolic timestamps is $\mathbb{V}$. A symbolic timed word over the finite alphabet Σ is a pair $\langle \sigma, v \rangle$ where σ is a finite word over Σ, and $v \in \mathbb{V}^*$

is a sequence of symbolic timestamps the same length as σ. We also write a sequence of pairs $(\sigma_0, v_0), (\sigma_1, v_1), \ldots, (\sigma_n, v_n)$ for a constrained symbolic timed word of length $n+1$. We write τ_i/v_i to denote that v_i takes the value τ_i.

We say that a concrete timed word *models* (written $\models$) a constrained symbolic timed word when both sequences of actions are equal, and the constraints on the symbolic timestamps are satisfied by the corresponding concrete timestamps. We use a partial order to relate actions instead of strict equality so that we can reuse the model's definition later with $\top_{\mathcal{I}}$ and $\top_{\mathcal{O}}$ as possible symbolic actions.

Definition 1 (Modeling of Symbolic Word). *Given a concrete timed word $\rho = \langle \sigma, \tau \rangle$ and a constrained symbolic timed word $\langle \mathcal{S}, \varphi \rangle$ where $\mathcal{S} = \langle \sigma', v \rangle$, we say that $\rho \models \langle \mathcal{S}, \varphi \rangle$ iff for all indices i we have $\sigma_i \sqsubseteq \sigma'_i$ and $\tau_0/v_0 \ldots \tau_n/v_n \models \varphi$.*

Example 1. In the brick-sorter example, suppose a constrained symbolic timed word $\langle \mathcal{S}, \varphi \rangle = \langle (\mathit{black}, v_0), (\mathit{eject}, v_1), v_0 + 3 \leq v_1 \rangle$ and a timed word that models it $\rho = (\mathit{black}, 0), (\mathit{eject}, 3)$. We see that $\rho \models \langle \mathcal{S}, \varphi \rangle$ since $\sigma_0 = \mathit{black} \sqsubseteq \mathcal{S}_0 = \mathit{black}$, $\sigma_1 = \mathit{eject} \sqsubseteq \mathcal{S}_1 = \mathit{eject}$, and $0 + 3 \leq 3$.

We concatenate constrained symbolic timed words $\langle \mathcal{S}_1, \varphi_1 \rangle$ and $\langle \mathcal{S}_2, \varphi_2 \rangle$ by concatenating the symbolic timed words $\mathcal{S}_1$ and $\mathcal{S}_2$ and conjoining the time constraints $\varphi_1 \wedge \varphi_2$, letting $\langle \mathcal{S}_1, \varphi_1 \rangle \cdot \langle \mathcal{S}_2, \varphi_2 \rangle \equiv \langle \mathcal{S}_1 \cdot \mathcal{S}_2, \varphi_1 \wedge \varphi_2 \rangle$.

Mealy Machines with One Timer

We learn Mealy machine models with one timer. The timer can be reset to values in $\mathbb{N}$ on transitions. We assume a special input **timeout** that triggers the expiration of the set timer and the corresponding change of a machine's state. We also assume a special output "-" that indicates no output on a transition. We first define the structure of these Mealy machines and then specify their semantics. Our definition extends the original definition by Vaandrager et al. [26] to model explicitly when a timer is reset or disabled and to allow a timer to be set already in the initial state. For a partial function $f : X \rightharpoonup Y$, we write $f(x)\downarrow$ to indicate that f is defined for x and $f(x)\uparrow$ to indicate that f is not defined for x. We fix a set of actions $\Sigma = \mathcal{I} \cup \mathcal{O}$ and use $\mathcal{I}_{\mathbf{to}}$ as a shorthand for $\mathcal{I} \cup \{\mathbf{timeout}\}$.

Definition 2 (Mealy Machine with One Timer). *A Mealy machine with one timer (MM1T) is a tuple $\mathcal{M} = \langle \mathcal{I}, \mathcal{O}, Q, q_0, \delta, \lambda, \kappa, t_0 \rangle$ with*

- *finite set $\mathcal{I}$ of inputs,*
- *finite set $\mathcal{O}$ of outputs disjoint from $\mathcal{I}_{\mathbf{to}}$,*
- *set of states $Q = Q_{\mathit{off}} \cup Q_{\mathit{on}}$, partitioned into states with and without a timer ($Q_{\mathit{off}} \cap Q_{\mathit{on}} = \varnothing$), respectively, with initial state $q_0 \in Q$,*
- *transition function $\delta : Q \times \mathcal{I}_{\mathbf{to}} \rightharpoonup Q$*
- *output function $\lambda : Q \times \mathcal{I}_{\mathbf{to}} \rightharpoonup \mathcal{O} \cup \{\text{-}\}$,*
- *timer reset $\kappa : Q \times \mathcal{I}_{\mathbf{to}} \rightharpoonup \{\infty, \bot\} \cup \mathbb{N}$, satisfying*
  - *$\delta(q, i) \in Q_{\mathit{off}} \iff \kappa(q, i) = \infty$, where no timer is set,*
  - *$q \in Q_{\mathit{off}} \wedge \delta(q, i) \in Q_{\mathit{on}} \iff \kappa(q, i) \in \mathbb{N}$, where the timer is set,*
  - *$q \in Q_{\mathit{on}} \wedge \delta(q, i) \in Q_{\mathit{on}} \iff \kappa(q, i) \in \{\bot\} \cup \mathbb{N}$, where the timer either continues or is set to a new value,*

- $\delta(q, \textbf{timeout}) \in Q_{on} \iff q \in Q_{on}$, *where timeouts only happen if the timer is running, and*

– *initial timer* $t_0 \in \{\infty\} \cup \mathbb{N}$ *s.t.* $t_0 = \infty$ *if* $q_0 \in Q_{off}$ *and* $t_0 \in \mathbb{N}$ *if* $q_0 \in Q_{on}$.

The transition function, output function, and timer reset have identical domains, i.e., $\delta(q,i)\uparrow$ *iff* $\lambda(q,i)\uparrow$ *iff* $\kappa(q,i)\uparrow$ *for* $q \in Q$ *and* $i \in \mathcal{I}$.

For a MM1T $\langle \mathcal{I}, \mathcal{O}, Q, q_0, \delta, \lambda, \kappa, t_0 \rangle$ we write $q \xrightarrow{i,o,t} q'$ for a transition from state q to q' for input i, output o, and new timer value t. If the given transition is possible, we must have that $\delta(q,i)\downarrow$.

Example 2. Figure 2 shows the MM1T for the brick-sorter example, as learned by our experiments, and illustrates the typical concepts of an MM1T. It shows MM1T $\mathcal{M} = \langle \mathcal{I}, \mathcal{O}, Q, q_0, \delta, \lambda, \kappa, t_0 \rangle$ with $\mathcal{I} = \{black, red\}, \mathcal{O} = \{pass, eject\}$, and $Q = \{q_0, q_1, q_2\}$, where $q_0 \in Q_{off}$ and $q_1, q_2 \in Q_{on}$. Additionally, we have that $\delta(q_0, red) = q_1, \lambda(q_0, red) =$ -, $\kappa(q_0, red) = 3$, and $t_0 = \infty$. We omit the remainder of transition, output, and timer reset functions for readability.

Untimed Semantics. The untimed semantics maps an untimed run to the last observed output on that run: The partial function $\mathcal{M} = \langle \mathcal{I}, \mathcal{O}, Q, q_0, \delta, \lambda, \kappa, t_0 \rangle$ $[\![\mathcal{M}]\!] : \mathcal{I}_{\mathbf{to}}^{+} \rightharpoonup \mathcal{O} \times (\{\infty, \bot\} \cup \mathbb{N})$ represents the behavior of the machine at the abstract level of how the timer is affected by the inputs. The function is defined for an *untimed word* $w = i_0, \ldots, i_n \in \mathcal{I}_{\mathbf{to}}^{*}$ if there exists a corresponding sequence of transitions in $\mathcal{M}$, i.e., let $[\![\mathcal{M}]\!](w)\downarrow$ if transitions $q_j \xrightarrow{i_j, o_j, t_j} q_{j+1}$ exist for $0 \leq j < n$, where q_0 is the initial state of $\mathcal{M}$. We call a sequence of such transitions an *untimed run*, as there is no information on exactly when transitions are taken. Finally, if we have that $[\![\mathcal{M}]\!](w)\downarrow$, the nth step of a sequence w can be found by $[\![\mathcal{M}]\!](w) = (o_n, t_n)$. Input-enabledness (i.e., totality of $[\![\mathcal{M}]\!]$) can easily be achieved by fixing a special *undefined* output, allowing us to use the active learning algorithms for Mealy machines in LearnLib [16].

Symbolic Runs. Before defining timed semantics on concrete timed words, we define symbolic runs as an intermediate construct that we will also use when generating MM1Ts from concrete traces. We need one auxiliary concept that we define inductively over the complete sequence of transitions: the current symbolic

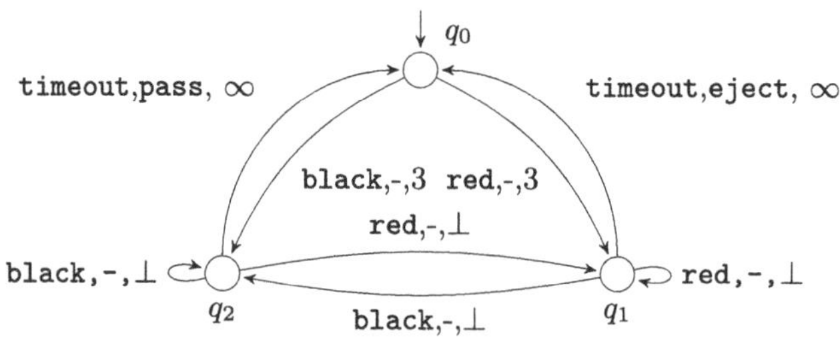

Fig. 2. Learned MM1T of the brick-sorter conveyor-belt example.

timer value θ_i at every transition. This has to be defined inductively as on some transitions a running timer is not reset. The initial timeout is $\theta_0 = v_0 + t_0$, for the start of the run at symbolic time v_0. Then, let

$$\theta_i = \begin{cases} \theta_{i-1} & \text{for } t_i = \bot \text{ (no reset)} \\ v_i + t_i & \text{otherwise (reset).} \end{cases}$$

The symbolic run is constructed from an untimed run of the form

$$q_0 \xrightarrow{i_1,o_1,t_1} q_1 , \dots, q_{n-1} \xrightarrow{i_n,o_n,t_n} q_n$$

The symbolic run is then represented by a constrained symbolic timed word and constructed as follows. In every step, we define a short constrained symbolic timed word $\langle \mathcal{S}_i, \varphi_i \rangle$ and concatenate these to form a constrained symbolic timed word for the whole sequence of transitions. For transition $q_{j-1} \xrightarrow{i_j,o_j,t_j} q_j$ let

$$\langle \mathcal{S}_j, \varphi_j \rangle = \begin{cases} \langle (o_j, v_j),\ v_j = \theta_{j-1} \rangle & \text{if } i_j = \textbf{timeout} \\ \langle (i_j, v_j),\ v_{j-1} < v_j < \theta_{j-1} \rangle & \text{else if } o_j = \texttt{-} \\ \langle (i_j, v_j)\ (o_j, v'_j),\ v_{j-1} < v_j = v'_j < \theta_{j-1} \rangle & \text{else.} \end{cases}$$

The complete symbolic run is then $\langle \mathcal{S}_1, \varphi_1 \rangle \cdot \dots \cdot \langle \mathcal{S}_n, \varphi_n \rangle$. Finally, every word in $w \in \mathcal{I}^*_{\textbf{to}}$ with $[\![\mathcal{M}]\!](w) \downarrow$ takes a unique sequence of transitions in $\mathcal{M}$ and consequently has a unique symbolic run, denoted by $\mathbf{sr}(w)$. We extend $\mathbf{sr}(\cdot)$ to sets of words by word-wise application and write $\mathbf{sr}(\mathcal{M})$ for the set of symbolic runs for words in the domain of $[\![\mathcal{M}]\!]$.

Timed Semantics. Our definition of the concrete timed semantics of $\mathcal{M}$ leverages symbolic runs. The concrete timed semantics of $\mathcal{M}$ then is the set $\mathbf{traces}(\mathcal{M}) \subseteq T\Sigma^*$ of timed words over actions $\Sigma = \mathcal{I} \cup \mathcal{O}$ such that

$$\rho \in \mathbf{traces}(\mathcal{M}) \Leftrightarrow \rho \models \langle \mathcal{S}, \varphi \rangle \text{ for some } \langle \mathcal{S}, \varphi \rangle \in \mathbf{sr}(\mathcal{M}).$$

Example 3. For the brick sorter, an untimed run could be

$$q_0 \xrightarrow{\mathit{red},\texttt{-},3} q_1 \xrightarrow{\mathit{black},\texttt{-},\bot} q_2 \xrightarrow{\mathit{timeout},\mathit{pass},\infty} q_3$$

Then, assuming $v_0 = 0$ and $t_0 = \infty$ would lead to the symbolic run

$$\langle (\mathit{red}, v_1), 0 < v_1 < 0+\infty \rangle \cdot \langle (\mathit{black}, v_2), v_1 < v_2 < v_1+3 \rangle \cdot \langle (\mathit{pass}, v_3), v_3 = v_1+3 \rangle$$

3 Trace Database

To learn an MM1T $\mathcal{M}$, we must find concrete timed words produced by the SUL that model constrained symbolic timed words in the symbolic runs of $\mathcal{M}$. However, we want to learn a model of a long-running black-box system to support more realistic logs. As such, we assume only a single timed word from which to learn[1], and we do not assume that the word begins or ends in an initial configuration. This makes learning more difficult since we cannot simply iterate over the recorded words starting from the initial state. Instead, we construct a *trace database* that is instantiated with a query to find *initial conditions*. The sub-words that model the initial conditions mark the positions in the timed word where the SUL has been reset to its initial state.

A symbolic query is an extension of a constrained symbolic timed word that supports queries for unknown inputs or outputs, and that can be modeled by timed words with *stuttering actions*. A stuttering action might occur in a concrete word several times in a row, all of which may be matched by one action in a symbolic query. We require stuttering to learn models where the initial state has transitions leading back to itself. These self-loops are common in many controllers, including our traffic controller case study, where an output is periodically triggered by a timer without any new inputs. We now describe symbolic queries before explaining how they are used to configure initial conditions.

Formally, a symbolic query is a triple $\langle \mathcal{S}, \varphi, \gamma \rangle$ where $\mathcal{S}$ is a pair $\langle \sigma, v \rangle$, φ is a constraint on the symbolic timestamps of $\mathcal{S}$, and $\gamma \in \mathbb{B}^*$ is a sequence of Booleans the same length as σ where truth indicates that stuttering is allowed for the action at the same index. Here, σ is a finite word over the alphabet $\Sigma \cup \{\top_{\mathcal{I}}, \top_{\mathcal{O}}\}$ and v is a series of symbolic timestamps the same length as σ. The special symbols $\top_{\mathcal{I}}$ and $\top_{\mathcal{O}}$ represent any *input* or *output* action, respectively. We use the convention that omitting γ when we write a symbolic query (i.e., writing $\langle \mathcal{S}, \varphi \rangle$) means that γ is *false* for all actions in $\mathcal{S}$.

We now define when a concrete trace models a symbolic query. The difference between a symbolic query and a constrained symbolic timed word is that a symbolic query may include the symbolic actions $\top_{\mathcal{I}}$ and $\top_{\mathcal{O}}$ and may permit stuttering on actions. Given an action σ_i and a symbolic timestamp v_i, the function $\textbf{\textit{repeat}}(\sigma_i, v_i) = \{(\sigma_i, v_{i,0}), \ldots, (\sigma_i, v_{i,j}), \bigvee v_{i,j} = v_i \mid j \geq 0\}$ produces a set of all constrained symbolic timed words with σ_i repeated finitely many times and constraints that require one symbolic timestamp $v_{i,j}$ to be equal to v_i.

Definition 3 (Modeling of Symbolic Query). *Given a concrete timed word ρ and a symbolic query$\langle \mathcal{S}, \varphi, \gamma \rangle$ where $\mathcal{S} = \langle \sigma, v \rangle$, $\rho \models \langle \mathcal{S}, \varphi, \gamma \rangle$ when there exists a constrained symbolic timed word u such that $\rho \models u$, where*

$$u \in \left\{ \langle \mathcal{S}'_0, \varphi'_0 \rangle \cdot \cdots \cdot \langle \mathcal{S}'_n, \varphi'_n \rangle \mid \langle \mathcal{S}'_i, \varphi'_i \rangle = \begin{cases} \textbf{\textit{repeat}}(\sigma_i, v_i) & \textit{if } \gamma_i \\ (\sigma_i, v_i), \varphi & \textit{otherwise} \end{cases} \right\}$$

Initial Conditions. A trace database is a timed word instantiated with an initial condition that serves to break it into smaller pieces and a special query to prepend to requests from the learner. The initial conditions are specified using a symbolic query and each index of the word is tested against the query to see if it satisfies the condition. If the query is satisfied, then the index is marked as a starting index for a word in the database. Subsequently, when the learner submits a symbolic query, it has no information about the initial conditions of

[1] Note that the approach also works with more than one word.

Table 1. Action statistics for our case studies. For the brick sorter, inputs are detected brick colors and outputs are sorting actions. For the intersection, inputs are lanes with detected cars and outputs are signalling configuration changes.

(a) Brick sorter

Input	Freq. [%]
red	49.5
black	50.5
Output	**Freq. [%]**
pass	49.5
reject	50.5

(b) Intersection

Input	Freq. [%]
A_2	41.8
A_1	39.2
B_{Left}	8.3
Output	**Freq. [%]**
$a_1 + a_2$	83.9
$b_1 + b_{\text{turn}}$	7.7

(c) Timing

Case	Symbols	Time Distance [s]
brick sorter	inputs	11.1 ±9.8
brick sorter	outputs	13.2 ±9.8
intersection	inputs	6.6 ±161.7
intersection	outputs	10.0 ±0.0

the trace database. As such, queries from the learner must be modified before testing against the trace database: they must be augmented with any additional actions matched by the initial condition.

Formally, a trace database is a triple $\mathcal{D} = \langle \rho, \langle \mathcal{S}_I, \varphi_I, \gamma_I \rangle, \langle \mathcal{S}_P, \varphi_P, \gamma_P \rangle \rangle$ where ρ is a concrete timed word, $\langle \mathcal{S}_I, \varphi_I, \gamma_I \rangle$ is a symbolic query that defines initial conditions, and $\langle \mathcal{S}_P, \varphi_P, \gamma_P \rangle$ is a symbolic query that is prepended to trace database queries to match the initial conditions and define the beginning of a word. We require that $\langle \mathcal{S}_P, \varphi_P, \gamma_P \rangle$ defines the symbolic timestamp v_0, thereby providing a relative timestamp from which offsets may be computed.

We can now define a function ***query*** that computes a response to a symbolic query from an instantiated trace database. Note that more than one sub-word of the database may match a query and, in that case, one such matching sub-word will be chosen non-deterministically. In practice, the choice of word does not matter since any fulfill the constraints of the query.

Definition 4. *Given a trace database* $\mathcal{D} = \langle \rho, \langle \mathcal{S}_I, \varphi_I, \gamma_I \rangle, \langle \mathcal{S}_P, \varphi_P, \gamma_P \rangle \rangle$ *where* $\rho = (\sigma, \tau)$ *and a symbolic query* $\langle \mathcal{S}, \varphi, \gamma \rangle$*, we define* $\textbf{query}(\mathcal{D}, \langle \mathcal{S}, \varphi, \gamma \rangle) = \rho_i, \ldots, \rho_n$ *where* $i \in \{ j \mid \exists k > j \cdot \rho_j, \ldots, \rho_k \models \langle \mathcal{S}_I, \varphi_I, \gamma_I \rangle \}$ *and* $\rho_i, \ldots, \rho_n \models \langle \mathcal{S}_P, \varphi_P, \gamma_P \rangle \cdot \langle \mathcal{S}, \varphi, \gamma \rangle$.

The initial conditions for a trace database are specific to each SUL and are a form of prior knowledge about which the learner has no information. However, in many cases the initial conditions can be safely assumed to be whatever happens when the SUL is fed no inputs for a long period of time. In this case, the only information provided by a human is how long to wait before the SUL can be assumed to have reset. This number need not be precise, only long enough that a reset occurs and short enough that the condition is met sufficiently often.

Example 4. Table 1 shows frequency and timing information for the most frequent inputs and outputs of our two case studies. Table 1a shows that bricks arrived and either passed or were rejected a similar number of times. Table 1c shows that the mean times between brick-sorter inputs and outputs diverged by about 2 s, but the standard deviation was the same. This tells us that the output timing is probably closely related to the input timing. We set initial conditions $\langle \mathcal{S}_I, \varphi_I, \gamma_I \rangle = \langle (\top_\mathcal{O}, v_0), (\top_\mathcal{I}, v_1), v_0 + 10 < v_1, (\mathit{true}, \mathit{false}) \rangle$ meaning that we search for any output (possibly stuttering) followed by any input after 10 (~ 9.8) seconds. We set the word beginnings with $\langle \mathcal{S}_P, \varphi_P, \gamma_P \rangle = \langle (\top_{\mathcal{O}}, v_0), \mathit{true}, (\mathit{true}) \rangle$. Table 1c shows the timing of inputs and outputs for the intersection appear largely unrelated, with outputs occurring at a fixed interval, and Table 1b shows that one output action dominates the others. We set initial conditions $\langle \mathcal{S}_I, \varphi_I, \gamma_I \rangle = \langle (a_1 + a_2, v_0), (\top_{\mathcal{I}}, v_1), v_0 + 10 < v_1, (\mathit{true}, \mathit{false}) \rangle$ meaning that we search for an $a1 + a2$ output (possibly stuttering) followed by any input after 10 s. We set the word beginnings with $\langle \mathcal{S}_P, \varphi_P, \gamma_P \rangle = \langle (a_1 + a_2, v_0), \mathit{true}, (\mathit{true}) \rangle$.

4 From Concrete Traces to Symbolic Runs

We use symbolic queries to construct a *symbolic observation tree* from a trace database. A symbolic observation tree is a tree-shaped MM1T. For a given set of actions $\Sigma = \mathcal{I} \cup \mathcal{O}$, we generate input sequences $w \in \mathcal{I}_{\mathbf{to}}^+$ and for these try to infer the corresponding symbolic runs of the target MM1T from which the trace database was recorded. The trace database provides a concrete timed word $\rho = (\sigma, \tau)$ for the symbolic query$\langle \mathcal{S}, \varphi, \gamma \rangle$ where we can use wildcards $\top_{\mathcal{I}}$ and $\top_{\mathcal{O}}$ to be matched by any input action and any output action, respectively. We do not use action stuttering when constructing the symbolic observation tree as this feature is needed only for specifying trace database initial conditions. As such, we omit γ when writing symbolic queries in this section. Intuitively, we mimic the inference process (i.e., interacting with the oracle) that is used for constructing an observation tree in [26]. However, while Vaandrager et al. can derive concrete timed queries for the symbolic relations and values they want to infer, we have to find adequate traces in the database, not having full control over timing. We leverage that, in general, a symbolic run is modeled by many timed words, most of which can be used interchangeably. One notable difference from an active learning setting is that the trace database may be incomplete. In this section, we focus on showing that the generated symbolic runs may be incomplete but will be consistent with all the information in the trace database. The quality of inferred models will depend on the quality of data in the database.

We initialize the symbolic observation tree $\langle \mathcal{I}, \mathcal{O}, Q, q_0, \delta, \lambda, \kappa, t_0 \rangle$ with initial state q_0, i.e., initially $Q = \{q_0\}$, and use a timed symbolic query $\langle (\top_{\mathcal{O}}, v_1), v_0 < v_1 \rangle$ to observe the initial timer τ_1 from timed word (o_1, τ_1), setting $t_0 = \tau_1$. Recall that v_0 will be defined in the initial conditions of the trace database. If we cannot find a concrete trace in the database, we assume that no timer is set initially, setting $t_0 = \infty$. This is consistent with the database as in this case all traces in the database start with an input.

Now, assume the path from the root q_0 of the tree leads to an unexplored state q, along already inferred transitions $q_0 \xrightarrow{i_1, o_1, t_1} q_1 \ \cdots \ q_{k-1} \xrightarrow{i_k, o_k, t_k} q_k = q$ (or empty sequence of transitions in the case of the initially unexplored state q_0). Let $\langle \mathcal{S}_q, \varphi_q \rangle$ denote the corresponding symbolic run. For q_0, we use symbolic run $\langle \varepsilon, \mathit{true} \rangle$, where ε denotes the empty word. The currently active symbolic timer (cf. Section 2) after the run is $\theta_q = v_i + t_i$ for the most recent set timer, i.e., such that $t_i \neq \bot$ and $t_j = \bot$ if $i < j$. If the sequence of transitions is empty or no such τ_i exists, then $\theta_q = v_0 + t_0$.

We generate a series of queries to the trace database and extend the symbolic tree based on the responses, adding new transitions from q to newly created states based on every input $i \in \mathcal{I}_{\mathbf{to}}$. We distinguish two basic cases: transitions for regular inputs and transitions on timeouts.

Timeouts. For $i = \mathbf{timeout}$, the symbolic tree only needs to be extended with a new state if a timer is currently running, i.e., if $t_i \neq \infty$ in active timer θ_q. In this case, we want to add new state r and new transition $q \xrightarrow{\mathbf{timeout},o,t} r$ and need to compute o and t. In the best case, both values can be computed from symbolic query $\langle \mathcal{S}_q, \varphi_q \rangle \cdot \langle (\top_\mathcal{O}, v_{k+1}),\ v_{k+1} = \theta_q \rangle \cdot \langle (\top_\mathcal{O}, v_{k+2}),\ v_{k+1} < v_{k+2} \rangle$.

If a corresponding concrete timed word exists in the database, then it ends with $\ldots, (o_{k+1}, \tau_{k+1}), (o_{k+2}, \tau_{k+2})$. The word immediately provides $o = o_{k+1}$ and $t = \tau_{k+2} - \tau_{k+1}$ is the time observed between the two subsequent timeouts. If no such word can be found, we can ask for the shorter $\langle \mathcal{S}_q, \varphi_q \rangle \cdot \langle (\top_\mathcal{O}, v_{k+1}),\ v_{k+1} = \theta_q \rangle$. A corresponding concrete timed word provides o and we assume that no new timer is set, i.e., that $t = \infty$. Here, we conflate the case that we do not have complete information with the case that no new timer is set. This is consistent with the trace database by the same argument given above: there can only be continuations with an input as the next action in the database.

In case the trace database also does not contain a concrete word for the second query, we do not add a new transition to the symbolic tree. Since we do not have enough information in the database for computing the transition, we stop exploring in this direction.

Regular Inputs. For $i \neq \mathbf{timeout}$, we want to add new state r and new transition $q \xrightarrow{i,o,t} r$ and need to observe o and infer t. This case is slightly more complex than timeouts since we have to account for the immediate output of the transition and the fact that input transitions can either continue the existing timer, reset it, or disable it. We start by asking symbolic query

$$\langle \mathcal{S}_q, \varphi_q \rangle \cdot \langle (i, v_{k+1}), v_{k+1} < \theta_q \rangle \cdot \langle (\top_\mathcal{O}, v'_{k+1}), v'_{k+1} = v_{k+1} \rangle \cdot \langle (\top_\mathcal{O}, v_{k+2}), v_{k+2} \neq \theta_q \rangle$$

which, answered with a timed word ending in $\ldots, (i, \tau_{k+1}), (o_{k+1}, \tau'_{k+1}), (o_{k+2}, \tau_{k+2})$, provides enough information. We set $o = o_{k+1}$ and $t = \tau_{k+2} - \tau'_{k+1}$. Since we observed a timeout that cannot be explained by the currently running timer (as $v_{k+2} \neq \theta_q$), we can infer that the new transition sets a timer.

If no matching timed word is found and there is a currently running timeout, i.e., if $t_i \neq \infty$ in θ_q, we alter the query slightly to

$$\langle \mathcal{S}_q, \varphi_q \rangle \cdot \langle (i, v_{k+1}), v_{k+1} < \theta_q \rangle \cdot \langle (\top_\mathcal{O}, v'_{k+1}), v'_{k+1} = v_{k+1} \rangle \cdot \langle (\top_\mathcal{O}, v_{k+2}), v_{k+2} = \theta_q \rangle$$

and try to observe the already running timer expiring. If a corresponding timed word is found, we set o as before and $t = \bot$. This may actually be wrong: the transition we observe could have reset the timer to a value that (accidentally) equals the remaining time on the previously running timer. However, from the unsuccessful first query, we know that our choice is consistent with the database.

If the second query also does not produce a timed word, we try the shorter query $\langle \mathcal{S}_q, \varphi_q \rangle \cdot \langle (i, v_{k+1}),\ v_{k+1} < \theta_q \rangle \cdot \langle (\top_{\mathcal{O}}, v'_{k+1}),\ v'_{k+1} = v_{k+1} \rangle$. If successful, we observe o as above and assume $t = \infty$, which, again, conflates missing information and disabling the timer but is consistent with the information in the trace database.

In case all three queries fail, we do not add a transition or new state.

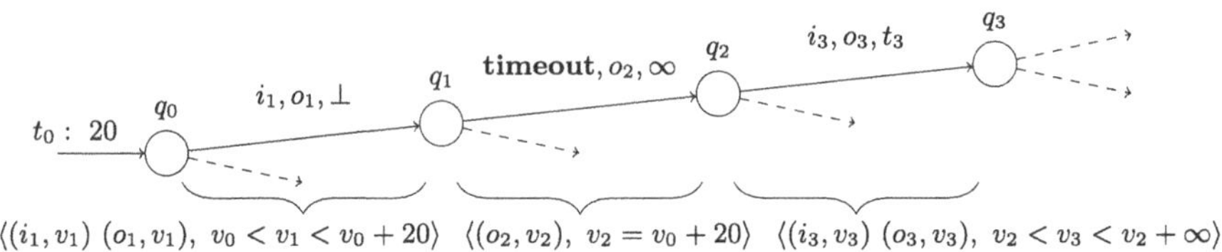

Fig. 3. Symbolic observation tree with symbolic run to q_3.

Example 5. Figure 3 shows a fragment of a symbolic observation tree and the corresponding symbolic run from the root q_0 to inner node q_3: The initial timer is set to 20. The transition from q_0 to q_1 does not reset the timer, the transition from q_1 to q_2 disables the timer, and the transition from q_2 to q_3 sets a timer to t_3. The corresponding symbolic run consists of all observed inputs and outputs along the sequence of transitions and constrains symbolic times to obey the active initial timer that is triggered by the second transition.

Consistency. For a trace database that could have been generated by a MM1T, i.e., with consistent timer behavior, the symbolic observation tree is consistent with the trace database: we only stop extending the tree when no concrete continuations to traces exist and in every single step we ensure that the symbolic representation is consistent with the trace database.

5 Application in Model Learning Scenarios

To evaluate the utility of our proposed symbolic abstraction in different learning pipelines, we define five pipelines and execute them on symbolic observations generated from single logs for the brick-sorter model and the intersection controller.[2] We report on their quantitative performance and discuss the human-readability of the created models.

Evaluation Setup. To identify the best learning setup, we assembled five learning pipelines, illustrated in Fig. 4: timed k-tails (TkT) without post-processing

[2] A note on the experiment design: since the symbolic abstraction is not learned (i.e., does not extrapolate beyond certain knowledge), we do not evaluate its performance but focus on the utility in model learning. We fix adequate initial conditions for computing the trace databases.

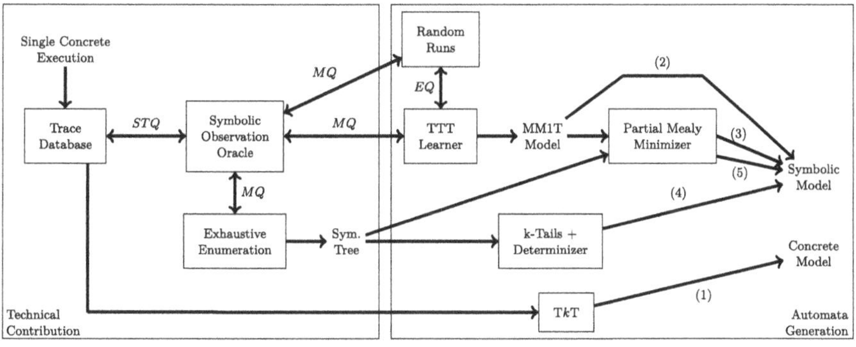

Fig. 4. The five evaluated learning pipelines.

(1), TTT without post-processing (2), TTT with subsequent refinement (3), symbolic tree recovery with subsequent k-tails (4), and symbolic tree recovery with subsequent refinement (5). We use the following three approaches to generate an initial model:

The *TkT* (baseline) approach performs passive learning on the trace database without symbolic abstraction using a modified version of the TkT algorithm [22,23]. We use a single non-resetting timer, no end events, $k = 2$, and a relaxed merge criterion (states are equal if one's k-tails are a subset of the other's).[3]

The *TTT* approach performs active learning of a Mealy machine using the novel symbolic abstraction oracle described in Sect. 4. We use the TTT [15] algorithm provided by LearnLib [16] and approximate equivalence queries with randomly generated runs with a fixed maximal length.

The *Symbolic Tree Recovery* queries the symbolic abstraction oracle exhaustively to recover a symbolic tree from the inputs.

We also implemented two post-processing steps that can be used in conjunction with the latter two learning approaches. The *k-Tails* approach performs an additional passive learning step on a set of symbolic runs by applying the k-tails passive learning algorithm [5]. Again, we use $k = 2$ and the relaxed merge criterion described above and follow this with a determinization step. The *Partial Mealy Minimizer* post-processing step performs greedy, partition-refinement-inspired minimization on a partial model.

Quantitative Evaluation. We executed the pipelines described above on both the brick-sorter and intersection logs. For the intersection, we also consider scenarios with a reduced input alphabet. E.g., "Intersection(A_i, B_i)" only considers vehicles on straight lanes. TkT does not support such scenarios since it operates on the concrete log where it is not obvious how to project to a subset of inputs.

[3] A problem with applying TkT to the intersection's logs is that an unbounded number of inputs can occur before a relevant output (i.e., cars being detected before the signal switches). As a result, no k can be chosen that would avoid overfitting.

Table 2. Performance of our learning pipelines on the different scenarios.

Scenario	Symb. Tree			TkT	TTT No Post-pr.		TTT Part. Ref.		Symbolic Tree k-Tails		Symbolic Tree Part. Ref.	
	$\|\mathcal{I}\|$	d	$\|\ell\|$	$\|Q\|$	acc. [%]	$\|Q\|$	acc. [%]	$\|Q\|$	acc. [%]	$\|Q\|$	acc. [%]	$\|Q\|$
Brick Sorter	2	7	139	7	100	3	100	3	100	3	100	3
Intersection(A_i, B_i)	4	6	581	n/a[1]	97	5	98	2	98	6	99	2
Intersection(A_i, B_{Left})	3	6	638	n/a[1]	99	2	99	2	100	4	86	19
Intersection(A_i, B_i, B_{Left})	5	6	970	n/a[1]	86	9	83	7	97	11	81	29
Intersection(A_i, B_i, A_{Turn})	8	6	1,351	n/a[1]	93	7	93	3	97	10	77	37
Intersection(complete)	11	6	1,839	749	81	13	81	13	94	23	77	50

[1] T*k*T cannot be used: projection of concrete trace to subset of inputs not obvious.

The results of the evaluation are shown in Table 2. For each scenario, the table provides some information about the symbolic tree: the number of inputs $|\mathcal{I}|$, the depth d to which the symbolic tree was explored and the number of resulting leaves $|\ell|$ (i.e., unique symbolic traces). For each learning pipeline, the accuracy in the model learning step (acc. [%]), i.e., the percentage of symbolic runs in the recovered symbolic tree that is correctly represented by the final model, and size of the resulting automaton $|Q|$ w.r.t. the traces contained in the symbolic tree are shown in the order described in the last section. By design, T*k*T always yields perfect accuracy, so this information is omitted.

The accuracy of the TTT-based approach degrades faster than using k-tails for post-processing in experiments with more inputs and sparser logs. There is a trade-off between learning extra states, distinguished from other states by missing information and querying the trace database more extensively during equivalence queries. As the experiments show, greedy minimization cannot effectively mitigate missing information (either on the models inferred with TTT or on the symbolic tree directly): obtained models are often less accurate than the original models.

Summarizing, post-processing the symbolic tree yields the best results: the approach scales to the complete intersection and the automata are not too large, while preserving very high accuracy.

Explainability. We also examined the human-readability of the generated models. To judge human-readability, we rendered the learned models using GraphViz [11] and examined them manually.

Since T*k*T operates on log entries, input and output actions are independent in the automaton and timeouts have to be inferred from the timing intervals. The resulting edge labels are non-symbolic, e.g., `<pass_through,[17,32]>`, indicating that the system can be expected to let the brick pass in 17–32 time units. Additionally, the number of generated locations is far greater than the underlying model's number of states, indicating that no semantic meaning can be assigned to the states. As a result, the model (available in the repeatability package [9]) is not easily comprehensible for a human reader.

In contrast, the workflows using the symbolic tree fully recover the correct automaton shown in Fig. 2. The symbolic tree generation yields MM1T transitions that combine input, output and timing behavior (e.g., `Timeout, pass_through // timer off`). One can comprehend the system's behavior "at a glance", e.g., the bug in the brick sorter's behavior can be seen in the generated model by following the execution path for insertion of two different-colored bricks.

These results extend to the intersection scenarios. One can see how the intersection controller behaves by inspection of the learned model: the signals change to accommodate arriving cars on blocked lanes. While the automata generated, e.g., by symbolic tree recovery with k-tails refinement do increase in size (up to 23 states) when the input alphabet is enlarged, their comprehensibility surpasses the 749-state automaton generated by TkT.

Threats to Validity. On the conceptual level, we assume that our scenarios can a) be correctly modeled using MM1Ts and b) initial conditions can be identified via queries. Vaandrager et al. [26] argue that MM1Ts are applicable to many real-life scenarios and we have anecdotally found that the quality of final learned models is not very sensitive to the precision of initial conditions. The primary internal threat is the parameterization of our k-tails, especially the choice of $k = 2$. We selected that value based on its frequent selection in the literature for similar use cases, e.g. in [6,7,10]. External validity may be threatened by our approach overfitting the two case studies. We designed our method to be as general as possible, and selected two dissimilar case studies to mitigate this risk.

6 Related Work

Many passive timed model learning methods construct and minimize trees. Pastore et al. [22,23] proposed the TkT algorithm for inference of timed automata with multiple clocks. It normalizes traces, turns them into Timed Automata (TAs) trees and merges locations to gain a general structure. Verwer et al. [28] proposed the RTI algorithm for learning deterministic real-time automata. It forms an "augmented" prefix tree with accepting/rejecting states, and merges and splits them to compress the trees into automata. Maier et al. [19] learned TAs online by constructing a prefix tree automaton and merging its states. Unlike RTI, their method does not require negative examples. Recently, Coranguer et al. [8] constructed tree-shaped automata, merged states (ignoring timing constraints) and then used timing information to split states. They presented promising results in comparison to TkT (in some respects) and RTI. Grinchtein et al. [12] learned event-recording TAs. They built timed decision trees, and then folded them into a compact automaton. Henry et al. [13] also proposed a method for learning event-recording TAs where not all transitions must reset clocks. Dematos et al. [20] presented a method and proof of concept for learning stochastic TAs by identifying an equivalence relation between states and merging them.

Other formalism used in passive approaches are as follows: Narayan et al. introduced a method to mine TAs using patterns expressed as Timed Regular Expressions (TREs) [21]. The technique passively mines variable bindings from system traces for TREs templates provided by a user. Verwer et al. [27] present an algorithm for the identification of deterministic one-clock TAs. The algorithm is efficient in the limit, i.e., it requires polyonomial time to identify the learned model. Tappler et al. [24] used genetic algorithms for learning TAs based on passive traces. Later, the approach was adapted to the active setting [2]. An et al. [3] proposed two methods for actively learning TAs. In one the learner needs to guess which transitions carry clock resets, and in the other the teacher has a method of telling if clock-resets occur. Recently, Tappler et al. [25] proposed a learning method for TAs that is based on SMT-solving. SMT-solving can handle cases with partial information (as experienced in the traffic controller), and still provide solutions satisfying the given constraints. However, the long traces we are dealing with will likely introduce too many variables and formulas to scale.

Aichernig et al. [1] compared active and passive learning approaches in a network protocol setting. They show that passive learning is competitive when utilizing sparse data, a result matching our observations when comparing TTT to passive learning-based symbolic tree post-processing.

A recent work by Vaandrager et al. defined MM1T and then used an adapter interface to actively mine them using existing Mealy machine mining algorithms in LearnLib [26]. This technique is used as one of the post-processing steps in our approach, and we use an equivalent definition of MM1Ts. We complement this approach via our symbolic observation oracle.

Jeppu et al. [18] recently introduced a method to construct automata from long traces by extracting counterexamples from attempting to prove that no such model exists. It found smaller models than traditional state-merging methods.

7 Conclusion

We presented a novel technique for abstracting a single concrete log of a timed system into a MM1T. The abstraction can be used as an oracle by active learning algorithms following the MAT framework such as TTT or to create a symbolic tree view of the system. We evaluate four approaches for learning a model of the system based on this abstraction in combination with different post-processing methods on two real-world-derived use cases, a brick sorting system and a traffic intersection signaling controller. We examined if our approach can be used to provide explainability for complex or machine learned black-box systems. We found that the proposed symbolic trees in combination with post-processing via k-tails yields concise and symbolic human-readable automata.

We plan to apply our approach to more use cases to verify its performance in more scenarios and on different automata classes (e.g., automata with data). Moreover, we can not yet formally relate the quality of our models to the input's completeness and aim at finding such a relation in future work.

Acknowledgements. This work was supported by the S40S Villum Investigator Grant (37819) from VILLUM FONDEN, the ERC Advanced Grant LASSO, DIREC, and the Deutsche Forschungsgemeinschaft (DFG, German Research Foundation) - 495857894 (STING).

References

1. Aichernig, B.K., Muškardin, E., Pferscher, A.: Active vs. passive: a comparison of automata learning paradigms for network protocols. Electron. Proc. Theor. Comput. Sci. **371**, 1–19 (2022). https://doi.org/10.4204/eptcs.371.1, FMAS/ASYDE 2022
2. Aichernig, B.K., Pferscher, A., Tappler, M.: From passive to active: learning timed automata efficiently. In: Lee, R., Jha, S., Mavridou, A., Giannakopoulou, D. (eds.) NFM 2020. LNCS, vol. 12229, pp. 1–19. Springer, Cham (2020). https://doi.org/10.1007/978-3-030-55754-6_1
3. An, J., Chen, M., Zhan, B., Zhan, N., Zhang, M.: Learning one-clock timed automata. In: TACAS 2020. LNCS, vol. 12078, pp. 444–462. Springer, Cham (2020). https://doi.org/10.1007/978-3-030-45190-5_25
4. Angluin, D.: Learning regular sets from queries and counterexamples. Inf. Comput. **75**(2), 87–106 (1987). https://doi.org/10.1016/0890-5401(87)90052-6
5. Biermann, A.W., Feldman, J.A.: On the synthesis of finite-state machines from samples of their behavior. IEEE Trans. Comput. **C-21**(6), 592–597 (1972). https://doi.org/10.1109/TC.1972.5009015
6. Busany, N., Maoz, S., Yulazari, Y.: Size and accuracy in model inference. In: 2019 34th IEEE/ACM International Conference on Automated Software Engineering (ASE), pp. 887–898, November 2019. https://doi.org/10.1109/ASE.2019.00087, ASE 2019
7. Cohen, H., Maoz, S.: The confidence in our k-tails. In: Proceedings of the 29th ACM/IEEE International Conference on Automated Software Engineering, pp. 605–610. Association for Computing Machinery, New York, NY, USA, September 2014. https://doi.org/10.1145/2642937.2642944, ASE '14
8. Cornanguer, L., Largouët, C., Rozé, L., Termier, A.: TAG: learning timed automata from logs. In: Proceedings of the AAAI Conference on Artificial Intelligence, vol. 36, no. 4, pp. 3949–3958 (2022). https://doi.org/10.1609/aaai.v36i4.20311
9. Dierl, S., et al.: Learning symbolic timed models from concrete timed data - data and replication package (2023). https://doi.org/10.5281/zenodo.7766789
10. Gabor, U.T., Dierl, S., Spinczyk, O.: Spectrum-based fault localization in deployed embedded systems with driver interaction models. In: Romanovsky, A., Troubitsyna, E., Bitsch, F. (eds.) SAFECOMP 2019. LNCS, vol. 11698, pp. 97–112. Springer, Cham (2019). https://doi.org/10.1007/978-3-030-26601-1_7
11. Gansner, E.R., North, S.C.: An open graph visualization system and its applications to software engineering. Softw. Pract. Exp. **30**(11), 1203–1233 (2000). https://doi.org/10.1002/1097-024X(200009)30:11⟨1203::AID-SPE338⟩3.0.CO;2-N
12. Grinchtein, O., Jonsson, B., Pettersson, P.: Inference of event-recording automata using timed decision trees. In: Baier, C., Hermanns, H. (eds.) CONCUR 2006. LNCS, vol. 4137, pp. 435–449. Springer, Heidelberg (2006). https://doi.org/10.1007/11817949_29

13. Henry, L., Jéron, T., Markey, N.: Active learning of timed automata with unobservable resets. In: Bertrand, N., Jansen, N. (eds.) FORMATS 2020. LNCS, vol. 12288, pp. 144–160. Springer, Cham (2020). https://doi.org/10.1007/978-3-030-57628-8_9
14. Howar, F., Steffen, B.: Active automata learning in practice. In: Bennaceur, A., Hähnle, R., Meinke, K. (eds.) Machine Learning for Dynamic Software Analysis: Potentials and Limits. LNCS, vol. 11026, pp. 123–148. Springer, Cham (2018). https://doi.org/10.1007/978-3-319-96562-8_5
15. Isberner, M., Howar, F., Steffen, B.: The TTT algorithm: a redundancy-free approach to active automata learning. In: Bonakdarpour, B., Smolka, S.A. (eds.) RV 2014. LNCS, vol. 8734, pp. 307–322. Springer, Cham (2014). https://doi.org/10.1007/978-3-319-11164-3_26
16. Isberner, M., Howar, F., Steffen, B.: The open-source LearnLib. In: Kroening, D., Păsăreanu, C.S. (eds.) CAV 2015. LNCS, vol. 9206, pp. 487–495. Springer, Cham (2015). https://doi.org/10.1007/978-3-319-21690-4_32
17. Iversen, T.K., et al.: Model-checking real-time control programs: verifying lego mindstorms tm systems using uppaal. In: Proceedings 12th Euromicro Conference on Real-Time Systems. Euromicro RTS 2000, pp. 147–155. IEEE (2000)
18. Jeppu, N.Y., Melham, T., Kroening, D., O'Leary, J.: Learning concise models from long execution traces. In: 2020 57th ACM/IEEE Design Automation Conference (DAC), pp. 1–6 (2020). https://doi.org/10.1109/DAC18072.2020.9218613
19. Maier, A.: Online passive learning of timed automata for cyber-physical production systems. In: IEEE International Conference on Industrial Informatics (INDIN 2014), pp. 60–66. IEEE (2014). https://doi.org/10.1109/INDIN.2014.6945484
20. de Matos Pedro, A., Crocker, P.A., de Sousa, S.M.: Learning stochastic timed automata from sample executions. In: Margaria, T., Steffen, B. (eds.) ISoLA 2012. LNCS, vol. 7609, pp. 508–523. Springer, Heidelberg (2012). https://doi.org/10.1007/978-3-642-34026-0_38
21. Narayan, A., Cutulenco, G., Joshi, Y., Fischmeister, S.: Mining timed regular specifications from system traces. ACM Trans. Embed. Comput. Syst. **17**(2), 46:1–46:21 (2018). https://doi.org/10.1145/3147660
22. Pastore, F., Micucci, D., Guzman, M., Mariani, L.: TkT: automatic inference of timed and extended pushdown automata. IEEE Trans. Softw. Eng. **48**(2), 617–636 (2022). https://doi.org/10.1109/TSE.2020.2998527
23. Pastore, F., Micucci, D., Mariani, L.: Timed k-tail: automatic inference of timed automata. In: 2017 IEEE International Conference on Software Testing, Verification and Validation (ICST), pp. 401–411. IEEE, New York, March 2017. https://doi.org/10.1109/ICST.2017.43, ICST 2017
24. Tappler, M., Aichernig, B.K., Larsen, K.G., Lorber, F.: Time to learn – learning timed automata from tests. In: André, É., Stoelinga, M. (eds.) FORMATS 2019. LNCS, vol. 11750, pp. 216–235. Springer, Cham (2019). https://doi.org/10.1007/978-3-030-29662-9_13
25. Tappler, M., Aichernig, B.K., Lorber, F.: Timed automata learning via SMT solving. In: Deshmukh, J.V., Havelund, K., Perez, I. (eds.) NASA Formal Methods. NFM 2022. LNCS, vol. 13260, pp. 489–507. Springer, Cham (2022). https://doi.org/10.1007/978-3-031-06773-0_26
26. Vaandrager, F., Bloem, R., Ebrahimi, M.: Learning mealy machines with one timer. In: Leporati, A., Martín-Vide, C., Shapira, D., Zandron, C. (eds.) LATA 2021. LNCS, vol. 12638, pp. 157–170. Springer, Cham (2021). https://doi.org/10.1007/978-3-030-68195-1_13

27. Verwer, S., de Weerdt, M., Witteveen, C.: One-clock deterministic timed automata are efficiently identifiable in the limit. In: Dediu, A.H., Ionescu, A.M., Martín-Vide, C. (eds.) LATA 2009. LNCS, vol. 5457, pp. 740–751. Springer, Heidelberg (2009). https://doi.org/10.1007/978-3-642-00982-2_63
28. Verwer, S., de Weerdt, M., Witteveen, C.: Efficiently identifying deterministic real-time automata from labeled data. Mach. Learn. **86**(3), 295–333 (2012). https://doi.org/10.1007/s10994-011-5265-4

Reward Shaping from Hybrid Systems Models in Reinforcement Learning

Marian Qian and Stefan Mitsch

Computer Science Department, Carnegie Mellon University, Pittsburgh, PA 15213, USA
marianq@andrew.cmu.edu, smitsch@cs.cmu.edu

Abstract. Reinforcement learning is increasingly often used as a learning technique to implement control tasks in autonomous systems. To meet stringent safety requirements, formal methods for learning-enabled systems, such as closed-loop neural network verification, shielding, falsification, and online reachability analysis, analyze learned controllers for safety violations. Besides filtering unsafe actions during training, these approaches view verification and training largely as separate tasks. We propose an approach based on logically constrained reinforcement learning to couple formal methods and reinforcement learning more tightly by generating safety-oriented aspects of reward functions from verified hybrid systems models. We demonstrate the approach on a standard reinforcement learning environment for longitudinal vehicle control.

Keywords: Theorem proving · Differential dynamic logic · Hybrid systems · Reinforcement learning · Reward shaping

1 Introduction

Complex (autonomous) systems increasingly often employ learning techniques to implement control tasks, which poses serious safety challenges. Formal methods for learning-enabled systems—such as closed-loop neural network verification (e.g., Verisig [15,16], NNV [27]), falsification [6], shielding [1,17], Neural Simplex [24], input-output behavior explanations [3], and online reachability analysis and hybrid systems monitoring [9,10,21]—address these challenges by analyzing trained controllers for safety violations and explanations of their behavior, or by filtering the actions proposed by controllers with formally verified artifacts. Besides filtering unsafe actions during training, the training setup itself typically is not supported with formal methods. A particularly attractive approach for training controllers is reinforcement learning, for its seemingly straightforward way of specifying desired behavior with a reward function. Designing reward functions, however, is challenging, not least because they need to balance safety-oriented requirements with goal-oriented ones.

This work was funded by the Federal Railroad Administration Office of Research, Development and Technology under contract number 693JJ620C000025.

K. Y. Rozier and S. Chaudhuri (Eds.): NFM 2023, LNCS 13903, pp. 122–139, 2023.
https://doi.org/10.1007/978-3-031-33170-1_8

In this paper, we base on ideas from logically constrained reinforcement learning [11–13] to develop a formal approach to generating the safety-oriented aspects of reward functions from verified predictive hybrid systems models. The main intuition behind our approach is that hybrid systems models describe safety envelopes that can be turned into formally verified runtime monitors [22]. These runtime monitors not only distinguish safe from unsafe behavior, but with an appropriate quantitative interpretation can be used to measure the robustness of actions with respect to such safety envelopes. The challenge in deriving a useful (for reinforcement learning) robustness measure from a formal model is that relative importance of safety aspects is not immediately obvious from the formal model alone, and that differences in units makes comparison of the magnitude of robustness values across different aspects of the formal model difficult. For example, an autonomous vehicle model may encode brake force limits and speed limits: as the vehicle approaches a speed limit, it is acceptable to experience decreased robustness in brake limit in order to not violate the posted speed limit. Another challenge is that measure-zero safety aspects can hide progress or regression in other requirements.

We address these challenges by adapting robustness measures from metric-temporal logic [7] and signal-temporal logic [5], and by developing signal rescaling [28] operators to adjust the relative importance of competing safety aspects.

The benefits of this approach are that the safety specification is rigorously checked for correctness and the resulting reward function inherits the predictive nature of the hybrid systems model and its safety guarantees. The contributions of this paper are threefold: based on [7,22] we develop a quantitative interpretation of hybrid systems models with an account for measure-zero requirements; we develop signal rescaling [28] operators to specify relative importance of (competing) safety aspects in the formal model; and we evaluate our approach on a standard reinforcement learning environment for longitudinal vehicle control [4].

2 Background

In this section, we summarize background theory and introduce notation.

2.1 Differential Dynamic Logic

Differential dynamic logic dL [25] is a formal language for hybrid systems written as hybrid programs. The syntax of *hybrid programs* (HP) is described by the following grammar where α, β are hybrid programs, x is a variable and $e, f(x)$ are arithmetic expressions (terms) in $+, -, \cdot, /$ over the reals, Q is a logical formula:

$$\alpha, \beta \ ::= \ x := e \mid x := * \mid ?Q \mid \{x' = f(x) \ \& \ Q\} \mid \alpha \cup \beta \mid \alpha ; \beta \mid \alpha^*$$

Assignment $x := e$ assigns the value of term e to x (e.g., compute acceleration to meet speed limit after T time $a := (v - v_{\text{des}})/T$), and nondeterministic assignment $x := *$ assigns any real value to x. Tests $?Q$ abort execution and discard the run if Q is not true, possibly backtracking to other nondeterministic alternatives. A typical modeling pattern combines nondeterministic assignments with tests to restrict the chosen values to some set (e.g., choose control within brake and acceleration limits: $a := *; ? -B \leq a \leq A$). Differential equations $\{x' = f(x) \ \& \ Q\}$ are followed along a solution of $x' = f(x)$ for any duration as long as the evolution domain constraint Q is true at every moment along the solution (e.g., speed changes according to acceleration/deceleration, but does not revert when hitting brakes $\{v' = a \ \& \ v \geq 0\}$). Nondeterministic choice $\alpha \cup \beta$ runs either α or β (e.g., either accelerate or brake), sequential composition $\alpha; \beta$ first runs α and then β on the resulting states of α (e.g., first control, then motion), and nondeterministic repetition α^* runs α any natural number of times (e.g., repeated control and environment loop).

The formulas of dL describe properties of hybrid programs and are described by the following grammar where P, Q are formulas, f, g are terms, $\sim \in \{<, \leq, =, \neq, \geq, >\}$, x is a variable and α is a hybrid program:

$$P, Q \ ::= \ f \sim g \mid \neg P \mid P \wedge Q \mid P \vee Q \mid P \rightarrow Q \mid P \leftrightarrow Q \mid \forall x \, P \mid \exists x \, P \mid [\alpha] \, P \mid \langle \alpha \rangle P$$

The operators of first-order real arithmetic are as usual with quantifiers ranging over the reals. For any hybrid program α and dL formula P, the formula $[\alpha] \, P$ is true in a state iff P is true after all runs of α. Its dual, $\langle \alpha \rangle P$ is true in a state iff P is true after at least one run of α.

The semantics of dL is a Kripke semantics in which the states of the Kripke model are the states of the hybrid system. A state is a map $\omega : \mathcal{V} \rightarrow \mathbb{R}$, assigning a real value $\omega(x)$ to each variable $x \in \mathcal{V}$ in the set of variables $\mathcal{V}$. We write $[\![Q]\!]$ to denote the set of states in which formula Q is true, $\omega \in [\![Q]\!]$ if formula Q is true at state ω, $\omega[\![e]\!]$ to denote the real value of term e in state ω, and ω_x^e to denote the state ν that agrees with ω except that $\nu(x) = \omega[\![e]\!]$. We write $\mathrm{FV}(P)$ for the set of free variables in formula P, and $\mathrm{BV}(\alpha)$ to denote the bound variables of program α, see [25]. The semantics of hybrid programs is expressed as a transition relation $[\![\alpha]\!]$ [25]. The differential equations and nondeterministic alternatives in hybrid programs make them an expressive specification language, but require computationally expensive methods similar to online reachability analysis for execution, which is detrimental to their use in reward functions in reinforcement learning. Next, we review ModelPlex [22] as a method to shift much of this computational complexity offline.

2.2 ModelPlex

ModelPlex [22] combines a universal offline safety proof $[\alpha] \, P$ with an existential reachability check whether two concrete states ω, ν are connected by the program α, i.e., whether $(\omega, \nu) \in [\![\alpha]\!]$. The safety proof witnesses that *all* states reachable by model α satisfy P, while passing the reachability check witnesses that the two concrete states ω, ν are connected by the program α, and so state ν inherits the safety proof, i.e., $\nu \in [\![P]\!]$. The reachability check is equivalently phrased in dL as a monitor specification $\langle \alpha \rangle \bigwedge_{x \in \mathrm{BV}(\alpha)} (x = x^+)$ [22]. The dL monitor specification allows ModelPlex, in contrast to online reachability analysis, to shift computation offline by using theorem proving to translate a hybrid systems model into a propositional ModelPlex formula over arithmetic expressions. Note that the reachability check is inherently a property of the runtime execution and, therefore, the dL monitor specification and the resulting ModelPlex formula are never valid (they introduce fresh variables x^+, which means the existential reachability proof will not succeed offline for all states). Instead, the proof can be finished at runtime for two concrete states (a state ω providing values for x and a state ν providing values for x^+) by plugging in concrete measurements for all variables of the ModelPlex formula.

The set $\mathcal{M}$ of ModelPlex formulas $\phi : \mathcal{S} \times \mathcal{S} \to \mathbb{B}$ is generated by the following grammar ($\sim \in \{\leq, <, =, \neq, >, \geq\}$ and θ, η form the arithmetic expressions of the set $\mathcal{T}$ of ModelPlex terms in $+, -, \cdot, /$ over the reals, i.e., $\theta : \mathcal{S} \times \mathcal{S} \to \mathbb{R}$):

$$\phi, \psi ::= \theta \sim \eta \mid \neg \phi \mid \phi \wedge \psi \mid \phi \vee \psi$$

When a ModelPlex formula $\phi \in \mathcal{M}$ is satisfied over states ω, ν, we write $(\omega, \nu) \models \phi$ as shorthand for $\omega_{x^+}^{\nu(x)} \in [\![\phi]\!]$, or in other words, $\phi(\omega, \nu)$ is true.

ModelPlex formulas are quantifier- and program-free, and are therefore easy (and computationally inexpensive) to evaluate from concrete measurements at runtime, which makes them attractive for use in reinforcement learning.

The predictive nature of ModelPlex monitors also makes them useful for safeguarding learned controllers during training and during operation [9,10], in a shielding-like approach [20] based on hybrid systems models. In this paper, we take a complementary approach to shielding by interpreting ModelPlex monitors quantitatively in rewards.

2.3 Reinforcement Learning and Reward Shaping

Reinforcement learning involves training an agent to reach a goal by allowing the agent to explore an environment while trying to maximize its reward. The agent attempts different actions from the set of actions $\mathcal{A}$. For every action the agent makes, the environment takes a transition from state $s \in \mathcal{S}$ to a new state $s' \in \mathcal{S}$. A reward function then signals to the agent how useful the outcome of action a is: a negative reward signals that taking action a to reach state s' is discouraged, while positive reward encourages action a. Put differently, negative rewards encourage leaving "bad" states, while positive rewards encourage dwelling in "good" states. In Sect. 4, we develop a principled approach to generate safety-oriented aspects of the reward function from hybrid systems models.

Often, the agent has to learn multiple (competing) aspects of control (e.g., reaching a destination fast while respecting posted speed limits and conserving energy). This process of augmenting the reward function with multiple aspects is referred to as reward shaping. The motivation behind reward shaping is to provide additional reward for accomplishing subtasks that could lead towards the goal in the hopes to improve convergence and efficiency of training.

3 Related Work

Shielding (e.g., [1,17], see [19] for a survey) prevents reinforcement learning agents during training and operation from taking actions that violate the specification. Specifications of shields are typically in linear temporal logic (LTL) and focus on discrete environments. Some approaches based on dL [9] target continuous environments, even from visual inputs [14]. Note that shields during training can be detrimental to safety in operation [20] if not specifically trained to return to safe states [9]. Neural Simplex [24] performs shielding with the additional feature of transferring control back to the learned controller when safe. In order to give feedback about compliance with shields to the learning agent during training and as a way of measuring robustness during operation, we follow logically constrained reinforcement learning (see e.g. [11–13]), but instead of LTL we use differential dynamic logic combined with signal rescaling [24] to shape safety-oriented rewards.

Previous works [2,18] involving logic-based rewards include using environment-based temporal logic formulas as additional award augmented through potential-based reward shaping. Results have shown faster convergence and optimal policy performance; however, these have been only tested for average-reward learning algorithms rather than discounted-reward [18]. Additionally, reward functions can be augmented with specifications in signal temporal logic for desired agent behavior [2].

4 Rewards from Hybrid Systems Models

We take a complementary approach to shielding by interpreting hybrid systems models quantitatively through their relational abstraction as ModelPlex monitors. To this end, we define a hybrid systems normal form that is designed to align states of the hybrid systems model with states in the training process.

Definition 1 (Time-triggered normal form). *A hybrid systems model* α *in time-triggered normal form is of the shape* $(u := \mathit{ctrl}(x); t := 0; \{x' = f(x,u),\ t' = 1 \ \&\ t \leq T\})^*$, *where* $u := \mathit{ctrl}(x)$ *is a discrete hybrid systems model not mentioning differential equations.*

A hybrid program in time-triggered normal form models repeated interaction between a discrete controller $u := \mathrm{ctrl}(x)$ that acts with a latency of at most time T and a continuous model $t := 0; \{x' = f(x,u),\ t' = 1 \ \&\ t \leq T\}$ that responds to the control choice u. Note that the discrete controller $u := \mathrm{ctrl}(x)$ typically focuses on safety-relevant features (such as collision avoidance) while abstracting from goal-oriented features (such as desired cruise speed). The goal of this section is to develop a principled approach to reward shaping to translate the safety-relevant insights of formal verification to reinforcement learning. Figure 1 illustrates how the states of a formal model correspond to states in reinforcement learning (note that unlike in usual RL notation, where states are responses of the environment and actions are drawn from a separate set, the states of the formal model include the values of actions).

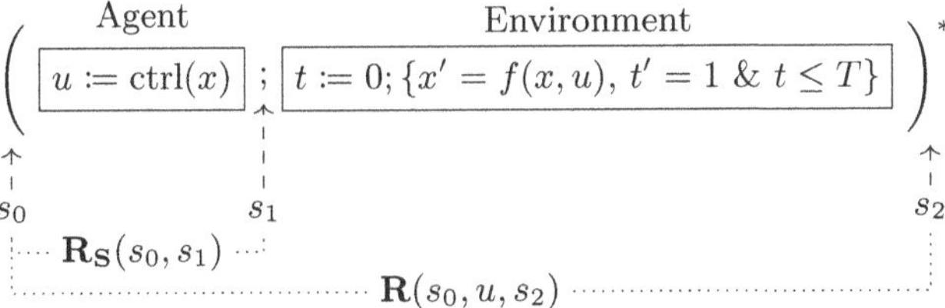

Fig. 1. Overview of aligning states in the formal model and the training process. The reward $\mathbf{R}(s_0, u, s_2)$ is given for the transition (s_0, u, s_2), whereas the states of a formal model include the values of actions, so taking action u traverses to intermediate state s_1 from which the environment responds by producing state s_2. Therefore, we can give separate reward $\mathbf{R_S}(s_0, s_1)$ from the predictive formal model for choosing action u in state s_0.

Let $s_0 \in \mathcal{S}$ be the state before executing $u := \text{ctrl}(x)$, $s_1 \in \mathcal{S}$ be the state after executing $u := \text{ctrl}(x)$ (and before executing $t := 0; \{x' = f(x, u),\ t' = 1 \,\&\, t \leq T\}$), and $s_2 \in \mathcal{S}$ be the state after executing $t := 0; \{x' = f(x, u),\ t' = 1 \,\&\, t \leq T\}$ (which becomes s_0 in the next loop iteration). These states relate to the training process in reinforcement learning as illustrated in Fig. 1: s_0 corresponds to the state before the agent picks an action, s_1 is the state after the agent chose an action $u \in \mathcal{A}$ (but before it is actuated in the environment), and s_2 is the result state of executing the action in the environment. In typical reinforcement learning setups, the reward associated with the transition (s_0, u, s_2) is computed by a reward function $\mathbf{R} : \mathcal{S} \times \mathcal{A} \times \mathcal{S} \to \mathbb{R}$. We provide separate reward $\mathbf{R_S} : \mathcal{S} \times \mathcal{S} \to \mathbb{R}$ directly for choosing action u in state s_0 from the *predictive* formal hybrid systems model, which requires a quantitative interpretation of ModelPlex formulas, as discussed next.

4.1 Quantitative Interpretation of ModelPlex Formulas

We adapt MTL/STL robustness measures [5,7,8] to define a quantitative interpretation of ModelPlex formulas, which describes *how robustly satisfied* a monitor is over two states.

Definition 2 (Quantitative ModelPlex). *The function $\mathbf{Q} : \mathcal{M} \to \mathcal{T}$ interprets a ModelPlex formula $\phi \in \mathcal{M}$ quantitatively as an arithmetic expression $\theta \in \mathcal{T}$ in $+, -, \cdot, /$ over the reals ($\theta : \mathcal{S} \times \mathcal{S} \to \mathbb{R}$):*

$$\mathbf{Q}(\theta \geq 0)(s_0, s_1) \rhd \theta(s_0, s_1)$$
$$\mathbf{Q}(\theta > 0)(s_0, s_1) \rhd \theta(s_0, s_1)$$
$$\mathbf{Q}(\theta = 0)(s_0, s_1) \rhd \mathbf{Q}(\theta \geq 0 \wedge -\theta \geq 0)(s_0, s_1)$$
$$\mathbf{Q}(\theta \neq 0)(s_0, s_1) \rhd \mathbf{Q}(\theta > 0 \vee -\theta > 0)(s_0, s_1)$$

$$\mathbf{Q}(\phi \wedge \psi)(s_0, s_1) \triangleright \begin{cases} \mathbf{Q}(\psi)(s_0, s_1) & \text{if } \phi \equiv \theta{=}0 \text{ and } (s_0, s_1) \models \theta{=}0 \\ -|\theta(s_0, s_1)| & \text{if } \phi \equiv \theta{=}0 \text{ and } (s_0, s_1) \not\models \theta{=}0 \\ (\mathbf{Q}(\phi) \sqcap \mathbf{Q}(\psi))(s_0, s_1) & \text{otherwise} \end{cases}$$

$$\mathbf{Q}(\phi \vee \psi)(s_0, s_1) \triangleright (\mathbf{Q}(\phi) \sqcup \mathbf{Q}(\psi))(s_0, s_1)$$

$$\mathbf{Q}(\neg\phi)(s_0, s_1) \triangleright -\mathbf{Q}(\psi)(s_0, s_1)$$

where $\sqcup$ *is* max, $\sqcap$ *is* min, *the atomic propositions in* ϕ *are normalized to* $\theta = 0, \theta \neq 0, \theta \geq 0, \theta > 0$, *and conjunctions are reordered to list all* $\theta = 0$ *before inequalities.*

Note that equalities $\theta = 0$ result in measure-zero robustness when they are satisfied: in a sense, their robustness is only meaningful when violated, since there is only a single way to satisfy $\theta = 0$. In conjunctions of the shape $\theta = 0 \wedge \phi$, the chosen robustness definition avoids unnecessary measure-zero robustness by evaluating to $\mathbf{Q}(\phi)$ when $\theta = 0$ is satisfied. In contrast, the naive phrasing $\mathbf{Q}(\theta = 0 \wedge \phi) \triangleright \min(\mathbf{Q}(\theta \geq 0), \mathbf{Q}(-\theta \geq 0), \mathbf{Q}(\phi))$ would evaluate to 0 when $\theta = 0$ is satisfied and thus hide changes in robustness in ϕ, which can be valuable reward signals to the agent. Quantitative ModelPlex maintains safety by overapproximating the original monitor verdict, see Lemma 1.

Lemma 1 (Mixed Quantitative ModelPlex Overapproximates Verdict). *The quantitative interpretation maintains the monitor verdict, i.e., the following formulas are valid:* $\mathbf{Q}(\phi) > 0 \rightarrow \phi$ *and* $\mathbf{Q}(\phi) < 0 \rightarrow \neg\phi$ *for all ModelPlex formulas* $\phi \in \mathcal{M}$.

Proof. By structural induction on ModelPlex formula and term operators. □

Mixed inequalities in Lemma 1 require for the quantitative interpretation to be conservative in the sense of causing false alarms on weak inequalities (a robustness measure of 0 is inconclusive). When comparisons are restricted to only weak inequalities or only strict inequalities, we maintain equivalence between the quantitative and the Boolean interpretation of ModelPlex, see Corollary 1.

Corollary 1 (Weak/Strict Quantitative ModelPlex Maintains Verdict). *When comparisons are restricted to weak/strict inequalities, the quantitative interpretation maintains the monitor verdict, i.e., the following formula is valid for weak inequalities* $\mathbf{Q}(\phi) \geq 0 \leftrightarrow \phi$ *(for strict inequalities* $\mathbf{Q}(\phi) > 0 \leftrightarrow \phi$*) for all ModelPlex formulas* $\phi \in \mathcal{M}$ *restricted to weak inequalities* $\geq, =$ *in atomic propositions (strict inequalities* $>, \neq$*, respectively) and Boolean connectives* $\wedge, \vee$.

Proof. By structural induction on ModelPlex formula and term operators. □

With a quantitative interpretation of how robustly the choices of a reinforcement learning agent satisfy the formal model, we next discuss several ways of combining the safety reward with other goal-oriented reward elements.

4.2 Logical Constraint Reward

In order to include feedback about the constraints of a formal model into the reward function, the agent receives goal-oriented reward when operating safely according to the model (safety monitor is satisfied), but receives the goal-oriented reward adjusted with a penalty from the monitor when operating unsafely.

Definition 3 (Logical Constraint Reward). *Let $P \in \mathcal{M}$ be a ModelPlex formula for $\langle u := ctrl(x)\rangle \bigwedge_{x \in BV(u:=ctrl(x))}(x = x^+)$, let $\mathbf{R_G}$ be a goal-oriented reward function, and $\mathbf{R_S} = \mathbf{Q}(P)$ be the safety reward function from the quantitative interpretation of P. Let s_0, s_1, s_2 be the states before the agent chooses an action, after it chooses an action, and after the action is executed in the environment, respectively. The logical constraint reward is defined as:*

$$\mathbf{R}(s_0, s_1, s_2) = \begin{cases} \mathbf{R_G}(s_0, s_2) & \textit{if } (s_0, s_1) \models P \\ \mathbf{R_G}(s_0, s_2) + \mathbf{R_S}(s_0, s_1) & \textit{otherwise} \end{cases}$$

Definition 3 discourages the agent to violate the assumptions of the formal model, while ignoring the safety reward when satisfied. The intuition behind this is that positive reward from the formal model is largest when robustly inside the boundary of the formal model's safety envelope, which may encourage the agent to make overly cautious (robust) action choices instead of making progress. Whether Definition 3 prioritizes goal-oriented reward or safety-oriented reward is entirely determined by the relative magnitude of $\mathbf{R_G}(s_0, s_2)$ vs. $\mathbf{R_S}(s_0, s_1)$. This can sometimes be undesirable since it does not necessarily encourage the agent to avoid safety violations. In order to emphasize safety and prioritize some aspects of the formal model over other aspects (e.g., satisfying a speed limit vs. satisfying deceleration assumptions) we introduce *reward scaling* to change the magnitude of rewards while preserving the safety verdict.

4.3 Reward Scaling

The logical constraint reward of Sect. 4.2 does not prioritize goal- vs. safety-oriented reward. Moreover, ModelPlex monitors do not distinguish between quantities of different units and sort in the formal model (e.g., a monitor conflates acceleration verdict, speed verdict, and position verdict into a single robustness measure). When used in a reward function, however, we may want to prioritize some safety aspects. For example, "violating" the brake assumptions of the formal model by having better brakes is acceptable and should not be penalized as hard as violating a speed limit. Here, we develop signal rescaling functions [28] to emphasize the verdict of the entire monitor or certain aspects of it.

Definition 4 (Scaling Function). *A scaling function $C : \mathbb{R} \to \mathbb{R}$ scales the result of a logical constraint reward function $\mathbf{R_S}$ such that the sign of its verdict remains unchanged, i.e., $C(0) = 0$ and $\forall r{\neq}0.\ C(r) \cdot r > 0$.*

Note that in the examples below we use $C(\theta)$ as a notation to indicate that the scaling function applies to a specific term θ.

Example 1 (Strong penalty). In order to emphasize that violating the formal model is highly undesirable, the following scaling function penalizes monitor violations while maintaining rewards for safety, see Fig. 2a:

$$C(\mathbf{R_S}(s_0, s_1)) = \begin{cases} \mathbf{R_S}(s_0, s_1) & \text{if } \mathbf{R_S}(s_0, s_1) > 0 \\ \mathbf{R_S}(s_0, s_1)^3 & \text{otherwise} \end{cases}$$

Example 2 (Boundary preference). In order to encourage behavior that follows close to a safety boundary (i.e. drive close to but not past a speed limit), the following scaling function gives more reward when the state's boundary distance is very small while giving less reward otherwise, see Fig. 2b:

$$C(\mathbf{R_S}(s_0, s_1)) = \begin{cases} \frac{1}{\mathbf{R_S}(s_0, s_1)} & \text{if } \mathbf{R_S}(s_0, s_1) > 0 \\ \mathbf{R_S}(s_0, s_1) & \text{otherwise} \end{cases}$$

Example 3 (Distance preference). In order to encourage behavior that follows a certain distance from a safety boundary (i.e. drive 10 km/h below but not past a speed limit), the following scaling function gives more reward when the state's boundary distance is close to the desired distance while giving less reward otherwise, see Fig. 2c:

$$C(\mathbf{R_S}(s_0, s_1)) = \begin{cases} e^{(-(\mathbf{R_S}(s_0, s_1) - 1.5)^2)} & \text{if } \mathbf{R_S}(s_0, s_1) > 0 \\ \mathbf{R_S}(s_0, s_1) & \text{otherwise} \end{cases}$$

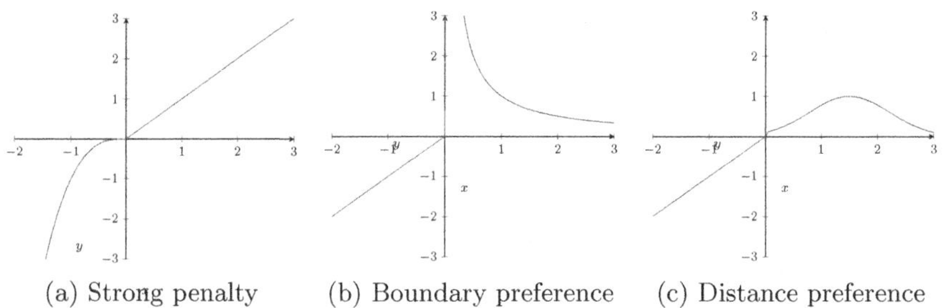

(a) Strong penalty (b) Boundary preference (c) Distance preference

Fig. 2. Reward scaling function illustrations.

Uniform scaling maintains the sign of the monitor verdict, but emphasizes its importance relative to the goal-oriented components of a reward function. If the goal-oriented reward is designed to encourage reaching a goal fast (i.e., $\mathbf{R_G}(s_0, s_2) \leq 0$ for all states $s_0, s_2 \in \mathcal{S}$), the logical constraint reward should be restricted to safety violations and offset to "exceed" the goal-oriented reward: $\min(\mathbf{R_S}(s_0, s_1), 0) - |\delta|$, where δ is the minimum attainable goal-oriented reward.

The states s checked with a monitor $\mathbf{R_S}$ are composed of different aspects of the environment and agent behavior that can be scaled component-wise within $\mathbf{R_S}$ so certain aspects are given more weight in the monitor verdict.

If desired, reward scaling can decrease the importance of safety through decreasing the penalty for unsafe behavior, implying that violating safety for brief moments in time is allowed. This behavior has shown up briefly in our experiments when penalization for violating safety constraints was too low.

Definition 5 (Component-wise Scaling). *Scaling $C_{\downarrow V} : \mathcal{T} \to \mathcal{T}$ applies scaling function C to components in variables V of a safety-reward function $\mathbf{R_S}$:*

$$C_{\downarrow V}(\mathbf{R_S}) = \begin{cases} \min(f,g) \rhd \min(C_{\downarrow V}(f), C_{\downarrow V}(g)) & \\ \max(f,g) \rhd \max(C_{\downarrow V}(f), C_{\downarrow V}(g)) & \\ f \rhd C(f) & \text{if } FV(f) \subseteq V \\ f \rhd f & \text{otherwise} \end{cases}$$

Component-wise scaling maintains the sign of safety-reward function $\mathbf{R_S}$:

$$\forall s_0, s_1 \in \mathcal{S}\big(\mathbf{R_S}(s_0,s_1) = 0 \land C_{\downarrow V}(\mathbf{R_S})(s_0,s_1) = 0 \\ \lor \mathbf{R_S}(s_0,s_1) \neq 0 \land C_{\downarrow V}(\mathbf{R_S})(s_0,s_1) \cdot \mathbf{R_S}(s_0,s_1) > 0\big).$$

Example 4 (Emphasizing speed). In order to emphasize that violating a speed limit is unsafe, while being close to it is desirable, we scale the difference between current speed v and speed limit v_{des} as follows.

$$C_1(v_{\text{des}} - v) = \begin{cases} (v_{\text{des}} - v) & \text{if } v_{\text{des}} - v > 0 \\ (v_{\text{des}} - v)^{1/3} & \text{if } 0 \geq v_{\text{des}} - v > -1 \\ (v_{\text{des}} - v)^3 & \text{otherwise} \end{cases}$$

$$C_2(v - v_{\text{des}}) = \begin{cases} (v - v_{\text{des}}) & \text{if } v - v_{\text{des}} > 0 \\ (v - v_{\text{des}})^3 & \text{if } 0 \geq v - v_{\text{des}} > -1 \\ (v - v_{\text{des}})^{1/3} & \text{otherwise} \end{cases}$$

We apply the scaling to reward components in $\{v, v_{\text{des}}\}$: $C_1(v - v_{\text{des}})_{\downarrow\{v,v_{\text{des}}\}}$ and $C_2(v_{\text{des}} - v)_{\downarrow\{v,v_{\text{des}}\}}$. The above functions scale two different speed verdicts, $v - v_{\text{des}}$ and $v_{\text{des}} - v$, which in a formal model and thus a monitor may arise for different control choices (e.g., requiring to slow down when current velocity, v, exceeds the speed limit, v_{des} vs. allowing to speed up when $v < v_{\text{des}}$). When $v_{\text{des}} - v \leq 0$, safety is violated and therefore C_1 scales the negative verdict more aggressively by applying an exponential function. When $v - v_{\text{des}} \leq 0$, safety is satisfied, but going much slower than v_{des} is undesirable; therefore, C_2 scales the negative verdict using a fractional exponential function, see Fig. 3.

4.4 Potential-Based Logical Constraint Reward

Reward shaping may cause unexpected behavior from the trained agent, as the reward directly influences what actions the agent takes and may cause the agent

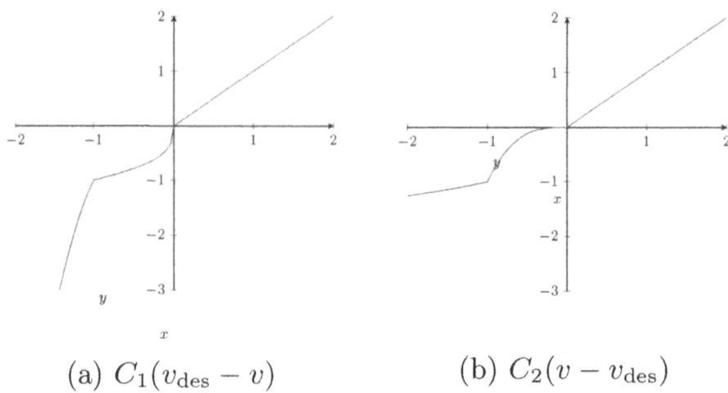

(a) $C_1(v_{\text{des}} - v)$ (b) $C_2(v - v_{\text{des}})$

Fig. 3. Component-wise scaling to emphasize speed rewards.

to learn a suboptimal policy [23]. To prevent unforeseen and unwanted behavior, potential-based reward shaping [23] provides additional reward to the agent while guaranteeing the agent will learn the optimal policy of the original reward function. The additional reward is specified using the transition from the current to the future state, and this transition is formalized as the difference in "potential" of the two states. Let $\Phi(s)$ characterize certain features of a state $s \in \mathcal{S}$ (e.g., safety). Potential-based reward is then $\mathbf{R_P}(s, a, s') = \gamma\Phi(s') - \Phi(s)$, where s is the current state, a is the action taken to reach a future state s', and γ is some discount factor, which gets added to the original reward: $\mathbf{R}(s, a, s') + \mathbf{R_P}(s, a, s')$. The main intuition [23] why the policy is still optimal under this modified reward function is that the potential function itself does not prefer one policy over the other. Therefore, the original optimal policy is still preferred when the potential difference is added to the original reward function.

Example 5 (Potential-based Logical Constraint Reward). The original reward function $\mathbf{R}(s, a, s')$ is augmented with additional reward that is calculated using the predictive formal model. We align the loop iterations of the model in time-triggered normal form with the learning states s and s' of the reward function: let $s_0, s_1, s_2{=}s$ be the states from the formal model leading up to learning state s, and let $s'_0{=}s_2{=}s, s'_1, s'_2{=}s'$ be the states of the formal model corresponding to the transition (s, a, s'). Since monitors are evaluated over two model states, the safety potential associated with learning state s is a function of the previous action $\Phi(s) = \mathbf{R_S}(s_0, s_1)$, whereas the safety potential associated with learning state s' is according to the safety of the current action $\Phi(s') = \mathbf{R_S}(s'_0, s'_1)$. Then, the additional reward is $\mathbf{R_P}(s, a, s') = \gamma\Phi(s') - \Phi(s)$ with $\gamma = 1$, and the final reward function is: $\mathbf{R'}(s, a, s') = \mathbf{R}(s, a, s') + \mathbf{R_P}(s, a, s')$.

5 Evaluation

Formal Model. In our evaluation, we adapt an existing formal model of a train protection system [26] and apply it to a standard reinforcement learning environment for longitudinal vehicle control [4]. The goal of the agent in longitudinal vehicle control is to drive forward as fast as possible while respecting posted

Model 1. Speed limit control, adapted from [26, Fig. 5]

spd	1	$((?v \leq v_{\mathrm{des}}; a := *; ?-B \leq a \leq A)$
	2	$\cup\, (?v \geq v_{\mathrm{des}}; a := *; ?-B \leq a \leq 0));$
atp	3	if $\left(e - p \leq \frac{v^2 - d^2}{2B} + \left(\frac{A}{B} + 1\right)\left(\frac{A}{2}\varepsilon^2 + v\varepsilon\right)\right)$ then $a := -B$ fi
drive	4	$t := 0;$
	5	$\{p' = v,\, v' = a,\, t' = 1 \ \&\ v \geq 0 \land t \leq \varepsilon\}$

speed limits. The speed limit control model (Model 1) comes with 3 components: a speed controller spd in lines 1–2 chooses acceleration to a desired cruising speed v_{des}, the automatic train protection atp in line 3 may override the choice of spd if the remaining distance to the speed limit d is unsafe, and the motion model drive in lines 4–5 describes how the vehicle position p and speed v change in response to the agent's acceleration choice.

From Model 1, we use [22] to obtain a ModelPlex formula, whose main components reflect the model structure:

$$\begin{aligned} \mathrm{slc} \equiv\ & 0 \leq v \leq v_{\mathrm{des}} \land -B \leq a^+ \leq A \land e - p > S \\ & \lor 0 \leq v_{\mathrm{des}} \leq v \land -B \leq a^+ \leq 0 \land e - p > S \\ & \lor 0 \leq v \land a^+ = -B \land e - p \leq S \\ & \qquad \text{where } S \equiv \frac{v^2 - d^2}{2B} + \left(\frac{A}{B} + 1\right)\left(\frac{A}{2}\varepsilon^2 + v\varepsilon\right) \end{aligned} \tag{1}$$

Environment. LongiControl [4] provides a longitudinal vehicle control environment with state space $[x(t), v(t), a(t), a_{\mathrm{prev}}(t), v_{\mathrm{lim}}(t), \boldsymbol{v}_{\mathrm{lim,fut}}(t), \boldsymbol{d}_{\mathrm{lim,fut}}(t)]$ of vehicle position $x(t)$, speed $v(t)$, acceleration $a(t)$, previous acceleration $a_{\mathrm{prev}}(t)$, current speed limit $v_{\mathrm{lim}}(t)$, upcoming two speed limits $\boldsymbol{v}_{\mathrm{lim,fut}}(t)$, and distances to the upcoming two speed limits $\boldsymbol{d}_{\mathrm{lim,fut}}(t)$. The action space is continuous acceleration in the interval $[-3, 3]\,\mathrm{m/s}^2$, and the sampling time is 0.1 s. The environment has posted speed limits of 50 km/h at $[0, 250)$ m, 80 km/h at $[250, 500)$ m, 40 km/h at $[500, 750)$ m, and 50 km/h after 750 m.

We map the environment to the ModelPlex formula (1) as follows: $x(t) \mapsto p, v(t) \mapsto v, a(t) \mapsto a^+, v_{\mathrm{lim}}(t) \mapsto v_{\mathrm{des}}, 3 \mapsto A, 3 \mapsto B, 0.1 \mapsto \varepsilon$ with two separate configurations in order to demonstrate how the formal model can influence the behavior of the trained reinforcement learning agent:

Configuration 1 encourages behavior similar to Model 1, satisfying a speed limit before the speed limit begins: $\boldsymbol{v}_{\mathrm{lim,fut}}(t)_1 \mapsto d, x(t) + \boldsymbol{d}_{\mathrm{lim,fut}}(t)_1 \mapsto e$, i.e., the first elements of the speed limit and speed limit position vectors are handed to the monitor

Configuration 2 to illustrate the effectiveness of the monitor in influencing learned behavior, this configuration encourages "unusual" behavior opposing

r_{forward} (2) by favoring meeting the posted speed limit by the end (rather than the beginning) of the speed limit: $v_{\text{lim}}(t) \mapsto d, x(t) + \boldsymbol{d}_{\text{lim,fut}}(t)_1 \mapsto e$

Reward Function. For evaluation, we use the reward function from [4, p. 1034] as a baseline, with weighted penalties for slow driving (r_{forward}), energy consumption (r_{energy}), jerk (r_{jerk}), and speeding (r_{safe}):

$$\underbrace{-\xi_{\text{forward}} r_{\text{forward}} - \xi_{\text{energy}} r_{\text{energy}} - \xi_{\text{jerk}} r_{\text{jerk}}}_{\mathbf{R_G}} - \underbrace{\xi_{\text{safe}} r_{\text{safe}}}_{\mathbf{R_S}} \tag{2}$$

We obtain a safety robustness measure $\mathbf{Q}(\text{slc})$ from formula (1), and then replace the speeding penalty with the (scaled) safety reward function as follows:

Logical constraint reward (LCR) with $\mathbf{R_S} = \min(0, \mathbf{Q}(\text{slc})(s_0, s_1)) - 1$ to ignore the safety robustness measure when satisfied and offset safety violations to exceed the largest magnitude of the $\mathbf{R_G}$ components in (2).
Logical constraint reward scaling (LCRS) applies the component-wise scaling of Example 4 to the safety robustness measure $\mathbf{Q}(\text{slc})$.
Potential-based reward shaping (PBRS) applies the potential-based reward shaping of Example 5 to the safety robustness measure $\mathbf{Q}(\text{slc})$.

We used reward function **LCR** with Configuration1 and reward functions **LCR**, **LCRS**, **PBRS** with Configuration 2.

Model Training. Using these different reward functions, we train several agents with the Soft Actor-Critic (SAC) method[1] and the hyperparameters of LongiControl [4, Table 4] with a learning rate of 1e-5. We trained the baseline agent with a learning rate of 1e-4.

Evaluation Metrics. We evaluate the training process in terms of number of epochs until convergence, and the safety of the resulting agents in terms of the number and magnitude of speed limit violations. We also quantify how successful the agents are in reaching the goal, which is to drive as fast and as close to the speed limit as possible, by measuring the accumulated reward per (2) and the difference between agent speed v and the posted speed limits v_{des} during an evaluation period. Note that training and evaluation episodes do not terminate early under unsafe behavior of the agent but instead invoke a negative reward as a penalty. Below are the results of our experiments.

Results. Figure 4 displays the average accumulated reward across several evaluation periods at every tenth epoch during training. Note, that during training we use different reward functions, which means their magnitude is not directly comparable. For the baseline reward function, we see that the reward converges to around −200 at 3000 epochs. The logical constraint reward using Configuration 1 converges to −300 at 1250 epochs. The following experiments using Configuration 2 converge to −325 at 1750 epochs for the logical constraint reward, −310

[1] GitHub of environment: https://github.com/dynamik1703/gym_longicontrol.

at 3000 epochs for logical constraint reward scaling, and −300 at 2250 epochs for potential-based reward shaping (faster or at the same rate as the baseline model). This helps with efficiency regarding how many epochs are required to finish training a reinforcement learning agent.

Figure 5a plots the accumulated reward according to the baseline reward function (2), so can be compared relative to each other. The baseline agent has the highest accumulated reward, indicating that it operates more aggressively (less robustly) than other agents. The robustness nature of the other agents can also be seen in Fig. 5b, which plots the $v_{\text{des}} - v$ to compare how well the agents achieve the goal of driving close to the speed limit.

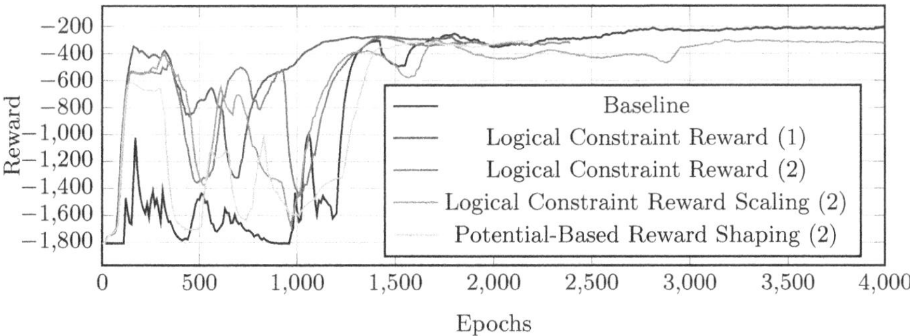

Fig. 4. Accumulated reward across evaluations during training; smoothed with exponential moving average.

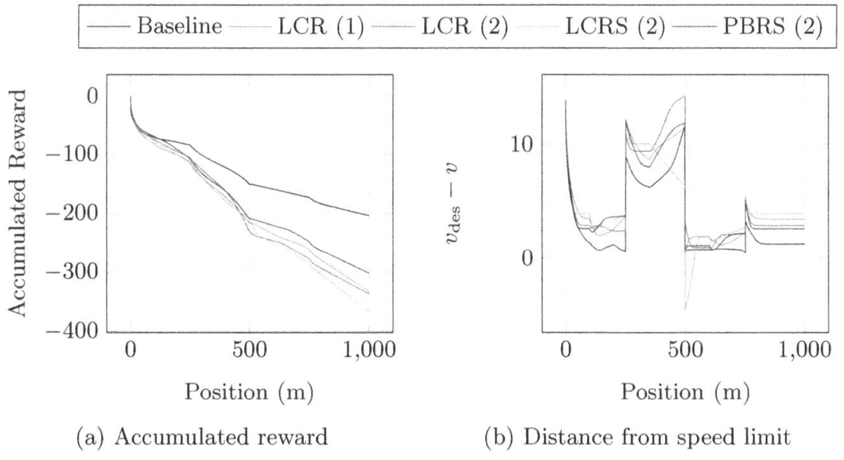

(a) Accumulated reward (b) Distance from speed limit

Fig. 5. Averaged reward and performance across five evaluation runs at end of training.

When evaluating the agents for Configuration 1, we compare **LCR(1)**, logical constraint reward, model against the baseline agent as their desired behavior is to drive as close to the speed limit as possible while satisfying the speed limit. After modifying the safety-oriented reward with the safety robustness measure from ModelPlex **Q**(slc), the resulting **LCR(1)** experiments resulted in agents that successfully satisfied the safety requirement by driving below the speed limit, while there were also some agents that violated safety when the upcoming speed limit was less than the current speed limit; using reward scaling to penalize unsafe behavior more can address this issue. The safe logical constraint reward agents had more robust behavior regarding maintaining safety as they left a larger gap to the desired speed limit as seen in Fig. 5b.

For the agents using Configuration 2, we also see that they are generally more robust compared to the baseline agent by the increased distance to desired speed in Fig. 5b. Note that for Configuration 2, the purpose was to demonstrate how the formal model can influence the behavior of the learned agent, which is most prominent when emphasizing speed with **LCRS(2)**, logical constraint reward scaling: the agent's behavior shows a preference for reaching the 80 km/h speed limit at the end of the speed limit at 500 m in Fig. 5b. This behavior extends into violating the monitor when passing into the subsequent 40 km/h speed limit.

The other Configuration 2 models, **LCR(2)** and **PBRS(2)** did not violate safety defined by the monitor.

In summary, the experiments suggest that training from modified reward functions **LCR(1)** converges faster, and **LCR(2)**, **PBRS(2)** generally satisfies safety. In addition, modifying aspects that correspond to the formal model can effectively change the agent's behavior **LCRS(2)**, which can help with designing the reward function for different goals of reinforcement learning problems.

6 Conclusion

We explored using predictive hybrid models with formalized safety specifications as an alternative to manually defining safety-oriented aspects of reward functions in reinforcement learning.[2] Based on logically constrained reinforcement learning, the agents we trained were implemented using dL-formalized safety rewards. The logical constraints of the safety-oriented reward are combined with the goal-oriented reward of the agent through reward scaling and potential-based reward shaping. We found that partly auto-generated reward functions produce agents that generally maintain the level of safety of hand-tuned reward functions and that reward scaling can be used to emphasize certain aspects of the generated reward functions. There were still agents that violated safety, specifically within logical constraint reward functions, and including dL-based shielding [9] can address these safety concerns. In addition, we observed faster convergence during training when using augmented reward functions, specifically for the logically constrained reward and the potential-based reward functions.

[2] GitHub for experiment code: https://github.com/marianqian/gym_longicontrol_formal_methods.

Future work includes generating goal-oriented rewards from liveness proofs, and extending the formal modeling language to specify scaling functions directly in the formal model, e.g., as design annotations. We also plan to use the predictive nature of the formal model for additional forms of reward shaping, e.g., to interpret the continuous dynamics of the formal model as a reward predictor for some reward aspects that are sustained over an extended time period, because they cannot be influenced instantaneously but only through affecting motion.

References

1. Alshiekh, M., Bloem, R., Ehlers, R., Könighofer, B., Niekum, S., Topcu, U.: Safe reinforcement learning via shielding. In: Proceedings of the Thirty-Second AAAI Conference on Artificial Intelligence, (AAAI-18), the 30th innovative Applications of Artificial Intelligence (IAAI 2018), and the 8th AAAI Symposium on Educational Advances in Artificial Intelligence (EAAI 2018), New Orleans, Louisiana, USA, 2–7 February 2018, pp. 2669–2678 (2018)
2. Balakrishnan, A., Deshmukh, J.V.: Structured reward shaping using signal temporal logic specifications. In: IEEE/RSJ International Conference on Intelligent Robots and Systems (IROS 2019), Macau, China, 4–8 November 2019, pp. 3481–3486 (2019). https://doi.org/10.1109/IROS40897.2019.8968254
3. Bayani, D., Mitsch, S.: Fanoos: multi-resolution, multi-strength, interactive explanations for learned systems. In: Finkbeiner, B., Wies, T. (eds.) VMCAI 2022. LNCS, vol. 13182, pp. 43–68. Springer, Cham (2022). https://doi.org/10.1007/978-3-030-94583-1_3
4. Dohmen, J., Liessner, R., Friebel, C., Bäker, B.: LongiControl: a reinforcement learning environment for longitudinal vehicle control. In: Proceedings of the 13th International Conference on Agents and Artificial Intelligence - Volume 2: ICAART, pp. 1030–1037. INSTICC, SciTePress (2021). https://doi.org/10.5220/0010305210301037
5. Donzé, A., Ferrère, T., Maler, O.: Efficient robust monitoring for STL. In: Sharygina, N., Veith, H. (eds.) CAV 2013. LNCS, vol. 8044, pp. 264–279. Springer, Heidelberg (2013). https://doi.org/10.1007/978-3-642-39799-8_19
6. Dreossi, T., Donzé, A., Seshia, S.A.: Compositional falsification of cyber-physical systems with machine learning components. J. Autom. Reason. **63**(4), 1031–1053 (2019). https://doi.org/10.1007/s10817-018-09509-5
7. Fainekos, G.E., Pappas, G.J.: Robustness of temporal logic specifications. In: Havelund, K., Núñez, M., Roşu, G., Wolff, B. (eds.) FATES/RV -2006. LNCS, vol. 4262, pp. 178–192. Springer, Heidelberg (2006). https://doi.org/10.1007/11940197_12
8. Fainekos, G.E., Pappas, G.J.: Robustness of temporal logic specifications for continuous-time signals. Theor. Comput. Sci. **410**(42), 4262–4291 (2009). https://doi.org/10.1016/j.tcs.2009.06.021
9. Fulton, N., Platzer, A.: Safe reinforcement learning via formal methods: toward safe control through proof and learning. In: Proceedings of the Thirty-Second AAAI Conference on Artificial Intelligence, (AAAI 2018), the 30th Innovative Applications of Artificial Intelligence (IAAI 2018), and the 8th AAAI Symposium on Educational Advances in Artificial Intelligence (EAAI 2018), New Orleans, Louisiana, USA, 2–7 February 2018, pp. 6485–6492 (2018)

10. Fulton, N., Platzer, A.: Verifiably safe off-model reinforcement learning. In: Vojnar, T., Zhang, L. (eds.) TACAS 2019. LNCS, vol. 11427, pp. 413–430. Springer, Cham (2019). https://doi.org/10.1007/978-3-030-17462-0_28
11. Hahn, E.M., Perez, M., Schewe, S., Somenzi, F., Trivedi, A., Wojtczak, D.: Faithful and effective reward schemes for model-free reinforcement learning of omega-regular objectives. In: Hung, D.V., Sokolsky, O. (eds.) ATVA 2020. LNCS, vol. 12302, pp. 108–124. Springer, Cham (2020). https://doi.org/10.1007/978-3-030-59152-6_6
12. Hammond, L., Abate, A., Gutierrez, J., Wooldridge, M.J.: Multi-agent reinforcement learning with temporal logic specifications. In: AAMAS 2021: 20th International Conference on Autonomous Agents and Multiagent Systems, Virtual Event, United Kingdom, 3–7 May 2021, pp. 583–592 (2021). https://doi.org/10.5555/3463952.3464024
13. Hasanbeig, M., Abate, A., Kroening, D.: Cautious reinforcement learning with logical constraints. In: Proceedings of the 19th International Conference on Autonomous Agents and Multiagent Systems, AAMAS 2020, Auckland, New Zealand, 9–13 May 2020, pp. 483–491 (2020). https://doi.org/10.5555/3398761.3398821
14. Hunt, N., Fulton, N., Magliacane, S., Hoang, T.N., Das, S., Solar-Lezama, A.: Verifiably safe exploration for end-to-end reinforcement learning. In: HSCC 2021: 24th ACM International Conference on Hybrid Systems: Computation and Control, Nashville, Tennessee, 19–21 May 2021, pp. 14:1–14:11 (2021). https://doi.org/10.1145/3447928.3456653
15. Ivanov, R., Carpenter, T.J., Weimer, J., Alur, R., Pappas, G.J., Lee, I.: Verifying the safety of autonomous systems with neural network controllers. ACM Trans. Embed. Comput. Syst. **20**(1), 7:1–7:26 (2021). https://doi.org/10.1145/3419742
16. Ivanov, R., Carpenter, T., Weimer, J., Alur, R., Pappas, G., Lee, I.: Verisig 2.0: verification of neural network controllers using Taylor model preconditioning. In: Silva, A., Leino, K.R.M. (eds.) CAV 2021. LNCS, vol. 12759, pp. 249–262. Springer, Cham (2021). https://doi.org/10.1007/978-3-030-81685-8_11
17. Jansen, N., Könighofer, B., Junges, S., Serban, A., Bloem, R.: Safe reinforcement learning using probabilistic shields (invited paper). In: 31st International Conference on Concurrency Theory, CONCUR 2020, 1–4 September 2020, Vienna, Austria (Virtual Conference), pp. 3:1–3:16 (2020). https://doi.org/10.4230/LIPIcs.CONCUR.2020.3
18. Jiang, Y., Bharadwaj, S., Wu, B., Shah, R., Topcu, U., Stone, P.: Temporal-logic-based reward shaping for continuing reinforcement learning tasks. In: Association for the Advancement of Artificial Intelligence (2021)
19. Könighofer, B., Bloem, R., Ehlers, R., Pek, C.: Correct-by-construction runtime enforcement in AI - a survey. CoRR abs/2208.14426 (2022). https://doi.org/10.48550/arXiv.2208.14426
20. Könighofer, B., Lorber, F., Jansen, N., Bloem, R.: Shield synthesis for reinforcement learning. In: Margaria, T., Steffen, B. (eds.) ISoLA 2020. LNCS, vol. 12476, pp. 290–306. Springer, Cham (2020). https://doi.org/10.1007/978-3-030-61362-4_16
21. Lin, Q., Mitsch, S., Platzer, A., Dolan, J.M.: Safe and resilient practical waypoint-following for autonomous vehicles. IEEE Control. Syst. Lett. **6**, 1574–1579 (2022). https://doi.org/10.1109/LCSYS.2021.3125717
22. Mitsch, S., Platzer, A.: ModelPlex: verified runtime validation of verified cyber-physical system models. Formal Methods Syst. Des. **49**(1–2), 33–74 (2016). https://doi.org/10.1007/s10703-016-0241-z

23. Ng, A.Y., Harada, D., Russell, S.: Policy invariance under reward transformations: Theory and application to reward shaping. In: Proceedings of the Sixteenth International Conference on Machine Learning (ICML 1999), Bled, Slovenia, 27–30 June 1999, pp. 278–287 (1999)
24. Phan, D.T., Grosu, R., Jansen, N., Paoletti, N., Smolka, S.A., Stoller, S.D.: Neural simplex architecture. In: Lee, R., Jha, S., Mavridou, A., Giannakopoulou, D. (eds.) NFM 2020. LNCS, vol. 12229, pp. 97–114. Springer, Cham (2020). https://doi.org/10.1007/978-3-030-55754-6_6
25. Platzer, A.: A complete uniform substitution calculus for differential dynamic logic. J. Autom. Reason. **59**(2), 219–265 (2017). https://doi.org/10.1007/s10817-016-9385-1
26. Platzer, A., Quesel, J.-D.: European train control system: a case study in formal verification. In: Breitman, K., Cavalcanti, A. (eds.) ICFEM 2009. LNCS, vol. 5885, pp. 246–265. Springer, Heidelberg (2009). https://doi.org/10.1007/978-3-642-10373-5_13
27. Tran, H., Cai, F., Lopez, D.M., Musau, P., Johnson, T.T., Koutsoukos, X.D.: Safety verification of cyber-physical systems with reinforcement learning control. ACM Trans. Embed. Comput. Syst. **18**(5s), 105:1–105:22 (2019). https://doi.org/10.1145/3358230
28. Zhang, Z., Lyu, D., Arcaini, P., Ma, L., Hasuo, I., Zhao, J.: On the effectiveness of signal rescaling in hybrid system falsification. In: Dutle, A., Moscato, M.M., Titolo, L., Muñoz, C.A., Perez, I. (eds.) NFM 2021. LNCS, vol. 12673, pp. 392–399. Springer, Cham (2021). https://doi.org/10.1007/978-3-030-76384-8_24

Conservative Safety Monitors of Stochastic Dynamical Systems

Matthew Cleaveland[1(✉)], Oleg Sokolsky[1], Insup Lee[1], and Ivan Ruchkin[2]

[1] University of Pennsylvania, Philadelphia, PA 19104, USA
{mcleav,sokolsky,lee}@seas.upenn.edu
[2] University of Florida, Gainesville, FL 32611, USA
iruchkin@ece.ufl.edu

Abstract. Generating accurate runtime safety estimates for autonomous systems is vital to ensuring their continued proliferation. However, exhaustive reasoning about future behaviors is generally too complex to do at runtime. To provide scalable and formal safety estimates, we propose a method for leveraging design-time model checking results at runtime. Specifically, we model the system as a probabilistic automaton (PA) and compute bounded-time reachability probabilities over the states of the PA at design time. At runtime, we combine distributions of state estimates with the model checking results to produce a bounded time safety estimate. We argue that our approach produces well-calibrated safety probabilities, assuming the estimated state distributions are well-calibrated. We evaluate our approach on simulated water tanks.

Keywords: Runtime Monitoring · Probabilistic Model Checking · Calibrated Prediction

1 Introduction

As autonomous systems see increased use and perform critical tasks in an open world, reasoning about their safety and performance is critical. In particular, it is vital to know if a system is likely to reach an unsafe state in the near future.

The field of predictive runtime monitoring offers ways for performing this reasoning. The basic idea is to reason about the expected future behaviors of the system and its properties. However, accurately computing future system states is computationally infeasible at runtime, as it requires running expensive reachability analysis on complex models. Previous works have computed libraries of reachability analysis results at design time and used them at runtime [9]. But these approaches require the system dynamics to have certain invariances to reduce the number of times reachability analysis must be called offline.

Other lines of work use system execution data to learn discrete probabilistic models of the system, which are then used to perform predictive runtime monitoring, as there is rich literature for runtime monitoring of discrete automata. These models range from discrete-time Markov chains (DTMCs) [2] to hidden Markov models (HMMs) [4] to Bayesian networks [17]. However, it is difficult

K. Y. Rozier and S. Chaudhuri (Eds.): NFM 2023, LNCS 13903, pp. 140–156, 2023.
https://doi.org/10.1007/978-3-031-33170-1_9

to provide guarantees relating the performance of the automata models to the real system, due to the fact that they are fit using finite data. Of particular interest is ensuring the models are conservative: it is essential to avoid run-time overconfidence in the safety of the dynamical system.

In this paper, we propose a method for predictive run-time monitoring of safety probabilities that builds on the strengths of the existing works. We use a mix of conservative modeling techniques and data-driven modeling techniques to transform the dynamical system into a probabilistic automaton (PA).[1] We then employ probabilistic model checking (PMC) to compute the safety of the model over all its states offline. Finally, we synthesize lightweight monitors that rely on the model checking results and a well-calibrated state estimator to compute the probability of system safety at runtime.

Under the assumption that the PA model is conservative and that the state estimator is well-calibrated, we prove that our runtime monitors are conservative. We demonstrate that our modeling technique is likely to result in conservative PA models. Finally, we show that our method produces well-calibrated, accurate, and conservative monitors on a case study using water tanks.

The contributions of this paper are threefold:

- We present a method for conservatively modeling dynamical systems as PAs and using PMC results at runtime to monitor the system's safety.
- We prove that if our PA models are conservative then the monitor safety estimates will be conservative.
- We demonstrate our approach on a case study of water tanks. We empirically show that our PA models and runtime monitors are both conservative.

The rest of the paper is structured as follows. We give an overview of the related work in Sect. 2, provide the necessary formal background in Sect. 3, and formulate the problem in Sect. 4. Section 5 goes over our proposed approach and Sect. 6 provides formal conservatism guarantees for the approach. We describe the results of our case study in Sect. 7 and conclude in Sect. 8.

2 Related Work

We divide the previous works in the area of predictive runtime monitoring into two bins. The first bin analyzes dynamical system models, while the second analyzes automata models.

Dynamical Systems Approaches. A large portion of the predictive monitoring for dynamical systems literature focuses on reasoning about the safety of autonomous vehicles. Prior work has employed reachability analysis to estimate the future positions of other cars to estimate the safety of a proposed vehicle trajectory [1]. In [18], the authors develop techniques to estimate the probability of

[1] In our scope, PAs are equivalent to Markov Decision Processes (MDPs) without rewards: both have finite states with probabilistic and non-deterministic transitions.

a proposed trajectory resulting in a collision with other vehicles, which are given as distributions of states predicted by neural networks (NNs). In [9], the authors use precomputed reachability analysis and Bayesian inference to compute the probability of an autonomous vehicle colliding with static obstacles. This approach requires the system dynamics to have certain invariances to ensure the reachability analysis can be feasibly run at design time. This approach is conceptually similar to ours, but we employ automata-based abstractions instead of making invariance assumptions about the system dynamics.

Previous works have also addressed the problem of synthesizing runtime monitors for signal temporal logic (STL) properties of dynamical systems. Approaches range from conformal prediction [8,25], design time forward reachability analysis [33], computing safe envelopes of control commands [32], online linear regression [15], and uncertainty aware STL monitoring [26].

Automata Approaches. The first works of this type developed predictive LTL semantics, also called LTL_3 [24,34], for discrete automata. The LTL_3 semantics allowed to the system to determine if every infinite extension of an observed finite trace would satisfy or not satisfy a specification. Recent work has extended these ideas to timed systems [28], multi-model systems [12], and systems with assumptions [10]. Another approach uses neural networks to classify if unsafe states of a hybrid automaton (HA) can be reached from the current state of the HA [5–7]. They additionally use conformal prediction to get guarantees about the accuracy of their predictions [31]. However, these frameworks give very coarse predictions, as they can only determine if a system is guaranteed to be safe, guaranteed to be unsafe, or not sure.

Another thread of work uses data to learn probabilistic models that can then be used in conjunction with predictive monitoring techniques. In [4], the authors learn an HMM model of the system from simulation data and perform bounded reachability analysis to determine the probability of an LTL specification being violated from each state of the HMM. This work was extended using abstraction techniques to simplify the learned models [3]. In [2], the same authors employ importance sampling to efficiently learn discrete-time Markov chain (DTMC) models from data, which they then use to synthesize predictive monitors. In [17], the authors use Bayesian networks to model temporal properties of stochastic timed automata. The Bayesian networks are updated online to improve their performance. Finally, in [13] the authors use process mining techniques to learn predictive models of systems, which are in turn used to synthesize predictive runtime monitors. An interesting line of future work for us is exploring applying our runtime monitoring technique using these models as they are updated from new observations online.

The most similar work to ours presents two methods for synthesizing predictive monitors for partially observable Markov decision processes (POMDPs) [19]. The first approach combines precomputed safety probabilities of each state with POMDP state estimators to estimate the probability that the system will remain safe. However, state estimation of POMDPs is computationally expensive since the set of potential state distributions increases exponentially due to the non-determinism in the model. The second approach uses model checking of conditional probabilities to directly compute the safety of the system based on the observation trace. A downside of this approach is that it requires running model checking at runtime. Our method, on the other hand, avoids expensive computations at run time while maintaining design-time scalability through abstraction.

3 Background

In the following Definitions 1 to 3, borrowed from Kwiatkowska et al. [23], we use $Dist(S)$ to refer to the set of probability distributions over a set S, η_s as the distribution with all its probability mass on $s \in S$, and $\mu_1 \times \mu_2$ to be the product distribution of μ_1 and μ_2.

Definition 1. *A* probabilistic automaton *(PA) is a tuple* $\mathsf{M} = (S, \bar{s}, \alpha, \delta, L)$, *where* S *is a finite set of states,* $\bar{s} \in S$ *is the initial state,* α *is an alphabet of action labels,* $\delta \subseteq S \times \alpha \times Dist(S)$ *is a probabilistic transition relation, and* $L : S \rightarrow 2^{AP}$ *is a labeling function from states to sets of atomic propositions from the set* AP.

If $(s, a, \mu) \in \delta$ then the PA can make a transition in state s with action label a and move based on distribution μ to state s' with probability $\mu(s')$, which is denoted by $s \xrightarrow{a} \mu$. If $(s, a, \eta_{s'}) \in \delta$ then we say the PA can transition from state s to state s' via action a. A state s is terminal if no elements of δ contain s. A path in M is a finite/infinite sequence of transitions $\pi = s_0 \xrightarrow{a_0, \mu_0} s_1 \xrightarrow{a_1, \mu_1} \dots$ with $s_0 = \bar{s}$ and $\mu_i(s_{i+1}) > 0$. A set of paths is denoted as Π. We use $\mathsf{M}(s)$ to denote the PA M with initial state s.

Reasoning about PAs also requires the notion of a *scheduler*, which resolves the non-determinism during an execution of a PA. For our purposes, a scheduler σ maps each state of the PA to an available action label in that state. We use $\Pi^{\sigma}_{\mathsf{M}}$ for the set of all paths through M when controlled by scheduler σ and Sch_{M} for the set of all schedulers for M. Finally, given a scheduler σ, we define a probability space Pr^{σ}_{M} over the set of paths $\Pi^{\sigma}_{\mathsf{M}}$ in the standard manner.

Given PAs M_1 and M_2, we define parallel composition as follows:

Definition 2. *The* parallel composition *of PAs* $\mathsf{M}_1 = (S_1, \bar{s}_1, \alpha_1, \delta_1, L_1)$ *and* $\mathsf{M}_2 = (S_2, \bar{s}_2, \alpha_2, \delta_2, L_2)$ *is given by the PA* $\mathsf{M}_1 \parallel \mathsf{M}_2 = (S_1 \times S_2, (\bar{s}_1, \bar{s}_2), \alpha_1 \cup \alpha_2, \delta, L)$, *where* $L(s_1, s_2) = L_1(s_1) \cup L_2(s_2)$ *and* δ *is such that* $(s_1, s_2) \xrightarrow{a} \mu_1 \times \mu_2$ *iff one of the following holds: (i)* $s_1 \xrightarrow{a} \mu_1, s_2 \xrightarrow{a} \mu_2$ *and* $a \in \alpha_1 \cap \alpha_2$, *(ii)* $s_1 \xrightarrow{a} \mu_1, \mu_2 = \eta_{s_2}$ *and* $a \in (\alpha_1 \setminus \alpha_2)$, *(iii)* $\mu_1 = \eta_{s_1}, s_2 \xrightarrow{a} \mu_2$ *and* $a \in (\alpha_2 \setminus \alpha_1)$.

In this paper, we are concerned with probabilities that the system will not enter an unsafe state within a bounded amount of time. These are represented as bounded-time safety properties, which we express using metric temporal logic (MTL) [21]. Following the notation from [20], we denote these properties as

$$\square^{\leq T} s \notin S_{unsafe},$$

where $S_{unsafe} \subset S$ is the set of unsafe states and $T \geq 0$ is the time bound.

Definition 3. *For MTL formula* ψ*, PA* M*, and scheduler* $\sigma \in Sch_{\mathsf{M}}$*, the* probability of ψ holding *is:*

$$Pr^{\sigma}_{\mathsf{M}}(\psi) := Pr^{\sigma}_{\mathsf{M}}\{\pi \in \Pi^{\sigma}_{\mathsf{M}} \mid \pi \models \psi\},$$

where $\pi \models \psi$ *indicates that the path* π *satisfies* ψ *in the standard MTL semantics [21]. We specifically consider MTL safety properties, which are MTL specifications that can be falsified by a finite trace though a model.*

Probabilistically verifying an MTL formula ψ against M requires checking that the probability of satisfying ψ meets a probability bound for all schedulers. This involves computing the minimum or maximum probability of satisfying ψ over all schedulers:

$$Pr^{min}_{\mathsf{M}}(\psi) := \inf_{\sigma \in Sch_{\mathsf{M}}} Pr^{\sigma}_{\mathsf{M}}(\psi)$$
$$Pr^{max}_{\mathsf{M}}(\psi) := \sup_{\sigma \in Sch_{\mathsf{M}}} Pr^{\sigma}_{\mathsf{M}}(\psi)$$

We call σ a min scheduler of M if $Pr^{\sigma}_{\mathsf{M}}(\psi) = Pr^{min}_{\mathsf{M}}(\psi)$. We use Sch^{min}_{M} to denote the set of min schedulers of M.

Remark. For the rest of this paper, we use Pr when referring to model-checking probabilities and P for all other probabilities.

Calibration and Conservatism. Consider a scenario where a probability estimator is predicting probability $\hat{p}$ that a (desirable) event E will occur (e.g., a safe outcome). We define the calibration for the probability estimates (adapted from Equation (1) of [16]):

Definition 4 (Calibration). *The probability estimates* $\hat{p}$ *of event* E *are* well-calibrated *if*

$$P(E \mid \hat{p} = p) = p, \quad \forall p \in [0, 1] \tag{1}$$

Next, we define conservatism for the probability estimates:

Definition 5 (Conservative Probability). *The probability estimates* $\hat{p}$ *of a desirable event* E *are* conservative *if*

$$P(E \mid \hat{p} = p) \geq p, \quad \forall p \in [0, 1] \tag{2}$$

In other words, the estimates $\hat{p}$ are conservative if they underestimate the true probability of event E. Note that any monitor that is well-calibrated (Definition 4) is guaranteed to be conservative (Definition 5), but not vice versa.

Two standard metrics for assessing the calibration of the $\hat{p}$ estimates are *expected calibration error* (ECE) [16] and *Brier score* [29]. The ECE metric is computed by dividing the $\hat{p}$ values into equally spaced bins in $[0, 1]$, within each bin taking the absolute difference between the average $\hat{p}$ and the empirical probability of event E, and weighted-averaging across bins with their sizes as weights. So ECE penalizes discrepancies between the estimator confidence and empirical probability of E within each bin. The Brier score is the mean squared error of the probability estimates

$$\sum_i (\hat{p}_i - \mathbf{1}_{E_i})^2$$

4 Problem Statement

Consider the following discrete-time stochastic system titled $\mathsf{M_{OS}}$ with dynamics:

$$\begin{aligned} X(t+1) &= f(X(t), U(t))), \\ Y(t) &= g(X(t), V(t)), \\ \bar{X}(t), \bar{Z}(t) &= h(\bar{Z}(t-1), Y(t), W(t)), \\ U(t) &= c(\bar{X}(t)), \end{aligned} \tag{3}$$

where $X(t) \in S \subset \mathbb{R}^n$ is the system state (with bounded S); $Y(t) \in \mathbb{R}^p$ are the observations; $\bar{X}(t) \in \mathbb{R}^n$ is the estimated state of the system; $\bar{Z}(t) \in \mathbb{R}^z$ is the internal state of the state estimator (e.g., a belief prior in a Bayesian filter); $U(t) \in \mathcal{U} \subset \mathbb{R}^m$ is the control output, which we discretize, resulting in a finite number $|\mathcal{U}|$ of control actions, the functions $f : \mathbb{R}^n \times \mathbb{R}^m \to \mathbb{R}^n$, $g : \mathbb{R}^n \times \mathbb{R}^v \to \mathbb{R}^p$, $h : \mathbb{R}^z \times \mathbb{R}^p \times \mathbb{R}^w \to \mathbb{R}^n \times \mathbb{R}^z$ describe the system dynamics, perception map, and state estimator respectively; the function $c : \mathbb{R}^p \to \mathbb{R}^m$ is a stateless controller; and $V(t) \in D_v \subseteq \mathbb{R}^v$ and $W(t) \in D_w \subseteq \mathbb{R}^w$ describe perception and state estimator noise. The $V(t)$ noise models inexact perception, such as an object detector missing an obstacle. The $W(T)$ noise accounts for state estimators that use randomness under the hood. A common example of this is particle filters randomly perturbing their particles so that they do not collapse to the exact same value.

Let $S_{unsafe} \subset S$ denote the set of unsafe states of $\mathsf{M_{OS}}$. At time t, we are interested in whether $\mathsf{M_{OS}}$ will lie in S_{unsafe} at some point in the next T time steps. This is represented by the bounded time reachability property

$$\psi_{\mathsf{M_{OS}}} = \square^{\leq T} (X \notin S_{unsafe}) \tag{4}$$

Let $P(\psi_{\mathsf{M_{OS}}} \mid \bar{Z}(t))$ denote the probability of $\mathsf{M_{OS}}$ satisfying $\psi_{\mathsf{M_{OS}}}$. Our goal is to compute calibrated (Definition 4) and conservative (Definition 5) estimates of $P(\psi_{\mathsf{M_{OS}}} \mid \bar{Z}(t))$ at runtime, which we denote as $\widehat{P}\left(\psi_{\mathsf{M_{OS}}} \mid \bar{Z}(t)\right)$.

5 Overall Approach

Our approach consists of a design time and runtime portion. At design time, a PA of the system (including its dynamics, perception, state estimation, and controller) is constructed using standard conservative abstraction techniques.

Then the bounded-time safety probability for each state of the model is computed using model checking and stored in a look-up table. At runtime, the estimated state (or distribution of states) from the real system's state estimator is used to estimate the abstract state (or distribution of abstract states) of the abstract system. This abstract state (or distribution of states) is used in conjunction with the lookup table to estimate the bounded-time safety of the real system.

5.1 Design Time

The design time aspect of our approach has two parts. First, we convert the original system M_{OS} into a probabilistic automaton M_{AS}. Then we use probabilistic model checking to compute the bounded time safety of M_{AS} for each state in the model.

Model Construction. To convert M_{OS} into a probabilistic automaton, M_{AS}, we first need to create probabilistic models of the perception g and state estimation h components of M_{OS}. To do this, we simulate M_{OS} and record the perception errors $X(t) - \bar{X}(t)$. We discretize the domain of these errors and estimate a categorical distribution over it. For example, this distribution would contain information such as "the perception will output a value that is between 2m/s and 3m/s greater than the true velocity of the car with probability 1/7."

To convert the system dynamics f and controller c to a probabilistic automaton, we use a standard interval abstraction technique. The high-level idea is to divide the state space S of M_{OS} into a finite set of equally sized hyperrectangles, denoted as S'. So every $s'_1 \in S'$ has a corresponding region $S_1 \subset S$. M_{AS} then has a transition from s'_1 to s'_2 (in M_{AS}) if at least one state in S_1 has a transition to a state in S_2 (in M_{OS}) under some control command $u \in \mathcal{U}$. Note that state s'_1 can non-deterministically transition to multiple states in S' because it covers an entire hyperrectangle of states in M_{OS}. This ensures that the interval abstraction is conservative, as it overapproximates the behaviors of M_{OS}.

Finally, the perception error model, controller, and interval abstraction are all parallel-composed into a single model as per Definition 2.

Remark. In describing the construction of the M_{AS}, we have not mentioned anything about initial states: we do not keep track of a singular initial state for M_{AS}. Instead, we will later run model checking for the full range of initial states of M_{AS} to anticipate all runtime scenarios. For our purposes, the "initial state-action space" of M_{AS} consists of every abstract state and control action. We include the control action in the initial state space because when using the model's safety probabilities online, we know what the next control action will be.

Safety Property. We need to transform the bounded time safety property on M_{OS} given in Eq. (4) into an equivalent property on M_{AS}. To do this, we compute the corresponding set of unsafe states on M_{AS}, which is defined as

$$S'_{unsafe} = \{s' \mid \exists s \in S_{unsafe}, s' \text{ corresponds to } s\}$$

Letting s' denote the state of M_{AS}, the bounded time safety property for M_{AS} is

$$\psi_{\mathsf{M}_{\mathsf{AS}}} := \square^{\leq T}\left(s' \notin S'_{unsafe}\right) \tag{5}$$

Probabilistic Model Checking. The final design-time step of our approach computes the safety probability of M_{AS} for every state in the model. This step amounts to computing the below values using standard model checking tools:

$$Pr^{min}_{\mathsf{M}_{\mathsf{AS}}(s',u)}(\psi_{\mathsf{M}_{\mathsf{AS}}}),\ \ \forall s' \in S',\ \forall u \in \mathcal{U}$$

This requires running model checking on M_{AS} for a range of initial states, which can be a time-consuming process. To mitigate this, we note that M_{AS} is simpler to analyze than M_{OS}, since the size of the state space gets reduced during the interval abstraction process. Additionally, one can lower the time bound T on the safety property to further speed up the model checking.

The probabilities from the model checking are stored in a lookup table, which we denote as $G(s', u)$. It will be used at runtime to estimate the likelihood of the system being unsafe in the near future.

Remark. This approach would work for any bounded time MTL properties, however more complex formulas may take longer to model check.

5.2 Runtime

At runtime, we observe the outputs of the state estimator and controller and run them through the lookup table to compute the probability of the system avoiding unsafe states for the next T time steps. We propose two different ways of utilizing the state estimator. The first way is to simply use the point estimate from the state estimator. In cases of probabilistic estimators, this means taking the mean of the distribution. The second way uses the estimated state distribution from the state estimator. This requires an estimator with a probabilistic output, but most common state estimators, such as particle filters and Bayesian filters, keep track of the distribution of the state. The second way takes full advantage of the available state uncertainty to predict safety.

Point Estimate. At time t, the state estimator outputs state estimate $\bar{X}(t)$. The controller then outputs control command $U(t) = c(\bar{X}(t))$. Finally, we get a safety estimate $\hat{P}^{mon}_{point}(\bar{X}(t), U(t))$ by plugging $\bar{X}(t)$ and $U(t)$ into G:

$$\hat{P}^{mon}_{point}(\bar{X}(t), U(t)) = G(\bar{X}(t), U(t)) \tag{6}$$

State Distribution. Now assume that at time t state estimator additionally outputs a state estimate $\bar{X}(t)$ and a finite, discrete distribution of the state, denoted as $P_{\bar{X}(t)}$. The controller still outputs control command $U(t) = c(\bar{X}(t))$.

To estimate the safety of the system, we compute a weighted sum of the safety of each state in $P_{\bar{X}(t)}$ using G and $U(t)$:

$$\hat{P}^{mon}_{dist}(P_{\bar{X}(t)}, U(t)) = \sum_{s \in Supp\left(P_{\bar{X}(t)}\right)} P_{\bar{X}(t)}(s) \cdot G(s', U(t)) \tag{7}$$

where $Supp\left(P_{\bar{X}(t)}\right)$ denotes the (finite) support of $P_{\bar{X}(t)}$, $P_{\bar{X}(t)}(s)$ denotes the estimated probability of M_{OS} being in state s according to $P_{\bar{X}(t)}$, and $s' \in S'$ is the state in M_{AS} that corresponds to state $s \in S$ in M_{OS}.

6 Conservatism Guarantees

This section proves that our state-distribution monitoring produces safety estimates that are *conservative* and *well-calibrated*; that is, we underestimate the probability of safety. We require two assumptions for that. The first assumption is the conservatism of abstract model M_{AS}, by which we mean that its probability of being safe is always less than that of M_{OS} for the same initial condition. The second assumption is the calibration of the state estimator, which means that it produces state probabilities that align with the frequencies of these states. Below we formalize and discuss these assumptions before proceeding to our proof.

Definition 6 (Model Conservatism). *Abstraction* M_{AS} *is* conservative *with respect to system* M_{OS} *if*

$$P_{\mathsf{M}_{OS}(s,u)}(\psi) \geq Pr^{min}_{\mathsf{M}_{AS}(s',u)}(\psi) \;\; \forall s \in S, u \in \mathcal{U} \tag{8}$$

where $s' \in S'$ *is the state in* M_{AS} *that corresponds to state* s *in* M_{OS}*.*

In general, it is difficult to achieve provable conservatism of M_{AS} by construction: the model parameters of complex components (e.g., vision-based perception) are estimated from data, and they may have complicated interactions with the safety chance. Instead, we explain why our approach is likely to be conservative in practice and validate this assumption in the next section.

Consider M_{OS} and M_{AS} as compositions of two sub-models: dynamics/control and perception/state estimation. We construct M_{AS} such that its dynamics/control component always overapproximates the dynamics/control portion of M_{OS}. That means that any feasible sequence of states and control actions from M_{OS} is also feasible in M_{AS}. This follows from the use of reachability analysis over the intervals of states to compute the transitions of M_{AS}.

It is unclear how to formally compare the conservatism of perception/state estimation portions of M_{AS} and M_{OS} when they are created from simulations of the perception/state estimation component of M_{OS}. First, these components are not modeled explicitly due to the high dimensionality of learning-based perception. Thus, when estimating probabilities from samples, we essentially approximate the average-case behavior of the component. Second, it is often unknown in which direction the probabilities need to be shifted to induce a conservative shift to the model. One opportunity is to use monotonic safety rules [11]; for now, this remains a promising and important future research direction.

To summarize, the dynamics/control portion of M_{AS} overapproximates that of M_{OS}, while the perception/state estimation portion of M_{AS} approximates the average-case behavior of M_{OS}. So one would expect, on average, M_{AS} to be conservative with respect to M_{OS}, even though we cannot formally prove that.

Next, we define the calibration for the state estimator (adapted from Equation (1) of [16]):

Definition 7 (Calibration). *Given the dynamical system from Eq.* (3) *and state estimator* h *that outputs a discrete, finite distribution of the estimated state, denoted* $P_{\bar{x}(t)}$, *we say that* h *is* well-calibrated *if*

$$P(x(t) = s \mid P_{\bar{x}(t)}(s) = p) = p, \quad \forall p \in [0, 1] \tag{9}$$

Intuitively, what this definition means is that if the state estimator says that there is probability p that the system is in state s, then the system will be in state s with probability p. Calibration is an increasingly common requirement for learning-based detectors [14,16,27,30] and we validate it in our experiments.

Now we are ready for our main theoretical result: assuming that M_{AS} is conservative with respect to M_{OS} and that the state estimator is well-calibrated, we show that the safety estimates of our monitoring are conservatively calibrated.

Theorem 1. *Let the system* M_{OS} *in Eq.* (3) *be given with a well-calibrated state estimator (Definition 7). Let* M_{AS} *be a conservative model of* M_{OS} *(Definition 6). Finally, assume that the safety of* M_{OS} *conditioned on the true state of the system is independent of the safety estimate from the monitor. Given state estimator distribution* $P_{\bar{X}(t)}$ *and control command* $U \in \mathcal{U}$, *the safety estimates from the state distribution monitor (Eq.* (7)*) are conservative:*

$$P(\psi_{\mathsf{M}_{OS}} \mid \hat{P}^{mon}_{dist}(P_{\bar{X}(t)}, U(t)) = p) \geq p \quad \forall p \in [0, 1] \tag{10}$$

Proof. We start with conditioning the safety of the system on the state of the system and proceed with equivalent transformations:

$$\begin{aligned}
&P(\psi_{\mathsf{M}_{\mathsf{OS}}} \mid \hat{P}^{mon}_{dist}(P_{\bar{X}(t)}, U(t)) = p) = \\
&\int_{s \in S} P\Big(\psi_{\mathsf{M}_{\mathsf{OS}}} \mid X(t) = s, \hat{P}^{mon}_{dist}(P_{\bar{X}(t)}, U(t)) = p\Big) \cdot \\
&\qquad P\Big(X(t) = s \mid \hat{P}^{mon}_{dist}(P_{\bar{X}(t)}, U(t)) = p\Big) ds = \\
&\int_{s \in S} P(\psi_{\mathsf{M}_{\mathsf{OS}}} \mid X(t) = s) \cdot P_{\bar{X}(t)}(s) ds = \\
&\sum_{s \in P_{\bar{X}(t)}} P(\psi_{\mathsf{M}_{\mathsf{OS}}} \mid X(t) = s) \cdot P_{\bar{X}(t)}(s) = \\
&\sum_{s \in P_{\bar{X}(t)}} P_{\mathsf{M}_{\mathsf{OS}}(s, U(t))}(\psi) \cdot P_{\bar{X}(t)}(s) \geq
\end{aligned}$$

$$\sum_{s \in P_{\bar{X}(t)}} Pr^{min}_{\mathsf{M_{AS}}(s_\downarrow, U(t))}(\psi) \cdot P_{\bar{X}(t)}(s) = p$$

□

The first step comes from marginalizing the state $X(t)$ into the left side of Eq. (10). The second step comes from the assumption that the safety of the system given the state is independent of the monitor output and the assumed calibration of the monitor from Eq. (9). The third step follows from the discrete, finite support of the state estimator output and the calibration. The fourth step comes from substituting and rearranging terms. The final step comes from the assumed conservatism of $\mathsf{M_{AS}}$ in Definition 6.

7 Case Study

Our experimental evaluation aims to demonstrate that the safety estimates from our monitoring approach are conservative and accurate. Additionally, we compare the effect of using the point-wise and distribution-wise state estimation. We perform the evaluation on a simulated water tank system and use the PRISM model checker [22] to perform the probabilistic model checking. The code and models for the experiments can be found on Github.

7.1 Water Tanks

Consider a system consisting of J water tanks, each of size TS, draining over time, and a central controller that aims to maintain some water level in each tank. With $w_i[t]$ as the water level in the ith tank at time t, the discrete-time dynamics for the water level in the tank is given by:

$$w_i[t+1] = w_i[t] - out_i[t] + in_i[t], \tag{11}$$

where $in_i[t]$ and $out_i[t]$ are the amounts of water entering ("inflow") and leaving ("outflow") respectively the ith tank at time t. The inflow is determined by the controller and the outflow is a constant determined by the environment.

Each tank is equipped with a noisy sensor to report its current perceived water level, $\hat{w}$, which is a noisy function of the true current water level, w. The noise on the sensor outputs is a Gaussian with zero mean and known variance. Additionally, with constant probability the perception outputs $\hat{w} = 0$ or $\hat{w} = TS$.

Each water tank uses a standard Bayesian filter as a state estimator. The filter maintains a discrete distribution over the system state. On each perception reading, the filter updates its state distribution using a standard application of the Bayes rule. The mean of the state distribution at this point is the estimator's point prediction, which is sent to the controller. Once the control action is computed, the filter updates its state distribution by applying the system dynamics.

The central controller has a single source of water to fill one tank at a time (or none at all) based on the estimated water levels. Then this tank receives a constant value $in > 0$ of water, whereas the other tanks receive 0 water. Each tank has a local controller that requests itself to be filled when its water level drops below the lower threshold LT and stops requesting to be filled after its water level reaches the upper threshold UT. If several tanks request to be filled, the controller fills the one with the lowest water level (or, if equal, it flips a coin).

At runtime, we are interested in the probability that a tank will neither be empty or overflowing, represented by the bounded-time safety property:

$$\psi_{wt}{:=}\Box^{\leq 10} \vee_{i=1..J} (wl_i > 0 \wedge wl_i < TS)$$

Model Construction. We construct the M_{AS} model for $J = 2$ water tanks, $in = 13.5$, $out_i[t] = 4.3$, $TS = 100$, $LT = 10$, $UT = 90$, and water level intervals of size 1 by following the description in Sect. 5.1. To model the combination of perception and state estimation, we estimated the state distributions with 100 trials of 50 time steps. Figure 1 shows a histogram of the state estimation errors.

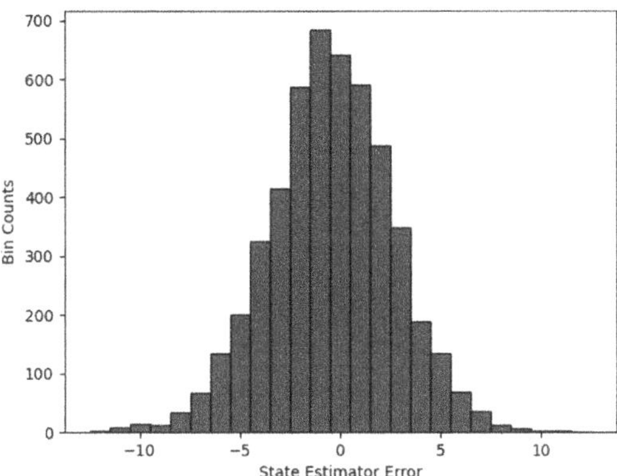

Fig. 1. Histogram of state estimation errors for the water tanks.

Model Checking. The initial state of M_{AS} comprises the water level of each tank, the low-level control command of each tank, and the filling command of the central controller. There are 101 discrete water levels in each tank and 5 possible configurations of the 3 control commands, for a total of 51005 different initial states of M_{AS}. We model-checked ψ_{wt} in these initial states on a server with 80 Intel(R) Xeon(R) Gold 6148 CPU @ 2.40GHz CPUs by running 50 parallel PRISM instances at a time. The full verification process took approximately 24 h, which is acceptable for the design-time phase.

7.2 Results

To test our approach, we ran 500 trials of the water tanks starting from water levels between 40 and 60. Each trial lasted for 50 time steps (recall that the model checking checked 10 time steps into the future) and 74 trials resulted in a water tank either over- or underflowing. We evaluated three different monitors in our approach. One used the point estimates from the Bayesian filter ("point estimate monitor"), another used the estimated distribution from the state estimator ("state distribution monitor"), and the last used the true state of the system ("true state monitor", for comparison only).

Qualitative Performance. Figure 2 shows the safety estimates of the monitors for one safe and one unsafe trial. The monitors keep high safety estimates for the entirety of the safe trial. In the unsafe trial, the failure occurred at time step 42 due to a tank overflowing. The safety estimates are high at first but then begin to drop around time step 30, predicting the failure with a 10-step time horizon.

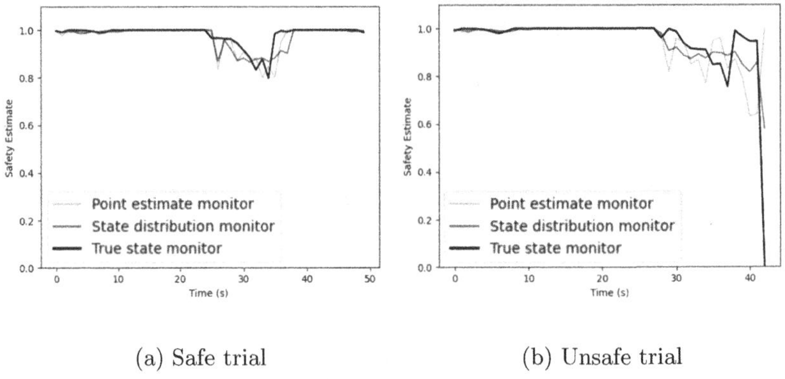

(a) Safe trial (b) Unsafe trial

Fig. 2. Monitor safety estimates for two water tank trials.

Calibration. Next, to examine the overall calibration of our safety estimates, we bin the safety estimates into 10 bins of width 0.1 ($[0-0.1, 0.1-0.2, \ldots, 0.9-1]$) and compute the empirical safety chance within each bin. The results are shown in Fig. 3, with the caveat that we only plot bins with at least 50 samples to ensure statistical significance. The point estimate monitor and true state monitor are conservative for all of their bins. On the other hand, the state distribution monitor has the best overall calibration. We also computed the ECE and Brier scores for the monitors, which are shown in Table 1. To assess the conservatism of the monitors, we introduce a novel metric called *expected conservative calibration error* (ECCE). It is similar to ECE, except that it only sums the bins where the average monitor confidence is greater than the empirical safety probability (i.e., the cases where the monitor is overconfident in safety). The ECCE values for the monitors are also shown in Table 1. Note that $ECE \geq ECCE$, because ECCE only aggregates a subset of the bins that ECE does. Our results show that the monitors are well-calibrated and conservative, and that the state distribution monitor manages to capture the uncertainty particularly well.

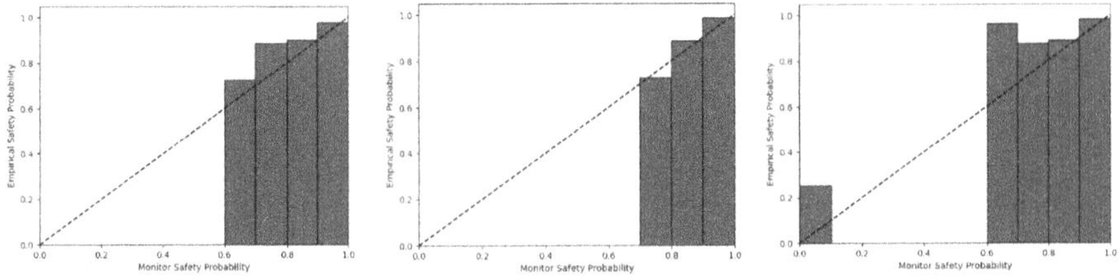

(a) Point estimate monitor (b) State distribution monitor (c) True state monitor

Fig. 3. Calibration plots for the three monitors. The x-axis shows the binned safety estimates reported by the monitor and the y-axis shows the empirical safety probability. The diagonal dashed line denotes perfect calibration. Bars higher than the dashed line represent under-confidence (i.e., conservatism) and bars lower than the dashed line represent over-confidence.

Accuracy. Finally, we are interested in the ability of the monitors to distinguish safe and unsafe scenarios. To do this, we computed a receiver operating characteristic (ROC) curve for the three monitors, shown in Fig. 4, and areas under curve (AUC) in Table 1. As expected, the state distribution monitor and true state monitor outperform the point estimate monitor. One surprising aspect is that the state distribution monitor performs about as well as the true state monitor. We hypothesize that this is because the state distribution contains information about how well the state estimator will perform in the near future. Investigating this potential phenomenon is another area of future work.

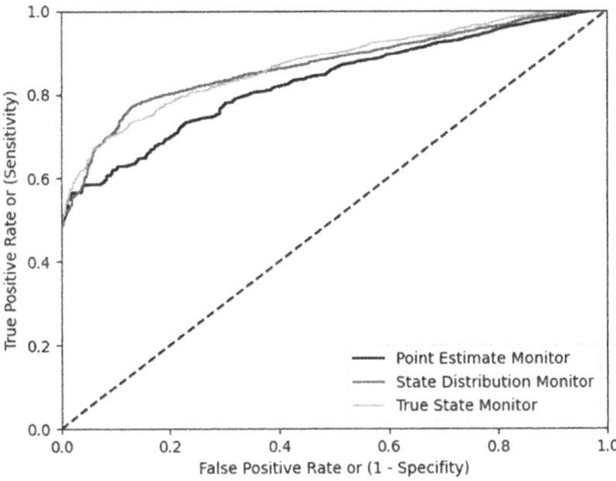

Fig. 4. ROC curves for the three monitors.

Table 1. Calibration and classification metrics for the monitors.

Monitor Type	ECE	ECCE	Brier Score	AUC
State estimate	0.0157	0.00818	0.0292	0.828
State distribution	0.00252	0.000899	0.0275	0.867
True state	0.0129	0.00459	0.0273	0.870

Validation of Assumptions. First, we empirically validate whether M_{AS} is conservative with respect to M_{OS}. Directly verifying this claim is infeasible, since it requires computing $P_{\mathsf{M}_{\mathrm{OS}}(s,u)}(\psi)$ for an infinite number of states $s \in S$. However, we can examine the performance of the true state monitor as a proxy for the conservatism of M_{AS}: the true state monitor obtains the probabilities from M_{AS} using the true state, avoiding any sensing and state estimation noise. The slightly underconfident true state monitor bins in Fig. 3 and the very low ECCE in Table 1 both provide strong evidence that M_{AS} is indeed conservative.

Second, we examine the calibration assumption of the state estimator. We computed its ECE across all water levels, resulting in the negligible value of 0.00656. We conclude that this state estimator gives calibrated results in practice.

8 Conclusion

This paper introduced a method for synthesizing conservative and well-calibrated predictive runtime monitors for stochastic dynamical systems. Our method abstracts the system as a PA and uses PMC to verify the safety of the states of the PA. At runtime, these safety values are used to estimate the true safety of the system. We proved that our safety estimates are conservative provided the PA abstraction is conservative and the system's state estimator is well-calibrated. We demonstrated our approach on a case study with water tanks. Future work includes applying our method to existing approaches that learn discrete abstractions directly from data, exploring how to construct conservative perception/state estimation abstractions, using our prior work in [11] to reduce the number of model checking calls, and investigating the effects of the estimated state distribution's variance on the future system safety.

Acknowledgments. This work was supported in part by DARPA/AFRL FA8750-18-C-0090 and by ARO W911NF-20-1-0080. Any opinions, findings and conclusions or recommendations expressed in this material are those of the authors and do not necessarily reflect the views of the Air Force Research Laboratory (AFRL), the Army Research Office (ARO), the Defense Advanced Research Projects Agency (DARPA), or the Department of Defense, or the United States Government.

References

1. Althoff, M., Stursberg, O., Buss, M.: Model-based probabilistic collision detection in autonomous driving. IEEE Trans. Intell. Transp. Syst. **10**(2), 299–310 (2009)

2. Babaee, R., Ganesh, V., Sedwards, S.: Accelerated learning of predictive runtime monitors for rare failure. In: Finkbeiner, B., Mariani, L. (eds.) RV 2019. LNCS, vol. 11757, pp. 111–128. Springer, Cham (2019). https://doi.org/10.1007/978-3-030-32079-9_7
3. Babaee, R., Gurfinkel, A., Fischmeister, S.: Predictive run-time verification of discrete-time reachability properties in black-box systems using trace-level abstraction and statistical learning. In: Colombo, C., Leucker, M. (eds.) RV 2018. LNCS, vol. 11237, pp. 187–204. Springer, Cham (2018). https://doi.org/10.1007/978-3-030-03769-7_11
4. Babaee, R., Gurfinkel, A., Fischmeister, S.: $\mathcal{P}$*revent*: a predictive run-time verification framework using statistical learning. In: Johnsen, E.B., Schaefer, I. (eds.) SEFM 2018. LNCS, vol. 10886, pp. 205–220. Springer, Cham (2018). https://doi.org/10.1007/978-3-319-92970-5_13
5. Bortolussi, L., Cairoli, F., Paoletti, N., Smolka, S.A., Stoller, S.D.: Neural predictive monitoring. In: Finkbeiner, B., Mariani, L. (eds.) RV 2019. LNCS, vol. 11757, pp. 129–147. Springer, Cham (2019). https://doi.org/10.1007/978-3-030-32079-9_8
6. Bortolussi, L., Cairoli, F., Paoletti, N., Smolka, S.A., Stoller, S.D.: Neural predictive monitoring and a comparison of frequentist and Bayesian approaches. Int. J. Softw. Tools Technol. Transfer **23**(4), 615–640 (2021)
7. Cairoli, F., Bortolussi, L., Paoletti, N.: Neural predictive monitoring under partial observability. In: Feng, L., Fisman, D. (eds.) RV 2021. LNCS, vol. 12974, pp. 121–141. Springer, Cham (2021). https://doi.org/10.1007/978-3-030-88494-9_7
8. Cairoli, F., Paoletti, N., Bortolussi, L.: Conformal quantitative predictive monitoring of STL requirements for stochastic processes. arXiv:2211.02375 (2022)
9. Chou, Y., Yoon, H., Sankaranarayanan, S.: Predictive runtime monitoring of vehicle models using Bayesian estimation and reachability analysis. In: 2020 IEEE/RSJ International Conference on Intelligent Robots and Systems (IROS), pp. 2111–2118. IEEE (2020)
10. Cimatti, A., Tian, C., Tonetta, S.: Assumption-based runtime verification of infinite-state systems. In: Feng, L., Fisman, D. (eds.) RV 2021. LNCS, vol. 12974, pp. 207–227. Springer, Cham (2021). https://doi.org/10.1007/978-3-030-88494-9_11
11. Cleaveland, M., Ruchkin, I., Sokolsky, O., Lee, I.: Monotonic safety for scalable and data-efficient probabilistic safety analysis. In: 2022 ACM/IEEE 13th International Conference on Cyber-Physical Systems (ICCPS), pp. 92–103 (2022)
12. Ferrando, A., et al.: Bridging the gap between single- and multi-model predictive runtime verification. Formal Methods Syst. Des. 1–33 (2022)
13. Ferrando, A., Delzanno, G.: Incrementally predictive runtime verification. In: Proceedings of the 36th Italian Conference on Computational Logic, Parma, Italy, 7–9 September 2021. CEUR Workshop Proceedings, vol. 3002, pp. 92–106 (2021)
14. Gong, Y., Lin, X., Yao, Y., Dietterich, T.G., Divakaran, A., Gervasio, M.T.: Confidence calibration for domain generalization under covariate shift. In: 2021 IEEE/CVF International Conference on Computer Vision, ICCV 2021, Montreal, QC, Canada, 10–17 October 2021, pp. 8938–8947. IEEE (2021)
15. Granig, W., Jakšić, S., Lewitschnig, H., Mateis, C., Ničković, D.: Weakness monitors for fail-aware systems. In: Bertrand, N., Jansen, N. (eds.) FORMATS 2020. LNCS, vol. 12288, pp. 283–299. Springer, Cham (2020). https://doi.org/10.1007/978-3-030-57628-8_17
16. Guo, C., Pleiss, G., Sun, Y., Weinberger, K.Q.: On calibration of modern neural networks. In: International Conference on Machine Learning, pp. 1321–1330. PMLR (2017)

17. Jaeger, M., Larsen, K.G., Tibo, A.: From statistical model checking to run-time monitoring using a Bayesian network approach. In: Deshmukh, J., Ničković, D. (eds.) RV 2020. LNCS, vol. 12399, pp. 517–535. Springer, Cham (2020). https://doi.org/10.1007/978-3-030-60508-7_30
18. Jasour, A., Huang, X., Wang, A., Williams, B.C.: Fast nonlinear risk assessment for autonomous vehicles using learned conditional probabilistic models of agent futures. Auton. Robot. **46**(1), 269–282 (2022)
19. Junges, S., Torfah, H., Seshia, S.A.: Runtime monitors for Markov decision processes. In: Silva, A., Leino, K.R.M. (eds.) CAV 2021. LNCS, vol. 12760, pp. 553–576. Springer, Cham (2021). https://doi.org/10.1007/978-3-030-81688-9_26
20. Katoen, J.P.: Model checking meets probability: a gentle introduction (2013)
21. Koymans, R.: Specifying real-time properties with metric temporal logic. Real-Time Syst. **2**(4), 255–299 (1990)
22. Kwiatkowska, M., Norman, G., Parker, D.: PRISM 4.0: verification of probabilistic real-time systems. In: Proceedings of 23rd International Conference on Computer Aided Verification (CAV 2011) (2011)
23. Kwiatkowska, M., Norman, G., Parker, D., Qu, H.: Compositional probabilistic verification through multi-objective model checking. Inf. Comput. **232**, 38–65 (2013)
24. Leucker, M.: Sliding between model checking and runtime verification. In: Qadeer, S., Tasiran, S. (eds.) RV 2012. LNCS, vol. 7687, pp. 82–87. Springer, Heidelberg (2013). https://doi.org/10.1007/978-3-642-35632-2_10
25. Lindemann, L., Qin, X., Deshmukh, J.V., Pappas, G.J.: Conformal prediction for STL runtime verification. arXiv abs/2211.01539 (2022)
26. Ma, M., Stankovic, J., Bartocci, E., Feng, L.: Predictive monitoring with logic-calibrated uncertainty for cyber-physical systems. ACM Trans. Embed. Comput. Syst. (TECS) **20**(5s), 1–25 (2021)
27. Minderer, M., et al.: Revisiting the calibration of modern neural networks. In: Advances in Neural Information Processing Systems, vol. 34, pp. 15682–15694. Curran Associates, Inc. (2021)
28. Pinisetty, S., Jéron, T., Tripakis, S., Falcone, Y., Marchand, H., Preoteasa, V.: Predictive runtime verification of timed properties. J. Syst. Softw. **132**, 353–365 (2017)
29. Ranjan, R., Gneiting, T.: Combining probability forecasts. J. Roy. Stat. Soc. Ser. B (Stat. Methodol.) **72**(1), 71–91 (2010)
30. Ruchkin, I., et al.: Confidence composition for monitors of verification assumptions. In: 2022 ACM/IEEE 13th International Conference on Cyber-Physical Systems (ICCPS), pp. 1–12 (2022)
31. Shafer, G., Vovk, V.: A tutorial on conformal prediction. J. Mach. Learn. Res. **9**(3) (2008)
32. Yoon, H., Chou, Y., Chen, X., Frew, E., Sankaranarayanan, S.: Predictive runtime monitoring for linear stochastic systems and applications to geofence enforcement for UAVs. In: Finkbeiner, B., Mariani, L. (eds.) RV 2019. LNCS, vol. 11757, pp. 349–367. Springer, Cham (2019). https://doi.org/10.1007/978-3-030-32079-9_20
33. Yu, X., Dong, W., Yin, X., Li, S.: Model predictive monitoring of dynamic systems for signal temporal logic specifications. arXiv:2209.12493 (2022)
34. Zhang, X., Leucker, M., Dong, W.: Runtime verification with predictive semantics. In: Goodloe, A.E., Person, S. (eds.) NFM 2012. LNCS, vol. 7226, pp. 418–432. Springer, Heidelberg (2012). https://doi.org/10.1007/978-3-642-28891-3_37

Code-Level Formal Verification of Ellipsoidal Invariant Sets for Linear Parameter-Varying Systems

Elias Khalife[1(✉)], Pierre-Loic Garoche[2], and Mazen Farhood[1]

[1] Kevin T. Crofton Department of Aerospace and Ocean Engineering, Virginia Tech, Blacksburg, VA 24061, USA
{eliask,farhood}@vt.edu

[2] Ecole Nationale de l'Aviation Civile, Toulouse, France
pierre-loic.garoche@enac.fr

Abstract. This paper focuses on the formal verification of invariant properties of a C code that describes the dynamics of a discrete-time linear parameter-varying system with affine parameter dependence. The C code is annotated using ACSL, and the Frama-C's WP plugin is used to transform the annotations and code into proof objectives. The invariant properties are then formally verified in both the real and float models using the polynomial inequalities plugin of the theorem prover Alt-Ergo. The challenges of verifying the invariant properties in the float model are addressed by utilizing bounds on numerical errors and incorporating them into the real model.

Keywords: Deductive Method · Static Analysis · Invariant Set · Linear Parameter-Varying System · Frama-C

1 Introduction

Ellipsoidal invariant sets constitute an important concept in the field of control theory, specifically in the context of dynamical systems and system stability analysis. These sets are defined by the property that all state trajectories starting from any point within the set remain inside the set for all future times. In other words, if the system's state lies initially inside an ellipsoidal invariant set, then the state evolution is guaranteed to stay within the boundaries of the set. Similarly, invariants in the field of formal methods refer to properties or conditions that hold true throughout the entire or part of the execution of a program, system, or algorithm [26]. The relationship between the two concepts is evident when considering that if a state is inside the ellipsoidal invariant set, then the next states will also be inside of this set. This situation is akin to an invariant property, where the current state being inside the ellipsoidal invariant

This work was supported by the Office of Naval Research under Award No. N00014-18-1-2627, the Army Research Office under Contract No. W911NF-21-1-0250, and the ANR-17-CE25-0018 FEANICSES project.

K. Y. Rozier and S. Chaudhuri (Eds.): NFM 2023, LNCS 13903, pp. 157–173, 2023.
https://doi.org/10.1007/978-3-031-33170-1_10

set acts as a precondition that implies the next states will remain within the set. There has been a significant amount of research on ellipsoidal invariant sets in the literature. Early work in this area focused on the use of ellipsoidal invariant sets for analyzing the stability of linear systems [5,20]. Several methods have been developed to construct invariant sets, including methods based on Lyapunov's stability theorem [18], linear matrix inequality (LMI) techniques [6], and sum-of-squares (SOS) programming [30]. Each of these methods has its own benefits and limitations, and the choice of method depends on the specific characteristics of the system being analyzed.

This paper focuses on the formal verification of some invariant properties of the C code describing the dynamics of a discrete-time linear parameter-varying (LPV) system with affine parameter dependence. Specifically, we formally verify that, if the state of the system lies in an ellipsoidal invariant set at the initial time, then it resides in this set at all time instants, and, further, the output of the system resides in another ellipsoid at all time instants as well for all permissible pointwise-bounded inputs and parameter trajectories. These sets are obtained by applying new results developed in [17] for computing state- and output-bounding sets for discrete-time uncertain linear fractional transformation (LFT) systems using pointwise integral quadratic constraints (IQCs) to characterize the uncertainties and the S-procedure. Uncertainties that admit pointwise IQC characterizations include static linear time-invariant and time-varying perturbations, sector-bounded nonlinearities, and uncertain time-varying time-delays. An affine LPV system can be expressed as an LFT on static linear time-varying perturbations, and so the aforementioned results are applicable in our case. The positive definite matrices defining the ellipsoids are obtained by solving semidefinite programs [7]. These solutions of the semidefinite programs, obtained by applying the IQC-based analysis approach, serve as a certificate that proves that the system satisfies the desired properties at the algorithmic level. Moreover, these solutions can be employed to annotate the C code describing the system dynamics with logical expressions, which indicate the set of reachable program states. The annotations are done in ACSL (ANSI/ISO C Specification Language) [3], Frama-C's formal annotation language. Additionally, we utilize WP, a Frama-C plugin based on the weakest precondition calculus and deductive methods, to transform annotations and code into proof objectives. Thus, the software verification in our case focuses on translating the guarantees obtained at the algorithmic level, using the analysis results from [17], and expressing them at the code level. Then, we revalidate the invariant properties at the code level using Alt-Ergo-Poly [28], an extension of the SMT solver Alt-Ergo [8] with a sound Sum-of-Squares solver [22,27], to discharge positive polynomial constraints. Last, we instrument the contract to account for floating-point errors in the code, ensuring the validity of our contracts despite the noise caused by floating-point inaccuracy.

One of the motivations for this work is analyzing the C code of gain-scheduled controllers, for instance, the robustly stable LPV path-following controller designed in [24] for a small, fixed-wing, unmanned aircraft system (UAS), where the scheduling parameter is the inverse of the radius of curvature of the path to be traversed. If the output-bounding ellipsoid in this case lies within the actuator saturation limits, then we have a guarantee that the actuators would not saturate for the considered pointwise-bounded measurements.

The paper is structured as follows. In Sect. 2, we introduce affine LPV systems and explain how to determine state and output invariant ellipsoids. In Sect. 3, we outline the steps for setting up the necessary Frama-C environment to formally verify the invariant properties at code level. In Sect. 4, we demonstrate the formal verification of these properties using the real model. In Sect. 5, we present the verification of these properties in the float model, which involves the use of bounds on numerical errors and their integration into the real model. The paper concludes with Sect. 6.

2 Affine LPV Systems and Ellipsoidal Invariant Sets

Consider a stable discrete-time LPV system G described by

$$\begin{aligned} x(k+1) &= A(\delta(k))x(k) + B(\delta(k))d(k), \\ y(k) &= C(\delta(k))x(k) + D(\delta(k))d(k), \end{aligned} \tag{1}$$

where $x(k) \in \mathbb{R}^{n_x}$, $y(k) \in \mathbb{R}^{n_y}$, $d(k) \in \mathbb{R}^{n_d}$, and $\delta(k) = (\delta_1(k), \ldots, \delta_{n_\delta}(k)) \in \mathbb{R}^{n_\delta}$ designate the values of the state, output, input, and scheduling parameters at the time instant k, respectively, where k is a nonnegative integer. The state-space matrix-valued functions of G are assumed to have affine dependence on the scheduling parameters; for instance, the state matrix $A(\delta(k))$ can be expressed as

$$A(\delta(k)) = A_0 + \sum_{i=1}^{n_\delta} \delta_i(k) A_i, \tag{2}$$

where the matrices A_i are known and constant for $i = 0, \ldots, n_\delta$, and the scheduling parameters $\delta_i(k) \in [\underline{\delta}_i, \bar{\delta}_i]$ for all integers $k \geq 0$ and $i = 1, \ldots, n_\delta$. The analysis results used in this paper also allow imposing bounds on the parameter increments $d\delta_i(k) = \delta_i(k+1) - \delta_i(k)$ for $i = 1, \ldots, n_\delta$ and all integers $k \geq 0$.

The analysis results in [17] are used to determine the state-invariant and output-bounding ellipsoids of system G. To apply these results, system G is first expressed as a linear fractional transformation (LFT) on uncertainties, where the uncertainties in this case are the static linear time-varying perturbations δ_i for $i = 1, \ldots, n_\delta$. That is, system G is expressed as an interconnection of a stable nominal linear time-invariant (LTI) system and an uncertainty operator. The set of allowable uncertainty operators is described using the so-called IQC multipliers. Namely, an IQC multiplier is used to define a quadratic constraint that the input and output signals of the uncertainty operator must satisfy. In the work [17], this quadratic constraint must be satisfied at every time instant and is hence referred to as a pointwise IQC. A pointwise IQC is more restrictive than the standard IQC [23], which involves an infinite summation of quadratic terms. However, the uncertainty set in our problem admits a pointwise IQC characterization. The approach in [17] allows representing the exogenous input d as a pointwise bounded signal, where its value lies in some closed, convex polytope Γ for all time instants or an ellipsoid $\mathcal{E}$. While the analysis conditions provided in [17] are generally nonconvex, they can be relaxed into convex conditions by applying the multiconvexity relaxation technique [1], along with gridding. Thus, the positive definite matrices defining the state-invariant and output-bounding ellipsoids can be obtained by solving semidefinite programs.

Let $\mathcal{D}$ be the set of admissible inputs of system G and $X \in \mathbb{S}^n_{++}$, where $\mathbb{S}^n_{++}$ denotes the set of $n \times n$ positive definite matrices. With every $X \in \mathbb{S}^n_{++}$, we associate an ellipsoid $\mathcal{E}_X := \{x \in \mathbb{R}^n \mid x^T X x \leq 1\}$, whose shape and orientation are determined by X. Let $\mathcal{E}_P$ and $\mathcal{E}_Q$ be the state-invariant and output-bounding ellipsoids, respectively, obtained by applying the results of [17], where $P \in \mathbb{S}^{n_x}_{++}$ and $Q \in \mathbb{S}^{n_y}_{++}$. This means that, if $x(k) \in \mathcal{E}_P$, then $x(k+1) \in \mathcal{E}_P$ and $y(k) \in \mathcal{E}_Q$ for any integer $k \geq 0$, all $d(k) \in \mathcal{D}$, and all admissible $\delta(k)$. The objective of this paper is to formally verify that the ellipsoids $\mathcal{E}_P$ and $\mathcal{E}_Q$ are state-invariant and output-bounding, respectively, for the affine LPV system G under all admissible inputs $\mathcal{D}$ and all possible scheduling parameters. These properties will be referred to as the state and output invariant properties in the rest of the paper.

3 Frama-C Setup

Frama-C is a suite of tools for the analysis of the source code of software written in C. These tools can be used for tasks such as static analysis, automatic proof generation, testing, and more [9]. In the following, we will use ACSL (ANSI/ISO C Specification Language), Frama-C's formal annotation language, as well as WP, a Frama-C plugin that relies on weakest precondition calculus and deductive methods, to transform annotations and code into proof objectives that are later solved by SMT solvers such as Z3 [12], CVC4 [2], or Alt-Ergo [8]. ACSL is a specification language that can be used to annotate C code and provide precise, machine-readable descriptions of the behavior of C functions and other code elements [4]. These annotations can be used by Frama-C and other tools to perform various kinds of analysis. In Frama-C, ACSL annotations can be used to specify properties of C code, such as preconditions and postconditions for functions, invariants for loops, and more. These annotations can then be checked by the Frama-C tools to ensure that the code adheres to the specified properties. This can be especially useful for developing safety-critical software, where it is important to ensure the code behaves correctly under all possible circumstances.

3.1 C Code of System Dynamics

To express the dynamics of a discrete-time system G in C, we define the function "`updateState`" that updates the state vector of the system and the function "`updateOutput`" that computes the output vector at the current time-step. These functions use the state and output equations in (1).

In the following code, the "`struct state`" defines a new data type that represents the state vector of the system. It has n_x fields: $\mathtt{x}_1, \ldots, \mathtt{x}_{n_x}$, which correspond to the n_x state variables of the system. Similarly, the "`struct output`" defines a new data type that has n_y fields: $\mathtt{y}_1$, ..., $\mathtt{y}_{n_y}$, which correspond to the n_y output variables of the system. The `updateOutput` function takes in the current state of the system `x`, the current input variables $\mathtt{d}_1$, ..., $\mathtt{d}_{n_d}$, and the current values of the scheduling parameters δ_1, ..., δ_{n_δ}. It computes the output vector of the system and stores the result in a "`struct output`" called `y`, following the output equation in (1). The `updateState` function takes in the same inputs as the previous function, stores the values of the current state variables in temporary variables (pre_$\mathtt{x}_1$, ..., pre_$\mathtt{x}_{n_x}$), and computes the next state of the system based on the difference state equation in (1). The state vector at the next time-step is then stored in the "`struct state`" `x`.

C

```
typedef struct { double x1, ..., xnx; } state;
typedef struct { double y1, ..., yny; } output;

void updateOutput(state *x, output *y, double d1, ...,
    double dnd, double δ1, ..., double δnδ){
    //Compute the output
    y->y1 = ...;
    y->yny = ...;}
void updateState(state *x, double d1, ..., double dnd, double
    δ1, ..., double δnδ){
    //Store the current state in temporary variables
    double pre_x1 = x->x1, ..., pre_xnx = x->xnx;
    //Compute the next state
    x->x1 = ...;
    x->xnx = ...;}
```

3.2 Invariant Set ACSL Annotation

Let $X \in \mathbb{S}^n_{++}$, then a vector $z \in \mathbb{R}^n \in \mathcal{E}_X$ if and only if

$$z^T X z = \sum_{i=1}^{n} X_{ii} z_i^2 + 2 \sum_{i=1}^{n-1} \sum_{j=i+1}^{n} X_{ij} z_i z_j \leq 1. \tag{3}$$

The invariant properties of the state-invariant ellipsoid $\mathcal{E}_P$ and the output-bounding ellipsoid $\mathcal{E}_Q$ must be annotated in ACSL to enable Frama-C to ensure that the codes adhere to them. This is achieved by defining the predicates `stateinv` and `outputinv` in ACSL as follows:

ACSL

```
//@ predicate stateinv(real x1, ..., real xnx, real λ) =
    (P11 * x1 * x1 + 2 * P12 * x1 * x2 + ... + Pnxnx * xnx * xnx
    <= λ);
//@ predicate outputinv(real y1, ..., real yny, real λ) =
    (Q11 * y1 * y1 + 2 * Q12 * y1 * y2 + ...+ Qnyny * yny * yny
    <= λ);
```

The predicate `stateinv` takes in the elements of the state vector at a given time instant along with a scalar λ. Similarly, `outputinv` takes in the elements of the output vector at a given time instant along with a scalar λ.

For λ equal to 1, the `stateinv` and `outputinv` predicates correspond to (3) with $X = P$ and $X = Q$, respectively. In this case, when true, these predicates imply that the vectors $x = \left[\mathtt{x}_1, \ldots, \mathtt{x}_{n_x}\right]^T$ and $y = \left[\mathtt{y}_1, \ldots, \mathtt{y}_{n_y}\right]^T$ belong to $\mathcal{E}_P$ and $\mathcal{E}_Q$, respectively.

Remark 1. The ACSL language allows predicates to be defined directly on C structs or pointers, but doing so may make it more difficult for automated solvers to prove the generated proof obligations. Based on our observation, it is more effective to define the predicate in a parameterized form, using all of the state/output variables as parameters. This approach may be more amenable to automated proofs and may improve the ability of automated solvers to prove the proof obligations. Note, however, that this observation may change with future versions of the tool or improvements in the solvers.

3.3 Contract-Based Verification

A contract is a set of preconditions, postconditions, and other specifications that describe the expected behavior of a piece of software. Preconditions are conditions that must be met in order for the software to be used correctly, and postconditions are conditions that must be satisfied after the software has been used. Contract-based verification is important for ensuring that the software behaves correctly and that certain properties are maintained under different possible circumstances. In ACSL, preconditions are expressed using the `requires` and `assumes` commands, while postconditions are expressed using the `ensures` command. Consider the simplest contract `// requires P; ensures E;`. It is equivalent to the contract `// requires \true; ensures \old(P) ==>E;`, where `\old(P)` denotes the evaluation of predicate `P` before the execution of the function.

As outlined in the ACSL manual [3, §2.3.3], we can rely on named behaviors to structure requirements. For example, the contract sketched in Fig. 1 amounts to requiring property `P` to hold for all cases but only requiring property `E1` to hold when the precondition `A1` is valid. It is syntactic sugar to express `// ensures \old(P) ==> ((\old(A1) ==> E1) && (\old(A2) ==> E2));`. This use of named behaviors allows to separate concerns and prevent a non-proven behavior from negatively impacting the analysis of other behaviors.

ACSL
```
/*@ requires P;
  @ behavior b1:
  @   assumes A1;
  @   ensures E1;
  @ behavior b2:
  @   assumes A2;
  @   ensures E2; */
```

Fig. 1. Behaviors in ACSL contracts.

Remark 2 (Beware of pointers and use of `\old()`*)* `\old()` must be used with care since `\old(x)->x0` denotes the value of field $\mathtt{x}_0$ for the previous value of the pointer `x`, while `\old(x->x0)` denotes the previous value of the field $\mathtt{x}_0$.

In the upcoming contracts, we assume that the scheduling parameter $\delta_i(k)$ belongs to $[\underline{\delta}_i, \bar{\delta}_i]$, for $i = 1, \ldots, n_\delta$ and a given time-step k. Now, we define the preconditions of our various contracts.

Zero Input Contract: The input set $\mathcal{D} = \{0\}$, i.e., for a given time-step k, if $d(k) \in \mathcal{D}$, then $d_i(k) = 0$ for $i = 1, \ldots, n_d$.

ACSL

```
/*@ behavior zero_input_contract:
     assumes d1 == 0 && ... && dnd == 0;
     assumes δ̲1 <= δ1 <= δ̄1 && ... && δ̲nδ <= δnδ <= δ̄nδ; */
```

Polytope Bounded Input Contract: The input set $\mathcal{D}$ is a polytope. Particularly, if $\mathcal{D}$ is a hyper-rectangle defined such that, given a time-instant k, $d_i(k)$ belongs to $[\underline{d}_i, \bar{d}_i]$ for $i = 1, \ldots, n_d$, we write the following contract:

ACSL

```
/*@ behavior polytope_input_contract:
     assumes d̲1 <= d1 <= d̄1 && ... && d̲nd <= dnd <= d̄nd;
     assumes δ̲1 <= δ1 <= δ̄1 && ... && δ̲nδ <= δnδ <= δ̄nδ; */
```

Ellipsoid Bounded Input Contract: The input set $\mathcal{D}$ is an ellipsoid $\mathcal{E}_M$, where $M \in \mathbb{S}^{n_d}_{++}$. In this case, the predicate `ellipinput` must be defined similarly to the `stateinv` and `outputinv` predicates in Sect. 3.2, and the contract is expressed as follows:

ACSL

```
//@ predicate ellipinput(real d1, ..., real dnd, real λ) =
   (M11 * d1 * d1 + 2 * M12 * d1 * d2 + ... + Mndnd * dnd * dnd
   <= λ);
/*@ behavior ellipsoid_input_contract:
     assumes ellipinput(d1, ..., dnd, 1);
     assumes δ̲1 <= δ1 <= δ̄1 && ... && δ̲nδ <= δnδ <= δ̄nδ; */
```

4 Validating Contracts: Real Model

In Frama-C, the real model is based on the mathematical model of real numbers. As a result, single and double precision floating-point numbers are mapped to real types in proof objectives. This simplification can make the proof process easier, but it does not take into account the actual computation that is performed using machine-code floating-point numbers. This means that the real model may not accurately reflect the behavior of the system when it is implemented in machine code. Nevertheless, in our setting, using the real model is a reasonable first step since the system analysis has been performed assuming real computation. The validity of the real model in our setting will be further addressed in the next section by taking into account the potential for numerical errors.

To validate the invariant properties of the system G, we combine the codes in Sects. 3.1, 3.2, and 3.3, and we add the missing preconditions and postconditions.

C+ACSL

```
typedef struct { double x1, ..., xnx; } state;
typedef struct { double y1, ..., yny; } output;
//@ predicate stateinv(real x1, ..., real xnx, real λ) =
    (P11 * x1 * x1 + 2 * P12 * x1 * x2 + ... + Pnxnx * xnx * xnx
    <= λ);
//@ predicate outputinv(real y1, ..., real yny, real λ) =
    (Q11 * y1 * y1 + 2 * Q12 * y1 * y2 + ...+ Qnyny * yny * yny
    <= λ);

/*@ requires \valid(x) && \valid(y);
    requires \separated(&(x->x1), ...,&(x->xnx),&(y->y1), ...,
     &(y->yny));
  assigns *y;
  behavior contract_name:
    assumes ...;
    ensures stateinv(\old(x->x1),..., \old(x->xnx),1) ==>
    outputinv(y->y1, ...,y->yny,1);
*/
void updateOutput(...) {...}

/*@ requires \valid(x);
    requires \separated(&(x->x1), ...,&(x->xnx));
    assigns *x;
    behavior contract_name:
      assumes ...;
      ensures stateinv(\old(x->x1), ..., \old(x->xnx),1) ==>
    stateinv(x->x1, ...,x->xnx,1);
*/
void updateState(...) {...}
```

In this code, the `\valid`, `\separated`, and `assigns` annotations are used for expressing constraints on the memory layout of the program and specifying which variables or memory locations may be modified by the code. Precisely, the `\valid` annotation is used to specify that a certain pointer or array refers to a valid, allocated region of memory, the `\separated` annotation is used to specify that certain variables or memory locations must be separated from each other in order for the code to be executed, and the `assigns` annotation is used to specify which variables or memory locations may be modified by the code. As shown in the above script, it is generally recommended to place an annotation before the code it is associated with.

To formally verify the invariant properties, we use the polynomial inequalities plugin of Alt-Ergo in the WP framework of Frama-C. This plugin, unlike other solvers, can deal with the type of predicates considered. The following command runs the formal verification process and returns the verification results:

```
frama-c -wp -wp-model real -wp-prover Alt-Ergo-Poly source_file.c
```

Many options and arguments can be used with the `frama-c -wp` command to customize and control the analysis process. For example, the `-wp-timeout` option is used to set a time limit for the analysis, which can be helpful in cases where the analysis is expected to take a long time. In our experiment, Alt-Ergo-Poly (the SOS plugin) was the only solver able to discharge any of our proof objectives. For instance, running the above command returned the following result:

```
[wp] 51 goals scheduled
[wp] Proved goals:    51 / 51
  Qed:               18  (2ms-7ms-14ms)
  Alt-Ergo-Poly :    33  (5ms-150ms-843ms) (3290)
```

The goals associated with the memory-related annotation were validated using the simpler internal solver Qed, while all the ellipsoid-related goals required the use of Alt-Ergo-Poly.

5 Validating Contracts: Float Model

In C, floating-point numbers are represented using a binary floating-point format, which is a method for representing real numbers with a fixed number of bits allocated to the mantissa (the fractional part of the number) and the exponent (the power of 2 by which the mantissa must be multiplied). The floating-point model in Frama-C adheres to the IEEE 754 standard for floating-point representation. This standard defines various floating-point formats for representing real numbers, including single-precision (32-bit) and double-precision (64-bit) formats.

5.1 Issues with Deductive Methods and the Floating-Point Model

While the float model is a more accurate representation of computation, it can produce proof goals that are more difficult to solve. This can be illustrated with the following simple example:

C+ACSL

```
/*@ requires x > 0 && x <= 10;
  @ ensures \result > 0; */
double f(double x) { return x + 0.25; }
```

This contract is easily solved using the real model:

```
% frama-c -wp -wp-model real -wp-prover z3,cvc4,alt-ergo simple.c
[wp] Proved goals:    1 / 1
------------------------------------------------------------
Prover Z3 4.11.2 returns Valid (Qed:0.81ms) (30ms) (21112)
Prover CVC4 1.8 returns Valid (Qed:0.81ms) (40ms) (5926)
Prover Alt-Ergo  returns Valid (Qed:0.81ms) (8ms) (8)
------------------------------------------------------------
```

However, if we analyze the same program using a more accurate encoding of floats, i.e., by omitting the option `-wp-model real`, we get

```
Prove: .0 < of_f64(add_f64(x, to_f64((1.0/4)))).
Prover Z3 4.11.2 returns Failed Unknown error
Prover CVC4 1.8 returns Timeout (Qed:2ms) (10s)
Prover Alt-Ergo  returns Timeout (Qed:2ms) (10s)
```

Given the limitations of automated provers in handling simple verification conditions involving floats, there are two primary alternatives to consider. One approach involves using proof assistants, like Gappa [11], which require more manual intervention but offer precise axiomatization of floating-point computations. Alternatively, static analysis tools such as FPTaylor [29], Fluctuat [13], and Rosa [10], which employ techniques like Taylor expansion or affine arithmetic, provide more systematic error bounding solutions.

In the following, instead of using the float model, we rely on such a static analysis to bound the numerical imprecision of the computation. For instance, in this example, using interval arithmetic, which will be discussed in Sect. 5.2, we can bound the values of `\result` by $[0.25, 10.25] + \pm 2.275958\text{E}{-15}$, where the first interval denotes the interval of double $[0.25, 10.25]$ and the term $\pm 2.275958\text{E}{-15}$ denotes the over-approximation of accumulated errors. The contract can then be instrumented, and the floating-point "noise" can be included in the `\ensures` statement as follows:

ACSL
```
/*@ requires x > 0 && x <= 10;
  @ ensures \forall real λ, -1 <= λ <= 1 ==> \result + λ *
    2.275958E-15 > 0; */
```

With this approach, we can use the real model for analysis to formally verify the postcondition in the float model:

```
% frama-c -wp -wp-model real -wp-prover z3,cvc4,alt-ergo simple2.c
[wp] Proved goals:    1 / 1
  Qed:               0  (2ms)
  Alt-Ergo :         1  (9ms) (12)
------------------------------------------------------------
Prover Alt-Ergo  returns Valid (Qed:2ms) (9ms) (12)
------------------------------------------------------------
```

$$([x_1, x_2], e) + ([y_1, y_2], f) = \left(\begin{array}{l} [\mathrm{fl}\,(x_1 + y_1)\,, \mathrm{fl}\,(x_2 + y_2)], e_{new} \\ \text{with } e_{new} = \max \begin{pmatrix} -\mathrm{fl}_{-\infty}\left(-e - f - e^+(x_1, y_1)\right), \\ \mathrm{fl}_{+\infty}\left(e + f + e^+(x_2, y_2)\right) \end{pmatrix} \end{array} \right),$$

$$([x_1, x_2], e) * ([y_1, y_2], f) = \left(\begin{bmatrix} \min(\mathrm{fl}\,(x_1 y_1)\,, \mathrm{fl}\,(x_1 y_2)\,, \mathrm{fl}\,(x_2 y_1)\,, \mathrm{fl}\,(y_1 y_2)), \\ \max(\mathrm{fl}\,(x_1 y_1)\,, \mathrm{fl}\,(x_1 y_2)\,, \mathrm{fl}\,(x_2 y_1)\,, \mathrm{fl}\,(y_1 y_2)) \end{bmatrix}, e_{new} \right),$$

where $e^+(a, b)$ is defined as $(|a| + |b|)\mathtt{eps}$ and $e^*(a, b)$ as $|a * b|\ \mathtt{eps} + \mathtt{eta}$ and with

$$e_{new} = \max \left(\begin{array}{l} -\mathrm{fl}_{-\infty} \begin{pmatrix} \min(\mathrm{fl}_{-\infty}(-ey_1)\,, \mathrm{fl}_{-\infty}(-ey_2)\,, \mathrm{fl}_{-\infty}(ey_1)\,, \mathrm{fl}_{-\infty}(ey_2)) \\ +\min(\mathrm{fl}_{-\infty}(-x_1 f)\,, \mathrm{fl}_{-\infty}(x_1 f)\,, \mathrm{fl}_{-\infty}(-x_2 f)\,, \mathrm{fl}_{-\infty}(x_2 f)) \\ -\min(e^*(x_1, y_1), e^*(x_1, y_2), e^*(x_2, y_1), e^*(x_2, y_2)) \end{pmatrix}, \\ \mathrm{fl}_{+\infty} \begin{pmatrix} \max(\mathrm{fl}_{+\infty}(-ey_1)\,, \mathrm{fl}_{+\infty}(ey_2)\,, \mathrm{fl}_{+\infty}(ey_1)\,, \mathrm{fl}_{+\infty}(ey_2)) \\ +\min(\mathrm{fl}_{+\infty}(-x_1 f)\,, \mathrm{fl}_{+\infty}(x_1 f)\,, \mathrm{fl}_{+\infty}(-x_2 f)\,, \mathrm{fl}_{+\infty}(x_2 f)) \\ +\min(e^*(x_1, y_1), e^*(x_1, y_2), e^*(x_2, y_1), e^*(x_2, y_2)) \end{pmatrix} \end{array} \right).$$

Fig. 2. Addition and multiplication on intervals with floating-point errors.

5.2 Bounding Numerical Errors

We refer the reader to [15,16,21] for more details on means to bound floating-point accumulated rounding errors. We recall the characterization of floating-point values for addition and multiplication of floating-point numbers:

$$(u + e^u) + (v + e^v) = (u + v) + (e^u + e^v + e^+(u, v)), \tag{4}$$
$$(u + e^u) * (v + e^v) = (u * v) + (e^u * v + e^v * u + e^*(u, v)), \tag{5}$$

with $|e^+(u, v)| \leq |u + v|\ \mathtt{eps}$ and $|e^*(u, v)| \leq |u * v|\ \mathtt{eps} + \mathtt{eta}$.

In the following discussions, $\mathrm{fl}\,(e)$ denotes the floating-point approximation of value e using a "round to the nearest" mode. Rounding towards $-\infty$ and $+\infty$ are denoted by $\mathrm{fl}_{-\infty}(\cdot)$ and $\mathrm{fl}_{+\infty}(\cdot)$, respectively. The constants eps and eta denote the precision of the floating-point format and its precision in case of underflows, respectively. For single precision floating-point numbers, $\mathtt{eps} = 2^{-22} \approx 10^{-7}$ and $\mathtt{eta} = 2^{-149} \approx 10^{-45}$, while for double precision, $\mathtt{eps} = 2^{-52} \approx 10^{-16}$ and $\mathtt{eta} = 2^{-1074} \approx 10^{-324}$.

Equations (4) and (5) can be adapted to intervals, as detailed in Fig. 2. The interval $[a, b]$ with additional error $\pm e$ is denoted by $([a, b], e)$. This method allows to characterize both the actual values, obtained by floating-point computation in the value part, and a safe error term. In case of a deterministic loopless code computing an expression exp, one would obtain the abstract value $[x, x] \pm e$ where the singleton interval for the value part denotes exactly the value x that would have been obtained when computing $\mathrm{fl}\,(\exp)$. Thanks to the handling of floating-point errors, the computation of exp with reals is guaranteed to lie within $[\mathrm{fl}_{-\infty}(x - e)\,, \mathrm{fl}_{+\infty}(x + e)]$.

5.3 Error Hyper-Rectangle Approach

For the analysis that follows, we will assume that the initial state of the system G is represented by a floating-point number that belongs to the state-invariant ellipsoid. The vector $z \in \mathbb{R}^n$ serves as a placeholder for both the updated state and output vectors of the system. The floating-point representation $\mathrm{fl}(z)$ of the exact vector z satisfies the following inequalities:

$$z - e \preceq \mathrm{fl}(z) \preceq z + e, \tag{6}$$

where $\preceq$ denotes the componentwise inequality and $e = [e_1, \ldots, e_n]^T$ is the "error" vector whose i^{th} element is an over-approximation of the accumulated error associated with the computation of the ith component of z using float model arithmetic. Consequently, it is clear that $\mathrm{fl}(z)$ belongs to a hyper-rectangle Γ that is symmetric about the exact vector z and that has 2^n vertices $\hat{z}_i$, where $i = 1, \ldots, 2^n$. Assume that $z \in \mathcal{E}_X$ is formally verified in the real model. Then, to prove that $\mathrm{fl}(z) \in \mathcal{E}_X$, it is sufficient to verify that $\Gamma \subset \mathcal{E}_X$. This sufficient condition can be established using either of the following two methods.

Method 1: Checking All Points in the Hyper-Rectangle. The first method to verify that $\Gamma \subset \mathcal{E}_X$ is to formally verify that all the points in Γ belong to $\mathcal{E}_X$, i.e., for all $z_e \in \Gamma$, $z_e \in \mathcal{E}_X$. To express this condition in ACSL, we first need to know how to express all the vectors that belong to Γ. We notice that the ith component of any vector z_e belonging to Γ can be expressed as $z_{e,i} = z + l_i e_i$, where $l_i \in [-1, 1]$ for $i = 1, \ldots, n$. This formulation of z_e can be expressed in ACSL using the universal quantifier $\forall$ (`\forall`) and n bound variables (`l_1`, ..., `l_n`), each belonging to $[-1, 1]$. For instance, in the case of formally verifying the state invariant property, the postcondition is the following:

ACSL
```
//State Invariant Postcondition
ensures \forall real l_1; ...;\forall real l_{n_x}; -1 <= l_1 <= 1
    ==> ... ==> -1 <= l_{n_x} <= 1 ==> stateinv(\old(x->x_1), ...,
    \old(x->x_{n_x}),1) ==> stateinv(x->x_1+l_1*e_1, ..., x->x_{n_x}+l_{n_x}*
    e_{n_x},1);
```

In this code, n_x bound variables are used with the universal quantifier `\forall` to represent all the vectors x_e belonging to Γ. Similarly, when formally verifying the output invariant property, the following postcondition is used:

ACSL
```
//Output Invariant Postcondition
ensures \forall real l_1; ...;\forall real l_{n_y}; -1 <= l_1 <= 1
    ==> ... ==> -1 <= l_{n_y} <= 1 ==> stateinv(\old(x->x_1), ...,
    \old(x->x_{n_x}),1) ==> outputinv(y->y_1+l_1*e_1, ..., y->y_{n_y}+l_{n_y}*
    e_{n_y},1);
```

Method 2: Checking Each Vertex. The second method to verify that $\Gamma \subset \mathcal{E}_X$ benefits from the convexity of the quadratic function $z^T X z$. Precisely, by leveraging the convexity of the quadratic function $z^T X z$, the following holds: $\Gamma \subset \mathcal{E}_X$ if and only if all the vertices $\hat{z}_i$, for $i = 1, \ldots, 2^n$, of Γ belong to $\mathcal{E}_X$. Therefore, to formally verify that $\mathrm{fl}(z) \in \mathcal{E}_X$, we must formally verify that the vertices of Γ belong to $\mathcal{E}_X$. The vertices $\hat{z}_i$, for $i = 1, \ldots, 2^n$, of Γ can be expressed in ACSL using the universal quantifier $\forall$ (`\forall`) and n bound variables (`l`$_1$, ..., `l`$_n$), each belonging to $\{-1, 1\}$. The postconditions for verifying the state and output invariant properties of the system using this method are similar to the ones used in the first method, with the exception that the bound variables' inequalities (`-1<=l`$_i$`<=1`) are replaced by (`l`$_i$`==-1` || `l`$_i$`==1`).

Assessment of Both Methods. While it is possible to formally verify that $\Gamma \subset \mathcal{E}_X$ using the methods described before, the use of quantifiers may lead to a proliferation of variables or constraints, which can make it difficult for the automated prover to discharge the proof: this may either lead to an extended time to prove the goals or to a solver failure. For instance, in our experiments, it was possible to verify the invariant properties of an LTI system with 16 state variables, 10 inputs, and 4 outputs in the float model using Method 1, but it was not possible to do so for any of the considered affine LPV systems with 4 state variables, 2 inputs, 2 outputs, and up to 2 scheduling parameters. On the other hand, using Method 2, it was possible to verify the invariant properties of these affine LPV systems and corresponding LTI systems in the float model, but it was not possible to do so for the large LTI system verified using Method 1. To address this issue, we present a different approach in the next section for formally verifying the invariant properties in the float model without the use of quantifiers.

5.4 Error Ball Approach

Consider the "error ball" $\mathcal{B}_e$ centered around the exact vector z with a radius r such that $\mathcal{B}_e$ covers the hyper-rectangle Γ. The ball $\mathcal{B}_e$ is defined as $\mathcal{B}_e = \{z_e \in \mathbb{R}^n |\, z_e = z + ru,\ \|u\|_2 \leq 1\}$, where $\|.\|_2$ is the standard Euclidean norm. Since $\mathrm{fl}(z) \in \Gamma$, it follows that $\mathrm{fl}(z) \in \mathcal{B}_e$ as well. Therefore, to verify that $\mathrm{fl}(z) \in \mathcal{E}_X$, it is sufficient to show that $\mathcal{B}_e \subset \mathcal{E}_X$. Clearly, $\mathcal{B}_e \subset \mathcal{E}_X$ if and only if all the points belonging to $\mathcal{B}_e$ also belong to $\mathcal{E}_X$. In other words, $\mathcal{B}_e \subset \mathcal{E}_X$ if and only if, for all $u \in \mathbb{R}^n$ such that $\|u\|_2 \leq 1$,

$$z_e^T X z_e = (z + ru)^T X (z + ru) = z^T X z + 2ru^T X z + r^2 u^T X u \leq 1.$$

It is not difficult to prove that the following inequality holds [7]:

$$z_e^T X z_e \leq z^T X z + 2r\|X\|_2 \|z\|_2 + r^2 \|X\|_2, \tag{7}$$

where $\|X\|_2$ is the matrix 2-norm induced by the vector Euclidean norm, i.e., $\|X\|_2 = \lambda_{\max}(X)$, where $\lambda_{\max}(X)$ is the maximum eigenvalue of X. We recall that, by assumption, it is formally verified in the real model that the exact vector z belongs to $\mathcal{E}_X$. Based on this assumption, we can find the maximum 2-norm of z such that $z \in \mathcal{E}_X$ by solving the following nonconvex optimization problem:

$$\begin{aligned} &\text{maximize} \quad z^T z \\ &\text{subject to} \quad z^T X z \leq 1. \end{aligned} \tag{8}$$

This optimization problem is a special case of a nonconvex problem discussed in [7, Chapter 5.2.4], for which strong duality holds [7,25], i.e., the optimal value, $\|z^*\|_2^2$, of the primal problem is equal to the optimal value of the following dual problem:

$$\begin{aligned} &\text{minimize} \quad \alpha \\ &\text{subject to} \quad X^{-1} \preceq \alpha I. \end{aligned} \tag{9}$$

The optimal value of the dual problem is $\alpha^* = \lambda_{\max}(X^{-1}) = \frac{1}{\lambda_{\min}(X)}$, where X^{-1} is the inverse of X and $\lambda_{\min}(X)$ is the minimum eigenvalue of X. Accordingly, the optimal value of the primal nonconvex problem is $\|z^*\|_2^2 = \alpha^* = (\lambda_{\min}(X))^{-1}$. Then, for all $z \in \mathcal{E}_X$, the following inequalities hold:

$$\begin{aligned} z_e^T X z_e &\leq z^T X z + 2r\|X\|_2\|z\|_2 + r^2\|X\|_2 \\ &\leq z^T X z + r\lambda_{\max}(X)\left(2\left(\lambda_{\min}(X)\right)^{-\frac{1}{2}} + r\right). \end{aligned} \tag{10}$$

Therefore, it is sufficient to formally verify that

$$z^T X z \leq 1 - r\lambda_{\max}(X)\left(2\left(\lambda_{\min}(X)\right)^{-\frac{1}{2}} + r\right) \tag{11}$$

to conclude that $z_e^T X z_e \leq 1$ for all $z_e \in \mathcal{B}_e$, and that $\mathcal{B}_e \subset \mathcal{E}_X$. In other words, if (11) is formally verified, then $\mathrm{fl}(z) \in \mathcal{E}_X$ and the ellipsoidal invariant property is verified in the float model. To formally verify (11), we need to compute the radius r of $\mathcal{B}_e$ such that $\Gamma \subset \mathcal{B}_e$, as well as the maximum and minimum eigenvalues of X. Since Γ is a symmetric hyper-rectangle about z, the smallest radius of $\mathcal{B}_e$ such that $\mathcal{B}_e$ covers Γ is $r = \|e\|_2$ [7], where e is the error vector satisfying (6). Then, for any $r \geq \|e\|_2$, $\mathcal{B}_e$ covers Γ. One acceptable choice of r is $r = n\|e\|_\infty$, where $\|e\|_\infty = \max_{i=1,\ldots,n} |e_i|$ is the ∞-norm of e. This choice is valid because $\|e\|_2 \leq \sqrt{n}\,\|e\|_\infty$. For our analysis, it is a better choice to set $r = n\|e\|_\infty$, as this computation only requires one operation compared to the $2n$ operations required for computing $\|e\|_2$, which minimizes the accumulated floating-point error during the computation of r. The error vector e is computed outside of Frama-C and injected in the contract. As for the computation of the maximum and minimum eigenvalues of X, there are several algorithms that can be used to compute the eigenvalues of a matrix, such as the diagonalization, power iteration, and QR algorithms, and singular value decomposition (SVD) methods [14,31]. These algorithms are generally reliable and can be expected to produce accurate results in most cases. For instance, iterative methods like the power iteration algorithm can be employed to compute the eigenvalues of a matrix, starting with a random initial vector [19]. This approach allows for an over-approximation of the converged value by estimating it from above. The over-approximation is then fed back into the algorithm as input for subsequent iterations, which refines the approximation and helps ensure its validity.

Hence, to formally verify the state and output invariant properties of the system G in the float model, we add `float_model` contracts to the code in Sect. 4 as follows:

C+ACSL

```
/*@ behavior contract_name_float_model:
      assumes ...;
      ensures stateinv(\old(x->x1), ..., \old(x->xnx),1) ==>
    outputinv(y->y1, ...,y->yny,1 - 2 * r_y * norm_Q *
    norm_y_max - r_y * r_y * norm_Q);*/
void updateOutput(...) {...}
/*@ behavior contract_name_float_model:
      assumes ...;
      ensures stateinv(\old(x->x1), ..., \old(x->xnx),1) ==>
    stateinv(x->x1, ...,x->xnx,1 - 2 * r_x * norm_P *
    norm_x_max - r_x * r_x * norm_P));*/
void updateState(...) {...}
```

In this code, the implied expressions in the postconditions correspond to inequality (11). The terms `norm_P`, `norm_Q`, `r_x`, `r_y`, `norm_x_max`, and `norm_y_max` correspond to $\|P\|_2$, $\|Q\|_2$, the radii of the error balls centered around the updated state and output vectors x and y, $(\lambda_{\min}(P))^{-\frac{1}{2}}$, and $(\lambda_{\min}(Q))^{-\frac{1}{2}}$, respectively. This approach allows for the formal verification of the invariant properties of all considered affine LPV and LTI systems in the float model.

6 Conclusion

This paper demonstrates a process for formally verifying the invariant properties of a C code describing the dynamics of a discrete-time LPV system with affine parameter dependence. The ACSL language and the WP plugin in Frama-C are used to express the invariant properties and generate proof obligations, and the polynomial inequalities plugin in Alt-Ergo is used discharge these proof obligations. The invariant properties were successfully verified in both the real and float models, with the latter requiring the use of bounds on numerical errors and their incorporation into the real model. This process can be applied to other systems with similar properties. The installation instructions of the tools used in this work along with the experiments are available at https://github.com/ploc/verif-iqc. Additionally, a dockerfile is also available at https://hub.docker.com/r/ekhalife/verif-iqc, and the instructions for using the dockerfile can be found in the same GitHub repository. In future work, we plan to extend this approach to more general classes of uncertain systems.

References

1. Apkarian, P., Tuan, H.D.: Parameterized LMIs in control theory. SIAM J. Control. Optim. **38**(4), 1241–1264 (2000)
2. Barrett, C., et al.: CVC4. In: Gopalakrishnan, G., Qadeer, S. (eds.) CAV 2011. LNCS, vol. 6806, pp. 171–177. Springer, Heidelberg (2011). https://doi.org/10.1007/978-3-642-22110-1_14
3. Baudin, P., et al.: ACSL: ANSI/ISO C specification language ACSL version 1.18, implementation in FRAMA-C 26.0
4. Baudin, P., Filliâtre, J.C., Marché, C., Monate, B., Moy, Y., Prevosto, V.: ACSL: ANSI C specification language. CEA-LIST, Saclay, France, Technical report, v1 2 (2008)
5. Blanchini, F.: Set invariance in control. Automatica **35**(11), 1747–1767 (1999)
6. Boyd, S., El Ghaoui, L., Feron, E., Balakrishnan, V.: Linear matrix inequalities in system and control theory. SIAM (1994)
7. Boyd, S., Vandenberghe, L.: Convex Optimization. Cambridge University Press, Cambridge (2004). http://www.stanford.edu/%7Eboyd/cvxbook/
8. Conchon, S., Iguernelala, M., Mebsout, A.: A collaborative framework for non-linear integer arithmetic reasoning in alt-ergo. In: Bjørner, N.S., et al. (eds.) 15th International Symposium on Symbolic and Numeric Algorithms for Scientific Computing, SYNASC 2013, Timisoara, Romania, 23–26 September 2013, pp. 161–168. IEEE Computer Society (2013). https://doi.org/10.1109/SYNASC.2013.29
9. Cuoq, P., Kirchner, F., Kosmatov, N., Prevosto, V., Signoles, J., Yakobowski, B.: Frama-C. In: Eleftherakis, G., Hinchey, M., Holcombe, M. (eds.) SEFM 2012. LNCS, vol. 7504, pp. 233–247. Springer, Heidelberg (2012). https://doi.org/10.1007/978-3-642-33826-7_16
10. Darulova, E., Kuncak, V.: Sound compilation of reals. SIGPLAN Not. **49**(1), 235–248 (2014). https://doi.org/10.1145/2578855.2535874
11. Daumas, M., Melquiond, G.: Certification of bounds on expressions involving rounded operators. ACM Trans. Math. Softw. **37**(1) (2010). https://doi.org/10.1145/1644001.1644003
12. de Moura, L., Bjørner, N.: Z3: an efficient SMT solver. In: Ramakrishnan, C.R., Rehof, J. (eds.) TACAS 2008. LNCS, vol. 4963, pp. 337–340. Springer, Heidelberg (2008). https://doi.org/10.1007/978-3-540-78800-3_24
13. Delmas, D., Goubault, E., Putot, S., Souyris, J., Tekkal, K., Védrine, F.: Towards an industrial use of FLUCTUAT on safety-critical avionics software. In: Alpuente, M., Cook, B., Joubert, C. (eds.) FMICS 2009. LNCS, vol. 5825, pp. 53–69. Springer, Heidelberg (2009). https://doi.org/10.1007/978-3-642-04570-7_6
14. Golub, G.H., Van Loan, C.F.: Matrix Computations. JHU Press (2013)
15. Goubault, E.: Static analyses of the precision of floating-point operations. In: Cousot, P. (ed.) SAS 2001. LNCS, vol. 2126, pp. 234–259. Springer, Heidelberg (2001). https://doi.org/10.1007/3-540-47764-0_14
16. Goubault, E., Putot, S.: Static analysis of finite precision computations. In: VMCAI, pp. 232–247 (2011)
17. Khalife, E., Abou Jaoude, D., Farhood, M., Garoche, P.L.: Computation of invariant sets for discrete-time uncertain systems. Int. J. Robust Nonlinear Control (2023, minor revision)
18. Khalil, H.K.: Nonlinear Systems, 3rd edn. Prentice-Hall, Upper Saddle River (2002). https://cds.cern.ch/record/1173048

19. Kuczyński, J., Woźniakowski, H.: Estimating the largest eigenvalue by the power and Lanczos algorithms with a random start. SIAM J. Matrix Anal. Appl. **13**(4), 1094–1122 (1992). https://doi.org/10.1137/0613066
20. Kurzhanski, A.B., Varaiya, P.: Ellipsoidal techniques for reachability analysis. In: Lynch, N., Krogh, B.H. (eds.) HSCC 2000. LNCS, vol. 1790, pp. 202–214. Springer, Heidelberg (2000). https://doi.org/10.1007/3-540-46430-1_19
21. Martel, M.: An overview of semantics for the validation of numerical programs. In: Cousot, R. (ed.) VMCAI 2005. LNCS, vol. 3385, pp. 59–77. Springer, Heidelberg (2005). https://doi.org/10.1007/978-3-540-30579-8_4
22. Martin-Dorel, É., Roux, P.: A reflexive tactic for polynomial positivity using numerical solvers and floating-point computations. In: Bertot, Y., Vafeiadis, V. (eds.) Proceedings of the 6th ACM SIGPLAN Conference on Certified Programs and Proofs, CPP 2017, Paris, France, 16–17 January 2017, pp. 90–99. ACM (2017). https://doi.org/10.1145/3018610.3018622
23. Megretski, A., Rantzer, A.: System analysis via integral quadratic constraints. IEEE Trans. Autom. Control **42**(6), 819–830 (1997)
24. Muniraj, D., Palframan, M.C., Guthrie, K.T., Farhood, M.: Path-following control of small fixed-wing unmanned aircraft systems with $\mathcal{H}_\infty$ type performance. Control. Eng. Pract. **67**, 76–91 (2017)
25. Nocedal, J., Wright, S.J.: Numerical Optimization. Springer, New York (1999). https://doi.org/10.1007/978-0-387-40065-5
26. Peled, D.A.: Software Reliability Methods. Springer, New York (2013). https://doi.org/10.1007/978-1-4757-3540-6
27. Roux, P.: Formal proofs of rounding error bounds - with application to an automatic positive definiteness check. J. Autom. Reason. **57**(2), 135–156 (2016). https://doi.org/10.1007/s10817-015-9339-z
28. Roux, P., Iguernlala, M., Conchon, S.: A non-linear arithmetic procedure for control-command software verification. In: Beyer, D., Huisman, M. (eds.) TACAS 2018. LNCS, vol. 10806, pp. 132–151. Springer, Cham (2018). https://doi.org/10.1007/978-3-319-89963-3_8
29. Solovyev, A., Baranowski, M., Briggs, I., Jacobsen, C., Rakamaric, Z., Gopalakrishnan, G.: Rigorous estimation of floating-point round-off errors with symbolic taylor expansions. ACM Trans. Program. Lang. Syst. (TOPLAS) **41**(1), 2:1–2:39 (2018). https://doi.org/10.1145/3230733
30. Topcu, U., Packard, A., Seiler, P.: Local stability analysis using simulations and sum-of-squares programming. Automatica **44**(10), 2669–2675 (2008). https://doi.org/10.1016/j.automatica.2008.03.010
31. Trefethen, L.N., Bau III, D.: Numerical linear algebra, vol. 50. SIAM (1997)

Reasoning with Metric Temporal Logic and Resettable Skewed Clocks

Alberto Bombardelli[1,2(✉)] and Stefano Tonetta[1]

[1] Fondazione Bruno Kessler, Via Sommarive, 18, 38123 Povo, TN, Italy
{abombardelli,tonettas}@fbk.eu
[2] University of Trento, Via Sommarive, 9, 38123 Povo, TN, Italy
alberto.bombardell-1@unitn.it

Abstract. The formal verification of distributed real-time systems is challenging due to the interaction between the local computation and the communication between the different nodes of a network. The overall correctness of the system relies on local properties and timing exchange of data between components. This requires to take into account the drift of local clocks and their synchronization. The reference time of local properties may be given by skewed and resettable (thus non-monotonic) clocks.

In this paper, we consider automated reasoning over MTLSK, a variant of MTL over Resettable Skewed Clocks. We focus on metric operators with lower and upper parametric bounds. We provide an encoding into temporal logic modulo the theory of reals and we solve satisfiability with SMT-based model checking techniques. We implemented and evaluated the approach on typical properties of real-time systems.

1 Introduction

Distributed Real-Time Systems (DRTS) consist of different real-time components connected by a communication network. Each component, therefore, responds to input data or events within a specified period of time or generates output data or events periodically. The correctness of the overall DRTS depends not only on the logic of the input/output functions but also on the timing constraints on the data/events. The formal verification of temporal properties of DRTS is thus very challenging due to the need for reasoning about both communication and timing constraints. Since local clocks of components are usually not perfect and drift from each other, DRTS employ various consensus algorithms to synchronize them.

In formal verification, the properties are typically specified in temporal logics such as Linear-time Temporal Logic (LTL) [19], which can specify temporal constraints on the succession of events or exchange of messages. When dealing with real-time systems, one of the most popular temporal logics is Metric Temporal Logics (MTL) [16], which enriches the temporal operators with bounds to constrain the time intervals in which formulas must be satisfied. Another variant, the Event Clock Temporal Logic (ECTL) [20] uses event clock constraints to

K. Y. Rozier and S. Chaudhuri (Eds.): NFM 2023, LNCS 13903, pp. 174–190, 2023.
https://doi.org/10.1007/978-3-031-33170-1_11

specify bounds on the time since the last time or until the next time a formula holds. Timed Propositional Temporal Logic (TPTL) [1], instead, uses freezing quantifiers to compare and constrain time at different points.

When these logics are used to formalize properties of DRTS, they must be extended in two directions. First, the local properties should use local clocks as the reference time for the timing constraints. Second, the local clocks should be possibly skewed and resettable to consider the potential drift and synchronization of clocks. Therefore, distributed variants of MTL and ECTL use local temporal operators that refer to local times (e.g., [18]). Moreover, in [4], the logic MTLSK was introduced where specific variants of the metric temporal operators overcome the issue of standard operators when the reference time is not monotonic as for resettable clocks.

In this paper, we address the problem of automated reasoning over MTLSK properties. We focus on metric operators with either lower or upper parametric bounds. We consider local properties of DRTS components that use local clocks that are occasionally reset for synchronization and, so, that may be not monotonic. We use assumptions on drift and synchronization mechanisms to entail global properties. This compositional reasoning is formalized into MTLSK.

The main contribution of the paper is a procedure that reduces the satisfiability of the new logic to Satisfiability Modulo Theories (SMT) of discrete-time First-Order LTL [9,23]. The encoding takes into account that a clock c may be not monotonic, which implies that interval constraints such as $c \leq p$ may be true in disjoint time intervals. Thus, differently from the monotonic case, it is not sufficient to guess the first point at which a subformula is satisfied. Guess variables are introduced to predict minimum/maximum values of the local clocks, for which subformulas hold. The correctness of the encoding exploits the assumptions that local clocks, although resettable, are diverging (i.e. do not converge to a finite value).

We implemented the approach on top of the timed features of nuXmv [8] using bounded model checking for finding traces and the k-zeno algorithm to prove the validity of formulas. We evaluated them on typical patterns of real-time properties real-time systems also showing scalability on tautologies derived from compositional reasoning.

The remainder of the paper is organized as follows: in Sect. 2, we describe a motivating example to explain the kind of automated reasoning addressed in the paper; in Sect. 3, we compare our approach with other related work; in Sect. 4, we provide preliminary knowledge about first-order LTL and temporal satisfiability modulo theory; in Sect. 5, we recall the definition of MTLSK; in Sect. 6 we show the reduction to satisfiability modulo theories; in Sect. 7 we provide the results of an experimental evaluation of our work; finally, in Sect. 8, we draw the conclusions and some future directions.

2 Motivating Example

2.1 Semantics with Resettable Skewed Clocks

In this section, we describe the type of compositional reasoning that we address in this paper. In the following, we use standard LTL operators such as G (always in the future) and F (eventually in the future), as well as their distributed metric variants. We informally recall the semantics and refer the reader to the next sections for a formal definition.

The formula $F^{c}_{\leq p}b$ is true in a time point t whenever b holds in some future point within p time units. The superscript c indicates that the time constraint must be evaluated using a clock c. Thus b must hold in a point t' such that $c(t') - c(t) \leq p$. The dual formula $G^{c}_{\leq p}b$ requires b to be true in all points t' such that $c(t') - c(t) \leq p$.

As an example, consider the plot in Fig. 1. Let us first refer to the perfect clock c (black line). The formula $F^{c}_{\leq 5}(y_1 \geq 2)$ is true in 0 because there is a point between time 4 and 5 where $y_1 \geq 2$. For the same reason, the formula $G^{c}_{\leq 5}(y_1 \leq 2)$ (which is equivalent to the negation of the first one) is false. If we consider instead y_2, the formula $G^{c}_{\leq 5}(y_2 \leq 2)$ is true.

Let us now consider the skewed clock sc (orange line), which runs too fast and is reset at points 2 and 5 to approximately the correct value (black line). If we consider again $F^{sc}_{\leq 5}(y_1 \geq 2)$, the formula is now false because of the drift as $y_1 \geq 2$ should hold before. Note however that thanks to the reset the points where $sc(t) \leq 5$ lie in disconnected intervals, namely $[0, 4]$ and $[5, 16/3]$. Thus, while $G^{c}_{\leq 5}(y_1 \leq 2)$ is true, $G^{c}_{\leq 5}(y_2 \leq 2)$ is false.

To better characterize the intended semantics over non-monotonic clocks, we consider the variant $\overline{F}^{c}_{\leq p}$ and $\overline{G}^{c}_{\leq p}$ introduced in [4], which consider only the first interval where $c(t') - c(t) \leq p$. Thus, in our example, $\overline{G}^{sc}_{\leq 5}(y_1 \leq 2)$ is true, $G^{c}_{\leq 5}(y_2 \leq 2)$ is true.

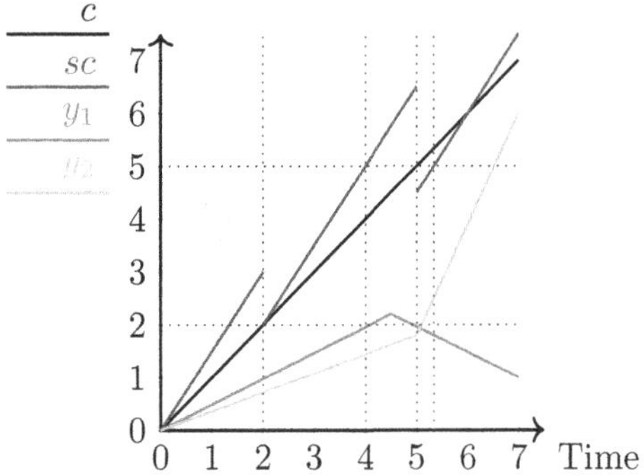

Fig. 1. Examples of real functions, including a perfect and a skewed resettable clock (Color figure online)

Finally, note that we are dealing with a super-dense model of time, which augments the interpretation of time over real numbers with instantaneous discrete steps such as resets and discrete variable updates. Thus, in the example above, there are two-time points where the real-time is 2: in the first point, sc is equal to 3, while in the second point, due to a reset, sc is equal to 2 even if real-time does not change. We use the functional symbol $next$ to refer to next value after a discrete step. For example, the above-mentioned reset point satisfies $next(sc) = sc - 1$.

2.2 Compositional Reasoning Example

Consider a system composed of two components. The first component sends an alive signal (variable *alv*) to the second component unless there is a fault (variable *flt*). The second component monitors the alive signal and, if absent, raises an alarm (variable *alm*). Globally, we expect that if there is a fault, an alarm is triggered in due time. The components use clocks *cl1* and *cl2*, while the global clock is *cl*.

The compositional reasoning is formalized with the following formula:

$$(G(flt \rightarrow G^{cl1}_{\leq p} \neg alv) \wedge G(G^{cl2}_{\leq p} \neg alv \rightarrow (F^{cl2}_{\leq p} alarm))) \rightarrow G(flt \rightarrow F^{cl}_{\leq p} alm)$$

The formula is valid if the clocks are not skewed. If instead the clocks diverge, the formulas $G^{cl1}_{\leq p} \neg alv$ and $G^{cl2}_{\leq p} \neg alv$ are not equivalent anymore (similarly for $F^{cl2}_{\leq p} alm$ and $F^{cl}_{\leq p} alm$). In this case, we need to consider safety margins in the guarantees of the two components. Let us assume that the error on the clock derivatives is bounded by ϵ. For simplicity, let us also consider for the moment no reset. In this case, given $= \tilde{\epsilon} = 1 + 2\epsilon/(1-\epsilon)$, we can prove that the following formula is valid:

$$(G(flt \rightarrow G^{cl1}_{\leq p\tilde{\epsilon}} \neg alv) \wedge G(G^{cl2}_{\leq p} \neg alv \rightarrow (F^{cl2}_{\leq p} alm))) \rightarrow G(flt \rightarrow F^{cl}_{\leq p\tilde{\epsilon}} alm)$$

Let us now consider resets. Intuitively, assuming that the clocks are reset with period q and that q is much smaller than p, we can reduce the safety margins. In particular, the resulting formula is:

$$\begin{aligned}&(G((Reset(cl1) \rightarrow next(cl1) = cl) \wedge (Reset(cl2) \rightarrow next(cl2) = cl) \wedge (\neg Reset(cl)\\&)) \wedge GF^{cl}_{\leq q}(next(cl) = cl1) \wedge GF^{cl}_{\leq q}(next(cl) = cl2) \wedge r \geq q(1 + 2\epsilon/(1-\epsilon)) \wedge\\&G(flt \rightarrow \overline{G}^{cl1}_{\leq p} \neg alv) \wedge G(\overline{G}^{cl2}_{\leq p-4r} \neg alv \rightarrow (\overline{F}^{cl2}_{\leq p} alm))) \rightarrow G(flt \rightarrow \overline{F}^{cl}_{\leq p+2r} alm)\end{aligned}$$

First, note that we use the "first-interval" variants. In fact, we require that after a fault the alive signal of the first component is down for an interval without discontinuity; similarly, when the second component sends an alarm it cannot rely on a future reset and must send it within the first interval in which the local clock is below the given bound.

Second, let us consider the assumptions on the resets. The first row says that whenever the clocks *cl*1 and *cl*2 are reset, they are set to the value of *cl*, and *cl* is never reset. The second row requires that at most every q time units the clocks are reset.

Summarizing, the logic addressed by the paper considers metric operators with parametric upper (or lower) bounds, super-dense semantics, resettable skewed clocks, and first-order constraints on the clocks and parameters.

3 Related Work

Various works customized the modal operators of temporal logics to better suit the specification of DRTS. TPTL was extended in [24] by using explicitly multiple local clocks and supporting inequalities to express constraints on the precedence between local clock readings. In [18], a distributed variant of ECTL is proposed. Similarly, [17] defines a distributed modal logic where the time varies independently in each component of the system, represented by a network of timed automata. In all these works, local times are assumed strictly increasing, thus, not addressing the semantic issues of the temporal operators when the time is not monotonic.

The problem of modelling DRTS with drifting and synchronized clocks was considered in [21], where specific patterns of timed automata were proposed and verified. Similarly, [5] considers the problem of parametrized verification of 8N1 and Biphase Mark protocols with skewed clocks using the SAL model checker [14]. These works focus on the modelling of clock drifts and synchronizations, but do not consider the specification of timed properties that refer to skewed synchronized clocks.

The problem of validating the correctness of drifted clocks synchronization algorithms have been studied in other works using theorem provers, e.g., [2,22].

The work closer to the problem addressed in this paper is focused on the satisfiability of MTL and TPTL over non-monotonic time, which has been studied in [7] in the more general context of data words. Timed words are considered a special case, although [7] considers only discrete time. A decision procedure is given for the fragment without negation and only temporal operators X and F. Instead, we address an undecidable fragment of MTLSK with SMT-based model checking.

Last, we mention [15], which focuses on runtime verification of MTL formulas in a distributed system. Here, the authors address the problem of monitoring global properties on all traces that are compatible with a given sequence of local observations with timestamps taking into account the possible drift of local clocks. Thus, the metric operators are not, as in our case, used in local properties and related to local clocks.

4 First-Order LTL over Discrete or Super-Dense Time

4.1 Discrete and Super-Dense Time

A time model is a structure $\tau = \langle T, <, \mathbf{0}, \upsilon \rangle$ with a temporal domain T, a total order $<$ over T, a minimum element $\mathbf{0} \in T$, and a function $\upsilon : T \to \mathbb{R}_0^+$ that represents the real-time of a time point in T. A *time point* is an element of T. A time interval sequence is a sequence $I_0, I_1, I_2, \dots$ of intervals of reals such that, for all $i \geq 0$, I_i and I_{i+1} are almost adjacent (subsequent intervals can overlap in at most one point) and $\bigcup_{i \geq 0} I_i = \mathbb{R}_0^+$.

- In discrete time models, $T = \mathbb{N}$, $\mathbf{0}$ and $<$ are the standard zero and order over natural numbers, $\upsilon(0) = 0$ and $\upsilon(0), \upsilon(1), \upsilon(2), \dots$ is a non-decreasing divergent sequence.
- In super-dense time models, 1) $T \subset \mathbb{N} \times \mathbb{R}_0^+$ such that the sequence of sets $I_0, I_1, I_2, \dots$ where, for all $i \geq 0$, the set $I_i := \{r \mid \langle i, r \rangle \in T\}$, is a time interval sequence, 2) $\langle i, r \rangle < \langle i', r' \rangle$ iff $i < i'$ or $i = i'$ and $r < r'$, 3) $\mathbf{0} = \langle 0, 0 \rangle \in \mathbb{N} \times \mathbb{R}_0^+$, and 4) $\upsilon(\langle i, r \rangle) = r$.

Intuitively, super-dense time models consist of the union of discrete sets of points in the form $\langle i, r\rangle, \langle i+1, r\rangle, \ldots$ (with the same timestamp r) and dense sets (containing an uncountable number of time points with different timestamps) of the form $\langle i, r\rangle, \langle i, r'\rangle, \langle i, r''\rangle, \ldots$ (with the same counter i). If $\langle i, r\rangle, \langle i+1, r\rangle \in T$, we say that there is a discrete step in $\langle i, r\rangle$ and we define a partial function *succ* as $succ(\langle i, r\rangle) = \langle i+1, r\rangle$ if there is a discrete step in $\langle i, r\rangle$.

4.2 Linear Temporal Logic

We consider First-Order Linear-time Temporal Logic that we denote as LTL for short. LTL formulas are interpreted over discrete and super-dense time models. Following [9], the "tomorrow"[1] operator X is generalized to the super-dense time case and we include its "dense counterpart" $\tilde{X}$. Intuitively, $X\phi$ holds in t whenever there is a discrete step in t and ϕ holds in $succ(t)$, while $\tilde{X}\phi$ holds in t whenever there is no discrete step in t and ϕ holds in a right neighborhood of t (formally defined below). It should be noted that $X\varphi$ is equivalent to $\bot\tilde{U}\varphi$ where $\tilde{U}$ is until with the "strict" semantics (in which $t' \geq t$ is replaced by $t' > t$ in the semantics). $\bot\tilde{U}\varphi$ disallow t' to have a point t'' such that $t < t'' < t'$; thus, t' must be $succ(t)$. Moreover, $\tilde{X}\varphi$ is equivalent to $\neg X\top \wedge \varphi\tilde{U}\top$: there is no discrete step and all points t'' preceding t' satisfy φ.

First-order formulae are composed of Boolean logic connectives, a given set of variables V and a first-order signature Σ.

Definition 1. *Given a signature Σ and a set of variables V, LTL formulas φ are built with the following grammar:*

$$\phi := pred(u, \ldots, u) \mid \phi \wedge \phi \mid \neg\phi \mid \phi U \phi \mid X\phi \mid \tilde{X}\phi$$
$$u := c \mid x \mid next(x) \mid f(u, \ldots, u) \mid ite(\varphi, u, u)$$

where c, f, and pred are respectively a constant, a function, and a predicate of the signature Σ and x is a variable in V.

Note that atomic formulas can constrain the "current" and "next" value of variables. We call a predicate with no occurrence of *next* a state predicate, otherwise an event predicate. Event predicates are evaluated between two states during discrete transitions, next symbols are evaluated considering the subsequent state while current symbols are evaluated in the current state.

We use standard abbreviations:

$$\varphi_1 \vee \varphi_2 := \neg(\neg\varphi_1 \wedge \neg\varphi_2),\ \varphi_1 \mathcal{R} \varphi_2 := \neg(\neg\varphi_1 U \neg\varphi_2),\ F\varphi := (\top U \varphi),\ G\varphi := \neg F \neg\varphi.$$

A state $s = \langle M, \mu\rangle$ is given by a first-order structure M and an assignment μ of variables of V into the domain of M. Given a state $s = \langle M, \mu\rangle$ and a symbol c in Σ or variable $x \in V$, we use $s(c)$ to denote the interpretation of c in M and $s(x)$ to denote the value $\mu(x)$ assigned by μ to x. Given M, let V^M be the set of states with first-order structure M. A trace $\pi = \langle M, \tau, \overline{\mu}\rangle$ is given by a first-order structure M, a time model τ, and a mapping $\overline{\mu}$ from the domain of τ to V^M.

[1] Note: "next" is used to refer to *next* instead of X.

Given a trace $\pi = \langle M, \tau, \overline{\mu} \rangle$ and $t \in \tau$, we denote by $\pi(t)$ the state $\langle M, \overline{\mu}(t) \rangle$. Note that the first-order structure M is shared by all time points, meaning that the interpretation of the symbols in the signature Σ is rigid (it does not vary with time). Terms that do not contain variables are called *parameters* and the interpretation does not depend on the time point.

We assume a Σ first-order theory $\mathcal{T}$ to be given. Given a Σ first-order structure M, an assignment μ to variables of V, and a Σ first-order formula ϕ over V, we use the standard notion of $\langle M, \mu \rangle \models_{\mathcal{T}} \phi$. In the rest of the paper, we omit the first-order signature Σ and theory $\mathcal{T}$ for simplicity.

Given a trace $\pi = \langle M, \tau, \overline{\mu} \rangle$, a time point t of τ, and a Σ formula ϕ, we define $\pi, t \models \phi$ as follows:

- if α is a state predicate, $\pi, t \models \alpha$ iff $\pi(t) \models \alpha$
- if α is an event predicate, $\pi, t \models \alpha$ iff there is a discrete step in t and $\pi(t) \cdot \pi(succ(t)) \models \alpha$
- $\pi, t \models \phi_1 \wedge \phi_2$ iff $\pi, t \models \phi_1$ and $\pi, t \models \phi_2$
- $\pi, t \models \neg\phi$ iff $\pi, t \not\models \phi$
- $\pi, t \models \phi_1 U \phi_2$ iff there exists $t' \geq t$ such that $\pi, t' \models \phi_2$ and for all $t'', t \leq t'' < t', \pi, t'' \models \phi_1$
- $\pi, t \models X\phi$ iff there is discrete step in t and $\pi, succ(t) \models \phi$
- $\pi, t \models \tilde{X}\phi$ iff there is not a discrete step in t and there exists $t' > t$, for all t'', $t < t'' < t'$, $\pi, t'' \models \phi$

Finally, $\pi \models \phi$ iff $\pi, \mathbf{0} \models \phi$. We say that ϕ is satisfiable iff there exists π such that $\pi \models \phi$. We say that ϕ is valid iff, for all π, $\pi \models \phi$.

5 MTL with Skewed Clocks and Resets

In this section, we define a variant of the logic MTLSK introduced in [4], where time constraints of metric operators use parametrized lower and upper bounds, as described in Sect. 2. Moreover, we consider only skewed clocks and superdense time, and we consider other standard logics as fragments (dense time and standard metric operators over perfect clocks).

We first formally define some assumptions on the clocks to ensure that, despite the resets, they are diverging. We assume to be given two constants ϵ and λ that are used as bounds for the drift and resets, respectively.

Definition 2. *A "resettable skewed clock" (henceforward, simply, "clock") is a real variable $c \in V$ such that, for every trace $\pi = \langle M, \tau, \overline{\mu} \rangle$ and $t = \langle i, r \rangle \in \tau$,*

1. *$\pi(t)(c)$ is differentiable in I_i with $\frac{d\pi(t)(c)}{dt} \in [1-\epsilon, 1+\epsilon]$.*
2. *If t is a discrete step $|\pi(succ(t))(c) - \nu(t)| \leq \lambda$.*

In particular, the clocks are piecewise continuous and strictly monotonic, with at most countably many resets where the clock can decrease.

Definition 3. *Given a signature Σ, a set of variables V, and a set of clock variables $C \subseteq V$, MTLSK formulas are built with the following grammar:*

$$\phi := pred(u, \ldots, u) \mid \phi \wedge \phi \mid \neg\phi \mid X\phi \mid \tilde{X}\phi \mid \phi U^c_{\lhd u}\phi \mid \phi U^c_{\rhd u}\phi \mid \phi \overline{U}^c_{\lhd u}\phi$$

where $c \in C$, $\lhd \in \{<, \leq\}$, $\rhd \in \{>, \geq\}$, and u is defined as in LTL but clock variables can occur only in event predicates.

Abbreviations are defined as in the standard case.

Note that metric operators use a clock variable in C as its reference for the timing constraints instead of the real-time, as done in [18] for ECTL.

We just define the semantics of metric operators, while the other cases are defined as for LTL. We assume here that the background first-order theory contains the theory of reals and that the clock variables and each parametric bound has real type.

- $\pi, t \models \varphi U^c_{\lhd p}\psi$ iff there exists $t' \geq t$ such that $\pi(t')(c) - \pi(t)(c) \lhd \pi(p)$ and $\pi, t' \models \psi$ and for all $t'', t \leq t'' < t', \pi, t'' \models \varphi$
- $\pi, t \models \varphi U^c_{\rhd p}\psi$ iff there exists $t' \geq t$ such that $\pi(t')(c) - \pi(t)(c) \rhd \pi(p)$ and $\pi, t' \models \psi$ and for all $t'', t \leq t'' < t', \pi, t'' \models \varphi$
- $\pi, t \models \varphi \overline{U}^c_{\lhd p}\psi$ iff there exists $t' \geq t$ such that $\pi(t')(c) - \pi(t)(c) \lhd \pi(p)$, $\pi, t' \models \psi$, and for all t'', $t \leq t'' < t'$, $\pi, t'' \models \varphi$ and $\pi(t'')(c) - \pi(t)(c) \lhd \pi(p)$

We recall the theorem proved in [4], which holds also for the parametric variant proposed here.

Theorem 1. *For all trace π, formulas φ, ψ: $\pi \models \varphi \overline{U}^c_{\lhd p}\psi \Rightarrow \pi \models \varphi U^c_{\lhd p}\psi$.*
If there is no reset (weakly monotonic case),

$$\pi \models \varphi \overline{U}^c_{\lhd p}\psi \Leftrightarrow \pi \models \varphi U^c_{\lhd p}\psi$$

Also, if there is no drift and no reset, i.e., $\epsilon = 0 \wedge \lambda = 0$ (perfect clocks), then

$$\pi \models \varphi \overline{U}^c_{\lhd p}\psi \Leftrightarrow \pi \models \varphi U_{\lhd p}\psi \Leftrightarrow \pi \models \varphi U^c_{\lhd p}\psi$$

Remark. As we discussed in Sect. 2, the non-monotonicity of the resettable clocks create some challenges as the time constraints defined by the metric operators are not simple intervals of $\mathbb{R}^+_0$. In fact, if we consider the formula $F^c_{\leq p} send$, Fig. 2a shows an execution in which *send* occurs in the near future but the clock difference is negative.

Most important, as shown in Sect. 2, the time intervals may be disconnected. Thus, it is not sufficient to look at the first occurrence of the subformulas, but we have to consider the minimum value of clocks. Consider for example the liveness property $\phi_{BR} := G(receive(msg) \rightarrow F^c_{\leq 1} send(ACK_{msg}))$ representing the bounded response of a component when it receives a message. Figure 2b shows an execution where the component receives the message at instant $t = 1$ while the local clock exits the time interval bounded by 1 but is later reset to a value lower than $c(t) + 1$. The component then sends the acknowledgement for the message msg within the time constraint and the property holds.

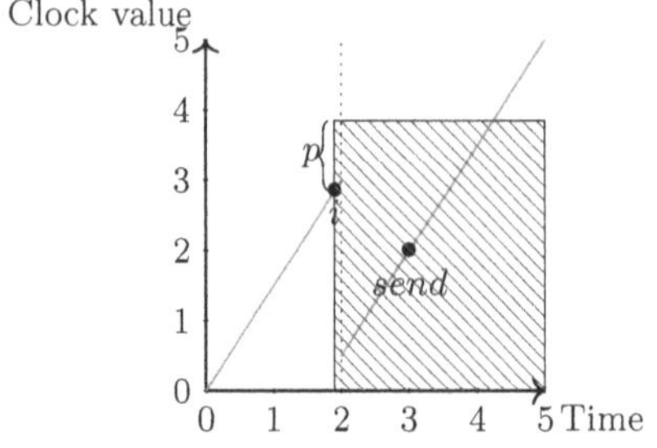

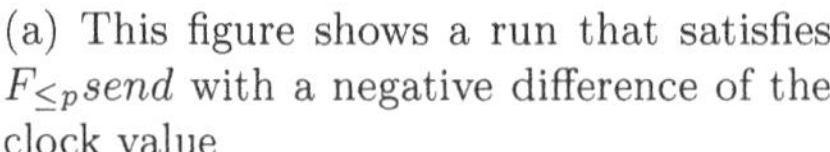
(a) This figure shows a run that satisfies $F_{\leq p} send$ with a negative difference of the clock value

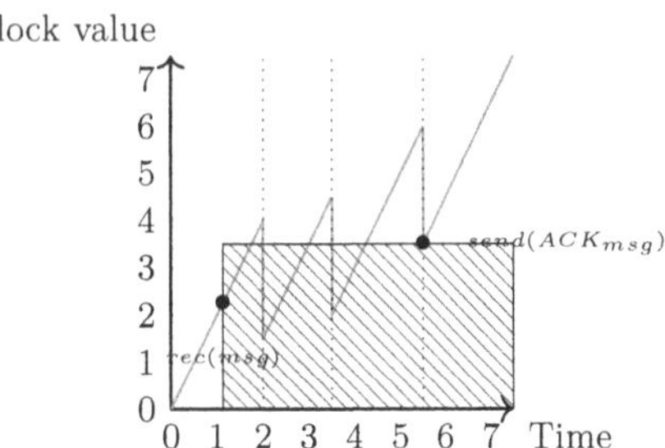

(b) Example trace satisfying ϕ_{BR} with an ack after a reset

Fig. 2. .

The key observation here is that it is sufficient to track the minimum value of c after t where the acknowledgement is sent and check if that is within the bound. With the operator $\overline{F}^c_{\leq p}$ instead we can express the property that the ack is sent within the *first* interval before $t + p$. In this case, we can therefore track the first point at which the acknowledgement is sent making sure that the time constraint was not violated before.

6 Encoding and Verification

In this section, we define an encoding[2] from MTLSK to first-order LTL. The encoding is divided into 3 parts: the first part considers a novel intermediate logic LTL-min-max that can express MTLSK properties through a straightforward rewriting Υ; the second part defines a discretization process of LTL-min-max based on the discretization proposed in [23]; the last part defines an encoding from LTL-min-max to First-order LTL.

6.1 LTL-min-max Definition and Rewriting

We construct a new intermediate logic LTL-min-max extending First-order LTL with minimum and maximum operators. The intuition behind this logic follows from the remark of Sect. 5: while the satisfaction of bounded operators in $MTL_{0,+\infty}$ can be achieved by looking at the value of time in the next occurrence of the formula, in MTLSK due to non-monotonicity of time we have to analyze the minimum and maximum time in which the property holds.

Definition 4. *Given a signature Σ, a set of variables V, and a set of clock variables $C \subseteq V$, LTL-min-max formulas are built with the following grammar:*

$$\phi := p(u, \dots, u) \mid tu \bowtie cu \mid \phi \wedge \phi \mid \neg\phi \mid \phi U \phi \mid X\phi \mid \tilde{X}\phi$$

[2] All the proofs can be found in https://es-static.fbk.eu/people/bombardelli/papers/nfm23/main_ext.pdf.

$$u := cu \mid x \mid f(u,\ldots,u) \mid ite(\phi,u,u) \mid next(u)$$
$$tu := time \mid c \mid min\Delta^c_{\phi U\phi} \mid f(tu,\ldots,tu) \mid next(c) \mid max\Delta^c_{\phi U\phi} \mid maxbef\Delta^c_{\phi}$$
$$cu := p \mid f(cu,\ldots,cu)$$

where $\bowtie \in \{\leq,\geq,<,>\}$ *and clock variables can occur only in event predicates and in min-max operator superscripts i.e.* $min\Delta^c_{\phi U\psi}$, $max\Delta^c_{\varphi U\psi}$ *and* $maxbef\Delta^c_{\varphi}$.

Definition 5. *The semantics of LTL-min-max new operators is defined as follows:*

$$\textit{If } \pi,t \models \varphi U\psi \textit{ then } \pi(t)(min\Delta^c_{\varphi U\psi}) = \min(\pi(t)(U^c_{\varphi U\psi})) - \pi(t)(c)$$
$$\textit{If } \pi,t \models (\varphi U\psi)\wedge \Phi_{finU} \textit{ then } \pi(t)(max\Delta^c_{\varphi U\psi}) = \max(\pi(t)(U^c_{\varphi U\psi})) - \pi(t)(c)$$
$$\textit{If } \pi,t \models F\varphi \textit{ then } \pi(t)(maxbef\Delta^c_{\varphi}) = \max(Bef^c_{\pi}(t,\varphi)) - \pi(t)(c)$$

where: $\Phi_{finU} := F(\neg\varphi \vee G\neg\psi)$,

$$\pi(t)(U^c_{\varphi U\psi}) := \{\pi(t')(c) \mid t' \geq t : \pi,t' \models \psi \textit{ and for all } t \leq t'' < t' : \pi,t'' \models \varphi\},$$
$$\pi(t)(Bef^c_{\varphi}) := \{\pi(t')(c) \mid t' \geq t : \textit{ for all } t < t'' < t' : \pi,t'' \not\models \varphi\}.$$

$\pi(t)(U^c_{\varphi U\psi})$ represents the value of each $\pi(t')(c)$ such that ψ holds at point t' and each point between t and t' (excluded) satisfies φ. This set takes all the witnesses of π satisfying $\varphi U\psi$ from point t; then, it extracts the value of c at point t' i.e. when ψ holds. $min\Delta^c_{\varphi U\psi}$ and $max\Delta^c_{\varphi U\psi}$ represent respectively the minimum and the maximum of that set. The existence of the minimum of $\pi(t)(U^c_{\varphi U\psi})$ is guaranteed if $\varphi U\psi$ holds. $\pi,t \models \varphi U\psi$ is a sufficient condition because clocks diverge (see Definition 2) and ψ contains clocks only inside event predicates. Similarly, the assumptions on $max\Delta$ guarantee that the maximum exists if the property holds and it holds only finitely many times. If Φ_{finU} does not hold, then the maximum does not exist because the clock diverges.

$\pi(t)(Bef^c_{\psi})$ is the set containing all clock values from point t to the first point such that ψ holds after t. $maxbef\Delta^c_{\psi}$ represents the maximum in that set. $F\varphi$ guarantees the existence of the maximum of that set.

Definition 6. *We define the rewriting* Υ *from MTLSK to LTL-min-max as follows:*

$$\Upsilon(\varphi U^c_{\lhd p}\psi) := \Upsilon(\varphi U\psi) \wedge min\Delta_{\Upsilon(\varphi U\psi)} \lhd p$$
$$\Upsilon(\varphi U^c_{\rhd p}\psi) := \Upsilon(G(\varphi \wedge F\psi)) \vee \Upsilon(\varphi U\psi) \wedge max\Delta_{\Upsilon(\varphi U\psi)} \rhd p$$
$$\Upsilon(\varphi \overline{U}^c_{\lhd p}\psi) := \Upsilon(\varphi U\psi) \wedge maxbef\Delta^c_{\Upsilon(\psi)} \lhd p$$

Theorem 2. φ *and* $\Upsilon(\varphi)$ *are equisatisfiable*

Proof (Sketch). $\varphi U^c_{\bowtie p}\psi$ is true at point t only if there exist a point t' such that ψ hold, $\pi(t')(c) - \pi(t)(c) \bowtie \pi(p)$ and all points from t to t' satisfy φ. Since $min\Delta^c_{\varphi U\psi}$ and $max\Delta^c_{\varphi U\psi}$ are respectively the minimum/maximum of the set containing the evaluation of c in each t' point minus $\pi(t)(c)$, then the translation holds. The same applies to $\varphi\overline{U}^c_{\lhd p}\psi$. In that case, the property holds iff $\varphi U\psi$ holds and each value of $\pi(t'')(c)$ with $t \leq t'' \leq t'$ is not greater than the upper bound $\pi(t)(c) + \pi(p)$. Thus, it is sufficient to verify that the $max(\pi(t)(Bef)) - \pi(t)(c) \lhd \pi(p)$.

6.2 LTL-min-max Discretization

We apply our discretization process based on the one defined in [23]. The discretization process defines time evolution as a sequence of open or singular intervals. The discretization process assumes that the satisfiability of each subformula of ϕ does not vary inside intervals. That assumption is ensured because MTLSK allows clocks only as part of event predicates.

Singular intervals are encoded by the fresh variable ι while the time elapsed in each interval is encoded by δ. The real variable ζ encodes an arbitrary accumulation of sums of δ. ζ is used to guarantee the divergence of the global time. For each skewed clock c, we introduce two fresh variables: δ_c and diff_c. δ_c encodes the clock time elapse in each transition while diff_c represents the difference between the global time and the current clock value c. We encode c using diff_c to guarantee the divergence of c relying on the divergence of global time.

The rewritten formula ϕ_D is composed of four parts: the constraints defining time and forcing discrete variables to stutter when time elapses (ψ_{time}), the constraints defining each clock c according to Definition 2 (ψ^c_{clock}), the constraint to define when an interval is open or when it is singular (ψ_ι) and the discretized formula ($\mathcal{D}(\phi)$). The whole transformation is as follows:

$$\phi_D := \psi_{time} \wedge \bigwedge_{c \in C} \psi^c_{clock} \wedge \psi_\iota \wedge \mathcal{D}(\phi)$$

$$\psi_{time} := time = 0 \wedge G(next(time) - time = \delta) \wedge G(\delta > 0 \rightarrow \bigwedge_{v \in V} (next(v) = v))$$

$$\begin{aligned} \psi^c_{clock} :=& \mathit{diff}_c = 0 \wedge G(next(\mathit{diff}_c) - \mathit{diff}_c = \delta_c - \delta) \wedge \\ & G((\delta > 0 \rightarrow \delta_c \in [\delta(1-\epsilon), \delta(1+\epsilon)]) \wedge (\delta = 0 \rightarrow |\mathit{diff}_c| \leq \lambda)) \\ \psi_\iota :=& \iota \wedge G((\iota \wedge \delta = 0 \wedge X\iota) \vee (\iota \wedge \delta > 0 \wedge X\neg\iota) \vee (\neg\iota \wedge \delta > 0 \wedge X\iota)) \wedge \\ & G((next(\zeta) - \zeta = \delta) \vee (\zeta \geq 1 \wedge \zeta = 0)) \wedge GF(\zeta \geq 1 \wedge next(\zeta) = 0) \end{aligned}$$

Definition 7. *The discretization rewriting $\mathcal{D}$ is defined as follows:*

$$\begin{aligned} & \mathcal{D}(X\varphi) := \iota \wedge X(\iota \wedge \mathcal{D}(\varphi)) \quad \mathcal{D}(\tilde{X}\varphi) := (\neg\iota \wedge \mathcal{D}(\phi)) \vee X(\neg\iota \wedge \mathcal{D}(\varphi)) \\ & \mathcal{D}(\varphi U \psi) := \mathcal{D}(\psi) \vee (\mathcal{D}(\varphi) U \tilde{\psi}) \quad \mathcal{D}(maxbef\,\Delta^c_\varphi) := maxbef\,\Delta^c_{\mathcal{D}(\varphi)} \\ & \mathcal{D}(min\Delta^c_{\varphi U \psi}) := ite(\mathcal{D}(\psi) \wedge 0 \leq min\Delta^c_{\mathcal{D}(\varphi) U \tilde{\psi}}, 0, min\Delta^c_{\mathcal{D}(\varphi) U \tilde{\psi}}) \\ & \mathcal{D}(max\Delta^c_{\varphi U \psi}) := ite(\mathcal{D}(\psi) \wedge 0 \geq max\Delta^c_{\mathcal{D}(\varphi) U \tilde{\psi}}, 0, max\Delta^c_{\mathcal{D}(\varphi) U \tilde{\psi}}) \\ & \textit{where } \tilde{\psi} = \mathcal{D}(\psi) \wedge (\iota \vee \mathcal{D}(\varphi)). \end{aligned}$$

$X\varphi$ is discretized forcing a discrete transition i.e. $\iota \wedge X\iota$. $\tilde{X}\varphi$ requires that either φ holds now in an open interval or it holds in the next state in an open interval. Until forces either ψ to hold now or φ has to hold until ψ holds; moreover, if ψ holds in an open interval also φ must hold in that point too. The discretization of $min\Delta^c_{\varphi U \psi}$ and $max\Delta^c_{\varphi U \psi}$ is similar to the one of until. It considers the current point in the minimum/maximum computation as a candidate min/max and then applies the discrete operator on the discretized until.

Theorem 3. *ϕ and ϕ_D are equisatisfiable*

6.3 LTL-min-max Discrete Encoding

The discrete setting enables recursive definitions of minimum and maximum. Consider for instance the set $S^v_{\top}$ which stores the values of variable v at each time point. $\pi(t)(S^v_{\top})$ can be defined by the following recursive definition: $\pi(t)(S^v_{\top}) = \{\pi(t)(v)\} \cup \pi(t+1)(S^v_{\top})$. Our discrete encoding of LTL-min-max exploits this inductive structure of $U^c_{\varphi U \psi}$ and Bef^c_{φ} to provide a sound translation to first-order LTL. Our encoding introduces new monitor variables representing $min\Delta^c_{\varphi U \psi}$, $max\Delta^c_{\varphi U \psi}$ and $maxbef\Delta^c_{\varphi}$. Each operator is replaced with the monitor in the formula and the formula is implied by the monitor constraints.

In the remainder of this section, we denote $\rho' := next(\rho)$, $\delta_c := c' - c$ and $\tilde{U}$ as the "strict" version of U operator (also expressible as $\varphi \tilde{U} \psi := \varphi \wedge X(\varphi U \psi)$ in the discrete setting).

$$\begin{aligned}Repl(\Psi, min\Delta^c_{\varphi U \psi}) := G(\varphi U \psi \rightarrow \rho_{min\Delta^c_{\varphi U \psi}} = \\ ite(\psi \wedge (\neg(\varphi \tilde{U} \psi) \vee 0 \leq \rho'_{min\Delta^c_{\varphi U \psi}} + \delta_c), 0, \rho'_{min\Delta^c_{\varphi U \psi}} + \delta_c) \wedge \\ (F(\psi \wedge \rho_{min\Delta^c_{\varphi U \psi}} = 0))) \rightarrow \Psi\lceil min\Delta^c_{\varphi U \psi} / \rho_{min\Delta^c_{\varphi U \psi}} \rfloor\end{aligned}$$

The value of $\rho_{min\Delta^c_{\varphi U \psi}}$ is evaluated as the minimum only when $\varphi U \psi$ holds; otherwise, $min(U^c_{\varphi U \psi})$ would be undefined. The ite expression evaluates the minimum between 0 and $\rho'_{min\Delta^c_{\varphi U \psi}} + \delta_c$ $(min(\pi(succ(t))(U^c_{\varphi U \psi}))$. Finally, $F(\psi \wedge \rho_{min\Delta^c_{\varphi U \psi}} = 0)$ guarantees that a minimum exists.

Theorem 4. *Ψ and $Repl(\Psi, min\Delta^c_{\varphi U \psi})$ are equisatisfiable*

$$\begin{aligned}Repl(\Psi, max\Delta^c_{\varphi U \psi}) := G((\varphi U \psi) \wedge \Phi_{finU} \rightarrow \rho_{max\Delta^c_{\varphi U \psi}} = \\ ite(\psi \wedge (\neg(\varphi \tilde{U} \psi) \vee 0 \geq \rho'_{max\Delta^c_{\varphi U \psi}} + \delta_c), 0, \rho'_{max\Delta^c_{\varphi U \psi}} + \delta_c) \wedge \\ (F(\psi \wedge \rho_{max\Delta^c_{\varphi U \psi}} = 0))) \rightarrow \Psi\lceil max\Delta^c_{\varphi U \psi} / \rho_{max\Delta^c_{\varphi U \psi}} \rfloor\end{aligned}$$

The encoding of $max\Delta$ is the same as the one of $min\Delta$ only flipping the sign and introducing the constraint Φ_{finU} from Definition 5 to evaluate the monitor only if the maximum exists i.e. the formula holds finitely often.

Theorem 5. *Ψ and $Repl(\Psi, max\Delta^c_{\varphi U \psi})$ are equisatisfiable*

$$\begin{aligned}&Repl(\Psi, maxbef\Delta^c_{\varphi}) := G(F\varphi \rightarrow \rho_{maxbef\Delta^c_{\varphi}} = \\ &ite(\varphi \vee 0 \geq \rho'_{maxbef\Delta^c_{\varphi}} + \delta_c, 0, \rho'_{maxbef\Delta^c_{\varphi}} + \delta_c)) \rightarrow \Psi\lceil maxbef\Delta^c_{\varphi} / \rho_{maxbef\Delta^c_{\varphi}} \rfloor\end{aligned}$$

The encoding of $maxbef\Delta$ evaluates the maximum of c before and including the first point in which φ holds.

Theorem 6. *Ψ and $Repl(\Psi, maxbef\Delta^c_{\psi})$ are equisatisfiable*

Table 1. Some MTLSK properties and their verification results.

Formula	Time in sec.	λ	ϵ	alg	valid
$G(\overline{F}^c_{\leq p}a \rightarrow F^c_{\leq p}a)$	2.81	any	any	ic3	True
$F(c = p) \rightarrow F(((\overline{G}^c_{\leq p}a) \wedge (\overline{G}^c_{\geq p}\neg a)) \rightarrow \bot)$	3.62	any	0.4	kzeno	True
$(q \geq p) \rightarrow G((\overline{G}^c_{\leq q}a) \rightarrow (\overline{G}^c_{\leq p}a))$	0.38	any	any	ic3	True
$G^c_{\leq p}a \rightarrow G(a \vee c > p)$	9.03	any	any	kzeno	True
$G^c_{\leq p}a \rightarrow G(a \vee c > p)$	1.09	any	any	ic3	True
$(q \geq p) \rightarrow G((G^c_{\geq p}a) \rightarrow (G^c_{\geq q}a))$	2.22	any	any	ic3	True
$\Phi_{exp} := q = p(2+\epsilon) + 2\lambda \wedge (G(fault \rightarrow G\neg alive) \wedge G(\overline{G}^{cl}_{\leq p}\neg alive \rightarrow (\overline{F}^{cl}_{\leq p}alarm))) \rightarrow G(fault \rightarrow F_{[0,q]}alarm)$	94.26	14.0	0.1	ic3	True
$(G((Reset(cl1) \rightarrow next(cl1) = cl) \wedge (\neg Reset(cl))) \wedge GF^{cl}_{\leq q}(next(cl) = cl1)) \rightarrow G(cl - cl1 \leq q * (1 + 2\epsilon/(1-\epsilon)))$	7.05	any	any	kzeno	True
$G(f \rightarrow \overline{G}^{cl1}_{\leq p}\neg alv) \wedge G(\overline{G}^{cl2}_{\leq p-4r}\neg alv \rightarrow (\overline{F}^{cl2}_{\leq p}alm))) \rightarrow G(f \rightarrow \overline{F}^{cl}_{\leq p+2r}alm)$	19.86	any	any	ic3	True
$G(F^c_{\leq p}a \rightarrow \overline{F}^c_{\leq p}a)$	0.27	any	any	bmc	False
$G((a \vee Xa) \rightarrow (F^c_{\leq 0}a \wedge F^c_{\geq 0}a))$	0.18	any	any	bmc	False
Bounded Response invalid with 11 clocks	1.36	any	any	bmc	False

7 Results

In this section, we present the implementation and experimental analysis of the procedure we described in the previous section to prove the validity and satisfiability of MTLSK formulas.

7.1 Implementation

We implemented MTLSK verification as an extension of timed nuXmv [8]. We used the following model-checking algorithms to verify the validity and satisfiability of the formulas: kzeno [11] in lockstep with bmc, ic3-ia [10], bmc [8] (with diverging variables). The algorithms used inside nuXmv are constructed on top of MathSAT5 [12] SMT-solver, which supports combinations of theories such as $\mathcal{LIA}$, $\mathcal{LRA}$ and $\mathcal{EUF}$. Unlike the logic definition of Sect. 5, our implementation permits the usage of formulas containing clocks in state predicates (e.g., $G(c - c1 \leq p)$ is allowed). Indeed, we introduced continuity constraints of [23] inside the discretization process to relax this syntactic restriction. Our implementation considers λ and ϵ constants from Sect. 5 to instantiate bounds for resettable clocks. These parameters are defined inside the SMV model either as scalar values (DEFINE) or as a parameter (FROZENVAR).

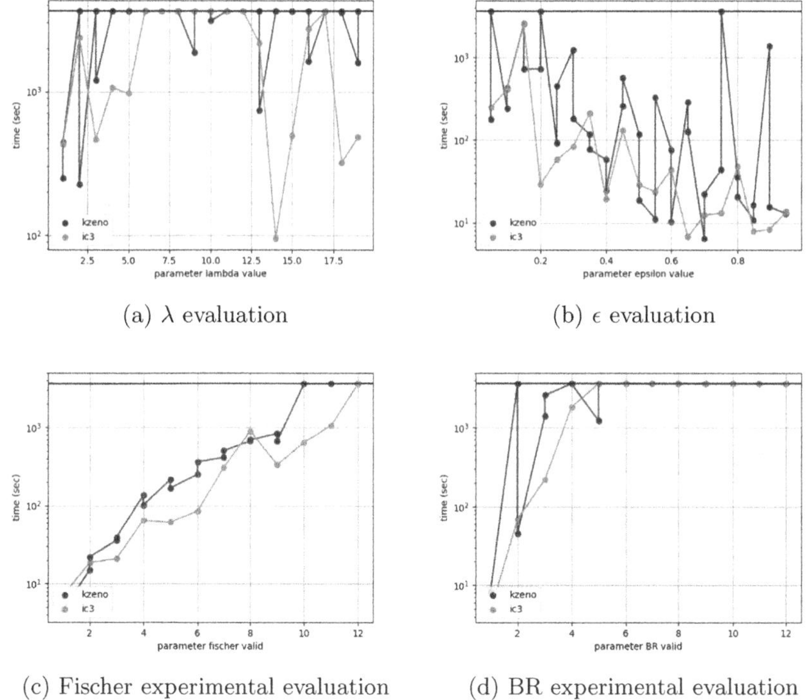

(a) λ evaluation

(b) ϵ evaluation

(c) Fischer experimental evaluation

(d) BR experimental evaluation

Fig. 3. Parametric experimental evaluations

7.2 Experimental Evaluation

We are not aware of other tools supporting MTLSK or other variations of MTL over resettable skewed clock; therefore, our experimental evaluation is performed only on our implementation. The experiments[3] were run in parallel on a cluster with nodes with Intel Xeon CPU running at 2.40 GHz with 12CPU, 64 GB. The timeout for each run was one hour and the memory cap was set to 1 GB. The experimental evaluation considers the scalability of the tool concerning λ, ϵ, formulas size and until bound.

Benchmarks. Our experiment is divided into the following groups:

The first group of formulas is composed of a chain of *bounded response* (BR) where each local component i sends to its successor message a_i in at most p time unit where p is a parameter and time is interpreted as the local clock c_i. Finally, given a parametrized maximum bound r between local clocks and the global clock, the bounded response chain guarantees that $q = 2n(p + r)$ is the right bound for the global bounded response.

$$G(\bigwedge_{0\leq i<n}((a_i \rightarrow \overline{F}^{c_i}_{\leq p} a_{i+1}) \wedge (c - c_i \leq r \wedge c_i - c \leq r))) \rightarrow G(a_0 \rightarrow \overline{F}^{c}_{\leq q} a_n)$$

[3] The results of the experimental evaluation can be found at https://es-static.fbk.eu/people/bombardelli/papers/nfm23/nfm23.tar.gz.

The second group of formulas is a Fischer algorithm benchmark taken from [8] MTL experimental evaluation and adapted for MTLSK. The pool of formulas is parametrized over the number of components. Each component has its skewed clock and a local formula representing its behaviour, the conjunction of all the formulas is used to imply a property of the first component.

The third group of formulas are a variation of the example proposed in Sect. 2 that instantiates the parameters p, λ and ϵ to study their impact on the validity checking performance. We also considered a timed and simplified version of a Wheel Brake System model of [13]. Given a redundant signal of the brake pedal, a redundant braking component, the property states that the hydraulic system should brake before a specified time threshold if the redundant components do not fail at the same time. This property has been translated to MTLSK and each component has been augmented with a local clock.

The last group is a collection of roughly 100 MTLSK specifications, 60 valid and 40 invalid, defined to validate the semantics and the implementation.

Experimental Results. Table 1 shows the results on a subset of formulas. The solver proves most of the tautologies of group 4 in less than 10 s and 38 properties were proved in less than 2 s. All the invalid properties of this group were disproved in less than 2 s with the bmc algorithm. Moreover, we performed an experimental evaluation using the example defined in Sect. 2. We were able to prove the example by splitting the property into two parts. First, we proved that q is an upper bound for the maximum distances between c and $c1$ if $c1$ is synchronized to c every r time unit. Second, we proved that assuming a maximum distance between c and the other clocks the property holds.

The experiments on λ and ϵ pointed out the instability brought by instantiating these parameters to an arbitrary value. In particular, Fig. 3a and Fig. 3b show the impact of the two constants increasing their values. The plots show a strong instability with jumps in execution time with both λ and ϵ.

Figure 3c shows the experimental evaluation of the Fischer algorithm formula. The IC3 algorithm proves the correctness of the formula with 11 components in less than one hour. Figure 3d shows the Bounded Response experimental evaluation. No algorithm can prove the formula with 6 components. Indeed, this model is challenging because to prove that the global component sees a_n before q time units we need to ensure that each component skewed does not delay too much the response. Moreover, this model is parametrized over λ, ϵ, p and r; thus, the solver needs to explore a larger state space.

8 Conclusions

In this paper, we addressed the problem of automated reasoning with MTLSK properties, a variant of MTL for DRTS with local clocks that are skewed and resettable. To cope with the non-monotonicity of timing constraints in the presence of resets, we introduce min/max operators that guess the min/max value of clocks when subformulas are satisfied. We described and implemented an encoding into LTL satisfiability modulo theory. The results show that the approach is feasible and can be used to assess the validity of formulas for different configurations of the skewed resettable clocks. In the future, we would like to investigate more efficient techniques to find counterexamples based on bounded model checking with different clocks as in [6]; we would study the impact of non-monotonic resets on the compositional reasoning with input/output data [3]; we would like to cover a deeper case study concerning real life examples such as 8N1 protocol and Biphase Mark protocol; we would like to relax the constraints of resettable clocks to match more realistic assumptions on the system; finally, we would extend distributed runtime verification as in [15] to MTLSK.

Acknowledgement. We acknowledge the support of the PNRR project FAIR - Future AI Research (PE00000013), under the NRRP MUR program funded by the NextGenerationEU.

References

1. Alur, R., Henzinger, T.A.: A really temporal logic. J. ACM **41**(1), 181–204 (1994)
2. Barsotti, D., Nieto, L.P., Tiu, A.: Verification of clock synchronization algorithms: experiments on a combination of deductive tools. Electron. Notes Theor. Comput. Sci. **145**, 63–78 (2006). Proceedings of the 5th International Workshop on Automated Verification of Critical Systems (AVoCS 2005)
3. Bombardelli, A., Tonetta, S.: Asynchronous composition of local interface LTL properties. In: Deshmukh, J.V., Havelund, K., Perez, I. (eds.) NFM 2022. LNCS, pp. 508–526. Springer, Cham (2022). https://doi.org/10.1007/978-3-031-06773-0_27
4. Bombardelli, A., Tonetta, S.: Metric temporal logic with resettable skewed clocks - version with proofs. In: DATE (2023, to appear). https://es-static.fbk.eu/people/bombardelli/papers/date23/extended_abstract.pdf
5. Brown, G.M., Pike, L.: Easy parameterized verification of Biphase mark and 8N1 protocols. In: Hermanns, H., Palsberg, J. (eds.) TACAS 2006. LNCS, vol. 3920, pp. 58–72. Springer, Heidelberg (2006). https://doi.org/10.1007/11691372_4
6. Bu, L., Cimatti, A., Li, X., Mover, S., Tonetta, S.: Model checking of hybrid systems using shallow synchronization. In: Hatcliff, J., Zucca, E. (eds.) FMOODS/FORTE -2010. LNCS, vol. 6117, pp. 155–169. Springer, Heidelberg (2010). https://doi.org/10.1007/978-3-642-13464-7_13
7. Carapelle, C., Feng, S., Fernández Gil, O., Quaas, K.: Satisfiability for MTL and TPTL over non-monotonic data words. In: Dediu, A.-H., Martín-Vide, C., Sierra-Rodríguez, J.-L., Truthe, B. (eds.) LATA 2014. LNCS, vol. 8370, pp. 248–259. Springer, Cham (2014). https://doi.org/10.1007/978-3-319-04921-2_20
8. Cimatti, A., Griggio, A., Magnago, E., Roveri, M., Tonetta, S.: Extending nuXmv with timed transition systems and timed temporal properties. In: Dillig, I., Tasiran, S. (eds.) CAV 2019. LNCS, vol. 11561, pp. 376–386. Springer, Cham (2019). https://doi.org/10.1007/978-3-030-25540-4_21
9. Cimatti, A., Griggio, A., Magnago, E., Roveri, M., Tonetta, S.: SMT-based satisfiability of first-order LTL with event freezing functions and metric operators. Inf. Comput. **272**, 104502 (2019)

10. Cimatti, A., Griggio, A., Mover, S., Tonetta, S.: IC3 modulo theories via implicit predicate abstraction. In: Ábrahám, E., Havelund, K. (eds.) TACAS 2014. LNCS, vol. 8413, pp. 46–61. Springer, Heidelberg (2014). https://doi.org/10.1007/978-3-642-54862-8_4
11. Cimatti, A., Griggio, A., Mover, S., Tonetta, S.: Verifying LTL properties of hybrid systems with K-Liveness. In: Biere, A., Bloem, R. (eds.) CAV 2014. LNCS, vol. 8559, pp. 424–440. Springer, Cham (2014). https://doi.org/10.1007/978-3-319-08867-9_28
12. Cimatti, A., Griggio, A., Schaafsma, B.J., Sebastiani, R.: The MathSAT5 SMT solver. In: Piterman, N., Smolka, S.A. (eds.) TACAS 2013. LNCS, vol. 7795, pp. 93–107. Springer, Heidelberg (2013). https://doi.org/10.1007/978-3-642-36742-7_7
13. Damm, W., Hungar, H., Josko, B., Peikenkamp, T., Stierand, I.: Using contract-based component specifications for virtual integration testing and architecture design, pp. 1–6 (2011)
14. de Moura, L., et al.: SAL 2. In: Alur, R., Peled, D.A. (eds.) CAV 2004. LNCS, vol. 3114, pp. 496–500. Springer, Heidelberg (2004). https://doi.org/10.1007/978-3-540-27813-9_45
15. Ganguly, R., et al.: Distributed Runtime Verification of Metric Temporal Properties for Cross-Chain Protocols. CoRR, abs/2204.09796 (2022)
16. Koymans, R.: Specifying real-time properties with metric temporal logic. Real-Time Syst. **2**(4), 255–299 (1990)
17. Ortiz, J., Amrani, M., Schobbens, P.-Y.: ML_{ν}: a distributed real-time modal logic. In: Badger, J.M., Rozier, K.Y. (eds.) NFM 2019. LNCS, vol. 11460, pp. 19–35. Springer, Cham (2019). https://doi.org/10.1007/978-3-030-20652-9_2
18. Ortiz, J., Legay, A., Schobbens, P.-Y.: Distributed event clock automata. In: Bouchou-Markhoff, B., Caron, P., Champarnaud, J.-M., Maurel, D. (eds.) CIAA 2011. LNCS, vol. 6807, pp. 250–263. Springer, Heidelberg (2011). https://doi.org/10.1007/978-3-642-22256-6_23
19. Pnueli, A.: The temporal logic of programs, pp. 46–57 (1977)
20. Raskin, J.-F., Schobbens, P.-Y.: The logic of event clocks - decidability, complexity and expressiveness. J. Autom. Lang. Comb. **4**(3), 247–286 (1999)
21. Rodríguez-Navas, G., Proenza, J.: Using timed automata for modeling distributed systems with clocks: challenges and solutions. IEEE Trans. Software Eng. **39**(6), 857–868 (2013)
22. Rushby, J.M., von Henke, F.W.: Formal verification of the interactive convergence clock synchronization algorithm using EHDM (1989)
23. Tonetta, S.: Linear-time temporal logic with event freezing functions. Electron. Proc. Theor. Comput. Sci. **256**, 09 (2017)
24. Wang, F., Mok, A.K., Emerson, E.A.: Distributed real-time system specification and verification in APTL. TOSEM **2**(4), 346–378 (1993)

Centralized Multi-agent Synthesis with Spatial Constraints via Mixed-Integer Quadratic Programming

Alexandra Forsey-Smerek[1(✉)], Ho Chit Siu[2], and Kevin Leahy[2]

[1] Massachusetts Institute of Technology, Cambridge, MA 02139, USA
aforsey@mit.edu

[2] MIT Lincoln Laboratory, Lexington, MA 02139, USA
{HoChit.Siu,Kevin.Leahy}@ll.mit.edu

Abstract. We address the challenge of centralized multi-agent motion planning for tasks described in Signal Temporal Logic (STL) which require both adherence to spatial constraints and simultaneous execution of team behaviors. Existing methods to satisfy STL specifications including spatial constraints use decentralized planning approaches. These decentralized methods are unable to enforce temporal constraints jointly across agents and therefore cannot require multiple agents to complete simultaneous team behaviors. We present a mixed-integer quadratic program (MIQP) encoding of the search for multi-agent trajectories to satisfy team STL specifications in a gridworld environment. We experimentally evaluate the solve time of the centralized MIQP encoding against a centralized mixed-integer linear program (MILP) encoding in scenarios with different types of spatial constraints. Numerical results uncover that the solve time for the MIQP encoding is more suitable for problems with inter-agent spatial constraints, such as collision avoidance constraints, while the MILP encoding better suits constraints between agents and static objects in the environment. Our findings provide valuable design recommendations for implementation of either approach according to the type of spatial constraints which must be supported.

Keywords: Multi-agent systems · Plan synthesis · Signal Temporal Logic

1 Introduction

Teams of mobile robots can have a powerful impact in many industry applications such as search and rescue, package delivery, agricultural surveillance, and

DISTRIBUTION STATEMENT A. Approved for public release. Distribution is unlimited. This material is based upon work supported by the Under Secretary of Defense for Research and Engineering under Air Force Contract No. FA8702-15-D-0001. Any opinions, findings, conclusions or recommendations expressed in this material are those of the author(s) and do not necessarily reflect the views of the Under Secretary of Defense for Research and Engineering.

K. Y. Rozier and S. Chaudhuri (Eds.): NFM 2023, LNCS 13903, pp. 191–206, 2023.
https://doi.org/10.1007/978-3-031-33170-1_12

warehouse management. Motion planning for a mobile robot team often requires enforcing safety and liveness properties that take the form of temporal and spatial constraints relating to the environment and other robots. These constraints enable team behaviors such as reaching goals while avoiding collisions. It is also often necessary for multiple robots to work together on a task, further imposing spatiotemporal constraints. Signal Temporal Logic (STL) provides a language for such rule specification using concrete timing over continuous signals [9].

The use of mixed-integer linear programming (MILP) is a popular choice for control synthesis to satisfy STL specifications [10]. However, since spatial constraints are often initially expressed as Euclidean distance inequalities, linear formulations are not always amenable to rapid plan generation due to the growth in the number of constraint variables required to reformulate the quadratic form of Euclidean distances into a linear form. Thus, a mixed-integer quadratic program (MIQP) formulation may be beneficial for centralized motion planning when encoding spatial constraints. It is not obvious when to select either option, since existing solvers are heavily optimized for solving linear problems.

We present the following contributions: 1) an MIQP encoding of multi-agent planning problems leveraging a MILP encoding of STL satisfaction, 2) experimental results showing the solve times for the MIQP encoding and an equivalent MILP encoding under differing environmental and objective conditions, and 3) recommendations for when to use each type of encoding for motion planning.

2 Related Work

There has been significant research interest in generating plans for mobile robots to satisfy complex goals. Temporal logics provide a useful tool for specifying plans for individual robots and teams of robots [1,5]. Many works for multi-agent synthesis have focused on Linear Temporal Logic (LTL) [7,8,11]. These works can handle many complex problems, such as large teams [11], heterogeneous agents [8] and collaborative tasks [7] for tasks with sequence-based specifications.

Nonetheless, planning problems that require properties involving continuous signals and concrete timing (rather than merely sequence) motivates the use of STL. In this work, we consider planning in a centralized manner for a multi-agent system to satisfy a global STL specification. In [6], a scalable method for solving large planning problems for heterogeneous agents was introduced. That method is based on a fragment of STL called Capability Temporal Logic (CaTL) whose semantics are defined over counts of agents. In this work, we present an extension of their approach that considers full STL and spatial constraints, both of which are not considered in that work. Two other closely-related works are [2,12]. In [2], the authors present a method for finding optimal trajectories for a team of agents while ignoring spatial constraints such as collision avoidance. Such constraints are handled in a sequential motion planning algorithm after a region-level plan has been synthesized from an STL formula. Additionally, their method assumes each agent has its own defined specification, assuming task assignment has already been completed. In this paper, we introduce an encoding for a team specification that allows us to solve such spatial constraints and task assignment directly as part of the synthesis problem. The authors of [12] similarly present a method for synthesizing team plans from a fragment of STL called Multi-Agent STL (MA-STL). While their approach can handle objectives such as collision avoidance, it restricts temporal operators to individual agent trajectories. This restriction makes it difficult to compactly specify goals that must be achieved simultaneously by different agents. Because it uses full STL, our method can specify simultaneous actions in a straightforward and compact manner. We demonstrate the ability of our method to synthesize plans given a team specification that includes spatial constraints and simultaneous task execution, a rich problem space that cannot be easily handled by related methods.

3 Problem Formulation

We address the problem of multi-agent synthesis for a homogeneous agent team which must complete individual tasks as well as simultaneously execute team tasks, all while abiding by spatial constraints. We focus our approach on a gridworld domain, with constraints inspired by military ground maneuvers as well as tasks that might be performed by a team of flying robots.

3.1 Environment

Definition 1. We adopt the definition presented in [6] as our *Environment*, given by the tuple $Env = (Q, E, W, AP, L)$ where:

1. Q is a finite set of states that corresponds to occupiable cells in the gridworld;
2. $E \subseteq Q \times Q$ is a set of edges such that $(q, q') \in E$ iff the two cells corresponding to states q and q' are non-diagonally adjacent in the gridworld;
3. $W : E \to \mathbb{R}$ is an edge weight such that $W(q, q')$ is the maximum amount of time required for an agent to travel from q before entering q';
4. AP is a set of atomic propositions that define environment state types;
5. $L : Q \to 2^{AP}$ is a mapping that labels each state of the environment according to its state type.

Un-occupiable cells in the gridworld, such as cells where obstacles are located, are omitted from Q, and transitions to and from those cells are omitted from E. We assume a gridworld where each edge weight W is equivalent.

The set of propositions AP corresponds to state types in the environment. We use three categories of state types to represent key environment features that are tracked in our problem formulation: objective state types, team action state types, and the static object state type. Objective state types represent locations where individual agent tasks must be completed. A mapping of $L(q) = \pi_{o_i}$ represents the ith objective is at state q. Team action state types represent states where execution of a certain team action is possible. The mapping $L(q) = \pi_{ta_\ell}$ represents the ℓth team action can be executed at state q. The existence of a static object at a state q is represented by the static object state type $L(q) = \pi_{ob}$.

3.2 Agents

We similarly adopt the definitions from [6] describing single agent and team trajectories, however with the assumption of homogeneous agent capability.

Definition 2. Let J be a finite index set representing all agents. An *Agent* $j \in J$ is given by a state $A_j = q_{0,j}$ where $q_{0,j} \in Q$ is the agent's initial state.

Definition 3. An *input signal* for agent j is defined as the mapping $u_j(t) = \mathbb{R} \to E \cup \{\emptyset\}$, where $u_j(t) = e$ specifies that agent j begins to travel on edge e at time t. An input signal $u_j(t) = e$, where $e = (q, q')$, describes an agent that is at state q at time t. An input signal has the property $u_j(t) = e \implies u_j(\tau) = \emptyset, \forall \tau \in (t, t+W(e))$. In other words, the input signal must be none while an agent is traveling on an edge. From the input signal we receive a piecewise constant *trajectory* of an agent $s_j(t) = \mathbb{R} \to Q \cup \{\emptyset\}$, which describes the agent's movement between environment states. The agent trajectory s_j has the properties $s_j(0) = q_{0,j}$, and $u_j(t) = (q, q') \implies s_j(\tau) = (q, q'), \forall \tau \in (t, t+W(e)) \wedge s_j(t+W(e)) = q'$.

Definition 4. The *team trajectory* is a mapping from each time t to the team state $s_J(t) = [n_Q(t), n_E(t)] \in \mathbb{Z}_{\geq 0}^{(|Q|+|E|)}$. The matrices $n_Q = [n_q(t)]_{q \in Q} \in \mathbb{Z}_{\geq 0}^{|Q|}$ and $n_E = [n_e(t)]_{e \in E} \in \mathbb{Z}_{\geq 0}^{|E|}$ are defined as

$$n_q(t) = \sum_{j \in J} I(s_j(t) = q) \tag{1a}$$

$$n_e(t) = \sum_{j \in J} I(s_j(t) = e) \tag{1b}$$

where I is the indicator function. Therefore, $n_q(t)$ and $n_e(t)$ represent the number of agents at state q and edge e, respectively. That is, the team trajectory represents the number of agents on each state and edge at each point in time.

3.3 Signal Temporal Logic

The syntax of STL [9] is given in Backus-Naur form as

$$\phi := \top | \mu | \neg \phi | \phi_1 \wedge \phi_2 | \phi_1 \mathcal{U}_{[a,b]} \phi_2 \,, \tag{2}$$

where $\top$ is the logical *True*; μ is a predicate; ϕ, ϕ_1, and ϕ_2 are STL formulas; $\neg$ and $\wedge$ are Boolean negation and conjunction; and $\mathcal{U}_{[a,b]}$ is the time-bounded until operator. Other common operators such as disjunction ($\phi_1 \vee \phi_2 := \neg(\neg\phi_1 \wedge \neg\phi_2)$), time-bounded eventually ($F_{[a,b]}\phi := \top \mathcal{U}_{[a,b]} \phi$), and time-bounded always ($G_{[a,b]}\phi := \neg F_{[a,b]\neg\phi}$) can be defined from these operators. In this work, we consider predicates of the form $\mu := f(x(t)) \geq c$, where $f : \mathbb{R}^n \to \mathbb{R}$ for an n-dimensional signal x and a constant c.

The semantics of an STL formula ϕ with respect to a trajectory s_J at time t are defined as

$$\begin{aligned}
(s_J,t) &\models \mu && \Leftrightarrow f(s_J(t)) \geq c \\
(s_J,t) &\models \neg\phi && \Leftrightarrow \neg((s_J,t) \models \phi) \\
(s_J,t) &\models \phi_1 \wedge \phi_2 && \Leftrightarrow (s_J,t) \models \phi_1 \wedge (s_J,t) \models \phi_2 \\
(s_J,t) &\models \phi_1 \mathcal{U}_{[a,b]} \phi_2 && \Leftrightarrow \exists t' \in [t+a, t+b] s.t. (s_J,t') \models \phi_2 \\
& && \wedge \forall t'' \in [0,t'](s_J,t'') \models \phi_1 \,.
\end{aligned} \tag{3}$$

In addition to the semantics defined above, STL also has the notion of quantitative semantics or *robustness degree*, ρ. The robustness of a signal s_J at time t with respect to formula ϕ is defined as [3]

$$\begin{aligned}
&\rho(s_J,t,\mu) = f(s_J(t)) - c \\
&\rho(s_J,t,\neg\phi) = -\rho(s_J,t,\phi) \\
&\rho(s_J,t,\phi_1 \wedge \phi_2) = \min(\rho(s_J,t,\phi_1), \rho(s_J,t,\phi_2)) \\
&\rho(s_J,t,\phi_1 \mathcal{U}_{[a,b]} \phi_2) = \\
&\qquad \max_{t' \in [t+a,t+b]} (\rho(s_J,t',\phi_2), \min_{t'' \in [t,t']} \rho(s_J,t'',\phi_1)).
\end{aligned} \tag{4}$$

3.4 Problem Statement

We address the challenge of multi-agent motion planning to satisfy spatial constraints in scenarios where agents must execute individual tasks and as well as team tasks. Table 1 lists the symbols used in problem formulation.

STL operators can be applied to specify the appropriate time bounds in which each objective must be achieved. For example, in the most general case we can specify that all n objectives must eventually be reached with

$$\phi_{objectives} = \bigwedge_{i=1}^{n} F_{[0,T]}(Objective_i) \,, \tag{5}$$

where T is the ending time of the scenario. The predicate $Objective_i$ is true if any agent is in state $q \in L^{-1}(\pi_{o_i})$.

Team actions refer to a team task which must be completed simultaneously by all agents on the team. The ℓth team action can only be executed when each agent is located in any state where the ℓth team action can be executed. STL operators can be used to enforce constraints such as requiring all m team actions to be performed at least once every time interval h with the formula

$$\phi_{team.action} = \bigwedge_{\ell=1}^{m} G_{[0,T]}(F_{[0,h]}(Team.Action_\ell)) \,, \tag{6}$$

where $Team.Action_\ell$ is true if each agent is located in any state $q \in L^{-1}(\pi_{ta_\ell})$.

Spatial constraints are grouped into two categories: dynamic (constraints on inter-agent distances) and static (constraints on distances between agents and static objects in the environment). Dynamic spatial constraints are placed on the Euclidean distance $d(j,j') \in \mathbb{R}$ between each pair of agents $(j,j') \in [J]^2$, where $[J]^2$ represents all subsets of J with cardinality 2.

A global upper bound, r^d_{max}, and lower bound, r^d_{min}, can be enforced on inter-agent distances with the constraints

$$\phi_{dynamic.lower}(r^d_{min}) = \bigwedge_{(j,j')\in[J]^2} G_{[0,T]}(d(j,j') \geq r^d_{min}) \tag{7a}$$

$$\phi_{dynamic.upper}(r^d_{max}) = \bigwedge_{(j,j')\in[J]^2} G_{[0,T]}(d(j,j') \leq r^d_{max}), \tag{7b}$$

where $\phi_{dynamic}(r^d_{min}, r^d_{max}) = \phi_{dynamic.lower}(r^d_{min}) \wedge \phi_{dynamic.upper}(r^d_{max})$.

A static spatial constraint on the distance between all agents and all static objects of type *ob* can be enforced as a global upper bound r^s_{max}, and lower bound, r^s_{min},

$$\phi_{static.lower}(r^s_{min}) = \bigwedge_{j\in J, q\in L^{-1}(\pi_{ob})} G_{[0,T]}(d(j,q) \geq r^s_{min}) \tag{8a}$$

$$\phi_{static.upper}(r^s_{max}) = \bigwedge_{j\in J, q\in L^{-1}(\pi_{ob})} G_{[0,T]}(d(j,q) \leq r^s_{max}), \tag{8b}$$

where $\phi_{static}(r^s_{min}, r^s_{max}) = \phi_{static.lower}(r^s_{min}) \wedge \phi_{static.upper}(r^s_{max})$. We represent the overall STL specification for the team of agents as

$$\Phi = \phi_{objectives} \wedge \phi_{team.action} \wedge \phi_{dynamic}(r^d_{min}, r^d_{max}) \wedge \phi_{static}(r^s_{min}, r^s_{max}), \tag{9}$$

and we aim to find a plan subject to agent dynamics which satisfies Φ.

Problem 1a (Satisfaction) Given a team of agents $\{A_j\}_{j\in J}$ operating in a shared environment $Env = (Q, E, W, AP, l)$, and a STL specification Φ, find a set of input signals $\{u_j\}_{j\in J}$ such that Φ is satisfied.

Problem 1b (Maximize robustness) Solve *Problem 1a* such that $\rho(s_J, t, \Phi)$ is maximized.

4 Mixed Integer Programming Encodings

We formulate Problem 1 as an equivalent MIQP, then as an equivalent MILP with a different spatial constraint encoding. We make the same assumption as in [6] that agent transitions between states can only happen at a set of discrete times, and all transition times are integer. Formally, we assume edge weight functions (transition times) are defined such that $W(q,q') = v\delta t, v \in \mathbb{N}$ where δt is a time step no larger than the minimum value of W, and $u_j(t) = \emptyset, \forall t \notin \{v\delta t\}_{v\in\mathbb{N}}$. We define a mapping $\mathcal{W} : Q\times Q \to \mathbb{N}$ which describes a discretized edge weight such that $W(q,q') = \mathcal{W}(q,q')\delta t,\ \forall q \neq q'$. We assume all discretized edge weights $\mathcal{W}(q,q') = 1$ for simplicity, however this is not a necessary assumption for the formulation. Additionally, a "self-loop" edge $\mathcal{W}(q,q) = 1$ is defined for each state to enable agents to remain at a state for a single time step. The planning horizon K denotes the total timesteps δt that we plan for our agents.

Table 1. Table of symbols corresponding to the problem variables and the MIQP/MILP variables. Symbols are listed in alphabetical order in each section.

Problem Variables	
AP	set of atomic propositions
$e \in E$	edge in the environment
J	index set of all agents
K	index set for discrete time horizon
$k \in K$	discrete time index
o_i	i^{th} objective
$q \in Q$	state in the environment
q_c	column location of state q
q_r	row location of state q
s_J	team trajectory
s_j	trajectory of agent j
ta_ℓ	ℓ^{th} team action
$W(q, q')$	environment edge weighting
$\mathcal{W}(q, q')$	discretized environment edge weighting
δt	environment discretization size
π_{ob}	static object proposition
π_{o_i}	i^{th} objective proposition
π_{ta_ℓ}	ℓ^{th} team action available proposition
MIQP/MILP Variables	
$d^d_{\max}(k)$	upper bound on distances between all agent pairs
$d^d_{\min}(k)$	lower bound on distances between all agent pairs
$d^s_{\max}(k)$	upper bound on distances between all agents and static objects
$d^s_{\min}(k)$	lower bound on distances between all agents and static objects
$u_{e,j}(k)$	binary encoding of if agent j is entering edge e at time k
$z_{c,j}(k)$	column location of agent j at time k
$z_{o_i}(k)$	satisfaction of ith objective at time k
$z_{q,j}(k)$	binary encoding of if agent j is in state q at time k
$z_{q,ta_\ell}(k)$	number of agents performing ℓ^{th} team action in state q at time k
$z_{r,j}(k)$	row location of agent j at time k
$z_{ta_\ell}(k)$	execution of ℓth team action at time k

4.1 Agent Dynamics

We apply the team dynamics encodings from [6] on the level of each agent in order to track individual agent locations required to incorporate spatial constraints. We define a variable $z_{q,j}(k) \in \{0, 1\}$ that we wish to be 1 if agent j is at state q at time k. The initial positions of each agent are set with equality constraints

$$z_{q,j}(0) = q_{0,j}, \; \forall j \in J. \tag{10}$$

where $q_{0,j}$ describes the known initial position of agent j. Agents' movement between nodes is governed by node and edge balance equations

$$z_{q,j}(k) = \sum_{(q',q)\in E} u_{(q',q),j}(k - \mathcal{W}(q',q)) \tag{11a}$$

$$\sum_{(q,q')\in E} u_{(q,q'),j}(k) = \sum_{(q',q)\in E} u_{(q',q),j}(k - \mathcal{W}(q',q)), \tag{11b}$$

$$\forall q \in Q, j \in J, k = 0, ..., K.$$

We define the location of each agent at each time step in order to enforce spatial constraints. Two variables are created to represent the integer value for the column location $z_{c,j}(k) \in \mathbb{N}$ and row location $z_{r,j}(k) \in \mathbb{N}$ of agent j at time t. The agent location variables are related to agent dynamics with the constraints

$$z_{c,j}(k) = \sum_{q\in Q} z_{q,j}(k) \cdot q_c \tag{12a}$$

$$z_{r,j}(k) = \sum_{q\in Q} z_{q,j}(k) \cdot q_r, \tag{12b}$$

$$\forall j \in J, k = 0, ..., K.$$

4.2 Objective Satisfaction

An objective at state q is reached at time k if any agent is in state q at time k. We define a variable $z_{o_i}(k) \in \{0, 1\}$, that we wish to be valued 1 if any agent is at the state where objective o_i is located at time k. This variable captures the satisfaction of objective o_i with the constraints

$$z_{o_i}(k) \le \sum_{j\in J} z_{q,j}(k) \tag{13a}$$

$$M \cdot z_{o_i}(k) \ge \sum_{j\in J} z_{q,j}(k), \tag{13b}$$

$$\forall q \in L^{-1}(\pi_{o_i}),\ k = 0, ...K,$$

where M is a sufficiently large number, i.e. $M \ge 1+|J|$. We assume $|L^{-1}(\pi_{o_i})| = 1$, in other words the ith objective is located in one state.

4.3 Team Actions

The ℓth team action can be executed at time k if each agent on the team is located in any state $q \in L^{-1}(\pi_{ta_\ell})$, not necessarily the same state. We first define a variable $z_{q,ta_\ell}(k) \in [0, |J|]$ which represents the number of agents performing the ℓth team action in state q at time k. We require an agent to be located at a state q and remain at state q for one time step while executing a team action with the constraints

$$z_{q,ta}(k) \le u_{(q,q)}(k),\ \forall q \in L^{-1}(\pi_{ta_\ell}), k = 0, ..., K. \tag{14}$$

We next define a variable $z_{ta_\ell}(k) \in \{0,1\}$ which we wish to be valued at least 1 if all agents are executing the ℓth team action at time k, thus capturing whether a team action is completed at time k with the constraints

$$-M \cdot z_{ta_\ell}(k) + \sum_{q \in L^{-1}(\pi_{ta})} z_{q,ta_\ell}(k) \geq |J| - M, \ \forall k = 0, ..., K. \tag{15}$$

4.4 Quadratic Spatial Constraint Encoding

Our quadratic encoding of spatial constraints requires the calculation of Euclidean distance using the integer values for agents' row and column location at a given time step. We use the function $d^{\text{quad}}(j,q)_k$ to represent the quadratic encoding of the Euclidean distance between an agent j and a state q at time k, where $d^{\text{quad}}(j,q)_k = \sqrt{|z_{c,j}(k) - q_c|^2 + |z_{r,j}(k) - q_r|^2}$. The same calculation and notation is used to represent the distance between two agents. Upper and lower bounds on the distance between each agent and each static object of a given type in the environment are encoded with constraints

$$d^s_{\text{min}}(k) \leq d^{\text{quad}}(j,q)_k \leq d^s_{\text{max}}(k), \ \forall j \in J, q \in L^{-1}(\pi_{ob}), k = 0, ..., K, \tag{16}$$

Upper and lower bounds on the distance between each pair of agents are similarly encoded with constraints

$$d^d_{\text{min}}(k) \leq d^{\text{quad}}(j,j')_k \leq d^d_{\text{max}}(k), \ \forall (j,j') \in [J]^2, k = 0, ...K. \tag{17}$$

4.5 Linear Spatial Constraints Encoding

We compare our quadratic encoding of spatial constraints to a linear encoding, which is much more common in the synthesis literature. Our linear formulation uses pre-calculated Euclidean distances between each pair of states, as well as the known state location of each agent at each time step. Bounds on the distance between each agent and static object are encoded with constraints

$$d^s_{\text{min}}(k) \leq \sum_{q \in Q} z_{q,j}(k) \cdot d(q,q') \leq d^s_{\text{max}}(k), \ \forall q' \in L^{-1}(\pi_{ob}), j \in J, k = 0, ..., K, \tag{18}$$

where $d(q,q')$ represents a precalculated Euclidean distance.

In order to linearly encode dynamic spatial constraints, we first define a binary variable $z_{q,q',j,j'}(k) \in \{0,1\}$ that we wish to be valued at least 1 if agent j is in state q and agent j' is in state q' at time k. We enforce this relationship with constraints

$$z_{q,q',j,j'}(k) \leq z_{q,j}(k) \tag{19}$$

$$z_{q,q',j,j'}(k) \leq z_{q',j'}(k) \tag{20}$$

$$M \cdot z_{q,q',j,j'}(k) \geq z_{q,j}(k) + z_{q',j'}(k) - 1, \tag{21}$$

$$\forall q \in Q, q' \in Q, (j,j') \in [J]^2, k = 0, ..., K.$$

The general intuition is that only one variable $z_{q,q',j,j'}(k)$ will be equal to 1 for each pair of agents (j, j') at time k. We can use a combination of these variables with the precalculated Euclidean distance to represent the distance between each agent pair at each time step. We place lower and upper bounds on the distance between each agent pair at each time step with the constraints

$$d^d_{\min}(k) \leq \sum_{q\in Q} \sum_{q'\in Q} z_{q,q',j,j'}(k) \cdot d(q,q') \leq d^d_{\max}(k),\ \forall (j,j') \in [J]^2, k = 0, ..., K. \tag{22}$$

4.6 Formula Satisfaction

The satisfaction of an STL formula can be converted to a set of mixed integer linear constraints using encodings given in [1]. Boolean and temporal operators are formulated recursively according to those encodings, while the formulations of predicates are given as follows. A binary variable is created for each $Objective_i$ predicate and for each $Team.Action_\ell$ predicate for each time step. The binary variables for a predicate $Objective_i$ at each time step are equated to a variable $z_{o_i}(k)$ such that $z_{o_i}(k) = 1 \iff (s_J, k\delta t) \models Objective_i$. The binary variables for a predicate $Team.Action_\ell$ at each time step are equated to a variable $z_{ta_\ell}(k)$ such that $z_{ta_\ell}(k) = 1 \iff (s_J, k\delta t) \models Team.Action_\ell$. An integer variable is be created for each $\phi_{dynamic.lower}, \phi_{dynamic.upper}, \phi_{static.lower}$, and $\phi_{static.upper}$ proposition for each time step. We equate these proposition variables respectively to the model variables $d^d_{min}(k), d^d_{max}(k), d^s_{min}(k)$, and $d^s_{max}(k)$ such that $(d^d_{min}(k) \geq r^d_{min}) \wedge (d^d_{max}(k) \leq r^d_{max}) \iff (s_J, k\delta t) \models \phi_{dynamic}$ and $(d^s_{min}(k) \geq r^s_{min}) \wedge (d^s_{max}(k) \leq r^s_{max}) \iff (s_J, k\delta t) \models \phi_{static}$.

5 Experiments

We present the results from experiments evaluating the solve times for the given encodings under different spatial constraint types and problem sizes.

5.1 Case Studies

We present three case studies on similarly-sized maps showcasing complex problems the centralized encodings can address, and we compare the solve times of both linear and quadratic spatial constraint encoding types (Table 2). Each case study map contains 100 or 105 cells, 2 agents, and 2 objectives. Each encoding model was solved 64 times using Gurobi 9.5.2 [4], and all reported solve times reflect Gurobi model solve times (excluding time to build the model). Timeouts are the number of solves exceeding 700 s, and all other reported statistics exclude the timeouts. Data greater than 1.5 times the interquartile range below the first quartile or above the third quartile are considered outliers. Case studies were solved for both problems: find a satisficing solution, and maximize robustness (referenced as '+R').

We use a *hostiles and objectives* domain to present our case studies. Agents (blue circles) are tasked with reaching objectives (green squares). The location of hostile objects (red diamonds) dictate the states in which agents are able to take cover (yellow squares). Taking cover ('x' on agent path) represents a team action executed by all agents simultaneously, and requires each agent to be in a covered state to execute the action. The example plans depicted on each map were all generated by the MIQP encoding to solve the problem of maximizing robustness. Similar to an expected practical workflow, an upper bound on time was estimated based on grid size, objective locations, and initial agent locations. All selected time bounds were at least 2 time steps longer than the length of the shortest satisficing solution.

Case Study 1 (Static Spatial Constraint). Agents are required to reach both objectives while maintaining a minimum distance from hostiles, which represent a static object. Additionally, agents must complete a team action (take cover) at least once. The STL formula used is

$$\Phi = F_{[0,12]}(Objective_1) \wedge F_{[0,12]}(Objective_2) \wedge F_{[0,20]}(Team.Action_1) \quad (23)$$
$$\wedge\, G_{[0,20]}(d^s_{min} \geq 2),$$

which gives an initial time window in which agents must reach both objectives, and a broader time frame for agents to perform a team action (take cover). The map used in the case study with an example plan overlaid is shown in Fig. 1, along with a comparison of the encoding solve times. The box plots clearly show that both linear encodings outperform the quadratic encodings in this case.

Case Study 2 (Inter-Agent Distance Upper Bound Constraint). Agents are required to reach both objectives while staying within a certain distance of

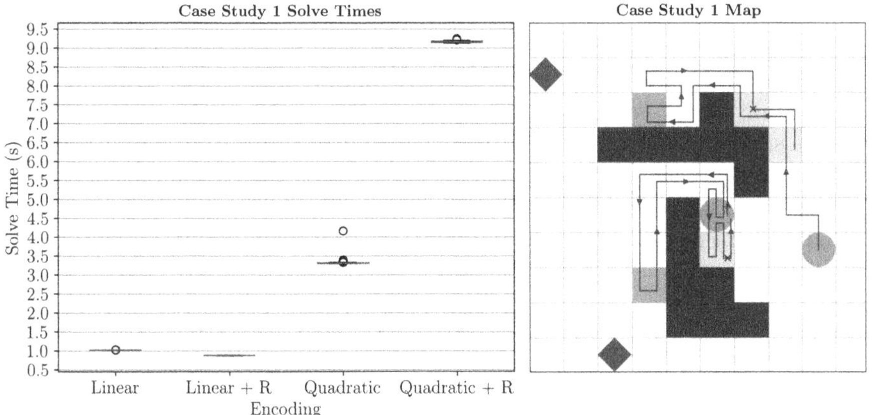

Fig. 1. Case Study 1 results. Agents remaining at a cell for a time step not shown on any case study map. Box plots depict median (red bar) and outliers (open circles). (Color figure online)

each other. This could exemplify a scenario where agents must maintain proximity to enable communication. The governing STL formula used

$$\Phi = F_{[0,20]}(Objective_1) \wedge F_{[0,20]}(Objective_2) \wedge G_{[0,20]}F_{[0,8]}(Team.Action_1) \wedge G_{[0,20]}(d^d_{max} \leq 10) \quad (24)$$

also requires agents to take cover at least once within a repeating time interval. Figure 2 provides the map and solve time comparisons; the separation between box plots show that both quadratic encodings outperform the linear encodings by about two orders of magnitude.

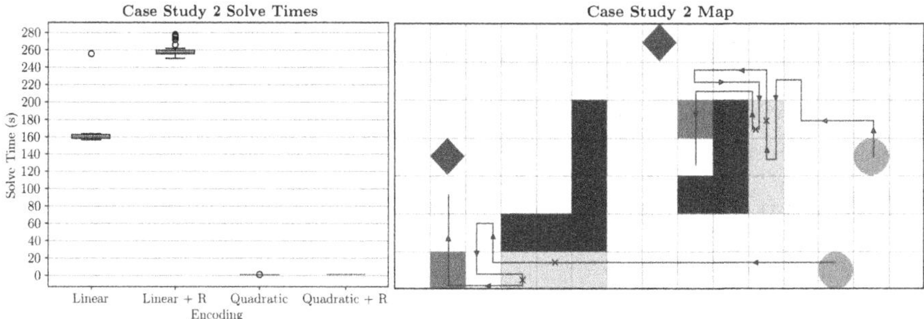

Fig. 2. Case Study 2 results. MILP solve timeouts are not included in box plots.

Case Study 3 (Inter-Agent Distance Lower Bound Constraint). Agents are required to reach both objectives, take cover at least once, and maintain a minimum inter-agent distance to avoid collision. The formula used

$$\Phi = F_{[0,21]}(Objective_1) \wedge F_{[0,21]}(Objective_2) \wedge F_{[0,21]}(Team.Action_1) \wedge G_{[0,21]}(d^d_{min} \geq 1.01) \quad (25)$$

indicates agents must maintain a minimum of 1.01 cells from each other. A 1.01 cell minimum distance (instead of a 1 cell minimum distance) prevents agent collision that would occur from a pair of agents switching cells with each other during a single time step. Figure 3 provides the map and solve time comparisons. All MILP solves resulted in timeouts. Hostiles are not included in the map; in this scenario the team action is any action that must be collaboratively completed by the agent team at pre-specified locations, not specifically the take cover action.

5.2 Scaling Experiments

We additionally evaluated encoding performance on maps of increasing size and number of agents. Experiments were conducted with maps of three sizes (without obstacles): 10×10 cells with 2 agents, 20×20 cells with 5 agents, and a 30×30

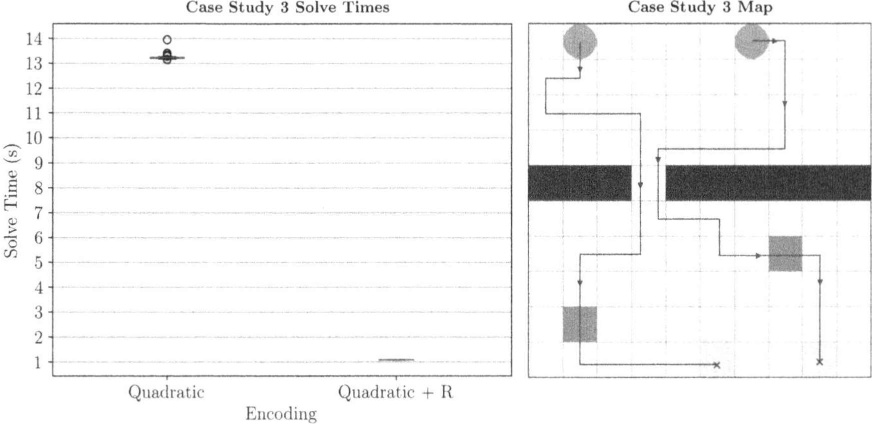

Fig. 3. Case Study 3 results. All MILP solves resulted in timeouts and are not shown. Agents travel through the narrow opening at different times.

Table 2. Case study (CS) experimental results for linear (L) and quadratic (Q) encodings when finding a satisficing solution and maximizing the degree of robustness (+R). Solve time statistics reference all 64 solves but exclude timeouts; $\tilde{t}$: median solve time; $\bar{t}$: mean solve time; t_1: minimum solve time; t_n: maximum solve time; $\#O$: number of outliers; $\#T$: number of timeouts. Model properties $\#\mathcal{V}_C$, $\#\mathcal{V}_I$, $\#\mathrm{C}_l$, and $\#\mathrm{C}_q$, respectively represent the numbers of continuous variables, integer variables, linear constraints, and quadratic constraints in each encoding. In Case Study 3, all 64 MILP solves for both problems resulted in a timeout and further statistics are not reported.

CS	Encoding	$\tilde{t}$ (s)	$\bar{t}$ (s)	t_1 (s)	t_n (s)	$\#T$	$\#O$	$\#\mathcal{V}_C$	$\#\mathcal{V}_I$	$\#\mathrm{C}_l$	$\#\mathrm{C}_q$
CS1	L	1.02	1.02	1.02	1.03	0	2	68	19672	8462	0
	L+R	0.88	0.88	0.87	0.88	0	0	69	19672	8462	0
	Q	3.31	3.33	3.30	4.17	0	10	68	19672	8378	84
	Q+R	9.16	9.16	9.13	9.24	0	3	69	19672	8378	84
CS2	L	160.42	162.09	156.77	255.52	5	1	92	211751	578193	0
	L+R	257.04	259.76	250.28	277.59	5	11	93	211751	578193	0
	Q	0.97	0.97	0.96	1.01	0	4	92	22226	9597	21
	Q+R	1.35	1.35	1.34	1.35	0	0	93	22226	9597	21
CS3	L	–	–	–	–	64	–	88	204673	555886	0
	L+R	–	–	–	–	64	–	89	204673	555886	0
	Q	13.23	13.24	13.15	13.95	0	6	88	22491	9318	22
	Q+R	1.09	1.09	1.08	1.09	0	0	89	22491	9318	22

cells with 10 agents. The same STL formula was used for each map, requiring agents to reach all objectives while avoiding collisions with the formula

$$\Phi = G_{[0,10]}(d^d_{min} \geq 1.01) \bigwedge_{i=1}^{n} F_{[0,10]}(Objective_i) \tag{26}$$

where n represents the number of objectives in a given map and is always equal to the number of agents in the map.

For each map size, 16 maps were randomly generated and used across both encodings. Maps had each agent and each objective placed more than 5 cells (Euclidean distance) away from every other agent and objective. This requires that each agent travel to an objective to satisfy Φ. Additionally, each objective was required to be reachable by at least two agents, and each agent was placed such that there were two possible objectives it could reach, though not that it could reach both in the same trajectory. Thus, a solution must exist, and an implicit task assignment problem must be solved for each map.

Experiment results are shown in Fig. 4 and Table 3. Each of the 16 maps was solved twice for each combination of encoding and problem type using Gurobi 9.5.2 and a solve time limit of 1000 s. Reported solve times exclude model construction. We ultimately did not measure the MILP encoding solve time on the 30×30 maps as all but eight MILP solves timed out for all 20×20 maps. The MILP model also becomes intractable to build for a 30×30 map with 10 agents.

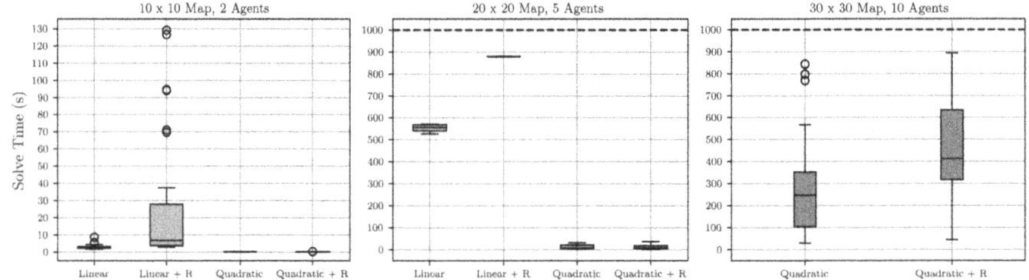

Fig. 4. Box plots of encoding solve times for both problem definitions across three map sizes. The MILP encoding is shown in pink and the MIQP encoding is shown in teal. The MILP encoding box plots for the 20×20 map only represent six data points (Linear) and two data points (Linear + R) due to timeouts. A red dashed line represents the solve timeout set at 1000 s (Color figure online).

Table 3. Scaling experiment results reported using same notation as Table 2. Map refers to map size and number of agents in parentheses. Solve time statistics are reported out of 32 total model solves (2 solves each for the 16 maps) and exclude outliers. All maps of the same size result in models with the same variable and constraint counts.

Map	Encoding	$\tilde{t}$ (s)	$\bar{t}$ (s)	t_1 (s)	t_n (s)	#T	#O	#$\mathcal{V}_C$	#$\mathcal{V}_I$	#$\mathcal{C}_l$	#$\mathcal{C}_q$
10×10 (2)	L	2.56	3.14	1.74	8.60	0	4	33	123321	335526	0
	L+R	6.79	26.82	2.85	129.18	0	6	34	123321	335526	0
	Q	0.18	0.18	0.07	0.30	0	0	33	13321	5515	11
	Q+R	0.08	0.12	0.05	0.05	0	4	34	13321	5515	11
20×20 (5)	L	555.55	552.53	526.31	570.87	26	0	66	17737383	52854142	0
	L+R	879.32	879.32	877.92	880.73	30	0	67	17737383	52854142	0
	Q	6.62	12.51	3.49	31.15	0	0	66	137383	54032	110
	Q+R	7.85	13.17	0.91	36.42	0	0	67	137383	54032	110
30×30 (10)	Q	247.39	314.42	29.69	844.94	0	6	121	624953	242627	495
	Q+R	412.18	450.62	44.29	894.00	2	0	121	624953	242627	495

6 Discussion

Our experiments demonstrate significant differences in the relative performance of the presented MILP and MIQP encodings depending on the type of spatial constraint required. Case Study 1 demonstrates that the linear encoding of spatial constraints solves faster than the quadratic encoding when the spatial constraints govern the relationship between agents and static objects. However, when inter-agent spatial constraints are required as in Case Study 2 and 3, the quadratic encoding of spatial constraints solves significantly faster than the linear encoding. In Case Study 3, when inter-agent distance was constrained to achieve collision avoidance, the MILP encoding was not even able find a solution for either problem type before timing out. These findings are further supported by our scaling experiment in which we found the quadratic encoding of spatial constraints to better support increases in map size and agent count when inter-agent constraints were required. The results demonstrate that the MIQP encoding can be solved quickly for maps sized 20×20 with five agents, and within a reasonable timeout for maps sized 30×30 with ten agents.

Our findings support key design recommendations for centralized multi-agent planning in domains that can be discretized into a gridworld environment. We demonstrate that problems containing inter-agent spatial constraints, such as collision avoidance constraints, can be solved faster by utilizing an MIQP encoding as opposed to a MILP encoding. However, in applications where spatial constraints are only required to govern the distance between agents and static objects, we find a MILP encoding to be better suited. We additionally show that the MIQP encoding solves much faster on static spatial constraints than the MILP encoding solves on dynamic spatial constraints. This suggests applications that require both constraint types may be best supported by an MIQP encoding, although future work could explore a combination of encoding types in the same model. Finally, the scaling experiment provides upper limits for feasible applications of the presented MILP and MIQP encodings.

7 Conclusion

In conclusion, we present an MIQP formulation of the search for multi-agent trajectories to satisfy team STL specifications which include spatial constraints and team actions. Through experimentation, we find the presented MIQP approach to outperform a MILP approach in applications where inter-agent spatial constraints are required, and we show application of the MIQP approach on maps sized up to 30×30 with 10 agents. We provide valuable design recommendations for the best applications of both approaches, and we demonstrate that the presented MIQP encoding can be a powerful tool for multi-agent planning to achieve coordinated team behaviors and adherence to inter-agent spatial constraints.

Acknowledgements. This work was supported by the Department of Defense (DoD) through the National Defense Science & Engineering Graduate (NDSEG) Fellowship Program.

References

1. Belta, C., Sadraddini, S.: Formal methods for control synthesis: an optimization perspective. Annu. Rev. Control Robot. Auton. Syst. **2**(1), 115–140 (2019). https://doi.org/10.1146/annurev-control-053018-023717
2. Büyükkoçak, A.T., Aksaray, D., Yazicioglu, Y.: Distributed planning of multi-agent systems with coupled temporal logic specifications. In: AIAA Scitech 2021 Forum, p. 1123 (2021). https://doi.org/10.2514/6.2021-1123
3. Donzé, A., Maler, O.: Robust satisfaction of temporal logic over real-valued signals. In: Chatterjee, K., Henzinger, T.A. (eds.) FORMATS 2010. LNCS, vol. 6246, pp. 92–106. Springer, Heidelberg (2010). https://doi.org/10.1007/978-3-642-15297-9_9
4. Gurobi Optimization, LLC: Gurobi Optimizer Reference Manual (2023). https://www.gurobi.com
5. Kress-Gazit, H., Lahijanian, M., Raman, V.: Synthesis for robots: guarantees and feedback for robot behavior. Annu. Rev. Control Robot. Auton. Syst. **1**, 211–236 (2018). https://doi.org/10.1146/annurev-control-060117-104838
6. Leahy, K., et al.: Scalable and robust algorithms for task-based coordination from high-level specifications (scratches). IEEE Trans. Robot. (2021). https://doi.org/10.1109/TRO.2021.3130794
7. Liu, Z., Guo, M., Li, Z.: Time minimization and online synchronization for multi-agent systems under collaborative temporal tasks. arXiv preprint arXiv:2208.07756 (2022). https://doi.org/10.48550/arXiv.2208.07756
8. Luo, X., Zavlanos, M.M.: Temporal logic task allocation in heterogeneous multi-robot systems. IEEE Trans. Robot. **38**(6), 3602–3621 (2022). https://doi.org/10.1109/TRO.2022.3181948
9. Maler, O., Nickovic, D.: Monitoring temporal properties of continuous signals. In: Lakhnech, Y., Yovine, S. (eds.) FORMATS/FTRTFT -2004. LNCS, vol. 3253, pp. 152–166. Springer, Heidelberg (2004). https://doi.org/10.1007/978-3-540-30206-3_12
10. Raman, V., Donzé, A., Maasoumy, M., Murray, R.M., Sangiovanni-Vincentelli, A., Seshia, S.A.: Model predictive control with signal temporal logic specifications. In: 53rd IEEE Conference on Decision and Control, pp. 81–87. IEEE (2014). https://doi.org/10.1109/CDC.2014.7039363
11. Sahin, Y.E., Nilsson, P., Ozay, N.: Multirobot coordination with counting temporal logics. IEEE Trans. Robot. **36**(4), 1189–1206 (2020). https://doi.org/10.1109/TRO.2019.2957669
12. Sun, D., Chen, J., Mitra, S., Fan, C.: Multi-agent motion planning from signal temporal logic specifications. IEEE Robot. Autom. Lett. **7**(2), 3451–3458 (2022). https://doi.org/10.1109/LRA.2022.3146951

A Framework for Policy Based Negotiation

Anna Fritz(✉) and Perry Alexander

Institute for Information Sciences, The University of Kansas, Lawrence, USA
{arfritzz,palexand}@ku.edu

Abstract. Semantic remote attestation is a process for gathering and appraising evidence to determine the state of a remote system. Remote attestation occurs at the request of an appraiser or relying party and proceeds with a target system executing an attestation protocol that invokes attestation services in a specified order to generate and bundle evidence. The appraiser may then reason about the evidence to establish trust in the target's state. *Attestation Protocol Negotiation* is the process of establishing a mutually agreed upon protocol that satisfies the appraiser's desire for comprehensive information and the target's desire for constrained disclosure. Here we explore formalization of negotiation focusing on a definition of system specifications through manifests, protocol sufficiency and soundness, policy representation, and negotiation structure. By using our formal models to represent and verify negotiation's properties we can statically determine that a provably sound, sufficient, and executable protocol is produced.

1 Introduction

Establishing trust in a networked peer is a difficult problem. Martin et al. (2008) state trust may be exhibited through unambiguous identification, unhindered operation, and direct observation of good behavior or indirect observation by a trusted third party. One possible technique allowing a communicating peer to establish trust in a target system's execution is semantic remote attestation (Haldar et al., 2004). Shown in Fig. 1 a *relying party* (RP) or *appraiser* (A) sends an attestation request ($r : (R, n, a)$) to a *target* (T) where attestation generates and returns evidence and meta-evidence ($e : (E, n)$) that can be appraised to determine trust.

Coker et al. (2011, 2008) define a remote attestation model where a target executes an *attestation protocol* that gathers evidence and generates meta-evidence. The protocol sequences the execution of attestation services that perform measurement, generate cryptographic signatures, and make requests of

This work is funded in part by the NSA Science of Security initiative contract #H98230-18-D-0009 and Defense Advanced Research Project Agency contract #HR0011-18-9-0001 and Honeywell FMT Purchase Order #N000422909. The views and conclusions contained in this document are those of the authors and should not be interpreted as representing the official policies, either expressed or implied, of the U.S. Government.

K. Y. Rozier and S. Chaudhuri (Eds.): NFM 2023, LNCS 13903, pp. 207–223, 2023.
https://doi.org/10.1007/978-3-031-33170-1_13

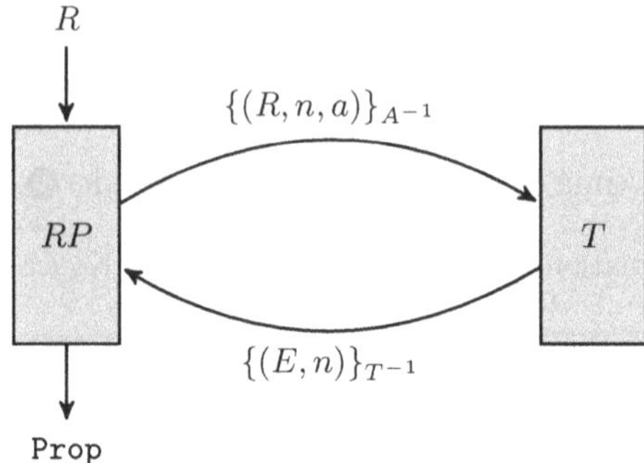

Fig. 1. Remote attestation architecture showing a *relying party* making an attestation request of a *target*.

other systems. These protocols are executed by one or many *attestation manager(s)* associated with the relying party and target.

The design of attestation systems are guided by the following five principles (Coker et al., 2011). Summarized here, these properties ensure evidence used by a relying party represents the system being appraised temporally and functionally:

1. Fresh information – Evidence gathered should reflect the system at the time it was gathered. This extends from boot-time evidence to run-time.
2. Comprehensive information – Evidence should provide a comprehensive view and attestation should access sufficient information about the target state.
3. Constrained disclosure – The target should control what is revealed to the relying party based on the relying party's identity and security context.
4. Semantic explicitness – Evidence should have a well-defined uniform and logical semantics.
5. Trustworthy mechanism – Evidence of attestation infrastructure trustworthiness must be provided to the relying party. Such evidence is called *meta-evidence*.

Most principles are upheld through the existing attestation infrastructure. However, the principles of comprehensive information and constrained disclosure require additional mechanisms to support their satisfaction. To meet the goal of comprehensive information, the relying party must have some idea of the target's measurement capabilities allowing them to select a comprehensive measurement. To meet the goal of constrained disclosure, the target must have some mechanism to distinguish measurements that would expose sensitive information. These contradictory goals can be difficult to mutually satisfy as the relying party would like the most descriptive evidence while the target would like to protect its information thus performing minimal measurements.

Our contributions can be summarized as follows. First, we introduce *negotiation*: a networked communication scheme whereby a target and relying party may mutually agree upon a protocol that satisfies conflicting goals of comprehensive information and constrained disclosure. We then formally define and prove important properties surrounding negotiation including protocol executability, soundness, and sufficiency. By establishing these properties are decidable, we show they can be checked during negotiation and produce decision procedures for that purpose.

Verified decision procedures for soundness and sufficiency criteria are critical to negotiation. Running a protocol that is unsound—not executable or in violation of local policy—will at best fail and waste resources or at worst result in erroneous attestation results. Running a protocol that is insufficient will not satisfy an appraiser's need for comprehensive information. Our results provide tools and models that prevent an ineffective negotiation procedure. All formal models are realized using the Coq (Bertot and Castéran, 2013) environment and are available publicly at `git@github.com:ku-sldg/nfm2023.git`

2 Background

Negotiation builds upon security associations (Maughan et al., 1998), attestation protocols Ramsdell et al. (2019); Coker et al. (2011), and attestation manager (AM) manifests. ISAKMP is a protocol for finding a security association among relying party and target that instantiates a common vocabulary and establishes a secure communication. Copland is a formally specified, domain-specific language for representing and reasoning about attestation protocols. Manifests are formally specified, abstract descriptions of attestation managers that define protocol execution capabilities and communication paths. Qualities of an attestation protocol can be determined by reasoning about it in the context of both a manifest and identities of the communicating peers.

2.1 ISAKMP

Negotiation begins with the establishment of a security association through the Internet Security Association and Key Management Protocol (ISAKMP) (Maughan et al., 1998). A security association (SA) is an agreement between communicating peers protecting all subsequent traffic. Within the security association, peers state their identities, define cryptographic primitives, identify the situation, and instantiate a domain of interpretation.

Identities and cryptographic primitives are trivial security services. More interestingly, the situation and domain of interpretation are unique, specialized fields critical to the success of negotiation. Within the situation, the relying party and target realize context specific information to instantiate policy. Additionally, the domain of interpretation solves any naming conflicts allowing the relying party and target a means to enforce a common understanding of measurement objects. A working implementation of ISAKMP is strongSwan (Steffen, 2021) which uses IKE for key management and authentication protocols (Carrel and Harkins, 1998).

2.2 Copland

Copland (Ramsdell et al., 2019; Helble et al., 2021) is a formally specified, domain specific language designed specifically for attestation protocols. Copland interpreters are available on multiple execution platforms (Petz and Alexander, 2019); Copland's formal semantics denotationally and operationally define protocol execution (Ramsdell et al., 2019) and are captured and verified in Coq (Bertot and Castéran, 2013). Copland is effectively *parameterized over work* allowing arbitrary, distributed measurements over complex systems (Helble et al., 2021).

The Copland grammar allows for Copland *phrases* to specify measurement place, measurement target, and any meta-evidence, such as signatures or nonces. It also allows for the combination of measurements through sequencing operators. The grammar appears as follows:

$$\begin{aligned} t &\leftarrow A \mid @_p\, t \mid (t \rightarrow t) \mid (t \overset{\pi}{\prec} t) \mid (t \overset{\pi}{\sim} t) \\ A &\leftarrow \mathsf{ASP}\ m\ \bar{a}\ p\ r \mid \mathsf{CPY} \mid \mathsf{SIG} \mid \mathsf{HSH} \mid \cdots \end{aligned}$$

Fig. 2. Copland Phrase Grammar

The terminal A is used to specify measurement operations and meta-evidence. Measurements are performed using attestation service providers (ASPs) which are minimal work units. Meta-evidence is an operation over evidence such as hashing or signing that enhances trustworthiness. The nonterminal t allows for terminal measurements combinations through sequencing ($\rightarrow$) and parallel operators ($\overset{\pi}{\prec}$ and $\overset{\pi}{\sim}$) (Ramsdell et al., 2019). $@_p\, t$ is necessary for dispatching measurement operations to distinct attestation managers present within the attestation system. A term in the language may appear as follows:

$$\texttt{@p (m } \bar{a} \texttt{ q t)}$$

where `p` is the measurement place, `m` is the specified ASP, $\bar{a}$ is a list of input arguments, and `q` is the place where the measurement target, `t` is located (Petz and Alexander, 2019). For the remainder of this work, we assume no measurements require input evidence and can therefore safely omit this field.

Layered attestation is the act of combining various measurements across platforms to provide a more comprehensive view of the target. For example, we can strengthen the previous Copland phrase by first measuring t's operational environment. Say this operational environment has an attestation manager located at place `s` with some ASP `aOS` that measures the operating system target `os`. We can linearly sequence the measurements to make stronger guarantees about `t` with the following Copland phrase:

$$\texttt{@os (aOS s os)} \rightarrow \texttt{@p (m q t)}$$

Helble et al. (2021) reasoned about a variety of measurement orderings for different attestation scenarios eventually coining them the flexible mechanisms.

These mechanisms are a collection of formally defined attestation scenarios where one such scenario is the certificate style attestation. In this case, a relying party wishes to determine trust in some attester through the appraisal of evidence where the result is summarized as a certificate.

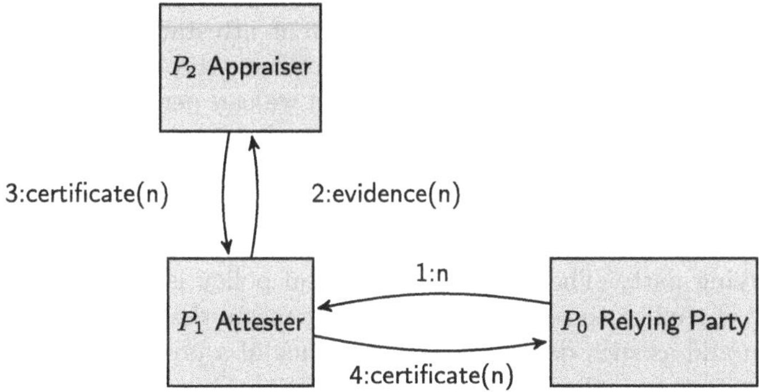

Fig. 3. Certificate-style remote attestation mechanism as seen in Helble et al. (2021).

In the certificate style presented in Fig. 3, the attester performs a measurement of their system (sys). The appraiser is some trusted party which the attester knows of but runs a separate attestation manager to verify the attester's evidence value(s). P_0 begins the attestation sequence by prompting P_1 with a nonce and some measurement request. It is important to note that, without negotiation, the requested measurement operation must be provisioned by a knowledgeable user who has identified said phrase as executable. P_1 performs the measurement request to generate evidence that is then sent to be appraised by P_2. P_2 appraises the evidence and generates a certificate that contains the appraisal result. The certificate is sent back to P_1 where it is forwarded to P_0. The Copland protocol for this scenario appears as follows (Helble et al., 2021):

```
*P0,n: @P1 [(attest P0 sys ) → @P2[(appraise P2sys) →
            (certificate P2 sys)]]
```

These flexible mechanisms are important not only because they distinguish attestation scenarios but they also introduce the idea that the attester and appraiser may be distinct. That is, in some situations, the appraiser and relying party are conflated but here they are disjoint. This motivates the need to capture each attestation component's capabilities in a formal way such that existing peers are able to realize their capabilities to formulate meaningful measurement.

2.3 Manifests

Manifests describe attestation manager-specific information and minimally include a list of existing and operational *ASPs*, a *context* relation, a *knows of* relation, and a *local policy*. The list of *ASPs* must be explicitly captured to realize measurement capabilities of an attestation manager. To understand the attestation manager's dependencies, we introduce the *context* relation (C) which lists all attestation managers which the current attestation manager depends on. This distinction is motivated by the idea that a trust decision of any higher level component depends on the assurance of the lower level components. To capture existing attestation managers which the current attestation manager is aware of and can request measurement from, we introduce the *knowsOf* relation (K). Capturing this relation is necessary to ensure we can perform @ operations to gain a comprehensive system view. The *local policy* is a context-specific policy that applies constraints to measurement operations. The target's local policy is their privacy policy. It is enforced to uphold the principle of constrained disclosure and as such is a means to distinguish sensitive information in the context of some relying party. The relying party's local policy is their selection policy. This policy is applied to select a protocol that meets the goal of comprehensive information and as such describes the sufficiency of a protocol in some context.

Below is our formalization of manifests using Coq. We abstractly reason about other attestation managers using *Plc*. Currently, policy here represents the privacy policy as such representation is necessary for reasoning during *refinement*. The policy is written relationally and states which ASPs can share measurements with other specified peers (represented as *Plc*).

```
Record Manifest := {
    ASPs : list ASP ;
    K : list Plc ;
    C : list Plc ;
    Policy : ASP → Plc → Prop ; }.
```

An *environment* is a set of AMs each defined by a manifest. The domain of an environment provides names for each manifest. A collection of environments is known as a *system*. Within Coq, we realize these structures formally below.

```
Definition Environment : Type := Plc → (option Manifest).
```

```
Definition System := list Environment.
```

For implementation purposes, a manifest also includes public keys, addresses, and trusted platform module (TPM) initialization information. A future goal is to abstractly write manifests and compile them into attestation components. This is currently out of scope.

3 Negotiation

We introduce negotiation to provide communicating peers a means to mutually determine an attestation protocol that correctly describes the target's infrastructure, is executable on the target system, and meets the target's goal of constrained disclosure. These three goals can be formally defined as sufficiency, executability, and soundness. Our negotiation procedure aims to satisfy these three properties through the following protocol presented in Fig. 4.

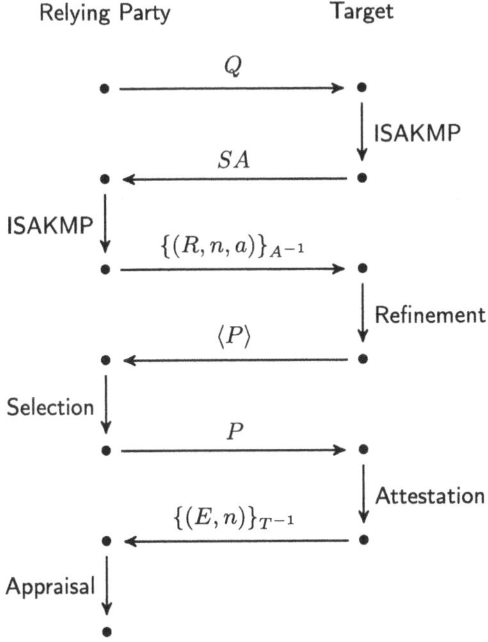

Fig. 4. Processing sequence for Negotiation, Selection, Attestation and Appraisal during remote attestation.

Negotiation begins with the establishment of a security association through ISAKMP. This multi-step procedure includes sharing necessary information, such as keys and identities, to establish a secure connection. Additional shared information includes instantiating the situation which is a function of identity and context. Together, these fields ultimately result in a security association (SA) which is valid for some predetermined length of time.

Once the network traffic is protected under the SA, the relying party sends a request ($\{(R, n, a)\}_{A^{-1}}$) which lists potentially many preferred measurement operations. The request is composed of the following four attributes:

- n – nonce
- R – list of protocols (Copland phrases)
- a – situational identifier
- $\{\cdot\}_{A^{-1}}$ – signature (by appraiser or relying party)

The most important piece of the request is R: a list of protocols which describe specific ASPs and measurement targets together as Copland phrases. Requesting evidence might be a useful concept but evidence reflects concrete values and we believe it is more useful to request abstract values in the form of Copland phrases. With the measurement operations abstractly outlined in R, the target can map requested operations to one or many suitable attestation components such that the request is satisfied. In addition to R, the request includes a situational identifier a previously determined during ISAKMP. a is necessary to describe the context of the attestation and may be used to help the communicating peers realize policy. The request also includes a nonce n and signature $\{\cdot\}_{A^{-1}}$ which are necessary for security purposes, namely freshness and authentication.

The process of mapping requested terms to existing, executable, and sound protocols is called *refinement*. Once the target receives a request, they may refine said request using specifications outlined in the $System$ to generate terms that are either specifically requested or variations of those requested. The target may reason about existing attestation components using the list of existing ASPs, the $knowsOf$ relation, and $context$ relation found within the manifest. The target may combine measurement operations within the manifests, within the environment, or within the system through Copland sequencing and parallel operators. As protocols are gathered for the proposal, the target recursively applies its privacy policy to ensure proposed protocols are sound. The target also recursively proves any proposed term is executable. Refinement ultimately produces the proposal $\langle P \rangle$ which is a collection of protocols that satisfy the request, are executable on the target system, and do not expose sensitive information.

Once the relying party receives the proposal, they must select the best protocol for attestation. To do so, the relying party orders the protocols based on some situationally determined criteria realized by the selection policy. One obvious ordering respects the goal of comprehensive information where the best protocol is the most comprehensive. Another possible ordering may be one that respects resource consumption and thus the best protocol is the one that consumes the fewest system resources. For any of these potential orderings, the arrangement of protocols naturally forms a lattice structure where the best protocol is at the top of the lattice and an empty protocol, or failed negotiation, is at the bottom.

The selection of a best protocol p ends the negotiation procedure. The relying party sends p to the target, signifying the beginning of the attestation sequence. Once received, the target performs measurement operations specified in p to generate some evidence E. The evidence is packaged ($\{(E, n)\}_{T^{-1}}$) and delivered to an appraiser for assessment. The evidence package consists of:

- n – nonce
- E – bundled evidence
- $\{\cdot\}_{T^{-1}}$ – signature (by the target)

where the nonce is the same nonce sent in the attestation request to ensure freshness. Bundled evidence (Rowe, 2016b) is evidence gathered by the appraisal and the signature ensures authenticity and integrity of the evidence.

4 Verification

The commuting diagram in Fig. 5 shows the relationship between attestation requirements and a correct implementation. At the requirements level a request is received and transformed by the attestation system into evidence as originally defined in Fig. 1. The evidence lattice $(E, \preceq, \top, \bot)$ captures evidence ordering reflecting the relying party's need for comprehensive information.

At the implementation level, a collection of ASPs run to generate measurements that are bundled into an evidence package and returned. If implementation is correct, the correct ASPs run on the correct places in the correct order.

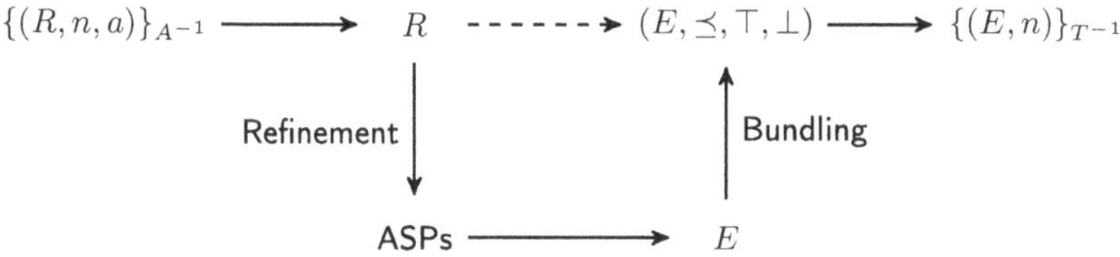

Fig. 5. Commuting diagram showing attestation correctness.

Verifying an implementation against requirements may be infeasible, thus we work step-wise from requirements to implementation through a series of refinement steps. The verification stack in Fig. 6 is a commuting diagram capturing attestation as defined in Fig. 1 at multiple abstractions. Using the canonical approach for compiler verification, we verify each refinement against its requirements. Because each refinement serves as requirements for the next refinement, the separate verification steps plug together into the stack from requirements to implementation shown in Fig. 6.

Figure 6 can be decomposed into two major activities. The request, R, through Selection producing P is *negotiation* while protocol P through ASPs is *execution*. Protocol execution is performed by compiling and running on an attestation manager. The attestation manager has been verified in earlier work by Petz and Alexander (2022). Thus, if we can verify a correct protocol results from negotiation, we will have a fully verified attestation process.

Primary requirements for negotiation are choosing a protocol that: (i) satisfies constrained disclosure requirements on the target; and (ii) satisfies comprehensive information requirements on the relying party. We refer to these properties as *soundness* and *sufficiency* respectively. Soundness is defined in terms of *executability* and *privacy policy enforcement*. Sufficiency is defined in terms of evidence ordering $(E, \preceq, \top, \bot)$.

Executability is a static guarantee that a proposed protocol can run on a target. This can be confirmed by knowing all protocol ASPs are available for execution on the target and all places referenced by dispatch commands are known. A manifest's `ASPs` list contains the set of available ASPs and its `knowsOf` list contains the set of attestation managers it can communicate with. The definition of executable is recursive implying that when a target dispatches a phrase to another attestation manager, that phrase must in turn be executable.

Definition 1 (Executability). *A protocol is* executable *with respect to a target, manifest, and environment if: (i) all necessary ASPs are available; (ii) all specified places are known, and (iii) all dispatched protocols are executable on their target.*

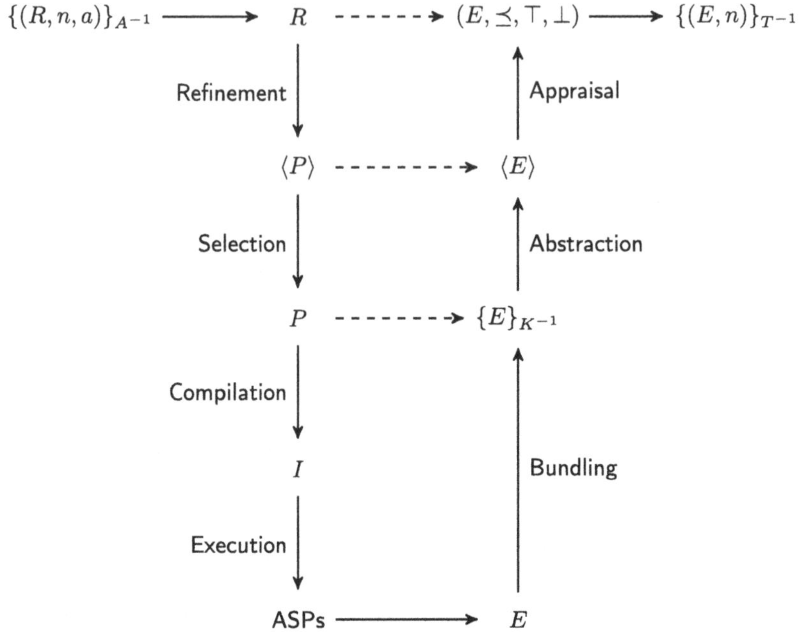

Fig. 6. Verification stack showing certification dependencies and execution path. Solid lines represent implementations while dashed lines represent mathematical definitions.

We formally represent executability with the Coq definition *executable*. One can see that given a term, place, and environment, any term may be recursively evaluated to determine executability. For any term with an ASP, executable checks that the environment has the ASP. For any $@p(t)$ operation, *executable* ensures that the requesting place knows of the receiving place and that the term is executable at the receiving place. For sequencing and parallel operations, executability recurses into subterms.

We prove the decidability of executable with the theorem *executable_dec* from Fig. 7.[1] *executable_dec* must produce a proof that *executable* is either true or false for every combination of term, place, and environment.

An executable protocol is *sound* if it does not violate the privacy policy of its target, including protocols dispatched to other attestation managers. To reason about soundness, we must first capture policy to realize if protocols expose sensitive information.

[1] For those unfamiliar with Coq, the type $\{p\} + \{\sim p\}$ is a sum type whose values are lifted proofs of p or $\sim p$.

```
Fixpoint executable(t:Term)(k:Plc)(e:Environment):Prop :=
match t with
| asp a ⇒ hasASPe k e a
| att p t ⇒ knowsOfe k e p → executable t p e
| lseq t1 t2 ⇒ executable t1 k e ∧ executable t2 k e
| bseq _ t1 t2 ⇒ executable t1 k e ∧ executable t2 k e
| bpar _ t1 t2 ⇒ executable t1 k e ∧ executable t2 k e
end.

Theorem executable_dec:∀ t k e,{(executable t k e)}+{~(executable t k e)}.
```

Fig. 7. Definition and decidability theorem for *executable*.

Definition 2 (Privacy Policy). *Privacy policy applies to the target and relationally defines the information that may be shared with a communicating peer.*

Local policy is specified by the manifest as a relation among ASPs and places. Local policy, for the target, is synonymous with privacy policy. If the relation (*Policy a p*) exists and is specified in the manifest then a protocol from place *p* may ask the current attestation manager to run *a*. If all ASPs referenced by a protocol are allowed by a place's local policy, then that protocol may run on that place.

Like executability, we prove that policy enforcement is decidable. Given any local policy, *p*, any place *plc*, and any requesting ASP *asp*, it is decidable whether the request is allowed:

$\forall\ p\ asp\ plc, \{(p\ asp\ plc)\}+\{\tilde{}(p\ asp\ plc)\}.$

Proving this theorem requires that the local policy relation be decidable. Specifically, for any ASP and place, it must be decidable whether the place can request an ASP's execution. When the local policy is defined as an inductive relation this proof is bulky, but straightforward. We have many examples of decidability proofs for individual policies and a rough Ltac tactic. However, when local policy is stated as an unqualified relation, we have not found a proof.

If we assume the local policy application is decidable we can prove decidability of access control checks over full protocols. The proof takes a form similar to the proof of executability:

```
Theorem checkTermPolicy_dec:∀ t k e,
    (∀ p0 a0, {(checkASPPolicy p0 e a0)} + {~(checkASPPolicy p0 e a0)}) →
    {(checkTermPolicy t k e)}+{~(checkTermPolicy t k e)}.
```

The trade-off is assuming local policy decidability places the burden of proof on the system implementer. Before a full protocol can be checked for policy adherence, the implementer needs to provide a proof that local policy defined over ASPs is decidable. With this assumption satisfied, policy enforcement over protocol terms is decidable and may be statically checked prior to execution.

With executability and policy enforcement proved decidable, it is a simple step to prove that *soundness* is decidable. Informally, soundness is defined as the combination of decidability and policy adherence:

Definition 3 (Soundness). *A protocol is* sound *with respect to a target manifest if: (i) it is executable; and (ii) it does not violate local privacy policy.*

The Coq definition of *soundness* and the associated theorem rely on the previously defined specifications for executability and policy adherence, as seen below.

```
Definition sound (t:Term)(k:Plc)(e:Environment) :=
  (executable t k e) ∧ (checkTermPolicy t k e).

Theorem sound_dec: ∀ t p e,
    (∀ p0 a0, {(checkASPPolicy p0 e a0)} + {~(checkASPPolicy p0 e a0)})
    → {sound t p e}+{~(sound t p e)}.
```

We have shown that for any protocol, place, and environment soundness is decidable and may be determined statically given local policy enforcement is statically decidable. Thus, our system can determine soundness during negotiation, prior to execution and use the result to help select a protocol. Furthermore, Curry-Howard allows using decidability proofs as functions (Howard, 1969). A call to *sound_dec* t p e will determine if protocol t running at place p in environment e is sound. The soundness check can be synthesized to CakeML for inclusion in our fielded attestation manager implementation (Barclay, 2022).

While soundness applies to the target, *sufficiency* applies to the relying party. If a protocol produces evidence that is *sufficient* for its trust assessment then the protocol is sufficient for the relying party.

Definition 4 (Sufficiency). *A protocol is* sufficient *with respect to a relying party if it meets the relying party's comprehensive information requirements.*

The evidence lattice $(E, \preceq, \top, \bot)$ shown in Fig. 5 captures comprehensive information requirements of the relying party as an ordering of evidence types producible by available protocols. The Copland semantics (Ramsdell et al., 2019) defines a formal evidence semantics that maps a protocol to its evidence type. Thus, given an evidence type we know which protocol(s) produced it and can use the evidence lattice to determine protocol sufficiency. Unfortunately, Rowe (2016a; 2016b) demonstrates that under certain conditions the same evidence type might be produced by different protocols. This problem can be avoided by restricting protocols considered, but the burden of this task falls to the user.

In the evidence lattice, E is the set of evidence produced by protocols considered in negotiation with a target. E is partially ordered by $\preceq$, a partial order we refer to informally as the evidence order. $\top$ and $\bot$ define all evidence and no evidence respectively as required by the lattice definition.

Every negotiation defines evidence type $e_{min} : E$ that specifies minimally sufficient comprehensive information for the relying party. Any evidence e such that $e_{min} \preceq e$ is acceptable to the relying party and satisfies its comprehensive information requirements. In turn, any protocol producing e is considered *sufficient* for the situation.

Protocol soundness and sufficiency are separate and potentially conflicting goals. A simple negotiation correctness definition requires producing a protocol that is both sound and sufficient.

Definition 5 (Negotiation Correctness). *Negotiation between a relying party and a target is* correct *if it produces a sound and sufficient protocol.*

This definition holds whenever negotiation produces a protocol that meets minimum requirements of a relying party while satisfying constrained disclosure and executability for the target.

While soundness and sufficiency are both statically predicted, Rowe (2016a; 2016b)'s result establishing that the same evidence can be generated by different protocols implies that we cannot infer from otherwise good evidence that the correct protocol ran. Similarly, we cannot infer from evidence that a target's privacy policy is actually enforced. Thus, we are obligated to gather meta-evidence of protocol execution in addition to evidence of system behavior. Thus the need for layered attestations and attestation protocols.

5 Example

An example attestation scenario used across our work is a relying party determining if an attester is running an acceptable, properly configured virus checker (Petz and Alexander, 2022). Figure 8 shows this architecture where P_0 is the location of the relying party, P_1 is the location of the attestation manager responsible for measurement of the virus checker and local signature file, and P_2 is the location of the attestation manager responsible for measuring the signature file server.

Manifests for this scenario are specified as (with reformatting for readability):

P_0`:={|asps:=[]; K:=[`P_1`]; C:=[]; Policy:={}|}`
P_1`:={|asps:=[aVC,aHSH]; K:=[`P_0`,`P_2`]; C:=[]; Policy:={(`P_0` aVC),(`P_0` aHSH)}|}`
P_2`:={|asps:=[aSFS]; K:=[`P_1`]; C:=[]; Policy:={(`P_1` aSFS)}|}`

Three Copland phrases describe potential attestation protocols available to P_0 for inclusion in proposals:

p_0 = `@`P_1 `[(aVC` P_1 `vc)]`
p_1 = `@`P_1 `[(aVC` P_1 `vc)` $\rightarrow$ `(aHSH` P_1 `sf)]`
p_2 = `@`P_1 `[(aVC` P_1 `vc)` $\rightarrow$ `(aHSH` P_1 `sf)` $\rightarrow$ `@`P_2 `(aSFS` P_2 `sfs)]`

In protocol p_0, the ASP `aVC` is used to measure `vc`, the virus checking target located at P_0. In p_1, the virus checking measurement is followed by `aHSH`, a measurement that hashes the signature file `sf` co-located at P_1. Finally, in p_2, the protocol invokes `aVC` and `aHSH` followed by a remote call to P_2 to invoke ASP `aSFS` to measure the signature file server `sfs` itself. While we are not limited to three protocols, this set defines a collection of increasingly informative attestations.

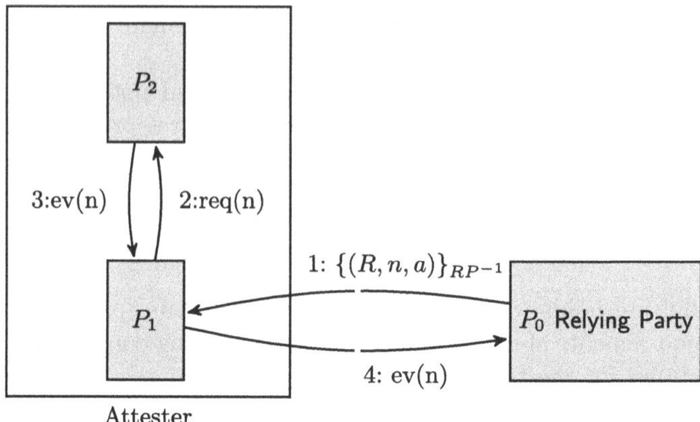

Fig. 8. Example remote attestation mechanism motivated by the flexible mechanisms presented in (Helble et al., 2021).

To begin negotiation the relying party sends the request $\{(R, n, a)\}_{RP^{-1}}$ to P_1 for a measurement of the target's virus checker. When P_1 receives the request, it returns a subset of its three protocols. The relying party selects protocols based on soundness. In the current configuration, all three protocols are executable and satisfy policy and are thus chosen. If the `aHSH` entry were removed from P_1's policy, protocols p_1 and p_2 would not be chosen because privacy policy will not allow them to run. Similarly, if `aSFS` were not available to P_2, protocol p_2 would not be selected because the required ASP is not available.

sound_dec determines the soundness of each protocol, but is unwieldy as defined. Two helper functions customize *sound_dec* for each system being examined. *sound_local_policies* takes a specific environment and ensures *checkASPPolicy* is decidable for each manifest. The resulting lemma is used to instantiate the assumption of *sound_dec* resulting in *sound_system_dec* that determines if a protocol is sound with respect to a place given. Specializing functions for a specific place simplifies exploration of the design space.

An alternative negotiation approach builds a proposal for each request. The *knowsOf* relation reveals P_1 knows of P_2 and therefore may request measurements involving the signature file server in addition to local measurements. The attester thus generates the proposal, $\langle p_0, p_1, p_2 \rangle$. Since p_2 is a more complex measurement, it may expose sensitive information not suitable for all appraisers. Privacy policy can be modified to prevent access to $aSFS$ making p_2 unsound and thus not included in the proposal. However, both p_0 and p_1 are sound and included in the proposal $\langle p_0,\ p_1 \rangle$. Again, our verified soundness decision procedure statically guarantees the soundness of each proposed protocol.

In this example, the evidence lattice used by the relying party is trivial. If comprehensive information is the goal, protocols should be ordered $p_0 \preceq p_1 \preceq p_2$ with $\top = p_2$ and $\bot = \emptyset$. The relying party then chooses e_{min} appropriately for the situation.

6 Related Work

Existing work in attestation protocol negotiation is minimal. Helble et al. (2021) briefly introduce the negotiation scheme stating that it is needed to mutually satisfy the situational requirements of the target and appraiser. The specific formalisms and overall scheme of negotiation are not considered in detail. Pendergrass et al. (2017) introduce Maat, a measurement and attestation platform that performs negotiation for security services such as cryptographic hashing and signing algorithms. Similar to the negotiation work done in Maat, Huang and Peng (2009) introduce an automated negotiation model which exchanges keys and identities to authenticate attesting peers. ISAKMP Maughan et al. (1998) and IKE Carrel and Harkins (1998) both perform limited negotiation for defining security associations, but at an earlier stage in the communication process.

Protocol analysis is a critical part of selecting a situationally best protocol. In works by Rowe (2016a), authors introduce a mathematical representation of protocols concluding that measurement order directly impacts the protocols vulnerability to an adversary. CHASE is a first order model finder used to reason about protocol ordering in the context of an attacker (Ramsdell, 2020). Petz et al. (2021) detail the process of using CHASE to instantiate such reasoning. Baez (2022) also reason about Copland protocols using CHASE. In both works by Petz et al. (2021) and Baez (2022),authors provision Copland phrases as knowledge system users rather than mutually agreed upon protocols.

VRASED (Nunes et al., 2019) and HYDRA Eldefrawy et al. (2017) are remote attestation systems using formal verification in their design. VRASED uses a co-design approach that results in formally verified attestation systems. Similarly, HYDRA uses a verified microkernel to achieve attestation guarantees. Both of these projects focus on attestations during boot and system initialization in contrast to this work that focuses on layered, runtime attestation.

7 Conclusions and Future Work

We propose a negotiation framework allowing communicating peers to establish a mutually agreed upon attestation protocol satisfying constrained disclosure and comprehensive information requirements. Using system manifests that describe attestation managers we derive a decision procedure for soundness and define an ordering relationship to establish sufficiency. Thus, for any communicating peers, an attestation protocol can be selected such that the goals of constrained disclosure and comprehensive information hold prior to execution.

This work represents an intermediate step in our longer term goal of verified attestation systems. Our current proofs are pedestrian and will not scale. We are using Coq proof engineering capabilities to construct simpler, reusable proof infrastructure. We are exploring synthesis and selection of a optimal attestation protocol that satisfies semantic appraisal goals in addition to soundness and sufficiency. Additionally, we are investigating techniques for automatically generating proposals to reduce protocol design and selection burden. Finally, we are developing techniques for verifying manifest compilation to ensure implementations satisfy assumptions made during design.

References

Baez, F.E.V.: Evaluating SGX's remote attestation security through the analysis of Copland phrases (2022)

Barclay, T.: Proof-producing synthesis of cakeml from coq. PhD Proposal (2022)

Bertot, Y., Castéran, P.: Interactive Theorem Proving and Program Development: Coq'Art: The Calculus of Inductive Constructions. Springer Science & Business Media, Berlin, Heidelberg (2013). https://doi.org/10.1007/978-3-662-07964-5

Carrel, D., Harkins, D.: The Internet Key Exchange (IKE). RFC 2409, November 1998. https://www.rfc-editor.org/info/rfc2409

Coker, G., et al.: Principles of remote attestation. Int. J. Inf. Secur. **10**(2), 63–81 (2011)

Coker, G., Guttman, J., Loscocco, P., Sheehy, J., Sniffen, B.: Attestation: evidence and trust. In: Chen, L., Ryan, M.D., Wang, G. (eds.) ICICS 2008. LNCS, vol. 5308, pp. 1–18. Springer, Heidelberg (2008). https://doi.org/10.1007/978-3-540-88625-9_1

Eldefrawy, K., Rattanavipanon, N., Tsudik, G.: Hydra: hybrid design for remote attestation (using a formally verified microkernel). In: Proceedings of the 10th ACM Conference on Security and Privacy in wireless and Mobile Networks, pp. 99–110 (2017)

Haldar, V., Chandra, D., Franz, M.: Semantic remote attestation - a virtual machine directed approach to trusted computing. In: Proceedings of the Third Virtual Machine Research and Technology Symposium. San Jose, CA, May 2004

Helble, S.C., Kretz, I.D., Loscocco, P.A., Ramsdell, J.D., Rowe, P.D., Alexander, P.: Flexible mechanisms for remote attestation. ACM Trans. Priv. Secur. (TOPS) **24**(4), 1–23 (2021)

Howard, W.A.: The formulae-as-types notion of construction (1969)

Huang, X., Peng, Y.: An effective approach for remote attestation in trusted computing. In: WISA 2009: Proceedings of the 2nd International Symposium on Web Information Systems and Applications, January 2009

Martin, A., et al.: The ten page introduction to trusted computing. Technical report CS-RR-08-11, Oxford University Computing Labratory, Oxford, UK (2008)

Maughan, D., Schertler, M., Schneider, M., Turner, J.: Internet security association and key management protocol RFC 2048 (ISAKMP). Technical report, The Internet Engineering Task Force of The Internet Society, November 1998

Nunes, I.D.O., Eldefrawy, K., Rattanavipanon, N., Steiner, M., Tsudik, G.: {VRASED}: a verified hardware/software co-design for remote attestation. In: 28th {USENIX} Security Symposium ({USENIX} Security 19), pp. 1429–1446 (2019)

Pendergrass, J.A., Helble, S., Clemens, J., Loscocco, P.: Maat: a platform service for measurement and attestation. arXiv preprint arXiv:1709.10147 (2017)

Petz, A., Alexander, P.: A copland attestation manager. In: Hot Topics in Science of Security (HoTSoS 2019). Nashville, TN, 8–11 April 2019

Petz, A., Alexander, P.: An infrastructure for faithful execution of remote attestation protocols. In: Dutle, A., Moscato, M.M., Titolo, L., Muñoz, C.A., Perez, I. (eds.) NFM 2021. LNCS, vol. 12673, pp. 268–286. Springer, Cham (2021). https://doi.org/10.1007/978-3-030-76384-8_17

Petz, A., Jurgensen, G., Alexander, P.: Design and formal verification of a copland-based attestation protocol. In: Proceedings of the 19th ACM-IEEE International Conference on Formal Methods and Models for System Design, pp. 111–117. MEMOCODE 2021, Association for Computing Machinery, New York, NY, USA (2021). https://doi.org/10.1145/3487212.3487340

Ramsdell, J., et al.: Orchestrating layered attestations. In: Principles of Security and Trust (POST 2019). Prague, Czech Republic, 8–11 April 2019

Ramsdell, J.: Chase: a model finder for finitary geometric logic (2020). https://github.com/ramsdell/chase

Rowe, P.D.: Confining adversary actions via measurement. In: Proceedings of the Third International Workshop on Graphical Models for Security, pp. 150–166 (2016a)

Rowe, P.D.: Bundling evidence for layered attestation. In: Franz, M., Papadimitratos, P. (eds.) Trust 2016. LNCS, vol. 9824, pp. 119–139. Springer, Cham (2016b). https://doi.org/10.1007/978-3-319-45572-3_7

Steffen, A.: strongswan, October 2021. https://www.strongswan.org/. Accessed 29 June 2022

Rewrite-Based Decomposition of Signal Temporal Logic Specifications

Kevin Leahy[1(✉)], Makai Mann[1], and Cristian-Ioan Vasile[2]

[1] MIT Lincoln Laboratory, 244 Wood St., Lexington, MA 02421, USA
{kevin.leahy,makai.mann}@ll.mit.edu
[2] Lehigh University, 27 Memorial Dr W, Bethlehem, PA 18015, USA
cvasile@lehigh.edu

Abstract. Multi-agent coordination under Signal Temporal Logic (STL) specifications is an exciting approach for accomplishing complex temporal missions with safety requirements. Despite significant progress, these approaches still suffer from scalability limitations. Decomposition into subspecifications and corresponding subteams of agents provides a way to reduce computation and leverage modern parallel computing architectures. In this paper, we propose a rewrite-based approach for jointly decomposing an STL specification and team of agents. We provide a set of formula transformations that facilitate decomposition. Furthermore, we cast those transformations as a rewriting system and prove that it is convergent. Next, we develop an algorithm for efficiently exploring and ranking rewritten formulae as decomposition candidates, and show how to decompose the best candidate. Finally, we compare to previous work on decomposing specifications for multi-agent planning problems, and provide computing and energy grid case studies.

1 Introduction

Coordination and control of multi-agent systems from high-level specifications is a challenging and active area of research. As with many areas of formal methods and multi-agent systems, scalability is often a limiting factor. Ideally, an operator would provide a single global specification for a large team of multi-agent systems, and the system would assign tasks and roles accordingly and synthesize a plan and controllers. Here, we aim to formalize a method for analyzing a signal temporal logic (STL) specification for a principled approach to jointly decompose and distribute the specification among a team of agents.

Most STL work in multi-agent systems assumes either centralized control from a global specification [4,11,15] or decentralized control from local

 The NASA University Leadership Initiative (grant #80NSSC20M0163) provided funds to assist the authors with their research, but this article solely reflects the opinions and conclusions of its authors and not any NASA entity.

Supplementary Information The online version contains supplementary material available at https://doi.org/10.1007/978-3-031-33170-1_14.

K. Y. Rozier and S. Chaudhuri (Eds.): NFM 2023, LNCS 13903, pp. 224–240, 2023.
https://doi.org/10.1007/978-3-031-33170-1_14

specifications [16,17]. In contrast, several methods for multi-agent planning with linear temporal logic (LTL) specifications have identified methods for automatically decomposing a specification into sub-specifications and assigning agents or sub-teams of agents to execute those sub-specifications [2,7,21,23].

Unlike LTL, STL has the advantage of specifying concrete timing requirements over continuous, real-valued signals, but there has been comparatively little work focused on decomposition of STL. [6] focused on decomposing an STL formula given an *a priori* set of disjoint sub-teams. In this work, we decompose the formula and team jointly, in an attempt to achieve a task-based set of sub-teams. We take inspiration from [14], but our approach is based on an abstract reduction system, providing guarantees on its convergence. We also perform formula transformation and assignment as two separate stages, reducing the search space of the assignment problem to those that are feasible for a given transformation. Additionally, our approach works for STL in general, whereas [14] focuses only on a fragment of STL. Another closely related work is [22], which looks at a multi-agent fragment of STL and assigns sub-formulae to individual agents. The assignment is an *implicit* part of their synthesis framework. Here, we focus only on an *explicit* assignment and decomposition, and we do not consider the synthesis problem. The method presented in this work could be used as a pre-processing step for their proposed synthesis and motion planning work, as well as most other existing multi-agent STL synthesis approaches.

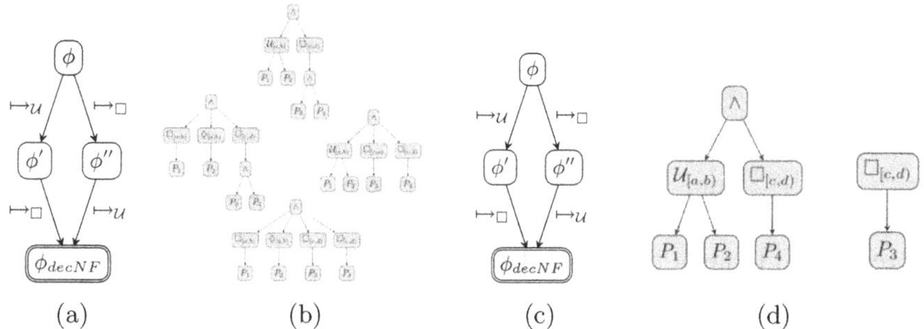

Fig. 1. Decomposition framework: build a DAG of all possible formula rewrites (1a, Sect. 3); build an AST for each resulting formula (1b, Sect. 4); score each node in the DAG according to its AST (1c, Sect. 4.3); and select best node and evaluate its decomposed specification (1d, Sect. 4.2).

The main contribution of this paper is an algorithm for simultaneous decomposition of STL formulae and heterogeneous agent subteam assignment consisting of 1) a rewriting system for reasoning about changes to STL formulae, with proof of termination and confluence; 2) a normal form of decomposed STL formulae that provides bounds on the ability to decompose a formula; and 3) an optimization approach for selecting the best decomposition and assignment based on a directed acyclic graph (DAG) constructed by the rewriting system.

2 Background and Problem Definition

In this work, we focus on requirements in the form of Signal Temporal Logic (STL) specifications [18]. The syntax of STL is given in Backus-Naur form as

$$\phi := \top \mid P \mid \neg\phi \mid \phi_1 \wedge \phi_2 \mid \phi_1 \mathcal{U}_{[a,b)} \phi_2 \ , \tag{1}$$

where ϕ, ϕ_1, and ϕ_2 are STL formulae; $\top$ is the symbol for logical *true*; P is a predicate of the form $\pi(\mathbf{x}(t)) \geq c$ for $\mathbf{x} \in \mathbb{R} \to \mathbb{R}^m$, $\pi \in \mathbb{R}^m \to \mathbb{R}$, and $c \in \mathbb{R}$; $\neg$ and $\wedge$ are Boolean negation and conjunction; and $\mathcal{U}_{[a,b)}$ is the temporal operator Until, with $a, b \in \mathbb{R}$ and $a \leq b$. Other operators $\vee$ (disjunction, $\neg(\neg\phi_1 \wedge \neg\phi_2)$), $\Diamond$ (finally, $\top\mathcal{U}_{[a,b)}\phi$), and $\Box$ (globally, $\neg\Diamond_{[a,b)}\neg\phi$) can be defined from the other operators. We use the notation *pred*(ϕ) to denote all predicates in ϕ, and *conj*(ϕ) for all the *top-level* conjuncts of formula ϕ.

Example 1. Let P_i be STL predicates, and $\phi := P_1\mathcal{U}_{[a,b)}P_2 \wedge \Box_{[c,d)}(P_3 \wedge P_4)$:

$$\begin{aligned} pred(\phi) &:= \{P_1, P_2, P_3, P_4\} \\ conj(\phi) &:= \{P_1\mathcal{U}_{[a,b)}P_2, \Box_{[c,d)}(P_3 \wedge P_4)\} \end{aligned}$$

Note that although $P_3 \wedge P_4$ contains a conjunction, it is not at the *top-level*.

The semantics of STL with respect to a signal $\mathbf{x}$ at time t are defined as

$$\begin{aligned} (\mathbf{x}, t) &\models \pi(\mathbf{x}(t)) \geq c && \Leftrightarrow \pi(\mathbf{x}(t)) \geq c \\ (\mathbf{x}, t) &\models \neg\phi && \Leftrightarrow (\mathbf{x}, t) \not\models \phi \\ (\mathbf{x}, t) &\models \phi_1 \wedge \phi_2 && \Leftrightarrow (\mathbf{x}, t) \models \phi_1 \text{ and } (\mathbf{x}, t) \models \phi_2 \\ (\mathbf{x}, t) &\models \phi_1\mathcal{U}_{[a,b)}\phi_2 && \Leftrightarrow \exists t' \in [t+a, t+b] s.t. (\mathbf{x}, t') \models \phi_2 \text{ and} \\ & && \qquad \forall t'' \in [0, t'](\mathbf{x}, t'') \models \phi_1 \ . \end{aligned} \tag{2}$$

In addition to the semantics defined above, STL also has the notion of quantitative semantics or *robustness degree*, ρ. The robustness of a signal $\mathbf{x}$ at time t with respect to formula ϕ is defined as [9]

$$\begin{aligned} \rho(\mathbf{x}, t, \pi(\mathbf{x}(t)) \geq c) &:= \pi(\mathbf{x}(t)) - c \\ \rho(\mathbf{x}, t, \neg\phi) &:= -\rho(\mathbf{x}, t, \phi) \\ \rho(\mathbf{x}, t, \phi_1 \wedge \phi_2) &:= \min(\rho(\mathbf{x}, t, \phi_1), \rho(\mathbf{x}, t, \phi_2)) \\ \rho(\mathbf{x}, t, \phi_1\mathcal{U}_{[a,b)}\phi_2) &:= \max_{t' \in [t+a, t+b]} (\rho(\mathbf{x}, t', \phi_2), \min_{t'' \in [t, t']} \rho(\mathbf{x}, t'', \phi_1)) \end{aligned} \tag{3}$$

The *horizon* of an STL formula is the maximum execution time before the satisfiability of the specification can be determined [8]. The formula horizon, *hzn*, is defined recursively as:

$$\begin{aligned} hzn(\pi(\mathbf{x}(t)) \geq c) &:= 0 \\ hzn(\neg\phi) &:= hzn(\phi) \\ hzn(\phi_1 \circ \phi_2) &:= max(hzn(\phi_1), hzn(\phi_2)) \text{ for } \circ \in \{\wedge, \vee\} \\ hzn(\phi_1\mathcal{U}_{[a,b)}\phi_2) &:= max(hzn(\phi_1) + b - 1, hzn(\phi_2) + b) \end{aligned} \tag{4}$$

Definition 1 (Agent). *An* agent *is a tuple $A = (x(t), u)$, where $x(t) \in \mathbb{R}^n$ is its n-dimensional state at time t, and $u \in \mathbb{R}^n$ serves as an element-wise upper bound on $x(t)$. The lower bound is assumed to be an n-dimensional zero vector.*

The upper- and lower-bounds on $x(t)$ do not change with time. Rather, they bound $x(t)$ across all time. For convenience, we often drop the explicit dependence of $x(t)$ on t and simply write x. We denote the signal for a team of agents as $\mathbf{x} \in \mathbb{R}^m$. This can be obtained via concatenation, summation or other operation over individual agent signals. We assume this can be done but are agnostic to how. We use the term *agent* to be consistent with the related robotics literature, but agents represent any entities or processes that can be controlled separately. We say that an agent "services" a predicate if it is responsible for maintaining a signal that satisfies that predicate (or contributes to its satisfaction).

For a team of agents indexed by set J, we denote the jth agent as A_j, where $j \in J$. If two agents have the same upper bound u, we consider them to belong to an equivalence class g_u. For a team of agents, we denote the set of all such equivalence classes as G.

Given a (sub)team of agents $\mathcal{A} = \{A_j\}_{j \in J}$, we define the robustness *upper bound*, ρ_{ub}, recursively as:

$$\begin{aligned}
\rho_{ub}(\pi(\mathbf{x}(t)) \geq c), \mathcal{A}) &:= (\Sigma_{a \in \mathcal{A}} \pi(a.u)) - c \\
\rho_{ub}(\neg\phi, \mathcal{A}) &:= -\rho_{ub}(\phi, \mathcal{A}) \\
\rho_{ub}(\phi_1 \wedge \phi_2, \mathcal{A}) &:= min(\rho_{ub}(\phi_1, \mathcal{A}), \rho_{ub}(\phi_2, \mathcal{A})) \\
\rho_{ub}(\phi_1 \vee \phi_2, \mathcal{A}) &:= max(\rho_{ub}(\phi_1, \mathcal{A}), \rho_{ub}(\phi_2, \mathcal{A})) \\
\rho_{ub}(\phi_1 \mathcal{U}_{[a,b)} \phi_2, \mathcal{A}) &:= min(\rho_{ub}(\phi_1, \mathcal{A}), \rho_{ub}(\phi_2, \mathcal{A}))
\end{aligned} \tag{5}$$

This is the typical robustness definition evaluated over the agent upper bounds for every agent in the given team. Note that it no longer depends on $\mathbf{x}$ or t. If the robustness upper bound is negative, there does not exist a synthesized plan for agents $\mathcal{A}$ that satisfies the formula.

Example 2. To illustrate our notion of agents, we consider an example from computing. For a large computing cluster, each compute node can be modeled as an agent, with the state x capturing its resource utilization between its CPU, GPU, and RAM. Different predicates in an STL formula ϕ might request different combinations of resources. For a node with 16 CPU cores, 800 GPU cores, and 64 GB of RAM, its state is 3-dimensional with upper bound $u = \{16, 800, 64\}$ representing 100% utilization. Let the class of this agent be denoted g_1. Any other agent with exactly the same values of u would also belong to g_1, otherwise, the agent would belong to a separate class. The team signal, $\mathbf{x}$, is a concatenation of the agent signals.

Assumption 1. *We assume the existence of a synthesis method,* **Synth**. *Given a team of agents J and an STL specification ϕ,* **Synth**(J, ϕ) *synthesizes a plan for the agent(s) J to satisfy ϕ, if such a plan exists.*

Synthesis is not the focus of this work, and there are many synthesis tools available depending on the specific problem under consideration. Assumption 1 simply states that a user of our proposed method has an appropriate synthesis tool available.

We are now ready to state the problem under consideration. We seek a method for decomposing a synthesis problem, consisting of a team of agents and an STL specification, into a set of smaller, disjoint subproblems that can each be solved independently. The goal of this decomposition is to achieve a faster solution than solving the original problem, without rendering the problem infeasible in the process of decomposing it. However, there is no known method for determining the feasibility of a synthesis problem without running the synthesis procedure, which is expensive. Therefore we rely on robustness upper bound, which is a necessary condition for feasibility.

Problem 1. Given a team of agents $\{A_j\}_{j \in J}$ and an STL formula ϕ, find a team partition R and a set of formulae $\{\phi_r\}_{r \in R}$ such that

1. ϕ is satisfied if each subteam $r \in R$ satisfies its specification ϕ_r;
2. Solving the set of synthesis problems $\texttt{Synth}(r, \phi_r)$, including the time to decompose, is faster than $\texttt{Synth}(J, \phi)$; and
3. Robustness upper bound for all teams is non-negative.

Assumption 2. *We assume that the original synthesis problem has a solution.*

The focus of this work is on decomposition of a problem into subproblems whose solution guarantees solution of the original problem. For our analysis, Assumption 2 restricts us to feasible problems, since every infeasible problem will yield at least one infeasible subproblem.

Our approach is depicted in Fig. 1. The first step generates various transformations of the original formula that are easier to decompose. Next, the technique builds an abstract syntax tree (AST) for each of these formulae, efficiently explores the possible transformations and scores each rewritten formula. Finally, it selects the best node and decomposes the specification into subspecifications and associated subteams. We cover each of these steps in the following sections.

3 An STL Rewriting System

We start by describing a technique for modifying STL formulae to be more amenable to decomposition, while still guaranteeing satisfaction of the original formula. We accomplish this by developing a rewriting system for STL. Rewriting operates on abstract syntax trees (ASTs). Every STL formula can be represented as an AST with each node representing an operator or predicate. See Definition 7 in the Supplementary Material for a formal definition.

Formulae consisting of top-level conjunctions are the easiest to decompose. Top-level conjuncts are represented in an AST as the children of the root node, which is a conjunction operator. Logically, if each top-level conjunct is satisfied, then the entire formula is satisfied. There is no logical dependence between any of the top-level conjuncts. In this section, we provide three formula transformations that can add top-level conjuncts to facilitate decomposition. Not all of these transformations produce an equisatisfiable formula. However, we ensure that the transformation only strengthens the formula. Let ϕ be an STL formula and τ a transformation operator, then we only consider transformations such that $\tau(\phi) \models \phi$. This ensures that any plan found for the transformed formula is guaranteed to satisfy the original formula.

Definition 2 (Rewriting System). *A rewriting system is a tuple,* $(T, \rightarrow)$, *where* T *is a set of* terms, *and* $\rightarrow \subseteq T \times T$ *is a rewriting relation on* T. *If the terms* y *and* z *are in* $\rightarrow$, *we write* $y \rightarrow z$.

We now define our rewriting system for STL, $(\mathbb{S}, \rightarrow_{STL})$, where $\mathbb{S}$ is the set of all STL formulae, and $\rightarrow_{STL} := \{\mapsto_{\Box}, \mapsto_{\Diamond}, \mapsto_{\mathcal{U}}\}$ is a collection of rewrite rules defined below. Let ϕ_1 and ϕ_2 be STL formulae, and $a \leq b$ be real-valued time instances. We consider the following rewriting rules in $\rightarrow_{STL}$:

$$\Box_{[a,b)}(\phi_1 \wedge \phi_2) \mapsto_{\Box} \Box_{[a,b)}(\phi_1) \wedge \Box_{[a,b)}(\phi_2) \qquad \text{(split-globally)}$$

$$\Diamond_{[a,b)}(\phi_1 \wedge \phi_2) \mapsto_{\Diamond} \Box_{[a,b)}(\phi_1) \wedge \Box_{[a,b)}(\phi_2) \qquad \text{(split-finally)}$$

$$\phi_1 \mathcal{U}_{[a,b)} \phi_2 \mapsto_{\mathcal{U}} \Box_{[0,b)}(\phi_1) \wedge \Diamond_{[a,b)}(\phi_2) \qquad \text{(split-until)}$$

Of these rewriting rules, only (split-globally) produces an equisatisfiable formula. The other two entail the original formula as required, but are not satisfied by every trace that satisfies the original formula.

Remark 1. Our (split-finally) transformation is the most conservative of several possible choices for splitting $\Diamond$ over a conjunction. Both $\Diamond_{[a,b)}(\phi_1) \wedge \Box_{[a,b)}(\phi_2)$ and $\Box_{[a,b)}(\phi_1) \wedge \Diamond_{[a,b)}(\phi_2)$ also entail the original formula. We choose the symmetric option for simplicity of presentation.

Remark 2. We include two other transformations that produce a formula equisatisfiable to the input. If two like temporal operators appear next to each other in the formula, we adjust their time bounds accordingly. That is, $\Box_{[a,b)}\Box_{[c,d)}\phi \mapsto_{\Box\Box} \Box_{[a+c,b+d)}\phi$ and likewise $\Diamond_{[a,b)}\Diamond_{[c,d)}\phi \mapsto_{\Diamond\Diamond} \Diamond_{[a+c,b+d)}\phi$. We omit these rewrite rules from our presentation for simplicity, but all subsequent proofs and analyses hold for these rewrites as well.

Theorem 1. *The rewriting system* $(\mathbb{S}, \rightarrow_{STL})$ *terminates.*

Proof (Sketch). By Lemma 2.3.3 of [1], a finitely branching rewriting system $(T, \rightarrow)$ terminates if there exists a monotone embedding φ from $(T, \rightarrow)$ into $(\mathbb{N}, >)$. In our case, φ has two components – the sum of distances of conjuncts and until operators from the root, and the number of occurrences of conjunction and until operators in the formula. Namely,

$$\varphi = \sum_{i=1}^{n_{\wedge,\mathcal{U}}} d_i + (n_{\wedge,\mathcal{U}} + 1)n_{\mathcal{U}} , \tag{6}$$

where $n_\wedge$ and $n_\mathcal{U}$ are the number of conjunction and until operators appearing in the formula, $n_{\wedge,\mathcal{U}} = n_\wedge + n_\mathcal{U}$, and d_i is the distance of the ith conjunction or until from the root in the formula AST. For all replacement rules we consider, φ is a monotone embedding into $(\mathbb{N}, >)$, and our rewriting system terminates. □

Let $\rightarrow$ be an arbitrary reduction system containing a nonempty set of reduction mappings $\mapsto_i$, and $\xrightarrow{*}$ be its reflexive, transitive closure. Terms y and w are *joinable*, denoted $y \downarrow w$, *iff* there is a z such that $y \xrightarrow{*} z \xleftarrow{*} w$.

Definition 3 (Confluence). *A reduction system is* confluent *if* $\forall y \;.\; w_1 \xleftarrow{*} y \xrightarrow{*} w_2 \implies w_1 \downarrow w_2$.

Theorem 2. *The reduction system generated by* (split-globally), (split-finally), *and* (split-until) *is confluent.*[1]

Proof (Sketch). To prove confluence, we break our formula rewriting reduction system into three independent reduction systems:

1. $\rightarrow_\Box := \{\mapsto_\Box\}$: reduction system for (split-globally)
2. $\rightarrow_\Diamond := \{\mapsto_\Diamond\}$: reduction system for (split-finally)
3. $\rightarrow_\mathcal{U} := \{\mapsto_\mathcal{U}\}$: reduction system for (split-until)

We prove confluence by proving that each individual reduction system is confluent and commutative, then building up to our full reduction system, $\rightarrow_{STL} := \{\mapsto_\Box, \mapsto_\Diamond, \mapsto_\mathcal{U}\}$. Each reduction system alone is trivially confluent. We now look at combinations of reduction systems.

$\rightarrow_\Box$ and $\rightarrow_\Diamond$ act on different temporal operators. Therefore each can be applied independently, making local changes to non-overlapping regions of the AST (see Sect. 4), and the final ASTs are the same. This implies that $\rightarrow_{\Box\Diamond} := \rightarrow_\Box \cup \rightarrow_\Diamond$ is confluent. The same logic applies to $\rightarrow_{\Box\Diamond}$ and $\rightarrow_\mathcal{U}$, and therefore $\rightarrow := \rightarrow_{\Box\Diamond} \cup \rightarrow_\mathcal{U} = \rightarrow_\Box \cup \rightarrow_\Diamond \cup \rightarrow_\mathcal{U}$ is also confluent. □

Complete proofs for Theorems 1 and 2 can be found in the Supplementary Materials. Because our STL formula rewriting system is terminating and confluent, it is *convergent*. This implies that any STL formula can be reduced to a unique normal form through the application of our rewriting rules. We will call this form *decomposition normal form* (decNF). Importantly, satisfaction of a formula in decNF form implies satisfaction of the original formula, but not vice-versa. The number of top-level conjuncts in an STL formula in decNF is an upper bound on the number of subteams our method will produce.

[1] We assume that there is a global subterm ordering that puts equivalent formulae in a normal form, i.e., $b \wedge a \rightarrow a \wedge b$ so that $a \wedge b$ and $b \wedge a$ are known to be identical.

3.1 Formula Rewrite DAG

Given $(\mathbb{S}, \rightarrow_{STL})$ and an STL formula, we can consider all possible formulae obtained by repeated application of the rewriting rules to subformulae.

Definition 4 (Rewrite DAG). *A Formula Rewrite DAG, $G := \langle \Phi, E \rangle$, is a directed acyclic graph where each node in Φ is an STL formula and each directed edge in E goes from ϕ_1 to ϕ_2 such that $\phi_1 \rightarrow_{STL} \phi_2$.*

We denote the Formula Rewrite DAG for a formula, ϕ, as $G(\phi)$. For all ϕ, $G(\phi)$ has a single source node (in-degree of 0) corresponding to the original formula, ϕ, and a single sink node (out-degree of 0) corresponding to the decNF form of ϕ.

Example 3. Let ϕ be the formula from Example 1. One edge in $G(\phi)$ would connect ϕ (the root) to $P_1\mathcal{U}_{[a,b)}P_2 \wedge \Box_{[c,d)}P_3 \wedge \Box_{[c,d)}P_4$. This edge would be tagged with the transformation $\rightarrow_\Box$ and the conjunct it was applied to, $\Box_{[c,d)}(P_3 \wedge P_4)$. Figure 2 shows the complete rewrite DAG.

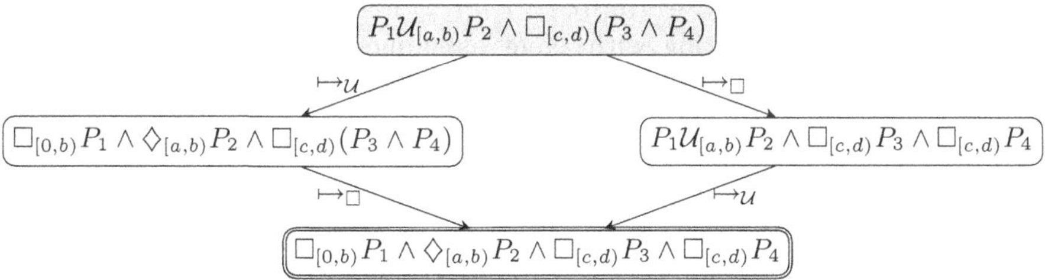

Fig. 2. Example of a rewrite DAG illustrating confluence and termination from the spec in Example 1. P_1, P_2, P_3, and P_4 represent STL predicates. a, b, c, and d are real-valued time bounds. The initial (root) formula is in the top gray box. Decomposition normal form is indicated by the double rectangle. Rewrite operations are indicated on the edges between formulae in the DAG.

Theorem 3. *Constructing a rewrite DAG by enumerating all possible formula transformations terminates with a finite graph.*

Proof. This follows directly from Theorem 1.

4 Decomposing STL

Having created a rewrite DAG as described in Sect. 3 above, we now describe how to analyze the candidate formula at each node in the DAG. For an STL formula at a given node in the DAG, we wish to assign agents to that formula in a way that is amenable to decomposition.

4.1 Agent Assignments

We now define agent assignments, followed by their use in STL decomposition.

Definition 5 (Agent Assignment). *An agent assignment for STL formula* ϕ *is a mapping* $\alpha : conj(\phi) \rightarrow 2^J$.

The mapping records agent assignments to top-level conjuncts of the specification. These are the children of the root AST node. The assignment is extended to all AST nodes by adopting the agent assignment of parent nodes. The root node agent assignment is defined to be all agents.

4.2 Decomposition

An agent assignment for a given STL specification induces a team partition R and a set of subspecifications, $\{\phi_r\}_{r\in R}$. Recall that J is the set of agent indices, thus R is a set of (nonempty) subsets that partition the agents. Formally, each element of R is a subset $r \subseteq J$ such that $\forall r \in R\ .\ |r| > 0$ and $\forall r_i, r_j \in R\ .\ i \neq j \rightarrow r_i \cap r_j = \emptyset$.

Given an agent assignment, α, R is computed as the largest valid partition such that $\forall r \in R\ \forall c \in conj(\phi)\ .\ \alpha(c) \subseteq r \vee \alpha(c) \cap r = \emptyset$. Intuitively, this is computed by starting with agent assignments for each top-level conjunct, and combining any conjuncts that have overlapping agent assignments. Let $match(r, \phi) := \{c | c \in conj(\phi) \wedge \alpha(c) \in r\}$. This denotes all top-level conjuncts associated with agent partition r. For each $r \in R$, there is a corresponding subspecification, $\phi_r := \bigwedge_{c \in match(r,\phi)} c$. Let a decomposition, $\mathcal{D}_R := \langle R, \{\phi_r\}_{r\in R}\rangle$, be a pair containing the agent partition and corresponding subspecifications.

A decomposition generates $|R|$ synthesis subproblems that can be solved independently with no coordination between them. Note that $\bigwedge_{r\in R} \phi_r \equiv \phi$. Thus, for $\phi := \tau(\psi)$, if $\texttt{Synth}(r, \phi_r)$ returns a valid solution for each subproblem, then the combined solutions satisfy the original specification ψ.

Remark 3. The decomposition method ensures that satisfied subproblems logically entail the original problem. However, we must also guarantee noninterference between signal generators of different teams, i.e., that two subteams do not have opposing goals when servicing predicates. This is problem-dependent: in our experimental results we have one case that avoids this via monotonicity (all goals are to increase signals), one that avoids it via mutual exclusion (never driving the same signal), and one that avoids it with an additional constraint that groups all relevant signals in the same subteam.

4.3 Comparison of Decomposition Candidates

There are many possible decompositions given a team of agents and an STL specification. Our main algorithm requires a method of ranking these candidate decompositions. The algorithm is fully parameterized by the choice of a score, ξ, for each decomposition. Here, we define our choice for this operator.

Since the robustness upper bound condition is necessary but not sufficient, we also introduce the costs c_{ap} and c_{pp} to produce a principled heuristic method for decomposition. These costs consist of a startup cost $c_{ap} : G \times pred(\phi) \rightarrow \mathbb{R}$, capturing the maximum initial cost for an agent of class $g \in G$ to begin servicing a predicate, and a switching cost $c_{pp} : G \times pred(\phi) \times pred(\phi) \rightarrow \mathbb{R}$, capturing the cost for switching from servicing one predicate to another. These costs abstract dynamics or other system properties that influence the feasibility of the synthesis process. The abstraction provides a way of incorporating some dynamics information while remaining computationally efficient (i.e., not solving the full synthesis problem).

For mobile robots, these costs might simply correspond to travel times between regions of the environment. We opt for this more general concept of costs to allow flexibility in the type of problem our framework can be applied to. We assume an analysis procedure that can either exactly or approximately determine these costs given the agent start state, dynamics, and predicate(s). In our experiments, costs are either provided explicitly, or agent states are nodes in a graph, for which we can use standard graph traversal algorithms to determine both startup and switching costs.

Example 4. Let us revisit the computing scenario from Example 2. Since starting from idle has little overhead, c_{ap} can be quite small, representing a few milliseconds to start any arbitrary computing request. However switching from a request that uses many GPU resources to one that requests many CPU resources typically has much higher overhead. Therefore c_{pp} would be higher for switching from GPU-intensive to CPU-intensive tasks or vice-versa.

To design a score, we start by defining the following metrics for a given decomposition:

1. N - number of subteams: $|R|$ (prefer larger)
2. C_{ap} - maximum startup cost: maximum value of c_{ap} over all agents and predicates in the subteam and corresponding subspecification (prefer smaller)
3. C_{pp} - maximum switching cost: maximum value of c_{pp} over all pairs of predicates in a subspecification (prefer smaller)
4. h - maximum horizon: the maximum subspecification horizon (prefer smaller)
5. ρ_{ub} - minimum robustness upper bound: minimum over all subproblem robustness upper bounds; relates predicates to maximum signal value with given decomposition (prefer larger)

Our primary goal is to maximize the number of subteams. More subteams results in smaller synthesis subproblems; however, we include the other metrics (defined in Sect. 2) to discourage "uneven" decompositions that contain subproblems of widely varying difficulty. If one subproblem is nearly as difficult as the original problem, then it still dominates the synthesis time.

Definition 6 (Decomposition Score). *For a given formula ϕ and its decomposition $\mathcal{D}_R$, our* heuristic decomposition score, $\xi := \langle N, -C_{ap}, -C_{pp}, -h, \rho_{ub} \rangle$ *collects the heuristic scores in a tuple.*

Let D_1 and D_2 be two possible decompositions for STL specification, ϕ. For each D_i, let our score choice be $\xi^i := \langle N^i, -C^i_{ap}, -C^i_{pp}, -h^i, \rho^i_{ub}\rangle$. Given these metrics, we compare D_1 and D_2 with $\xi^1 >_L \xi^2$, where $>_L$ is a lexicographic comparison. Note that metrics which are preferred to be smaller are negated to prioritize smaller values in the greater-than comparison. We prefer decompositions with a higher score. A decomposition D_i is guaranteed to be infeasible if $\rho^i_{ub} < 0$. Beyond a cheap feasibility check, we included ρ^i_{ub} in our decomposition score to break ties between otherwise equally scored decomposition candidates.

5 Exploring the Formula Rewrite DAG

We now describe an algorithm for decomposing an STL planning task into sub-specifications and agent subteams. We directly explore all possible formula transformations using a Formula Rewrite DAG and choose the formula that gives the best decomposition according to heuristic measures. For efficiency, we also avoid processing nodes of the DAG that do not add a top-level conjunct (and thus cannot increase the number of subteams). Furthermore, we leverage the following theorem to prune nodes that are not worth visiting.

Theorem 4. *Let ϕ be the formula at a node in a Formula Rewrite DAG such that $conj(\phi) = N$. If ϕ has no decomposition into N subteams (one subteam per top-level conjunct) with a nonnegative robustness, then its children do not have decompositions into $N+1$ subteams. See the Supplementary Materials for a proof sketch.*

Intuitively, Algorithm 1 explores the Formula Rewrite DAG starting from the root and attempting to decompose each transformed formula ϕ into $conj(\phi)$ subteams. It stops the search at nodes with guaranteed infeasible decompositions and compares the decomposition candidates using $>_L$.

Lines 1–2 initialize empty data structures used for tracking nodes to process and infeasible nodes, respectively. Lines 3–4 initialize the candidate to a null value, and the score to the worst possible score. Line 5 pushes the root node of the Formula Rewrite DAG as the start of the search. The loop starting at line 6 processes nodes in the DAG in a breadth-first order until all nodes have been processed or skipped. We assume the queue automatically caches and skips nodes that have already been processed. Lines 7–9 obtain the next node to process and skip it if it is known to be infeasible. Lines 10–13 check if the node has the same number of conjuncts as the parent. If so, it cannot have a greater number of subteams and is skipped. Note that the number of conjuncts only stays the same or increases with formula transformations, so we must still process its children. Line 14 obtains a decomposition assignment and robustness upper bound for the formula. The number of subteams is the number of top-level conjuncts, because we assume each conjunct is assigned a unique subteam. The algorithm still works without this assumption. However, this restriction allows the algorithm to conclude that a formula and all its descendants are infeasible in lines 15–18, by leveraging Theorem 4. If the robustness upper bound is negative,

Algorithm 1. Main decomposition algorithm

Input: Formula Rewrite DAG G, Set of agents $\mathcal{A}$
Output: Decomposition $\mathcal{D}_R$

1: $Q \leftarrow$ *empty queue* ▷ Nodes to explore
2: $D \leftarrow \emptyset$ ▷ Set to store dropped nodes
3: $c \leftarrow$ *null* ▷ Start with a null candidate
4: $\xi \leftarrow$ *worst* ▷ Initialize score with worst possible values
5: $push(Q, G.root)$
6: **while** $\neg empty(Q)$ **do**
7: $\quad n \leftarrow pop(Q)$
8: $\quad$ **if** $n \in D$ **then**
9: $\quad\quad$ **continue** ▷ Formula is known to be infeasible
10: $\quad$ **if** $|conj(n)| = |conj(Parent(n))|$ **then**
11: $\quad\quad push(Q, children(n))$
12: $\quad\quad push(D, n)$
13: $\quad\quad$ **continue** ▷ Cannot improve on parent
14: $\quad \mathcal{D}_n, \rho_{ub}^n \leftarrow compute\_assignment(n, \mathcal{A})$
15: $\quad$ **if** $\rho_{ub}^n < 0$ **then** ▷ Infeasibility condition
16: $\quad\quad push(D, Descendants(n))$ ▷ Descendants are all infeasible
17: $\quad\quad push(D, n)$
18: $\quad\quad$ **continue**
19: $\quad push(Q, Children(n))$
20: $\quad \xi^n \leftarrow compute\_score(\mathcal{D}_n, \mathcal{A})$
21: $\quad$ **if** $\xi^n >_L \xi$ **then** ▷ lexicographic comparison
22: $\quad\quad \xi \leftarrow \xi^n$
23: $\quad\quad c \leftarrow \mathcal{D}_n$
return c

all descendants are marked as infeasible to avoid processing them unnecessarily in case they appear on another path of the DAG. Line 19 adds all the node's children onto the end of the queue for future processing and line 20 computes the heuristic score. Lines 21–23 update the best score and candidate decomposition if this is the best score seen thus far according to a lexicographic comparison. Finally, the best decomposition is returned after processing or skipping all nodes in the Formula Rewrite DAG.

The implementation of *compute_score* is specific to the particular heuristic score choice. Depending on the score, there could be additional early-stopping checks before computing the entire decomposition. We efficiently compute the decomposition and score by solving mixed-integer linear programs (MILPs). We provide further information on our MILP encodings for *compute_decomp* and *compute_score* in the Supplementary Material.

Limitations. Our assumption that decomposition assigns a unique subteam to each top-level conjunct allows us to prune descendants. However, it might also rule out solutions that combine top-level conjunctions of a more heavily rewritten formula and achieve a higher number of subteams overall. Although we might miss alternative decompositions, it is important that the decomposition procedure runs quickly. Our goal is to cheaply find a decent decomposition, and let the synthesis procedure proceed from there. Too much upfront computation can be counterproductive for the larger synthesis problem. Empirically, this approach works well.

Despite the computed score, it is still possible that the best decomposition contains an infeasible subproblem that is only revealed during the synthesis procedure. In this case, we can return to the DAG and recover a different decomposition that does not contain the same infeasible subproblem. Future work can investigate weaker transformations that present less risk of creating infeasible problems. Note that between two decomposition options with the same score, the algorithm will pick the one closer to the root node by design of the search procedure. This is desirable because transformations only strengthen the formula, making it harder to satisfy. That is another reason that our restriction to decomposition assignments with one subteam per conjunct is a reasonable heuristic. It tends to stop the search earlier in the DAG even if it produces fewer subteams overall.

Table 1. Results from computing and energy grid case studies. Note that runtime for decomposition is by solving the resulting synthesis problems serially.

Example	Runtime (s)		% Speedup	$\|R\|$	DAG Size	N Agents	Decomp Time (s)	Largest Subproblem Time (s)
	No Decomp	With Decomp						
Computing	8.05	1.51	81.2	11	5	12	0.59	0.12
Energy Grid	329.37	165.90	49.6	10	128	45	19.74	35.09

6 Experiments and Results

We now provide evidence that this approach surpasses the state-of-the-art, and give two case studies of its application in practical domains. Our implementation is written in Python and encodes MILPs using the `PuLP` Python linear programming toolkit [19]. We instantiate `Synth` with a MILP-based synthesis approach for STL [3]. All results were obtained on a 2.10 GHz Intel Xeon Silver 4208 with 64 GB of memory. We used `Gurobi` 9.5.1 [12] as the underlying solver for both decomposition and synthesis. Gurobi had access to 16 physical cores with hyperthreading. All comparisons include the time to solve all decomposed subproblems serially. This is an upper bound on the real time, assuming in practice some would be solved in parallel. See the Supplementary Material for more information on our experiments, including an evaluation with the SCIP optimizer 7.0.3 [10] where decomposition has an even larger impact.

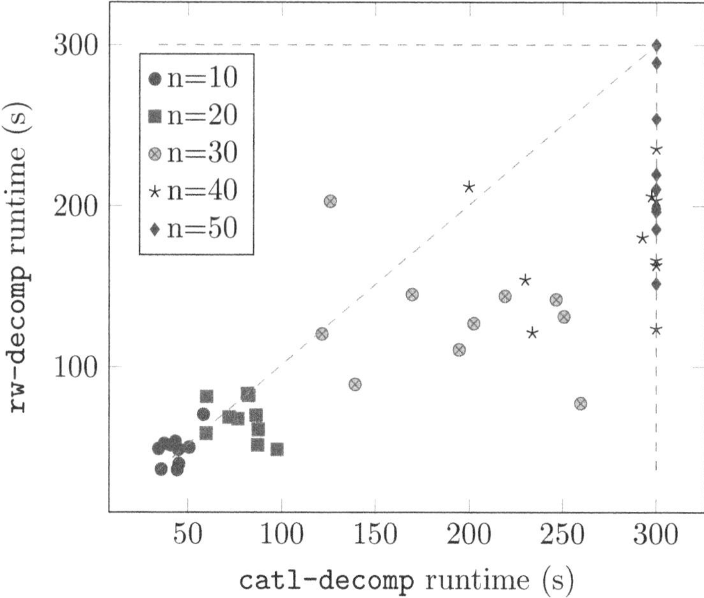

Fig. 3. Comparison of our approach `rw-decomp` to the SMT-based CaTL decomposition approach. Runtime includes the time to decompose and solve each of the subproblems serially.

6.1 CaTL Example

First, we compare against the decomposition technique of [14] for a fragment of STL, Capability Temporal Logic (CaTL). Their approach uses a Satisfiability Modulo Theories (SMT) solver to find agent assignments, and only makes formula transformations after obtaining an assignment. We evaluate our algorithm against theirs on the same set of template formulae used in their paper which vary from 10 to 50 (by tens) randomly-generated agents on a randomly-generated environment. We run 10 trials for each number of agents seeded with the trial number (0–9). We use a timeout of 5 min. Figure 3 depicts our results. Our technique is faster for any value below the diagonal. We define a *degenerate* decomposition as a decomposition with only a single subteam. Our approach had no degenerate solutions and one timeout. The other technique had 2 degenerate solutions and 15 timeouts.

Their technique is faster to decompose than ours (up to 1 s vs. up to 13 s), but finds less desirable decompositions. This is expected because their technique does not optimize or explore the space of formula rewrites. Both techniques improve the runtime compared to monolithic synthesis.

6.2 Case Studies

We now apply decomposition to two case studies. Table 1 summarizes the results.

Computing Example. We consider a computing cluster whose processor nodes are each equipped with either a CPU or GPU. Each processor has a number of cores available, and can be assigned to process jobs. There is a startup cost associated with sending jobs to processors, and a switching cost for switching from a serial job to parallel and vice versa. The overall formula for a day's requests is

$$\phi_{cluster} = \Diamond_{[0,12)}\phi_{batch} \wedge \Box_{[3,12)}\phi_{admin}, \tag{7}$$

where ϕ_{batch} captures the overnight batch jobs, ϕ_{admin} captures administrative events that must be performed periodically. Both ϕ_{batch} and ϕ_{admin} are conjunctions over sets of individual requests. These requests may specifically ask for a number of CPU cores, a number of GPU cores, or may specify that the job can be accomplished with a CPU and/or GPU. We assume that if a job is running on a node, no other job can start on that node until the previous job has finished. This mitigates the interference concerns in Remark 3.

Energy Grid. We develop an energy grid problem. There are ten towns and a daily specification over half-hour increments. There are two energy companies and each has a power station for each type of energy: coal, natural gas, wind, nuclear, and solar. The specification ensures that each town receives the required power along with additional constraints imposed by each town for cost or green initiatives, such as limiting the amount of coal. Each agent represents 1 GWh from a particular power plant. Since this specification has both less-than and greater-than predicates, we must directly mitigate the interference concerns of Remark 3. We accomplish this with an additional constraint that all signals for a given town must be grouped in the same subteam. This may require bundling several top-level conjuncts into a single conjunct by editing the AST. This prevents the situation in which one subteam is trying to increase a signal while another subteam attempts to decrease it. This specification has a natural geographic decomposition, but the specification needs to be rewritten so that this is possible. Due to the predicate grouping constraint, the original formula can only be decomposed into 3 subteams, but after rewriting we obtain 10 subteams.

7 Conclusions

This work proposed an abstract rewriting system for STL, with proofs of termination and confluence. The rewriting system forms the basis for a method of decomposing an STL specification and distributing it among a heterogenous team of agents. It outperforms a closely related method on a fragment of STL, and is effective on general STL case studies.

Future work includes investigating refinement of formula time bounds in the rewriting system, further formalization of the decomposition procedure, and potential relaxations of the noninterference condition mentioned in Remark 3.

References

1. Baader, F., Nipkow, T.: Term Rewriting and All That. Cambridge University Press, Cambridge (1999)
2. Banks, C., Wilson, S., Coogan, S., Egerstedt, M.: Multi-agent task allocation using cross-entropy temporal logic optimization. In: 2020 IEEE International Conference on Robotics and Automation (ICRA), pp. 7712–7718. IEEE (2020)
3. Belta, C., Sadraddini, S.: Formal methods for control synthesis: an optimization perspective. Annu. Rev. Control Robot. Auton. Syst. **2**(1), 115–140 (2019). https://doi.org/10.1146/annurev-control-053018-023717
4. Buyukkocak, A.T., Aksaray, D., Yazıcıoğlu, Y.: Planning of heterogeneous multi-agent systems under signal temporal logic specifications with integral predicates. IEEE Robot. Autom. Lett. **6**(2), 1375–1382 (2021)
5. Castanon, D., Drummond, O., Bellovin, M.: Comparison of 2-D assignment algorithms for rectangular, floating point cost matrices. In: Proc. Os SDI Panels on tracking, No. 4 (1990)
6. Charitidou, M., Dimarogonas, D.V.: Signal temporal logic task decomposition via convex optimization. IEEE Contr. Syst. Lett. **6**, 1238–1243 (2021)
7. Chen, Y., Ding, X.C., Stefanescu, A., Belta, C.: Formal approach to the deployment of distributed robotic teams. IEEE Trans. Rob. **28**(1), 158–171 (2011)
8. Dokhanchi, A., Hoxha, B., Fainekos, G.: On-line monitoring for temporal logic robustness. In: Bonakdarpour, B., Smolka, S.A. (eds.) RV 2014. LNCS, vol. 8734, pp. 231–246. Springer, Cham (2014). https://doi.org/10.1007/978-3-319-11164-3_19
9. Donzé, A., Maler, O.: Robust satisfaction of temporal logic over real-valued signals. In: Chatterjee, K., Henzinger, T.A. (eds.) FORMATS 2010. LNCS, vol. 6246, pp. 92–106. Springer, Heidelberg (2010). https://doi.org/10.1007/978-3-642-15297-9_9
10. Gamrath, G., et al.: The SCIP optimization suite 7.0. Technical report, Optimization Online (2020). http://www.optimization-online.org/DB_HTML/2020/03/7705.html
11. Gundana, D., Kress-Gazit, H.: Event-based signal temporal logic synthesis for single and multi-robot tasks. IEEE Robot. Autom. Lett. **6**(2), 3687–3694 (2021)
12. Gurobi Optimization, LLC: Gurobi optimizer reference manual (2022). https://www.gurobi.com
13. Jonker, R., Volgenant, A.: A shortest augmenting path algorithm for dense and sparse linear assignment problems. Computing **38**(4), 325–340 (1987). https://doi.org/10.1007/BF02278710
14. Leahy, K., Jones, A., Vasile, C.I.: Fast decomposition of temporal logic specifications for heterogeneous teams. IEEE Robot. Autom. Lett. **7**(2), 2297–2304 (2022)
15. Leahy, K., et al.: Scalable and robust algorithms for task-based coordination from high-level specifications (ScRATCHeS). IEEE Trans. Robot. **38**(4), 2516–2535 (2021)
16. Lindemann, L., Dimarogonas, D.V.: Feedback control strategies for multi-agent systems under a fragment of signal temporal logic tasks. Automatica **106**, 284–293 (2019)
17. Liu, S., Saoud, A., Jagtap, P., Dimarogonas, D.V., Zamani, M.: Compositional synthesis of signal temporal logic tasks via assume-guarantee contracts. arXiv preprint arXiv:2203.10041 (2022)
18. Maler, O., Nickovic, D.: Monitoring temporal properties of continuous signals. In: Lakhnech, Y., Yovine, S. (eds.) FORMATS/FTRTFT -2004. LNCS, vol. 3253, pp.

152–166. Springer, Heidelberg (2004). https://doi.org/10.1007/978-3-540-30206-3_12
19. Mitchell, S., O'Sullivan, M., Dunning, I.: PuLP: a linear programming toolkit for Python (2011)
20. Munkres, J.R.: Algorithms for the assignment and transportation problems. J. Soc. Ind. Appl. Math. **10**, 196–210 (1957)
21. Schillinger, P., Bürger, M., Dimarogonas, D.V.: Decomposition of finite LTL specifications for efficient multi-agent planning. In: Groß, R., et al. (eds.) Distributed Autonomous Robotic Systems. SPAR, vol. 6, pp. 253–267. Springer, Cham (2018). https://doi.org/10.1007/978-3-319-73008-0_18
22. Sun, D., Chen, J., Mitra, S., Fan, C.: Multi-agent motion planning from signal temporal logic specifications. IEEE Robot. Autom. Lett. **7**(2), 3451–3458 (2022)
23. Zhou, Z., Lee, D.J., Yoshinaga, Y., Guo, D., Zhao, Y.: Reactive task allocation and planning of a heterogeneous multi-robot system. arXiv preprint arXiv:2110.08436 (2021)

Quantitative Verification and Strategy Synthesis for BDI Agents

Blair Archibald, Muffy Calder, Michele Sevegnani, and Mengwei Xu(✉)

University of Glasgow, Glasgow, UK
{blair.archibald,muffy.calder,michele.sevegnani,
mengwei.xu}@glasgow.ac.uk

Abstract. Belief-Desire-Intention (BDI) agents feature probabilistic outcomes, *e.g.* the chance an agent tries but fails to open a door, and non-deterministic choices: what plan/intention to execute next? We want to reason about agents under both probabilities and non-determinism to determine, for example, probabilities of mission success and the *strategies* used to maximise this. We define a Markov Decision Process describing the semantics of the Conceptual Agent Notation (CAN) agent language that supports non-deterministic event, plan, and intention selection, as well as probabilistic action outcomes. The model is derived through an encoding to Milner's Bigraphs and executed using the BigraphER tool. We show, using probabilistic model checkers PRISM and Storm, how to reason about agents including: probabilistic and reward-based properties, strategy synthesis, and multi-objective analysis. This analysis provides verification and optimisation of BDI agent design and implementation.

Keywords: BDI Agents · Quantitative Verification · Strategy Synthesis · Markov Decision Process · Bigraphs · PRISM · Storm

1 Introduction

BDI agents [1] are a popular architecture for developing rational agents where (B)eliefs represent what an agent knows, (D)esires what the agent wants to bring about, and (I)ntentions the desires the agent is currently acting on. BDI agents have inspired many agent programming languages including AgentSpeak [2], CAN [3], 3APL [4], and 2APL [5] along with a collection of mature software including JACK [6], Jason [7], and Jadex [8].

In BDI languages, desires and intentions are represented implicitly by defining a plan library where the plans are written by programmers in a modular fashion. Plans describe how, and under what conditions (based on beliefs), an agent can react to an event (a desire). The set of intentions are those plans that are currently being executed. A desirable feature of agent-based systems is that they are reactive [9]: an agent can respond to new events even while already dealing with existing events. To allow this, agents pursue multiple events and execute intentions in an interleaved manner. This requires a decision making

K. Y. Rozier and S. Chaudhuri (Eds.): NFM 2023, LNCS 13903, pp. 241–259, 2023.
https://doi.org/10.1007/978-3-031-33170-1_15

process: which event to handle first (event selection) and which intention to progress next (intention selection). When handling events, we must also decide on which plan is selected from a set of possible plans (plan selection).

The deployment of BDI-based systems raises concerns of trustworthiness. For example, erroneous plans can cause incorrect behaviour. Even with a correct plan library, careless decisions for interleaving intention progression can result in failures/conflicts, *e.g.* the execution of one intention can make it impossible to progress another. This negative tension between modularised plan design and interleaved execution is difficult to identify using traditional non-exhaustive testing approaches as there is no guarantee we see all interleavings. Furthermore, the outcome of an action may be probabilistic due to imprecise actuation. As a result, there is a growing need for formal techniques that can handle quantitative properties of agent-based systems [10]. Given the number of decisions faced by an agent, we may want to synthesise a strategy to determine ahead-of-time the decisions an agent should make *e.g.* to avoid the worst-case execution.

Verifying BDI agent behaviours through model checking and theorem proving has been well explored. For example, the authors apply the Java PathFinder model-checker (resps. Isabelle/HOL proof assistant) to verify BDI programs in the work [11] (resp. [12]). Unfortunately, they do not adequately represent agent behaviours in cyber-physical robotics systems (*e.g.* surveyed in [13]) with imprecise actuators. To reason with the quantitative behaviours of BDI agents, the authors of [14] investigate the probabilistic semantics and resulting verification of BDI agents with imprecise actuators by resolving non-determinism in various selections through manually specified strategies (fixed orders, round-robin fashion, or probabilistic distribution). However, these hand-crafted strategies may not be optimal. Determining effective strategies is complex and often requires advanced planning algorithms [15,16].

We show how to combine and apply quantitative verification and strategy synthesis [17,18] within BDI agents allowing us to both determine, *e.g.* the probability an agent successfully completes a mission under environmental uncertainty, and also a method to resolve the non-determinism required for intention/event/-plan selection. We focus on the Can language [3,19] which features a high-level agent programming language that captures the essence of BDI concepts without describing implementation details such as data structures. As a superset of most well-known AgentSpeak [2], Can includes advanced BDI agent behaviours such as reasoning with *declarative goals* and *failure recovery*, which are necessary for our examples discussed in Sect. 4. Importantly, although we focus on Can, the language features are similar to those of other mainstream BDI languages, and the same modelling and verification techniques would apply to other BDI programming languages.

We build on our previous work [14] developing an executable *probabilistic* semantics of Can [3], based on Milner's Bigraphs [20]. Specifically, we use probabilistic bigraphs [21], that assigns probabilities to transitions (graph rewrites). Previously, we used manually-crafted strategies (*e.g.* fixed schedule) to resolve non-determinism. Instead, we keep these selections as non-deterministic choices and encode them using action bigraphs [21] (which supports modelling non-deterministic actions). This provides a model of CAN based on a Markov decision process (MDP) [22], that we denote as CAN^m. The MDP formalisation of agent behaviours enables us to model certain unknown aspects of a system's behaviour *e.g.* the scheduling between intentions executing in parallel and represent uncertainty arising from, for example, imprecise actuator. For analysis, we export, using BigraphER [23], the underlying MDP to the popular probabilistic model checkers PRISM [24] and Storm [25]. This includes probabilistic and reward-based properties, strategy synthesis, and multi-objective analysis. In particular, temporal logics provide an expressive means of formally specifying the requirement properties when synthesising strategies that are guaranteed to be correct (at least with respect to the specified model and properties).

We make the following research contributions:

- an MDP model of the CAN semantics, supporting non-deterministic selections and probabilistic action outcomes;
- an executable MDP model of CAN with BigraphER for quantitative verification and (optimal) strategy synthesis through PRISM and Storm;
- a simple example of smart manufacturing computes the probability analysis of mission success and strategy synthesis, and a simple example of a rover computes the reward probability of mission success and strategy synthesis.

Outline. In Sect. 2 we recall BDI agents and an MDP. In Sect. 3 we propose our approach. In Sect. 4 we evaluate our approach to smart manufacturing and rover examples. We discuss related work in Sect. 5 and conclude in Sect. 6.

2 Background

2.1 CAN

CAN language formalises a classical BDI agent consisting of a belief base $\mathcal{B}$ and a plan library Π. The belief base $\mathcal{B}$ is a set of formulas encoding the current beliefs and has belief operators for entailment (*i.e.* $\mathcal{B} \models \varphi$), and belief atom addition (resp. deletion) $\mathcal{B} \cup \{b\}$ (resp. $\mathcal{B} \setminus \{b\}$)[1]. A plan library Π is a collection of plans of the form $e : \varphi \leftarrow P$ with e the triggering event, φ the context condition, and P the plan-body. The triggering event e specifies why the plan is relevant, while the context condition φ determines *when* the plan-body P is applicable.

The CAN semantics are specified by two types of transitions. The first, denoted $\rightarrow$, specifies *intention-level* evolution on intention-level configurations $\langle \mathcal{B}, P \rangle$ where $\mathcal{B}$ is the belief base, and P the plan-body currently being executed. The second type, denoted $\Rightarrow$, specifies *agent-level* evolution over agent-level configurations $\langle E^e, \mathcal{B}, \Gamma \rangle$, detailing how to execute a complete agent where E^e is the set of pending external events to address (desires) and Γ a set of partially executed plan-bodies (intentions). The intention-level CAN configurations $\langle \mathcal{B}, P \rangle$ can be seen a special case of $\langle E^e, \mathcal{B}, \Gamma \rangle$ where E^e is an arbitrary set of event and $P \in \Gamma$. We denote configurations as $\mathcal{C}$.

[1] Any logic is allowed providing entailment is supported.

$$\frac{act : \psi \leftarrow \langle \phi^-, \phi^+ \rangle \quad \mathcal{B} \vDash \psi}{\langle \mathcal{B}, act \rangle \rightarrow \langle (\mathcal{B} \setminus \phi^- \cup \phi^+), nil \rangle} \; act \qquad \frac{\varphi : P \in \Delta \quad \mathcal{B} \models \varphi}{\langle \mathcal{B}, e : (\!| \Delta |\!) \rangle \rightarrow \langle \mathcal{B}, P \triangleright e : (\!| \Delta \setminus \{\varphi : P\} |\!) \rangle} \; select$$

$$\frac{\langle \mathcal{B}, P_1 \rangle \rightarrow \langle \mathcal{B}', P_1' \rangle}{\langle \mathcal{B}, (P_1 \| P_2) \rangle \rightarrow \langle \mathcal{B}', (P_1' \| P_2) \rangle} \; \|_1 \qquad \frac{\langle \mathcal{B}, P_2 \rangle \rightarrow \langle \mathcal{B}', P_2' \rangle}{\langle \mathcal{B}, (P_1 \| P_2) \rangle \rightarrow \langle \mathcal{B}', (P_1 \| P_2') \rangle} \; \|_2$$

Fig. 1. Examples of intention-level CAN semantics.

$$\frac{e \in E^e}{\langle E^e, \mathcal{B}, \Gamma \rangle \Rightarrow \langle E^e \setminus \{e\}, \mathcal{B}, \Gamma \cup \{e\} \rangle} \; A_{event} \qquad \frac{P \in \Gamma \quad \langle \mathcal{B}, P \rangle \rightarrow \langle \mathcal{B}', P' \rangle}{\langle E^e, \mathcal{B}, \Gamma \rangle \Rightarrow \langle E^e, \mathcal{B}', (\Gamma \setminus \{P\}) \cup \{P'\} \rangle} \; A_{step}$$

$$\frac{P \in \Gamma \quad \langle \mathcal{B}, P \rangle \nrightarrow}{\langle E^e, \mathcal{B}, \Gamma \rangle \Rightarrow \langle E^e, \mathcal{B}, \Gamma \setminus \{P\} \rangle} \; A_{update}$$

Fig. 2. Agent-level CAN semantics.

Figure 1 gives some semantics rules for evolving an intention. For example, *act* handles the execution of an action (in the form of $act = \psi \leftarrow \langle \phi^-, \phi^+ \rangle$), when the pre-condition ψ is met, resulting in a belief state update ($\mathcal{B} \setminus \phi^- \cup \phi^+$). Rule *select* chooses an applicable plan from a set of relevant plans (*i.e.* $\mathcal{B} \models \varphi$ and $\varphi : P \in \Delta$) while retaining un-selected plans as backups (*i.e.* $P \triangleright e : (\!| \Delta \setminus \{\varphi : P\} |\!)$). Rules $\|_1$ and $\|_2$ specify how to execute (interleaved) concurrent programs (within an intention). The full intention-level semantics is given in Appendix A. The agent-level semantics are given in Fig. 2. The rule A_{event} handles external events, that originate from the environment, by adopting them as intentions. Rule A_{step} selects an intention and evolves a single step w.r.t. the intention-level transition, while A_{update} discards unprogressable intentions (either succeeded, or failed).

2.2 Markov Decision Processes

A Markov decision process (MDP) [22] is a tuple $\mathcal{M} = (S, \bar{s}, \alpha, \delta)$ where S is a set of states, $\bar{s}$ an initial state, α a set of actions (atomic labels), and $\delta : S \times \alpha \rightarrow Dist(S)$ a (partial) probabilistic transition function where $Dist(S)$ is the set of the probability distribution over states S. Each state s of an MDP $\mathcal{M}$ has a (possibly empty) set of *enabled* actions $A(s) \stackrel{\text{def}}{=} \{a \in \alpha \mid \delta(s, a) \text{ is defined}\}$. When action $a \in A(s)$ is taken in state s, the next state is determined probabilistically according to the distribution $\delta(s, a)$, *i.e.* the probability that a transition to state s' occurs is $\delta(s, a)(s')$. An MDP may have an action reward structure *i.e.* a function of the form $R : S \times \alpha \rightarrow \mathbb{R}_{\geq 0}$ that increments a counter when an action is taken. An *adversary* (also known as a strategy or policy) resolves non-determinism by determining a single action choice per state, and optimal adversaries are those that *e.g.* minimise the probability some property holds. This can be used to ensure, for example, the chance of system failure events is minimised.

3 An MDP Model of CAN Semantics

MDPs model systems with nondeterministic and probabilistic behaviour. To use an MDP with the CAN semantics we associate CAN rules with MDP actions and CAN states to MDP states. We refer to the MDP model of CAN as CAN^m.

States in CAN^m are given by the agent-level configuration $\langle E^e, \mathcal{B}, \Gamma\rangle$ of CAN. The state space is $S \subseteq 2^{E^e} \times 2^{\mathcal{B}} \times 2^{\Gamma}$ where the exact subset of states is determined by the specific program we are modelling[2]. An initial state of a CAN^m is $\bar{s} = \langle E^e_0, \mathcal{B}_0, \Gamma_0\rangle$. In practice, including our examples in Sect. 4, this usually has the form $E^e_0 = \{e_1, \cdots, e_j\}$ (a set of tasks), $\mathcal{B}_0 = \{b_1, \cdots, b_k\}$ (an initial set of beliefs, *e.g.* about the environment), $\Gamma_0 = \emptyset$ (no intentions yet), and $j, k \in \mathbb{N}^+$.

The CAN semantics are defined using operational semantics with transitions over configurations $\mathcal{C} \rightarrow \mathcal{C}'$ (see Sect. 2.1). As we reason with probabilistic action outcomes of agents, we instead use probabilistic transitions $\mathcal{C} \rightarrow_p \mathcal{C}'$, *i.e.* this transition happens with probability p [26]. In our case, probabilities are introduced by uncertain action outcomes of the agents (see Sect. 3.1).

To translate a (probabilistic) semantic rule named *rule* (Eq. (1)) to an MDP action, we include an MDP action a_{rule} in the set of all MDP action labels and define the transition function δ such that Eqs. (2) and (3) hold:

$$\frac{\lambda_1 \quad \lambda_2 \quad \cdots \quad \lambda_n}{\mathcal{C} \rightarrow_p \mathcal{C}'}\ rule \tag{1}$$

$$\delta(\mathcal{C}, a_{rule}) \text{ is defined iff } \lambda_i \text{ holds in } \mathcal{C} \text{ with } i \in \{1, 2, \cdots, n\} \tag{2}$$

$$\delta(\mathcal{C}, a_{rule})(\mathcal{C}') = p \tag{3}$$

Condition (2) says a transition of CAN^m is only enabled if the transition would be enabled in CAN, *i.e.* the premises λ_i of *rule* are all met. Condition (2) defines the probability of transitioning from $\mathcal{C}$ to $\mathcal{C}'$ in CAN^m as the same as the probability of transitioning in CAN. The mapping of semantic rules to MDP actions is applied to both intention and agent-level rules from CAN.

The overview of our translation from CAN to an MDP is depicted in Fig. 3. CAN features non-deterministic transition, *e.g.* for plan selection and choices appear throughout both the agent and intention level transitions. Furthermore, agent actions have probabilistic outcomes sampled from a distribution. The right-hand of Fig. 3 presents our MDP model of CAN with translated MDP actions for each semantic rules. We detail this translation in the next sections.

3.1 Probabilistic Action Outcomes

Probabilistic transitions occur when we add support for probabilistic action outcomes for agents. In CAN, the semantic rule *act* gives a fixed outcome (belief changes in the semantics; but also environment changes in real application) when an agent action is executed. In practice agent actions often fail, *e.g.* there is a chance an agent tries to open a door but cannot. To capture these uncertain outcomes in agent actions, we introduce a new *probabilistic* semantic rule (same

[2] We determine this by symbolically executing the program as we convert to an MDP.

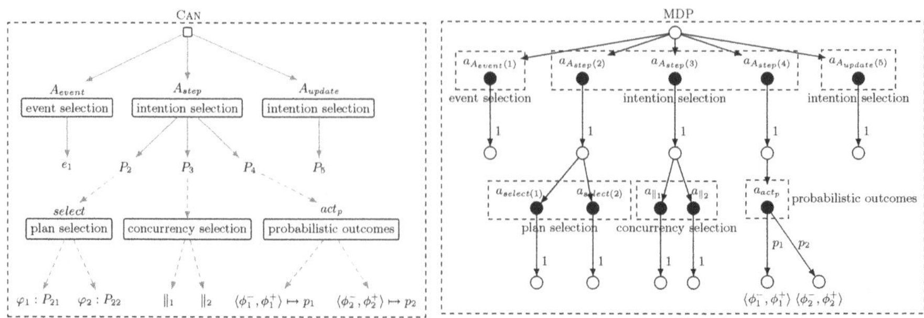

Fig. 3. Left: CAN semantic rule possibilities highlighting event, intention, plan, and concurrency selection, and probabilistic agent action outcomes. Solid lines are agent-level transitions and dashed lines are intention-level. Right: Corresponding MDP model of CAN semantic rules with empty circles as states and solid circles as MDP actions.

as in [14]) act_p where $\mu = [(\phi_1^-, \phi_1^+) \mapsto p_1, \ldots, (\phi_n^-, \phi_n^+) \mapsto p_n]$ is a user-specified outcome distribution where $\mu(\phi_i^-, \phi_i^+) = p_i$ and $\sum_{i=1}^{n} p_i = 1$.

$$\frac{act : \psi \leftarrow \mu \quad \mu(\phi_i^-, \phi_i^+) = p_i \quad \mathcal{B} \models \psi}{\langle \mathcal{B}, act \rangle \rightarrow_{p_i} \langle (\mathcal{B} \setminus \phi_i^- \cup \phi_i^+), nil \rangle}\ act_p$$

For mapping intention-level CAN configurations to MDP states we use the fact that $\langle \mathcal{B}, P \rangle$ is a special case of $\langle E^e, \mathcal{B}, \Gamma \rangle$ where E^e is an arbitrary set of event and $P \in \Gamma$ allowing us to translate the intention-level semantic rules to MDP actions according to the rule translation template in Eqs. (2) and (3). The probabilistic nature of act_p is reflected in the MDP action a_{act_p}:

$$\delta(\mathcal{C}, a_{act_p})(\mathcal{C}') = p_i \text{ s.t. } \mathcal{C} = \langle \mathcal{B}, act \rangle,\ act : \psi \leftarrow \mu,\ \mathcal{B} \models \psi,$$
$$\mu(\phi_i^-, \phi_i^+) = p_i, \text{ and } \mathcal{C}' = \langle \mathcal{B} \setminus \phi_i^- \cup \phi_i^+, nil \rangle$$

3.2 Intention-Level Semantics

The intention-level semantics (Fig. 1) specify how to evolve any single intention. Most rules have deterministic outcomes with the exception of some rules such as *select* (Fig. 1) which is non-deterministic, *i.e.* when we select a single applicable plan from the set of relevant plans. To use rules like this in CAN^m we need to lift the non-determinism, hidden *within* the rules, to non-determinism *between* rules. We do this by introducing a new rule for each possible choice, *e.g.* a rule for each possible plan that can be selected. As notation, we describe this set of rules via a parameterised rules, *e.g.* *select*(n) as follows:

$$\frac{\langle n, \varphi : P \rangle \in \Delta \quad \mathcal{B} \models \varphi}{\langle \mathcal{B}, e : (\!|\ \Delta\ |\!) \rangle \rightarrow_1 \langle \mathcal{B}, P \rhd e : (\!|\ \Delta \setminus \{\langle n, \varphi : P \rangle\}\ |\!) \rangle}\ select(n)$$

where n is an identifier for the plan and can be trivially assigned using positions in the plan library (*i.e.* $1 \leq n \leq |\Pi|$). Once we chose a plan rule, it is always successful ($p = 1$) and it can be similarly translated into an MDP action, denoted as $a_{select(n)}$, using the previous translation template.

3.3 Agent-Level Semantics

Agent-level CAN rules (Fig. 2) determine how an agent responds to events and progresses/completes intentions. There are three rules and each has a non-deterministic outcome: A_{event} that selects one event to handle from a set of pending events; A_{step} that progresses one intention from a set of partially executed intentions; and A_{update} that removes an unprogressable intention from a set of unprogressable intentions. As with *select* in Sect. 3.2, to use these in the CAN^m model we need to move from non-deterministic rules to a set of deterministic rules parameterised by the outcome. The new rules are:

$$\frac{\langle n, e\rangle \in E^e}{\langle E^e, \mathcal{B}, \Gamma\rangle \Rightarrow_1 \langle E^e \setminus \{\langle n, e\rangle\}, \mathcal{B}, \Gamma \cup \{\langle n, e\rangle\}\rangle} A_{event}(n)$$

$$\frac{\langle n, P\rangle \in \Gamma \quad \langle \mathcal{B}, \langle n, P\rangle\rangle \rightarrow_p \langle \mathcal{B}', \langle n, P'\rangle\rangle}{\langle E^e, \mathcal{B}, \Gamma\rangle \Rightarrow_p \langle E^e, \mathcal{B}', (\Gamma \setminus \{\langle n, P\rangle\}) \cup \{\langle n, P'\rangle\}\rangle} A_{step}(n)$$

$$\frac{\langle n, P\rangle \in \Gamma \quad \langle \mathcal{B}, \langle n, P\rangle\rangle \not\rightarrow_1}{\langle E^e, \mathcal{B}, \Gamma\rangle \Rightarrow_1 \langle E^e, \mathcal{B}, \Gamma \setminus \{\langle n, P\rangle\}\rangle} A_{update}(n)$$

Event parameters are specified by numbering them based on an ordering on the full set of events, e.g. $\langle n, e\rangle$ with $n \in \mathbb{N}^+$ as an identifier. We identify (partially executed) intentions based on the identifier of the top level plan that led to this intention, *e.g.* for $P \in \Gamma$ we assign a label $n \in \mathbb{N}^+$ that is passed alongside the intention. This style of labelling assumes only one instance of an event can be handled at once (this is enough to imply the top level plans are also unique). As with *select* the transition probability is 1 in the cases of $A_{event}(n)$ and $A_{update}(n)$ as the rule, if selected, always succeeds. The (omitted) MDP actions for rules $A_{event}(n)$ and $A_{update}(n)$ can be similarly given as $a_{A_{event}(n)}$ and $a_{A_{update}(n)}$, respectively. The rule $A_{step}(n)$ says that agent-level transitions depend on the intention-level transitions and we need to account for this in the transition probabilities. Formally, we have:

$$\begin{aligned}\delta(\langle E^e, \mathcal{B}, \Gamma\rangle, a_{A_{step}(n)})(\langle E^e, \mathcal{B}', \Gamma \setminus \{\langle n, P\rangle\}) \cup \{\langle n, P'\rangle\}) = p \text{ iff}\\ \langle n, P\rangle \in \Gamma \text{ and } \delta(\langle \mathcal{B}, \langle n, P\rangle\rangle, a_{rule})(\langle \mathcal{B}', \langle n, P'\rangle\rangle) = p\end{aligned}$$

where a_{rule} denotes the MDP action for the equivalent semantic rule in CAN that handles the intention-level transition of $\langle \mathcal{B}, \langle n, P\rangle\rangle \rightarrow_p \langle \mathcal{B}', \langle n, P'\rangle\rangle$.

3.4 Rewards

While an MDP allows action rewards to be assigned to any action, and therefore CAN rule, they are particularly useful for the parameterised rules. In practice, as it is difficult to specify all current states of an agent (needed for the configuration), we apply rewards based only on the action chosen, *e.g.* $R(\mathcal{C}, a_{rule}) = R(a_{rule}) = r_{rule}$. With this, we can choose preferred parameters by assigning higher reward values, *e.g.* $R(a_{select(1)}) < R(a_{select(2)})$. Usually we give non-zero rewards to MDP actions that correspond to selection (*e.g.* plan selection) for strategy synthesis later on. For other MDP actions the reward is 0.

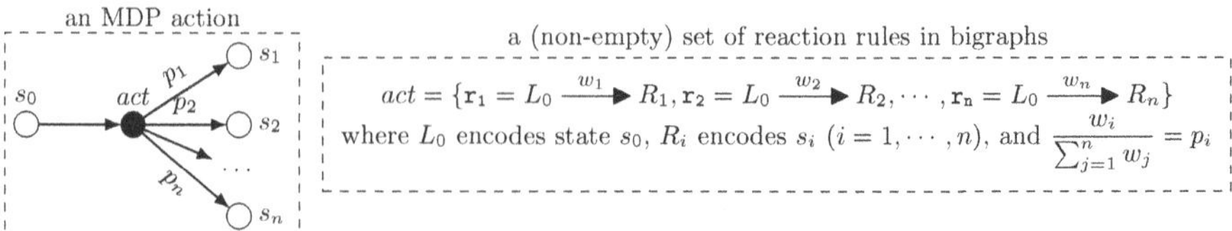

Fig. 4. Left: MDP action *act* applying to state s_0 with a probability p_i reaching to the state s_i $((i \in \{1, \cdots, n\})$. Right: corresponding bigraph reaction rules to encode *act*.

4 Implementation and Examples

Using a simple smart manufacturing and rover example, we show how our approach can quantitatively analyse/verify agent programs and synthesise the (optimal) strategies. Specifically, we evaluate the probabilistic properties for smart manufacturing and reward-based properties for the rover example together with their optimal strategy synthesis. The results show we can detect undesired executions (that result in mission failure) and generate different optimal strategies that can maximise either probability-based or reward-based objective. While we only give details of two simple cases, users of the executable model can "run" models with different external events and plan libraries. The examples shown in this paper and instructions on reproducibility are open available in [27].

4.1 Bigraph Encoding of CAN^m Model

We use Milner's bigraphs [20]—a graph-based rewriting formalism—to encode our CAN^m model. As a graph-based rewriting formalism, over customised rules called *reaction rules*, bigraphs provide an intuitive diagrammatic representation to model the execution process of the systems. Applying a reaction rule, $L \longrightarrow R$, replaces an occurrence of bigraph L (in a bigraph) with bigraph R. Given an initial bigraph (*i.e.* initial system state) and a set of reaction rules (*i.e.* system dynamics), we obtain a transition system capturing system behaviours for formal verification. Bigraphs allow reaction rules to be weighted, *e.g.* $\mathtt{r} = L \xrightarrow{3} R$ and $\mathtt{r}' = L \xrightarrow{1} R'$, such that if both (and only) $\mathtt{r}$ and $\mathtt{r}'$ are applicable then $\mathtt{r}$ is three times as likely to apply as $\mathtt{r}'$. Non-deterministic choices (*e.g.* an MDP action) can be modelled as a non-empty set of reaction rules. For example, we can have an MDP action $\mathtt{a} = \{\mathtt{r}, \mathtt{r}'\}$ and once it is executed, it has a distribution of 75% transition from L to R and 25% from L to R'. Figure 4 depicts how to encode any MDP action in bigraphs. To execute our bigraph model, we employ BigraphER [23], an open-source language and toolkit for bigraphs. It allows exporting transition systems of an MDP, and states may be labelled using bigraph patterns that assign a state *predicate* label if it contains (a match of) a given bigraph. The labelled MDP transition systems are exported for quantitative analysis and strategy synthesis in PRISM and Storm. We use PRISM[3] (for

[3] PRISM currently does not support reward import.

non-reward properties) and Storm (for reward-based properties) by importing the underlying MDPs produced by BigraphER. We reason about the minimum or maximum values of properties such as $\mathcal{P}_{max=?}\mathbf{F}[\phi]$ in Probabilistic Computation Tree Logic (PCTL) [28]. $\mathcal{P}_{max=?}\mathbf{F}[\phi]$ expresses the maximum probability of ϕ holding *eventually* in all possible resolutions of non-determinism.

4.2 Example: Smart Manufacturing

We revisit the robotic packaging scenario from [14] where a robot packs products and moves them to a storage area. Previously, this example was quantitatively analysed using probabilistic model checking, but all non-determinism was resolved using pre-defined strategies (fixed, round-robin, probabilistic choice). Here, we wish to *find* a good strategy without assuming one.

The example is as follows: a robot is designed to pick a product from a production line, insulate them with either cheap or expensive wrapping bags (to prevent decay) and then move them to storage. Complexity arises from: (1) success depends on *when* a product is packed (*e.g.* before it decays), (2) *when* a product is packed determines which wrappings are applicable as earlier packing means cheaper bags, and (3) both wrappings introduce uncertainty as they may fail to insulate or break.

The agent program for a scenario with two initial products is given in Listing 1.1. We assume the agent uses a propositional logic with numerical comparisons. Products awaiting processing are captured by external events in line 4. The agent responds to the events using a declarative goal on line 6 stating it wants to achieve the state success1 (*i.e.* wrapped and moved) through addressing the (internal) event process_product1; failing if failure1 (*i.e.* dropped or decayed) ever becomes true. Two plans (in lines 7–8), representing the different wrappings, handle the event process_product1 depending on the deadline for the product. Event product2 is handled similarly (line 9–11). We encode (discrete) temporal information for the deadline as agent belief atoms. This should not be viewed as general support clocks in an MDP. Instead, these temporal information is simply modelled as numerical belief atoms and we update these belief atoms in the background, without executing any explicit MDP action. The deadline decreases after a step of *any* intention or the selection of *any* event. We have $deadline_1 = 10$ and $deadline_2 = 14$ as initial deadlines of product1 and product2 in line 2. The choice of these initial values was made by the agent designer. Our approach enables the analysis of alternative values quantitatively before deploying the agent. There is a probabilistic outcome for the agent action of both wrap_standard1 and move_product_standard1, such that they carry a 30% chance of causing the belief failure1 to hold by failing to insulate and dropping the product accidentally. Meanwhile, there is only 10% change of causing insulation failure or product dropping by action wrap_premium1 and move_product_premium1. Due to space limits, we omit the action descriptions. Full agent examples are online [27].

Listing 1.1. CAN agent for smart manufacturing

```
// Initial belief bases
deadline_1 = 10, deadline_2 = 14
// External events
product1, product2
// Plan library
product1 : true <- goal(success1,process_product1,failure1).
process_product1 : deadline_1 ≥ 3 <- wrap_standard1; move_product_standard1.
process_product1 : deadline_1 ≥ 0 <- wrap_premium1; move_product_premium1.
product2 : true <- goal(success2,process_product2,failure2).
process_product2 : deadline_2 ≥ 3 <- wrap_standard2; move_product_standard2.
process_product2 : deadline_1 ≥ 3 <- wrap_premium2; move_product_premium2.
```

Listing 1.2. A list of properties with its associated value for smart manufacturing where PS1 and PS2 denote product1 and product2 successfully being processed, and Pch1 and Pch2 denote cheap bag selected for product1 and product2, respectively.

$\mathcal{P}_{min=?}\mathsf{F}[\mathsf{PS1} \wedge \mathsf{PS2}]$ (value 0)
$\mathcal{P}_{max=?}\mathsf{F}[\mathsf{PS1} \wedge \mathsf{PS2}]$ (value 0.6561)
$\mathcal{P}_{max=?}\mathsf{F}[\mathsf{PS1} \wedge \mathsf{PS2} \wedge \mathsf{Pch1} \wedge \mathsf{Pch2}]$ (value 0)
$\mathcal{P}_{max=?}\mathsf{F}[\mathsf{PS1} \wedge \mathsf{PS2} \wedge (\mathsf{Pch1} \vee \mathsf{Pch2})]$ (value 0.3969)

Quantitative Verification and Strategy Synthesis. For analysis we label states where properties of interest hold. We use PS1 and PS2 to denote product1 and product2 being successfully processed by the robot. Pch1 and Pch2 hold when the cheaper bag was selected to handle product1 and product2 respectively. A full list of properties checked for this example is in Listing 1.2.

Property $\mathcal{P}_{min=?}\mathbf{F}[\mathsf{PS1} \wedge \mathsf{PS2}]$ checks the minimum probability of both products being processed successfully over all possible adversaries. This property returns a value of 0 meaning there is a possible situation where the robot fails to handle both products, *e.g.* careless decision making causes failed deadlines. Property $\mathcal{P}_{max=?}\mathbf{F}[\mathsf{PS1} \wedge \mathsf{PS2}]$ determines the best possible outcome (both products processed) and returns a value of 0.6561[4], which implies there exists an adversary that the robot can handle both products with moderate success. Given this property, PRISM can automatically synthesise an adversary (strategy) for achieving this property. That is, a list of MDP actions to be taken in each state. Here the optimal adversary instructs the robot to wrap more urgent products (*i.e.* product1) first until it is packed and then switch to wrap the other product. As expected, in both cases the expensive bag is used. Only after both are wrapped does the robot move them to storage.

The property $\mathcal{P}_{max=?}\mathbf{F}[\mathsf{PS1} \wedge \mathsf{PS2} \wedge \mathsf{Pch1} \wedge \mathsf{Pch2}]$ checks if there is a way to successfully handle both products while using cheap bags for both of them. The value is 0, confirming it is impossible to do so. We can use the property $\mathcal{P}_{max=?}\mathbf{F}[\mathsf{PS1} \wedge \mathsf{PS2} \wedge (\mathsf{Pch1} \vee \mathsf{Pch2})]$ to determine if it is possible to use a cheap bag for either product. This is possible ($p = 0.3969$) by adapting the optimal strategies from before to use a cheap bag for product1.

[4] This probability is never 1 as there is always a chance bags fail regardless of type.

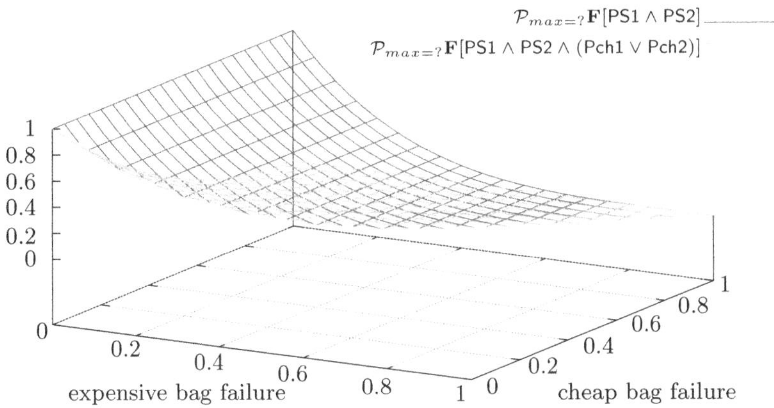

Fig. 5. Value of the property $\mathcal{P}_{max=?}\mathbf{F}[\mathsf{PS1} \land \mathsf{PS2}]$ and $\mathcal{P}_{max=?}\mathbf{F}[\mathsf{PS1} \land \mathsf{PS2} \land (\mathsf{Pch1} \lor \mathsf{Pch2})]$ with increasing failure probability in cheap and expensive bags.

Action Outcome Analysis. The effects of different failure probability for cheap and expensive bag are shown in Fig. 5 where the probability of bag failing to insulate or breaking is increased from 0 to 1. We can see that the value of the property $\mathcal{P}_{max=?}\mathbf{F}[\mathsf{PS1} \land \mathsf{PS2}]$ and $\mathcal{P}_{max=?}\mathbf{F}[\mathsf{PS1} \land \mathsf{PS2} \land (\mathsf{Pch1} \lor \mathsf{Pch2})]$ shows a decreasing trend with increasing failure probability in both cheap and expensive bag. When the failure probability of both types of bags equals to 0 or 1, the values of these two properties coincide with each other with either total success of probability 1 or total failure of probability 0. As expected, the probability of successfully handling two products is always higher than the one which requires cheap bags to be used because of the larger failure probability from the cheap bag than the expensive bag.

4.3 Example: Rover

We consider a rover scenario where the rover travels to a set of sites assigned by the mission centre for scientific experiments, *e.g.* to collect rocks or analyse soil. Given multiple sites to visit, the rover must *choose* one. Once chosen, the robot must then decide the route to use: some routes are shorter than others (plan selection). The mission is to successfully visit all sites, perform required experiments, and return to base.

To illustrate how much impact careless interleavings can make to the resulting agent behaviours, we use a very simplified scenario with only two sites to visit (*i.e.* a very small plan library). The agent program is in Listing 1.3. The rover has two sites to visit, which are captured by external events site1 and site2 in line 4, and is initially at the base (at_base in line 2). To address event site1, the plan on line 6 instructs the rover to pursue two ordered (internal) events,

Listing 1.3. CAN agent for rover.

```
1  // Initial belief bases
2  at_base
3  // External events
4  site1, site2
5  // Plan library
6  site1 : true <- experiment_site1;return_to_base.
7  site2 : true <- experiment_site2;return_to_base.
8  experiment_site1 : at_base <- move_base_to_site1; perform_experiment_site1.
9  experiment_site1 : at_site1 <- perform_experiment_site1.
10 experiment_site1 : at_site2 <- move_site2_to_site1; perform_experiment_site1.
11 experiment_site2 : at_base <- move_base_to_site2; perform_experiment_site2.
12 experiment_site2 : at_site1 <- move_site1_to_site2; perform_experiment_site1.
13 experiment_site2 : at_site2 <- perform_experiment_site2.
14 return_to_base: at_base <- do_nothing.
15 return_to_base: at_site1 <- move_site1_to_base.
16 return_to_base: at_site2 <- move_site2_to_base.
```

namely experiment_site1 and return_to_base. The first event experiment_site1 can be achieved by plans from lines 8 to 10 depending on where the rover is. For example, if the rover is at the base, the plan on line 8 instructs it to move to site 1 and perform necessary experiments. After successfully performing experiments the rover returns to base (return_to_base) through plans in lines 14–16. Event site2 can be handled in a similar way. In this case, we assume each moving agent action (*e.g.* move_base_to_site1) always succeeds. It allows us to easily reason about reward-based properties as any state with the reachability probability of less than 1 will always give an infinite reward. Full agent examples including action descriptions are online [27]. We use SS1 and SS2 to denote site1 and site2 successfully being processed by the rover and use Storm for model analysis.

We first check property $\mathcal{P}_{min=?}\mathbf{F}[\mathsf{SS1} \wedge \mathsf{SS2}]$ to see if there is a case where neither site visit is successful and, unexpectedly, the return value of 0 confirms this is possible. This shows, even in such a simple case, careless interleaving can cause issues: in this case movements back and forth between different locations without processing. For example, the rover may have moved to site 1, but before performing the experiment at site 1, it decides to address event site2 and moves to site 2. This behaviour then repeats in reverse. As the CAN semantics (semantic rule $\rhd_\perp$ in Appendix A) remove used plans on failure, the rover can enter a situation where there is no plan left to move and the mission cannot continue. We then check the property $\mathcal{P}_{max=?}\mathbf{F}[\mathsf{SS1} \wedge \mathsf{SS2}]$ whose value is 1, confirming there is a way to analyse both sites. However, the optimal adversary (regarding the probability) returned by Storm makes unnecessary, but non-detrimental, movement between locations. To ensure the rover achieves the tasks while minimising travelling distance, we use rewards properties $\mathcal{R}_{min=?}\mathbf{F}[\mathsf{SS1} \wedge \mathsf{SS2}]$ and the expected strategy (visit and process each in turn and then return) is synthesised.

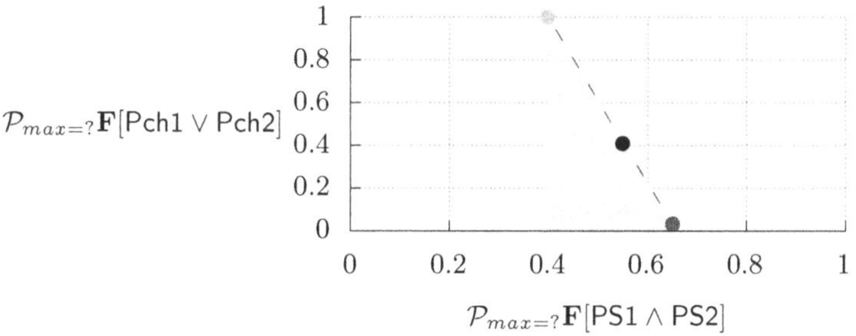

Fig. 6. Trade-offs between property $\mathcal{P}_{max=?}\mathbf{F}[\mathsf{PS1} \wedge \mathsf{PS2}]$ (successfully handling two products) and $\mathcal{P}_{max=?}\mathbf{F}[\mathsf{Pch1} \vee \mathsf{Pch2}]$ (using cheap bag for either product). The red and blue point stand for two possible deterministic adversaries that always make the same choice in a given state of the model. Any point (*e.g.* black one) in the line between red and blue point represents a pair of mission objectives having randomised adversaries. (Color figure online)

4.4 Discussion

Our framework gives agent designers an indication of the type of strategies that may be needed for a given application. For example, it gives confidence to either use a fixed strategy, such as the ordered schedule in the rover example, or justify the need for advanced planning capability. As we target the *semantics* rather than a specific implementation, it is possible to modify these in future to determine if other languages might be more suitable before implementation. For instance, in the rover example, the decision by CAN to throw away failed plans caused issue, while a different language design could avoid this pitfall.

The framework also allows verifying several, possibly conflicting, quantitative properties of an agent system. For example, we can ask how to maximise the probability of achieving the packing tasks while using cheap bags. PRISM can compute (approximately) the Pareto curve [29] shown in Fig. 6, which provides a useful visualization of trade-offs between different mission objectives and can help the agent designers prioritize objectives. Once the agent designer selects a combination of mission objective values in the line, a corresponding strategy can be automatically synthesized. In detail, the blue and red points stand for two pairs of objective values that have deterministic adversaries *i.e.* they always make the same choice in a state of the model. Any point (*e.g.* the black dot) on the line (except blue and red points) represents the pair of objective values that can be achieved by randomised strategy that makes an initial one-off random non-deterministic choice. However, it remains unclear how to interpret these randomised strategies, and this is an interesting area for future work.

We also note it is difficult to reason about the accumulated rewards for reaching some target set of states if these states cannot be eventually reached with probability 1. A good example would be to maximise the probability of achieving a mission state while minimising the cost of reaching it. It is due to a choice that both PRISM and Storm made when designing the reward property specification. They assume that if there is a non-zero probability of not reaching the target state (*i.e.* the probability of reaching it is less than 1), it is reasonable to say the path continues indefinitely without reaching the target state (*i.e.* the overall expected reward for being infinite). A potential solution is to use the state reward (a certain amount of rewards is assigned if a certain state holds). Then the reward information can be specified as a temporal formula in property specifications. (*e.g.* what is the maximum probability of reaching this state which gives some certain reward). Unfortunately, this makes modelling and reasoning more cumbersome, and future work is required to investigate this.

5 Related Work

Optimal decision-making under uncertainty is a core problem in Artificial Intelligence (AI). A prime example is planning [15,16]: studying how to find good or optimal strategies to maximise rewards or the probability of reaching a goal and MDPs are also used as a fundamental mathematical models for planning. Formal verification coincides with planning when formulas in temporal logic express reachability goals (*i.e.* a set of final desired states) and verification methods are used to extract a particular evolution of the system that makes temporal formulas true. That is, verification focuses on checking if (reachability) properties hold for a system and obtaining strategies is a side effect. Our aim is not to compete with AI planning, but to use planning-like benefits in our verification framework for BDI agents. A prominent sub-field for finding good strategies is through reinforcement learning (RL) [30]. RL automatically trains agents to take actions to maximise a reward in an uncertain environment. Here, a concise specification of an MDP (capturing both the agent and the environment) is executed in an initially random manner and over time RL improves the reward of every state-action pair executed to yield good strategies. There has been promising work unifying planning, learning and verification [31].

The BDI community is interested in event, plan and intention selection strategies and this is usually done through modifying or replacing the original BDI reasoning entirely with other decision-making techniques. Although most BDI agent languages specify selection choices (*e.g.* plan selection) made by the agent in non-deterministic fashion, it is typical in practice to constrain the overwhelming non-determinism through ordering—either statically [7] or at run-time [32]—to enforce simple deterministic behaviours. While desirable to exploit the highest ordered choices, it may be worthwhile exploring other non-highest order ones every now and then to avoid being stuck in a local maximum. Some selection strategies use advanced planning algorithms [33,34]. For example, in [35] agent programs are compiled to TÆMS framework to represent the coordination relations *e.g.* "enables" and "hinders" between tasks and employ the Design-To-Criteria scheduler for intention selection. Other works show many of the intention progress issues can be modelled as AI planning problems and resolved through suitable planners [36]. An increasingly popular topic is intention progression [37], *e.g.* the contest [38], that helps the agent to make better decisions on event/plan/intention selection. Our approach not only ensures the safety of agent behaviours through formal verification, but also the quality of agent decision-making through optimal adversary generation. Finally, it is not a new idea to integrate advanced decision-making techniques into BDI. There is a large body of work [33] to employ planning to synthesise new plans to achieve an event when no pre-defined plan worked or exists. For example, work [39] shows how the integration of planning and BDI can be done at the semantic level.

Verifying BDI agents using model checking, via Java PathFinder [11], and theorem proving, using Isabelle/HOL [12] has also been explored. However, these use fixed schedulers for agent selections strategies, *e.g.* first-in-first-out for intention selection, and do not allow probabilistic action outcomes for the agents. Verification and strategy synthesis have also been successfully applied to many traditional probabilistic systems (*e.g.* security systems or protocols) overviewed in [18]. The contribution of our work applied both verification and strategy synthesis to ensure correct and optimal BDI agent behaviours (which features non-deterministic choices and probabilistic action outcomes) with the potentiality such as for multi-objective analysis.

6 Conclusions

Quantitative verification is a powerful technique for analysing systems that exhibits non-deterministic and probabilistic behaviours, allowing us to verify and synthesise strategies for autonomous agents operating in uncertain environments.

We have translated the CAN language, which formalises the behaviour of a classical BDI agent, to an Markov Decision Process model. This supports both non-deterministic decision-making (*e.g.* which plan to select) and probabilistic agent action outcomes (*e.g.* imprecise actuators). The resulting model, CAN^m, is encoded and executed using Milners bigraphs and the BigraphER tool. This allows quantitative analysis and strategy synthesis using popular probabilistic model checking tools including PRISM and Storm.

Through two simple examples, we have shown our approach can help the agent developers to reason about probability and reward-based properties and synthesise optimal strategies. We also reflect on how quantitative verification and strategy synthesis can aid or improve BDI agent system design and implementation, and propose some future work (*e.g.* multi-objective analysis).

Acknowledgements. This work is supported by the EPSRC, under PETRAS SRF grant MAGIC (EP/S035362/1), S4: Science of Sensor Systems Software (EP/N007565/1), and an Amazon Research Award on Automated Reasoning.

A Appendix

The language used in the plan-body in CAN is defined by the grammar:

$$\pm b \mid act \mid e \mid P_1; P_2 \mid P_1 \triangleright P_2 \mid P_1 \parallel P_2 \mid goal(\varphi_s, P, \varphi_f)$$

where $\pm b$ stands for belief addition and deletion, *act* a primitive agent action, and e is a sub-event (i.e. internal event). Actions *act* take the form $act = \psi \leftarrow \langle \phi^+, \phi^- \rangle$, where ψ is the pre-condition, and ϕ^+ and ϕ^- are the addition and deletion sets (resp.) of belief atoms, i.e. a belief base $\mathcal{B}$ is revised to be $(\mathcal{B} \setminus \phi^-) \cup \phi^+$ when the action executes. To execute a sub-event, a plan (corresponding to that event) is selected and the plan-body added in place of the event. In this way we allow plans to be nested (similar to sub-routine calls in other languages). In addition, there are composite programs $P_1; P_2$ for sequence, $P_1 \triangleright P_2$ that executes P_2 in the case that P_1 fails, and $P_1 \parallel P_2$ for interleaved concurrency. Finally, a declarative goal program $goal(\varphi_s, P, \varphi_f)$ expresses that the declarative goal φ_s should be achieved through program P, failing if φ_f becomes true, and retrying as long as neither φ_s nor φ_f is true (see in [19] for details).

Figure 7 gives the complete set of semantic rules for evolving an intention. For example, *act* handles the execution of an action, when the pre-condition ψ is met, resulting in a belief state update. Rule *event* replaces an event with the set of relevant plans, while rule *select* chooses an applicable plan from a set of relevant plans while retaining un-selected plans as backups. With these backup plans, the rules for failure recovery $\triangleright_;$, $\triangleright_\top$, and $\triangleright_\bot$ enable new plans to be selected if the current plan fails (*e.g.* due to environment changes). Rules ; and $;_\top$ allow executing plan-bodies in sequence, while rules $\parallel_1$, $\parallel_2$, and $\parallel_\top$ specify how to execute (interleaved) concurrent programs (within an intention). Rules G_s and G_f deal with declarative goals when either the success condition φ_s or the failure condition φ_f become true. Rule G_{init} initialises persistence by setting the program in the declarative goal to be $P \triangleright P$, *i.e.* if P fails try P again, and rule $G_;$ takes care of performing a single step on an already initialised program. Finally, the derivation rule $G_\triangleright$ re-starts the original program if the current program has finished or got blocked (when neither φ_s nor φ_f is true).

$$\frac{act : \psi \leftarrow \langle \phi^-, \phi^+ \rangle \quad \mathcal{B} \models \psi}{\langle \mathcal{B}, act \rangle \rightarrow \langle (\mathcal{B} \setminus \phi^- \cup \phi^+), nil \rangle} \; act$$

$$\frac{\Delta = \{\varphi : P \mid (e' = \varphi \leftarrow P) \in \Pi \wedge e' = e\}}{\langle \mathcal{B}, e \rangle \rightarrow \langle \mathcal{B}, e : (\mid \Delta \mid) \rangle} \; event$$

$$\frac{\varphi : P \in \Delta \quad \mathcal{B} \models \varphi}{\langle \mathcal{B}, e : (\mid \Delta \mid) \rangle \rightarrow \langle \mathcal{B}, P \rhd e : (\mid \Delta \setminus \{\varphi : P\} \mid) \rangle} \; select$$

$$\frac{\langle \mathcal{B}, P_1 \rangle \rightarrow \langle \mathcal{B}', P_1' \rangle}{\langle \mathcal{B}, P_1 \rhd P_2 \rangle \rightarrow \langle \mathcal{B}', P_1' \rhd P_2 \rangle} \; \rhd_; \qquad \frac{}{\langle \mathcal{B}, (nil \rhd P_2) \rangle \rightarrow \langle \mathcal{B}', nil \rangle} \; \rhd_\top$$

$$\frac{P_1 \neq nil \; \langle \mathcal{B}, P_1 \rangle \nrightarrow \quad \langle \mathcal{B}, P_2 \rangle \rightarrow \langle \mathcal{B}', P_2' \rangle}{\langle \mathcal{B}, P_1 \rhd P_2 \rangle \rightarrow \langle \mathcal{B}', P_2' \rangle} \; \rhd_\bot$$

$$\frac{\langle \mathcal{B}, P \rangle \rightarrow \langle \mathcal{B}', P' \rangle}{\langle \mathcal{B}, (nil; P) \rangle \rightarrow \langle \mathcal{B}', P' \rangle} \; ;_\top \qquad \frac{\langle \mathcal{B}, P_1 \rangle \rightarrow \langle \mathcal{B}', P_1' \rangle}{\langle \mathcal{B}, (P_1; P_2) \rangle \rightarrow \langle \mathcal{B}', (P_1'; P_2) \rangle} \; ;$$

$$\frac{\langle \mathcal{B}, P_1 \rangle \rightarrow \langle \mathcal{B}', P_1' \rangle}{\langle \mathcal{B}, (P_1 \| P_2) \rangle \rightarrow \langle \mathcal{B}', (P_1' \| P_2) \rangle} \; \|_1 \qquad \frac{\langle \mathcal{B}, P_2 \rangle \rightarrow \langle \mathcal{B}', P_2' \rangle}{\langle \mathcal{B}, (P_1 \| P_2) \rangle \rightarrow \langle \mathcal{B}', (P_1 \| P_2') \rangle} \; \|_2$$

$$\frac{}{\langle \mathcal{B}, (nil \| nil) \rangle \rightarrow \langle \mathcal{B}, nil \rangle} \; \|_\top$$

$$\frac{\mathcal{B} \models \varphi_s}{\langle \mathcal{B}, goal(\varphi_s, P, \varphi_f) \rangle \rightarrow \langle \mathcal{B}, nil \rangle} \; G_s \qquad \frac{\mathcal{B} \models \varphi_f}{\langle \mathcal{B}, goal(\varphi_s, P, \varphi_f) \rangle \rightarrow \langle \mathcal{B}, ?false \rangle} \; G_f$$

$$\frac{P \neq P_1 \rhd P_2 \quad \mathcal{B} \not\models \varphi_s \quad \mathcal{B} \not\models \varphi_f}{\langle \mathcal{B}, goal(\varphi_s, P, \varphi_f) \rangle \rightarrow \langle \mathcal{B}, goal(\varphi_s, P \rhd P, \varphi_f) \rangle} \; G_{init}$$

$$\frac{\mathcal{B} \not\models \varphi_s \quad \mathcal{B} \not\models \varphi_f \quad \langle \mathcal{B}, P_1 \rangle \rightarrow \langle \mathcal{B}', P_1' \rangle}{\langle \mathcal{B}, goal(\varphi_s, P_1 \rhd P_2, \varphi_f) \rangle \rightarrow \langle \mathcal{B}', goal(\varphi_s, P_1' \rhd P_2, \varphi_f) \rangle} \; G_;$$

$$\frac{\mathcal{B} \not\models \varphi_s \quad \mathcal{B} \not\models \varphi_f \quad \langle \mathcal{B}, P_1 \rangle \nrightarrow}{\langle \mathcal{B}, goal(\varphi_s, P_1 \rhd P_2, \varphi_f) \rangle \rightarrow \langle \mathcal{B}, goal(\varphi_s, P_2 \rhd P_2, \varphi_f) \rangle} \; G_\rhd$$

Fig. 7. Complete intention-level CAN semantics.

References

1. Bratman, M.: Intention, Plans, and Practical Reason. Harvard University Press (1987)
2. Rao, A.S.: AgentSpeak(L): BDI agents speak out in a logical computable language. In: Van de Velde, W., Perram, J.W. (eds.) MAAMAW 1996. LNCS, vol. 1038, pp. 42–55. Springer, Heidelberg (1996). https://doi.org/10.1007/BFb0031845
3. Winikoff, M., Padgham, L., Harland, J., Thangarajah, J.: Declarative and procedural goals in intelligent agent systems. In: The 8th International Conference on Principles of Knowledge Representation and Reasoning. Morgan Kaufman (2002)
4. Hindriks, K.V., De Boer, F.S., Van der Hoek, W., Meyer, J.-J.Ch.: Agent programming in 3APL. Auton. Agents Multi-Agent Syst. **2**(4), 357–401 (1999)

5. Dastani, M.: 2APL: a practical agent programming language. Auton. Agent. Multi-Agent Syst. **16**(3), 214–248 (2008)
6. Winikoff, M.: Jack^{TM} intelligent agents: an industrial strength platform. In: Bordini, R.H., Dastani, M., Dix, J., El Fallah Seghrouchni, A. (eds.) Multi-Agent Programming. MSASSO, vol. 15, pp. 175–193. Springer, Boston (2005). https://doi.org/10.1007/0-387-26350-0_7
7. Bordini, R.H., HüJomi, J.F., Wooldridge, M.: Programming Multi-agent Systems in AgentSpeak Using Jason, vol. 8. Wiley, Hoboken (2007)
8. Pokahr, A., Braubach, L., Jander, K.: The Jadex project: programming model. In: Ganzha, M., Jain, L. (eds.) Multiagent Systems and Applications, pp. 21–53. Springer, Cham (2013). https://doi.org/10.1007/978-3-642-33323-1_2
9. Wooldridge, M.: An Introduction to Multiagent Systems. Wiley, Hoboken (2009)
10. Luckcuck, M., Farrell, M., Dennis, L.A., Dixon, C., Fisher, M.: Formal specification and verification of autonomous robotic systems: a survey. ACM Comput. Surv. (CSUR) **52**(5), 1–41 (2019)
11. Dennis, L.A., Fisher, M., Webster, M.P., Bordini, R.H.: Model checking agent programming languages. Autom. Softw. Eng. **19**(1), 5–63 (2012)
12. Jensen, A.B.: Machine-checked verification of cognitive agents. In: Proceedings of the 14th International Conference on Agents and Artificial Intelligence, pp. 245–256 (2022)
13. Chen, H.: Applications of cyber-physical system: a literature review. J. Ind. Integr. Manag. **2**(03), 1750012 (2017)
14. Archibald, B., Calder, M., Sevegnani, M., Xu, M.: Probabilistic BDI agents: actions, plans, and intentions. In: Calinescu, R., Păsăreanu, C.S. (eds.) SEFM 2021. LNCS, vol. 13085, pp. 262–281. Springer, Cham (2021). https://doi.org/10.1007/978-3-030-92124-8_15
15. Ghallab, M., Nau, D., Traverso, P.: Automated Planning: Theory and Practice. Elsevier (2004)
16. Geffner, H., Bonet, B.: A concise Introduction to Models and Methods for Automated Planning. Synthesis Lectures on Artificial Intelligence and Machine Learning, vol. 8, no. 1, pp. 1–141 (2013)
17. Abdeddaı, Y., Asarin, E., Maler, O., et al.: Scheduling with timed automata. Theor. Comput. Sci. **354**(2), 272–300 (2006)
18. Kwiatkowska, M., Parker, D.: Automated verification and strategy synthesis for probabilistic systems. In: Van Hung, D., Ogawa, M. (eds.) ATVA 2013. LNCS, vol. 8172, pp. 5–22. Springer, Cham (2013). https://doi.org/10.1007/978-3-319-02444-8_2
19. Sardina, S., Padgham, L.: A BDI agent programming language with failure handling, declarative goals, and planning. Auton. Agents Multi-Agent Syst. **23**, 18–70 (2011)
20. Milner, R.: The Space and Motion of Communicating Agents. Cambridge University Press, Cambridge (2009)
21. Archibald, B., Calder, M., Sevegnani, M.: Probabilistic bigraphs. Formal Aspects Comput. **34**(2), 1–27 (2022)
22. Bellman, R.: A Markovian decision process. J. Math. Mech. 679–684 (1957)
23. Sevegnani, M., Calder, M.: BigraphER: rewriting and analysis engine for bigraphs. In: Chaudhuri, S., Farzan, A. (eds.) CAV 2016. LNCS, vol. 9780, pp. 494–501. Springer, Cham (2016). https://doi.org/10.1007/978-3-319-41540-6_27
24. Kwiatkowska, M., Norman, G., Parker, D.: PRISM 4.0: verification of probabilistic real-time systems. In: Gopalakrishnan, G., Qadeer, S. (eds.) CAV 2011. LNCS,

vol. 6806, pp. 585–591. Springer, Heidelberg (2011). https://doi.org/10.1007/978-3-642-22110-1_47

25. Hensel, C., Junges, S., Katoen, J.P., Quatmann, T., Volk, M.: The probabilistic model checker storm. Int. J. Softw. Tools Technol. Transfer 1–22 (2021)
26. Di Pierro, A., Wiklicky, H.: An operational semantics for probabilistic concurrent constraint programming. In: The 1998 International Conference on Computer Languages, pp. 174–183. IEEE (1998)
27. Xu, M.: Bigraph models of smart manufacturing and rover example in can (2022). https://doi.org/10.5281/zenodo.7441574
28. Hansson, H., Jonsson, B.: A logic for reasoning about time and reliability. Formal Aspects Comput. **6**(5), 512–535 (1994)
29. Forejt, V., Kwiatkowska, M., Parker, D.: Pareto curves for probabilistic model checking. In: Chakraborty, S., Mukund, M. (eds.) ATVA 2012. LNCS, pp. 317–332. Springer, Heidelberg (2012). https://doi.org/10.1007/978-3-642-33386-6_25
30. Sutton, R.S., Barto, A.G.: Reinforcement Learning: An Introduction. MIT Press, Cambridge (2018)
31. Hartmanns, A., Klauck, M.: The modest state of learning, sampling, and verifying strategies. In: Margaria, T., Steffen, B. (eds.) ISoLA 2022. LNCS, vol. 13703, pp. 406–432. Springer, Heidelberg (2022). https://doi.org/10.1007/978-3-031-19759-8_25
32. Padgham, L., Singh, D.: Situational preferences for BDI plans. In: The 2013 International Conference on Autonomous Agents and Multi-agent Systems, pp. 1013–1020 (2013)
33. Meneguzzi, F., De Silva, L.: Planning in BDI agents: a survey of the integration of planning algorithms and agent reasoning. Knowl. Eng. Rev. **30**(1), 1–44 (2015)
34. De Silva, L., Meneguzzi, F.R., Logan, B.: BDI agent architectures: a survey. In: The 29th International Joint Conference on Artificial Intelligence (2020)
35. Bordini, R.H., Bazzan, A.L.C., Jannone, R.D.O., Basso, D.M., Vicari, R.M., Lesser, V.R.: AgentSpeak (XL) efficient intention selection in BDI agents via decision-theoretic task scheduling. In: The First International Joint Conference on Autonomous Agents and Multiagent Systems: Part 3, pp. 1294–1302 (2002)
36. Xu, M., McAreavey, K., Bauters, K., Liu, W.: Intention interleaving via classical replanning. In: 2019 IEEE 31st International Conference on Tools with Artificial Intelligence, pp. 85–92. IEEE (2019)
37. Logan, B., Thangarajah, J., Yorke-Smith, N.: Progressing intention progression: a call for a goal-plan tree contest. In: AAMAS, pp. 768–772 (2017)
38. Intention progression competition. https://www.intentionprogression.org/
39. Xu, M., Bauters, K., McAreavey, K., Liu, W.: A formal approach to embedding first-principles planning in BDI agent systems. In: Ciucci, D., Pasi, G., Vantaggi, B. (eds.) SUM 2018. LNCS (LNAI), vol. 11142, pp. 333–347. Springer, Cham (2018). https://doi.org/10.1007/978-3-030-00461-3_23

Multi-objective Task Assignment and Multiagent Planning with Hybrid GPU-CPU Acceleration

Thomas Robinson and Guoxin Su(✉)

University of Wollongong, Wollongong, NSW 2522, Australia
tmr463@uowmail.edu.au, guoxin@uow.edu.au

Abstract. Allocation and planning with a collection of tasks and a group of agents is an important problem in multiagent systems. One commonly faced bottleneck is scalability, as in general the multiagent model increases exponentially in size with the number of agents. We consider the combination of random task assignment and multiagent planning under multiple-objective constraints, and show that this problem can be decentralised to individual agent-task models. We present an algorithm of point-oriented Pareto computation, which checks whether a point corresponding to given cost and probability thresholds for our formal problem is feasible or not. If the given point is infeasible, our algorithm finds a Pareto-optimal point which is closest to the given point. We provide the first multi-objective model checking framework that simultaneously uses GPU and multi-core acceleration. Our framework manages CPU and GPU devices as a load balancing problem for parallel computation. Our experiments demonstrate that parallelisation achieves significant run time speed-up over sequential computation.

Keywords: Multiagent System · Task Assignment · Planning · Probabilistic Model Checking · GPU and Multi-Core Acceleration

1 Introduction

Markov Decision Processes (MDPs) [26] are a fundamental model for multiagent planning in stochastic environments, where actions of an agent at a state may lead to uncertain outcomes. Multiagent task allocation and planning is concerned with enabling a group of agents to divide up tasks amongst themselves and carry out their planning and execution. Scalability is a commonly faced bottleneck for this kind of problems, as in general an MDP that models a multiagent system (MAS) increases exponentially in size with a linear increment in the number of agents in the system [5].

Probabilistic model checking (PMC) is a verification technique to establish rigorous guarantees about the correctness of real-life stochastic systems [1]. PMC

This work was partially supported by Australian Defence Science and Technology Group under the Artificial Intelligence for Decision Making 2022 Initiative scheme.

K. Y. Rozier and S. Chaudhuri (Eds.): NFM 2023, LNCS 13903, pp. 260–277, 2023.
https://doi.org/10.1007/978-3-031-33170-1_16

provides methods to compute the optimal values of reachability rewards for an MDP, and the optimal probabilities that an MDP satisfies properties formalised with Linear Temporal Logic (LTL). A fragment of LTL, called co-safe LTL, has a deterministic finite-state automaton (DFA) representation [19], and thus is suitable to specify tasks that must be completed in finite time. Task execution in finite time is important in multiagent planning because we typically want to re-use the agents to execute further tasks.

In practice, coordination of agents usually involves conflicting solutions to the multiple objectives that an MAS is required to satisfy, for example, agents may need to balance execution time with energy consumption. When simultaneous verification of multiple objectives is concerned, we require the multi-objective MDP (MOMDP) [30] whose reward structure specifies reward vectors (rather than scalars). The solution space of an MOMDP is a convex polytope [10,13], which makes the MOMDP model checking problem tractable. Currently three kinds of queries are considered in MOMDP model checking [14]: The achievability query is the most basic query, which asks whether there exists a scheduler to meet all objective thresholds; the numerical query is a numerical variant of the first query, which computes the optimal value of one objective while meeting all other objective thresholds; the Pareto query is the most expensive query, which computes approximately the Pareto curve of all objectives.

The classical assignment problem finds an assignment, namely a one-to-one mapping from tasks to agents, which results in a maximal assignment reward. The multi-objective assignment problem is to determine an assignment such that the vectorised assignment reward is Pareto optimal. The classical assignment problem can be solved efficiently (e.g., using the Hungarian algorithm [18]), but the multi-objective assignment problem is much harder [33]. The multi-objective random assignment (MORA) problem pursues a randomised distribution over assignments such that the expected assignment reward is Pareto optimal.

The combination of (single-objective) task assignment and multiagent planning has been considered for non-stochastic agent models (i.e., transition systems) [32] and stochastic agent models (i.e., MDPs) [11]. In this paper, we extend MOMDP model checking to a setting of multi-objective random assignment and planning (MORAP) in an MAS, and present a novel implementation with hybrid GPU-CPU acceleration. Our main contributions are as follows:

- We show the convexity of our formal problem (MORAP), and that a practical approach to solve this problem can rely on a decentralised model, which avoids the exponential model size growth with agent-task numbers.
- Our main algorithm is a new point-oriented Pareto computation complementing the existing achievability and Pareto queries [13]. For a given point corresponding to cost and probability thresholds, our algorithm finds a point which is feasible for the MORAP problem and closest to the given point under a general vector norm.
- To the best of our knowledge, we provide the first multi-objective model checking framework that utilises simultaneous GPU and multi-core acceleration. Our framework manages CPU and GPU devices as a load balancing problem

for parallel computation. We evaluate the performance of our implementation in a smart-warehouse example.

The remainder of this paper is organised as follows: Sect. 2 provides the preliminaries for the problem; Sect. 3 gives the approach to the problem, model construction and algorithms; Sect. 4 provides details on the hybrid implementation and parallel architecture; Sect. 5 analyses the performance of our approach; Sect. 6 provides related work; and finally Sect. 7 concludes the paper. Formal proofs of theorems are included in the appendix of the long version of this paper [28].

2 Preliminaries

Deterministic Finite Automata. A *deterministic finite automaton* (DFA) $\mathcal{A}$ is given by the tuple $(Q, q_0, Q_F, \Sigma, \delta)$ where (i) Q is a set of locations, (ii) $q_0 \in Q$ is an initial location, (iii) $Q_F \subseteq Q$ is a set of accepting locations, (iv) $\Sigma = 2^{AP}$ (where AP is a non-empty set of atomic propositions) is the alphabet, and (v) $\delta : S \times \Sigma \to S$ is the transition function. If $\delta(q, W) = q'$ for some $W \subseteq AP$, we call q a *predecessor* of q' and q' a *successor* of q. Let $\text{pre}(q)$ and $\text{suc}(q)$ denote the set of predecessors or successors of q, respectively. A location q is a *sink* if $\text{suc}(q) = \{q\}$. In this paper, it suffices to consider DFAs whose accepting locations are sinks. A run in $\mathcal{A}$ is a sequence of locations $q_1, \ldots, q_m$ such that $q_{i+1} \in \text{suc}(q_i)$ for all $1 \leq i \leq m-1$. We call q a *trap* if there is no run to any $q' \in Q_F$ from it. Let Q_R be the set of traps in $\mathcal{A}$.

Co-Safe LTL. LTL is a compact representation of linear time properties. The syntax of LTL is $\varphi ::= \top \mid \mathsf{a} \mid \neg\varphi \mid \varphi \wedge \varphi \mid \mathsf{X}\,\varphi \mid \varphi\,\mathsf{U}\,\varphi$, where $\mathsf{a} \in AP$. The operators X and U stand for "next" and "until", respectively. Let $\mathsf{F}\,\varphi := \top\,\mathsf{U}\,\varphi$, and $\mathsf{G}\,\varphi := \neg\,\mathsf{F}\,\neg\varphi$. The semantic relationship $\sigma \models \varphi$ where $\sigma \in \Sigma^\omega$ is standard where Σ^ω denotes the set of all infinite words over Σ. We are interested in the *co-safe* fragment of LTL formulas. Informally, φ is co-safe if any σ such that $\sigma \models \varphi$ includes some *good prefix* (which is accepting in some DFA) $pref_{good}(\varphi)$ denoted $acc(\mathcal{A})$. Syntactically, any LTL formula containing only the temporal operators X (*next*), U (*until*), and F (*eventually*) in *positive normal form* (PNF) is co-safe. A formal characterisation in the semantic level is included the appendix of [28].

Markov Decision Process. A (labelled) MDP is given by the tuple $\mathcal{M} = (S, s_0, A, P, L)$ where (i) S is a finite nonempty state space, (ii) $s_0 \in S$ is an initial state, (iii) A is a set of actions, (iv) $P : S \times A \times S \to [0,1]$ is a transition probability function such that $\sum_{s' \in S} P(s, a, s') \in \{0, 1\}$, and (v) $L : S \to \Sigma$ is a labelling function. Let $A(s) = \{a \in A \mid \sum_{s' \in S} P(s, a, s') = 1\}$, i.e., $A(s)$ is the set of *enabled* actions at s. The size of $\mathcal{M}$ is $|\mathcal{M}| = |S| + |P|$, where $|P| = |\{(s, a, s') \in S \times A \times S \mid P(s, q, s') > 0\}|$. A *reward function or structure* for $\mathcal{M}$ is a function $\rho : \{(s, a) \in S \times A \mid a \in A(s)\} \to \mathbb{R}$. We write $\mathcal{M}[\rho]$ to explicitly indicate the reward structure ρ for $\mathcal{M}$. An (infinite) *path* π is a sequence $s_1 a_1 s_2 a_2 \ldots$ such that $P(s_i, a_i, s_{i+1}) > 0$ for all $i \geq 1$. Let $L(\pi)$ denote the word $L(s_1)L(s_2)\ldots \in$

Σ^ω. Let IPath be the set of paths in $\mathcal{M}$ and IPath(s) be the subset of IPath containing the paths originating from s. The set of probability distributions over A is denoted by $Dist(A)$. A memoryless *scheduler* (or scheduler for short) for $\mathcal{M}$, is a mapping $\mu : s \mapsto Dist(A(s))$ for all $s \in S$. If μ is a *simple* (or pure) if $\mu(s)(a) = 1$ for each $s \in S$ and some $a \in A(s)$. The set of schedulers (resp., simple schedulers) is denoted by $Sch(\mathcal{M})$ (resp., $Sch_S(\mathcal{M})$).

Reachability Reward. Given any LTL formula $\mathsf{F}B$ with B being a Boolean formula, let $\rho(\pi|\,\mathsf{F}B) = \sum_{i=1}^{n} \rho(s_i, a_i)$ where $\pi = s_1 a_1 s_2 a_2 \ldots \in \text{IPath}(s_1)$ and n is the smallest number such that $L(s_n) \models B$ and $L(s_i) \not\models B$ for all $i < n$; if such n does not exist, let $\rho(\pi|\,\mathsf{F}B) = \infty$. Let $\mathbf{Pr}^{\mathcal{M},\mu}$ be the probability measure over paths in IPath(s).[1] The expectation $\mathbf{E}^{\mathcal{M}[\rho],\mu}(\mathsf{F}\,B) \doteq \int_\pi \rho(\pi|\,\mathsf{F}B)\mathrm{d}\mathbf{Pr}^{\mathcal{M},\mu}$, a.k.a. *reachability reward* [21], is the expected reward accumulated in a path of $\mathcal{M}$ under μ until reaching states satisfying B. We say $\mathcal{M}[\rho]$ is *reward-finite* w.r.t. $\mathsf{F}B$ if $\sup_{\mu \in Sch(\mathcal{M})} \mathbf{E}^{\mathcal{M}[\rho],\mu}(\mathsf{F}\,B) < \infty$.

Product MDP. Given $\mathcal{M} = (S, s_0, A, P, L)$ and $\mathcal{A} = (Q, q_0, Q_F, \Sigma, \delta)$, a *product MDP* is a tuple $\mathcal{M} \otimes \mathcal{A} = (S \times Q, (s_0, q_0), A, P', L')$ where (i) $P' : S \times Q \times A \times S \times Q \to [0,1]$ is a transition probability function such that

$$P'(s, q, a, s', q') = \begin{cases} P(s, a, s') & \text{if } q' = \delta(q, L(s')) \\ 0 & \text{otherwise} \end{cases}$$

and (ii) $L' : S \times Q \to 2^\Sigma$ is a labelling function s.t. $L'(s, q) = L(s)$. Let $\mathcal{M}[\rho] \otimes \mathcal{A}$ refer to $(\mathcal{M} \otimes \mathcal{A})[\rho]$ where $\rho(s, q, a) = \rho(s, a)$ for all $(s, q) \in S \times Q, a \in A(s)$.

Geometry. For a point (i.e., vector) $\boldsymbol{v} \in \mathbb{R}^n$ for some n, let v_i denote the ith element of $\boldsymbol{v}$. A *weight vector* $\boldsymbol{w}$ is a vector such that $w_i \geq 0$ and $\sum_{i=1}^{n} w_i = 1$. The *dot product* of $\boldsymbol{v}$ and $\boldsymbol{u}$, denoted $\boldsymbol{v} \cdot \boldsymbol{u}$, is the sum $\sum_{i=1}^{n} v_i u_i$. For a set $\Phi = \{\boldsymbol{v}_1, \ldots, \boldsymbol{v}_m\} \subseteq \mathbb{R}^n$, a *convex combination* in Φ is $\sum_{i=1}^{m} w_i \boldsymbol{v}_i$ for some weight vector $\boldsymbol{w} \in \mathbb{R}^m$. The *downward closure* of the *convex hull* of Φ, denoted $down(\Phi)$, is the set of vectors such that for any $\boldsymbol{u} \in down(\Phi)$ there is a convex combination $\boldsymbol{v} = w_1 \boldsymbol{v}_1 + \ldots + w_m \boldsymbol{v}_m$ such that $u_i \leq v_i$. Let $\Psi \subseteq \mathbb{R}^n$ be any downward closure of points. We say $\boldsymbol{u}$ *dominates* $\boldsymbol{v}$ *from above*, denoted $\boldsymbol{v} \leq \boldsymbol{u}$, if $v_i \leq u_i$ for all $1 \leq i \leq n$. A vector $\boldsymbol{u} \in \Psi$ is *Pareto optimal* if $\boldsymbol{u}$ is no point in Ψ dominates it from above. A *Pareto curve* in Ψ is the set of Pareto optimal vectors in Ψ. The following lemma follows from the *separating hyperplane* and *supporting hyperplane theorems*.

Lemma 1 ([6]). *Let $\Psi \subseteq \mathbb{R}^n$ be any downward closure of a convex hull constructed from a set of points $\boldsymbol{x} \in \mathbb{R}^n$. For any $\boldsymbol{v} \notin \Psi$, there is a weight vector $\boldsymbol{w}$ such that $\boldsymbol{w} \cdot \boldsymbol{v} > \boldsymbol{w} \cdot \boldsymbol{x}$ for all $\boldsymbol{x} \in \Psi$. We say that $\boldsymbol{w}$* separates *$\boldsymbol{v}$ from Ψ. Also, for any $\boldsymbol{u}$ on the Pareto curve of Ψ, there is a weight vector $\boldsymbol{w}'$ such that $\boldsymbol{w}' \cdot \boldsymbol{u} \geq \boldsymbol{w}' \cdot \boldsymbol{x}$ for all $\boldsymbol{x} \in \Psi$. We say that $\{\boldsymbol{x} \in \mathbb{R}^n \mid \boldsymbol{w}' \cdot \boldsymbol{x} = \boldsymbol{w}' \cdot \boldsymbol{u}\}$ is a* supporting hyperplane *of Ψ.*

---

[1] This probability measure is defined on the discrete-time Markov chain induced by the scheduler μ of $\mathcal{M}$ (c.f. Definition 10.92 in [2]).

Bistochastic Matrix. For a matrix $\boldsymbol{U} \in \mathbb{R}^{n \times n}$ for some n, let $u_{i,j}$ denote the element of $\boldsymbol{U}$ in the ith row and j^{th} column. $\boldsymbol{U}$ is *bistochastic* if $u_{i,j} \geq 0$ and $\sum_{i'=1}^{n} u_{i',j} = \sum_{j'=1}^{n} u_{i,j'} = 1$ for all $1 \leq i, j \leq n$. A bistochastic matrix $\boldsymbol{U}$ is a *permutation matrix* if $\boldsymbol{U}$ has exactly one element with value 1 in each row and each column. We recall the following Birkhoff-von Neumann Theorem:

Lemma 2 ([3]). *A bistochastic matrix* $\boldsymbol{U}$ *of order* n *is equivalent to a convex combination of permutation matrices* $\boldsymbol{U}_1, \ldots, \boldsymbol{U}_k$ *for some* $k \leq n^2 - 2n + 2$.

Random Assignment. Given a set I (resp., J) of agents (resp., tasks) with $|I| = |J|$, a (balanced) *assignment* is a bijective function $f : J \to I$. Denote the set of assignments of J to I by $\mathcal{F}$. A *random assignment* ν is a randomised distribution over $\mathcal{F}$ (or, equivalently, a convex combination of assignments in $\mathcal{F}$). For convenience, let $I = J = \{1, \ldots, n\}$. Let $\nu_{j \to i} = \nu(\{f \in \mathcal{F} \mid f(j) = i\})$, namely, the marginal probability of assigning task j to agent i according to ν. Clearly, any assignment is equivalent to a permutation matrix. Moreover, by Lemma 2 any bistochastic matrix $\boldsymbol{U}$ is equivalent to a random assignment ν such that $u_{i,j} = \nu_{j \to i}$.

3 Problem and Approach

3.1 Problem Statement

In our MAS setting, each agent is an MDP (with a reward structure) and each task is a DFA (equivalently, a co-safe LTL formula), and the rewards are the probabilities of accomplishing the tasks and the costs (as negative rewards) of agents executing tasks. Therefore, we aim to compute a random task assignment and schedulers for all agents and tasks, which must meet multiple probability and cost requirements. Intuitively, we consider the task assignment and agent planning scenario satisfying the following two conditions [32]:

C1. The tasks are mutually independent.
C2. The behaviours of agents do not impact each other.

For each $(i, j) \in I \times J$,[2] we define an *agent-task* (product) MDP $\mathcal{M}_{i \otimes j}[\rho_i] \doteq \mathcal{M}_i[\rho_i] \otimes \mathcal{A}_j$ and include an atomic proposition $\texttt{done}_j$ such that

$$L_{i,j}(s, q) \models \texttt{done}_j \text{ iff } q \in Q_{j,F} \cup Q_{j,R}$$

which indicates "task j is ended (either accomplished or failed)." For each $j \in J$ we define a designated reward function $\rho_{j+|I|} : \dot{\bigcup}_{i \in I}(S_i \times Q_j \times A_i) \to \{0, 1\}$ such that $\rho_{j+|I|}(s, q, a) = 1$ iff $q \notin Q_{j,F}$ and $\text{suc}(q) \subseteq Q_{j,F}$. If such a pre-sink q does not exist, we can modify $\mathcal{A}_j$ to include q without altering $acc(\mathcal{A}_j)$. In words, $\rho_{j+|I|}$ provides a one-off unit reward whenever an accepting location will be traversed *for the first time*. Informally, $\rho_{j+|I|}$ expresses "the probability of

[2] Throughout the paper we assume $I = J = \{1, \ldots, n\}$ for some n (unless explicitly stated otherwise) but still use I, J to indicate the agent or task references.

Maximise

$$\begin{cases} \sum_{j\in J}\sum_{(s,q)\in S_i\times Q_j}\sum_{a\in A_i(s)}\rho_i(s,q,a)x_{s,q,a} & \forall i\in I\\ \sum_{i\in I}\sum_{(s,q)\in S_i\times Q_j}\sum_{a\in A_i(s)}\rho_{j+|I|}(s,q,a)x_{s,q,a} & \forall j\in J\end{cases}$$

Subject to $\forall i\in I, j\in J, (s,q)\in S_i\times Q_j$:

$$\begin{cases} \sum_{a\in A_i(s)}x_{s,q,a} - \mathrm{I}_{(s,q)=(s_{i,0},q_{j,0})}x_{i,j} \\ \quad = \sum_{(s',q')\in S_i\times Q_j}\sum_{a'\in A_i(s')}P_{i,j}(s',q',a',s,q)x_{s',q',a'}\\ x_{s,q,a}\ge 0;\ x_{i,j}\ge 0;\ \sum_{i'\in I}x_{i',j}=1;\ \sum_{j'\in I}x_{i,j'}=1\end{cases}$$

Fig. 1. The multi-objective linear program for MORAP

accomplishing task j." As the atomic proposition done_j is fixed for each $\mathcal{M}_{i\otimes j}$, we *abbreviate* $\mathbf{E}^{\mathcal{M}_{i\otimes j}[\rho_k],\mu_{i,j}}(\mathsf{F}\,\mathsf{done}_j)$ *as* $\mathbf{E}^{\mathcal{M}_{i\otimes j}[\rho_k],\mu_{i,j}}$ where $k=j$ or $k=j+|I|$. As the reachability rewards for agents may be infinite and cause instability in computation, similar to the multi-objective verification literature [13,15], we require that $\mathcal{M}_{i\otimes j}[\rho_i]$ is reward-finite (w.r.t. $\mathsf{F}\,\mathsf{done}_j$) for all $(i,j)\in I\times J$.

Definition 1 (MORAP). *A multi-objective random assignment and planning (MORAP) problem is finding a bistochastic matrix* $(x_{i,j})_{i\in I,j\in J}$ *and a set of schedulers* $\{\mu_{i,j}\in Sch(\mathcal{M}_{i\otimes j})\mid i\in I, j\in J\}$ *such that the following two kinds of requirements, namely R1 and R2, are satisfied:*

(R1. Probability) $\sum_{i\in I}x_{i,j}\mathbf{E}^{\mathcal{M}_{i\otimes j}[\rho_{j+|I|}],\mu_{i,j}}\ge p_j$ *for all* $j\in J$,
(R2. Cost) $\sum_{j\in J}x_{i,j}\mathbf{E}^{\mathcal{M}_{i\otimes j}[\rho_i],\mu_{i,j}}\ge c_i$ *for all* $i\in I$,

where the probability thresholds $(p_j)_{j\in J}\in[0,1]^{|J|}$ *and the cost thresholds* $(c_i)_{i\in I}\in\mathbb{R}^{|I|}$ *are given. If the above requirements are satisfied, we say that the MORAP problem is* feasible *with given thresholds or just that the thresholds are* feasible.

Definition 1 is an adequate formulation in the presence of conditions C1 and C2. First, since tasks are mutually independent (C1), the probability requirements only need to address the successful probability of each task. Second, since the execution of any task by each agent does not impact other agents (C2), the cost requirements only need to consider the cost of each agent. In practice, we can relax the condition $|I|=|J|$ to $|I|\ge|J|$ (e.g., adding dummy tasks whose probability threshold is 0).

3.2 Convex Characterisation and Centralised Model

An essential characteristic of our MORAP problem is *convexity*, namely, the downward closure of feasible probability and cost thresholds is a convex polytope (i.e., the downward convex hull of some finite set of points). This follows from the fact that the MORAP problem can be expressed as a multi-objective linear program (LP) by using a similar technique which underpins multi-objective verification of MDPs [10,13,24]. Figure 1 includes the multi-objective LP for MORAP. Intuitively, for each $(i, j) \in I \times J$, $x_{i,j}$ represents the probability of assigning j to i (c.f., Lemma 2), and for each $(s, q) \in S_i \times Q_i$, $x_{s,q,a}$ is the expected frequency of visiting (s, q) and taking action a. A memoryless scheduler can be defined as follows: $\mu_{i,j}(s, q)(a) = x_{s,q,a}/x_{s,q}$ where $x_{s,q} = \sum_{a \in A_i(s)} x_{s,q,a}$. Thus, a MORAP problem has the following time complexity:

Theorem 1. *The feasibility of a MORAP problem is decidable in time polynomial in* $\sum_{i \in I, j \in J} |\mathcal{M}_{i \otimes j}|$.

LP is not efficient for large problems, and value- and policy-iteration methods are more scalable methods in practice. For this purpose, we define a new MDP which combines all agent-task MDPs and includes an additional variable indicating which agents have been assigned with tasks. This MDP is targeted directly at solving the random assignment problem in a centralised way

Definition 2 (Centralised MDP). *A centralisd MDP is* $\mathcal{M}^{ct} = (S^{ct}, s_0^{ct}, A^{ct}, P^{ct}, L^{ct})$ *where (i)* $S^{ct} = \biguplus_{i \in I} \biguplus_{j \in J} S_i \times Q_j \times 2^I$, *(ii)* $s_0^{ct} = (s_{1,0}, q_{1,0}, \emptyset)$, *(iii)* $A^{ct} = \bigcup_{i \in I} A_i \uplus \{b_1, b_2, b_3\}$, *(iv)* $P^{ct} = S^{ct} \times A^{ct} \times S^{ct} \to [0, 1]$ *such that:*

- $P^{ct}(s, q, \sharp, a, s', q', \sharp) = P_{i,j}(s, q, a, s', q')$ *if* $s, s' \in S_i$, $q, q' \in Q_j$, $a \in A_i(s)$ *and* $i \in \sharp$ *for some* i, j,
- $P^{ct}(s, q, \sharp, b_1, s, q, \sharp \cup \{i\}) = 1$ *if* $s = s_{i,0}$, $q = q_{j,0}$ *and* $i \notin \sharp$ *for some* i, j,
- $P^{ct}(s, q, \sharp, b_2, s', q, \sharp) = 1$ *if* $s = s_{i,0}$, $q = q_{j,0}$ *and* $s' = s_{i',0}$ *with* $i' = \min\{i'' \in I \mid i'' > i, i'' \notin \sharp\}$ *for some* i, j,
- $P^{ct}(s, q, \sharp, b_3, s', q', \sharp) = 1$ *if* $s \in S_i$, $q \in Q_{j,F} \cup Q_{j,R}$, $i \in \sharp$, $s' = s_{i',0}$ *with* $i' = \min\{i'' \in I \mid i'' \notin \sharp\}$, *and* $q' = q_{j+1,0}$ *for some* i, $j < |J|$,

(v) $L^{ct} : S^{ct} \to 2^{\{\mathsf{done}\}}$ *such that* $L^{ct}(s, q) \models \mathsf{done}$ *iff* $q \in Q_{j,F} \cup Q_{j,R}$.

Intuitively, $\sharp \subseteq I$ indicates agents who have worked on some tasks; b_1 indicates "a task is assigned to the current agent"; b_2 indicates "a task is forwarded to the next agent"; and b_3 indicates "the next task is considered". The model behaves as an individual product MDP when working on the assigned tasks.

Given any reward structure ρ for $\mathcal{M}_{i \otimes j}$, we view ρ as a reward structure for $\mathcal{M}^{ct}$ by letting $\rho(s, q, \sharp, a) = \rho(s, q, a)$ if $a \in A_i(s)$ and $\rho(s, q, \sharp, a) = 0$ otherwise for all $(s, q, \sharp, a)$. Similarly, given any reward structure ρ for $\mathcal{M}^{ct}$, a restriction of ρ on $S_i \times Q_j \times A_i$ is a reward structure for $\mathcal{M}_{i \otimes j}$. Similar to agent-task MDPs, we abbreviate $\mathbf{E}^{\mathcal{M}^{ct}[\rho],\mu}(\mathsf{F}\,\mathsf{done})$ as $\mathbf{E}^{\mathcal{M}^{ct}[\rho],\mu}$ for a given ρ.

Theorem 2. *The MORAP problem in Definition 1 is feasible with respect to* $(p_j)_{j \in J}$ *and* $(c_i)_{i \in I}$ *if and only if there is* $\mu \in Sch(\mathcal{M}^{ct})$ *such that* $\mathbf{E}^{\mathcal{M}^{ct}[\rho_{j+|J|}],\mu} \geq p_j$ *and* $\mathbf{E}^{\mathcal{M}^{ct}[\rho_i],\mu} \geq c_i$ *for all* $i \in I, j \in J$.

With the above theorem, one can work on the centralised MDP $\mathcal{M}^{ct}$ (e.g., by using value-iteration) to solve a MORAP problem. Therefore, existing probabilistic model checking tools for multi-objective MDP verification (e.g., Prism

Algorithm 1: Point-oriented Pareto computation

Input: $\{\mathcal{M}_{i \otimes j}\}_{(i,j) \in I \times J}$, $\boldsymbol{\rho} = \{\rho_k\}_{k=1}^{|I|+|J|}$, $\boldsymbol{t}$ (a concatenation of $\boldsymbol{c}$ and $\boldsymbol{p}$), $\varepsilon \geq 0$

1 $\boldsymbol{t}_\uparrow := -\infty$; $\boldsymbol{t}_\downarrow := \boldsymbol{t}$; $\Phi := \emptyset$; $\Lambda := \emptyset$; $\boldsymbol{w} := (1, 0, \ldots, 0)$;
2 **while** $\|\boldsymbol{t}_\downarrow - \boldsymbol{t}_\uparrow\| > \varepsilon$ **do**
3   **if** $\Phi \neq \emptyset$ **then**
4   Find $\boldsymbol{x} \in \mathit{down}(\Phi)$ minimising $\|\boldsymbol{t} - \boldsymbol{x}\|$;
5         $\boldsymbol{t}_\uparrow := \boldsymbol{x}$;
6         $\boldsymbol{w} := \boldsymbol{M}(\boldsymbol{t} - \boldsymbol{t}_\uparrow)/\|\boldsymbol{M}(\boldsymbol{t} - \boldsymbol{t}_\uparrow)\|_1$;
7   Find $\boldsymbol{r}$ s.t. $\{\boldsymbol{y} \mid \boldsymbol{w} \cdot \boldsymbol{y} = \boldsymbol{w} \cdot \boldsymbol{r}\}$ is a supporting hyperplane of $\mathscr{C}$;
8     $\Phi := \Phi \cup \{\boldsymbol{r}\}$; $\Lambda := \Lambda \cup \{(\boldsymbol{w}, \boldsymbol{r})\}$;
9   **if** $\boldsymbol{w} \cdot \boldsymbol{r} < \boldsymbol{w} \cdot \boldsymbol{t}_\downarrow$ **then**
10   Find $\boldsymbol{z}$ minimising $\|\boldsymbol{t} - \boldsymbol{z}\|$ s.t. $\boldsymbol{w}' \cdot \boldsymbol{r}' \geq \boldsymbol{w}' \cdot \boldsymbol{z}$ for all $(\boldsymbol{w}', \boldsymbol{r}') \in \Lambda$;
11         $\boldsymbol{t}_\downarrow := \boldsymbol{z}$;

[20] and Storm [17]) can be employed. However, the state space of $\mathcal{M}^{\mathrm{ct}}$ is exponential with respect to the agent team size $|I|$. Therefore, this approach is hard to scale to a relatively large $|I|$.

3.3 Point-Oriented Pareto Computation by Decentralised Model

We present a decentralised method solve a given MORAP problem, especially when the agent number (i.e., task number) is large. Besides deciding whether the problem is feasible or not, for a non-feasible problem our method also computes a new feasible threshold vector on the Pareto curve of the problem, and nearest the original threshold vector up to some numerical tolerance.

Let $\mathscr{C}_0 = \{(\mathbf{E}^{\mathcal{M}^{\mathrm{ct}}[\rho_k],\mu})_{1 \leq k \leq |I|+|J|} \mid \mu \in \mathit{Sch}(\mathcal{M}^{\mathrm{ct}})\}$. The reward-finiteness implies that $\mathscr{C}_0$ is non-empty and bounded. Let $\mathscr{C}$ be the downward closure of $\mathscr{C}_0$, i.e., namely, $\mathscr{C}$ is *the set of feasible threshold vectors* in Definition 1. The main algorithm for our method is presented in Algorithm 1 with the supporting hyperplane computation (i.e., Line 7) detailed in Algorithm 2. Algorithm 1 works by iteratively refining a *lower approximation*, encoded as Φ, and an *upper approximation*, encoded as Λ, for $\mathscr{C}$. It computes a vector $\boldsymbol{t}_\uparrow$ (resp., $\boldsymbol{t}_\downarrow$) which is the closest point from the origin threshold vector $\boldsymbol{t}$ to the lower (resp., upper) approximation such that $\boldsymbol{t}_\uparrow$ and $\boldsymbol{t}_\downarrow$ converge eventually.

The algorithm uses a general norm $\|\cdot\|$ to measure the distance between vectors, as in practice one may prefer to differentiate the importance of probability and cost thresholds. An *inner product* of $\boldsymbol{v}, \boldsymbol{u} \in \mathbb{R}^m$ (m a positive integer), denoted $\langle \boldsymbol{v}, \boldsymbol{u} \rangle$, is the matrix-vector multiplication $\boldsymbol{v}^T \boldsymbol{M} \boldsymbol{u}$, where $\boldsymbol{M}$ is a symmetric positive-definite matrix. Note that if $\boldsymbol{M}$ is the identity matrix then $\langle \boldsymbol{v}, \boldsymbol{u} \rangle$ is $\boldsymbol{v} \cdot \boldsymbol{u}$. Then, $\|\boldsymbol{v}\| = \langle \boldsymbol{v}, \boldsymbol{v} \rangle$. Let $\|\cdot\|_1$ denote vector 1-norm. The weight vector $\boldsymbol{w}$ computed in Line 6 is the (opposite) direction of projecting $\boldsymbol{t}$ onto $\mathit{down}(\Phi)$. Moreover, $\boldsymbol{w} \cdot \boldsymbol{\rho}$ denotes a weighted combination of reward functions in $\boldsymbol{\rho}$.

Algorithm 2: Supporting hyperplane computation in Line 7 of Alg. 1

Input: $\{\mathcal{M}_{i\otimes j}\}_{(i,j)\in I\times J}$, $\boldsymbol{\rho}=\{\rho_k\}_{k=1}^{|I|+|J|}$, $\boldsymbol{w}$
1 **foreach** $(i,j)\in I\times J$ **do**
   `/* Line 2 is computed by policy iteration. */`
2    $c_{i,j} := \mathbf{E}^{\mathcal{M}_{i\otimes j}[\boldsymbol{w}\cdot\boldsymbol{\rho}],\mu_{i,j}}$ with $\mu_{i,j} := \arg\max_{\mu} \mathbf{E}^{\mathcal{M}_{i\otimes j}[\boldsymbol{w}\cdot\boldsymbol{\rho}],\mu}$;
3 Find an assignment $f\in\mathcal{F}$ maximising $\sum_{j\in J} c_{f(j),j}$;
4 **foreach** $j\in J$ **do**
   `/* Lines 5-6 are computed by value iteration. */`
5    $r_{j+|I|} := \mathbf{E}^{\mathcal{M}_{f(j)\otimes j}[\rho_{j+|I|}],\mu_{f(j),j}}$;
6    $r_{f(j)} := \mathbf{E}^{\mathcal{M}_{f(j)\otimes j}[\rho_{f(j)}],\mu_{f(j),j}}$;
7 **return** $(r_k)_{k=1}^{|I|+|J|}$;

Theorem 3. *Algorithm 1 terminates for any $\varepsilon\geq 0$. Throughout the execution of Algorithm 1, the following properties hold: (i) $\boldsymbol{t}_\uparrow\in\mathscr{C}$. (ii) If $\boldsymbol{t}\in\mathscr{C}$ then $\boldsymbol{t}_\downarrow=\boldsymbol{t}$. (iii) $\|\boldsymbol{t}-\boldsymbol{t}_\downarrow\|\leq\min_{\boldsymbol{u}\in\mathscr{C}}\|\boldsymbol{t}-\boldsymbol{u}\|\leq\|\boldsymbol{t}-\boldsymbol{t}_\uparrow\|$.*

Corollary 1. *Suppose $\varepsilon=0$. After Algorithm 1 terminates, the following properties hold: (i) $\boldsymbol{t}_\uparrow=\boldsymbol{t}_\downarrow$. (ii) $\boldsymbol{t}\in\mathscr{C}$ if and only if $\boldsymbol{t}_\downarrow=\boldsymbol{t}$. (iii) If $\boldsymbol{t}\notin\mathscr{C}$ then $\boldsymbol{t}_\downarrow$ is on the Pareto curve of $\mathscr{C}$.*

Algorithm 2 finds a supporting hyperplane of $\mathscr{C}$ for a given orientation $\boldsymbol{w}$. As probabilistic model checking is employed in the two inner loops, it is usually an expensive computation. To see the significance of Algorithm 2, we point out that $\mathscr{C}$ is a convex set defined on the centralised model $\mathcal{M}^{\mathrm{ct}}$ whose size is $O(2^{|I|})$. But instead of dealing with $\mathcal{M}^{\mathrm{ct}}$, Algorithm 2 works on a decentralised model consisting of $\{\mathcal{M}_{i\otimes j}\}_{(i,j)\in I\times J}$. The first inner loop includes $|I|\times|J|$ (i.e., $|I|^2$) policy-iteration processes to compute optimal schedulers and reachability rewards. The second inner loop uses $2|I|$ value-iteration processes under a fixed scheduler.[3] The model selection is computed by using the Hungarian algorithm [18] (Line 3) whose run time is $O(|I|^3)$. Another important implication of using a decentralised model is the parallel execution of the two inner loops, which we elaborate on in Sect. 4. Also notice that if $\mathcal{M}_{i\otimes j}=\mathcal{M}_{i'\otimes j'}$ for some $(i,j)\neq(i',j')$, then some models can be skipped in the two inner loops.

In the implementation we should choose some positive ε for the following three reasons: First, the policy and value iterations for computing the two inner loops are approximate. Second, small numerical inaccuracy (e.g., rounding) usually occurs in the solving optimisation problems in the algorithm. Third, as the worst-case number of iterations in Algorithm 1 is exponential on the model size and agent number [13], a suitable ε can terminate the algorithm earlier with an approximate threshold vector whose precision is acceptable in practice.

For synthesis purposes, we can extract a random assignment and a collection of schedulers. Assume that the while loop iterates ℓ times in total. Let $\{\mu^{\iota}_{i,j}\mid i\in$

[3] The methods for computing the two inner loops are detailed in the appendix of [28].

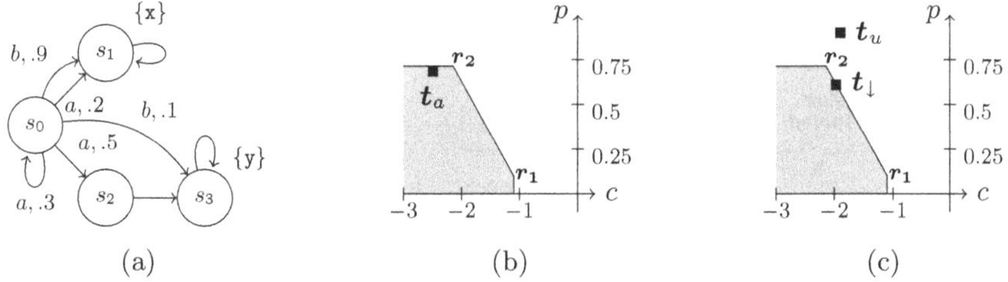

Fig. 2. Example MOMDP agent and corresponding execution of Algorithm 1.

$I, j \in J, \}$ and f_ι be generated in Lines 2–3 in Algorithm 2, respectively, in the ιth iteration. Let $v_1 \boldsymbol{r}_1 + \ldots + v_\ell \boldsymbol{r}_\ell \geq \boldsymbol{t}_\uparrow$ for some weight vector $\boldsymbol{v}$ (this $\boldsymbol{v}$ exists since $\boldsymbol{t}_\uparrow \in down(\Phi)$). The convex combination of assignments $v_1 f_1 + \ldots + v_\ell f_\ell$ defines a random assignment (i.e., bistochastic matrix). After an assignment f_ι is chosen randomly according to probability v_ι, the schedulers for planning are those from $\{\mu^\iota_{i,j} \mid j \in J, f_\iota(j) = i\}$.

Example. Figure 2 is a simple example consisting of one agent and one task to demonstrate an execution of Algorithm 1. Figure 2a shows the agent MDP, where $\rho(s, a) = -1$ for each $a \in A(s)$ and $s \in S$, and the task is $\varphi := \neg \mathsf{x} \,\mathsf{U}\, \mathsf{y}$. Let $\varepsilon = 0.001$. Figure 2b shows the computation with a feasible threshold vector $\boldsymbol{t}_a = (-2.5, 0.7)$. Initially, $\boldsymbol{w} = (1, 0)$, which results in $\boldsymbol{r}_1 = (-1.1, 0.1)$ and the hyperplane $\boldsymbol{w} \cdot \boldsymbol{x} = \boldsymbol{w} \cdot \boldsymbol{r}_1 = -1.1$. Here, $\|\boldsymbol{t}_\downarrow - \boldsymbol{t}_\uparrow\| = 0.6$ and so another iteration is needed. The algorithm finds $\boldsymbol{w} = (0.4, 0.6)$ and the corresponding $\boldsymbol{r}_2 = (-2.1, 0.71)$. As $\boldsymbol{t}_a$ is contained in $down(\{\boldsymbol{r}_1, \boldsymbol{r}_2\})$, the algorithm terminates. Figure 2c shows the case with a non-feasible $\boldsymbol{t}_u = (-1.8, 0.9)$. Similar to the previous case, the algorithm finds $\boldsymbol{w} = (1, 0)$ and $\boldsymbol{r}_1$, and then $\boldsymbol{w} = (0.4, 0.6)$ and $\boldsymbol{r}_2$. As $\boldsymbol{w} \cdot \boldsymbol{r}_2 < \boldsymbol{w} \cdot \boldsymbol{t}_u$, it finds a new threshold vector $\boldsymbol{t}_\downarrow = (-1.97, 0.61)$ in Line 10. Now as $\|\boldsymbol{t}_\downarrow - \boldsymbol{t}_\uparrow\| < \varepsilon$, the algorithm terminates.

4 Hybrid GPU-CPU Implementation

In modern systems, GPU and multi-core CPU hardware is readily available. We developed an implementation for our MORAP framework, which utilises heterogeneous GPU and multi-core CPU resources to accelerate the computation. The acceleration is based on non-shared data within the two probabilistic model checking loops in Algorithm 2, which takes up the majority of run time for Algorithm 1 in practice. Parallel execution on GPU and CPU is by allocating models to each available GPU device and CPU core. For GPU, further (massive) parallelisation can be achieved on the low-level matrix operations for probabilistic model checking.

Implementation Goal. The main goal of our framework is to maximise throughput and parallelism. Combination of multiple devices is a load balancing problem in which we can effectively schedule model checking problems to

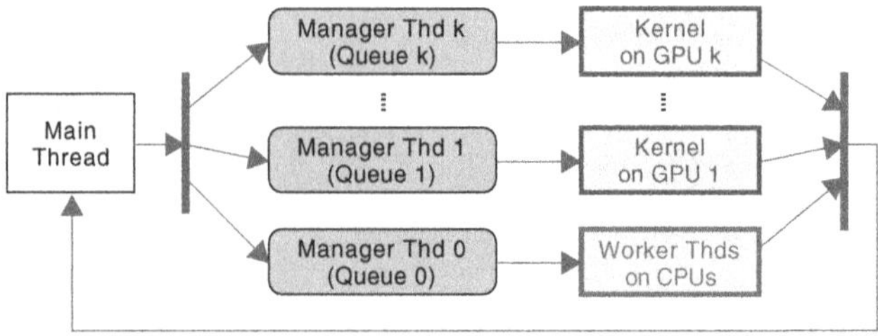

Fig. 3. Parallel architecture of MORAP framework.

Table 1. Thread roles in MORAP implementation

Component	Functionality
Main Thread	Loading models to the main memory and running all computation except the two (inner) loops in Alg. 2; generating and allocating models to queues for worker threads and kernels
Manager Thread	Managing the bounded FIFO queues; (one thread) spawning CPU Worker Threads; (the other threads) calling GPU kernels, incl. copying data between the host memory and GPU device memory; communicating with each other via a messaging channel for load balancing
Worker Thread	Computing the loops in Alg. 2; each thread bounded on one CPU core and handling one model each time
Kernel on GPU	Computing the loops in Alg. 2; each kernel running on one GPU device and handling one model each time

keep all devices optimally busy, and reduce run time. We say that computations run on GPU are called *device* operations. A multi-core processor can leverage shared memory with negligible latency before computing. The main concern with parallelism when using a multi-core processor is *thread-blocking* and *context switching* overhead which should be avoided. Moreover, because low level computations are sequential a processor's execution run time will correspond to the size of a model's state space. On the other hand, the major issue with computing on GPU is data transfer between the host and the device.

Design. Figure 3 shows the parallel architecture of our framework, and Table 1 explains the roles of thread types. In particular, there are $k+1$ manager threads controlling $k+1$ FIFO queues of agent-task models $\mathcal{M}_{i\otimes j}$, where k is the number of available GPU devices. One particular manager thread is responsible for spawning worker threads bound on each available CPU-core, while the others call kernel functions on the GPU. As each worker thread is dedicated to computing one $\mathcal{M}_{i\otimes j}$, response time and context switching overhead are minimised. Manager threads are not required to be bound to any CPU core as program management is not demanding. The computation workload between GPU devices and CPU cores is controlled through a *work stealing* approach [4], that is, if a processor or device is idle and its queue is empty then its manager thread will request (i.e., *steal*) a model from another queue. In this way, hardware is optimally loaded with work, and all threads operate asynchronously.

Programming and Data Structure. We implemented our framework with multiple languages including Rust (framework API), CUDA C (GPU device control), and a Python user interface, where the Rust API calls to C, and Python via a foreign function interface (FFI). Our implementation uses the *affine* property [25] of the type system in Rust [22] to ensure that owned variables can be used at most once in the application with move-only types. This feature is particularly useful in a parallel architecture, as $\mathcal{M}_{i\otimes j}$ can be owned by at most one thread at a time, and thread computation side-effects are inconsequential to any other thread. Isolating data access to each $\mathcal{M}_{i\otimes j}$ mitigates the requirement of shared memory access, freeing the framework from data races and data starving. Consequently, the problem is *embarrassingly* parallel. Constructing the architecture in this way ensures that our implementation approaches the upper-bound of parallelism. Our implementation uses explicit data structures (i.e., sparse matrices) to store the transition probability function and reward structures for each $\mathcal{M}_{i\otimes j}$. Parallel low-level matrix operations on GPU are implemented using the CUDA cuSPARSE API, which guarantees thread-safety. The reduce operation of state-action values for finding an optimal policy in Line 2 is also computed in parallel with one kernel launch. Optimal occupancy for a GPU kernel is managed through a kernel launcher and a call to CUDA `cudaOccupancyMaxPotentialBlockSize`.

5 Experiments

One realistic example for our MORAP problem is a smart-warehousing or robotic mobile fulfilment system (RMFS), which usually controls tasks centrally with limited communication between robots [35]. The environment, as depicted in Fig. 4, is a $W \times H$ two-dimensional grid typically consisting of movable racks (shelves), storage locations, and workstations where order picking and replenishment can take place [23]. Robots maneuver in the warehouse to carry out tasks such as order picking and replenishment.

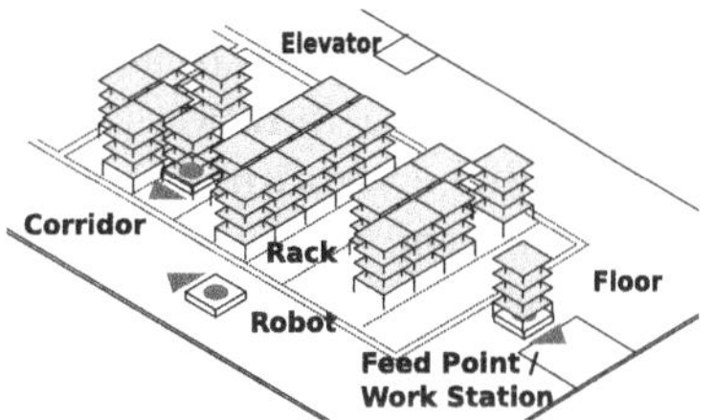

Fig. 4. A smart warehouse layout

The state of robots is described by the robot position, the internal robot state (e.g., carrying a rack or not) and the environment parameters (e.g., the rack locations) and is discrete. Robots can perform such actions as Rotate Left/Right, Go Forward, Load/Unload Rack. The MORAP problem in this example is (random) assignment n tasks to n robots, and task planning for robots, under the multi-objective requirements of running costs and task fulfilment probabilities. We considered *replenishment tasks* for agents, which are informally described as follows: "While not carrying anything, go to a rack position in the warehouse, get the rack and carry it to the feed for replenishment, then carry the rack and drop back at a specific rack position." Formally, each replenishment task can be specified as a co-safe LTL formula or as a DFA. Other tasks such as picking tasks can be specified in a similar way.

Table 2. Evaluation of average run time (sec.) per iteration in Algorithm 1 for centralised and decentralised models, where states and transitions refer to reachable states and reachable transitions, respectively.

W.H. size $W \times H$	agent (task) num. n	Decentralised						Centralised			
		Dec. Model Size		Time per iter.				Cent. Model Size		Time per iter.	
		states	trans	Hybrid	Mult CPU	GPU	CPU	states	trans	CPU	GPU
6×6	2	17k	104k	0.016	**0.01**	0.037	0.025	21.2K	136K	0.059	0.017
	5	106k	652k	0.023	**0.02**	0.2	0.36	3.5M	22.5M	6.1	2.35
	6	152K	940K	0.03	**0.022**	0.96	0.38	24.9M	162M	`timeout`	15.2
	50	10.6M	65.3M	1.36	**1.0**	27.2	11.1	`memerr`	`memerr`	-	-
	100	42.4M	261M	4.8	**3.9**	90.8	31.9	-	-	-	-
12×12	2	254k	1.5M	0.18	0.14	0.13	**0.09**	190k	1.2M	1.08	1.5
	4	1.0M	6.1M	**0.36**	0.38	0.33	1.78	635k	4.2M	9.8	2.1
	6	2.2M	13.8M	**0.7**	0.9	0.7	4.0	`memerr`	`memerr`	-	-
	8	4.1M	24.5M	**1.1**	1.6	1.2	7.2	-	-	-	-
	10	6.4M	38.3M	**1.8**	4.23	2.46	11.7		-	-	-
	20	25.4M	153M	**6.5**	17.3	9.8	45.7	-	-	-	-
	30	57.2M	345M	**15.3**	38.8	22.1	`timeout`	-	-	-	-

We conducted two experiments to evaluated our MORAP implementation using Algorithm 1 in our smart warehousing example with different warehouse dimensions $W \times H$ and different agent (task) numbers n. Notice that we evaluated run time per iteration (rather than its end-to-end run time) for our main algorithm (i.e., Algorithm 1). **Experiment 1** included two comparisons : First, it compared the model size of the centralised and decentralised models. Second, it compared the run time of hybrid GPU-CPU, (pure) GPU, multi-core CPU and single-core CPU computation. Note that the hybrid GPU-CPU and multi-core CPU computation is applicable to the decentralised model only. To benchmark the performance of our implementation with the probabilistic model checking tools Prism and Storm which do not support task assignment problems, **Experiment 2** compared the verification-only average run time for the centralised model for our implementation, against Prism and Storm. Prism, and Storm work in a similar way to Algorithm 1 by iteratively generating a weight vector $\boldsymbol{w}$ and computing a new Pareto point. In all cases which we had performed, the number of iterations ranged from 2 to 16.

All experiments were conducted on Debian with an AMD 2970WX 24 Core 3.0GHz Processor PCIe 3.0 32Gbps bandwidth, 3070Ti 1.77GHz 8Gb 6144 CUDA Cores GPU, and 32Gb of RAM. An artefact to reproduce the experiments is available online[4]. A single GPU was used and therefore $k = 1$ for the number of GPU management threads. Prism configuration included using explicit data structures, the Java heap size and hybrid `maxmem` were set to 32Gb to avoid memory exceptions. The default configuration was sufficient for Storm.

[4] https://github.com/tmrob2/hybrid-motap.

Table 3. Comparison of verification-only average run time (sec.) per iteration for a centralised model with one agent and one task

W.H. Size $W \times H$	Model Size		Time per iter.			
	states	trans	CPU	GPU	Prism	Storm
3×3	334	2.17k	**1e-4**	0.03	0.005	0.038
6×6	4.2k	18.8k	**0.004**	0.038	0.025	0.058
8×8	12.9k	78.5k	**0.017**	0.041	0.081	0.114
10×10	30.9k	187k	0.048	**0.046**	0.17	0.33

The value iteration stopping threshold was set to 10^{-6}. Running time cut-off was set to 180 s, if the run time exceeds the cut-off time a `timeout` error was recorded. If the GPU device runs out of memory, a `memerr` was recorded. The Pareto curve threshold ε (see line 2 in Algorithm 1) was set to 0.01.

The results for Experiment 1 are included in Table 2. It can be observed that, in general, the run time performance of the decentralised model is significantly improved over the centralised model. As expected, the centralised model run time grows exponentially with the increment on the agent and task numbers, while the growth for the decentralised model is linear. Table 2 also shows that parallel implementation of some form achieved improved run time performance. For a 6×6 warehouse size, multiple CPU achieved almost 10 times improvement over single-CPU. For a 12×12 warehouse size, the hybrid GPU-CPU achieved a similar performance increase. When conducting this experiment, we observed that one performance indicator is the ratio of model checking time to model (data) copying time: A higher (resp., lower) ratio implies more (resp., less) effective GPU acceleration. This ratio was higher in a 12×12 warehouse than in a 6×6 warehouse, as the former size led larger individual agent-task models than the latter size. In particular, we observed that a high ratio is important to the hybrid GPU-CPU approach. For larger individual agent-task models, the hybrid approach achieved significant improvement over both pure GPU acceleration and multi-core CPU acceleration.

Experiment 2 compared the performance of our implementation and the multi-objective model checking function in Prism and Storm. This experiment was conducted on a centralised model regarding one agent and one task, which was essentially a standard MOMDP model acceptable by those two tools. For our implementation, we restricted the MORAP problem to the *verification-only* setting, achieved by replacing Lines 10–11 in Algorithm 1 with a *break* statement to terminate the algorithm. (Thus, the *break* statement is executed if and only if the verification returns *false*.) For Prism and Storm, we specified the same problem as an achievabilty query. The comparison included model checking time only and excluded the model building time. The results, as shown in Table 3, indicate that our implementation can still achieve competitive performance compared against the existing tools. It can be seen that, even without utilising the parallelism of the decentralised model, our implementation is an efficient framework for multi-objective probabilistic model checking.

6 Related Work

Multi-objective optimisation considers the domain of planning where objectives may be conflicting, and Pareto-optimal solutions are of interest. These problems are often the focus of multi-objective model checking [30]. Efficient synthesis of a set of Pareto optimal schedulers maximising expected total rewards for multi-objective model checking are covered in [7,9,10,12,13,29]. While step and reward bounded reachability probabilities are covered in [13,16]. Recently, a computationally efficient procedure for multi-objective model checking of long-run average and total mixed rewards is presented in [27], a generalisation of [13]. Our point-oriented Pareto computation is a new method complementing the existing multi-objective queries in [13] specifically targeting scalability in multi-agent systems. Different from existing approaches, if a given threshold point is non-feasible, our algorithm computes a Pareto-optimal point which is nearest the given point.

GPU acceleration for MOMDP is studied in [8], but is problem specific without task verification. A parallel GPU accelerated sparse value iteration algorithms are presented in [31,34]. The implementation in [31] is similar to ours, particularly value iteration within Line 2 of Algorithm 2 including the reduce kernel operation for action comparison, but does not consider multiple objectives, or task specification. The GPU acceleration considered in [34], requires specific strongly connected component topologies to achieve optimal parallel performance. In contrast, our parallel implementation takes advantage of multi-agent and task factorisation, and are always present in our problem.

The approach in [11] aims to reduce the redundant complexity in the multi-agent MDP [5] for problems in which agents do not collaborate on tasks, only that an agent optimally completes its allocated tasks. We consider the classical random assignment problem for which agents may only work independently on a single task. The model generated in [11] is not suitable for solving our problem as no mechanism exists for tracking which agents have been assigned a particular task. Moreover, by decentralising the task allocation model, this work achieves linear scalability with respect to the numbers of agents and tasks.

7 Conclusion

In this paper, we presented an approach addressing the problem of simultaneous random task assignment and planning in an MAS under multi-objective constraints. We demonstrated that our problem is convex and solvable in polynomial time, and that an optimal random assignment and schedulers can be computed in a decentralised way. We provided a hybrid GPU-CPU multi-objective model checking framework which optimally manages the computational load on GPU devices and multiple CPU-cores. We conducted two experiments to show that decentralising the problem results in a parallel implementation which can achieve linear scaling and significant run time improvement. Our experiments also demonstrated that the multi-objective model checking performance of our framework is competitive compared with the probabilistic model checkers Prism and Storm. Future work consists of further optimisation of the implementation utilising CUDA streams to alleviate the PCI bottleneck for small individual agent-task models. We are also interested to extend our MORAP problem to include tasks expressed as ω-regular temporal properties and limiting behaviours (e.g., mean pay-offs).

References

1. Baier, C., Hermanns, H., Katoen, J.-P.: The 10,000 facets of MDP model checking. In: Steffen, B., Woeginger, G. (eds.) Computing and Software Science. LNCS, vol. 10000, pp. 420–451. Springer, Cham (2019). https://doi.org/10.1007/978-3-319-91908-9_21
2. Baier, C., Katoen, J.P.: Principles of Model Checking. The MIT Press, Cambridge, Mass (2008)
3. Birkhoff, G.: Three observations on linear algebra. Univ. Nac. Tacuman, Rev. Ser. A **5**, 147–151 (1946)
4. Blumofe, R.D., Leiserson, C.E.: Scheduling multithreaded computations by work stealing. J. ACM (JACM) **46**(5), 720–748 (1999)
5. Boutilier, C.: Planning, learning and coordination in multiagent decision processes. In: Proceedings of the 6th Conference on Theoretical Aspects of Rationality and Knowledge, pp. 195–210 (1996)
6. Boyd, S., Boyd, S.P., Vandenberghe, L.: Convex Optimization. Cambridge University Press, Cambridge (2004)
7. Chatterjee, K., Majumdar, R., Henzinger, T.A.: Markov decision processes with multiple objectives. In: Durand, B., Thomas, W. (eds.) STACS 2006. LNCS, vol. 3884, pp. 325–336. Springer, Heidelberg (2006). https://doi.org/10.1007/11672142_26
8. Chowdhury, R., Navsalkar, A., Subramani, D.: GPU-accelerated multi-objective optimal planning in stochastic dynamic environments. J. Mar. Sci. Eng. **10**(4), 533 (2022)
9. Delgrange, F., Katoen, J.P., Quatmann, T., Randour, M.: Simple strategies inmulti-objective mdps. In: Tools and Algorithms for the Construction and Analysis of Systems: 26th International Conference, TACAS 2020, Held as Part of the European Joint Conferences on Theory and Practice of Software, ETAPS 2020, Dublin, Ireland, 25–30 April 2020, Proceedings, Part I 26, pp. 346–364. Springer, Cham (2020). https://doi.org/10.1007/978-3-030-45190-5_19
10. Etessami, K., Kwiatkowska, M., Vardi, M.Y., Yannakakis, M.: Multi-objective model checking of Markov decision processes. In: Grumberg, O., Huth, M. (eds.) TACAS 2007. LNCS, vol. 4424, pp. 50–65. Springer, Heidelberg (2007). https://doi.org/10.1007/978-3-540-71209-1_6
11. Faruq, F., Parker, D., Laccrda, B., Hawes, N.: Simultaneous task allocation and planning under uncertainty. In: 2018 IEEE/RSJ International Conference on Intelligent Robots and Systems (IROS), pp. 3559–3564. IEEE, Madrid (2018)
12. Forejt, V., Kwiatkowska, M., Norman, G., Parker, D., Qu, H.: Quantitative multi-objective verification for probabilistic systems. In: Abdulla, P.A., Leino, K.R.M. (eds.) TACAS 2011. LNCS, vol. 6605, pp. 112–127. Springer, Heidelberg (2011). https://doi.org/10.1007/978-3-642-19835-9_11

13. Forejt, V., Kwiatkowska, M., Parker, D.: Pareto curves for probabilistic model checking. In: Chakraborty, S., Mukund, M. (eds.) ATVA 2012. LNCS, pp. 317–332. Springer, Heidelberg (2012). https://doi.org/10.1007/978-3-642-33386-6_25
14. Forejt, V., Kwiatkowska, M., Norman, G., Parker, D.: Automatic verification techniques for probabilistic systems. Formal Meth. Eternal Netw. **6659**, 60–120 (2011)
15. Hahn, E.M., Hashemi, V., Hermanns, H., Lahijanian, M., Turrini, A.: Multi-objective robust strategy synthesis for interval Markov decision processes. In: Bertrand, N., Bortolussi, L. (eds.) QEST 2017. LNCS, vol. 10503, pp. 207–223. Springer, Cham (2017). https://doi.org/10.1007/978-3-319-66335-7_13
16. Hartmanns, A., Junges, S., Katoen, J.P., Quatmann, T.: Multi-cost bounded trade-off analysis in MDP. J. Autom. Reason. **64**(7), 1483–1522 (2020)
17. Hensel, C., Junges, S., Katoen, J.P., Quatmann, T., Volk, M.: The probabilistic model checker storm. Int. J. Softw. Tools Technol. Transfer **24**(4), 589–610 (2022)
18. Kuhn, H.W.: The Hungarian method for the assignment problem. Naval Res. Logistics Quart. **2**(1–2), 83–97 (1955)
19. Kupferman, O., Vardi, M.Y.: Model checking of safety properties. Formal Meth. Syst. Des. **19**(3), 291–314 (2001)
20. Kwiatkowska, M., Norman, G., Parker, D.: PRISM 4.0: verification of probabilistic real-time systems. In: Gopalakrishnan, G., Qadeer, S. (eds.) CAV 2011. LNCS, vol. 6806, pp. 585–591. Springer, Heidelberg (2011). https://doi.org/10.1007/978-3-642-22110-1_47
21. Kwiatkowska, M., Norman, G., Parker, D.: Probabilistic model checking and autonomy. Ann. Rev. Control Robot. Auton. Syst. **5**(1), 385–410 (2022). https://doi.org/10.1146/annurev-control-042820-010947
22. Matsakis, N.D., Klock, F.S.: The rust language. ACM SIGAda Ada Lett. **34**(3), 103–104 (2014)
23. Merschformann, M., Xie, L., Li, H.: RAWsim-o: a simulation framework for robotic mobile fulfillment systems. Logistics Res. **11**(1) (2018)
24. Papadimitriou, C.H., Yannakakis, M.: On the approximability of trade-offs and optimal access of web sources. In: Proceedings 41st Annual Symposium on Foundations of Computer Science, pp. 86–92. IEEE (2000)
25. Pierce, B.C.: Advanced Topics in Types and Programming Languages. MIT press, Cambridge (2004)
26. Puterman, M.L.: Markov Decision Processes: Discrete Stochastic Dynamic Programming. Wiley, Hoboken (2014)
27. Quatmann, T., Katoen, J.P.: Multi-objective optimization of long-run average and total rewards. In: Tools and Algorithms for the Construction and Analysis of Systems: 27th International Conference, TACAS 2021, Held as Part of the European Joint Conferences on Theory and Practice of Software, ETAPS 2021, Luxembourg City, Luxembourg, March 27-April 1, 2021, Proceedings, Part I 27. pp. 230–249. Springer, Cham (2021). https://doi.org/10.1007/978-3-030-72016-2_13
28. Robinson, T., Su, G.: Multi-objective task assignment and multiagent planning with hybrid GPU-CPU acceleration. https://github.com/tmrob2/hybrid-motap/blob/master/GPU_MOTAP_NFM23_LONG.pdf
29. Roijers, D., Scharpff, J., Spaan, M., Oliehoek, F., De Weerdt, M., Whiteson, S.: Bounded approximations for linear multi-objective planning under uncertainty. In: Proceedings of the International Conference on Automated Planning and Scheduling, vol. 24, pp. 262–270 (2014)
30. Roijers, D.M., Vamplew, P., Whiteson, S., Dazeley, R.: A survey of multi-objective sequential decision-making. J. Artif. Intell. Res. **48**, 67–113 (2013)

31. Sapio, A., Bhattacharyya, S.S., Wolf, M.: Efficient solving of Markov decision processes on GPUs using parallelized sparse matrices. In: 2018 Conference on Design and Architectures for Signal and Image Processing (DASIP), pp. 13–18. IEEE (2018)
32. Schillinger, P., Bürger, M., Dimarogonas, D.V.: Simultaneous task allocation and planning for temporal logic goals in heterogeneous multi-robot systems. Int. J. Robot. Res. **37**(7), 818–838 (2018)
33. Ulungu, E.L., Teghem, J.: Multi-objective combinatorial optimization problems: a survey. J. Multi-Criteria Decis. Anal. **3**(2), 83–104 (1994). https://doi.org/10.1002/mcda.4020030204
34. Wu, Z., Hahn, E.M., Günay, A., Zhang, L., Liu, Y.: GPU-accelerated value iteration for the computation of reachability probabilities in MDPS. In: ECAI 2016, pp. 1726–1727. IOS Press (2016)
35. Wurman, P.R., D'Andrea, R., Mountz, M.: Coordinating hundreds of cooperative, autonomous vehicles in warehouses. AI Mag. **29**(1), 9–9 (2008)

Reasoning over Test Specifications Using Assume-Guarantee Contracts

Apurva Badithela[1], Josefine B. Graebener[1(✉)], Inigo Incer[1,2], and Richard M. Murray[1]

[1] California Institute of Technology, Pasadena, USA
{apurva,jgraeben,inigo}@caltech.edu, murray@cds.caltech.edu
[2] University of California, Berkeley, Berkeley, USA

Abstract. We establish a framework to reason about test campaigns described formally. First, we introduce the notion of a test structure—an object that carries i) the formal specifications of the system under test, and ii) the test objective, which is specified by a test engineer. We build on test structures to define test campaigns and specifications for the tester. Secondly, we use the algebra of assume-guarantee contracts to reason about constructing tester specifications, comparing test structures and test campaigns, and combining and splitting test structures. Using the composition operator, we characterize the conditions on the constituent tester specifications and test objectives for feasibly combining test structures. We illustrate the different applications of the quotient operator to split the test objective, the system into subsystems, or both. Finally, we illustrate test executions corresponding to the combined and split test structures in a discrete autonomous driving example and an aircraft formation-flying example. We anticipate that reasoning over test specifications would aid in generating optimal test campaigns.

Keywords: Testing Autonomous Systems · Assume-Guarantee Reasoning · Contracts

1 Introduction

Rigorous test campaigns have to be designed, implemented, and executed to aid in certification of safety-critical autonomous systems [30]. Testing complex autonomous systems is a key challenge that remains to be solved to achieve human confidence in the system's behavior in a real world setting, ranging from autonomous driving to military and space missions and beyond [9,12,19,32]. Currently, test campaigns are designed by test engineers, who rely on their product know-how and experience, and the resulting test scenarios are fine-tuned using simulation-based falsification to find the desired test execution [4,15]. Executing these test campaigns in real-world settings can be prohibitive for some systems, such as those involved in space missions, due to the immense cost and

A. Badithela, J. B. Graebener and I. Incer—These authors contributed equally to this work.

K. Y. Rozier and S. Chaudhuri (Eds.): NFM 2023, LNCS 13903, pp. 278–294, 2023.
https://doi.org/10.1007/978-3-031-33170-1_17

impracticality of the tests. Thus, carefully choosing the constituent tests of a test campaign is necessary. Instead of the test engineer designing the entire test manually, we require them to specify the objective of the test. For example, an autonomous car required to operate safely at a busy T-intersection, while two tester cars arrive at the same time as the system, could be the test objective. Prior work in [2,17], takes this high-level input from the test engineer, and provides algorithms for synthesizing test environments and tester strategies that meet the test objective.

We provide a brief overview of prior work that has used assume-guarantee reasoning for testing safety-critical systems. In [11], assume-guarantee contracts have been used for compositional verification of system models, and verified components have been reused in the certification process for new system architectures. In [7,16], the authors use assume-guarantee reasoning to (i) generate component-level tests that convey system-level information, (ii) limit the scope of component testing by focusing on tests that meet a component's assumptions, and (iii) perform predictive testing. In [8], assume-guarantee reasoning is used in the context of input output conformance testing [31]. Assume-guarantee methodologies have been provided for testing web-services [10,13,18], and to distribute the burden of testing by augmenting subsystems with the ability to test their environment and neighboring subsystems during runtime [1].

We propose a framework grounded in assume-guarantee contract algebra to aid the test engineer in reasoning over a test campaign. We make use of a test objective in the form of a specification, which together with the system specification is used to characterize an assume guarantee contract for the test environment. This allows us to define tests as pairs of contracts, and reason over these tests using operators from contract theory. This approach reasons over the specifications for the system and the tester to construct a test specification which is then used in synthesizing a test environment. Overall, our approach is complementary to falsification—test environments synthesized for the tester specifications discussed in this paper could be used to seed falsification algorithms to find a worst-case test execution. We seek to address the following questions by using operators from contract algebra to reason over test objectives and system specifications.

(Q1) *Constructing Tests:* How do we generate a specification for the test environment so that a desired behavior, characterized by the test objective, is demonstrated? See Sect. 3.
(Q2) *Comparing Tests:* When can we say that one test is a refinement of the other, and define an ordering of tests? See Sect. 5.
(Q3) *Combining Tests:* Is it possible to check for multiple unit test objectives in a single test execution? See Sect. 4.
(Q4) *Splitting Tests:* Is it possible to derive unit test objectives from a more complex test objective? See Sect. 6.

The focus of this paper is on reasoning about tests at the specification level, not on synthesizing tests from these specifications. We illustrate different possible test executions for a combined and a split test on a discrete autonomous car example and a formation flying example.

2 Background

To reason about the specifications, we will make use of the contract-based-design framework first introduced as a design methodology for modular software systems [14,23,24] and later extended to complex cyber-physical systems [5,26,29]. We will adopt the mathematical framework presented by Benveniste et al. [6] and Passerone et al. [27].

Definition 1 (Assume-Guarantee Contract)**.** Let $\mathcal{B}$ be a universe of behaviors, then a *component* M is a set of behaviors $M \subseteq \mathcal{B}$. A *contract* is the pair $\mathcal{C} = (A, G)$, where A are the assumptions and G are the guarantees. A component E is an *environment* of the contract $\mathcal{C}$ if $E \models A$. A component M is an *implementation* of the contract, $M \models \mathcal{C}$ if $M \subseteq G \cup \neg A$, meaning the component provides the specified guarantees if it operates in an environment that satisfies its assumptions. There exists a partial order of contracts, we say $\mathcal{C}_1$ is a refinement of $\mathcal{C}_2$, denoted $\mathcal{C}_1 \leq \mathcal{C}_2$, if $(A_2 \leq A_1)$ and $(G_1 \cup \neg A_1 \leq G_2 \cup \neg A_2)$. We say a contract $\mathcal{C} = (A, G)$ is in canonical, or saturated, form if $\neg A \subseteq G$.

Multiple operations are known for assume guarantee contracts—see [21]. Assume the following contracts are in canonical form. The meet or conjunction of two contracts exists [5] and is given by $\mathcal{C}_1 \wedge \mathcal{C}_2 = (A_1 \cup A_2, G_1 \cap G_2)$. Composition [6] yields the specification of a system given the specifications of the components: $\mathcal{C}_1 \parallel \mathcal{C}_2 = ((A_1 \cap A_2) \cup \neg(G_1 \cap G_2), G_1 \cap G_2)$. Given specifications $\mathcal{C}$ and $\mathcal{C}_1$, the quotient is the largest specification $\mathcal{C}_2$ such that $\mathcal{C}_1 \parallel \mathcal{C}_2 \leq \mathcal{C}$. It is given by [20]: $\mathcal{C}/\mathcal{C}_1 = (A \cup G_1, (G \cap A_1) \cup \neg(A \cup G_1))$. Strong merging [27] yields a specification obeyed by a system that obeys two given specifications $\mathcal{C}_1$ and $\mathcal{C}_2$: $\mathcal{C}_1 \bullet \mathcal{C}_2 = (A_1 \cap A_2, (G_1 \cap G_2) \cup \neg(A_1 \cap A_2))$. The reciprocal (or mirror) [25,27] is a unary operation which inverts assumptions and guarantees: $\mathcal{C}^{-1} = (G, A)$. The relationships among contract operations are illustrated in Fig. 1.

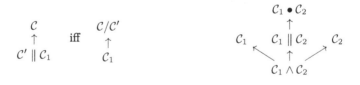

(a) Composition and quotient. (b) Order of operations.

Fig. 1. Contract operators and the partial order of their resulting objects.

To state the requirements on the system and the test, we will make use of linear temporal logic (LTL), although any specification formalism can be used. LTL is a temporal logic describing linear-time properties, allowing reasoning over the timing of events, where each point in time has a single successor. The use of LTL for formally verifying properties of computer programs was first introduced by Pnueli in 1977 [28].

Definition 2 (Linear Temporal Logic (LTL) [3]). The syntax of *linear temporal logic (LTL)* is given as:

$$\varphi ::= \top \mid a \mid \varphi_1 \wedge \varphi_2 \mid \neg\varphi \mid \bigcirc \varphi \mid \varphi_1 \mathcal{U} \varphi_2,$$

with $a \in AP$, where AP are the set of atomic propositions, the Boolean connectors conjunction $\wedge$ and negation $\neg$, and the temporal operators 'next' $\bigcirc$ and 'until' $\mathcal{U}$. From conjunction and negation, we can derive the entirety of propositional logic including disjunction $\vee$, implication $\rightarrow$, and equivalence $\leftrightarrow$. The temporal operators 'always' $\square$ and 'eventually' $\lozenge$ can be derived from $\mathcal{U}$ as

$$\lozenge\varphi = \top \,\mathcal{U}\, \varphi, \quad \square\varphi = \neg\lozenge\neg\varphi.$$

From these temporal operators we can derive 'always eventually' $\square\lozenge$ and 'eventually always' $\lozenge\square$, which specify that a proposition will be true infinitely often (progress) or eventually forever (stability) respectively. Let φ be an LTL formula over AP. The semantics of LTL formula φ are defined over an infinite word $\sigma = s_0 s_1 \cdots$ as follows

$\sigma \models \top$,
For $a \in AP$, $\sigma \models a$ iff $\sigma_0 \models a$,
$\sigma \models \varphi_1 \wedge \varphi_2$ iff $\sigma \models \varphi_1$ and $\sigma \models \varphi_2$,
$\sigma \models \neg\varphi$,
$\sigma \models \bigcirc\varphi$ iff $\sigma[1, \cdots] = s_1 s_2 \cdots \models \varphi$,
$\sigma \models \varphi_1 \mathcal{U} \varphi_1$ iff $\exists j \geq 0, \sigma[j, \cdots] \models \varphi_2$ and $\sigma[i, \cdots] \models \varphi_1$, for all $0 \leq i < j$,

where $\sigma[j, \cdots]$ denotes the word fragment $s_j s_{j+1} \cdots$.

3 Test Structures and Tester Specifications

For conducting a test, we need i) the system under test and its specification to be tested and ii) specifications for the test environment that ensure that a set of behaviors (specified by the test engineer) can be observed during the test. These sets of desired test behaviors are characterized by the test engineer in the form of a specification. The system specifications make some assumptions about the test environment. The test objective, together with the system specification, is used to synthesize a test environment and corresponding strategies of the tester agents. As a result, the test objective is not made known to the system since doing so would reveal the test strategy to the system. These concepts are formally defined below.

Definition 3. The *system specification* is the assume-guarantee contract denoted by $\mathcal{C}^{\text{sys}} = (A^{\text{sys}}, G^{\text{sys}})$, where A^{sys} are the assumptions that the system makes on its operating environment, and G^{sys} denotes the guarantees that it is expected to satisfy if A^{sys} evaluates to $\top$. In particular, A^{sys} are the assumptions requiring a safe test environment, and $\neg A_i^{\text{sys}} \cup G_i^{\text{sys}}$ are the guarantees on the specific subsystem that will be tested.

$$\mathcal{C}^{\text{sys}} = (A^{\text{sys}}, \neg A^{\text{sys}} \cup \bigcap_i (\neg A_i^{\text{sys}} \cup G_i^{\text{sys}})).$$

Definition 4. A *test objective* $\mathcal{C}^{\text{obj}} = (\top, G^{\text{obj}})$, where G^{obj} characterizes the set of desired test behaviors, is a formal description of the specific behaviors that the test engineer would like to observe during the test.

These contracts can be refined or relaxed using domain knowledge. Using Definitions 3 and 4, we define a *test structure*, which is the unitary object that we use to establish our framework and for the analysis in the rest of the paper.

Definition 5. A *test structure* is the tuple $\mathfrak{t} = (\mathcal{C}^{\text{obj}}, \mathcal{C}^{\text{sys}})$ comprising of the test objective and the system requirements for the test.

Given the system specification and the test objective, we need to determine the specification for a valid test environment, which will ensure that if the system meets its specification, the desired test behavior will be observed. The resulting test execution will then enable reasoning about the capabilities of the system. If the test is executed successfully, the system passed the test, and conversely, if the test is failed, it is because the system violated its specification and not due to an erroneous test environment.

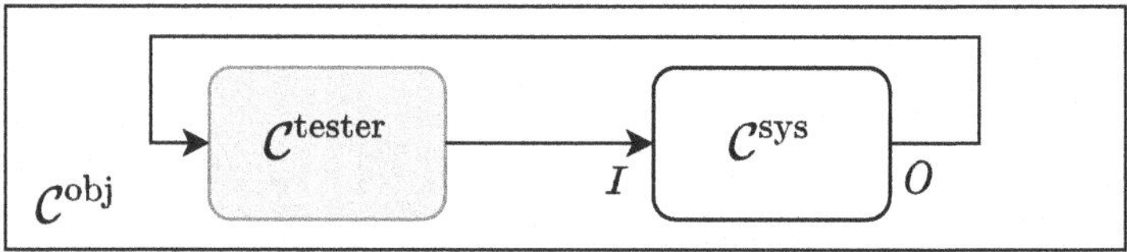

Fig. 2. Block diagram showing contracts specifying the system specification $\mathcal{C}^{\text{sys}}$, the test objective $\mathcal{C}^{\text{obj}}$, and the test environment $\mathcal{C}^{\text{tester}}$.

Now we need to find the specification of the test environment, the tester contract $\mathcal{C}^{\text{tester}}$, in which the system can operate and will satisfy the test objective according to Fig. 2, with I, O denoting the inputs and outputs of the system contract. This contract can be computed as the mirror of the system contract, merged with the test objective, which is equivalent to computing the quotient of $\mathcal{C}^{\text{obj}}$ and $\mathcal{C}^{\text{sys}}$ [21]:

$$\mathcal{C}^{\text{tester}} = (\mathcal{C}^{\text{sys}})^{-1} \bullet \mathcal{C}^{\text{obj}} = \mathcal{C}^{\text{obj}} / \mathcal{C}^{\text{sys}}.$$

The tester contract can therefore directly be computed as

$$\mathcal{C}^{\text{tester}} = (G^{\text{sys}}, G^{\text{obj}} \cap A^{\text{sys}} \cup \neg G^{\text{sys}}). \tag{1}$$

Remark: Since it is the tester's responsibility to ensure a safe test environment, A^{sys}, a test is synthesized with respect to the following specification,

$$\bigcap_i (\neg A_i^{\text{sys}} \cup G_i^{\text{sys}}) \rightarrow A^{\text{sys}} \cap G^{\text{obj}}. \tag{2}$$

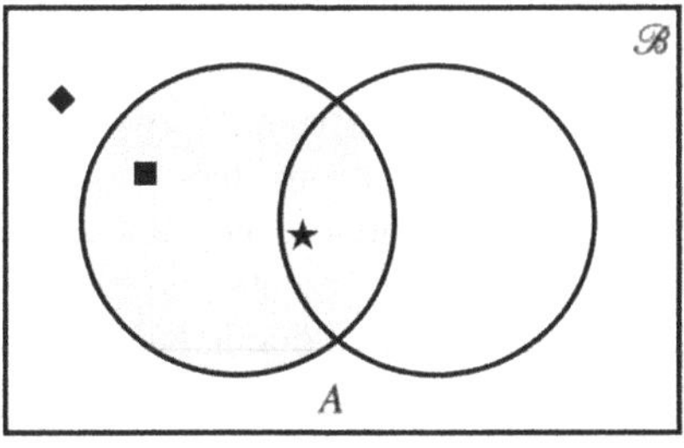

(a) Assumptions A of the contract.

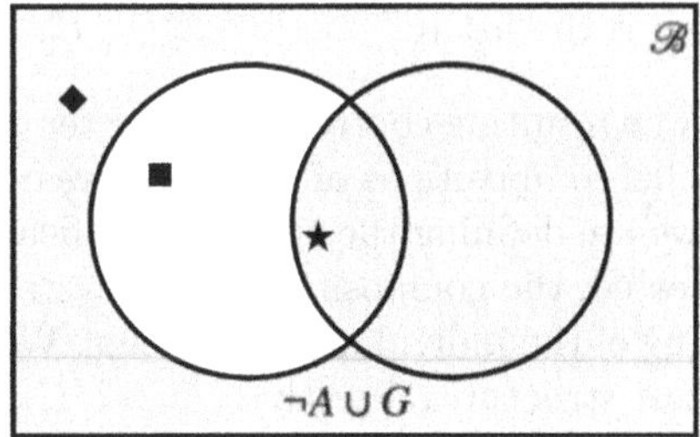

(b) Guarantees $\neg A \cup G$ of the contract.

Fig. 3. Geometric interpretation of an assume-guarantee contract (A, G) as a pair of sets of behaviors. The first element of the pair describes the set of behaviors for which the assumptions A hold, and the second element describes the set of behaviors for which G holds or A does not hold. The tester failing to provide the guarantees G (square) does not satisfy the contract. The set of desired test executions is in the intersection of the assumptions and guarantees (star), and the set of test executions that fall outside the assumptions (diamond) are because the system under test failed to satisfy its requirements.

A successful test execution lies in the set of behaviors $A^{\mathrm{sys}} \cap G^{\mathrm{sys}} \cap G^{\mathrm{obj}}$, and an unsuccessful test execution is the sole responsibility of the system being unable to satisfy its specification. Thus, any implementation of $\mathcal{C}^{\mathrm{tester}}$ will be an environment in which the system can operate and satisfy $\mathcal{C}^{\mathrm{obj}}$ if the system satisfies its specification, a geometric interpretation is shown in Fig. 3.

4 Combining Tests

We now provide a framework to combine unit test campaigns into a single system-level test structure. Suppose we have test structures $(\mathcal{C}_i^{\mathrm{obj}}, \mathcal{C}_i^{\mathrm{sys}})$ for $i \in \{1, 2\}$ with test environment (tester) contracts $\mathcal{C}_i^{\mathrm{tester}}$. We interpret the specifications $\mathcal{C}_i^{\mathrm{tester}}$ as viewpoints of the tester that apply to different specifications of the system. When we merge the tester specifications, we obtain a single test structure given as follows:

Proposition 1. *$\mathcal{C}_1^{tester} \bullet \mathcal{C}_2^{tester} = (\mathcal{C}_1^{obj} \parallel \mathcal{C}_2^{obj}) / (\mathcal{C}_1^{sys} \parallel \mathcal{C}_2^{sys})$.*

Proof. Merging tester contracts yields

$$\begin{aligned}
\mathcal{C}_1^{\mathrm{tester}} \bullet \mathcal{C}_2^{\mathrm{tester}} &= (\mathcal{C}_1^{\mathrm{obj}}/\mathcal{C}_1^{\mathrm{sys}}) \bullet (\mathcal{C}_2^{\mathrm{obj}}/\mathcal{C}_2^{\mathrm{sys}}) \\
&= (\mathcal{C}_1^{\mathrm{obj}} \bullet (\mathcal{C}_1^{\mathrm{sys}})^{-1}) \bullet (\mathcal{C}_2^{\mathrm{obj}} \bullet (\mathcal{C}_2^{\mathrm{sys}})^{-1}) && \text{([22], Sect. 3.1)} \\
&= (\mathcal{C}_1^{\mathrm{obj}} \bullet \mathcal{C}_2^{\mathrm{obj}}) \bullet ((\mathcal{C}_1^{\mathrm{sys}})^{-1}) \bullet ((\mathcal{C}_2^{\mathrm{sys}})^{-1})) \\
&= (\mathcal{C}_1^{\mathrm{obj}} \bullet \mathcal{C}_2^{\mathrm{obj}}) \bullet (\mathcal{C}_1^{\mathrm{sys}} \parallel \mathcal{C}_2^{\mathrm{sys}})^{-1} && \text{([21], Table 6.1)} \\
&= (\mathcal{C}_1^{\mathrm{obj}} \bullet \mathcal{C}_2^{\mathrm{obj}}) / (\mathcal{C}_1^{\mathrm{sys}} \parallel \mathcal{C}_2^{\mathrm{sys}}) \\
&= (\mathcal{C}_1^{\mathrm{obj}} \parallel \mathcal{C}_2^{\mathrm{obj}}) / (\mathcal{C}_1^{\mathrm{sys}} \parallel \mathcal{C}_2^{\mathrm{sys}}), && (A_1^{\mathrm{obj}} = A_2^{\mathrm{obj}} = \top))
\end{aligned}$$

which is the list $(\mathcal{C}_1^{\text{obj}} \parallel \mathcal{C}_2^{\text{obj}}, \mathcal{C}_1^{\text{sys}} \parallel \mathcal{C}_2^{\text{sys}})$. □

The resulting contract is the tester contract for the test structure given by the parallel compositions of the objective contracts and system contracts, separately. As we are defining the system specification as requirements on the subsystem to be tested, the composition of the system specifications represents a system consisting of the individual subsystems. We use Proposition 1 to define an operation on test structures directly:

Definition 6. Given test structures $\mathfrak{t}_i = (\mathcal{C}_i^{\text{obj}}, \mathcal{C}_i^{\text{sys}})$ for $i \in \{1, 2\}$, we define their *composition* $\mathfrak{t}_1 \parallel \mathfrak{t}_2$ as

$$(\mathcal{C}_1^{\text{obj}}, \mathcal{C}_1^{\text{sys}}) \parallel (\mathcal{C}_2^{\text{obj}}, \mathcal{C}_2^{\text{sys}}) = (\mathcal{C}_1^{\text{obj}} \parallel \mathcal{C}_2^{\text{obj}}, \mathcal{C}_1^{\text{sys}} \parallel \mathcal{C}_2^{\text{sys}}).$$

For the composition of the test structures to correspond to a valid test, we require the composed test objective and the resulting tester contract to be satisfiable.

Example 1. Consider a test setup with a single lane road and a pedestrian on a crosswalk. The agent under test is an autonomous car, which has to detect the pedestrian and come to a stop in front of the crosswalk under different visibility conditions. These requirements are encoded in the system specification and the test objective. The setup for this test is shown in Fig. 4. Three unit test objective contracts are specified by the test engineer. The first test objective is as follows:

$$\mathcal{C}_1^{\text{obj}} = \left(\top, \quad \varphi_{\text{init}}^{\text{car}} \wedge \Box \varphi_{\text{low}}^{\text{vis}} \wedge \Diamond \varphi_{\text{cw}}^{\text{ped}} \wedge \varphi_{\text{cw}}^{\text{ped}} \rightarrow \Diamond \varphi_{\text{cw}}^{\text{stop}}\right),$$

where $\varphi_{\text{low}}^{\text{vis}} := \varphi^{\text{vis}} \models \text{low}$, denotes low visibility conditions, $\varphi_{\text{init}}^{\text{car}}$ the initial conditions of the car (position x_{car} and velocity v_{car}), $\varphi_{\text{cw}}^{\text{ped}}$ denotes the pedestrian being on the crosswalk, and $\varphi_{\text{cw}}^{\text{stop}} := x_{\text{car}} \leq C_{\text{cw}-1} \wedge v_{\text{car}} = 0$ the stopping maneuver at least one cell in front of the crosswalk cell C_{cw}. The second test objective is given as

$$\mathcal{C}_2^{\text{obj}} = \left(\top, \quad \varphi_{\text{init}}^{\text{car}} \wedge \Box \varphi_{\text{high}}^{\text{vis}} \wedge \Diamond \varphi_{\text{cw}}^{\text{ped}} \wedge \varphi_{\text{cw}}^{\text{ped}} \rightarrow \Diamond \varphi_{\text{cw}}^{\text{stop}}\right),$$

where $\varphi_{\text{high}}^{\text{vis}} := \varphi^{\text{vis}} \models \text{high}$ denotes high visibility conditions; and lastly the third test objective is given as:

$$\mathcal{C}_3^{\text{obj}} = \left(\top, \quad \exists k : (v_{\text{car}} = V_{\text{max}} \wedge x_{\text{car}} = C_k) \rightarrow \Diamond \varphi_{k+d_{\text{braking}}}^{\text{stop}}\right),$$

where the car has to drive at a specified speed of V_{max} in an arbitrary cell C_k and stop within the allowed braking distance d_{braking}. This test represents the mechanical requirement of stopping without specifying any interaction with a pedestrian. Note that neither of the test objective contracts hold information about the system's capabilities to detect a pedestrian, only that the system needs to stop in front of a pedestrian.

The system capabilities are encoded in the system specifications, which are provided by the system and test engineers. For each test objective, we are given the corresponding system specification, which describes the required capabilities of the system for that test objective (e.g. perception, mechanical requirements, etc.). Each system specification relies on the system being in a safe environment, where the transitions of the environment agents are ensured to be safe. This is denoted as $A^{\text{sys}} = \Box\varphi^{\text{ped}}_{\text{dyn}} \wedge \Box\varphi^{\text{vis}}_{\text{dyn}}$, where $\varphi^{\text{ped}}_{\text{dyn}}$, and $\varphi^{\text{vis}}_{\text{dyn}}$ denote the dynamics of the pedestrian, and the visibility conditions, respectively. We use the same notation for the set and formula A^{sys}, which can be inferred from context. The system contract $\mathcal{C}^{\text{sys}}_1$ corresponding to the first test objective is given as

$$\mathcal{C}^{\text{sys}}_1 = \Big(A^{\text{sys}}, \quad \Box\varphi^{\text{car}}_{\text{dyn}} \wedge \Box\left(\varphi^{\text{vis}}_{\text{low}} \rightarrow v \leq V_{\text{low}}\right) \wedge \\ \Box\left(\texttt{detectable}^{\text{ped}}_{\text{low}} \rightarrow \Diamond\varphi^{\text{stop}}_{\text{ped}}\right) \vee \neg A^{\text{sys}}\Big),$$

where $\varphi^{\text{car}}_{\text{dyn}}$, describes the dynamics of the car. The maximum speed that the car is allowed to drive at in low visibility conditions is V_{low}, and $\texttt{detectable}^{\text{ped}}_{\text{low}}$ is defined as

$$\texttt{detectable}^{\text{ped}}_{\text{low}} := x_{\text{car}} + dist^{\text{low}}_{\text{min}} \leq x_{\text{ped}} \leq x_{\text{car}} + dist^{\text{low}}_{\text{max}},$$

which describes the pedestrian being in the 'buffer' zone in front of the car, where $dist^{\text{low}}_{\text{min}}$ denotes the minimum distance such that the car can come to a full stop, and $dist^{\text{low}}_{\text{max}}$ denotes the maximum distance at which the car can detect a pedestrian in low visibility conditions. The system specification for the second test objective, the system contract $\mathcal{C}^{\text{sys}}_2$, is given as

$$\mathcal{C}^{\text{sys}}_2 = \Big(A^{\text{sys}}, \quad \Box\varphi^{\text{car}}_{\text{dyn}} \wedge \Box\left(\varphi^{\text{vis}}_{\text{high}} \rightarrow v \leq V_{\text{max}}\right) \wedge \\ \Box\left(\texttt{detectable}^{\text{ped}}_{\text{high}} \rightarrow \Diamond\varphi^{\text{stop}}_{\text{ped}}\right) \vee \neg A^{\text{sys}}\Big),$$

describing driving in high visibility conditions with a maximum speed of V_{max} and $\texttt{detectable}^{\text{ped}}_{\text{high}}$ denoting the pedestrian being detectable in the 'buffer' zone for high visibility conditions. The third system specification $\mathcal{C}^{\text{sys}}_3$ is given as

$$\mathcal{C}^{\text{sys}}_3 = \Big(A^{\text{sys}}, \quad \Box\varphi^{\text{car}}_{\text{dyn}} \vee \neg A^{\text{sys}}\Big),$$

with the braking distance as a function of speed being part of the car's dynamics denoted by $\varphi^{\text{car}}_{\text{dyn}}$. For each pair of system specifications and test objectives, we can synthesize the test environment according to Eq. (2). Now we will find combinations of these tester structures $\mathfrak{t}_i = (\mathcal{C}^{\text{obj}}_i, \mathcal{C}^{\text{sys}}_i)$, that we can use instead of executing all tests individually. We will start by computing the combined test structure $\mathfrak{t} = \mathfrak{t}_2 \parallel \mathfrak{t}_3$. The combined test objective contract $\mathcal{C}^{\text{obj}}$ is computed as

$$\mathcal{C}^{\text{obj}} = \mathcal{C}^{\text{obj}}_2 \parallel \mathcal{C}^{\text{obj}}_3 = \big(\top, \quad \varphi^{\text{car}}_{\text{init}} \wedge \Box\varphi^{\text{vis}}_{\text{low}} \wedge \Diamond\varphi^{\text{ped}}_{\text{cw}} \wedge \varphi^{\text{ped}}_{\text{cw}} \rightarrow \Diamond\varphi^{\text{stop}}_{\text{cw}} \wedge \\ \exists k : (v_{\text{car}} = V_{\text{max}} \wedge x_{\text{car}} = C_k) \rightarrow \Diamond\varphi^{\text{stop}}_{k+d_{\text{braking}}}\big). \tag{3}$$

The combined system contract is computed as

$$\mathcal{C}^{\text{sys}} = \mathcal{C}^{\text{sys}}_2 \parallel \mathcal{C}^{\text{sys}}_3 = \left(A^{\text{sys}} \cup \neg(G^{\text{sys}}_2 \cap G^{\text{sys}}_3), \quad G^{\text{sys}}_2 \cap G^{\text{sys}}_3\right).$$

We will relax this system contract by removing $\neg(G_2^{\rm sys} \cap G_3^{\rm sys})$ from the assumptions to ensure that the assumptions are in the same form as we require for the system contract in Definition 3. Consequently, the tester contract resulting from this system contract is more refined. So the system contract becomes

$$\begin{aligned}\mathcal{C}^{\rm sys} =\big(A^{\rm sys},\quad & \Box\varphi_{\rm dyn}^{\rm car} \wedge \Box\left(\varphi_{\rm high}^{\rm vis} \rightarrow v \leq V_{\max}\right) \wedge \\ & \Box(\texttt{detectable}_{\rm high}^{\rm ped} \rightarrow \Diamond\varphi_{\rm ped}^{\rm stop}) \vee \neg A^{\rm sys}\big).\end{aligned} \tag{4}$$

From Eqs. (3) and (4), we construct the test structure $\mathfrak{t} = (\mathcal{C}^{\rm obj}, \mathcal{C}^{\rm sys})$, where every implementation that satisfies to Eq. (2) describes a valid test environment for this combined test. This merged tester specification describes a test environment where we will see the car decelerate from $V_{\max}$ and stop in front of the crosswalk in high visibility conditions.

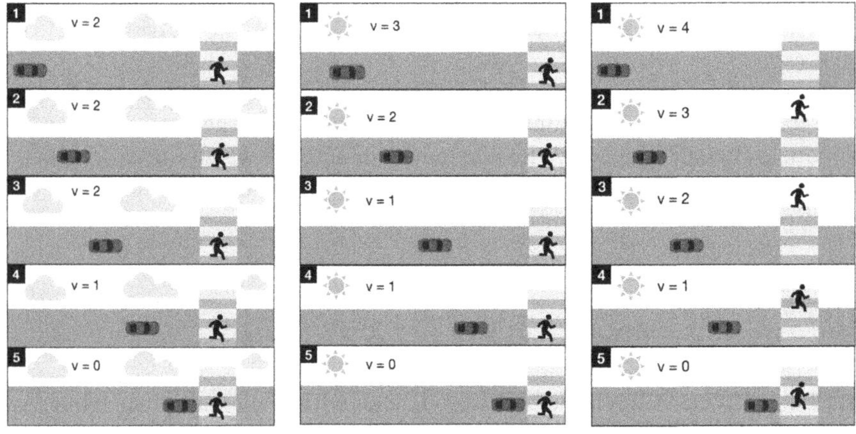

(a) Low visibility with a stationary pedestrian. (b) High visibility with a stationary pedestrian. (c) High visibility with a reactive pedestrian.

Fig. 4. Test execution snapshots of the car stopping for a pedestrian. Figure (a) shows a test execution satisfying $\mathcal{C}_1^{\rm tester}$, Figure (b) satisfies $\mathcal{C}_2^{\rm tester}$ and Figure (c) satisfies $\mathcal{C}_2^{\rm tester}$ and $\mathcal{C}_3^{\rm tester}$.

To ensure that test structures can be combined, we need to check whether the resulting test objective, and the corresponding tester contract are satisfiable. We will now explain which combinations of the given test structures cannot be implemented for either of these reasons. Computing the composition $\mathfrak{t}_1 \parallel \mathfrak{t}_2$ is not possible, as the composition of the test objectives $\mathcal{C}_1^{\rm obj} \parallel \mathcal{C}_2^{\rm obj}$ results in a contract with empty guarantees. This is the case, because $\Box\varphi_{\rm low}^{\rm vis}$ and $\Box\varphi_{\rm high}^{\rm vis}$ are disjoint, as the visibility conditions cannot be *high* and *low* at the same time. Thus these two test structures are not composable with each other. The composition $\mathfrak{t}_1 \parallel \mathfrak{t}_3$, does not result in a feasible test—the test objective requires a maximum speed of V_{max}, but the system is constrained to a maximum speed of $V_{\mathrm{low}} < V_{\mathrm{max}}$ in low visibility conditions, resulting in $G^{\mathrm{sys}} \cap G^{\mathrm{obj}} = \emptyset$.

Figure 4 shows snapshots of manually constructed test executions satisfying the tester contracts corresponding to $\mathfrak{t}_1, \mathfrak{t}_2$, and $\mathfrak{t}_2 \parallel \mathfrak{t}_3$. The simulation is in a grid world setting, where the car will move one cell forward if it has a positive speed v, and can accelerate or decelerate by one unit during every time step, meaning if the car is driving at a higher speed, it will take more cells to come to a stop. In the low visibility setting, the car can drive at a maximum speed of $v = 2$ and it can detect a pedestrian up to two cells away. So in Fig. 4a it is able to detect the pedestrian and come to a full stop in front of the crosswalk. In a high visibility setting, the car can drive at a maximum speed of $v_{\mathrm{max}} = 4$, and it can detect the pedestrian up to 5 cells ahead. In Fig. 4b we can see that the pedestrian is detected and the car slows down gradually until is reaches the cell in front of the crosswalk. Figure 4c shows a test for the tester contract corresponding to $\mathfrak{t}_2 \parallel \mathfrak{t}_3$, where we see the pedestrian entering the crosswalk in high visibility conditions when the car is driving at its maximum speed of $v = 4$ and is exactly $d_{\mathrm{braking}} = 4$ cells away from the pedestrian. This test execution now checks the test objective of detecting a pedestrian in high visibility conditions and executing the braking maneuver with the desired constant deceleration from its maximum speed down to zero. ■

Remark: Sometimes in addition to the combined test contract, the test executions must satisfy further constraints, informed by domain knowledge, to provide useful information to the test engineer. In the case of combining tests, a metric can be useful in determining whether we get the desired information from the execution of the combined test. In [17], to ensure that a merged test execution respects causality in satisfying all unit guarantees, temporal constraints are added to refine the merged test objective. Instead of refining the test structure, such additional constraints can also be handled during test environment synthesis. This can be helpful in determining if and how tests can be combined for a given available environment and the desired test information.

5 Comparing Test Campaigns

Justifying the choice of a test campaign from a list of possibilities requires a method of comparing test campaigns. A more refined test campaign is preferable to execute, because the system will be tested for a more refined set of test objectives and possibly for a more stringent set of system specifications. Let $\mathfrak{t}_i = (\mathcal{C}_i^{\mathrm{obj}}, \mathcal{C}_i^{\mathrm{sys}})$ be test structures for $1 \leq i \leq n$. When generating tests for $\mathfrak{t}_i$, we want to ensure that our test execution satisfies the constraints set out by $\mathcal{C}_i^{\mathrm{obj}}$ in the context of system behaviors defined by $\mathcal{C}_i^{\mathrm{sys}}$. As seen in Sect. 3, the tester contract can be computed using the quotient operator. We characterize a test campaign, $\mathtt{TC} = \{\mathfrak{t}_i\}_{i=1}^n$, as a finite list of test structures specified by the test engineer. Definition 7 allows us to generate a single test structure from a test campaign.

Definition 7. Given a test campaign $\mathtt{TC} = \{\mathfrak{t}_i\}_{i=1}^n$, the *test structure generated by this campaign*, denoted $\tau(\mathtt{TC})$, is

$$\tau(\mathtt{TC}) = \mathfrak{t}_1 \parallel \ldots \parallel \mathfrak{t}_n.$$

To define a notion of order for test campaigns, we need a notion of order for test structures. Comparing two test structures becomes important for defining the quotient of test structures (see Sect. 6) for splitting tests.

Definition 8. We say that the test structure $(\mathcal{C}_1^{\mathrm{obj}}, \mathcal{C}_1^{\mathrm{sys}})$ *refines* the structure $(\mathcal{C}_2^{\mathrm{obj}}, \mathcal{C}_2^{\mathrm{sys}})$, written $(\mathcal{C}_1^{\mathrm{obj}}, \mathcal{C}_1^{\mathrm{sys}}) \leq (\mathcal{C}_2^{\mathrm{obj}}, \mathcal{C}_2^{\mathrm{sys}})$, if contract refinement occurs element-wise, i.e., if $\mathcal{C}_1^{\mathrm{sys}} \leq \mathcal{C}_2^{\mathrm{sys}}$ and $\mathcal{C}_1^{\mathrm{obj}} \leq \mathcal{C}_2^{\mathrm{obj}}$.

We use the order between test structures (see Definition 8) to know when a test campaign is more refined than another (see Definition 9). A test campaign can be replaced by a more refined test campaign because the refined test campaign includes more stringent specifications in more stringent settings.

Definition 9. Given two test campaigns $\mathtt{TC}$ and $\mathtt{TC}'$, we say that $\mathtt{TC} \leq \mathtt{TC}'$ if $\tau(\mathtt{TC}) \leq \tau(\mathtt{TC}')$.

6 Splitting Tests

In this section, we explore the notion of splitting test structures. One of our motivations for doing this is failure diagnostics, in which we wish to look for root causes of a system-level test failure. To split test structures, we look for the existence of a quotient—see [22]. Suppose there exists a test structure $\mathfrak{t}$ that we want to split, and suppose one of the pieces of this decomposition, $\mathfrak{t}_1$, is given to us. Our objective is to find $\mathfrak{t}_2$ such that $\mathfrak{t}_1 \parallel \mathfrak{t}_2 \leq \mathfrak{t}$. The following result tells how to compute the optimum $\mathfrak{t}_2$. This optimum receives the name *quotient of test structures.*

Proposition 2. *Let* $\mathfrak{t} = (\mathcal{C}^{obj}, \mathcal{C}^{sys})$ *and* $\mathfrak{t}_1 = (\mathcal{C}_1^{obj}, \mathcal{C}_1^{sys})$ *be two test structures and let* $\mathfrak{t}_q = (\mathcal{C}^{obj}/\mathcal{C}_1^{obj}, \mathcal{C}^{sys}/\mathcal{C}_1^{sys})$. *For any test structure* $\mathfrak{t}_2 = (\mathcal{C}_2^{obj}, \mathcal{C}_2^{sys})$, *we have*

$$\mathfrak{t}_2 \parallel \mathfrak{t}_1 \leq \mathfrak{t} \quad \textit{if and only if} \quad \mathfrak{t}_2 \leq \mathfrak{t}_q.$$

We say that $\mathfrak{t}_q$ *is the quotient of* $\mathfrak{t}$ *by* $\mathfrak{t}_1$, *and we denote it as* $\mathfrak{t}/\mathfrak{t}_1$.

Proof. $\mathfrak{t}_2 \leq \mathfrak{t}_q \Leftrightarrow \mathcal{C}_2^{\mathrm{sys}} \leq \mathcal{C}^{\mathrm{sys}}/\mathcal{C}_1^{\mathrm{sys}}$ and $\mathcal{C}_2^{\mathrm{obj}} \leq \mathcal{C}^{\mathrm{obj}}/\mathcal{C}_1^{\mathrm{obj}} \Leftrightarrow (\mathcal{C}_2^{\mathrm{obj}} \parallel \mathcal{C}_1^{\mathrm{obj}}, \mathcal{C}_2^{\mathrm{sys}} \parallel \mathcal{C}_1^{\mathrm{sys}}) \leq (\mathcal{C}^{\mathrm{obj}}, \mathcal{C}^{\mathrm{sys}}) \Leftrightarrow \mathfrak{t}_2 \parallel \mathfrak{t}_1 \leq \mathfrak{t}$. □

Remark: The method of constructing the quotient test structure in Proposition 2 involves taking the quotient of the system contracts as well as the test objectives, meaning that we remove a subsystem from the overall system, and remove a part of the test objective. Depending on the use case, we can consider two further situations, where we can define the test structure $\mathfrak{t}_1$ such that:

i) only removing a subsystem from the overall system, which gives the quotient $\mathfrak{t}_q = (\mathcal{C}^{\text{obj}}, \mathcal{C}^{\text{sys}}/\mathcal{C}_1^{\text{sys}})$; and ii) only separating a part of the test objective: $\mathfrak{t}_q = (\mathcal{C}^{\text{obj}}/\mathcal{C}_1^{\text{obj}}, \mathcal{C}^{\text{sys}})$. The quotient test structures of type (i) could be useful in adding further test harnesses to monitor sub-systems under for the same test objective, and test structures of type (ii) could be useful in monitoring overall system behavior under a more unit test objective. In future work, we will study automatically choosing the relevant quotient test structure for specific use cases.

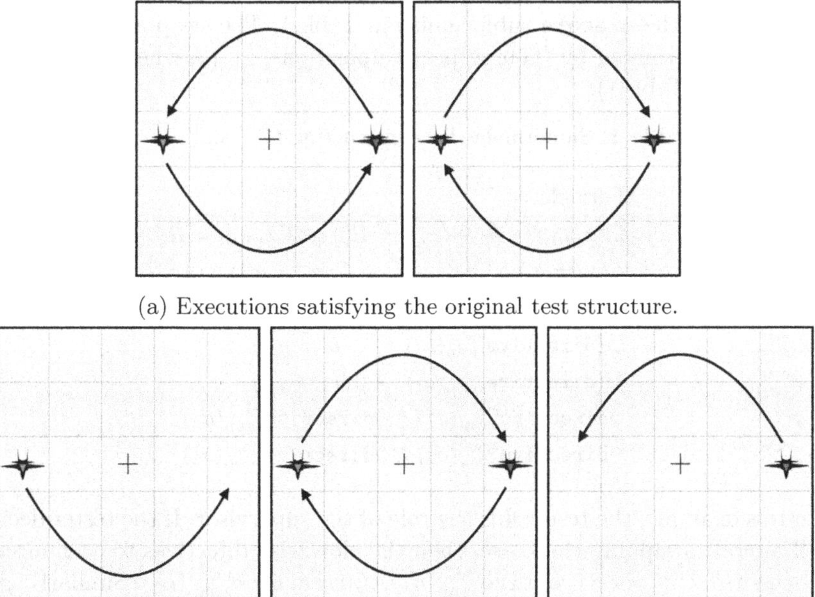

(a) Executions satisfying the original test structure.

(b) Left: Given unit test. Center and right: Possible executions for the split test.

Fig. 5. Front view of test executions satisfying the original test structure and the split test structure.

Example 2. Consider two aircraft, a_1 and a_2, flying parallel to each other undergoing a formation flying test shown in Fig. 5a where two aircraft need to swap positions longitudinally in a clockwise or counterclockwise spiral motion. Assume that during this test execution a system-level failure has been observed, but it is unknown which aircraft is responsible for the failure during which stage of the maneuver. We will make use of our framework to split test structures to help identify the subsystem responsible for the failure. The aircraft communicate with a centralized computer that issues waypoint directives to each aircraft in a manner consistent to the directives issued to other aircraft to ensure that there are no collisions. The dynamics of aircraft a_i on the gridworld is specified by G_i^{dyn}, and the safety or no collision requirement on all aircraft is given in

G^{safe}. The swap requirement, G_i^{swap}, specifies the maneuver that each aircraft must take in the event that a directive is issued.

$$G_i^{\text{swap}} = \Box\big(\texttt{directive}^{\text{cw}}_{\text{swap}}(a_i) \rightarrow \texttt{execute}^{\text{cw}}_{\text{swap}}(a_i)\big)\wedge \\ \Box\big(\texttt{directive}^{\text{ccw}}_{\text{swap}}(a_i) \rightarrow \texttt{execute}^{\text{ccw}}_{\text{swap}}(a_i)\big). \tag{5}$$

For example, in the case of a counter-clockwise swap directive issued to aircraft a_1 starting in region R_1, the aircraft must eventually reach the counter-clockwise swap goal, R_2, by traveling in the counter-clockwise direction, and upon reaching the goal must stay there as long as no new directive is issued. These maneuvers are specified in the **execute** subformulas in Table 1. The swap goals, g_i, for the aircraft are determined by their respective positions, $x_{\text{init,i}}$, when the directives are issued (see Table 1).

Table 1. Subformulas for constructing G^{sys} and G^{obj}.

Label	Formula
φ_{setgoal}	$\Box(x_{init,i} = R_1 \rightarrow x_{g,i} = R_2) \wedge \Box(x_{init,i} = R_2 \rightarrow x_{g,i} = R_1)$
$\texttt{execute}^{\text{ccw}}_{\text{swap}}(a_i)$	$\Diamond(x_i = g_i) \wedge \Box(x_i = g_i \rightarrow \bigcirc(x_i = g_i)) \wedge \Box\varphi^{\text{ccw}}_{\text{traj,i}}$
$\texttt{execute}^{\text{cw}}_{\text{swap}}(a_i)$	$\Diamond(x_i = g_i) \wedge \Box(x_i = g_i \rightarrow \bigcirc(x_i = g_i)) \wedge \Box\varphi^{\text{cw}}_{\text{traj,i}}$
$\varphi^{\text{cw}}_{\text{swap,i}}$	$\Box\big(\texttt{directive}^{\text{cw}}_{\text{swap}}(a_i) \rightarrow \Diamond(x_i = g_i)\big)$
$\varphi^{\text{ccw}}_{\text{swap,i}}$	$\Box\big(\texttt{directive}^{\text{ccw}}_{\text{swap}}(a_i) \rightarrow \Diamond(x_i = g_i)\big)$
φ^{cw}	$\Diamond\texttt{directive}^{\text{cw}}_{\text{swap}}(a_1) \wedge \Diamond\texttt{directive}^{\text{cw}}_{\text{swap}}(a_2)$
φ^{ccw}	$\Diamond\texttt{directive}^{\text{ccw}}_{\text{swap}}(a_1) \wedge \Diamond\texttt{directive}^{\text{ccw}}_{\text{swap}}(a_2)$

In this example, the tester fills the role of the supervisor. If the tester decides on all aircraft swapping clockwise, then the clockwise directives to each aircraft will be issued: $\varphi^{\text{cw}} = \Diamond\texttt{directive}^{\text{cw}}_{\text{swap}}(a_1) \wedge \Diamond\texttt{directive}^{\text{cw}}_{\text{swap}}(a_2)$. Similarly, φ^{ccw} denotes the eventual issue of counter-clockwise swap directives to both aircraft. All the temporal logic formulas required to construct the test structure associated with this example are summarized in Table 1. Moreover, no new directives are issued until all current directives are issued and all aircraft have completed the swap executions corresponding to the current directives (labeled as $G^{\texttt{dir}}_{\text{limit}}$). Finally, the aircraft are never issued conflicting swap directions—all aircraft are instructed to go clockwise or counterclockwise (labeled as $G^{\texttt{dir}}_{\text{safe}}$). For simplicity, we choose not to write out $G^{\texttt{dir}}_{\text{limit}}$ and $G^{\texttt{dir}}_{\text{safe}}$ in their extensive forms. Thus, the requirements for the system under test are as follows:

$$\mathcal{C}^{\text{sys}} = (A^{\text{sys}}, G^{\text{sys}}) = (G^{\texttt{dir}}_{\text{limit}} \wedge G^{\texttt{dir}}_{\text{safe}}, G^{\text{safe}} \wedge \bigwedge_i G_i^{\text{swap}} \wedge G_i^{\text{dyn}}). \tag{6}$$

That is, assuming that the supervisor issues consistent directives, and issues new directives only when all aircraft have completed the executions corresponding to the current round of directives, the aircraft system is required to guarantee safety and successful execution of the swap maneuver corresponding to the current directive. If we were to write the system requirements for a single aircraft, the corresponding contract would be similar:

$$\mathcal{C}_i^{\text{sys}} = (A_i^{\text{sys}}, G_i^{\text{sys}}) = (G_{\text{limit}}^{\text{dir}} \wedge G_{\text{safe}}^{\text{dir}}, G_i^{\text{swap}} \wedge G_i^{\text{dyn}}). \tag{7}$$

$$\begin{aligned} \mathcal{C}^{\text{obj}} &= (\top, G^{\text{obj}}), \quad \text{where} \\ G^{\text{obj}} &= (\varphi^{\text{cw}} \wedge \neg\varphi^{\text{ccw}}) \vee (\varphi^{\text{ccw}} \wedge \neg\varphi^{\text{cw}}). \end{aligned} \tag{8}$$

Observe that G^{obj} represents the tester issuing either clockwise or counter-clockwise swap directives. One of the unit tests is to the have the aircraft a_1 starting at $x_{init,1} = R_1$ (and as a result, $x_g = R_2$) get the counter-clockwise swap directive to reach $x_g = R_2$. The corresponding unit test structure $\mathfrak{t}_1 = (\mathcal{C}_1^{\text{obj}}, \mathcal{C}_1^{\text{sys}})$ can be written as follows,

$$\mathcal{C}_1^{\text{obj}} = (\top, G_1^{\text{obj}}) = (\top, \Diamond\texttt{directive}_{\text{swap}}^{\text{ccw}}(a_1)) \tag{9}$$

$$\mathcal{C}_1^{\text{sys}} = (A_1^{\text{sys}}, G_1^{\text{sys}}) = (G_{\text{limit}}^{\text{dir}} \wedge G_{\text{safe}}^{\text{dir}}, G_1^{\text{swap}} \wedge G_1^{\text{dyn}}). \tag{10}$$

Following Proposition 2, the second unit test structure can be derived by separately applying the quotient operator on the test objectives and the system contract. Applying the quotient on the test objective, we substitute $\top$ for the assumptions to simplify, and we refine the quotient contract $\mathcal{C}^{\text{obj}}/\mathcal{C}_1^{\text{obj}}$ by replacing its assumptions with $\top$:

$$\begin{aligned} \mathcal{C}^{\text{obj}}/\mathcal{C}_1^{\text{obj}} &= (A \cap G_1^{\text{obj}}, G \cap A_1^{\text{obj}} \cup \neg(A \cap G_1^{\text{obj}})) \\ &= (G_1^{\text{obj}}, G \cup \neg G_1^{\text{obj}}) \geq (\top, G^{\text{obj}} \cup \neg G_1^{\text{obj}}). \end{aligned}$$

Designer input is important for refining this contract resulting from applying the quotient; a similar observation has been documented for quotient operators in previous work [20]. Domain knowledge can be helpful in refining the contracts. Using $\neg G_1^{\text{obj}}$ as context, the contract $(\top, G^{\text{obj}} \cup \neg G_1^{\text{obj}})$ can be simplified to $(\top, \neg G_1^{\text{obj}} \vee \varphi_1 \vee \varphi_2)$, where $\varphi_1 = (\Diamond\texttt{directive}_{\text{swap}}^{\text{ccw}}(a_2) \wedge \neg\varphi^{\text{cw}})$ and $\varphi_2 = \varphi^{\text{cw}} \wedge \neg\varphi^{\text{ccw}}$. Then, $\neg G_1^{\text{obj}}$ is discarded and the test objective of the second unit test can be defined as a refinement of this simplified contract arising from the quotient:

$$\mathcal{C}_{a_2}^{\text{obj}} = (\top, \varphi_1 \vee \varphi_2) \leq (\top, \neg G_1^{\text{obj}} \vee \varphi_1 \vee \varphi_2). \tag{11}$$

In Eq. (11), there are two types of test executions that would be the unit contract obtained by applying the quotient operator: i) A counter-clockwise directive is issued to aircraft a_2 and no clockwise directives are issued to either aircraft, or ii) Both aircraft are issued clockwise directives and no counter-clockwise directives. Note that φ_1 and φ_2 cannot be implemented in the same test by construction. Finally, the unit system contract can also by found by applying the quotient operator:

$$\begin{aligned} \mathcal{C}^{\text{sys}}/\mathcal{C}_1^{\text{sys}} &= (A^{\text{sys}} \cap G_1^{\text{sys}}, G^{\text{sys}} \cap A_1^{\text{sys}} \cup \neg(A^{\text{sys}} \cap G_1^{\text{sys}})) \\ &= (G_{\text{limit}}^{\text{dir}} \wedge G_{\text{safe}}^{\text{dir}} \wedge G_1^{\text{swap}} \wedge G_1^{\text{dyn}}, (G^{\text{safe}} \wedge G_2^{\text{swap}} \wedge G_2^{\text{dyn}}) \\ &\quad \vee \neg(G_1^{\text{swap}} \wedge G_1^{dyn} \wedge G_{\text{limit}}^{\text{dir}} \wedge G_{\text{safe}}^{\text{dir}})) \\ &= (G_{\text{limit}}^{\text{dir}} \wedge G_{\text{safe}}^{\text{dir}} \wedge G_1^{\text{swap}} \wedge G_1^{\text{dyn}}, (G^{\text{safe}} \wedge G_2^{\text{swap}} \wedge G_2^{\text{dyn}})). \end{aligned} \tag{12}$$

Remark: Observe that Eq. (12) carries the swap and dynamics requirements of aircraft a_1 in its assumptions. Since we choose to separate aircraft a_1 from the overall aircraft system, this quotient contract can be satisfied by making aircraft a_1 a part of the tester. For a test execution of $\mathfrak{t}_2$, the tester can choose to keep aircraft a_1 as a part of the test harness for the operational test involving aircraft a_2, or choose to not deploy a_1 during the test execution.

The system requirement $\mathcal{C}_2^{\text{sys}} = \mathcal{C}^{\text{sys}}/\mathcal{C}_1^{\text{sys}}$ and the test objective together result in the following possible tester specifications,

$$\begin{aligned}\mathcal{C}_{\varphi_1}^{\text{tester}} = \Big(G^{\text{safe}} \wedge G_2^{\text{swap}} \wedge G_2^{\text{dyn}},\ G_{\text{limit}}^{\text{dir}} \wedge G_{\text{safe}}^{\text{dir}} \wedge G_1^{\text{swap}} \wedge G_1^{\text{dyn}} \\ \wedge \Diamond \mathtt{directive}_{\text{swap}}^{\text{ccw}}(a_2) \wedge \neg\varphi^{\text{cw}}\Big).\end{aligned} \tag{13}$$

$$\begin{aligned}\mathcal{C}_{\varphi_2}^{\text{tester}} = \Big(G^{\text{safe}} \wedge G_2^{\text{swap}} \wedge G_2^{\text{dyn}},\ G_{\text{limit}}^{\text{dir}} \wedge G_{\text{safe}}^{\text{dir}} \wedge G_1^{\text{swap}} \wedge G_1^{\text{dyn}} \\ \wedge \Diamond \mathtt{directive}_{\text{swap}}^{\text{cw}}(a_1) \wedge \Diamond \mathtt{directive}_{\text{swap}}^{\text{cw}}(a_2) \wedge \neg\varphi^{\text{ccw}}\Big).\end{aligned} \tag{14}$$

From Eq. (13), we see that the tester does not require aircraft a_1 for any dynamic maneuvers, so it need not be deployed. In Eq. (14), even though aircraft a_1 would be a part of the test harness, it needs to be deployed for the tester contract, $\mathcal{C}_{\varphi_2}^{\text{tester}}$, to be satisfied. These tests resulting from the quotient test structure will help with determining the source of the failure that arose in the more complex test. ■

7 Conclusion and Future Work

We have developed formal notions for constructing, comparing, combining, and splitting test structures. We reason at the specification level of the test structures to find more refined test campaigns, and derive the tester specification from which a test environment can be synthesized. We give the conditions for when test structures are composable, allowing for simultaneous execution of test objectives when possible.

We briefly discussed the use of splitting tests for the application of failure diagnosis to find the root cause of a system-level test failure. Using the splitting operation on the test structure, we can isolate the components and verify their operation, assuming we can make use of a test harness, allowing us to monitor certain subsystem inputs and outputs. For future work, we can annotate which sub-component was used in context to satisfy a formula and thus use this additional information to track potential sources of a system-level failure. Additionally, we aim to construct an algorithm that will find a refined test campaign from a given test campaign that is optimal for a certain user-defined metric, e.g., test time or cost or coverage, while also accounting for test environment constraints.

Acknowledgements. The authors acknowledge funding from AFOSR Test and Evaluation program, grant FA9550-19-1-0302, and NSF and ASEE through an eFellows postdoctoral fellowship. The contents are solely the responsibility of the authors and do not necessarily represent the views of the sponsors.

References

1. Atkinson, C., Groß, H.G.: Built-in contract testing in model-driven, component-based development. In: Proceedings of ICSR-7 Workshop on Component-Based Development Processes (2002)
2. Badithela, A., Graebener, J.B., Ubellacker, W., Mazumdar, E.V., Ames, A.D., Murray, R.M.: Synthesizing reactive test environments for autonomous systems: testing reach-avoid specifications with multi-commodity flows. In: 2023 International Conference on Robotics and Automation (ICRA), London, UK. IEEE, arXiv preprint arXiv:2210.10304 (2023, to appear)
3. Baier, C., Katoen, J.P.: Principles of Model Checking. MIT Press, Cambridge (2008)
4. Beer, A., Ramler, R.: The role of experience in software testing practice. In: 2008 34th Euromicro Conference Software Engineering and Advanced Applications. pp. 258–265. IEEE (2008)
5. Benveniste, A., Caillaud, B., Ferrari, A., Mangeruca, L., Passerone, R., Sofronis, C.: Multiple viewpoint contract-based specification and design. In: de Boer, F.S., Bonsangue, M.M., Graf, S., de Roever, W.-P. (eds.) FMCO 2007. LNCS, vol. 5382, pp. 200–225. Springer, Heidelberg (2008). https://doi.org/10.1007/978-3-540-92188-2_9
6. Benveniste, A., et al.: Contracts for system design. Found. Trends® Electron. Design Autom. **12**(2–3), 124–400 (2018)
7. Blundell, C., Giannakopoulou, D., Pundefinedsundefinedreanu, C.S.: Assume-guarantee testing, SAVCBS 2005, p. 1-es. Association for Computing Machinery, New York (2005). https://doi.org/10.1145/1123058.1123060
8. Brandán Briones, L.: Assume-guarantee reasoning with ioco testing relation. On testing software and systems: short papers, p. 103 (2010)
9. Brat, G., Jonsson, A.: Challenges in verification and validation of autonomous systems for space exploration. In: Proceedings of 2005 IEEE International Joint Conference on Neural Networks, vol. 5, pp. 2909–2914. IEEE (2005)
10. Bruno, M., Canfora, G., Di Penta, M., Esposito, G., Mazza, V.: Using test cases as contract to ensure service compliance across releases. In: Benatallah, B., Casati, F., Traverso, P. (eds.) ICSOC 2005. LNCS, vol. 3826, pp. 87–100. Springer, Heidelberg (2005). https://doi.org/10.1007/11596141_8
11. Cofer, D., Gacek, A., Miller, S., Whalen, M.W., LaValley, B., Sha, L.: Compositional verification of architectural models. In: Goodloe, A.E., Person, S. (eds.) NFM 2012. LNCS, vol. 7226, pp. 126–140. Springer, Heidelberg (2012). https://doi.org/10.1007/978-3-642-28891-3_13
12. Dahm, W.J.: Technology horizons vision for the air force during 2010–2030 (video). Technical report, Chief Scientist (Air Force) Washington, DC (2011)
13. Dai, G., Bai, X., Wang, Y., Dai, F.: Contract-based testing for web services. In: 31st Annual International Computer Software and Applications Conference (COMPSAC 2007), vol. 1, pp. 517–526 (2007). https://doi.org/10.1109/COMPSAC.2007.100
14. Dijkstra, E.W.: Guarded commands, nondeterminacy and formal derivation of programs. Commun. ACM **18**(8), 453–457 (1975)

15. Fremont, D.J., et al.: Formal scenario-based testing of autonomous vehicles: from simulation to the real world. In: 2020 IEEE 23rd International Conference on Intelligent Transportation Systems (ITSC), pp. 1–8. IEEE (2020)
16. Giannakopoulou, D., Păsăreanu, C., Blundell, C.: Assume-guarantee testing for software components. IET Softw. **2**(6), 547–562 (2008)
17. Graebener, J.B., Badithela, A., Murray, R.M.: Towards better test coverage: Merging unit tests for autonomous systems. In: Deshmukh, J.V., Havelund, K., Perez, I. (eds.) NFM 2022. LNCS, vol. 13260, pp. 133–155. Springer, Cham (2022). https://doi.org/10.1007/978-3-031-06773-0_7
18. Heckel, R., Lohmann, M.: Towards contract-based testing of web services. Electron. Notes Theor. Comput. Sci. **116**, 145–156 (2005). https://doi.org/10.1016/j.entcs.2004.02.073, https://www.sciencedirect.com/science/article/pii/S1571066104052831. Proceedings of the International Workshop on Test and Analysis of Component Based Systems (TACoS 2004)
19. Helle, P., Schamai, W., Strobel, C.: Testing of autonomous systems-challenges and current state-of-the-art. In: INCOSE International Symposium, vol. 26, pp. 571–584. Wiley Online Library (2016)
20. Incer, I., Sangiovanni-Vincentelli, A.L., Lin, C.W., Kang, E.: Quotient for assume-guarantee contracts. In: 16th ACM-IEEE International Conference on Formal Methods and Models for System Design, MEMOCODE 2018, pp. 67–77 (2018). https://doi.org/10.1109/MEMCOD.2018.8556872
21. Incer, I.: The algebra of contracts. Ph.D. thesis, EECS Department, University of California, Berkeley (2022)
22. Incer, I., Mangeruca, L., Villa, T., Sangiovanni-Vincentelli, A.: The quotient in preorder theories. arXiv:2009.10886 (2020)
23. Lamport, L.: Win and sin: predicate transformers for concurrency. ACM Trans. Program. Lang. Syst. (TOPLAS) **12**(3), 396–428 (1990)
24. Meyer, B.: Applying 'design by contract'. Computer **25**(10), 40–51 (1992)
25. Negulescu, R.: Process Spaces. In: Palamidessi, C. (ed.) CONCUR 2000. LNCS, vol. 1877, pp. 199–213. Springer, Heidelberg (2000). https://doi.org/10.1007/3-540-44618-4_16
26. Nuzzo, P., Sangiovanni-Vincentelli, A.L., Bresolin, D., Geretti, L., Villa, T.: A platform-based design methodology with contracts and related tools for the design of cyber-physical systems. Proc. IEEE **103**(11), 2104–2132 (2015)
27. Passerone, R., Incer, I., Sangiovanni-Vincentelli, A.L.: Coherent extension, composition, and merging operators in contract models for system design. ACM Trans. Embed. Comput. Syst. (TECS) **18**(5s), 1–23 (2019)
28. Pnueli, A.: The temporal logic of programs. In: 18th Annual Symposium on Foundations of Computer Science (SFCS 1977), pp. 46–57. IEEE (1977)
29. Sangiovanni-Vincentelli, A.L., Damm, W., Passerone, R.: Taming Dr. Frankenstein: contract-based design for cyber-physical systems. Eur. J. Control **18**(3), 217–238 (2012). https://doi.org/10.3166/ejc.18.217-238
30. Seshia, S.A., Sadigh, D., Sastry, S.S.: Towards verified artificial intelligence. arXiv preprint arXiv:1606.08514 (2016)
31. Tretmans, J.: Model based testing with labelled transition systems. In: Hierons, R.M., Bowen, J.P., Harman, M. (eds.) Formal Methods and Testing. LNCS, vol. 4949, pp. 1–38. Springer, Heidelberg (2008). https://doi.org/10.1007/978-3-540-78917-8_1
32. Weiss, L.G.: Autonomous robots in the fog of war. IEEE Spectr. **48**(8), 30–57 (2011)

From the Standards to Silicon: Formally Proved Memory Controllers

Felipe Lisboa Malaquias[1(✉)], Mihail Asavoae[2], and Florian Brandner[1]

[1] LTCI, Télécom Paris, Institut Polytechnique de Paris, Palaiseau, France
{flisboa,florian.brandner}@telecom-paris.fr
[2] Université Paris Saclay, CEA List, Gif-sur-Yvette, France
mihail.asavoae@cea.fr

Abstract. Recent research in both academia and industry has successfully used deductive verification to design hardware and prove its correctness. While tools and languages to write formally proved hardware have been proposed, applications and use cases are often overlooked. In this work, we focus on *Dynamic Random Access Memories* (DRAM) controllers and the DRAM itself – which has its expected temporal and functional behaviours described in the standards written by the *Joint Electron Device Engineering Council* (JEDEC). Concretely, we associate an existing *Coq DRAM controller framework* – which can be used to write DRAM scheduling algorithms that comply with a variety of correctness criteria – to a back-end system that generates proved logically equivalent hardware. This makes it possible to simultaneously enjoy the trustworthiness provided by the Coq framework and use the generated synthesizable hardware in real systems. We validate the approach by using the generated code as a plug-in replacement in an existing DDR4 controller implementation, which includes a host interface (AXI), a physical layer (PHY) from Xilinx, and a model of a memory part *Micron MT40A1G8WE-075E:D*. We simulate and synthesise the full system.

Keywords: Coq · DRAM · Hardware Design · Code Generation

1 Introduction

The limitations of approaches such as model checking and satisfiability solving – widely adopted in industrial *hardware* (HW) verification – are well-known [6]: 1) Verification effort is focused on (relatively) small components of full systems; 2) Relatively weak properties are proved, with considerable abstraction gaps from the natural correctness criteria described in the specifications; and 3) The *state-space-explosion* problem. Conversely, proof assistants (i.e., deductive verifiers, or theorem provers) rely on the functional paradigm and on rich expressive high-order logic specification languages to describe systems at a high abstraction

This research was supported by Labex DigiCosme (project ANR11LABEX0045DIGICOSME) operated by ANR as part of the program "Investissement d'Avenir" Idex ParisSaclay (ANR11IDEX000302).

K. Y. Rozier and S. Chaudhuri (Eds.): NFM 2023, LNCS 13903, pp. 295–311, 2023.
https://doi.org/10.1007/978-3-031-33170-1_18

level – allowing programmers to implement systems and state correctness theorems naturally, without scalability constraints. The most significant caveats are arguably a higher entry bar, given the complexity of specification languages and proof scripts, and the lack of automation. Proof assistants, like Coq, also allow users to *extract* proved programs, which can then be compiled and executed.

In this work, we use Coq to propose a trustworthy design workflow for *Dynamic Random Access Memory* (DRAM) controllers – whose timing and functional correctness is essential for a variety of computing systems (e.g., critical real-time systems, our main focus, but also parallel and distributed systems). The correct behaviour of DRAM modules, and thus that of DRAM controllers, is described in standards [10] written by the *Joint Electron Device Engineering Council* (JEDEC). Furthermore, given that the standards use textual natural language (English) to describe correctness criteria along with timing diagrams, choosing Coq to model such systems is highly convenient – given the expressivity provided by its functional high-order logic specification language.

Precisely, we connect an existing Coq framework used to develop correct DRAM scheduling algorithms [13] – which in this work will be referred to as *CoqDRAM* for brevity – to a *back-end* that generates logically equivalent *Register Transfer Level* (RTL) representations in SystemVerilog. The back-end, which will be referred to as *CavaDRAM*, is developed in Cava,[1] a *Domain Specific Language* (DSL) written in Coq for designing and proving properties about circuits.

The connection between CoqDRAM and CavaDRAM plays a vital role in the design workflow proposed in this work – presented below as a list of steps:

1. Describe a DRAM scheduling algorithm in CoqDRAM and prove its correctness against the JEDEC standards;
2. Describe the controller circuit in Cava;
3. Prove bisimilarity between the two representations;
4. Extract a SystemVerilog circuit from the Cava controller (automatically), which can then be used as a plug-in replacement in existing hardware designs.

On the one hand, CoqDRAM – written in plain Coq – has been conceived to design, explore, model, and finally prove the correctness of DRAM arbitration **algorithms**, abstracting from actual HW implementations. It has little to no size constraints, a fact that allows users to use powerful abstractions to prove strong properties. On the other hand, CavaDRAM derives real memory controller HW implementations. This means that HW limitations become relevant, e.g., CoqDRAM uses queues that can grow to arbitrary sizes to store incoming requests, which is evidently not possible in a HW model. Therefore, a logical equivalence proof will require the queue to be limited in size. This duality is formalised through a series of assumptions – which are presented further – that allow us to limit the scope of CoqDRAM algorithms.

In summary, this work proposes the following **contributions**:

- A design workflow to design correct-by-construction DRAM controllers, going from correctness criteria described in the JEDEC standards to RTL code;

[1] https://github.com/project-oak/silveroak.

- A proved proof-of-concept controller implementation, corresponding to one of the controllers originally proposed in CoqDRAM;
- A methodology to validate the generated RTL code in an existing design, and consequently, validate both the CoqDRAM and CavaDRAM models;
- An extension of the CoqDRAM to include REFRESH commands and its underlying correctness criteria.

The remainder of the paper is organised as follows: Sect. 2 gives a concise background on the two building blocks of our work: CoqDRAM and Cava; besides presenting some fundamental concepts about DRAM systems; Sect. 3 introduces our novel contributions with an architectural overview of the system and presents how memory controllers (and transition systems, more generally) that are logically equivalent to CoqDRAM implementations can be written in Cava; Sect. 4 elaborates on our use of the term "logical equivalence", which is de facto a *bisimilarity* relationship. Moreover, it presents the theorem and key insights of the proof procedure; Sect. 5 details the RTL generation phase, explains how the generated code is plugged into the existing DDR4 controller implementation (written in SystemVerilog), and presents the setup and the results regarding both simulation and synthesis; Sect. 6 reviews and compares the state-of-the-art with our work; and Sect. 7 concludes by revisiting our contributions and giving pointers for future research directions.

2 Background

2.1 DRAM Basics

DRAM controllers are responsible for servicing memory requests by issuing commands to the DRAM module (among other tasks, such as translating addresses into DRAM bank groups, banks, rows, and columns; and applying some scheduling algorithm to service requests). Moreover, each bank in a DRAM module has a row-sized buffer (the row-buffer) that serves as a "cache" for the bank, storing chunks of data that can be accessed with lower latency. Although several types of commands exist, the main ones used to directly service requests are: **ACT** (Activate), used to transfer one row of a bank into the row-buffer; **PRE** (Precharge), used to re-write the content of the row-buffer back into the matrix of memory cells; and **CAS** (Column Address Strobe), used to access one of the columns from the row-buffer (a **CAS** can be either a **RD** or a **WR**). Additionally, the controller has to issue **REF** (Refresh) commands periodically to restore the charge of cell capacitors.

2.2 CoqDRAM

CoqDRAM [13] models DRAM devices as command traces. Correctness criteria coming from the JEDEC standards [10] are modelled as *proof obligations* (POs) over traces and cover both functional and timing properties. Listing 1 shows such modelling: `Trace_t` is a record (much like structures in C), with constructor mkTrace. The trace itself is the member Commands (of type Commands_t). It is implemented as a standard Coq list type, where elements of the list are of type Command_t, the type of DRAM commands (not shown here).

```
Record Trace_t := mkTrace {
 Commands : Commands_t;
 Time     : nat;
 (* PO: Ensures that the time between an ACT and a CAS commands to the
     same bank respects T_RCD *)
 Cmds_T_RCD_ok : forall a b, a \in Commands → b \in Commands →
 isACT a → isCAS b → Same_Bank a b → Before a b
 → a.(CDate) + T_RCD <= b.(CDate); }
```

Listing 1. Command trace.

The record member Time is the trace length, and Cmds_T_RCD_ok is one of many POs: it states that for any two commands a and b members of the list, if a is an ACT command, b is a CAS command, they both target the same DRAM bank, a is issued before b, then the proposition a.(CDate) + T_RCD <= b.(CDate) must hold, where T_RCD is a constraint defined in the JEDEC standards. In other words, T_RCD is a lower bound between the issue dates of a and b. Besides JEDEC properties, essential characteristics of real-time systems are also modelled, such as non-starvation and controller semantics (e.g., memory consistency models).

Listing 2 shows CoqDRAM's definition of a memory controller. It is made of a function (Arbitrate) that, for a given request arrival model (Arrival_function_t), produces a trace of DRAM commands (Trace_t) of length defined by a nat parameter (the number of clock cycles). The class member Requests_handled is a proof obligation: it states that any request that has arrived will eventually have a corresponding CAS command in the trace (i.e., requests cannot starve).[2]

```
Class Controller_t {AF : Arrival_function_t} := mkController {
 Arbitrate : nat → Trace_t;

 Requests_handled : forall ta req, req \in (Arrival_at ta)
   → exists tc, (CAS_of_req req tc) \in (Arbitrate tc).(Commands); }.
```

Listing 2. Memory controller definition.

```
Class Implementation_t := mkImplementation {
 (* Init takes a set of incoming requests and produces a state *)
 Init : Requests_t → State_t;
 (* Next takes a set of incoming requests, a state, and produces a new
     state, a command and the request currrently being serviced *)
 Next : Requests_t → State_t → State_t * (Command_kind_t * Request_t); }.
```

Listing 3. Implementation interface for memory controllers.

[2] CAS commands tell the memory to start the data transfer – its issue date is considered to be the completion date of the corresponding request.

Concretely, memory controllers are implemented as *transition systems* (TS). The user of CoqDRAM has to implement the type class `Implementation_t` (shown in Listing 3), made of functions `Init` and `Next`. The `Next` function, for instance, takes a set of arriving requests (`Requests_t`) at an arbitrary clock cycle, an arbiter state (`State_t`), and produces a new state and an output pair made of a DRAM command (`Command_kind_t`) and the request currently being serviced (`Request_t`). These functions together define a canvas, in some sense, for implementing controllers as transition systems.

Furthermore, it is typical of high-level abstraction models of memory controllers to ignore REF commands and its impact on timing. This is however not possible in a HW implementation. Hence, we extend CoqDRAM to model REF commands, including POs that guarantee timing and functional correctness.

2.3 Cava

Cava is a DSL written in Coq designed to specify, implement and prove circuits, greatly inspired by Lava [2]. It was developed by researchers at Google as part of the *Silver Oak project*, which focuses on the verification of high assurance components of the OpenTitan[3] silicon root of trust, i.e., a set of inherently trusted functions within a platform. Cava, much like other recent Coq DSLs for hardware design (e.g., *Kami* [6] and *Kôika* [4]), follows the highly automated proof and design style proposed by Adam Chlipala in his book *Certified Programming with Dependent Types* [5]. We choose Cava over other Coq DSLs for a few reasons: 1) Cava circuit simulations generate a list of values, where each element represents the value of a wire at a given clock cycle – this emulates *time*, a key element of command traces in CoqDRAM; 2) Cava is relatively simpler and faster to get acquainted to; and 3) Cava designs resemble classic RTL design style in some sense, whereas other DSLs take an approach closer to the rule-based design of Bluespec SystemVerilog [15].

Cava combines shallow and deep embedding techniques to describe combinational and sequential circuits, respectively. In other words, sequential circuits are implemented as inductive types (which includes a wrapper to combinational circuits). Thanks to its inductive nature, circuits can be interpreted in different ways [2], a feature that allows Cava users to prove correctness, simulate, and generate a netlist from a single circuit definition. Furthermore, sequential circuits in Cava are transition systems, much like controllers in CoqDRAM.

While we lack the space to formally present Cava's syntax and semantics, we will try to give the reader an intuitive understanding of how sequential circuits – and transition systems, more generally – can be designed with the DSL. Listing 4 is a sequential circuit definition in Cava (Fig. 1). Circuit `Foo` takes an input `i` of type `inputType` and produces an outout `o` of type `outputType`. Possible signal types in Cava are: `Void`, an empty type; `Bit`, which is interpreted in Coq as a boolean; `Vec`, which takes another Cava signal type and the vector's size; and `ExternalType`, which is a non-interpreted type. Moreover, circuit `Foo` has an

[3] https://opentitan.org/.

internal state of type `stateType`, a register with initial value `s_init`. The loop body `f` is a combinational function with type (`stateType,inputType`)→ (`stateType ,outputType`). In other words, although the internal state `s` (a given name) is not visible from outside `Foo`, the loop body `f` takes a pair of type (`stateType * inputType`) as input and produces another pair of type (`stateType,outputType`). Lastly, Cava loops can be nested in order to form circuits that have multiple internal state signals.

```
Definition Foo : Circuit
 (i : inputType) (o : outputType) :=
 LoopInit (s_init : stateType) (
  Comb (f)
  (* f : (stateType * inputType) →
  (stateType,outputType) *)
 ).
```

Listing 4. Sequential circuit in Cava.

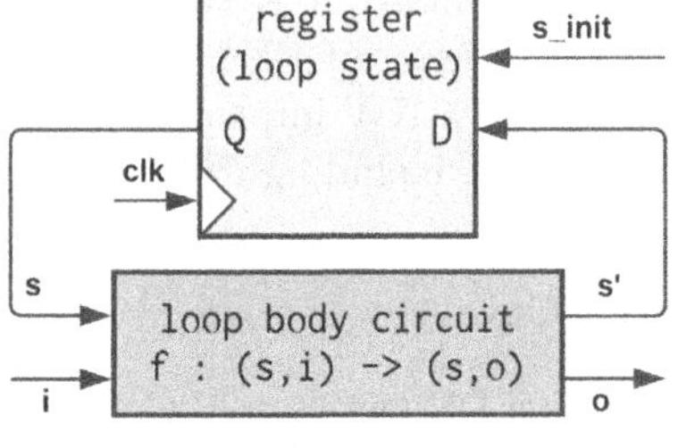

Fig. 1. Sequential circuit diagram.

3 Coupling CoqDRAM and CavaDRAM

Figure 2 illustrates the coupling between CoqDRAM and CavaDRAM. The design path starts at the JEDEC standards, modelled by `Trace_t` in CoqDRAM (c.f. Listing 1). Specifically, the CoqDRAM specification covers the DDR3 and DDR4 JEDEC standards. Next, for scheduling algorithms implemented in CoqDRAM, we introduce *provably equivalent* controllers in CavaDRAM (equivalence is defined in Sect. 4). The RTL code produced from a controller implementation (using Cava's code extraction) can be used in existing designs. In our case, it is used as a plug-in replacement in an existing DDR4 controller implementation [20]. From a framework point of view, the additional workload introduced by the back-end coupling consists solely of writing the equivalent controllers in Cava and the equivalence proof with the representation in CoqDRAM.

3.1 Controller Implementation Constraints

Hardware controller implementations impose constraints that are not captured by CoqDRAM. The setup we use for simulation and synthesis, for instance, is equipped with an AXI bus interface, which expects an interface to communicate with the memory controller. As a consequence, CavaDRAM controllers have to implement an interface containing the following input and output signals: a) the arrival of a new request is signalled by a 1-bit `pending_i` input signal; b) a *single* `request_i` is provided as a bit vector input; and c) the circuit has to produce a 1-bit `ack_o` signal as output. The `pending_i`/`ack_o` signals allow to perform a handshake (used in many bus implementations besides AXI).

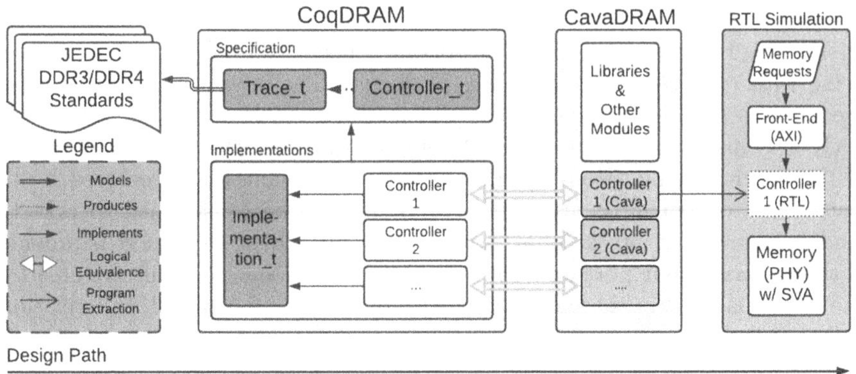

Fig. 2. System architecture (Figure 2 omits several components and does not represent a complete architecture, as its goals are to ease comprehension and provide an overview of the system). ■ CoqDRAM classes, ■ Introduced workload, ■ DDR4 hardware simulation setup.

This interface is less *generic* than the CoqDRAM implementation. An equivalence proof thus can only succeed by introducing two additional assumptions that constrain the arrival model of CoqDRAM:

Assumption 1. The arrival function needs to be constrained to a *single incoming request per cycle.* In Coq, we model this constraint with a PO that limits the number of requests in the incoming arrival list; the PO is denoted by `HW_single` in Listing 5. For one, this models the limitation of the AXI bus mentioned in the interface above. In addition, this reflects a fundamental limitation on memories, which are typically used to implement queues in hardware: the implementation cost of memories increases drastically with the number of read/write ports. In our case (Distributed/BRAM of FPGAs), it is limited to a single read/write port each. Bear in mind that the proofs in CoqDRAM are valid for all possible arrival functions without any limitations, including `HW_Arrival_function`.

```
Class HW_Arrival_function_t {AF : Arrival_function_t} := mkHW_AF {
 HW_single : forall t, size (Arrival_at t) <= 1; (* Assumption 1 *)

 (* Assumption 2 consisting of two POs *)
 pending_i : nat → signal Bit; (* pending input for controller circuit *)
 request_i : nat → signal request_t; (* request as input *)
 HW_arrived : forall t, size (Arrival_at t) = 1 ↔ (ack_o t) ∧ (pending_i t);
 HW_request : forall t, size (Arrival_at t) = 1 →
       EqReq (Arrival_at t) (request_i t);
}.
```

Listing 5. Assumption reflecting hardware-level implementation constraints.

Assumption 2. Note that Assumption 1 does not constrain the number of outstanding requests from the requestors, it is just a constraint on the bus interfacing with requestors and memories of queues. The interface described before also comprises a handshake protocol, which allows a controller to accept (or not) newly in-coming requests. CoqDRAM only considers requests that are *accepted* by the controller, i.e., from the moment that the request is processed by the controller. Consequently, arrival functions have to be constrained to take the handshake protocol into account: a request arrives when the request is provided on the `request` input port and both the `pending` and `ack_o` signals are asserted. The two POs `HW_arrived` and `HW_request` from Listing 5 establish this relation.

3.2 From CoqDRAM to CavaDRAM Implementation

As a Proof-of-Concept, we implement a controller based on the *First-In-First-Out* (FIFO) scheduling policy, as originally proposed in CoqDRAM. The controller serves an arbitrary number of requestors. Requests are served in arrival order, without distinction between requestors. Each request is processed in a *slot* large enough to fit every necessary DRAM command while respecting all timing constraints. The controller issues DRAM commands following a *closed-page policy*, i.e., it always issues the same sequence of commands: PRE-ACT-CAS.

Representing States. Listing 6 shows CoqDRAM's FIFO state definition, an inductive type with three possible values: `IDLE`, `RUNNING`, and `REFRESHING`. Additionally, each value carries a series of arguments that extends the set of states: `Cnt_t` is a counter used to count clock cycles within a FIFO slot; `Cnt_ref_t` is another counter used to manage memory REFRESH operations, i.e., keep track of clock cycles until a REF command is needed; and `Reqs_t` is the infinite sequence of requests in the queue, i.e., waiting to be serviced. Note also that the `RUNNING` state carries an additional value of type `Req_t`, used to remember the request currently being processed by the controller. The counters are implemented in Coq as bounded integers (which carry a proof stating that the counter value is always strictly smaller than its bound) and the queue is a standard Coq list (of arbitrary size). `Reqs_t` being an unbounded list is obviously not possible in a HW model. Assumptions 1 and 2 (presented in Sect. 3.1) mitigate this problem, as they make it impossible for `Reqs_t` to grow arbitrarily. In connection with Listing 3, `FIFO_state_t` is a valid instance of `State_t`.

```
Inductive FIFO_state_t :=
| IDLE    : Cnt_t → Cnt_ref_t → Reqs_t → FIFO_state_t
| RUNNING : Cnt_t → Cnt_ref_t → Reqs_t → Req_t → FIFO_state_t
| REFRESHING : Cnt_ref_t → Reqs_t → FIFO_state_t.
```

Listing 6. CoqDRAM FIFO state.

Cava Implementation. A simplified version of the FIFO CavaDRAM implementation can be seen in Listing 7.[4] Figure 3 is a diagram of the resulting circuit.[5] A few points are worth emphasising:

```
Definition FIFO : Circuit (pending * request) (ack * request * command) :=
 Loop (Loop (Loop ( (* one loop for each resigster *)
  ReadLogic >==>Queue >==>NextCR >==>CmdGen >==>Update)))
```

Listing 7. Simplified version of the FIFO implementation in CavaDRAM.

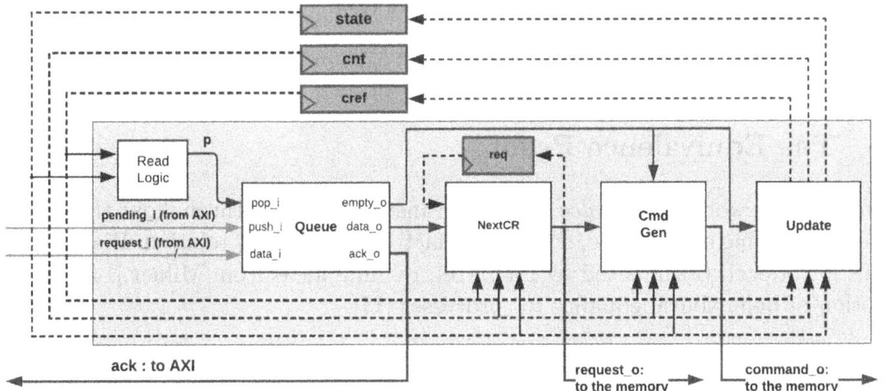

Fig. 3. FIFO circuit implementation in Cava.

1. We use nested `Loop` constructors to manipulate multiple internal state signals, allowing us to mimic CoqDRAM states. A correspondence can be established between elements of Listing 7/Fig. 3 and CoqDRAM's FIFO state definition (Listing 6): the register `state` corresponds to the state identifier (`IDLE` /`RUNNING`/`REFRESHING`); register `cnt` corresponds to the counter `Cnt_t`, and has as many bits as necessary to count up to the counter's bound; similarly, register `cref` corresponds to `Cnt_ref_t`. The request queue in CoqDRAM (`Reqs_t`) corresponds to `Queue`. Lastly, `Req_t` in `RUNNING` is a register of circuit `NextCR`.

2. `Queue` is implemented as a dual-ported memory (one port for reads and one for writes, recall Assumption 1), with additional combinational logic to determine whether the queue is full or empty using internal write and read pointers.

3. The signals `pending_i` and `request_i` (highlighted in green on the left hand side of Fig. 3) are the circuit's inputs: both signals are fed directly to the queue. The `pop_i` signal, however, comes from the `Read Logic` module, which is based on the register values and on the state of the queue itself, will produce a read enable signal. The queue produces three outputs: `empty_o`, used in the following

[4] In the listing, the notation >==> stands for circuit composition.

[5] Initial register values are omitted from the figure.

modules; `data_o`, the request at the head of the queue; and `ack_o`, a signal used to complete the handshake with the bus arbiter and possibly stall the arrival of incoming requests (recall Assumption 2).

4. Besides `ack_o`, the circuit produces two output signals: a) `request_o` is the request currently being serviced by the controller and is eventually fed to the DRAM address bus, it contains the target bank, row, and column; and b) `command_o`, generated by `CmdGen`. These output signals are similar to those produced by CoqDRAM algorithms (see Listing 3). They are generated by circuits `NextCR` and `CmdGen`, respectively, and take as input the register values, i.e., the current state, as well as the signals `empty_o` and `data_o` from `Queue`.

5. `Update` implements the transition function: it is made of three separate combinational functions that calculate the next value of each register and thus determine the next state.

4 The Equivalence Proof

We used the word *equivalence* between transition systems throughout the paper. Here, we define equivalence, which is de facto a *bisimilarity* relation. Bisimilarity was introduced (formulated by Park [16], refining ideas from Milner [14]) as the notion of behavioural equality for processes [17].

Definition 1 (Bisimulation and Bisimilarity [18]**).** Given an LTS $(S, \Lambda, \rightarrow)$, where S is a set of states, Λ is a set of labels, and $\rightarrow \subseteq (S \times \Lambda \times S)$ is a transition relation, written $P \xrightarrow{\mu} Q$ for $\langle P, \mu, Q \rangle \in \rightarrow$. A binary relation $\mathcal{R}$ on the states of the LTS is a bisimulation if whenever $P \mathcal{R} Q$:

1. for all P', with $P \xrightarrow{\mu} P'$, there is Q' such that $Q \rightarrow Q'$ and $P' \mathcal{R} Q'$;
2. the converse, on the transitions emanating from Q: for all Q', with $Q \rightarrow Q'$, there is P' such that $P \rightarrow P'$ and $P' \mathcal{R} Q'$;

Bisimilarity, written $\sim$, is the union of all bisimulations; thus $P \sim Q$ holds if there is a bisimulation $\mathcal{R}$ with $P \mathcal{R} Q$.

Remark [18]. Note that although bisimulation and bisimilarity are defined on a single LTS, it is also a valid definition for distinct LTS with the same alphabet of actions; as the union of two LTSs is again an LTS.

Intuitively, two bisimilar systems match each other's moves, i.e., if we assume that two agents were playing a game according to some rules, the agents could not be distinguished from the other by an observer.

In Coq, we start by giving meaning to the $\mathcal{R}$ binary relation of Definition 1. Listing 8 shows the definition of `State_Eq`, a predicate that defines the equality between CoqDRAM and CavaDRAM states for the FIFO controller. In the listing, `fs` is the state coming from CoqDRAM (defined as shown in Listing 6), and `cs` is the Cava FIFO state (of type `State_t`). The identifiers with prefix `cs_` come from `get_` functions applied to `cs` (as in Line 2). These functions retrieve individual signals/registers from `cs`, which contains every other internal signal.

```
1 Definition State_Eq (fs : FIFO_state_t) (cs : State_t) : bool :=
2 let cs_state := get_state cs in ... (* every cs_ variable comes from cs *)
3 match fs with
4 | IDLE cnt cref P ⇒ (cs_state =? STATE_IDLE_VEC) && (cs_cnt =? cnt2Bv
     cnt)
5   && (cs_cref =? cref2Bv cref) && (EqMem P cs_mem) && (EqQueue P wra
       rda)
6 | RUNNING cnt cref P r ⇒ ... (* similar *)
7 | REFRESHING cref P ⇒ ... (* similar *)
8 end.
```

Listing 8. Predicate for state equality.

Note the pattern matching on `fs` in Line 3. If, for instance, the `fs` state is an `IDLE` state, has a `Cnt_t` denoted by `cnt`, `Cref_t` denoted by `cref`, and `Reqs_t` denoted by `P`, then, the predicate should evaluate to `true` only if a series of conjunctions are satisfied: `cs_state` – the register carrying the information if the circuit is either `IDLE`, `RUNNING`, or `REFRESHING` – has to evaluate to `STATE_IDLE_VEC`, a literal representing the idle state; `cs_cnt` has to be numerically equivalent to `cnt`, `cs_cref` has to be numerically equivalent to `cref`, et cetera.

The predicates `EqMem` and `EqQueue` are recursive functions that establish a connection between both representations of the request queue. A simplified definition of `EqMem` is shown in Listing 9. The predicate states that each element in `CoqDRAM_Q` has a logical correspondence in `CavaDRAM_Q`. The correspondence is defined by the predicate `EqReq`, which takes as arguments a `CoqDRAM` request and a `CavaDRAM` request and outputs `true` if they are equal. Note that `x`, the element at the head of `CoqDRAM_Q`, maps to `nth rda CavaDRAM_Q`, the element of `CavaDRAM_Q` at index `rda`, the read address, where `nth` is a function used to access indexed list elements. The following element maps to index `rda` + 1, and so on. We omit the definition of `EqQueue` and `nth` for brevity.

```
Fixpoint EqMem_ {W} CoqDRAM_Q CavaDRAM_Q (rda : Bvector W) :=
 match CoqDRAM_Q with
 | [::] ⇒ true
 | x :: x0 ⇒ (EqReq x (nth rda CavaDRAM_Q)) && (EqMem_ x0 (rda + 1)
     CavaDRAM_Q)
 end.
```

Listing 9. Equality of memories/request queues.

Listing 10 shows the Coq version of Definition 1 applied to our problem. Consider an arbitrary Cava FIFO state (`c_state`) and an arbitrary CoqDRAM FIFO state (`f_state`) – obtained through `t` calls to `HW_Default_arbitrate`. The reason for having `t` – the number of clock cycles (i.e., the trace length) – explicit is to access the incoming request at time `t`, denoted by `R := Arrival_at t` and `c_req := request_i` for CoqDRAM and CavaDRAM respectively.

```
Theorem TS_Bisimulation : forall c_state (t : nat),
 let f_state := (HW_Default_arbitrate t).(Implementation_State) in
 let R := Arrival_at t in let c_req := request_i t in
 State_Eq f_state c_state →
 let f_nextstate := fst (Next_state R f_state) in
 exists c_nextstate,
   (c_nextstate = fst (step FIFOSM c_state (pending_i t,c_req))) ∧
   State_Eq f_nextstate c_nextstate.
Proof. ... (* Proof script not shown *) Qed.
```

Listing 10. The bisumulation theorem.

The rest of the theorem is equivalent to clause (1) of Definition 1, it reads: if whenever `State_Eq f_state c_state`, then, for all derivative states of `f_state`, denoted by `f_nextstate`, there exists a derivative state of `c_state`, denoted by `c_nextstate`, such that `State_Eq f_nextstate c_nextstate` holds. Note that the universal quantifier of Definition 1 is encoded into `f_nextstate` itself. Furthermore, `f_nextstate` and `c_nextstate` are respectively obtained through calls to `Next_state` – an implementation of `Next` (c.f. Listing 3) – and `step`, a Cava function that produces a new circuit state given the previous state and inputs. The converse theorem, corresponding to clause (2) of Definition 1, i.e., a challenge of `c_state` (with universally quantified transitions) against `f_state`, is also true (we omit the converse lemma for brevity). We recall that from Definition 1, proving that a bisimulation exists proves that the *two transition systems are bisimilar*.

The main strategy used to drive the proof is case analysis on CoqDRAM state definitions (such as the one in Listing 6). Moreover, the `step` function in Listing 10 is unfolded and applied to every sub-circuit in a composite circuit. As a consequence, the proof of `TS_Bisimulation` is structured with lemmas stating the equivalence of individual circuits, such as in Listing 11. It states that the `step` function applied to the `CmdGen` circuit with an input containing a `cref` value equal to `CNT_REF_PREA`, a literal containing the counter value that dictates when the controller should issue a PREA command,[6] will indeed output a `PREA`.

```
Lemma CmdGen_equiv_idle_to_ref (c : circuit_state CmdGen) cnt cref:
(cref =? CNT_REF_PREA) = true → (* when cref reaches CNT_REF_PREA *)
snd (step CmdGen c (STATE_IDLE_VEC,true,cnt,cref,REQUEST_NIL)) = PREA_VEC.
Proof. ... (* Proof script not shown *) Qed.
```

Listing 11. A lemma part of the proof tree: Equivalence of CmdGen.

We use Coq's `Ltac` language extensively in order to build automated proof procedures and thus facilitate the proofs for future implementations. The methodology for writing and proving different memory controller implementations is similar and/or follow a very specific pattern; hence, the implementation provided here, although simple, can be effectively used as a template.

[6] PREA commands are PRE commands sent to every bank at once.

Lastly, for the FIFO controller, the proof of Theorem `TS_Bisimulation` has a total of 3117 *lines of code*, and checking the proof takes an average of 22.54 min on a system with the following specifications: Intel(R) Core(TM) i5-10210U CPU @ 1.60 GHz, 8 GB RAM, and Ubuntu 22.04. The memory usage during proof checking peaks at 5.83 GB, measured with `time`. The high computational load required to check proofs about Cava circuits comes from design choices of Cava itself – Cava circuit states are large tuples that result in lengthy terms in the goals, therefore reducing the performance of reduction and rewriting tactics.

5 Simulation and Synthesis

With the goal validating our methodology in a "real world" setup, we start by (certifiably) extracting the CavaDRAM code to Haskell, using standard Coq extraction. Then, an additional Haskell script, part of the Cava tool-chain, analyses the circuit AST to generate a gate-level netlist in SystemVerilog. Next, as a host "hardware environment" for the generated code, we choose a DDR4 controller implementation for Transprecision Computing [20], which is publicly available[7] and will be referred to as *DDR4cntrl* for brevity.

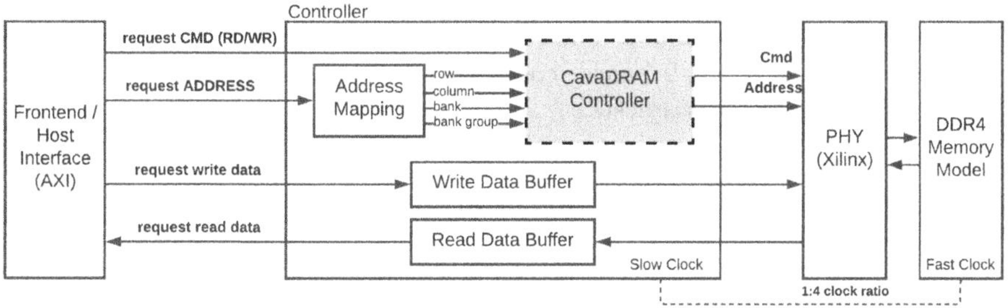

Fig. 4. An illustration of *DDR4cntrl* [20] with our modifications highlighted.

Figure 4 illustrates the *DDR4cntrl* architecture, with our modifications highlighted. In summary, we replace a module called `rank machine` with the CavaDRAM controller. Originally, `rank machine` was responsible for scheduling requests, generating and issuing DRAM commands, as well as managing REF commands; the same tasks performed by the CavaDRAM controller.

Every other functionality is kept unchanged: the AXI logic and its interface to the controller, the logic to control the read and write data buffers, the PHY, and the memory model. The PHY, a Xilinx IP in this case, generates the signal timing and sequencing required to interface to the memory device, e.g. phase

[7] https://github.com/oprecomp/DDR4_controller.

alignment between DQ and DQs signals, logic for initialising the DRAM after power-up, and conversion of slow clock to fast clock.[8]

Simulation. We validate the approach with the two testbenches provided in *DDR4cntrl*. The simulation is filled with SVA, which trigger if timing constraints are not respected, invalid commands are issued, or transactions do not complete. The simulation goes through with no assertions triggered.

We emphasise that achieving good performance is not the goal of this work, but rather present the methodology and provide a proof-of-concept. Considering that, although RTL code generated from Cava performs as well as standard SystemVerilog designs,[9] both simulation time and controller bandwidth worsen, for two straightforward reasons: 1) The CavaDRAM controller was not designed to exploit the ratio between the different clock domains of the system and the memory; therefore, it only operates at 1/4 of the available bandwidth in *DDR4cntrl*. 2) The FIFO algorithm does not offer competitive bandwidth compared to state-of-the-art memory controllers.

Synthesis. Using a testbench, which is part of the *DDR4cntrl* source code, we synthesise the FIFO CavaDRAM controller. A comparison of synthesis utilisation metrics between the original *DDR4cntrl* and the modified *CavaDRAM* version can be seen in Table 1. The results were obtained with a Xilinx Virtex UltraScale 095FFVB2104-2 board, considering a request queue in CavaDRAM that can store up to 256 requests.

Table 1. Key metrics from the synthesis report showing the resource utilisation on a Xilinx Virtex UltraScale 095FFVB2104-2.

		LUTs	Flip-Flops	bram_fifo_52x4
DDR4cntrl	`rank_machine`	8195	4644	16
	Full Design	9263	6129	16
CavaDRAM	`CavaDRAM`	5312	8605	0
	Full Design	6344	9832	0

[8] Inasmuch as the PHY runs at the system clock frequency (1/4 of the DRAM clock frequency), it expects four command/address per system clock and issues them serially on consecutive DRAM clock cycles on the DRAM bus. This means that the PHY interface provides four command slots: 0,1,2, and 3, which it accepts each system clock. To cope with the different clock domains, we insert CavaDRAM commands always in the first slot. The proofs in CoqDRAM do not lose validity, as lower-bounds still hold. The only proofs that need adapting are REF related proofs, as they are upper bounds on the spacing between REF commands. We write modified version of such constraints considering the different clock domains.

[9] https://silm-seminar.gitlabpages.inria.fr/season2/episode5/singh.pdf.

Unsurprisingly, the CavaDRAM version uses fewer LUTs, since the FIFO scheduling logic is simpler than what had been originally proposed in *DDR4cntrl*. The total number of Flip-Flops (FFs) in the design augments, since the Vivado synthesizer chooses to represent Cava queues with FFs rather than native FPGA FIFOs (accessible through the *bram_fifo_52x4* macro). Note also that *DDR4cntrl* took 88,46% and 75,77% of the total amount of LUTs and FFs in the design, respectively. For *CavaDRAM*, these percentages are 83,73% and 87,52%, respectively. These results show that the generated code introduces only a negligible imbalance w.r.t. resource utilisation, compared to the replaced module.

6 Related Work

DRAM and Formal Methods. The idea of applying formal methods to verify that DRAM controllers comply to the standards was first introduced by Datta et al. [7]. The authors perform a manual translation of the DDR2 standards into *SystemVerilog Assertions* (SVA). Kayed et al. [11] improves this idea by automatically deriving SVA from timing diagrams in the standards. More recently, Steiner et al. [19] go further by proposing automatic generation of SVA from *DRAMml* scripts, a DSL that models the functional and timing properties from JEDEC standards as *Petri nets*. While these approaches have incrementally succeeded at automatically capturing and formally verifying JEDEC properties, they cannot be used to verify broader aspects, such as latency bounds, controller semantics, and security properties.

Li et al. [12] use the Uppaal model checker [1] to analyse memory controller models described as *Timed Automata* (TA). However, in order to keep the state-space manageable, they assume that each requestor has at most one outstanding request, i.e., they constrain how requests arrive in the system. Moreover, there is a large abstraction gap from the standards to the TA models, as they are complex and written by hand [13]. Moreover, Hassan et al. [9] use Linear Temporal Logic (LTL) formulas to specify the correctness of DRAM controllers. However, the specification is not used to prove the actual implementation correct. Instead, counterexamples are obtained from models by bounded model checking, which are then used to build a test bench for the validation of the implementation. This latter approach can be seen as complimentary.

Hardware and Deductive Verification. The idea of describing circuits using functional programming languages was first introduced by Bjesse et al. in Lava [2], a DSL written in Haskell. The verification part of Lava, however, was limited, since logical formulas extracted from circuit definitions were exported to automatic theorem provers (ATPs), and therefore limited to decidable properties. Cava implements the key concepts of Lava in Coq, allowing its user to prove circuit properties directly from its definitions. Cava's most notable use case is an *Advanced Encryption Standard* (AES) implementation proven correct against the AES NIST standard [8].

Other DSLs for hardware design in Coq are Kami [6] and Kôika [4]. The former has been used to verify a RISC-V implementation against simple ISA semantics [3]. In short, the latter extends Kami by providing mechanisms to enhance per-cycle performance of designs. In this work, we use Cava – which, like the other DSLs, is built to describe circuits at a low level – to bridge the gap from a high-level framework (CoqDRAM, written in plain Coq) to actual synthesizable RTL. CoqDRAM captures correctness criteria directly from the standards in their most natural form and is mainly used to prove algorithms, using general Coq abstractions and ignoring HW limitations. Conversely, proving the properties captured by CoqDRAM directly from a Cava or Kami circuit definition would be certainly more difficult. In our approach, by doing a single equivalence proof, the properties ensured by CoqDRAM are inherited by the CavaDRAM HW implementations (under some assumptions modelling HW limitations).

7 Conclusion

We developed a framework for designing correct-by-design, standard-compliant DRAM controllers. The feasibility of the methodology is demonstrated by one proof-of-concept implementation. We use the generated RTL as a plug-in replacement in an existing hardware design – the simulation and synthesis results provide confidence in the correctness of the Coq models. In the future, we plan to implement state-of-the-art bus arbiters and memory controllers using this methodology. Another research path would be to develop a DSL tailored to the needs of DRAM controller algorithms (handling of queues and DRAM requests/commands) that allows an automatic translation to Cava, while maintaining the versatility of plain Coq used in the current version of CoqDRAM.

Acknowledgement. We acknowledge and are grateful for the contributions of Sumantha Chaudhuri, who provided help setting up the simulation environment; Chirag Sudarshan, who made himself available for discussing the implementation of *DDR4cntrl*; and Lirida Naviner for insightful discussions. This work is supported by the European Union's Horizon 2020 research and innovation program under grant agreement No. 101070627 (REWIRE).

References

1. Behrmann, G., et al.: Uppaal 4.0 (2006)
2. Bjesse, P., Claessen, K., Sheeran, M., Singh, S.: Lava: hardware design in Haskell. ACM SIGPLAN Notices **34**(1), 174–184 (1998)
3. Bourgeat, T., Clester, I., Erbsen, A., Gruetter, S., Wright, A., Chlipala, A.: A multipurpose formal RISC-V specification. arXiv preprint arXiv:2104.00762 (2021)
4. Bourgeat, T., Pit-Claudel, C., Chlipala, A.: The essence of Bluespec: a core language for rule-based hardware design. In: 41st ACM SIGPLAN Conference on Programming Language Design and Implementation, pp. 243–257 (2020)

5. Chlipala, A.: Certified Programming with Dependent Types: A Pragmatic Introduction to the Coq Proof Assistant. MIT Press, Cambridge (2022)
6. Choi, J., Vijayaraghavan, M., Sherman, B., Chlipala, A., et al.: Kami: a platform for high-level parametric hardware specification and its modular verification (2017)
7. Datta, A., Singhal, V.: Formal verification of a public-domain DDR2 controller design. In: 21st International Conference on VLSI Design, pp. 475–480. IEEE (2008)
8. Dworkin, M.J., et al.: Advanced encryption standard (AES) (2001)
9. Hassan, M., Patel, H.: MCXplore: automating the validation process of DRAM memory controller designs. IEEE Trans. Comput. Aided Des. Integr. Circuits Syst. **37**(5), 1050–1063 (2017)
10. Joint Electron Device Engineering Council: DDR4 SDRAM standard (2021)
11. Kayed, M.O., Abdelsalam, M., Guindi, R.: A novel approach for SVA generation of DDR memory protocols based on TDML. In: 2014 15th International Microprocessor Test and Verification Workshop, pp. 61–66. IEEE (2014)
12. Li, Y., Akesson, B., Lampka, K., Goossens, K.: Modeling and verification of dynamic command scheduling for real-time memory controllers. In: Real-Time and Embedded Technology and Applications Symposium (RTAS), pp. 1–12. IEEE (2016)
13. Lisboa Malaquias, F., Asavoae, M., Brandner, F.: A Coq framework for more trustworthy DRAM controllers. In: Proceedings of the 30th International Conference on Real-Time Networks and Systems, pp. 140–150. ACM (2022)
14. Milner, R. (ed.): A Calculus of Communicating Systems. LNCS, vol. 92. Springer, Heidelberg (1980). https://doi.org/10.1007/3-540-10235-3
15. Nikhil, R.: Bluespec system verilog: efficient, correct RTL from high level specifications. In: Proceedings 2nd ACM and IEEE International Conference on Formal Methods and Models for Co-Design, pp. 69–70. IEEE (2004)
16. Park, D.: A new equivalence notion for communicating systems. EATCS Bull. **14**, 78–80 (1981)
17. Pous, D., Sangiorgi, D.: Bisimulation and coinduction enhancements: a historical perspective. Form. Asp. Comput. **31**(6), 733–749 (2019)
18. Sangiorgi, D.: Introduction to Bisimulation and Coinduction. Cambridge University Press, Cambridge (2011)
19. Steiner, L., Sudarshan, C., Jung, M., Stoffel, D., Wehn, N.: A framework for formal verification of DRAM controllers. arXiv preprint arXiv:2209.14021 (2022)
20. Sudarshan, C., Lappas, J., Weis, C., Mathew, D.M., Jung, M., Wehn, N.: A lean, low power, low latency DRAM memory controller for transprecision computing. In: Pnevmatikatos, D.N., Pelcat, M., Jung, M. (eds.) SAMOS 2019. LNCS, vol. 11733, pp. 429–441. Springer, Cham (2019). https://doi.org/10.1007/978-3-030-27562-4_31

Formalising Liveness Properties in Event-B with the Reflexive EB4EB Framework

P. Rivière(✉), N. K. Singh(✉), Y. Aït-Ameur(✉), and G. Dupont(✉)

INPT-ENSEEIHT/IRIT, University of Toulouse, Toulouse, France
{peter.riviere,nsingh,yamine,guillaume.dupont}@enseeiht.fr

Abstract. The correct-by-construction state-based Event-B formal method lacks the ability to express liveness properties using temporal logic. To address this challenge, two approaches can be envisioned. First, embed Event-B models in another formal method supporting liveness properties verification. This method is cumbersome and error-prone, and the verification result is not guaranteed on the source model. Second, extend Event-B to support the expression of and reasoning on liveness properties, and more generally temporal properties. Following the second approach, in [20], J.-R. Abrial and T. S. Hoang proposed an axiomatisation of linear temporal logic (LTL) for Event-B with a set of proof obligations (POs) allowing to verify these properties. These POs are mathematically formalised, but are neither implemented nor generated automatically. In this paper, using the reflexive EB4EB framework [37,38] allowing for manipulation of the core concepts of Event-B, we propose to formalise and operationalise the automatic generation of proof obligations associated to liveness properties expressed in LTL. Furthermore, relying on trace-based semantics, we demonstrate the soundness of this formalisation, and provide a set of intermediate and generic theorems to increase the rate of proof automation for these properties. Finally, a case study is proposed to demonstrate the use of the defined operators for expressing and proving liveness properties.

Keywords: Proof and state-based methods · Event-B and Theories · Meta-theory · Reflexive EB4EB framework · Temporal logic · Liveness properties · Traces and soundness

1 Introduction

Event-B is a formal method based on explicit state expression, refinement and formal proof. It enables the design of complex systems using a correct by construction approach. This method has been used successfully for the design of many complex systems in various engineering areas such as aeronautics [42], railway systems [8,9], health and medicine [40], etc. In particular, it has shown its

The authors thank the ANR-19-CE25-0010 *EBRP:EventB-Rodin-Plus* project.

K. Y. Rozier and S. Chaudhuri (Eds.): NFM 2023, LNCS 13903, pp. 312–331, 2023.
https://doi.org/10.1007/978-3-031-33170-1_19

effectiveness in establishing properties related to system functionalities, safety, security, reachability, compliance with some temporal requirements, and so on.

Event-B models are machines that express state-transition systems using set theory and first-order logic (FOL). A mechanism of proof by induction enables the demonstration of inductive properties based on the preservation of properties at initialization and by each transition (event). Refinement, on the other hand, is defined by a weak simulation relation in which proof obligations guarantee the preservation of behaviours between levels of abstraction. The Rodin platform supports the development of Event-B models. It offers an environment for model editing, automatic and interactive proofs, animation, model checking, etc.

However, Event-B, like every formal methods, lacks some capabilities. It supports the verification of a fragment of temporal logic properties: $\Box$ using invariants and theorem clauses and $\Diamond$ using variants and convergence proof obligations. However, there is a lack of composition of temporal logic operators, as well as the ability to express and reason about liveness properties. To remedy this absence, two solutions are possible in general. The first solution consists in embedding an Event-B model in another formal method offering the possibility of expressing and reasoning about liveness properties such as TLA^+ [25], NuSMV [12], PRISM [23], PAT [43], Spin [22], Uppaal [3], ProB [27] etc. However, tracing the verification results on the source Event-B models is difficult and care must be taken to guarantee the correctness of this embedding. This approach is very popular and is followed by many authors who use other formal methods allowing to express and verify this type of property without worrying about the correctness of the transformation. However, there exist several approaches to ensuring the transformation's correctness [7,18,26,35]. The second solution consists in extending the Event-B method to allow the expression of and reasoning on liveness properties. This second approach requires the expression of the semantics and the proof system of the temporal logic in Event-B, as well as establishing the soundness of this extension.

Based on the second approach, JR. Abrial and TS. Hoang [20] proposed an axiomatisation of linear temporal logic (LTL) for Event-B in their article entitled *"Reasoning about liveness properties in Event-B"*. This work has defined a set of proof obligations allowing to establish temporal properties such as reachability, progress, persistence or until. However, these proof obligations are mathematically formalised in that paper but are neither implemented nor generated automatically. They must be explicitly described in Event-B by the developer for each model, thus leading to formalization errors. Moreover, their proofs are cumbersome and require too much manual effort to proving them.

Relying on the reflexive EB4EB framework [37–39] defined in Event-B, we propose to formalise and operationalise the automatic generation of proof obligations associated with liveness properties expressed in LTL temporal logic. We define an extension of EB4EB including a set of operators expressing these properties on traces. In addition, we demonstrate the soundness of these properties on model traces. Finally, a set of intermediate and generic theorems are also proposed to increase the rate of proof automation.

Table 1. Global structure of Event-B Contexts, Machines and Theories

Context	Machine	Theory
CONTEXT Ctx	**MACHINE** M	**THEORY** Th
SETS s	**SEES** Ctx	**IMPORT** Th1, ...
CONSTANTS c	**VARIABLES** x	**TYPE PARAMETERS** E, F, ...
AXIOMS A	**INVARIANTS** $I(x)$	**DATATYPES**
THEOREMS T_{ctx}	**THEOREMS** $T_{mch}(x)$	**Type1**(E, ...)
END	**VARIANT** $V(x)$	**constructors**
	EVENTS	**cstr1**(p_1: T_1, ...)
	EVENT evt	**OPERATORS**
	ANY α	**Op1** <nature> (p_1: T_1, ...)
	WHERE $G_i(x, \alpha)$	**well−definedness** $WD(p_1, ...)$
	THEN	**direct definition** D_1
	x :| $BAP(\alpha, x, x')$	**AXIOMATIC DEFINITIONS**
	END	**TYPES** A_1, ...
	...	**OPERATORS**
	END	**AOp2** <nature> (p_1: T_1, ...): T_r
		well−definedness $WD(p_1, ...)$
		AXIOMS A_1, ...
		THEOREMS T_1, ...
		PROOF RULES R_1, ...
		END
(a)	(b)	(c)

Note that our proposed approach is non-intrusive (self-contained) and does not require the use of any other formal techniques or tools; it is fully formalised in Event-B and mechanised on the Rodin platform.

This paper is organised as follows. Section 2 describes the Event-B modelling language and its Theory plugin extension. Section 3 recalls linear temporal logic, and the EB4EB framework is described in Sect. 4. Section 5 presents the trace-based semantics of Event-B, and its soundness properties. Section 6 describes a case study that will be used as a running example to show how to use defined LTL operators. Section 7 presents the temporal logic proof rules encoded as EB4EB proof obligations. Their correctness is discussed in Sect. 8. Section 9 summarises related work, and Sect. 10 concludes the paper.

2 Event-B

Event-B [1] is a state-based, *correct-by-construction* formal method, where systems are modelled with a set of events representing state changes, using first-order logic (FOL) and set theory.

Contexts and Machines (Tables 1.a and 1b). `Contexts` (Table 1.a) encompass the model's *static* part: *carrier sets* s and *constants* c, as well as their properties, through *axioms* A and *theorems* T_{ctx}. `Machines` (Table 1.b) describe the model's behaviour, using a set of *events* evt, each of which may be guarded G and/or parameterized by α. An event models the evolution of a set of variables x using a Before-After Predicate (BAP) that links the before (x) and after (x') value of the variables. Safety properties are encoded using *invariants* $I(x)$ and *theorems* $T_{mch}(x)$, and *variants* $V(x)$ may be defined to demonstrate the machine's convergence. Model consistency is established by discharging a number of automatically generated POs (Table 2).

Refinements. One strength of Event-B is its *refinement* operation, which is used to transform an abstract model into a more concrete one, adding infor-

Table 2. Relevant Proof Obligations for Event-B contexts and machines

(1) Ctx Theorems (ThmCtx)	$A(s,c) \Rightarrow T_{ctx}$ `(For contexts)`
(2) Mch Theorems (ThmMch)	$A(s,c) \wedge I(x) \Rightarrow T_{mch}(x)$ `(For machines)`
(3) Initialisation (Init)	$A(s,c) \wedge BAP(x') \Rightarrow I(x')$
(4) Invariant preservation (Inv)	$A(s,c) \wedge I(x) \wedge G(x,\alpha) \wedge BAP(x,\alpha,x') \Rightarrow I(x')$
(5) Event feasibility (Fis)	$A(s,c) \wedge I(x) \wedge G(x,\alpha) \Rightarrow \exists x' \cdot BAP(x,\alpha,x')$
(6) Variant progress (Var)	$A(s,c) \wedge I(x) \wedge G(x,\alpha) \wedge BAP(x,\alpha,x') \Rightarrow V(x') < V(x)$

mation (refined states) and behavioural (refined events) details gradually, while retaining a similar observational behaviour (simulation relationship). Refinement correctness is established with the help of a gluing invariant, and ensures properties are preserved from the abstract to the concrete model.

Extension with Theories. Being based on set theory and FOL, the Event-B formalism is mathematically low-level and thus very expressive. However, it lacks features to build up more complex structures. The theory extension has been proposed to address this issue [10]. A theory is a type of component that makes it possible to define new type-generic datatypes together with constructive and axiomatic operators, specific theorems and axioms and even proof rules (see Table 1.c). The resulting theories consistency can be established by providing witnesses for axioms and definitions, ensuring conservative extensions of Event-B. Once defined, elements of a theory become seamlessly available in an Event-B model and its proofs.

This extension is central for embedding, as data types, *concepts that are unavailable in core Event-B*, similar to Coq [4], Isabelle/HOL [32] or PVS [33]. Many theories have been defined, for supporting real numbers, lists, differential equations and so on.

Well-Definedness (WD). Beyond machine-related POs, one key aspect of model consistency is the *well-definedness* (WD) of the expressions involved in it. This notion supplements the one of syntactical correctness with the idea of a formula being "meaningful", i.e. it can always be safely evaluated (e.g., dividing by a term that is provably non 0). Each formula of a model is associated to a WD PO, usually consisting in checking that operators are correctly used and combined. Once proven, WDs are added to set of hypotheses of other POs.

Note that theories allow designers to provide custom WD conditions for partially defined operators in order to precisely characterise their proper use.

The Rodin Platform. Rodin is an open source integrated development platform for designing, editing and proving Event-B models. It also supports model checking and animation with ProB, as well as code generation. Being based on Eclipse, it also allows the definition of *plug-ins*, including theory extensions. Many provers for first-order logic as well as SMT solvers are plugged to Rodin for helping the proof process.

3 Linear Temporal Logic

This section recalls the principles of linear temporal logic (LTL) following the definition of Manna and Pnueli [28]. Linear temporal logic is defined syntactically as an extension of propositional logic. A valid LTL formula consists of literals (usually, predicates on the state of the system), the usual logical connectors ($\wedge$, $\vee$, $\neg$ and $\Rightarrow$) as well as *modal operators* $\Box$, $\Diamond$ and $\mathcal{U}$. The semantics of LTL is expressed in terms of *traces* of a system. Given a trace $tr = s_0 \mapsto s_1 \mapsto \ldots$, then tr_i ($i \in \mathbb{N}$) denotes the *suffix* trace of tr, starting from s_i, $tr_i = s_i \mapsto s_{i+1} \mapsto \ldots$

A state that satisfies a predicate P is called a P-state. LTL semantics are given with the following rules:

1. For any state predicate P, $tr \models P$ iff s_0 is a P-state.
2. $tr \models \phi_1 \wedge \phi_2$ iff $tr \models \phi_1$ and $tr \models \phi_2$
3. $tr \models \phi_1 \vee \phi_2$ iff $tr \models \phi_1$ or $tr \models \phi_2$
4. $tr \models \neg\phi$ iff not $tr \models \phi$
5. $tr \models \phi_1 \Rightarrow \phi_2$ iff not $tr \models \phi_1$ or $tr \models \phi_2$
6. $tr \models \Box\phi$ iff for all k, $tr_k \models \phi$
7. $tr \models \Diamond\phi$ iff there exists a i such that $tr_i \models \phi$
8. $tr \models \phi_1 \mathcal{U} \phi_2$ iff there exists a i such that $tr_i \models \phi_2$, and for all $j < i$, $tr_j \models \phi_1$

A machine M satisfies a property ϕ, denoted $M \models \phi$ if and only if for all traces tr of M, that trace satisfies ϕ ($tr \models \phi$).

4 The EB4EB Framework

The EB4EB framework [37,38] proposes to extend the reasoning capabilities of Event-B by enabling the access of Event-B components as first-class citizens within Event-B models (reflection), thereby making it possible to express new reasoning mechanism at the meta-level.

```
THEORY EvtBTheo
TYPE PARAMETERS St, Ev
DATATYPES Machine(St ,Ev)
 CONSTRUCTORS
    Cons_machine(
       Event : ℙ(Ev),
       State : ℙ(St),
       Init : Ev,Progress : ℙ(Ev)
       Variant : ℙ(St × ℤ),
       AP : ℙ(St),
       BAP : ℙ(Ev × (St × St)),
       Grd : ℙ(Ev × St),
       Inv : ℙ(St) ,
       ...)
```

Listing 1: Machine Data type

```
Event_WellCons <predicate>
      (m : Machine(St, Ev))
   direct definition
      partition(Event(m), {Init(m)}, Progress(m))
...
Machine_WellCons <predicate>
      (m : Machine(St, Ev))
   direct definition
      Event_WellCons(m) ∧ ...
```

Listing 2: Operators to check well-defined data type (static semantics)

Machine Structure. Event-B is formalised in an Event-B theory. A machine is represented using the data-type `Machine` (see Listing 1) parameterised by generic types with event labels (`Ev`) and states (`St`). Constructor `Cons_machine` gathers the components of a machine, such as `Event`, `State`, `Grd`, `Inv`, `BAP`, etc.

Well-Construction. A machine built using `Cons_machine` may not be consistent, despite being syntactically correct. Thus, additional operators are defined to encode the *well-construction* of a machine, i.e. the consistency of its components with regard to each others (Listing 2). For instance, `Event_WellCons` ensures that events are partitioned between initialisation and progress events.

Machine Proof Obligations. For any machine expressed in the framework, its associated proof obligations are provided under the form of operators (see Listing 3). Such operators are predicates that rely on the set-theoretical definition of the machine and guarded transition system semantics.

In particular, for a given machine m the predicate `Mch_INV`(m) holds if and only if the invariants of m hold with regard to m's behaviour, corresponding to PO INV (see Table 2). Following similar principles, every machine-related POs of the Event-B method is formalised in the theory.

```
Mch_INV_Init <predicate> (m : Machine(St, Ev))
  direct definition   AP(m) ⊆ Inv(m)
Mch_INV_One_Ev <predicate> (m : Machine(St, Ev), e : Ev)
  well-definedness e ∈ Progress(m)
  direct definition  BAP(m)[{e}][Inv(m) ∩ Grd(m)[{e}]] ⊆ Inv(m)
Mch_INV <predicate> (m : Machine(St, Ev))
  direct definition
      Mch_INV_Init(m) ∧ (∀e · e ∈ Progress(m) ⇒ Mch_INV_One_Ev(m, e))
...
```

Listing 3: Well-defined data type operators (behavioural semantics)

Finally, the PO operators are all gathered in a conjunctive expression within the `check_Machine_Consistency` operator (Listing 4), which thus encode the correctness condition for the machine. It uses `Machine_WellCons` as WD condition. At instantiation, it is used as a theorem to ensure machine correctness.

```
check_Machine_Consistency <predicate> (m : Machine(St, Ev))
  well-definedness Machine_WellCons(m)
  direct definition  Mch_INV(m) ∧ ...
```

Listing 4: Operator for Event-B machine consistency

Remark. The EB4EB framework makes accessible all the features of Event-B machines, and thus enables the formalisation and verification of the fragment of temporal logic properties already supported by classical Event-B machines: $\Box$ using invariants and theorem clauses and $\Diamond$ using variants and convergence proof obligations. However, it does not support the composition of these operators nor any of the other temporal logic properties.

Instantiation of the meta-theory is used to define specific Event-B machines (instantiation) using the `Cons_machine` constructor. An Event-B context where values for the type parameters `St` and `Ev` are provided.

5 Trace-Based Semantics of Event-B

Establishing the *correctness* of the POs provided in the EB4EB framework requires modelling of Event-B trace-based semantics. We express traces in an Event-B theory and relate them to an EB4EB machine. It becomes possible to prove that a PO defined in EB4EB encodes correctly the property it formalises.

5.1 Semantics: Traces of Event-B Machines in EB4EB

A machine m consists of state variables and events describing their evolution. A trace tr of m is a sequence of states $tr = s_0 \mapsto s_1 \mapsto \ldots \mapsto s_n \mapsto \ldots$ such that:

1. the initial state s_0 satisfies the after predicate (AP) of the initialisation event
2. each pair of consecutive states s_i, s_{i+1} corresponds to the activation of an event e of m, i.e.: 1) s_i verifies the guard, and 2) $s_i \mapsto s_{i+1}$ verifies the BAP
3. if tr is *finite*, its final state deadlocks (i.e., system cannot progress any more)

In EB4EB, traces are encoded in a theory (Listing 5) extending `EvtBTheo`. They are linked to machines. A trace is a partial function $tr \in \mathbb{N} \nrightarrow St$ such that, for any n in the domain, $tr(n) = s_n$ is the n-th state of the trace.

```
THEORY EvtBTraces IMPORT EvtBTheo
TYPE PARAMETERS St , Ev
OPERATORS
   IsANextState predicate (m : Machine(St, Ev) , s : St , sp : St)
      direct definition
            ∃e · e ∈ Progress(m) ∧ s ∈ Grd(m)[{e}] ∧ s ↦ sp ∈ BAP(m)[{e}]
   IsATrace predicate (m : Machine(St, Ev) , tr : ℙ(ℕ × St))
      direct definition
         (tr ∈ ℕ → St ∨ (∃n · n ∈ ℕ ∧ tr ∈ 0..n → St ∧ tr(n) ∉ Grd(m)[Progress(m)]))∧
         tr(0) ∈ AP(m)∧
         (∀i, j · i ∈ dom(tr) ∧ j ∈ dom(tr) ∧ j = i + 1 ⇒ IsANextState(m, tr(i), tr(j)))
   ...
END
```

Listing 5: Theory of Event-B Traces

The operator `IsATrace` captures the relation between machines and traces. A transition associated to an event in a trace is defined by the `IsANextState` operator. Considering a machine m and two states s and sp, the operator checks that there exists an event e such that: 1) s verifies the guard of e ($s \in Grd(m)[\{e\}]$), and 2) the pair $s \mapsto sp$ verifies the BAP of e ($s \mapsto sp \in BAP(m)[\{e\}]$).

5.2 Correctness Principle

Soundness properties can be expressed with the formalisation of the semantics using traces, in particular the correctness of the newly defined POs [38]. A generic principle can be stated as follows.

In Listing 6, each PO `[PO]` is associated with a `thm_of_Correctness_of_[PO]` soundness theorem in the `Theo4[PO]Correctness` theory. It states that the `[PO]` predicate definition (see Sect. 7) implies the PO predicate definition expressed on traces using the `PO_Spec_On_Traces` expression. Such theorems have been proved for each PO introduced in the EB4EB framework.

```
THEORY Theo4[PO]Correctness IMPORT EvtBTraces, Theo4[PO]
TYPE PARAMETERS St, Ev
THEOREMS
   thm_of_Correctness_of_[PO] :
        ∀m, tr · m ∈ Machine(St, Ev) ∧ Machine_WellCons(m)∧
     IsATrace(tr, m) ∧ ... ∧ [PO](m, args) ⇒ PO_Spec_On_Traces(...)
```

Listing 6: Liveness Analyses Correctness

Example: Soundness of the Invariant PO (INV). The theorem of Listing 7 states that for any well-constructed machine m, if the invariant PO holds ($Mch\_INV(m)$) then for any trace tr associated to this machine ($IsATrace(tr, m)$), each state of that trace is in the invariant of the machine ($tr(i) \in Inv(m)$).

It has been proved, by induction on the indexes of the traces, using the Rodin platform provers. This principle is applied for all the newly introduced POs, in particular for the temporal logic properties POs introduced in this paper.

```
THEORY EvtBCorrectness IMPORT EvtBTraces, EvtBPO
TYPE PARAMETERS St, Ev
THEOREMS
   thm_of_Correctness_of_Invariant_PO : ∀m, tr · m ∈ Machine(St, Ev)∧
     Machine_WellCons(m) ∧ IsATrace(tr, m) ∧ Mch_INV(m)
              ⇒ (∀i · i ∈ dom(tr) ⇒ tr(i) ∈ Inv(m))
END
```

Listing 7: Theorem of correction of the proof obligation

This approach follows the work presented in [2]. It has been used in particular for hybrid systems as well [13].

6 A Case Study: A Read Write Machine

In the original paper [20], the authors used the read-write case study to illustrate their approach. For comparison purposes, we use the same case study.

```
MACHINE RdWrMch
VARIABLES r, w
INVARIANTS
   inv1-2: r ∈ ℕ, w ∈ ℕ
   inv3-4: 0 ≤ w − r, w − r ≤ 3
EVENTS
   INITIALISATION
   THEN
      act1: r, w := 0, 0
   END

   read
   WHERE grd1: r < w
   THEN act1: r := r + 1
   END

   write
   WHERE grd1: w < r + 3
   THEN act1: w := w + 1
   END

END
```

(a)

```
CONTEXT RdWr
SETS Ev
CONSTANTS rdwr, init, read, write
AXIOMS
   axm1: partition(Ev, {init}, {read}, {write})
   axm2: rdwr ∈ Machine(ℤ × ℤ, Ev)
   axm3: Event(rdwr) = Ev
   axm5: State(rdwr) = ℤ × ℤ
   axm6: Init(rdwr) = init
   axm7: Inv(rdwr) = {r ↦ w | r ∈ ℕ ∧ w ∈ ℕ∧
                        0 ≤ w − r ∧ w − r ≤ 3}
   axm8: AP(rdwr) = {0 ↦ 0}
   axm9: BAP(rdwr) = {e ↦ (
                  (r ↦ w) ↦ (rp ↦ wp)) |
               (e = read ∧ rp = r + 1 ∧ wp = w)
             ∨(e = write ∧ rp = r ∧ wp = w + 1)}
   axm10: Grd(rdwr) = {e ↦ (r ↦ w) |
                  (e = read ∧ r < w)∨
                  (e = write ∧ w < r + 3)}
   axm11: Progress(rdwr) = {read, write}
   ...
   thm1: check_Machine_Consistency(rdwr)
END
```

(b)

Listing 8: Read write machine in Event-B (a) and instantiation with EB4EB (b)

The system requirements are: **Req1** – The reader process reads data from the buffer; **Req2** – The writer process writes data to the buffer; **Req3** – The reader and the writer share the same buffer; **Req4** – The shared buffer has a fixed size of 3; **Req5** – The system does not stop when data is written and not read; and **Req6** – The reader eventually reads L, $L \in \mathbb{N}$, pieces of data.

Listing 8.a proposes the `RdWrMch` Event-B machine fulfilling the above requirements. The reader (resp. writer) is modelled by variable r (resp. w) corresponding to its position in the buffer and by event *read* (resp. *write*) that represents the associated input/output operation and increments the pointer (**Req1** and **Req2**). The shared buffer is captured by interval $r + 1..w$ (**Req3**). The correct formalisation of the events, i.e. data that has not been written yet is not read and the amount of data in the buffer does not exceed 3 (**Req4**), is guaranteed by invariants *inv3-4*. Listing 8.b shows the context obtained when instantiating the `EvtBTheo` theory (Listing 1) of the EB4EB framework. The `thm1` theorem guarantees the consistency of the `RdWrMch` Event-B machine.

Missing Requirements. **Req5** and **Req6** are not *safety properties* in the usual sense and are not present in the current model. Event-B does not natively provide explicit constructs for handling them. Additional modelling effort is necessary, like introducing variants and new theorems and altering events.

7 Temporal Logic Proof Rules as EB4EB POs

To support temporal logic properties and handle the missing requirements, we propose an Event-B extension relying on the EB4EB framework. This section presents the formalisation of the liveness properties, introduced in [20], that are missing in core Event-B. For this purpose, we extend the EB4EB framework to introduce the corresponding PO definitions. All the definitions are formalised in the Theo4Liveness theory (see Listings 9) extending the EvtBTheo theory of EB4EB using a set of operators, defined for each proof rule defined in [20]. Each of these definitions is introduced below. Note that each of the following tables contain two parts, where (a) is from [20] and (b) our corresponding formalization.

```
THEORY Theo4Liveness
IMPORT EvtBTheo
TYPE PARAMETERS Ev ,St
...
```

Listing 9: Liveness operators Theory

Notations. For a predicate P on states of St, we define the subset $\hat{P}$ of states satisfying the property P as $\hat{P} = \{x \in St \mid P(x)\}$.

7.1 Liveness Properties

This section presents core definitions for expressing formal definition of liveness properties. We first describe the basic building operators.

Machine M Leads From P_1 to P_2, $P_1 \curvearrowright P_2$ (TLLeads_From_P1_To_P2 Operator). For a machine M, given two state formulas P_1 and P_2, we state that M leads from P_1 to P_2 if for every trace of M with two successor states such that $s_i \in \hat{P_1}$ then $s_{i+1} \in \hat{P_2}$. The given property of Table 3(a) is formally defined by the operator TLLeads_From_P1_To_P2 with a machine m and two set of states $\hat{P_1}$ and $\hat{P_2}$ as parameters. Its direct definition is a predicate $BAP(m)[\{e\}][\hat{P_1} \cap Grd(m)[\{e\}] \cap Inv(m)] \subseteq \hat{P_2}$ stating that for all progress events of machine m that preserve invariant, states of $\hat{P_1}$ lead to $\hat{P_2}$.

Table 3. Leads from P1 to P2 encoded in EB4EB

The Sequent Rule for $\curvearrowright$	Associated Operator in EB4EB
$P_1 \curvearrowright P_2 \equiv \forall v, v', x \cdot$ $P_1(v) \wedge G(x, v) \wedge A(x, v, v') \Rightarrow P_2(v')$	**TLLeads_From_P1_To_P2** <*predicate*> $(m : Machine(St, Ev),\ \hat{P_1} : \mathbb{P}(St), \hat{P_2} : \mathbb{P}(St))$ **direct definition** $\forall e \cdot e \in Progress(m) \Rightarrow$ $BAP(m)[\{e\}][\hat{P_1} \cap Grd(m)[\{e\}] \cap Inv(m)] \subseteq \hat{P_2}$
(a)	(b)

Machine M is Convergent in P, $\downarrow P$ (TLConvergent_In_P Operator). For a given property P, a machine M is convergent in P if it does not allow for an infinite sequence of P-states (i.e. states satisfying the property P). It is formalised in Table 4(a) by the predicate operator TLConvergent_In_P on machine m, set of states $\hat{P}$ and variant v. The operator's WD condition ensures that the variant

Table 4. Convergence in P encoded in EB4EB

The Sequent Rule of $\downarrow$	Associated Operator in EB4EB
$\downarrow P \equiv \forall x, v, v' \cdot$ $(P(v) \wedge G(x, v) \Rightarrow V(v) \in \mathbb{N}) \wedge$ $(P(v) \wedge G(x, v) \wedge A(x, v, v') \Rightarrow V(v') < V(v))$	**TLConvergent_In_P** *<predicate>* $(m : Machine(St, Ev),\ \hat{P} : \mathbb{P}(St), v : \mathbb{P}(St \times \mathbb{Z}))$ **well−definedness** $v \in St \rightarrow \mathbb{Z}$ **direct definition** $\forall e \cdot e \in Progress(m) \Rightarrow ($ $v[\hat{P} \cap Grd(m)[\{e\}] \cap Inv(m)] \subseteq \mathbb{N} \wedge$ $(\forall s, s' \cdot s \in Inv(m) \wedge s \in \hat{P} \wedge$ $s \in Grd(m)[\{e\}] \wedge s' \in BAP(m)[\{e\}][\{s\}]$ $\Rightarrow v(s') < v(s)))$
(a)	(b)

is associated to each state. The operator states that, for all progress events e, when its before-after-states s and s' satisfy P, variant v decreases ($v(s') < v(s)$).

Machine M is Divergent in P, $\nearrow P$ (`TLDivergent_In_P` Operator). Divergence property guarantees that any infinite trace of a machine M ends with an infinite sequence of P-states. The operator `TLDivergent_In_P` of Table 5(a) is identical to the previous convergent operator, except that the variant does not decrease *strictly* ($v(s') \leq v(s)$) allowing divergent sequences of P-states.

Table 5. Divergence in P encoded in EB4EB

The Sequent Rule of $\nearrow$	Associated Operator in EB4EB
$\nearrow P \equiv \forall x, v, v' \cdot$ $(\neg P(v) \wedge G(x, v) \Rightarrow V(v) \in \mathbb{N}) \wedge$ $(\neg P(v) \wedge G(x, v) \wedge A(x, v, v') \Rightarrow$ $V(v') < V(v)) \wedge$ $(P(v) \wedge G(x, v) \wedge A(x, v, v') \wedge V(v') \in \mathbb{N} \Rightarrow$ $V(v') \leq V(v))$	**TLDivergent_In_P** *<predicate>* $(m : Machine(St, Ev),\ \hat{P} : \mathbb{P}(St), v : \mathbb{P}(St \times \mathbb{Z}))$ **well−definedness** $v \in St \rightarrow \mathbb{Z}$ **direct definition** $TLConvergent\_In\_P(m, St \setminus \hat{P}, v) \wedge$ $\forall e \cdot e \in Progress(m) \Rightarrow ($ $(\forall s, s' \cdot s \in Inv(m) \wedge s \in \hat{P} \wedge s \in Grd(m)[\{e\}]$ $\wedge s' \in BAP(m)[\{e\}][\{s\}] \wedge v(s') \in \mathbb{N}$ $\Rightarrow v(s') \leq v(s)))$
(a)	(b)

Machine M is Deadlock-free in P, $\circlearrowleft P$ (`TLDeadlock_Free_In_P` Operator). The deadlock-freeness states that a trace of a machine M never reaches a P-state where no event is enabled. It requires that, in a P-state, at least one event of M is enabled. This property is defined in Table 6(a) and is formalised by the operator `TLDeadlock_Free_In_P` in Table 6(b).

The expression $\hat{P} \cap Inv(m) \subseteq Grd(m)[\ Progress(m)]$ ensures that at least one progress event of the $Progress(m)$ set is enabled in a P-state satisfying the invariant.

Table 6. Deadlock-freeness in P encoded in EB4EB

The Sequent Rule of $\circlearrowleft$	Associated Operator in EB4EB
$\circlearrowleft P \equiv \forall v \cdot P(v) \Rightarrow \bigvee_i (\exists x \cdot G_i(x, v))$	**TLDeadlock_Free_In_P** <*predicate*> $(m : Machine(St, Ev), \hat{P} : \mathbb{P}(St))$ **direct definition** $\hat{P} \cap Inv(m) \subseteq Grd(m)[Progress(m)]$
(a)	(b)

7.2 *Deadlock Freeness* $\circlearrowleft$ *P* applied to the Read-Write machine

We illustrate how the operators defined above work in the extended EB4EB framework on the read write case study, with the case of the deadlock-freeness property ensuring requirement **Req5**.

```
CONTEXT RdWrDeadlockFree
EXTENDS RdWr
THEOREMS
  thmDeadlockFreeInP:
    TLDeadlock_Free_In_P(rdwr ,
      {r ↦ w | w ∈ ℤ ∧ r ∈ ℤ ∧ r < w})
END
```

Listing 10: Generation of Proof Obligation of Deadlock_Free_In_ P

A context `RdWrDeadlockFree`, extending the context `RdWr` of Listing 8 is defined with a theorem, `thmDeadlockFreeInP`. This theorem uses the predicate operator `Deadlock-_Free_In_P`, previously formalised. Here, the $\hat{P}$ parameter is composed of the pair of state variables $r \mapsto w$ and the property P defined by $w \in \mathbb{Z} \land r \in \mathbb{Z} \land r < w$. Indeed, the machine does not deadlock if it reads less data than it writes. Remember that when a theorem is stated, a PO is automatically generated requiring to prove it.

7.3 Temporal Operator Proof Rules

Section 7.1 presents a formalisation of the basic temporal operators allowing to define liveness properties. This section is devoted to the formalisation of more complex temporal properties, relying on the operators previously defined, like `TLGlobally`, `TLExistence` `TLUntil`, `TLProgress`, and `TLPersistence`. Each of them is defined in the same manner as the previous ones.

Invariance, $\Box I$ (`TLGlobally` Operator). In Event-B, safety properties are commonly described as invariants. Although this property is already available in core Event-B, it can be formalised in EB4EB as well.

Table 7(a) expresses this property using two sequents. The first one is the inductive invariant proof rule and the second one defines, as theorems, all of the entailed stronger invariants. The `TLGlobally` operator of Table 7(b) defines this property as $Inv(m) \subseteq \hat{I}$; it reuses the native invariant PO of EB4EB.

Table 7. Invariance encoded in EB4EB

The Sequent Rule of $\Box$	Associated Operator in EB4EB
$\dfrac{\vdash\ init \Rightarrow I \qquad M\ \vdash\ I \curvearrowright I}{M\ \vdash\ \Box I}$ $\dfrac{\vdash\ J \Rightarrow I \qquad M\ \vdash\ \Box J}{M\ \vdash\ \Box I}$	**TLGlobally** <*predicate*> $(m : Machine(St, Ev),\ \hat{I} : \mathbb{P}(St))$ **direct definition** $Inv(m) \subseteq \hat{I}$
(a)	(b)

Existence, $\Box\Diamond P$ (`TLExistence` Operator). The existence temporal property states that a property P *always eventually* holds for machine M. To express existence $\Box\Diamond P$ in a machine M, we rely on convergence and deadlock-freeness. Indeed, the machine shall be convergent on $\neg P$-states, i.e., sometimes $\neg P$ does not hold and $\neg P$-states are not deadlocks. The defined `TLExistence` predicate operator is defined as the conjunction of the two corresponding previously defined operators on a set $\hat{P}$ and a variant v (Table 8).

Table 8. Existence encoded in EB4EB

The Sequent Rule of $\Box\Diamond$	Associated Operator in EB4EB
$\dfrac{M\ \vdash \downarrow \neg P \qquad M\ \vdash \circlearrowleft \neg P}{M\ \vdash\ \Box\Diamond P}$	**TLExistence** <*predicate*> $(m : Machine(St, Ev),\ \hat{P} : \mathbb{P}(St), v : \mathbb{P}(St \times \mathbb{Z})$ **well−definedness** $v \in St \rightarrow \mathbb{Z}$ **direct definition** $TLConvergent\_In\_P(m, St \setminus \hat{P}, v) \wedge$ $TLDeadlock\_Free\_In\_P(m, St \setminus \hat{P})$
(a)	(b)

Until, $\Box(P_1 \Rightarrow (P_1 \mathcal{U} P_2))$ (`TLUntil` Operator). The *Until* property states that a P_1-state is *always followed eventually* by a P_2-state. Its definition relies on the *leads-to* and *existence* properties we have introduced. The *Until* property requires two antecedents, a leads to from $P_1 \wedge \neg P_2$ to $P_1 \vee P_2$ in the next state and the second is the existence of $\neg P_1 \vee P_2$ (see Table 9(a)). This proof rule is directly formalises using the `TLUntil` operator (see Table 9(b)). It requires two properties P_1 ($\hat{P}_1$ set) and P_2 ($\hat{P}_2$ set) and a variant v. It is defined as the conjunction of the `TLLeads_From_P1_To_P2` and `TLExistence` predicate operators.

Table 9. Until encoded in EB4EB

The Sequent Rule of $\Box(P_1 \Rightarrow (P_1 \mathcal{U} P_2)$	Associated Operator in EB4EB
$A \equiv (P_1 \wedge \neg P_2) \curvearrowright (P_1 \vee P_2)$ $B \equiv \Box\Diamond(\neg P_1 \vee P_2)$ $\dfrac{M \vdash A \qquad M \vdash B}{M \vdash \Box(P_1 \Rightarrow (P_1 \mathcal{U} P_2))}$	**TLUntil**<*predicate*> $(m : Machine(St, Ev),$ $\hat{P_1} : \mathbb{P}(St), \hat{P_2} : \mathbb{P}(St),\ v : \mathbb{P}(St \times \mathbb{Z})$ **well−definedness** $v \in St \rightarrow \mathbb{Z}$ **direct definition** $Leads\_From\_P1\_To\_P2($ $m, \hat{P_1} \cap (St \setminus \hat{P_2}), \hat{P_1} \cup \hat{P_2})$ $\wedge\ TLExistence(m, (St \setminus \hat{P_1}) \cup \hat{P_2}, v)$
(a)	(b)

Progress, $\Box(P_1 \Rightarrow (\Diamond P_2))$ **(`TLProgress` Operator).** Close to the *Until* property, a more general property, namely *Progress* can be defined. It states that always P_1-states reaches $P2$-states. This property does not require P_1 to always hold before reaching P_2-states. To describe this property, an intermediate property P_3 holding before P_2 holds is introduced. It acts as a local invariant between P_1-states and P_2-states.

Table 10. Progress encoded in EB4EB

The Sequent Rule of $\Box(P_1 \Rightarrow \Diamond P_2)$	Associated Operator in EB4EB
$A \equiv \Box(P_1 \wedge \neg P_2 \Rightarrow P_3)$ $B \equiv \Box(P_3 \Rightarrow (P_3 \mathcal{U} P_2))$ $\dfrac{M \vdash A \qquad M \vdash B}{M \vdash \Box(P_1 \Rightarrow (\Diamond P_2))}$	**TLProgress**<*predicate*> $(m : Machine(St, Ev),$ $\hat{P_1} : \mathbb{P}(St), \hat{P_2} : \mathbb{P}(St), \hat{P_3} : \mathbb{P}(St), v : \mathbb{P}(St \times \mathbb{Z})$ **well−definedness** $v \in St \rightarrow \mathbb{Z}$ **direct definition** $TLGlobally(m, \hat{P_3} \cup \hat{P_2} \cup (St \setminus \hat{P_1})) \wedge$ $TLUntil(m, variant, \hat{P_3}, \hat{P_2})$
(a)	(b)

The *Progress* proof rule of Table 10(a) has two antecedents. One states that always $P_1 \wedge \neg P_2 \Rightarrow P_3$ and the second uses the previously defined *Until* property as $\Box(P_3 \Rightarrow (P_3 \mathcal{U} P_2))$. The `TLProgress` predicate operator is the conjunction of the application of the two predicate operators, `Leads_From_P1_To_P2` and `TLUntil` on the $\hat{P_1}$, $\hat{P_2}$ and $\hat{P_3}$ sets and the variant v, encoding the antecedents.

Persistence, $\Diamond\Box P$ **(`TLPersistence` Operator).** *Persistence* is the last property we formalise. It states that a predicate P must eventually hold forever ($\Diamond\Box P$). The two antecedents of the associated proof rule, presented in Table 11(a), state that P-states are divergent $\neg P$-states are deadlock-free. The `TLPersistence` predicate operator is defined as a conjunctive expression of `TLDivergent_In_P` and `TLDeadlock_Free_In_P` operators with the $\hat{P}$ for the property P and the variant v as input parameters.

Table 11. Persistence encoded in EB4EB

The Sequent Rule of $\Diamond\Box$	Associated Operator in EB4EB
$$\frac{M \vdash \nearrow P \qquad M \vdash \circlearrowleft \neg P}{M \vdash \Diamond\Box P}$$	**TLPersistence** <*predicate*> $(m : Machine(St, Ev), \hat{P} : \mathbb{P}(St), v : \mathbb{P}(St \times \mathbb{Z})$ **well−definedness** $v \in St \to \mathbb{Z}$ **direct definition** $TLDivergent\_In\_P(m, \hat{P}, variant) \wedge$ $TLDeadlock\_Free\_In\_P(m, St \setminus \hat{P})$
(a)	(b)

7.4 *Existence* $\Box\Diamond P$ applied to the read write machine

The temporal operators defined in [20] have been successfully formalised in the EB4EB as predicate operators used as theorems to be proved for any Event-B machine.

```
CONTEXT RdWrExistence
EXTENDS RdWrDeadlockFree
CONSTANTS L
AXIOMS
   axm1: L ∈ ℕ
   thmExistence: TLExistence(
        rdwr, {r ↦ w | w ∈ ℤ ∧ r ≥ L},
        {(r ↦ w) ↦ v |
             v = ((L − r) + (L + 3 − w))})
END
```

Listing 11: Generation of Proof Obligation of Existence

Here, we show how **Req6** (the reader eventually reads L, $L \in \mathbb{N}$, pieces of data) expressed for the read write case study is fulfilled thanks to the `TLExistence` operator. Like for deadlock freeness in Sect. 7.2, we introduce a new Event-B context `RdWrExistence` (see Listing 11), extending the `RdWr` context of Listing 8, with a theorem stating the existence property. The existence operator is used with a set of states $\{r \mapsto w \mid w \in \mathbb{Z} \wedge r \geq L\}$ and a variant $v = ((L - r) + (L + 3 - w))\})$.

8 Correctness of the Temporal Logic Properties Proof Rules

The last step establishes the correctness of our formalisation with respect to the semantics of trace, i.e. the defined proof rules actually hold on the traces of the Event-B machines. The verification principle of Sect. 5.2 is set up for this purpose.

```
THEORY Theo4LivenessCorrectness
  IMPORT Theo4Liveness , EvtBTraces
  TYPE PARAMETERS St, Ev
  ...
```

Listing 12: Theory of correctness

A theory `Theo4LivenessCorrectness` (Listing 12) provides a list of correctness theorems for each of the defined operators. It imports the previously developed theories related to liveness properties `Theo4Liveness` and Event-B traces `EvtBTraces`.

Below, we present the correctness theorem for the `TLExistence` property. All the other theorems are formalised[1] and proved using the Rodin Platform.

[1] https://www.irit.fr/~Peter.Riviere/models/.

Existence in Pcorrectness theorem $\Box\Diamond P$ (`TLExistence`). The correctness of the existence property follows the principle of Sect. 5.2. It is supported by the proved `thm_of_correctness_of_Existence` theorem stating that a property P always eventually holds in traces of a machine m. It states that for any well constructed ($Machine\_WellCons(m)$) and consistent ($check\_Machine\_Consistency(m)$) machine, and for any trace tr of this machine satisfying the existence property $TLExistence(m, \hat{P}, variant)$, then for all i there exists j with $j \geq i$ where $tr(j)$ satisfies the property P.

THEOREMS

$thm\_of\_Correctness\_of\_Existence:\ \forall m, tr, v, \hat{P} \cdot v \in STATE \rightarrow \mathbb{Z} \wedge$
$\quad m \in Machine(STATE, EVENT) \wedge Machine\_WellCons(m) \wedge$
$\quad check\_Machine\_Consistency(m) \wedge IsATrace(m, tr) \wedge TLExistence(m, \hat{P}, v)$
$\qquad \Rightarrow (\forall i \cdot i \in dom(tr) \Rightarrow (\exists j \cdot j \geq i \wedge j \in dom(tr) \wedge tr(j) \in \hat{P}))$
...

Listing 13: Theorem of correctness of the operators Existence

9 Related Work

Reflexive modelling is present under various forms in formal methods. For instance, the *ASM-Metamodel* API (AsmM) for Abstract State Machines (ASM) has been developed to be able to handle ASM-related concepts. This leads to several extensions, analyses and tools for ASMs [36]. This is also the case when using Mural to modify a VDM specification [5]. Furthermore, the reflexive modelling is also addressed with proof assistants like Coq with MetaCoq [41], Agda [34], PVS [31], HOL [15] and Lean [14] and Event-B with EB4EB [37,38].

Correctness of the Event-B method and its modelling components has been tackled in various previous work. A meta-level study of Event-B context structure is proposed in particular to validate the expected properties of theorem instantiation [6]. Event-B has also been formalised as an *institution* in category theory [16,17], with the aim to facilitate and enable composition of heterogeneous semantics and of different model specifications. Similarly, Event-B has been embedded in Coq [11] in order to establish the correctness of refinement, i.e. that the refinement POs entail the validity of refinement in the trace-based semantics. Last, a form of shallow embedding of Event-B in itself has been proposed and serves as the basis of a methodology for proving the correctness of decomposition and re-composition of Event-B machines [19].

Event-B's methodology is mainly aimed at defining and proving safety properties (that must always hold), or possible convergence. Expressing liveness properties (that must hold at some point [24]) is not as trivial, and many authors address this issue. For Event-B, the ProB model-checker [27] handles Event-B models and enables the expression and verification of liveness properties. Some liveness operators have been formalised to be used in Event-B, together with their related hypotheses [20], making it possible to express *some* liveness properties. However, it is to be noted that liveness properties are not generally preserved by refinement. To address this latter issue, additional conditions on the refinement must be posed, leading to the definition of particular refinement strategies [21], which are proven to preserve liveness properties through to the concrete model. In addition, the problem of *fairness* has also been studied. For instance, the work of [30] proposes to check fairness of Event-B machines in TLA (on a per-machine basis). Refinement strategies have been defined as well to ensure that fairness and liveness properties are preserved [44].

Our proposed approach is based on the reflexive modelling of Event-B on itself, which is fully integrated into Rodin development environment using the Theory Plugin [10]. Our framework is fully formalised in Event-B and relies solely on FOL and set theory, similar to other approach like MetaCoq [41] with dependent type. Such characteristic makes it possible to *export* models expressed using the framework to any other formalism based on FOL and set theory while preserving the state-transition semantics of the model. Therefore, the issue of the translation of the universe and the semantics' preservation are not related to our work due to the reflexive modelling.

10 Conclusion

This paper has presented a formalisation of liveness properties for Event-B models by encoding LTL temporal logic expressions on the Rodin platform using the reflexive EB4EB framework. LTL logic expressions of properties are formalised within the defined framework. Automatic generation of proof obligations related to the expressed properties and the soundness of the defined proof rules using a trace based semantics have been addressed as well. The proposed approach relies on the definition of algebraic theories offering the capability to define new operators. The read write machine case study was borrowed from [20] to illustrate our approach. Other case studies have been developed as well (Peterson algorithm [39] and behavioural analyses in human computer interaction [29]).

The proposed framework supports non-intrusive analysis for Event-B models, allowing liveness properties to be expressed and verified on any size Event-B formal model and at any refinement level without resorting to any other formal methods. Since our framework allows checking temporal properties at any refinement level, it avoids dealing with the preservation of temporal properties by refinement. Furthermore, the proof process has been enhanced with relevant and proven rewrite rules, which have been incorporated into Rodin tactics, resulting in a high level of proof automation. All the developments illustrated in this paper have been fully formalised and proved using the Rodin platform. They can be accessed on https://www.irit.fr/~Peter.Riviere/models/

This work leads to several perspectives. First, we plan to study the capability to allow compositional definitions of LTL properties relying on the defined basic operators. In addition, the proposed approach makes it possible to define other Event-B model analyses or domain specific theories shared by many Event-B models. Last, we believe that our approach can be scaled up to other state based methods provided that a reflexive meta-model is available.

References

1. Abrial, J.R.: Modeling in Event-B: System and Software Engineering. Cambridge University Press, Cambridge (2010)
2. Aït Ameur, Y. et al.: Empowering the Event-B method using external theories. In: ter Beek, M.H., Monahan, R. (eds.) Integrated Formal Methods. IFM 2022. LNCS, vol. 13274, pp. 18–35. Springer, Cham (2022). https://doi.org/10.1007/978-3-031-07727-2_2
3. Behrmann, G., David, A., Larsen, K.G.: A tutorial on UPPAAL . In: Bernardo, M., Corradini, F. (eds.) Formal Methods for the Design of Real-Time Systems. SFM-RT 2004. LNCS, vol. 3185. Springer, Berlin, Heidelberg (2004). https://doi.org/10.1007/978-3-540-30080-9_7
4. Bertot, Y., Castéran, P.: Interactive Theorem Proving and Program Development - Coq'Art: The Calculus of Inductive Constructions. Texts in Theoretical Computer Science. An EATCS Series. Springer Berlin, Heidelberg (2004). https://doi.org/10.1007/978-3-662-07964-5
5. Bicarregui, J.C., Ritchie, B.: Reasoning about VDM developments using the VDM support tool in mural. In: Prehn, S., Toetenel, W.J. (eds.) VDM 1991. LNCS, vol. 551, pp. 371–388. Springer, Heidelberg (1991). https://doi.org/10.1007/3-540-54834-3_23
6. Bodeveix, J.-P., Filali, M.: Event-B formalization of Event-B contexts. In: Raschke, A., Méry, D. (eds.) ABZ 2021. LNCS, vol. 12709, pp. 66–80. Springer, Cham (2021). https://doi.org/10.1007/978-3-030-77543-8_5
7. Bodeveix, J., Filali, M., Garnacho, M., Spadotti, R., Yang, Z.: Towards a verified transformation from AADL to the formal component-based language FIACRE. Elsevier SCP **106**, 30–53 (2015)
8. Butler, M., et al.: Formal modelling techniques for efficient development of railway control products. In: Fantechi, A., Lecomte, T., Romanovsky, A. (eds.) Reliability, Safety, and Security of Railway Systems. Modelling, Analysis, Verification, and Certification. RSSRail 2017. LNCS, vol. 10598, pp. 71–86. Springer, Cham (2017). https://doi.org/10.1007/978-3-319-68499-4_5
9. Butler, M., et al.: The first twenty-five years of industrial use of the B-Method. In: ter Beek, M.H., Ničković, D. (eds.) FMICS 2020. LNCS, vol. 12327, pp. 189–209. Springer, Cham (2020). https://doi.org/10.1007/978-3-030-58298-2_8
10. Butler, M., Maamria, I.: Practical theory extension in Event-B. In: Liu, Z., Woodcock, J., Zhu, H. (eds.) Theories of Programming and Formal Methods. LNCS, vol. 8051, pp. 67–81. Springer, Heidelberg (2013). https://doi.org/10.1007/978-3-642-39698-4_5
11. Castéran, P.: An explicit semantics for event-b refinements. In: Ait-Ameur, Y., Nakajima, S., Méry, D. (eds.) Implicit and Explicit Semantics Integration in Proof-Based Developments of Discrete Systems, pp. 155–173. Springer, Singapore (2021). https://doi.org/10.1007/978-981-15-5054-6_8

12. Cimatti, A., et al.: NuSMV 2: an opensource tool for symbolic model checking. In: Brinksma, E., Larsen, K.G. (eds.) CAV 2002. LNCS, vol. 2404, pp. 359–364. Springer, Heidelberg (2002). https://doi.org/10.1007/3-540-45657-0_29
13. Dupont, G., Aït Ameur, Y., Singh, N.K., Pantel, M.: Event-B hybridation: a proof and refinement-based framework for modelling hybrid systems. ACM TECS **20**(4), 35:1–35:37 (2021)
14. Ebner, G., Ullrich, S., Roesch, J., Avigad, J., de Moura, L.: A metaprogramming framework for formal verification. ACM PACMPL **1**(ICFP), 34:1–34:29 (2017)
15. Fallenstein, B., Kumar, R.: Proof-producing reflection for HOL. In: Urban, C., Zhang, X. (eds.) ITP 2015. LNCS, vol. 9236, pp. 170–186. Springer, Cham (2015). https://doi.org/10.1007/978-3-319-22102-1_11
16. Farrell, M., Monahan, R., Power, J.F.: An institution for Event-B. In: James, P., Roggenbach, M. (eds.) WADT 2016. LNCS, vol. 10644, pp. 104–119. Springer, Cham (2017). https://doi.org/10.1007/978-3-319-72044-9_8
17. Farrell, M., Monahan, R., Power, J.F.: Building specifications in the Event-B institution. Log.Methods Comput. Sci. **18**(4) (2022). https://doi.org/10.46298/lmcs-18(4:4)2022
18. Halchin, A., Ameur, Y.A., Singh, N.K., Ordioni, J., Feliachi, A.: Handling B models in the PERF integrated verification framework: formalised and certified embedding. Sci. Comput. Program. Elsevier **196**, 102477 (2020)
19. Hallerstede, S., Hoang, T.S.: Refinement of decomposed models by interface instantiation. Elsevier SCP **94**, 144–163 (2014)
20. Hoang, T.S., Abrial, J.-R.: Reasoning about liveness properties in Event-B. In: Qin, S., Qiu, Z. (eds.) ICFEM 2011. LNCS, vol. 6991, pp. 456–471. Springer, Heidelberg (2011). https://doi.org/10.1007/978-3-642-24559-6_31
21. Hoang, T.S., Schneider, S., Treharne, H., Williams, D.M.: Foundations for using linear temporal logic in Event-B refinement. Formal Aspects Comput. **28**(6), 909–935 (2016). https://doi.org/10.1007/s00165-016-0376-0
22. Holzmann, G.: Spin Model Checker, The: Primer and Reference Manual, first edn. Addison-Wesley Professional, Boston (2003)
23. Kwiatkowska, M., Norman, G., Parker, D.: PRISM 4.0: verification of probabilistic real-time systems. In: Gopalakrishnan, G., Qadeer, S. (eds.) CAV 2011. LNCS, vol. 6806, pp. 585–591. Springer, Heidelberg (2011). https://doi.org/10.1007/978-3-642-22110-1_47
24. Lamport, L.: Proving the correctness of multiprocess programs. IEEE TSE **3**(2), 125–143 (1977)
25. Lamport, L.: Specifying Systems: The TLA+ Language and Tools for Hardware and Software Engineers. Addison-Wesley Longman Publishing Co., Inc., Boston (2002)
26. Leroy, X., Blazy, S., Kästner, D., Schommer, B., Pister, M., Ferdinand, C.: CompCert - a formally verified optimizing compiler. In: Embedded Real Time Software and Systems (ERTS). SEE (2016)
27. Leuschel, M., Butler, M.J.: ProB: an automated analysis toolset for the B method. Springer Int. J. STTT **10**(2), 185–203 (2008)
28. Manna, Z., Pnueli, A.: Adequate proof principles for invariance and liveness properties of concurrent programs. Elsevier SCP **4**(3), 257–289 (1984)
29. Mendil, I., Riviere, P., Ameur, Y.A., Singh, N.K., Méry, D., Palanque, P.A.: Non-intrusive annotation-based domain-specific analysis to certify event-b models behaviours. In: 29th Asia-Pacific Software Engineering Conference, APSEC, pp. 129–138. IEEE (2022)

30. Méry, D., Poppleton, M.: Towards an integrated formal method for verification of liveness properties in distributed systems: with application to population protocols. SoSyM **16**(4), 1083–1115 (2017)
31. Mitra, S., Archer, M.: PVS strategies for proving abstraction properties of automata. In: International Workshop on Strategies in Automated Deduction. ENTCS, vol. 125, pp. 45–65. Elsevier (2004)
32. Nipkow, T., Wenzel, M., Paulson, L.C.: Isabelle/HOL - A Proof Assistant for Higher-Order Logic, LNCS, vol. 2283. Springer, Heidelberg (2002). https://doi.org/10.1007/3-540-45949-9
33. Owre, S., Rushby, J.M., Shankar, N.: PVS: a prototype verification system. In: Kapur, D. (ed.) CADE 1992. LNCS, vol. 607, pp. 748–752. Springer, Heidelberg (1992). https://doi.org/10.1007/3-540-55602-8_217
34. Paul van der Walt: Reflection in Agda. Master's thesis, University of Utrecht, Department of Computing Science (2012)
35. Pnueli, A., Siegel, M., Singerman, E.: Translation validation. In: Steffen, B. (ed.) TACAS 1998. LNCS, vol. 1384, pp. 151–166. Springer, Heidelberg (1998). https://doi.org/10.1007/BFb0054170
36. Riccobene, E., Scandurra, P.: Towards an interchange language for ASMs. In: Zimmermann, W., Thalheim, B. (eds.) ASM 2004. LNCS, vol. 3052, pp. 111–126. Springer, Heidelberg (2004). https://doi.org/10.1007/978-3-540-24773-9_9
37. Riviere, P., Singh, N.K., Aït Ameur, Y.: EB4EB: a framework for reflexive Event-B. In: International Conference on Engineering of Complex Computer Systems, ICECCS 2022, pp. 71–80. IEEE (2022)
38. Riviere, P., Singh, N.K., Aït Ameur, Y.: Reflexive Event-B: semantics and correctness the EB4EB framework. IEEE Transactions on Reliability, pp. 1–16 (2022)
39. Riviere, P., Singh, N.K., Aït Ameur, Y., Dupont, G.: Standalone Event-B models analysis relying on the EB4EB meta-theory. In: Glässer, U., Campos, J.C., Méry, D., Palanque, P. (eds.) International Conference on Rigorous State Based Methods, ABZ 2023. LNCS, vol. 14010. Springer, Cham (2023). https://doi.org/10.1007/978-3-031-33163-3_15
40. Singh, N.K.: Using Event-B for Critical Device Software Systems. Springer, London (2013). https://doi.org/10.1007/978-1-4471-5260-6
41. Sozeau, M., et al.: The MetaCoq project. Springer J. Autom. Reason. **64**(5), 947–999 (2020)
42. Su, W., Abrial, J.: Aircraft landing gear system: approaches with Event-B to the modeling of an industrial system. Springer Int. J. STTT **19**(2), 141–166 (2017)
43. Sun, J., Liu, Y., Dong, J.S., Pang, J.: PAT: towards flexible verification under fairness. In: Bouajjani, A., Maler, O. (eds.) CAV 2009. LNCS, vol. 5643, pp. 709–714. Springer, Heidelberg (2009). https://doi.org/10.1007/978-3-642-02658-4_59
44. Zhu, C., Butler, M., Cirstea, C., Hoang, T.S.: A fairness-based refinement strategy to transform liveness properties in Event-B models. Elsevier SCP **225**, 102907 (2023)

Formalized High Level Synthesis with Applications to Cryptographic Hardware

William Harrison[(✉)], Ian Blumenfeld, Eric Bond, Chris Hathhorn, Paul Li, May Torrence, and Jared Ziegler

Two Six Technologies, Inc., 901 N. Stuart Road, Arlington, VA 22203, USA
william.harrison@twosixtech.com

Abstract. Verification of hardware-based cryptographic accelerators connects a low-level RTL implementation to the abstract algorithm itself; generally, the more optimized for performance an accelerator is, the more challenging its verification. This paper introduces a verification methodology, *model validation*, that uses a formalized high-level synthesis language (FHLS) as an intermediary between algorithm specification and hardware implementation. The foundation of our approach to model validation is a mechanized denotational semantics for the ReWire HLS language. Model validation proves the faithfulness of FHLS models to the RTL implementation and we summarize a model validation case study for a suite of pipelined Barrett multipliers.

Keywords: Programming languages and models · Verifying cryptographic systems · Automated theorem proving

1 Introduction

This paper presents the mechanized semantics for the functional high-level synthesis (HLS) language ReWire [48,53], where ReWire is an embedded DSL in Haskell for expressing synchronous hardware designs. This semantics is the cornerstone of a hardware verification methodology called *model validation* that we also introduce with the verification case study of a family of cryptographic accelerators for fully homomorphic encryption. With model validation, ReWire plays a dual role as a language for both formal modeling and implementation.

Model validation (Fig. 1) establishes that a Verilog design produces the same results as a verified correct ReWire model. The first path (model; embed; verify) creates a ReWire model, embeds it in

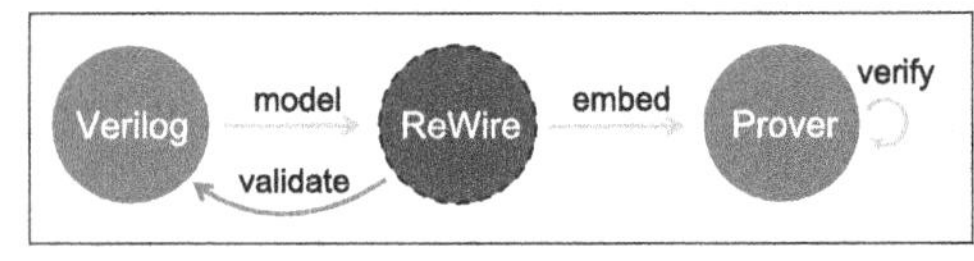

Fig. 1. Model Validation Methodology.

This research was developed with funding from the Defense Advanced Research Projects Agency (DARPA). The views, opinions and/or findings expressed are those of the author and should not be interpreted as representing the official views or policies of the Department of Defense or the U.S. Government.

K. Y. Rozier and S. Chaudhuri (Eds.): NFM 2023, LNCS 13903, pp. 332–352, 2023.
https://doi.org/10.1007/978-3-031-33170-1_20

a theorem prover via ReWire's formalized semantics, and verifies its functional correctness. The second path (model ; validate) validates the fidelity of the ReWire model to the Verilog design by establishing functional equivalence using the model-checking capabilities in YoSys [59].

Synchronous circuitry never terminates and, consequently, neither do ReWire programs. ReWire syntax and semantics are structured by reactive resumption monads over state (RRS), where computations in RRS monads [18,34,43,45, 57] resemble potentially infinite sequences of stateful actions. Non-terminating computation can be challenging to mechanize with a theorem prover and, for the ReWire semantics, this challenge is overcome by an alternative representation of RRS monads using infinite streams. This stream-based RRS representation allows an embedding of ReWire directly into any prover with a stream library—we provide example embeddings of the semantics in Isabelle, Coq, and Agda [12]. The semantics resembles a Reynolds-style definitional interpreter [52], although our semantics targets theorem prover object languages rather than a general-purpose functional programming language as Reynolds' classic paper did. The shallow embedding uses effect labels [41] to distinguish between the termination behavior of ReWire terms and to selectively pick the appropriate denotations.

This focus of this paper is primarily on the embed arrow in Fig. 1 and we leave a broader discussion of model validation and its uses for follow-on publications. The remainder of this section introduces background on ReWire. Section 2 presents the formalization of ReWire as a typed λ-calculus and the embedding of this semantics in three theorem proving systems: Isabelle, Coq, and Agda. It is with the Isabelle embedding that we perform the formal verification of the family of pipelined Barrett multipliers in Sect. 3. Section 3 describes the BMM case study at a high-level due to lack of space. Section 4 reviews related work and Sect. 5 summarizes our results and outlines future directions for this research.

ReWire is a domain-specific language (DSL) embedded in Haskell for expressing, implementing, and verifying hardware designs. All ReWire programs are Haskell programs (but not necessarily vice versa). We assume of necessity that the reader is familiar with functional languages and especially with the use of monads to model effects in functional programming (see Appendix A for an overview). We first illustrate ReWire syntax and semantics in terms of two simple examples: Mealy machines and carry-save adders.

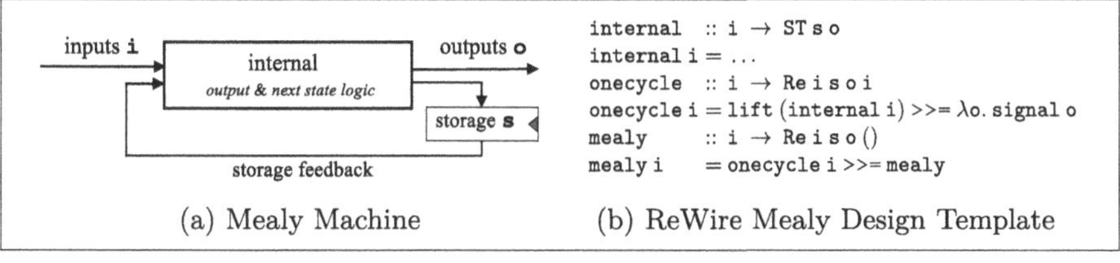

(a) Mealy Machine (b) ReWire Mealy Design Template

Fig. 2. Mealy Machines (a); Corresponding Mealy Template in ReWire (b).

Mealy machines (Fig. 2a) are a common mental model for designers of sequential circuitry [26,35]. Given current values of the input (`i`), internal storage (`s`), and output (`o`), the internal combinational logic of the Mealy machine computes the storage and output values for the next clock cycle. Figure 2b presents a ReWire template encoding the Mealy machine. The type constructors, `Re i s o` and `ST s`, refer, respectively, to a reactive resumption monad over state and to the state monad. The type variables `i`, `s`, and `o` in `Re i s o` correspond directly to the Mealy machine's input, storage, and output types. Monads like `Re i s o` and `ST s` possess their respective monadic unit (`return`) and bind (`>>=`) operators (that are typically overloaded in both Haskell and ReWire). Operations in `ST s` read and write storage typed in `s`. The `Re` operation `lift` injects a stateful computation into `Re` and `signal` performs synchronous input-output.

It is possible to describe what `mealy` does intuitively before presenting any formal semantics (although readers experienced with monadic semantics may find Fig. 4 useful at this point). Calls to `onecycle` describe exactly one clock cycle of circuit execution, while calls to `mealy` describe an entire circuit computation itself. The internal action of a cycle, `lift (internal i)`, in combination with the current internal storage (of type `s`), updates that storage, and computes the next output `o`. The `signal` operator sends its argument to the output ports and, then, returns the next input. Producing a signal, (`signal o`), sends the computed output to the output port, and signifies the completion of a clock cycle; `mealy` then continues, ad infinitum. `ST` (resp., `Re`) operations will ultimately be compiled into combinational (resp., sequential) circuitry by the ReWire compiler.

```
f :: W8 → W8 → W8 → (W8, W8)
f a b c = (((a & b) | (a & c) | (b & c)) << 1 , a ⊕ b ⊕ c)
data Ans a = DC | Val a   — resp., "don't care" and "valid"

csa :: (W8, W8, W8) → Re (W8, W8, W8) () (W8, W8)
csa (a, b, c) = signal (f a b c) >>= csa

scsa :: (W8, W8, W8) → Re (W8, W8, W8) (W8, W8) (W8, W8) ()
scsa abc = save abc >>= λcs. signal cs >>= scsa
  where
    thread :: (W8, W8) → ST (W8, W8) (W8, W8)
    thread cs = set cs >> get
    save :: (W8 , W8 , W8) → Re (W8 , W8 , W8) (W8, W8) (W8, W8) (W8, W8)
    save (a , b , c) = lift (thread (f a b c))

pcsa :: W8 → Re W8 () (Ans (W8, W8)) ()
pcsa a = signal DC >>= λb. signal DC >>= λc. signal (Val cs) >>= pcsa
                 where cs = f a b c

bad  :: i → Re i i o ()   — Haskell, not ReWire; not signal-productive
bad i = lift (set i) >>= bad
```

Fig. 3. ReWire source code for Carry-Save Adder Functions. The operators &, |, and ⊕ are bitwise and, inclusive or, and exclusive or. Operator `<<` is shift-left.

A carry-save adder (CSA) is a function which takes in three n-bit words a, b, and c, and computes two n-bit words s and c′, such that $\mathtt{a} + \mathtt{b} + \mathtt{c} = \mathtt{s} + \mathtt{c}'$. Figure 3 presents three ReWire functions for CSA circuits for $n = 8$. The function f defines the carry-save operation, so that, for example, f 40 25 20 $=$ $(48, 37)$, representing W8 words as integers for readability. The answer Ans data type indicates whether an output is valid. Function csa accepts inputs a, b, and c on each clock cycle, computes their carry-save sum, and sends that sum to the outport port before starting again. The behavior of scsa is the same as csa, but scsa also stores the result in a local store of type (W8, W8)—this difference is reflected in the types of csa and scsa in Fig. 3. Function pcsa is pipelined, accepting inputs on successive clock cycles and computing the carry-save sum when the third input, c, is available. While it waits, DC is signaled, and, once all three arguments are available, Val of the carry-save sum is signaled.

The bad function in Fig. 3 is not valid ReWire because it is not *signal-productive*—i.e., there is no output-producing call to signal. Signal-productivity means that ReWire programs regularly produce outputs analogously to how synchronous circuits (e.g., mealy in Fig. 2a) produce outputs on every clock signal. Signal-productivity is enforced by the type system below in Sect. 2 (e.g., so that bad does not type check).

The ReWire compiler can translate functions like mealy, csa, scsa, and pcsa into synthesizable VHDL or Verilog (as shorthand, we call such functions *devices*). But not every Haskell function with codomain Re i s o a is a device—there are three main provisos arising from the nature of synchronous hardware—and none of these provisos is enforced by the Haskell type system. The first proviso limits recursion in devices to tail recursion, because tail recursion only requires a fixed memory footprint. Arbitrary recursive Haskell functions may require a stack and heap and such dynamic allocation is anathema to hardware. The second proviso requires that devices never terminate—i.e., just like a synchronous circuit, they should (in principle) never terminate on any inputs. The third proviso is that they be signal-productive—the Haskell function bad in Fig. 3 is not signal-productive and, hence, is not a ReWire device. The effect type system described in Sect. 2 enforces each these requirements so that $\mathtt{Re}^{\infty}$ ($\mathtt{Re}^{+}$) is the type for devices (resp., signal-productive, terminating terms).

A conventional formulation of Re appears in Fig. 4. In ReWire, Re is constructed using Haskell monad transformers, but rather than introducing that notational overhead here, we define Re directly in Fig. 4. The functor part of Re is written in a categorical style followed by the definitions of its unit (return) and bind (>>=). Additional structure includes lift (which lifts a stateful computation into Re) and signal (which sends o to the "output port"). We include these definitions for reference and to make the article self-contained.

2 Formalizing ReWire

The ReWire formalization is a conventionally structured denotational semantics of the form, $[\![-]\!] : (\Gamma \vdash \mathtt{t}) \rightarrow \mathtt{Env}\Gamma \rightarrow \ulcorner \mathtt{t} \urcorner$, mapping a well-typed term and suitable environment into a domain of values. We first present the term and type

```
Re i s o a = μX. ST s (a + (o × (i → X)))      lift     :: ST s a → Re i s o a
return    :: a → Re i s o a                     lift f   = λ s. let
return a  = λ s. (inj₁ a , s)                                 (a , s′) = f s
(>>=) :: Re i s o a          →                              in
         (a → Re i s o b) →                                 (inj₁ a , s′)
         Re i s o b                              signal   :: o → Re i s o i
(x >>= f) s₀ = case (x s₀) of                    signal o = λ s. (inj₂ (o , return) , s)
  (inj₁ a, s₁)      → f a s₁                     ST s a   = s → (a × s)
  (inj₂(o, κ), s₁) →                             get :: ST s s      set :: s → ST s ()
      (inj₂(o, λi. κ i >>= f) , s₁)              get = λs.(s, s)    set s′ = λs.((), s′)
```

Fig. 4. *Reactive Resumption Monads over State.* Re is a synchronous concurrency monad allowing expression of both terminating and non-terminating threads; it constitutes a core part of ReWire's syntax and semantics. The codebase includes a Haskell rendering of this semantics [12].

syntax of the formalized ReWire effect calculus and then the mechanization of RRS monads. RRS monads originated in the denotational semantics of concurrent and parallel languages [18,34,43,45,57]; much of the challenge of formalizing ReWire originates in representing them in a theorem prover.

We use the term *denotational* advisedly for our semantics, because the term may evoke expectations in some readers of some explicit form of CPO semantics. The ReWire semantics takes the form of, to borrow a term from Reynolds [52], a *definitional interpreter*—i.e., an embedding of a source language into a conventional functional programming language. Here, however, the embedding maps a typed syntax for ReWire into the object language of a theorem prover (specifically Isabelle, Agda, and Coq). The domain semantics displayed in Fig. 6a is based on infinite streams of snapshots and this enabled the straightforward definitional embedding of ReWire into Isabelle, Coq, and Agda, because each of these provers possesses a stream library. This obviated the need for a deep embedding of the denotational semantics in the manner of, for example, Huffman et al. [24,25] or Schröder [54]. We present the Agda formalization because Agda's syntax is simpler to read than either that of Coq or Isabelle [12], and within that code, several syntactic simplifications have been made to improve readability (e.g., removing certain quantifiers or implicitly-passed variables, etc.).

ReWire is a computational λ-calculus (in the sense of Moggi [37]) with monadic constructs corresponding to the Re and ST monads from Fig. 4. The type language in Fig. 5a includes effect labels indicating the termination and productivity behavior of expressible programs. The intrinsically-typed term syntax encodes typing rules in the constructors. The type language contains base types specific to hardware: bit and the standard logic vector type constructor (slv) that takes a natural number representing bit vector size. We elide operations on low-level data types in Fig. 5a because they are not remarkable.

The syntax is parameterized by productivity labels, 0, +, and ∞, which are ordered linearly so that $\mathtt{p} \sqcup \mathtt{q}$ returns the maximum of labels p and q. Terms

```
data Ty : Set where
  nat   : Ty
  bool  : Ty
  unit  : Ty
  bit   : Ty
  slv   : ℕ → Ty
  _⇒_   : Ty → Ty → Ty
  _⊗_   : Ty → Ty → Ty
  _⊕_   : Ty → Ty → Ty
  ST    : Ty → Ty → Ty
  Re⁰   : Ty → Ty →
          Ty → Ty → Ty
  Re⁺   : Ty → Ty →
          Ty → Ty → Ty
  Re∞   : Ty → Ty →
          Ty → Ty

Effects
  p, q ∈ {0 , + , ∞}
  0 ⊔ 0 = 0     + ⊔ + = +
  0 ⊔ + = +     + ⊔ 0 = +
```

```
data _⊢_ : Cxt Ty → Ty → Set where
  var       : a ∈ Γ → Γ ⊢ a
  lam       : a :: Γ ⊢ b → Γ ⊢ (a ⇒ b)
  app       : Γ ⊢ a ⇒ b → Γ ⊢ a → Γ ⊢ b
                  ... elided ...
  return^ST : Γ ⊢ a ⇒ ST s a
  _>>=^ST_  : Γ ⊢ ST s a →
                Γ ⊢ a ⇒ ST s b →
                Γ ⊢ ST s b
  get       : Γ ⊢ ST s s
  set       : Γ ⊢ s ⇒ ST s unit
  lift^r    : Γ ⊢ ST s a ⇒ Re⁰ i s o a
  _>>=^pq_  : Γ ⊢ Re^p i s o a ⇒
                (a ⇒ Re^q i s o b) ⇒
                Re^(p⊔q) i s o b
  return^r  : Γ ⊢ a ⇒ Re⁰ i s o a
  signal^r  : Γ ⊢ o ⇒ Re⁺ i s o i
  loop      : Γ ⊢ (a ⇒ Re⁺ i s o a) ⇒
                (a ⇒ Re∞ i s o)
```

(a) Type and Effect Syntax (left) and intrinsically-typed term syntax (right).

```
⌜_⌝             : Ty → Set
⌜nat⌝           = ℕ
⌜bool⌝          = Bool
⌜unit⌝          = ⊤
⌜bit⌝           = Bool
⌜slv n⌝         = Vec Bool n
⌜t₁ ⇒ t₂⌝       = ⌜t₁⌝ → ⌜t₂⌝
⌜t₁ ⊗ t₂⌝       = ⌜t₁⌝ × ⌜t₂⌝
⌜t₁ ⊕ t₂⌝       = ⌜t₁⌝ ⊎ ⌜t₂⌝
⌜ST s a⌝        = State ⌜s⌝ ⌜a⌝
⌜Re⁰ i s o a⌝ =
  DomRe⁰ ⌜i⌝ ⌜s⌝ ⌜o⌝ ⌜a⌝
⌜Re⁺ i s o a⌝ =
  DomRe⁺ ⌜i⌝ ⌜s⌝ ⌜o⌝ ⌜a⌝
⌜Re∞ i s o⌝ =
  DomRe∞ ⌜i⌝ ⌜s⌝ ⌜o⌝
```

```
⟦ - ⟧               : (Γ ⊢ t) → Env Γ → ⌜t⌝
⟦ var x ⟧ ρ         = lookup∈ ρ x
⟦ lam f ⟧ ρ         = λv. ⟦ f ⟧ (v ◁ ρ)
⟦ app f e ⟧ ρ       = (⟦ f ⟧ ρ) (⟦ e ⟧ ρ)
        ⋮
⟦ return^ST ⟧ ρ     = λv. SM(λs. (v , s))
⟦ e >>=^ST f ⟧ ρ    = (⟦ e ⟧ ρ) <>=^00 (⟦ f ⟧ ρ)
⟦ get ⟧ ρ           = SM (λs. (s , s))
⟦ set ⟧ ρ           = λs. SM (λ_. (() , s))
⟦ lift^r ⟧ ρ        = λφ. φ
⟦ return^r ⟧ ρ      = λv. SM(λs. (v , s))
⟦ e >>=^pq f ⟧ ρ    = (⟦ e ⟧ ρ) <>=^pq (⟦ f ⟧ ρ)
⟦ signal ⟧ ρ        = λo. λ(_ , s , _). λis.
                        let
                          i   = shd is
                          is′ = stl is
                        in
                          (i , s , o) ▷ [(i , is′)]
⟦ loop f ⟧ ρ        = iterRe (⟦ f ⟧ ρ)
```

(b) Denotational Semantics for the ReWire Calculus

Fig. 5. ReWire as an Effect Calculus.

of 0-productivity are created with $\texttt{lift}^{\texttt{r}}$ and $\texttt{return}^{\texttt{r}}$ or binds of 0-productive computations. Such computations correspond to computations by combinational circuitry between clock cycles. Terms of +-productivity are created with `signal` or binds, `x >>= f`, in which at least one of `x` or `f` is a +-productive computations. Computations typed in $\texttt{Re}^{+}$ correspond to signal-productive, terminating computations spanning at least one clock cycle. One could define $\texttt{>>=}^{pq}$ for cases in which p and/or q is ∞, but we have not done so here. In Haskell, for example, `x>>=f` is identical to `x` when `x` is non-terminating; such terms are not of use in expressing hardware designs in ReWire. Terms of ∞-productivity—i.e., what we previously called devices—may be only created with the recursion-binder `loop`. To represent the `mealy` program from Fig. 2b in the ReWire Calculus, one would refactor its definition with `loop` so that $\texttt{mealy} : \texttt{i} \rightarrow \texttt{Re}^{\infty}\texttt{i s o}$ and $\texttt{mealy} = \texttt{loop onecycle}$. Refactoring with a recursion operator is a common syntactic change of representation in denotational semantics.

Figure 5b defines the denotational semantics of the ReWire calculus. It is worth remarking on its structure and organization now, but detailed discussion is deferred until the end of this section. The domain semantics ($\ulcorner - \urcorner$) maps each type `Ty` into a corresponding Agda `Set`. For the RRS monadic type constructors, there are corresponding constructions indexed by effect labels and these are defined in the next section. Most of the cases in the semantics of terms ($[\![-]\!]$) are similarly not remarkable except in the monadic cases. Corresponding to syntactic binds (i.e., $\texttt{>>=}^{pq}$) are semantic binds (i.e., $\texttt{<>=}^{pq}$) and corresponding to recursive syntactic operator (`loop`) is the semantic recursive operator (`iterRe`).

Reynolds et al. [53] formulated a small-step, operational semantics for ReWire in Coq. A deep embedding formalizing ReWire's denotational semantics [47] in terms of mechanized domain theory (e.g., Huffman [24,25], Benton et al. [5], or Schröder [54]) is possible as well. However, both the deep embedding and the small-step operational approaches seemed too unwieldy at the scale of our case studies. Recent work [22] introduced the Device Calculus, a λ-calculus with types and operations for constructing Mealy machines and our semantics extends the Device Calculus semantics to RRS monads.

Figure 6a presents the semantics for reactive resumption monads over state in which the productivity-labelled constructors are expressed in terms of "snapshots" of the form $(\texttt{i}, \texttt{s}, \texttt{o})$. `State s` is the familiar state monad over `s`. A $(\texttt{Writer}^{+}\ \texttt{s a})$ is a list-like structure for which the constructor $\triangleright$ corresponds to list cons—intuitively, it is a non-empty list that ends in an `a`-value—and is used to model ReWire terms typed in $\texttt{Re}^{+}$. It is used to represent terminating *signal-productive* hardware computations—i.e., those that operate over multiple clock cycles, produce snapshots and terminate. A hardware computation typed in $\texttt{Re}^{\infty}$ corresponds to sequential circuitry. The intuition is that, given the current snapshot of a circuit (Fig. 2a) and a stream of all its future inputs, the result is a stream of all snapshots (i.e., a $\texttt{Stream}\ (\texttt{i} \times \texttt{s} \times \texttt{o})$).

Signal-productive computations (i.e., those corresponding to terms of type $\texttt{Re}^{+}\texttt{i s o a}$) are represented in the domain $\texttt{DomRe}^{+}\ \ulcorner\texttt{i}\urcorner\ \ulcorner\texttt{s}\urcorner\ \ulcorner\texttt{o}\urcorner\ \ulcorner\texttt{a}\urcorner$. The intuition underlying this structure is that, given an initial snapshot $(\texttt{i}, \texttt{s}, \texttt{o})$ and a

```
data State (s : Set) (a : Set) : Set where
  SM : (s → (a×s)) → State s a

data Writer⁺ (w : Set) (a : Set) : Set where
  _▷[_] : w → a → Writer⁺ w a
  _▷_   : w → Writer⁺ w a → Writer⁺ w a

DomRe⁰ i s o a = State s a
DomRe⁺ i s o a = (i×s×o) → Stream i → Writer⁺ (i×s×o) (a × Stream i)
DomRe∞ i s o   = (i×s×o) → Stream i → Stream (i×s×o)
```

(a) Domain Semantics

```
  _<>=⁰⁰_  : ST s a → (a → ST s b) → ST s b
  _<>=⁰⁺_  : ST s a → (a → DomRe⁺ i s o b) → DomRe⁺ i so b
  _<>=⁺⁺_  : DomRe⁺ i s o a → (a → DomRe⁺ i s o b) → DomRe⁺ i s o b
  iterRe   : (a → DomRe⁺ i s o a) → (a → DomRe∞ i s o a)
```

(b) Type Declarations of Effect-labeled Bind & Co-Recursion Operators

Fig. 6. Domain Semantics & Semantic Operators.

stream of inputs in i, signal-productive computations will express a finite, non-zero number of additional snapshots, represented in $\texttt{Writer}^{+}(\texttt{i} \times \texttt{s} \times \texttt{o})\texttt{a}$. The intuition underlying $\texttt{DomRe}^{\infty}$ ⌜i⌝ ⌜s⌝ ⌜o⌝ ⌜a⌝ is similar, except that it produces a stream expressing the entire circuit as a "transcript" of snapshots. The intuition underlying a value in $\texttt{DomRe}^{0}$ ⌜i⌝ ⌜s⌝ ⌜o⌝ ⌜a⌝ is simple—it produces no snapshots because it represents computation that occurs between clock cycles; hence it is simply a state monad computation.

The type declarations for effect-labeled bind operators are shown in Fig. 6b. The monad laws for these were verified in Coq [12]. We chose to verify these laws in Coq and, although this choice was somewhat arbitrary, it does however illustrate the utility of Reynold-style definitional shallow embedding of the ReWire formalization. The Coq syntax below is different from the Agda syntax we have adopted throughout; e.g., bindRePP stands for ($\texttt{>>=}^{++}$), etc. A typical theorem, showing the associativity of ($\texttt{>>=}^{++}$), is below:

```
Theorem AssocPP {i s o a b c} : forall (x : RePlus i s o a),
 forall (f : a -> RePlus i s o b), forall (g : b -> RePlus i s o c),
   bindRePP x (fun va => bindRePP (f va) g) = bindRePP (bindRePP x f) g.
```

Figure 6b presents the type declaration of the corecursion operator, iterRe. ReWire devices typically take the form of mutually recursive co-equations and such co-equations may be encoded in the ReWire calculus using a standard approach from denotational semantics. Two ReWire co-equations (left) are represented in the calculus by (iterRe f), where f is defined as (right):

$$\begin{array}{ll} \texttt{f}_i \;\; :: \mathtt{a}_i \to \mathtt{Re\ i\ s\ o\ ()} & \texttt{f} : (\mathtt{a}_1 \oplus \mathtt{a}_2) \to \mathtt{Re}^+\ \mathtt{i\ s\ o} \\ \texttt{f}_1\ \mathtt{a}_1 = \mathtt{x}_1 \texttt{ >>= } \texttt{f}_2 & \texttt{f}\ (\texttt{inl}\ \mathtt{a}_1) = \mathtt{x}_1 \texttt{ >>=}^{+0}\ (\texttt{return}^r \circ \texttt{inr}) \\ \texttt{f}_2\ \mathtt{a}_2 = \mathtt{x}_2 \texttt{ >>= } \texttt{f}_1 & \texttt{f}\ (\texttt{inr}\ \mathtt{a}_2) = \mathtt{x}_2 \texttt{ >>=}^{+0}\ (\texttt{return}^r \circ \texttt{inl}) \end{array}$$

Figure 5b presents the mechanized denotational semantics for ReWire. It closely resembles the Device Calculus semantics referred to previously [22], except for the monadic fragment of the calculus, which is represented by the constructions of Fig. 6a. The state monadic operators ($\texttt{return}^{ST}$, $\texttt{>>=}^{ST}$, `get`, and `set`) have an unremarkable semantics. Lifting and unit (respectively, $\texttt{lift}^r$ and $\texttt{return}^r$) are treated as state monad computations as one would expect from the type semantics in Fig. 6a. Lifting is the identity function and the denotation for $\texttt{return}^r$ is identical to that of $\texttt{return}^{ST}$. The productivity-labelled bind is mapped to the appropriate operator from Fig. 6b. The denotation of `signal` computes a snapshot `(i , s , o)` based on the current internal state (`s`), the head of the input stream (`i`), and the output argument it has been passed (`o`), returning the next input and the remaining stream of inputs. The semantics of `loop` applies `iterRe` to the denotation of `f`.

3 Case Study: Cryptographic Hardware Verification

We performed the model validation process on a substantial case study: a family of pipelined Barrett modular multipliers (BMM) that are based on hardware algorithms published by Zhang et al. [62]. The formal methods team was provided with Verilog designs created by hand by a team of hardware engineers and it was our task was to formally verify the correctness of these designs. The designs in question were highly optimized using a variety of techniques (e.g., specialized encodings for compression/decompression) to enhance area and time performance of the synthesized circuits. The technical focus heretofore has been on the embed arrow from Fig. 1. This section summarizes the BMM case study (i.e., the verify arrow in Fig. 1) and we provide sufficient information to understand the its essentials, although the presentation is necessarily at a high-level due to space limitations. A complete description is left for future publications.

It is important to note that the Verilog designs for BMM were not designed with formal verification in mind. Model validation is a hybrid approach mixing interactive theorem-proving with user-guided, but otherwise, fully automated equivalence checking. We developed this approach, in part, because we were concerned that a fully-automated approach would not scale up to the large size of several of the designs. All of the relevant materials to this case study are available [12]; these include Verilog designs for the multipliers, the Isabelle proof scripts that specify and verify the hardware designs, as well as the semantics for ReWire formalized in Isabelle, Coq, and Agda.

***BMM Case Study* (model).** Creating a ReWire model of the BMM Verilog design constitutes the model phases of the model validation process illustrated in Fig. 1. The task required formally verifying instances of this input RTL for word sizes: W = 64, 128 , 256, 512, and 1024. This section illustrates this process using

```
module BMM (CLK, A_IN, B_IN, M_IN
           , mu_IN, km3_IN, Z_OUT);

 parameter N     = 128;
 parameter LOG_N = 7;
 input               CLK;
 input   [N-1      : 0] A_IN, B_IN, M_IN;
 input   [N+2      : 0] mu_IN;
 input   [LOG_N-1 : 0] km3_IN;
 output [N-1     : 0] Z_OUT;
 reg [2*N-1 : 0] stage0_XY_reg; // stage 0 reg
 reg [N+2    : 0] stage0_mu_reg;
 reg [N-1    : 0] stage0_M_reg;
 reg [LOG_N-1:0] stage0_km3_reg;
 reg [N      : 0] stage1_XY_reg; // stage 1 reg
 reg [N-1    : 0] stage1_q_reg;
 reg [N-1    : 0] stage1_M_reg;
 reg [N      : 0] stage2_XY_reg; // stage 2 reg
              ...
```

(a) Input Verilog for BMM

```
type Inp = ( BV(N)         -- A_IN
           , BV(N)         -- B_IN
           , BV(N)         -- M_IN
           , BV(N + 3)     -- mu_IN
           , BV(LOG_N) )   -- km3_IN
type Out = BV(N)           -- Z_OUT

bmm :: Inp → Re Inp Reg Out ()
bmm i = do lift (internal i)
           i' ← signal (obs reg)
           bmm i'
   where
      internal :: Inp → ST Reg Out
      internal i = do r ← get
                      put (trans i r)
                      returnST (obs r)
      trans :: Inp → Reg → Reg
      trans i r = ...
      obs :: Reg → Out
      obs r     = ...
```

(b) Corresponding ReWire Mimic

Fig. 7. Case Study: Modeling Hardware Designs in ReWire. The bmm function (b) is an instance of the ReWire's Mealy pattern that mimics the original hardware design (a). Haskell's do notation is syntactic sugar for >>=.

relevant parts of the BMM case study. An excerpt of the input BMM Verilog code is presented in Fig. 7a. The top-level input and output declarations are displayed (not all register declarations are included for reasons of space).

The Verilog I/O port declarations that are captured as ReWire tuple types, Inp and Out, in Fig. 7b. The Verilog register declarations are encoded as the ReWire tuple type, Reg, although it does not appear in the figure. The ReWire compiler unfolds boolean vector types to built-in ReWire types (e.g., for N = 128, BV(N) becomes the built-in ReWire word type W128).

One notable difference between the Verilog input ports and the ReWire type Inp in Fig. 7 is the absence of a clock type in the latter. This reflects the implicit timing inherent in the Re monad. Figure 7b excerpts the ReWire formal model that mimics the input Verilog BMM design—this is a ReWire function, bmm, that has type Inp →Re Inp Reg Out. The ReWire function bmm is an instance of the Mealy design pattern from Fig. 2b. In our experience, most of the effort in the model phase of model validation derives from specifying the input, storage, and output types (e.g., Inp, Reg, and Out) and, also, from the formulation of the internal function that represents the combinational output and next-state logic. Developing the ReWire model was, for the case study presented here, entirely by hand, although we believe that future work can automate (at least parts of) the process (see Sect. 5 for further discussion).

***BMM Case Study* (embed).** The final part of the embed arrow in Fig. 1 for this case study is the semantic translation of the ReWire model into the logic of the Isabelle theorem prover. (Some liberties have been taken with Isabelle syntax for readability.) The semantic foundation expressed in Figs. 5 and 6 was developed as a theory file in Isabelle. This development was along the lines of Reynold's notion of definitional interpreters [52] as remarked upon in the previous section—i.e., because Isabelle possesses a stream library, the definitional embedding of the ReWire semantics was straightforward. For example, the semantic domain DomRe$^{\infty}$ i s o is formulated in Isabelle in Fig. 8. Given this semantic foundation formulated as an Isabelle theory, a translation into this theory based on the denotational semantics from Fig. 5b was written in Haskell. This translation, in most respects, simply transliterates ReWire abstract syntax into the constructions of the Isabelle semantic theory, making use of the built-in monadic syntax in Isabelle/HOL. Figure 8 presents the Isabelle translation of the ReWire mimic of the original BMM design (from Fig. 7b). Note the structural similarity between body and onecycle from Fig. 2b. Note also that body is typed in the Isabelle version of DomRe+ from Fig. 6a. The translator analyses recursive definitions (e.g., the original bmm from Fig. 7b) and reformulates them using iterRe, but, otherwise, the translations of ReWire definitions in Fig. 8 are unremarkable. The use of Oxford brackets emphasizes that this Isabelle declaration defines the denotational semantics of bmm from Fig. 7b.

```
type_synonym ('i,'s,'o) DomRe_INF =
           "('i × 's × 'o) ⇒ 'i stream ⇒ (('i × 's × 'o) stream)"
fun body :: "Inp ⇒ (Inp, Reg, Out, Inp) Dom_Re_Plus" where
   "body (i) = retdo { reg ← liftR get;
                       liftR (set (trans i reg)); signalR (obs reg) }"
definition ⟦bmm⟧ :: "Inp ⇒ (Inp, Reg, Out) Dom_Re_INF"
  where "⟦bmm⟧ i = iterRe body (i)"
```

Fig. 8. Embedding of bmm from Fig. 7b in Isabelle.

***BMM Case Study* (verify).** This section presents the verify phase of the model validation process illustrated in Fig. 1. The compute_bmm function in Fig. 9 defines the calling convention for the bmm ReWire device. In the figure, the initial values, i0, s0, and o0, are tuples of zeros, represented as bit vectors of appropriate sizes (e.g., o0 is just W128). The function applies ⟦bmm⟧ to the appropriate inputs thereby producing a stream of snapshots. The computed bmm value is the output of the fifth such snapshot (calculated with projection π_3, stream take stake, and the list indexing operation "!"). The correctness theorem embedding_eq in Fig. 9 is expressed in Isabelle as an equation relating the results computed by the compute_bmm Isabelle embedding (lhs) to the value computed by the high-level algorithm, barrett_fws_word (rhs).

***BMM Case Study* (validate).** This section overviews the validate phase of the model validation process illustrated in Fig. 1 as applied to the BMM case study. The successful proof of the correctness theorem embedding_eq in Isabelle verifies the functional correctness of the ReWire representation of the BMM target design. This alone provides a strong assurance story, but there remains a question as to the accuracy of the hand translation of Verilog BMM design into ReWire model—what evidence is there that the ReWire model faithfully represents the input design? Model validation goes further and demonstrates the soundness of the model through the use of model checking technology.

```
fun compute_bmm :: "128 word ⇒ 128 word ⇒ 128 word ⇒ 131 word ⇒ 7 word ⇒ 128 word"
 where
  "compute_bmm a b m mu km3 =
    π3 (stake 5 (⟦bmm⟧ (a,b,m,mu,km3) (i0,s0,o0)  (repeat (a,b,m,mu,km3))) ! 4)"

theorem embedding_eq : "compute_bmm a b m mu km3 = barrett_fws_word a b m mu km3"
```

Fig. 9. Formal Specification of bmm.

The *yosys* (Yosys Open SYnthesis Suite) toolchain [59] supports the synthesis of Verilog (and, through an extension, VHDL) designs, providing an array of options for transformation, optimization, and model checking. In particular for our use case, *yosys* integrates the ABC system [9] for sequential logic synthesis and formal verification. Here, we use *yosys* to carry out an equivalence check between two circuits: those synthesized from the input Verilog BMM design and the Verilog output by compiling the verified ReWire model.

The ReWire compiler provides a Verilog backend and we can thus perform an apples-to-apples comparison of the two Verilog circuits using *yosys*. Because the ReWire model mimics the modular and algorithmic structure of the hand-written circuit, *yosys* can quickly identify common substructures in support of automatic equivalence verification of the two circuits. Even with the high degree of similarity between the two circuits, some of the more complex equivalence checks proved challenging for the automated tooling. To break down the problem further, we applied *compositional verification*, in which subcomponents are verified individually and those results are used to verify higher-level components. After we verify equivalence for a submodule, we instruct *yosys* to treat references to that submodule by both the implementation and ReWire specification as a blackbox library. "Blackboxing" modules can streamline equivalence checking.

The *yosys* scripts we used may be found in the codebase [12]. Our initial experimentation focused on purely combinational circuits, provable using the *yosys* `equiv_simple` command. This worked "out of the box" for a number of submodules. However, much of the target design consists of sequential circuits, which require additional configuration to manage timing and state. In this case, with the `equiv_induct` command, *yosys* proves such circuits equivalent by temporal induction over clock cycles.

4 Related Work

We coined the term *model validation* because of its similarities to translation validation [17,40,44,46]. Translation validation begins with a given source program and compiler and, then, establishes the correctness relation between the source and its implementation (i.e., the compiled source program). Translation validation establishes the correctness of individual compiler translations rather than verifying the whole compiler itself. Model validation starts from a given implementation (i.e., the HDL circuit design) and high-level correctness criteria (e.g., an algorithm given in pseudocode) and, then, establishes the equivalence of the two to a ReWire formal model that mimics the circuit design. The (model ; validate) path in model validation proceeds in the "opposite direction" from translation validation. Translation validation for HLS has been applied before (e.g., Kundu [29] and Ramanathan et al. [49,50]), but model validation is novel to the best knowledge of the authors.

High-level synthesis (HLS) adapts software high-level languages to hardware development. The motivation to do so has been to bring software engineering virtues—e.g., modularity, comprehensibility, reusability, etc.—to the whole hardware development process [2] but also more recently to translate software formal methods into a hardware context [7,14,53]. Herklotz and Wickerson [23] and Du et al. [13] make compelling arguments for applying software formal methods to HLS languages and compilers as a means of bringing a level of maturity and reliability to HLS that justifies its use in critical systems. Formal methods applied to *software* compilers have been explored for at least five decades now [38] and the state of the art is at a high-level of sophistication [30].

Gordon outlined the challenges of semantic specification of hardware definition languages [19], focusing specifically on Verilog, although his analysis applies equally to VHDL. There have been previous attempts to formalize VHDL as well [28,58] that have succeeded only on small parts of the language. One way of coping with the lack of formal semantics for commodity HDLs is to identify a formalizable subset of the language in question. Gordon [20], Zhu et al. [63], Meredith et al. [36], Khan [27], and Lööw and Myreen [32] do so for Verilog. Another approach creates a new hardware language and compiler with formalization as a specific requirement (e.g., Kami [11], Bluespec [7], and CHERI [42]). HLS generally seeks to adapt software languages to hardware—ReWire, being a DSL embedded in Haskell, is in this camp.

The original motivation for high-level synthesis was to promote software-like development to hardware design by introducing software-like abstractions and methodologies. In particular, functional language approaches to high-level synthesis have a long pedigree, including muFP [55], CλaSH [15], ForSyDe, Lava [6], Kiwi [56], and Chisel [4]. There is a growing awareness of the utility of language-based approaches (including HLS) for hardware formal methods (e.g., a sample of very recent publications [3,7,8,21,22,31,32,42,53] can be found in the references). This language-based approach has been particularly successful in formal development of instruction set architectures [3,42,51].

There has been work formalizing monads with theorem provers as a basis for verifying functional programs [1,10,16,33,39]. Simple monads (e.g., Haskell's `Maybe`) can be transliterated into a theorem prover, but more complex monads—e.g., RRS monads—require more care [24,25,53,54]; their mechanization here is, by comparison, a shallow embedding. Effect labels in the ReWire calculus type system were essential because they allow fine-grained distinctions with respect to signal-productivity and non-termination to be made in the construction of terms that, in turn, determine the appropriate denotation domain.

5 Summary, Conclusions, and Future Work

The research described here was performed as part of a project to develop formally verified hardware accelerators to improve upon the existing algorithmic gains to fully-homomorphic encryption (FHE). ReWire's role is to bridge the gap between the hardware design and algorithm by establishing 1) the equivalence of the algorithm to the model and 2) the equivalence of the model to the circuit design. Equivalence between the algorithm and the ReWire model is verified with a ReWire semantics formalized in the Isabelle theorem prover. Equivalence between the ReWire model and the input circuit design is established by producing binary circuits from each (using commodity synthesis tools and the ReWire compiler) and applying an automated binary equivalence checker.

Model validation addresses the following kind of scenario. A team of hardware engineers produces a circuit design C in a commodity HDL (e.g., VHDL or Verilog) to implement an algorithm A (written in informal, imperative style pseudocode) in hardware and then a formal methods team is given the task of evaluating whether C implements A correctly. There is significant distance between the notions of computation underlying A (i.e., store-passing in some form) and C (i.e., clocked, synchronous parallelism) and so formally relating the two is non-trivial and requires care. We have shown how a formalized HLS language like ReWire can bridge this gap to reduce this conceptual distance.

The first path of model validation—the composite arrow (model; embed; verify) in Fig. 1—is, in some respects, a conventional hardware verification flow with a theorem prover: a formal model is abstracted from an HDL design, encoded in the prover logic, and then properties of that model are verified. The interposed formalized HLS language may provide some benefits with respect to proof engineering via libraries of theorems that may be reused later. We have developed such libraries of theorems and tactics over the course of this project that will be shared as open source. The second path of the model validation process—the composite arrow (model ; validate)—speaks to the fidelity of the formal model itself to the input circuit design. Establishing the fidelity of a formal model to the object it models addresses a broad issue in formal methods research that can be difficult to explore: how can we gauge the accuracy of a formal model itself?

The class of high-level algorithms of which the BMM case study is a member are generally informally specified as C-style pseudocode (see, for instance, Zhang et al. [62]). One approach for future work would be to develop a formalized domain-specific language for this class of high-level algorithms that can be lifted automatically into ReWire. This would accelerate the model validation process as it would automate the otherwise time-consuming, by-hand model phase. Such a language-based approach would support, among other things, a correct-by-construction approach to hardware development based in program transformation. Another potential accelerator applies recent work by Zeng et al. [60,61]

that seeks to automatically generate update functions of type `i → s → (o × s)` from Verilog designs. Automatic recovery of such update functions would go a long way towards automating the model phase of model validation.

We have successfully applied the model validation methodology to several substantial case studies, including the BMM case study from Sect. 3 and another on a 4096-bit iterative Montgomery modular multiplier (MMM) that we will describe in future work. Why develop a new methodology at all? Several members of the formal methods team have extensive experience with Cryptol, for example, and we did experiment with it. For example, we specified some of the basic encoder components from the MMM in Cryptol, but the automated equivalence check of these against the relevant components failed to terminate after several days. It seemed unlikely, then, that this fully automated approach would scale up to a 4096-bit multiplier. One of the key reasons for our success in these case studies is the extensive automation available in Isabelle—that motivated our choice of Isabelle over Coq. ReWire is open source and the success of the (model ; validate) path in Fig. 1 relied on our ability to make customizations to its Verilog code generator in support of Yosys equivalence checking.

Table 1. Performance Comparison: ReWire vs. Handwritten Barrett Multipliers.

	Fmax (GHz)			Area (μm^2)		
Width	ReWire	Original	Δ%	ReWire	Original	Δ%
64	1.588	2.127	+25%	13399	12126	+10%
128	1.357	2.134	+36%	42970	41650	+3%
256	1.229	1.952	+37%	150463	157214	-4%
512	1.074	1.789	+40%	554612	578506	-4%
1024	0.954	1.473	+35%	2109037	2106714	+0.1%

Comparing the performance of the compiled ReWire models in Sect. 3 against those of the original Verilog designs was in some respects surprising to us. Table 1 displays performance numbers (maximum clock frequency and area) for the case study for each word size of pipelined Barrett multipliers. The columns labeled "Original" are those for the original Verilog design created by hand and those labeled "ReWire" are for the mimic designs created as formal models. While the maximum clock frequency numbers for the ReWire models are between 25%–40% slower than the Original designs, the area of the circuits is roughly equivalent and, in some cases, slightly better than those produced for the handwritten designs. Future work will explore the optimization of the ReWire compiler to bring these performance characteristics into line with hand-written Verilog and VHDL designs as much as possible.

A Monads, Monad Transformers, and Reactive Resumption Monads over State in Haskell

This appendix includes background material on reactive resumption monads over state and, specifically, their representation in Haskell.

A.1 Monads in Haskell

A Haskell monad is a type constructor `m` with associated operations `return` and `>>=` with types:

```
return :: a → m a
(>>=)  :: m a → (a → m b) → m b
(>>)   :: m a → m b → m b     — "null" bind
x >> y  = x >>= λ_. y
```

A term of type `m a` is referred to as a *computation of* `a`, whereas a term of type `a` is a *value*—the distinction between values and computations is fundamental to monadic denotational semantics [37]. The `return` operation creates an `a`-computation from an `a`-value. The (`>>=`) operation is a kind of "backwards application" for `m`, meaning that, in `x>>=f`, an `a`-value is computed by `x` and then `f` is applied to that value. Null bind performs computation `x`, ignores its result, and then performs computation `y`.

Monadic return and bind operations are overloaded in Haskell and this overloading is resolved via the type class system.

The return and bind of a monad generally obey the "monad laws" that signify that `>>=` is associative and that `return` is a left and right unit of `>>=`. What makes monads useful in language semantics and functional programming, however, is not this basic infrastructure, but rather the other operations definable in terms of the monad (e.g., the state monad has operations for reading and writing to and from state).

A.2 `Identity` Monad

The type constructor for the identity monad is given by:

```
data Identity a = Identity a
```

It is conventional in Haskell to use `Identity` for both the type and data constructors for the identity monad. For `Identity`, return and bind are defined by:

```
return              = Identity
(Identity a) >>= f  = f a
```

A.3 Monad Transformers in Haskell

A *monad transformer* is a construction `t` such that, for any monad `m`, `t m` is a monad. Monads created through applications of monad transformers to a base monad (e.g., `Identity`) are referred to as *modular* monads. For example, `(Re i s o)` from Fig. 4 is a modular monad; see Appendix A.6 below. For each monad transformer `t`, there is a lifting operation `lift` :: `ma` → `tma` used to redefine `m`'s operations for `t m`.

A.4 StateT Monad Transformer

Return and bind for the monad `StateT s m` are defined in terms of `m`:

```
return a          = StateT (return_m a)
(StateT x) >>= f  = StateT (x >>=_m λ(a , s). deStateT (f a) s)
```

The return and bind operations are disambiguated by attaching an `m` subscript to `m`'s operations.

In addition to the standard return and bind operations, the state monad transformers also defines three other operations: `get` (to read the current state), `set` (to set the current state), and the overloaded `lift` (that redefines `m` computations as `StateT s m` computations):

```
get    :: StateT s m s
get    = StateT (λs. return_m (s , s))
set    :: s → (StateT s m ())
set s  = StateT (λ_. return_m (() , s))
lift   :: m a → StateT s m a
lift x = StateT (λs. x >>=_m λa. return_m (a , s))
```

A.5 ReacT Monad Transformer

The reactive resumption monad transformer is given by:

```
data ReacT i o m a = ReacT (m (Either a (o , i → ReacT i o m a)))
```

Return and bind for the monad `ReacT i o m` are defined in terms of `m`:

```
return a         = ReacT (return_m (Left a))
(ReacT x) >>= f  = ReacT (x >>=_m λr. case r of
                                         Left a       → f a
                                         Right (o , k) → return_m (o , λi. (k i) >>= f) )
```

The additional operations in `ReacT i o m` are:

```
signal   :: o → ReacT i o m i
signal o = ReacT (return_m (o , return)))
lift     :: m a → ReacT i o m a
lift x   = ReacT (x >>=_m (Left ∘ return_m))
```

A.6 Reactive Resumption Monads over State in Haskell

In ReWire, device specifications have a type constructed using monad transformers defined above. The type constructor for devices is given by the type synonym `Re`—this is the Haskell definition equivalent to that from Fig. 4.

```
type Re i s o = ReacT i o (StateT s Identity)
```

ReWire allows a slightly more flexible formulation in which there are multiple `StateT` applications, although one such application as above suffices for the purposes of this work.

There are also projections from the monad transformer type constructors:

```
deStateT            :: StateT s m a → s → m (a, s)
deStateT (StateT x) = x
deReacT             :: ReacT i o m a → m (Either a (o , i → ReacT i o m a))
deReacT (ReacT x)   = x
```

References

1. Affeldt, R., Nowak, D., Saikawa, T.: A hierarchy of monadic effects for program verification using equational reasoning. In: Hutton, G. (ed.) Mathematics of Program Construction, pp. 226–254 (2019)
2. Andrews, D.: Will the future success of reconfigurable computing require a paradigm shift in our research community's thinking?, keynote address, Applied Reconfigurable Computing (2015)
3. Armstrong, A., et al.: The state of sail. In: SpISA 2019: Workshop on Instruction Set Architecture Specification (2019)
4. Bachrach, J., et al.: Chisel: constructing hardware in a scala embedded language. In: DAC, pp. 1216–1225 (2012)
5. Benton, N., Kennedy, A., Varming, C.: Some domain theory and denotational semantics in Coq. In: Berghofer, S., Nipkow, T., Urban, C., Wenzel, M. (eds.) TPHOLs 2009. LNCS, vol. 5674, pp. 115–130. Springer, Heidelberg (2009). https://doi.org/10.1007/978-3-642-03359-9_10
6. Bjesse, P., Claessen, K., Sheeran, M., Singh, S.: Lava: hardware design in haskell. ACM SIGPLAN Not. **34** (2001)
7. Bourgeat, T., Pit-Claudel, C., Chlipala, A.A.: The essence of Bluespec: a core language for rule-based hardware design. In: Proceedings of the 41st ACM SIGPLAN Conference on Programming Language Design and Implementation, pp. 243–257. PLDI 2020 (2020)
8. Bourke, T., Brun, L., Pouzet, M.: Mechanized semantics and verified compilation for a dataflow synchronous language with reset. Proc. ACM Program. Lang. **4**(POPL) (2019)
9. Brayton, R., Mishchenko, A.: ABC: an academic industrial-strength verification tool. In: Computer Aided Verification, pp. 24–40 (2010)
10. Breitner, J., Spector-Zabusky, A., Li, Y., Rizkallah, C., Wiegley, J., Weirich, S.: Ready, set, verify! applying hs-to-coq to real-world haskell code (experience report). Proc. ACM Program. Lang. (2018)

11. Choi, J., Vijayaraghavan, M., Sherman, B., Chlipala, A.A.: Kami: a platform for high-level parametric hardware specification and its modular verification. PACMPL **1**, 24:1–24:30 (2017)
12. Model Validation Codebase. https://www.dropbox.com/s/r59xg34qzh0arri/codebase_paper4262.tar.gz?dl=0 (2022)
13. Du, Z., Herklotz, Y., Ramanathan, N., Wickerson, J.: Fuzzing high-level synthesis tools. In: The 2021 ACM/SIGDA International Symposium on Field-Programmable Gate Arrays, FPGA 2021, p. 148. Association for Computing Machinery, New York (2021)
14. Flor, J.P.P., Swierstra, W., Sijsling, Y.: Π-Ware: hardware description and verification in agda. In: Proceedings of TYPES (2015)
15. Gerards, M., Baaij, C., Kuper, J., Kooijman, M.: Higher-order abstraction in hardware descriptions with CλaSH. In: Proceedings of the 2011 14th EUROMICRO Conference on Digital System Design, DSD 2011, pp. 495–502. IEEE Computer Society, Washington, DC (2011). https://doi.org/10.1109/DSD.2011.69
16. Gibbons, J., Hinze, R.: Just do it: Simple monadic equational reasoning. In: Proceedings of the 16th ACM SIGPLAN International Conference on Functional Programming, ICFP 2011, pp. 2–14 (2011)
17. Goldberg, B., Zuck, L., Barrett, C.: Into the loops: Practical issues in translation validation for optimizing compilers. Electron. Notes Theor. Comput. Sci. **132**(1), 53–71 (2005)
18. Goncharov, S., Schröder, L.: A coinductive calculus for asynchronous side-effecting processes. In: Proceedings of the 18th International Conference on Fundamentals of Computation Theory, pp. 276–287 (2011)
19. Gordon, M.J.C.: The semantic challenge of Verilog HDL. In: Proceedings of 10th Annual IEEE LICS, pp. 136–145 (1995)
20. Gordon, M.J.C.: Relating event and trace semantics of hardware description languages. Comput. J. **45**(1), 27–36 (2002)
21. Harrison, W.L., Allwein, G.: Verifiable security templates for hardware. In: Proceedings of the Design, Automation, and Test Europe (DATE) Conference (2020)
22. Harrison, W.L., Hathhorn, C., Allwein, G.: A mechanized semantic metalanguage for high level synthesis. In: 23rd International Symposium on Principles and Practice of Declarative Programming (PPDP 2021) (2021)
23. Herklotz, Y., Wickerson, J.: High-level synthesis tools should be proven correct. In: Workshop on Languages, Tools, and Techniques for Accelerator Design (LATTE) (2021)
24. Huffman, B.: HOLCF 2011: A Definitional Domain Theory for Verifying Functional Programs. Ph.D. thesis, Portland State University (2012)
25. Huffman, B.: Formal verification of monad transformers. In: Proceedings of the 17th ACM SIGPLAN International Conference on Functional Programming, ICFP 2012, pp. 15–16 (2012)
26. Katz, R.H.: Contemporary Logic Design, 2nd edn. Addison-Wesley Longman Publishing Co. Inc., Boston (2000)
27. Khan, W., Tiu, A., Sanan, D.: Veriformal: an executable formal model of a hardware description language. In: Roychoudhury, A., Liu, Y. (eds.) A Systems Approach to Cyber Security: Proceedings of the 2nd Singapore Cyber-Security R&D Conference (SG-CRC 2017), pp. 19–36. IOS Press (2017)
28. Kloos, C., Breuer, P. (eds.): Formal Semantics for VHDL. Kluwer Academic Publishers (1995)

29. Kundu, S., Lerner, S., Gupta, R.K.: Translation Validation of High-Level Synthesis, pp. 97–121. Springer, New York (2011). https://doi.org/10.1007/978-1-4419-9359-5_7
30. Leroy, X.: Formal verification of a realistic compiler. Commun. ACM **52**(7), 107–115 (2009)
31. Lööw, A.: Lutsig: a verified verilog compiler for verified circuit development. In: Proceedings of the 10th ACM SIGPLAN International Conference on Certified Programs and Proofs, CPP 2021, pp. 46–60. Association for Computing Machinery, New York (2021)
32. Lööw, A., Myreen, M.O.: A proof-producing translator for verilog development in HOL. In: 2019 IEEE/ACM 7th International Conference on Formal Methods in Software Engineering (FormaliSE), pp. 99–108 (2019)
33. Maillard, K., et al.: Dijkstra monads for all. Proc. ACM Program. Lang. **3**(ICFP) (2019)
34. Marlow, S., Brandy, L., Coens, J., Purdy, J.: There is no fork: an abstraction for efficient, concurrent, and concise data access. In: Proceedings of the 19th ACM SIGPLAN International Conference on Functional Programming, ICFP 2014, pp. 325–337. ACM, New York (2014). https://doi.org/10.1145/2628136.2628144
35. Mealy, G.H.: A method for synthesizing sequential circuits. Bell Syst. Techn. J. **34**(5), 1045–1079 (1955)
36. Meredith, P., Katelman, M., Meseguer, J., Roşu, G.: A formal executable semantics of Verilog. In: Eighth ACM/IEEE International Conference on Formal Methods and Models for Codesign (MEMOCODE 2010), pp. 179–188 (2010)
37. Moggi, E.: Notions of computation and monads. Inf. Comput. **93**(1), 55–92 (1991)
38. Morris, F.L.: Advice on structuring compilers and proving them correct. In: Proceedings of the 1st Annual ACM SIGACT-SIGPLAN Symposium on Principles of Programming Languages, POPL 1973, pp. 144–152. Association for Computing Machinery, New York (1973)
39. Mu, S.C.: Calculating a backtracking algorithm: an exercise in monadic program derivation. Technical Report, TR-IIS-19-003, Institute of Information Science, Academia Sinica (June 2019)
40. Necula, G.C.: Translation validation for an optimizing compiler. In: Proceedings of the ACM SIGPLAN 2000 Conference on Programming Language Design and Implementation, pp. 83–94 (2000)
41. Nielson, F., Nielson, H.R., Hankin, C.: Principles of Program Analysis. Springer, Heidelberg (2010). https://doi.org/10.1007/978-3-662-03811-6
42. Nienhuis, K., et al.: Rigorous engineering for hardware security: formal modelling and proof in the CHERI design and implementation process. In: 2020 IEEE Symposium on Security and Privacy, pp. 1003–1020 (2020)
43. Papaspyrou, N.S.: A resumption monad transformer and its applications in the semantics of concurrency. In: Proceedings of the 3rd Panhellenic Logic Symposium (2001). expanded version available as a tech. report from the author by request
44. Perez, I., Goodloe, A.: Copilot 3. Technical Report. 20200003164, National Aeronautics and Space Administration (NASA) (2020)
45. Piróg, M., Gibbons, J.: The coinductive resumption monad. Electron. Notes Theor. Comput. Sci. **308**, 273 – 288 (2014). https://doi.org/10.1016/j.entcs.2014.10.015, http://www.sciencedirect.com/science/article/pii/S1571066114000826
46. Pnueli, A., Siegel, M., Singerman, E.: Translation validation. In: Steffen, B. (ed.) TACAS 1998. LNCS, vol. 1384, pp. 151–166. Springer, Heidelberg (1998). https://doi.org/10.1007/BFb0054170

47. Procter, A.: Semantics-Driven Design and Implementation of High-Assurance Hardware. Ph.D. thesis, University of Missouri (2014)
48. Procter, A., Harrison, W., Graves, I., Becchi, M., Allwein, G.: A principled approach to secure multi-core processor design with ReWire. ACM TECS **16**(2), 33:1–33:25 (2017)
49. Ramanathan, N., Constantinides, G.A., Wickerson, J.: Concurrency-aware thread scheduling for high-level synthesis. In: 2018 IEEE 26th Annual International Symposium on Field-Programmable Custom Computing Machines (FCCM), pp. 101–108 (2018). https://doi.org/10.1109/FCCM.2018.00025
50. Ramanathan, N., Fleming, S.T., Wickerson, J., Constantinides, G.A.: Hardware synthesis of weakly consistent C concurrency. In: Proceedings of the 2017 ACM/SIGDA International Symposium on Field-Programmable Gate Arrays, FPGA 2017, pp. 169–178. Association for Computing Machinery, New York (2017). https://doi.org/10.1145/3020078.3021733
51. Reid, A.: Trustworthy specifications of ARM®v8-a and v8-m system level architecture. In: 2016 Formal Methods in Computer-Aided Design (FMCAD), pp. 161–168 (2016). https://doi.org/10.1109/FMCAD.2016.7886675
52. Reynolds, J.C.: Definitional interpreters for higher-order programming languages. In: Proceedings of the ACM Annual Conference, vol. 2, pp. 717–740. ACM (1972)
53. Reynolds, T.N., Procter, A., Harrison, W., Allwein, G.: The mechanized marriage of effects and monads with applications to high-assurance hardware. ACM TECS **18**(1), 6:1–6:26 (2019)
54. Schröder, L.: Bootstrapping inductive and coinductive types in hascasl. Log. Methods Comput. Sci. **4**(4:17), 1–27 (2008)
55. Sheeran, M.: muFP, a language for VLSI design. In: LISP and Functional Programming, pp. 104–112 (1984)
56. Singh, S., Greaves, D.J.: Kiwi: synthesis of FPGA circuits from parallel programs. In: 2008 16th International Symposium on Field-Programmable Custom Computing Machines, pp. 3–12 (2008). https://doi.org/10.1109/FCCM.2008.46
57. Swierstra, W., Altenkirch, T.: Beauty in the beast. In: Proceedings of the ACM SIGPLAN Workshop on Haskell Workshop, Haskell 2007, pp. 25–36. ACM, New York (2007). https://doi.org/10.1145/1291201.1291206
58. Umamageswaran, K., Pandey, S.L., Wilsey, P.A.: Formal Semantics and Proof Techniques for Optimizing VHDL Models. Kluwer Academic Publishers, Boston (1999)
59. Wolf, C.: Yosys Open SYnthesis Suite. https://yosyshq.net/yosys/
60. Zeng, Y., Gupta, A., Malik, S.: Automatic generation of architecture-level models from RTL designs for processors and accelerators. In: Design, Automation & Test in Europe (DATE), pp. 460–465 (2022). https://doi.org/10.23919/DATE54114.2022.9774527
61. Zeng, Y., Huang, B.Y., Zhang, H., Gupta, A., Malik, S.: Generating architecture-level abstractions from RTL designs for processors and accelerators part i: Determining architectural state variables. In: 2021 IEEE/ACM International Conference On Computer Aided Design (ICCAD), pp. 1–9 (2021)
62. Zhang, B., Cheng, Z., Pedram, M.: A high-performance low-power barrett modular multiplier for cryptosystems. In: 2021 IEEE/ACM International Symposium on Low Power Electronics and Design (ISLPED), pp. 1–6 (2021)
63. Zhu, H., He, J., Bowen, J.: From algebraic semantics to denotational semantics for Verilog. In: 11th IEEE International Conference on Engineering of Complex Computer Systems (ICECCS 2006), p. 341–360 (2006)

From Natural Language Requirements to the Verification of Programmable Logic Controllers: Integrating FRET into PLCverif

Zsófia Ádám[1(✉)], Ignacio D. Lopez-Miguel[3(✉)], Anastasia Mavridou[4(✉)], Thomas Pressburger[5], Marcin Bęś[2], Enrique Blanco Viñuela[2], Andreas Katis[4], Jean-Charles Tournier[2], Khanh V. Trinh[4], and Borja Fernández Adiego[2(✉)]

[1] Department of Measurement and Information Systems, Budapest University of Technology and Economics, Budapest, Hungary
adamzsofi@edu.bme.hu

[2] European Organization for Nuclear Research (CERN), Geneva, Switzerland
borja.fernandez.adiego@cern.ch

[3] TU Wien, Vienna, Austria
ignacio.lopez@tuwien.ac.at

[4] KBR at NASA Ames Research Center, Moffett Field, Moffett Field, CA, USA
anastasia.mavridou@nasa.gov

[5] NASA Ames Research Center, Moffett Field, Moffett Field, CA, USA
tom.pressburger@nasa.gov

Abstract. PLCverif is an actively developed project at CERN, enabling the formal verification of Programmable Logic Controller (PLC) programs in critical systems. In this paper, we present our work on improving the formal requirements specification experience in PLCverif through the use of natural language. To this end, we integrate NASA's FRET, a formal requirement elicitation and authoring tool, into PLCverif. FRET is used to specify formal requirements in structured natural language, which automatically translates into temporal logic formulae. FRET's output is then directly used by PLCverif for verification purposes. We discuss practical challenges that PLCverif users face when authoring requirements and the FRET features that help alleviate these problems. We present the new requirement formalization workflow and report our experience using it on two critical CERN case studies.

1 Introduction

Over the past few years, formal verification has become a crucial part in the process of software development for critical applications. To this end, CERN's open-source tool PLCverif [3] opened the door for the verification of Programmable

Z. Ádám and I. D. Lopez-Miguel—Work performed while at CERN.

K. Y. Rozier and S. Chaudhuri (Eds.): NFM 2023, LNCS 13903, pp. 353–360, 2023.
https://doi.org/10.1007/978-3-031-33170-1_21

Logic Controller (PLC) programs [6,12,13] and it has successfully been used to verify several safety-critical applications [7–9].

Given PLC code and a set of requirements formalized in either computation tree logic (CTL) or future-time linear temporal logic (LTL), PLCverif automatically transforms these to an intermediate mathematical model, i.e., control flow automata (CFA) [5]. Once the intermediate model is obtained, PLCverif supports its translation into the input language of various model checkers for verification. Finally, analysis results are presented to the user in a convenient and easy-to-understand format.

The aforementioned process relies on control and safety engineers formalizing requirements. Prior to this work, PLCverif already supported the use of natural language templates, which are a set of pre-made templates with "blanks" where expressions containing variables of the PLC program can be added (e.g., "{expression1} is always true at the end of the PLC cycle"). During formalization, pattern instantiations are translated to LTL or CTL based on the pre-made templates. However, the expressive power of the existing templates is limited.

In this paper, we present the integration of NASA Ames' Formal Requirements Elicitation Tool (FRET [1]) into PLCverif, which provides a structured natural requirements language with an underlying temporal logic semantics. The integration of FRET within PLCverif helps users express and formalize a greater range of requirements and understand their semantics. The toolchain was successfully used in two critical CERN case studies: a safety program of a superconducting magnet test facility and a module of a process control library.

2 Integrating FRET into PLCverif

FRET is an open source project for writing, understanding, formalizing, and analyzing requirements [1,10,11]. FRET's user interface was designed with usability in mind; engineers with varying levels of experience in formal methods can express requirements using a restricted natural language plus standard Boolean/arithmetic expressions, called FRETish with precise, unambiguous meaning. For a FRETish requirement, FRET produces textual and diagrammatic explanations of its exact meaning and temporal logic formalizations in LTL. FRET also supports interactive simulation of the generated logical formulae to increase confidence that they capture the intended semantics.

2.1 Limitations of Requirement Formulation in PLCverif

As already anticipated in the introduction, *patterns* have significant limitations:

1. they offer a *limited set of 9 pre-made templates* only,
2. they do not offer any tool for *validation* of complex requirements; i.e., methods for checking if the created requirement is the same as the intended one.

FRET is able to improve on the current limitations the following ways:

Expressive Power. Users are able to formulate requirements in FRETish as constrained and unambiguous sentences, which are then automatically transformed to LTL expressions.

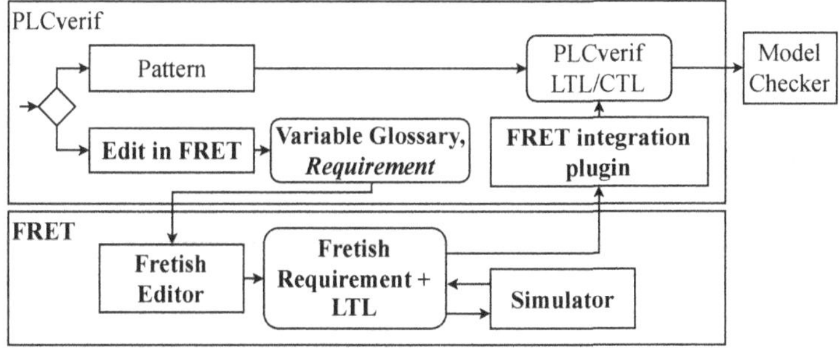

Fig. 1. Requirement formalization workflow in PLCverif. Features integrated into PLCverif in this work are shown in bold.

Validation. FRET has a built-in simulator, allowing the user to check different temporal variable valuations. Furthermore, FRET generates a textual and diagrammatic description of the requirement to further help precise understanding.

2.2 Realization of the New Workflow with FRET

The bold parts of Fig. 1 show how FRET fits into the workflow of PLCverif. If "Edit in FRET" is chosen, FRET is opened and the user can work in the requirement editor. Once the requirement is written in FRETISH and formalized, it is then sent back to PLCverif.

The External Mode of FRET. The feature set of FRET covers much more than what PLCverif could currently utilize (e.g., requirement hierarchies). PLCverif handles each requirement in a separate verification case, thus only the following features are utilized: the requirement editor, the formalization component and the requirements simulator. To facilitate integration with external tools including PLCverif, we developed a Node.js script for running the aforementioned features as a standalone tool. This new mode also implements the ability to import a variable glossary into the requirement editor of FRET.

Variable Glossary. PLCverif extracts the list of variable names and types by parsing the PLC code. Now the resulting *variable glossary* can also be exported to a JSON file for FRET to use. This enables features such as *autocompletion* of variable names in the FRET requirement editor. It also facilitates the process of creating formalized properties that can be directly used by PLCverif for verification as these requirement variables directly match PLC code variables.

Since variable names used in PLC code may include other characters besides alphanumeric, we extended the FRET editor to support identifiers with periods, percents, or double-quoted identifiers that can contain any special character.

The supported data types differ between the two tools (e.g., PLC programs might use arrays, while FRET only has scalar types). Assigning a data type to a variable is not mandatory in FRET and in this work it is only utilized by the simulator to show what possible values a variable can be assigned. Thus implementing a best-effort mapping proved to be adequate (e.g., sending each array element as a separate variable).

Preparing FRET for PLCs. The working principle of a PLC is described by the so-called *PLC Scan Cycle*, consisting of three steps: (1) read sensor values, (2) execute the PLC program and (3) write the actuator values. PLC requirements must be able to express cycles, e.g. "next cycle" or "at the end of the cycle".

To enable this, FRET's formalization algorithm was extended to express new built-in predicates `nextOcc(p,q)` and `prevOcc(p,q)`, and FRETISH was extended with the phrases *"at the next/previous occurrence of* `p`, `q`" meaning: at the next (previous) time point where `p` holds (if there is such), `q` also holds. These are expanded into the following LTL formulae, where L (R) is the formula that specifies the left (right) endpoint of the scope interval:

- Future for nextOcc
  `($R$ | (X (((!p & !$R$) U p) => ((!p & !$R$) U (p & q)))))`
- Past for prevOcc
  `($L$ | (Y (((!$L$ & !p) S p) => ((!$L$ & !p) S (p & q)))))`

Based on our experience, many PLC program requirements are checked at the end of PLC cycles. This is the most critical moment since the calculated values are sent to the actuators of the system. In the FRET PLC requirements, a variable called `PLC_END` can be used to express this exact moment.

In addition, FRET allows the creation of templates to help users write common requirements. For this work, we have created new FRET templates for PLCverif (e.g., ***In PLC_END*** *[COMPONENT]* `shall` *always* ***satisfy [RESPONSE]***). For further details on the workflow, we refer readers to our technical report [14].

3 Case Studies

The integration has been used in two CERN critical systems. The PLC programs and the properties are real cases at CERN. The first case study utilizes the validation capabilities, while the second employs the improved expressiveness. Only two properties per case study are shown due to a lack of space.

We give a brief description of the FRETISH syntax used in the case studies. For a complete description please refer to [11]. A FRETISH requirement is composed of six sequential fields: *scope*, *condition*, *component*, shall, *timing* and *response*. The optional *condition* field is a Boolean expression preceded by the word *when* that triggers the *response* Boolean expression to be satisfied when the condition expression becomes true from false. FRETISH provides a variety of timings. In this case study, we use *always* and *eventually*.

3.1 Safety PLC Program

The safety PLC program of the *SM18 Cluster F*, a superconducting magnet test facility at CERN, is meant to protect the personnel and the equipment

```
F_MAIN shall always satisfy if (PLC_END & (!MTBF_WCC_PCLSW20_FSL | !MTBF_WCC_PCLSW20_TSH |
    (MTBF1_LSW20_POS & (!MTBF1_WCC_LSW20_FSL | !MTBF1_WCC_LSW20_TSH)) | (MTBF2_LSW20_POS &
    (!MTBF2_WCC_LSW20_FSL | !MTBF2_WCC_LSW20_TSH)))) then SIF01_DB.SIF01_PC20K
```

(a) Property of SIF01_PC20K in FRETISH.

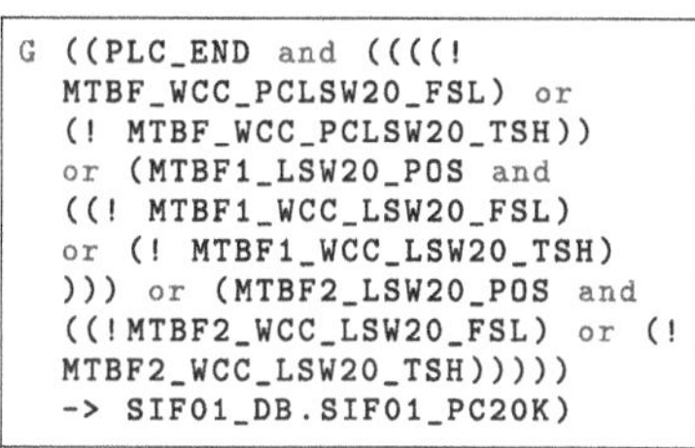

```
G ((PLC_END and ((((!
  MTBF_WCC_PCLSW20_FSL) or
  (! MTBF_WCC_PCLSW20_TSH))
  or (MTBF1_LSW20_POS and
  ((! MTBF1_WCC_LSW20_FSL)
  or (! MTBF1_WCC_LSW20_TSH)
  ))) or (MTBF2_LSW20_POS and
  ((!MTBF2_WCC_LSW20_FSL) or (!
  MTBF2_WCC_LSW20_TSH)))))
  -> SIF01_DB.SIF01_PC20K)
```

(b) Generated LTL property by FRET.

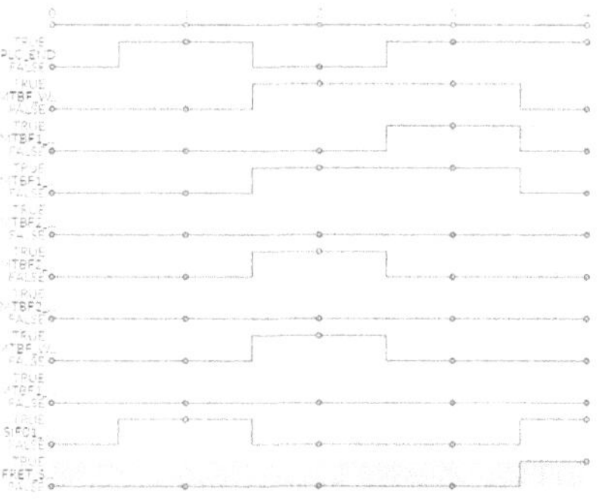

(c) Future LTL simulation

Fig. 2. Property of the SIF01_PC20K safety function.

of this installation. The *SM18 cluster F* is dedicated to test the new superconducting magnet technology for the High Luminosity Large Hadron Collider (HL-LHC) [2], an upgrade of the existing LHC particle accelerator. Its main risks are related to the cryogenic system and the powerful power converters up to 20.000 Amps.

Error Property. The property of this case study corresponds to the expected logic of one of the safety functions (*SIF01_PC20K*):

if at the end of the PLC cycle (PLC_END) the flow (*_FSL) or thermo (*_TSH) switches monitoring the cooling system detect a low flow or a high temperature, and the power converter (PC20k) is connected to the magnet (*_LSW20_POS), then the safety function should shut down the power converter (SIF01_PC20K).

Figure 2 shows how the property is expressed in FRETISH and in LTL.

Validation. Before verifying this property with PLCverif, the user should make sure that the formalized property behaves as expected. The main challenge is the number of operators and parentheses, making manual validation difficult. FRET's simulator aids by allowing the user to check any temporal valuation and whether it satisfies the property or not as shown in Fig. 2c.

3.2 Standard PLC Program

This case study is concerned with UNICOS [4], a CERN framework for the development of hundreds of industrial control systems. The selected program library is called the *OnOff* object. Its purpose is to control physical equipment driven by digital signals, which can be composed of different types of devices. This makes its PLC program highly configurable and its associated logic complex.

Error Property. The property presented here is related to the transitions between two operation modes shown in Fig. 3: (1) *Auto mode*, where the *OnOff* object is driven by the control logic of a higher object of the hierarchy of the program, and (2) *Manual mode*, where the operator drives the object.

The property extracted from the specification is: When the OnOff object is in Manual mode (MMoSt) and the control logic requests to move to Auto mode (AuAuMoR) at any point in the PLC cycle, the OnOff object should move to the Auto mode (AuMoSt). Figure 4 shows the property in FRETISH and the LTL formula.

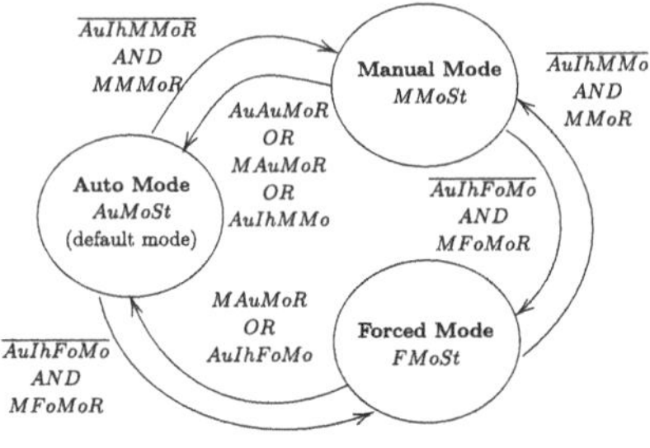

Fig. 3. OnOff operation modes specification.

```
When (MMoSt & AuAuMoR) the
    CPC_FB_OnOff shall eventually
    satisfy AuMoSt & PLC_END
```

(a) Property expressed in FRETISH.

```
(G (((!(MMoSt and AuAuMoR)) and (X (MMoSt
  and AuAuMoR))) -> (X(F(AuMoSt and
  PLC_END))))) and ((MMoSt and
  AuAuMoR) -> (F(AuMoSt and PLC_END)))
```

(b) Generated LTL property by FRET

Fig. 4. PLCverif property for the *OnOff* object.

```
the CPC_FB_OnOff shall always satisfy
    if (MMoSt & AuAuMoR & !PLC_END)
    then at the next occurrence of
    PLC_END, AuMoSt
```

(a) Property expressed in FRETISH.

```
G (((MMoSt and AuAuMoR) and (! PLC_END)) ->
  (X ((((! PLC_END) ) U PLC_END) ->
  (((! PLC_END)) U (PLC_END and AuMoSt)))))
```

(b) Generated LTL property by FRET

Fig. 5. PLCverif property for the *OnOff* object using the `nextOcc` predicate

Thanks to the new *"at the next occurrence of"* phrase, we can verify that this property is satisfied at the end of the current cycle (which is more precise and strict), as shown in Fig. 5.

These properties can not be expressed with the current PLCverif patterns, but they are expressible with the restricted natural language of FRET. Now PLCverif users can express a large variety of requirements in a natural language and validate these in the simulator.

4 Conclusion

The creation of requirements in FRET fits well into the verification workflow and improves both usability and expressiveness, as shown by the case studies. PLCverif [3] and FRET [1] are both open source.

Plans for improvements include the support of verification of time properties in PLCverif and the support for different type widths in the FRET simulator (*e.g. 16/32 bit integers*).

To the best of our knowledge, this is the first attempt to specify formal requirements using a structured natural language for PLC program verification.

References

1. FRET: Formal requirements elicitation tool. https://github.com/NASA-SW-VnV/fret
2. High luminosity large hadron collider webpage. https://home.cern/science/accelerators/high-luminosity-lhc
3. PLCverif: A tool to verify PLC programs based on model checking techniques. https://gitlab.com/plcverif-oss
4. UNICOS webpage. https://unicos.web.cern.ch/
5. Beyer, D., Henzinger, T.A., Jhala, R., Majumdar, R.: The software model checker Blast. Int. J. Softw. Tools Technol. Transf. **9**(5-6), 505–525 (2007). https://doi.org/10.1007/s10009-007-0044-z
6. Darvas, D., Fernández Adiego, B., Blanco Viñuela, E.: PLCverif: a tool to verify PLC programs based on model checking techniques. In: Proceedings of the ICALEPCS 2015, October 2015. https://doi.org/10.18429/JACoW-ICALEPCS2015-WEPGF092
7. Fernández Adiego, B., Blanco Viñuela, E.: Applying model checking to critical PLC applications: an ITER case study. In: Proceedings of the ICALEPCS 2017, October 2017. https://doi.org/10.18429/JACoW-ICALEPCS2017-THPHA161
8. Fernández Adiego, B., et al.: Applying model checking to industrial-sized PLC programs. IEEE Trans. Ind. Inform. **11**, 1400–1410 (2015). https://doi.org/10.1109/TII.2015.2489184
9. Fernández Adiego, B., Lopez-Miguel, I.D., Tournier, J.C., Blanco Viñuela, E., Ladzinski, T., Havart, F.: Applying model checking to highly-configurable safety critical software: the SPS-PPS PLC program. In: Proceedings of the ICALEPCS'21, March 2022. https://doi.org/10.18429/JACoW-ICALEPCS2021-WEPV042
10. Giannakopoulou, D., Pressburger, T., Mavridou, A., Rhein, J., Schumann, J., Shi, N.: Formal requirements elicitation with FRET. In: REFSQ Tools (2020)
11. Giannakopoulou, D., Pressburger, T., Mavridou, A., Schumann, J.: Automated formalization of structured natural language requirements. Inf. Softw. Technol. **137**, 106590 (2021)
12. Lopez-Miguel, I.D., Tournier, J.C., Fernández Adiego, B.: PLCverif: status of a formal verification tool for programmable logic controller. In: Proceedings of the ICALEPCS'21, March 2022. https://doi.org/10.18429/JACoW-ICALEPCS2021-MOPV042

13. Viñuela, E.B., Darvas, D., Molnár, V.: PLCverif re-engineered: an open platform for the formal analysis of PLC programs. In: Proceedings of the ICALEPCS'19, pp. 21–27. No. 17 in International Conference on Accelerator and Large Experimental Physics Control Systems, JACoW Publishing, Geneva, Switzerland, August 2020. https://doi.org/10.18429/JACoW-ICALEPCS2019-MOBPP01, https://jacow.org/icalepcs2019/papers/mobpp01.pdf
14. Ádám, Z., et al.: Automated verification of programmable logic controller programs against structured natural language requirements. Technical report NASA/TM 0230003752 (2023)

Automata-Based Software Model Checking of Hyperproperties

Bernd Finkbeiner[1], Hadar Frenkel[1], Jana Hofmann[2], and Janine Lohse[3(✉)]

[1] CISPA Helmholtz Center for Information Security, Saarbrücken, Germany
[2] Azure Research, Microsoft, Cambridge, UK
[3] Saarland University, Saarbrücken, Germany
s8jalohs@stud.uni-saarland.de

Abstract. We develop model checking algorithms for Temporal Stream Logic (TSL) and Hyper Temporal Stream Logic (HyperTSL) modulo theories. TSL extends Linear Temporal Logic (LTL) with memory cells, functions and predicates, making it a convenient and expressive logic to reason over software and other systems with infinite data domains. HyperTSL further extends TSL to the specification of hyperproperties – properties that relate multiple system executions. As such, HyperTSL can express information flow policies like noninterference in software systems. We augment HyperTSL with theories, resulting in HyperTSL(T), and build on methods from LTL software verification to obtain model checking algorithms for TSL and HyperTSL(T). This results in a sound but necessarily incomplete algorithm for specifications contained in the $\forall^*\exists^*$ fragment of HyperTSL(T). Our approach constitutes the first software model checking algorithm for temporal hyperproperties with quantifier alternations that does not rely on a finite-state abstraction.

1 Introduction

Hyperproperties [20] generalize trace properties [2] to system properties, i.e., properties that reason about a system in its entirety and not just about individual execution traces. Hyperproperties comprise many important properties that are not expressible as trace properties, e.g., information flow policies [20], sensitivity and robustness of cyber-physical systems, and linearizability in distributed computing [11]. For software systems, typical hyperproperties are program refinement or fairness conditions such as symmetry.

For the specification of hyperproperties, Linear Temporal Logic [50] (LTL) has been extended with trace quantification, resulting in Hyper Linear Temporal Logic [19] (HyperLTL). There exist several model checking algorithms for HyperLTL [19,23,37], but they are designed for finite-state systems and are therefore

This work was partially supported by the European Research Council (ERC) Grant HYPER (No. 101055412).

J. Hofmann—Research carried out while at CISPA Helmholtz Center for Information Security.

K. Y. Rozier and S. Chaudhuri (Eds.): NFM 2023, LNCS 13903, pp. 361–379, 2023.
https://doi.org/10.1007/978-3-031-33170-1_22

not directly applicable to software. Existing algorithms for software verification of temporal hyperproperties (e.g., [1,9]) are, with the exception of [10], limited to universal hyperproperties, i.e., properties without quantifier alternation.

In this paper, we develop algorithms for model checking software systems against $\forall^*\exists^*$ hyperproperties. Our approach is complementary to the recently proposed approach of [10]. They require to be given a finite-state abstraction of the system, based on which they can both prove and disprove $\forall^*\exists^*$ hyperproperties. We do not require abstractions and instead provide sound but necessarily incomplete approximations to detect counterexamples of the specification.

The class of $\forall^*\exists^*$ hyperproperties contains many important hyperproperties like program refinement or *generalized noninterference* [47]. Generalized noninterference states that it is impossible to infer the value of a high-security input by observing the low-security outputs. Unlike *noninterference*, it does not require the system to be deterministic. Generalized noninterference can be expressed as $\varphi_{gni} = \forall\pi\exists\pi'.\Box(i_{\pi'} = \lambda \land c_\pi = c_{\pi'})$. The formula states that replacing the value of the high-security input i with some dummy value λ does not change the observable output c.

The above formula can only be expressed in HyperLTL if i and c range over a finite domain. This is a real limitation in the context of software model checking, where variables usually range over infinite domains like integers or strings. To overcome this limitation, our specifications build on Hyper Temporal Stream Logic (HyperTSL) [22]. HyperTSL replaces HyperLTL's atomic propositions with memory cells together with predicates and update terms over these cells. Update terms use functions to describe how the value of a cell changes from the previous to the current step. This makes the logic especially suited for specifying software properties.

HyperTSL was originally designed for the synthesis of software systems, which is why all predicates and functions are uninterpreted. In the context of model checking, we have a concrete system at hand, so we should interpret functions and predicates according to that system. We therefore introduce HyperTSL(T) – HyperTSL with interpreted theories – as basis for our algorithms.

Overview. Following [41], we represent our system as a symbolic automaton labeled with program statements. Not every trace of such an automaton is also a valid program execution: for example, a trace $assert(n = 0)\,; n{-}{-}; \,(assert(n = 0))^{\omega}$[1] cannot be a program execution, as the second assertion will always fail. Such a trace is called *infeasible*. In contrast, in a feasible trace, all assertions can, in theory, succeed. As a first step, we tackle TSL model checking (Sect. 4) by constructing a program automaton whose feasible accepted traces correspond to program executions that violate the TSL specification. To do so, we adapt the algorithm of [27], which constructs such an automaton for LTL, combining the given program automaton and an automaton for the negated specification.

We then extend this algorithm for HyperTSL(T) formulas without quantifier alternation (Sect. 5.1) by applying *self-composition*, a technique commonly used for the verification of hyperproperties [5,6,30].

[1] The superscript ω denotes an infinite repetition of the program statement.

Next, in Sect. 5.2, we further extend this algorithm to finding counterexamples for $\forall^*\exists^*$-HyperTSL(T) specifications (and, dually, witnesses for $\exists^*\forall^*$ formulas). We construct an automaton that over-approximates the combinations of program executions that satisfy the existential part of the formula. If some program execution is not included in the over-approximation, this execution is a counterexample proving that the program violates the specification.

More concretely, for a HyperTSL(T) formula $\forall^m\exists^n\psi$, we construct the product of the automaton for ψ and the n-fold self-composition of the program automaton. Every feasible trace of this product corresponds to a choice of executions for the variables $\pi_1, \ldots, \pi_n$ such that ψ is satisfied. Next, we remove (some) spurious witnesses by removing infeasible traces. We consider two types of infeasibility: *k-infeasibility*, that is, a local inconsistency in a trace appearing within k consecutive timesteps; and infeasibility that is not local, and is the result of some *infeasible accepting cycles* in the automaton. In the next step, we project the automaton to the universally quantified traces, obtaining an over-approximation of the trace combinations satisfying the existential part of the formula. Finally, all that remains to check is whether the over-approximation includes all combinations of feasible traces.

Lastly, in Sect. 6, we demonstrate our algorithm for two examples, including generalized noninterference.

Contributions. We present an automata-based algorithm for software model checking of $\forall^*\exists^*$-hyperproperties. We summarize our contributions as follows.

- We extend HyperTSL with theories, a version of HyperTSL that is suitable for model checking.
- We adapt the approach of [27] to TSL(T) and alternation-free HyperTSL(T), and thereby suggest the first model checking algorithm for both TSL(T) and HyperTSL(T).
- We further extend the algorithm for disproving $\forall^*\exists^*$ hyperproperties and proving $\exists^*\forall^*$ hyperproperties using a feasibility analysis.

Related Work. Temporal stream logic extends linear temporal logic [50] and was originally designed for synthesis [35]. For synthesis, the logic has been successfully applied to synthesize the FPGA game 'Syntroids' [39], and to synthesize smart contracts [34]. To advance smart contract synthesis, TSL has been extended to HyperTSL in [22]. The above works use a version TSL that leaves functions and predicates uninterpreted. While this choice is very well suited for the purpose of synthesis, for model checking it makes more sense to use the interpretation of the program at hand. TSL was extended with theories in [33], which also analyzed the satisfiability problem of the logic. Neither TSL nor HyperTSL model checking has been studied so far (with or without interpreted theories).

For LTL, the model checking problem for infinite-state models has been extensively studied, examples are [13,16,25,27,38]. Our work builds on the automata-based LTL software model checking algorithm from [27]. There are also various algorithms for verifying universal hyperproperties on programs, for example, algorithms based on type theory [1,9]. Major related work is [10], which (in contrast to our approach) requires on predicate abstractions to model check software against $\forall^*\exists^*$ HyperLTL specifications. They can also handle asynchronous hyperproperties, which is currently beyond our scope. Another proposal for the verification of $\forall\exists$ hyperproperties on software is [52]. Here, generalized constrained horn clauses are used to verify functional specifications. The approach is not applicable to reactive, non-terminating programs. Recently, it was also proposed to apply model checkers for TLA (a logic capable of expressing software systems as well as their properties) to verify $\forall^*\exists^*$ hyperproperties [45].

Beyond the scope of software model checking, the verification of hyperproperties has been studied for various system models and classes of hyperproperties. Model checking has been studied for ω-regular properties [21,31,37] and asynchronous hyperproperties [7,12] in finite-state Kripke structures, as well as timed systems [43], real-valued [49] and probabilistic hyperproperties [3,28,29] (some of which study combinations of the above).

2 Preliminaries

A Büchi Automaton is a tuple $\mathcal{A} = (\Sigma, Q, \delta, q_0, F)$ where Σ is a finite alphabet; Q is a set of states; $\delta \subseteq Q \times \Sigma \times Q$ is the transition relation; $q_0 \in Q$ is the initial state; and $F \subseteq Q$ is the set of accepting states. A *run* of the Büchi automaton $\mathcal{A}$ on a word $\sigma \in \Sigma^\omega$ is an infinite sequence $q_0\ q_1\ q_2 \cdots \in Q^\omega$ of states such that for all $i \in \mathbb{N}, (q_i, \sigma_i, q_{i+1}) \in \delta$. An infinite word σ is *accepted* by $\mathcal{A}$ if there is a run on σ with infinitely many $i \in \mathbb{N}$ such that $q_i \in F$. The language of $\mathcal{A}$, $\mathcal{L}(\mathcal{A})$, is the set of words accepted by $\mathcal{A}$.

2.1 Temporal Stream Logic Modulo Theories TSL(T)

Temporal Stream Logic (TSL) [35] extends Linear Temporal Logic (LTL) [50] by replacing Boolean atomic propositions with predicates over memory cells and inputs, and with *update terms* that specify how the value of a cell should change.

We present the formal definition of TSL modulo theories – TSL(T), based on the definition of [33], which extends the definition [35]. The definition we present is due to [46] and it slightly differs from the definition of [33]; The satisfaction of an update term is not defined by syntactic comparison, but relative to the current and previous values of cells and inputs. This definition suites the setting of model checking, where a concrete model is given.

TSL(T) is defined based on a set of *values* $\mathbb{V}$ with *true*, *false* $\in \mathbb{V}$, a set of inputs $\mathbb{I}$ and a set of memory cells $\mathbb{C}$. Update terms and predicates are interpreted with respect to a given theory. A *theory* is a tuple $(\mathbb{F}, \varepsilon)$, where $\mathbb{F}$ is a set of function symbols; $\mathbb{F}_n$ is the set of functions of arity n; and $\varepsilon : \left(\bigcup_{n\in\mathbb{N}} \mathbb{F}_n \times \mathbb{V}^n\right) \to \mathbb{V}$ is the interpretation function, evaluating a function with arity n. For our purposes, we assume that every theory $(\mathcal{T}_{\mathcal{F}}, \varepsilon)$ contains at least $\{=, \vee, \neg\}$ with their usual interpretations.

A *function term* τ_F is defined by the grammar

$$\tau_F ::= c \mid i \mid f(\tau_F,\ \tau_F,\ \ldots\ \tau_F)$$

where $c \in \mathbb{C}, i \in \mathbb{I}, f \in \mathbb{F}$, and the number of elements in f matches its arity. An *assignment* $a : (\mathbb{I} \cup \mathbb{C}) \to \mathbb{V}$ is a function assigning values to inputs and cells. We denote the set of all assignments by A. Given a concrete assignment, we can compute the value of a function term.

The *evaluation function* $\eta : \mathcal{T}_\mathcal{F} \times \mathsf{A} \to \mathbb{V}$ is defined as

$$\begin{aligned} \eta(c, a) &= a(c) && \text{for } c \in \mathbb{C} \\ \eta(i, a) &= a(i) && \text{for } i \in \mathbb{I} \\ \eta(f\ (\tau_{F1}, \tau_{F2}, \dots, \tau_{Fn}), a) &= \varepsilon(f, (\eta(\tau_{F1}), \eta(\tau_{F2}), \dots, \eta(\tau_{Fn}))) && \text{for } f \in \mathbb{F} \end{aligned}$$

A *predicate term* τ_P is a function term only evaluating to *true* or *false*. We denote the set of all predicate terms by $\mathcal{T}_P$.

For $c \in \mathbb{C}$ and $\tau_F \in \mathcal{T}_\mathcal{F}$, $[\![c \leftarrowtail \tau_F]\!]$ is called an *update term*. Intuitively, the update term $[\![c \leftarrowtail \tau_F]\!]$ states that c should be updated to the value of τ_F. If in the previous time step τ_F evaluated to $v \in \mathbb{V}$, then in the current time step c should have value v. The set of all update terms is $\mathcal{T}_U$. TSL formulas are constructed as follows, for $c \in \mathbb{C}, \tau_P \in \mathcal{T}_P, \tau_F \in \mathcal{T}_\mathcal{F}$.

$$\varphi ::= \tau_P \mid [\![c \leftarrowtail \tau_F]\!] \mid \neg\varphi \mid \varphi \wedge \varphi \mid \bigcirc\varphi \mid \varphi\mathcal{U}\varphi$$

The usual operators $\vee, \diamondsuit$ ("eventually"), and $\square$ ("globally") can be derived using the equations $\varphi \vee \psi = \neg(\neg\varphi \wedge \neg\psi)$, $\diamondsuit\varphi = \mathit{true}\ \mathcal{U}\varphi$ and $\square\varphi = \neg\diamondsuit\neg\varphi$.

Assume a fixed initial variable assignment ζ_{-1} (e.g., setting all values to zero). The satisfaction of a TSL(T) formula with respect to a *computation* $\zeta \in \mathsf{A}^\omega$ and a time point t is defined as follows, where we define $\zeta \vDash \varphi$ as $0, \zeta \vDash \varphi$.

$$\begin{aligned} t, \zeta &\vDash \tau_P && \Leftrightarrow \eta(\tau_P, \zeta_t) = \mathit{true} \\ t, \zeta &\vDash [\![c \leftarrowtail \tau_F]\!] && \Leftrightarrow \eta(\tau_F, \zeta_{t-1}) = \zeta_t(c) \\ t, \zeta &\vDash \neg\varphi && \Leftrightarrow \neg(t, \zeta \vDash \varphi) \\ t, \zeta &\vDash \varphi \wedge \psi && \Leftrightarrow t, \zeta \vDash \varphi \text{ and } t, \zeta \vDash \psi \\ t, \zeta &\vDash \bigcirc\varphi && \Leftrightarrow t + 1, \zeta \vDash \varphi \\ t, \zeta &\vDash \varphi\mathcal{U}\psi && \Leftrightarrow \exists t' \geq t.\ t', \zeta \vDash \psi \text{ and } \forall t \leq t'' < t'.\ t'', \zeta \vDash \varphi \end{aligned}$$

3 HyperTSL Modulo Theories

In this section, we introduce HyperTSL(T), HyperTSL with theories, which enables us to interpret predicates and functions depending on the program at hand. In [22], two versions of HyperTSL are introduced: HyperTSL and HyperTSL$_{rel}$. The former is a conservative extension of TSL to hyperproperties, meaning that predicates only reason about a single trace. In HyperTSL$_{rel}$, predicates may relate multiple traces, which opens the door to expressing properties like noninterference in infinite domains. Here, we build on HyperTSL$_{rel}$, allowing, in addition, update terms ranging over multiple traces. Furthermore, we extend the originally uninterpreted functions and predicates with an interpretation over theories. We denote this logic by HyperTSL(T).

$\pi := (c = 0)\ (c = 1)^\omega,\ \pi' := ((c = 0)\ (c = 1)\ (c = 2))^\omega$
$\hat{a}_1 : \{c_\pi \mapsto 0, c_{\pi'} \mapsto 0\}, \hat{a}_2 : \{c_\pi \mapsto 1, c_{\pi'} \mapsto 1\}$
$\hat{a}_3 : \{c_\pi \mapsto 1, c_{\pi'} \mapsto 2\}, \hat{a}_4 : \{c_\pi \mapsto 1, c_{\pi'} \mapsto 0\}$

Fig. 1. Left: A program automaton. Right: two traces π and π' of the program automaton. We interpret each trace as a computation. When executing both traces simultaneously, every time point has a corresponding hyper-assignment that assigns values to c_π and $c_{\pi'}$. Those for the first four time steps are shown on the right. Together, they define the hyper-computation $\hat{\varsigma} := \hat{a}_1(\hat{a}_2\ \hat{a}_3\ \hat{a}_4)^\omega$, matching π and π'.

The syntax of HyperTSL(T) is that of TSL(T), with the addition that cells and inputs are now each assigned to a trace variable that represents a computation. For example, c_π now refers to the memory cell c in the computation represented by the trace π. Formally, let Π be a set of trace variables. We define a *hyper-function term* $\hat{\tau_F} \in \hat{\mathcal{T}_F}$ as a function term using $(\mathbb{I} \times \Pi)$ as the set of inputs and $(\mathbb{C} \times \Pi)$ as the set of cells.

Definition 1. *A* hyper-function term $\hat{\tau_F}$ *is defined by the grammar*

$$\hat{\tau_F} ::= c_\pi \mid i_\pi \mid f(\hat{\tau_F},\ \hat{\tau_F},\ \ldots\ \hat{\tau_F})$$

where $c_\pi \in \mathbb{C} \times \Pi, i_\pi \in \mathbb{I} \times \Pi, f \in \mathbb{F}$, *and the number of the elements in the tuple matches the function arity. We denote by* $\hat{\mathcal{T}_F}$ *the set of all hyper-function terms.*

Analogously, we define *hyper-predicate terms* $\hat{\tau_P} \in \hat{\mathcal{T}_P}$ as hyper-function terms evaluating to *true* or *false*; *hyper-assignments* $\hat{\mathsf{A}} = (\mathbb{I} \cup \mathbb{C}) \times \Pi \to \mathbb{V}$ as functions mapping cells and inputs of each trace to their current values; *hyper-computations* $\hat{\varsigma} \in \hat{\mathsf{A}}^\omega$ as hyper-assignment sequences. See Fig. 1 for an example.

Definition 2. *Let* $c_\pi \in \mathbb{C} \times \Pi, \hat{\tau_P} \in \hat{\mathcal{T}_P}, \hat{\tau_F} \in \hat{\mathcal{T}_F}$. *A* HyperTSL(T) formula *is defined by the following grammar:*

$$\varphi ::= \psi \mid \forall \pi.\ \varphi \mid \exists \pi.\ \varphi$$
$$\psi ::= \hat{\tau_P} \mid [\![c_\pi \leftarrowtail \hat{\tau_F}]\!] \mid \neg\psi \mid \psi \wedge \psi \mid \bigcirc\psi \mid \psi\,\mathcal{U}\,\psi$$

To define the semantics of HyperTSL(T), we need the ability to extend a hyper-computation to new trace variables, one for each path quantifier. Let $\hat{\varsigma} \in \hat{\mathsf{A}}^\omega$ be a hyper-computation, and let $\pi, \pi' \in \Pi, \varsigma \in \mathsf{A}^\omega$ and $x \in (\mathbb{I} \cup \mathbb{C})$. We define the extension of $\hat{\varsigma}$ by π using the computation ς as $\hat{\varsigma}[\pi, \varsigma]\ (x_{\pi'}) = \hat{\varsigma}(x_{\pi'})$ for $\pi' \neq \pi$, and $\hat{\varsigma}[\pi, \varsigma]\ (x_\pi) = \varsigma(x_\pi)$ for π.

Definition 3. *The* satisfaction of a HyperTSL(T)-Formula *w.r.t. a hyper- computation* $\hat{\varsigma} \in \hat{\mathsf{A}}^\omega$, *a set of computations* Z *and a time point* t *is defined by*

$$t, Z, \hat{\varsigma} \vDash \forall \pi.\ \varphi \qquad \Leftrightarrow \forall \varsigma \in Z.\ t,\ Z,\ \hat{\varsigma}[\pi, \varsigma] \vDash \varphi$$
$$t, Z, \hat{\varsigma} \vDash \exists \pi.\ \varphi \qquad \Leftrightarrow \exists \varsigma \in Z.\ t,\ Z,\ \hat{\varsigma}[\pi, \varsigma] \vDash \varphi$$

The cases that do not involve path quantification are analogous to those of TSL(T) as defined in Sect. 2.1. We define $Z \models \varphi$ *as* $0, Z, \varnothing^\omega \models \varphi$.

4 Büchi Product Programs and TSL Model Checking

We now describe how we model the system and specification as Büchi automata, adapting the automata of [27] to the setting of TSL. Then, we introduce our model checking algorithm for TSL(T). In Sect. 5.2 we build on this algorithm to propose an algorithm for HyperTSL(T) model checking.

We use a symbolic representation of the system (see, for example, [41]), where transitions are labeled with program statements, and all states are accepting.

Definition 4. *Let* $c \in \mathbb{C}, \tau_P \in \mathcal{T}_P$ *and* $\tau_F \in \mathcal{T}_\mathcal{F}$. *We define the set of* (basic) program statements *as*

$$s_0 ::= assert(\tau_P) \mid c := \tau_F \mid c := *$$
$$s ::= s_0 \mid s; s$$

We call statements of the type s_0 basic program statements, *denoted by* $Stmt_0$*; statements of type* s *are denoted by* $Stmt$. *The assignment* $c := *$ *means that any value could be assigned to* c.

A *program automaton* $\mathcal{P}$ is a Büchi automaton with $\Sigma = Stmt$, that is, $\mathcal{P} = (Stmt, Q, q_0, \delta, F)$ and $\delta \subseteq Q \times Stmt \times Q$. When modeling the system we only need basic statements, thus we have $Stmt = Stmt_0$; and $F = Q$ as all states are accepting. See Fig. 3 for an illustration.

Using a program automaton, one can model `if` statements, `while` loops, and non-deterministic choices. However, not every trace of the program automaton corresponds to a program execution. For example, the trace $(n := input_1); assert(n > 0); assert(n < 0); assert(true)^\omega$ does not – the second assertion will always fail. Such a trace is called *infeasible*. We call a trace *feasible* if it corresponds to a program execution where all the assertions may succeed. We now define this formally.

Definition 5. *A computation* ζ matches *a trace* $\sigma \in Stmt_0^\omega$ *at time point* t, *denoted by* $\zeta \triangleleft_t \sigma$, *if the following holds:*

$$\begin{array}{ll} \textit{if } \sigma_t = assert(\tau_P): & \eta(\tau_P, \zeta_{t-1}) = true \quad \textit{and} \quad \forall c \in \mathbb{C}.\ \zeta_t(c) = \zeta_{t-1}(c) \\ \textit{if } \sigma_t = c := \tau_F: & \eta(\tau_F, \zeta_{t-1}) = \zeta_t(c) \quad \textit{and} \quad \forall c' \in \mathbb{C}\backslash\{c\}.\ \zeta_t(c') = \zeta_{t-1}(c') \\ \textit{if } \sigma_t = c := *: & \forall c \in \mathbb{C}\backslash\{c\}.\ \zeta_t(c) = \zeta_{t-1}(c) \end{array}$$

where ζ_{-1} *is the initial assignment. A computation* ζ *matches a trace* $\sigma \in Stmt_0^\omega$, *denoted by* $\zeta \triangleleft \sigma$, *if* $\forall t \in \mathbb{N}.\ \zeta \triangleleft_t \sigma$.

Definition 6. *A program automaton $\mathcal{P}$ over $Stmt_0$ satisfies a TSL(T)-formula φ, if for all traces σ of P we have $\forall \zeta \in \mathbb{A}^\omega.\ \zeta \triangleleft \sigma \Rightarrow \zeta \vDash \varphi$.*

We now present an algorithm to check whether a program automaton $\mathcal{P}$ satisfies a TSL(T) formula. It is an adaption of the automaton-based LTL software model checking approach by [27], where the basic idea is to first translate the negated specification φ into an automaton $\mathcal{A}_{\neg\varphi}$, and then combine $\mathcal{A}_{\neg\varphi}$ and $\mathcal{P}$ to a new automaton, namely the *Büchi program product*. The program satisfies the specification iff the Büchi program product accepts no feasible trace.

In [27], the Büchi program product is constructed similarly to the standard product automata construction. To ensure that the result is again a program automaton, the transitions are not labeled with pairs $(s, l) \in Stmt_0 \times 2^{AP}$, but with the program statement $(s;\ assert(l))$. A feasible accepted trace of the Büchi program product then corresponds to a counterexample proving that the program violates the specification. In the following, we discuss how we adapt the construction of the Büchi program product for TSL(T) such that this property – a feasible trace corresponds to a counterexample – remains true for TSL(T).

Let φ be a TSL(T) specification. For the construction of $\mathcal{A}_{\neg\varphi}$, we treat all update and predicate terms as atomic propositions, resulting in an LTL formula $\neg\varphi_{LTL}$, which is translated to a Büchi automaton.[2] For our version of the Büchi program product, we need to merge a transition label s from $\mathcal{P}$ with a transition label l from $\mathcal{A}_{\neg\varphi_{LTL}}$ into a single program statement such that the assertion of the combined statement succeeds iff l holds for the statement s. Note that l is a set of update and predicate terms. For the update terms $[\![c \leftarrowtail \tau_F]\!]$ we cannot just use an assertion to check if they are true, as we need to 'save' the value of τ_F before the statement s is executed.

Our setting differs from [27] also in the fact that their program statements do not reason over input streams. We model the behavior of input streams by using fresh memory cells that are assigned a new value at every time step. In the following, we define a function *combine* that combines a program statement s and a transition label l to a new program statement as described above.

Definition 7. *Let $\upsilon = \{[\![c_1 \leftarrowtail \tau_{F1}]\!], \ldots, [\![c_n \leftarrowtail \tau_{Fn}]\!]\}$ be the set of update terms appearing in φ, let ρ be the set of predicate terms appearing in φ. Let $l \subseteq (\upsilon \cup \rho)$ be a transition label of $\mathcal{A}_{\neg\varphi}$. Let $(tmp_j)_{j\in\mathbb{N}}$ be a family of fresh cells. Let $\mathbb{I} = \{i_1, \ldots i_m\}$. We define the function combine : $Stmt \times \mathcal{P}(\mathcal{T}_P \cup \mathcal{T}_U) \rightarrow Stmt$ as follows. The result of combine(s, l) is composed of the program statements in save_values$_l$, s, new_inputs, check_preds$_l$ and check_updates$_l$. Then we have:*

$$save\_values := tmp_1 := \tau_{F1};\ \ldots; tmp_n := \tau_{Fn}$$

$$new\_inputs := i_1 := *;\ \ldots\ ; i_m := *$$

$$check\_preds_l := assert\left(\bigwedge_{\tau_P \in l} \tau_P \wedge \bigwedge_{\tau_P \in \rho \setminus l} \neg\tau_P\right)$$

[2] For the translation of LTL formulas to Büchi automata, see, for example, [4,48,51].

$$check\_updates_l := assert\left(\bigwedge_{[\![c_j \twoheadleftarrow \tau_{Fj}]\!] \in v} \begin{cases} c_j = tmp_j & if\ [\![c_j \twoheadleftarrow \tau_{Fj}]\!] \in l \\ c_j \neq tmp_j & else \end{cases} \right)$$

$$combine(s,l) := save\_values;\ s;\ new\_inputs;\ check\_preds_l;\ check\_updates_l$$

We can extend this definition to combining traces instead of single transition labels. This leads to a function $combine : Stmt^\omega \times \mathcal{P}(\mathcal{T}_P \cup \mathcal{T}_U)^\omega \to Stmt^\omega$. Note that the result of *combine* is again a program statement in *Stmt* (or a trace $Stmt^\omega$) over the new set of cells $\mathbb{C} \cup \mathbb{I} \cup (tmp_j)_{j \in \mathbb{N}}$, which we call $\mathbb{C}^*$.

Example 1. Let $\mathbb{I} = \{i\}$. Then the result of $combine(n := 42, \{[\![n \twoheadleftarrow n+7]\!], n > 0\})$ is $tmp_0 := n + 7;\ n := 42;\ i := *;\ assert(n > 0);\ assert(n = tmp_0)$.

As *combine* leads to composed program statements, we now need to extend the definition of feasibility to all traces. To do so, we define a function $flatten : Stmt^\omega \to {Stmt_0}^\omega$ that takes a sequence of program statements and transforms it into a sequence of basic program statements by converting a composed program statement into multiple basic program statements.

Definition 8. *A trace $\sigma \in Stmt^\omega$* matches *a* computation *ζ, denoted by $\zeta \lhd \sigma$ if $\zeta \lhd flatten(\sigma)$. A trace σ is* feasible *if there is a computation ζ such that $\zeta \lhd \sigma$.*

Definition 9 ***(Combined Product).*** *Let $\mathcal{P} = (Stmt, Q, q_0, \delta, Q)$ be a program automaton and $\mathcal{A} = (\mathcal{P}(\mathcal{T}_P \cup \mathcal{T}_U), Q', q'_0, \delta', F')$ be a Büchi automaton (for example, the automaton $\mathcal{A}_{\neg\varphi_{LTL}}$). The combined product $\mathcal{P} \otimes \mathcal{A}$ is an automaton $\mathcal{B} = (Stmt, Q \times Q', (q_0, q'_0), \delta_B, F_B)$, where*

$$F_B = \{(q, q') \mid q \in Q \wedge q' \in F'\}$$
$$\delta_B = \{((p,q), combine(s,l), (p',q')) \mid (p,s,p') \in \delta \wedge (q,l,q') \in \delta'\}$$

Theorem 1. *Let $\mathcal{P}$ be a program automaton over $Stmt_0$. Let φ be a TSL(T) formula. Then $\mathcal{P}$ satisfies φ if and only if $\mathcal{P} \otimes \mathcal{A}_{\neg\varphi_{LTL}}$ has no feasible trace.*

Proof (sketch). If $\zeta \lhd \sigma$ is a counterexample, we can construct a computation $\tilde{\zeta}$ that matches the corresponding combined trace in $\mathcal{P} \otimes \mathcal{A}_{\neg\varphi_{LTL}}$, and vice versa. See the full version [32] for the formal construction.

We can now apply Theorem 1 to solve the model checking problem by testing whether $\mathcal{P} \otimes \mathcal{A}_{\neg\varphi_{LTL}}$ does not accept any feasible trace, using the feasibility check in [27] as a black box. The algorithm of [27] is based on counterexample-guided abstraction refinement (CEGAR [18]). Accepted traces are checked for feasibility. First, finite prefixes of the trace are checked using an SMT-solver. If they are feasible, a ranking function synthesizer is used to check whether the whole trace eventually terminates. If the trace is feasible, it serves as a counterexample. If not, the automaton is refined such that it now does not include the spurious counterexample trace anymore, and the process is repeated. For more details, we refer to [27]. The limitations of SMT-solvers and ranking function synthesizers also limit the functions and predicates that can be used in both the program and in the TSL(T) formula.

5 HyperTSL(T) Model Checking

We now turn to the model checking problem of HyperTSL(T). We start with alternation-free formulas and continue with $\forall^*\exists^*$ formulas.

5.1 Alternation-Free HyperTSL(T)

In this section, we apply the technique of self-composition to extend the algorithm of Sect. 4 to alternation-free HyperTSL(T). First, we define what it means for a program automaton to satisfy a HyperTSL(T) formula.

Definition 10. *Let $\mathcal{P}$ be a program automaton over $Stmt_0$, let φ be a HyperTSL(T) formula and let $Z = \{\zeta \in \mathsf{A}^\omega \mid \exists\sigma.\ \zeta \triangleleft \sigma$ and σ is a trace of $\mathcal{P}\}$. We say that $\mathcal{P}$* satisfies *φ if $Z \models \varphi$.*

Definition 11. *Let $\mathcal{P} = (Stmt, Q, q_0, \delta, Q)$ be a program automaton. The n*-fold self-composition *of $\mathcal{P}$ is $\mathcal{P}^n = (Stmt', Q^n, q_0^n, \delta^n, Q^n)$, where $Stmt'$ are program statements over the set of inputs $\mathbb{I} \times \Pi$ and the set of cells $\mathbb{C} \times \Pi$ and where $Q^n = Q \times \cdots \times Q$, $q_0^n = (q_0, \ldots, q_0)$ and*

$$\begin{aligned}\delta^n = &\{((q_1, \ldots, q_n), ((s_1)_{\pi_1}; \ldots; (s_n)_{\pi_n}), (q_1', \ldots, q_n'))\\ &\mid \forall 1 \leq i \leq n.\ (q_i, s_i, q_i') \in \delta\}\end{aligned}$$

where $(s)_\pi$ renames every cell c used in s to c_π and every input i to i_π.

Theorem 2. *A program automaton $\mathcal{P}$ over $Stmt_0$ satisfies a universal HyperTSL(T) formula $\varphi = \forall\pi_1. \ldots \forall\pi_n.\ \psi$ iff $\mathcal{P}^n \otimes \mathcal{A}_{\neg\psi_{LTL}}$ has no feasible trace.*

Theorem 3. *A program automaton P over $Stmt_0$ satisfies an existential HyperTSL(T) formula $\varphi = \exists\pi_1. \ldots \exists\pi_n.\ \psi$ iff $\mathcal{P}^n \otimes \mathcal{A}_{\psi_{LTL}}$ has some feasible trace.*

The proofs of are analogous to the proof of Theorem 1, see the full version of this paper [32] for details.

5.2 $\forall^*\exists^*$ HyperTSL(T)

In this section, we present a sound but necessarily incomplete algorithm for finding counterexamples for $\forall^*\exists^*$ HyperTSL(T) formulas.[3] Such an algorithm can also provide witnesses $\exists^*\forall^*$ formulas. As HyperTSL(T) is built on top of HyperLTL, we combine ideas from finite-state HyperLTL model checking [37] with the algorithms of Sect. 4 and Sect. 5.1.

Let $\varphi = \forall^m\exists^n.\psi$. For HyperLTL model checking, [37] first constructs an automaton containing the system traces satisfying $\psi_\exists := \exists^n.\psi$, and then applies

[3] Note that the algorithms of Sect. 4 and Sect. 5.1 are also incomplete, due to the feasibility test. However, the incompleteness of the algorithm we provide in this section is inherent to the quantifier alternation of the formula.

complementation to extract counterexamples for the $\forall\exists$ specification. Consider the automaton $\mathcal{P}^n \otimes \mathcal{A}_{\psi_{LTL}}$ from Sect. 4, whose feasible traces correspond to the system traces satisfying $\psi_\exists$. If we would be able to remove all infeasible traces, we could apply the finite-state HyperLTL model checking construction. Unfortunately, removing all infeasibilities is impossible in general, as the result would be a finite-state system describing exactly an infinite-state system. Therefore, the main idea of this section is to remove parts of the infeasible traces from $\mathcal{P}^n \otimes \mathcal{A}_{\psi_{LTL}}$, constructing an over-approximation of the system traces satisfying $\psi_\exists$. A counterexample disproving φ is then a combination of system traces that is not contained in the over-approximation.

We propose two techniques for removing infeasibility. The first technique removes *k-infeasibility* from the automaton, that is, a local inconsistency in a trace, occurring within k consecutive time steps. When choosing k, there is a trade-off: if k is larger, more counterexamples can be identified, but the automaton construction gets exponentially larger.

The second technique removes *infeasible accepting cycles* from the automaton. It might not be possible to remove all of them, thus we bound the number of iterations. We present an example and then elaborate on these two methods.

Example 2. The trace t_1 below is 3-infeasible, because regardless of the value of n prior to the second time step, the assertion in the fourth time step will fail.

$$t_1 = (n--;\ assert(n >= 0))\ (n := 1;\ assert(n >= 0))\ (n--;\ assert(n >= 0))^\omega$$

In contrast, the trace $t_2 = (n := *)\ (n--;\ assert(n >= 0))^\omega$ is not k-infeasible for any k, because the value of n can always be large enough to pass the first k assertions. Still, the trace is infeasible because n cannot decrease forever without dropping below zero. If such a trace is accepted by an automaton, $n--;\ assert(n >= 0)$ corresponds to an infeasible accepting cycle.

Removing k-Infeasibility. To remove k-infeasibility from an automaton, we construct a new program automaton that 'remembers' the $k-1$ previous statements. The states of the new automaton correspond to paths of length k in the original automaton. We add a transition labeled with l between two states p and q if we can extend the trace represented by p with l such that the resulting trace is k-feasible. Formally, we get:

Definition 12. *Let $k \in \mathbb{N}$, $\sigma \in Stmt^\omega$. We say that σ is k-*infeasible *if there exists $j \in \mathbb{N}$ such that $\sigma_j\sigma_{j+1}\dots\sigma_{j+k-1}; assert(true)^\omega$ is infeasible for all possible initial assignments ζ_{-1}. We then also call the subsequence $\sigma_j\sigma_{j+1}\dots\sigma_{j+k-1}$ infeasible. If a trace is not k-infeasible, we call it k-feasible.*[4]

Definition 13. *Let $\mathcal{P} = (Stmt, Q, q_0, \delta, F)$ be a program automaton. Let $k \in \mathbb{N}$. We define $\mathcal{P}$ without k-infeasibility, as $\mathcal{P}_k = (Stmt, Q', q_0, \delta', F')$ where*

$$Q' := \{(q_1, s_1, q_2 \dots, s_{k-1}, q_k) \mid (q_1, s_1, q_2) \in \delta \wedge \dots \wedge (q_{k-1}, s_{k-1}, q_k) \in \delta\} \cup$$

[4] Whether a subsequence $\sigma_j\sigma_{j+1}\dots\sigma_{j+k-1}$ is a witness of k-infeasibility can be checked using an SMT-solver, e.g., [14,15,17,26].

$$\{(q_0, s_0, q_1 \dots, s_{k'-1}, q_{k'}) \mid k' < k-1 \wedge (q_0, s_0, q_1) \in \delta \wedge \dots \wedge (q_{k'-1}, s_{k'-1}, q_{k'}) \in \delta\}$$

$$\begin{aligned}\delta' := &\{((q_1, s_1, q_2 \dots, s_{k-1}, q_k), s_k, (q_2, s_2, \dots, q_k, s_k, q_{k+1})) \in Q' \times \mathit{Stmt} \times Q' \\ &\quad \mid s_1 \dots s_k \ \mathit{feasible}\} \cup \\ &\{((q_0, s_0, q_1 \dots, s_{k'-1}, q_{k'}), s_{k'}, (q_0, s_0, \dots, q_{k'}, s_{k'}, q_{k'+1})) \in Q' \times \mathit{Stmt} \times Q' \\ &\quad \mid k' < k-1 \wedge s_0 \dots s_{k'} \ \mathit{feasible}\}\end{aligned}$$

$$\begin{aligned}F' := &\{(q_1, s_1, q_2 \dots, s_{k-1}, q_k) \in Q' \mid q_k \in F\} \cup \\ &\{(q_0, s_0, q_1 \dots, s_{k'-1}, q_{k'}) \in Q' \mid k' < k-1 \wedge q_{k'} \in F\}\end{aligned}$$

Theorem 4. *$\mathcal{P}_k$ accepts exactly the k-feasible traces of $\mathcal{P}$.*

The proof follows directly from the construction above. For more details, see full version [32].

Removing Infeasible Accepting Cycles. For removing infeasible accepting cycles, we first enumerate all simple cycles of the automaton (using, e.g., [44]), adding also cycles induced by self-loops. For each cycle ϱ that contains at least one accepting state, we test its feasibility: first, using an SMT-solver to test if ϱ is locally infeasible; then, using a ranking function synthesizer (e.g., [8,24,40]) to test if ϱ^ω is infeasible. If we successfully prove infeasibility, we refine the model, using the methods from [41,42]. This refinement is formalized in the following.

Definition 14. *Let $\mathcal{P} = (\mathit{Stmt}, Q, q_0, \delta, F)$ be a program automaton. Let $\varrho = (q_1, s_1, q_2)(q_2, s_2, q_3) \dots (q_n, s_n, q_1)$ be a sequence of transitions of $\mathcal{P}$. We say that ϱ is an* infeasible accepting cycle *if there is a $1 \leq j \leq n$ with $q_j \in F$ and $(s_1 s_2 \dots s_{n-1})^\omega$ is infeasible for all possible initial assignments ζ_{-1}.*

Definition 15. *Let $\mathcal{P}$ be a program automaton and $C \subseteq (Q \times \mathit{Stmt} \times Q)^\omega$ be a set of infeasible accepting cycles of $\mathcal{P}$. Furthermore, let*

$$\varrho = (q_1, s_1, q_2)(q_2, s_2, q_3) \dots (q_{n-1}, s_{n-1}, q_n) \in C.$$

The automaton $\mathcal{A}_\varrho$ for ϱ is $\mathcal{A}_\varrho = (\mathit{Stmt}, Q = \{q_0, q_1, \dots q_n\}, q_0, \delta, Q \backslash \{q_0\})$ where

$$\begin{aligned}\delta \;=\; &\{(q_0, s, q_0) \mid s \in \mathit{Stmt}\} \\ &\cup \{(q_j, s_j, q_{j+1}) \mid 1 \leq j < n\} \cup \{(q_0, s_1, q_2), (q_n, s_n, q_1)\}.\end{aligned}$$

Then, $\mathcal{A}_\varrho$ accepts exactly the traces that end with ϱ^ω, without any restriction on the prefix. See Fig. 2 for an example. To exclude the traces of $\mathcal{A}_\varrho$ from $\mathcal{P}$, we define $\mathcal{P}_C := \mathcal{P} \backslash \left(\bigcup_{\varrho \in C} \mathcal{A}_\varrho\right)$.[5] This construction can be repeated to exclude infeasible accepted cycles that are newly created in $\mathcal{P}_C$. We denote the result of iterating this process k' times by $\mathcal{P}_{C(k')}$.

Finding Counterexamples for $\forall^*\exists^*$ HyperTSL(T)-Formulas. Consider now a HyperTSL(T) formula $\varphi = \forall^{1 \cdots m} \exists^{m+1 \cdots n}. \psi$ and a program automaton $\mathcal{P}$.

[5] For two automata $\mathcal{A}_1, \mathcal{A}_2$ we use $\mathcal{A}_1 \backslash \mathcal{A}_2$ to denote the intersection of $\mathcal{A}_1$ with the complement of $\mathcal{A}_2$, resulting in the language $\mathcal{L}(\mathcal{A}_1) \setminus \mathcal{L}(\mathcal{A}_2)$.

For finding a counterexample, we first construct the combined product $\mathcal{P}^n \otimes \mathcal{A}_\psi$. Each feasible accepted trace of $\mathcal{P}^n \otimes \mathcal{A}_\psi$ corresponds to a combination of n feasible program traces that satisfy ψ. Next, we eliminate k-infeasibility and remove k'-times infeasible accepting cycles from the combined product, resulting in the automaton $(\mathcal{P}^n \otimes \mathcal{A}_\psi)_{k,C(k')}$. Using this modified combined product, we obtain an over-approximation of the program execution combinations satisfying the existential part of the specification. Each trace of the combined product is a combination of n program executions and a predicate/update term sequence. We then project the m universally quantified program executions from a feasible trace, obtaining a tuple of m program executions that satisfy the existential part of the formula. Applying this projection to all traces of $(\mathcal{P}^n \otimes \mathcal{A}_\psi)_{k,C(k')}$ leads to an over-approximation of the program executions satisfying the existential part of the specification. Formally:

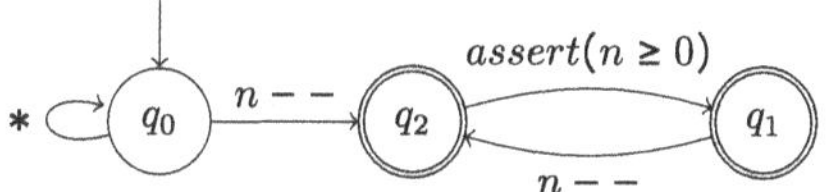

Fig. 2. Automaton $\mathcal{A}_\varrho$ for the infeasible cycle $\varrho = (q_1,\ n--,\ q_2)(q_2,\ assert(n > 0),\ q_1)$. Label $*$ denotes an edge for every (relevant) statement.

Definition 16. *Let $\mathcal{P}$ be a program automaton, let $m \leq n \in \mathbb{N}$, and let $\mathcal{A}_\psi$ be the automaton for the formula ψ. Let $(\mathcal{P}^n \otimes \mathcal{A})_{k,C(k')} = (Stmt, Q, q_0, \delta, F)$. We define the* projected automaton $(\mathcal{P}^m \otimes \mathcal{A})^{\forall}_{k,C(k')} = (Stmt, Q, q_0, \delta^{\forall}, F)$ *where* $\delta^{\forall} = \{(q, (s_1; \ldots;\ s_m), q') \mid \exists s_{m+1}, \ldots s_n, l.\ (q, combine(s_1; \ldots;\ s_n, l), q') \in \delta\}$.

The notation $s_1; s_2$ refers to a sequence of statements, as given in Definition 4. For more details on the universal projection we refer the reader to [36].

Now, it only remains to check whether the over-approximation contains all tuples of m feasible program executions. If not, a counterexample is found. This boils down to testing if $\mathcal{P}^m \backslash (\mathcal{P}^n \otimes \mathcal{A}_\psi)^{\forall}_{k,C(k')}$ has some feasible trace. Theorem 5 states the soundness of our algorithm. For the proof, see full version [32].

Theorem 5. *Let $\varphi = \forall^{1 \cdots m} \exists^{m+1 \cdots n}.\psi$ be a HyperTSL(T) formula. If the automaton $\mathcal{P}^m \backslash (\mathcal{P}^n \otimes \mathcal{A}_\psi)^{\forall}_{k,C(k')}$ has a feasible trace, then $\mathcal{P}$ does not satisfy φ.*

6 Demonstration of the Algorithm

In this section, we apply the algorithm of Sect. 5.2 to two simple examples, demonstrating that removing some infeasibilities can already be sufficient for identifying counterexamples.

Generalized Noninterference Recall the formula $\varphi_{gni} = \forall \pi.\ \exists \pi'.\ \square(i_{\pi'} = \lambda \wedge c_\pi = c_{\pi'})$ introduced in Sect. 1, specifying generalized noninterference. We model-check φ_{gni} on the program automaton $\mathcal{P}$ of Fig. 3 (left), setting $\lambda = 0$. The program $\mathcal{P}$ violates φ_{gni} since for the trace $(assert(i < 0)\ c := 0)^\omega$ there is no other trace where on which c is equal, but $i = 0$. The automaton for $\psi = \square(i_{\pi'} = 0 \wedge c_\pi = c_{\pi'})$ consists of a single accepting state with the self-loop labeled with $\tau_P = (i_{\pi'} = 0 \wedge c_\pi = c_{\pi'})$. For this example, it suffices to choose $k = 1$.

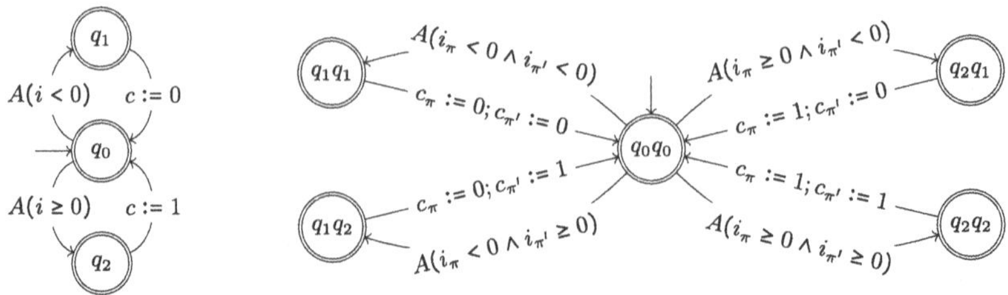

Fig. 3. Left: The program automaton $\mathcal{P}$ used in the first example. Right: The program automaton $\mathcal{P}^2$. For brevity, we use A for *assert* and join consecutive assertions.

To detect 1-inconsistencies we construct $\mathcal{P}^2$ (Fig 3, right). Then, $(\mathcal{P}^2 \otimes \mathcal{A}_\psi)_k$ is the combined product with all 1-inconsistent transitions removed (see Fig. 5 for the combined product).

The automaton $(\mathcal{P}^2 \otimes \mathcal{A}_\psi)_k^\forall$ is shown in Fig. 4. It does not contain the trace $\sigma = assert(i < 0)\ (c := 0)^\omega$ which is a feasible trace of $\mathcal{P}$. Therefore, σ is a feasible trace accepted by $\mathcal{P} \backslash (\mathcal{P}^2 \otimes \mathcal{A}_\psi)_k^\forall$ and is a counterexample proving that $\mathcal{P}$ does not satisfy generalized noninterference – there is no feasible trace that agrees on the value of the cell c but has always $i = 0$.

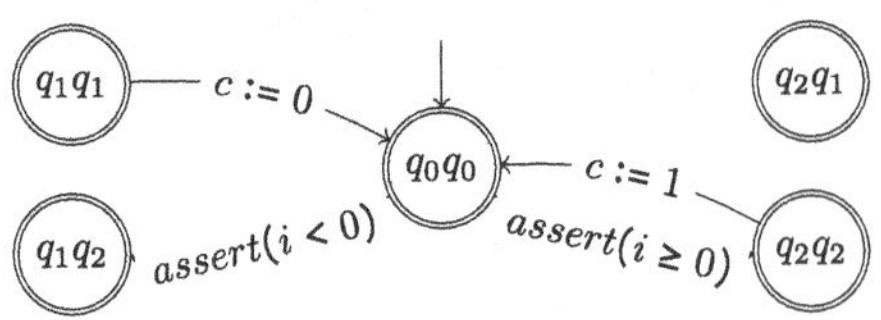

Fig. 4. program automaton $(\mathcal{P}^2 \otimes \mathcal{A}_\psi)_k^\forall$

The Need of Removing Cycles. We now present an example in which removing k-infeasibility is not sufficient, but removing infeasible accepting cycles leads to a counterexample. Consider the specification $\varphi = \forall\pi\exists\pi'.\square(p_\pi \neq p_{\pi'} \wedge n_\pi < n_{\pi'})$ and the program automaton $\mathcal{P}_{cy}$ of Fig. 6. The formula φ states that for every trace π, there is another trace π' which differs from π on p, but in which n is always greater. The trace $\pi = (n := *); (p := *); assert(p = 0); (n - -)^\omega$ is a counterexample for φ in $\mathcal{P}_{cy}$ as any trace π' which differs on p will decrease its n by 2 in every time step, and thus $n_{\pi'}$ will eventually drop below n_π.

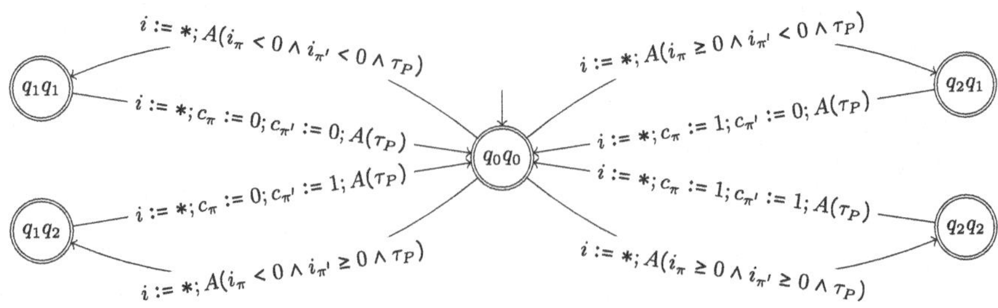

Fig. 5. The combined product $(\mathcal{P}^2 \otimes \mathcal{A}_\psi)$

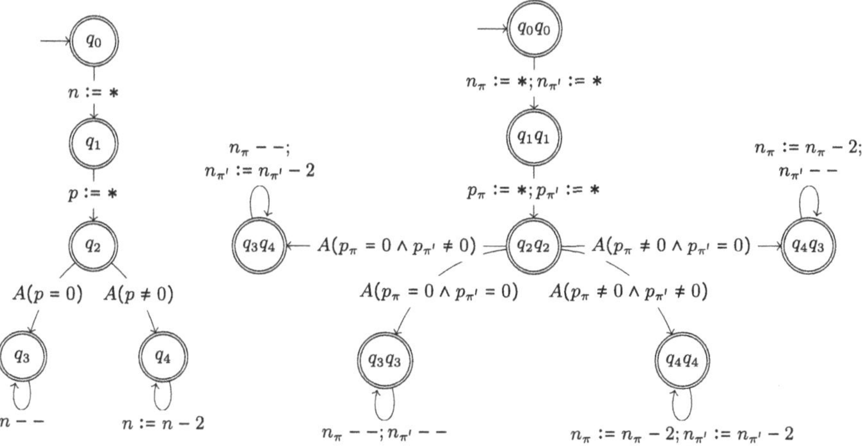

Fig. 6. Left: The program automaton $\mathcal{P}_{cy}$, Right: The program automaton $\mathcal{P}_{cy}^2$.

The automaton $\mathcal{P}_{cy}^2$ is shown in Fig. 6. In the combined product, the structure of the automaton stays the same, and $assert(p_\pi \neq p_{\pi'} \wedge n_\pi < n'_\pi)$ is added to every state. Removing local k-infeasibilities is not sufficient here; assume $k = 1$. The only 1-infeasible transition is the transition from q_2q_2 to q_3q_3, and this does not eliminate the counterexample π. Greater k's do not work as well, as the remaining traces of the combined product are not k infeasible for any k.

However, the self-loop at q_3q_4 is an infeasible accepting cycle – the sequence $(n_\pi--;\ n_{\pi'} := n_{\pi'}-2;\ assert(n_\pi < n_{\pi'}))^\omega$ must eventually terminate. We choose $k' = 1$ removing all traces ending with this cycle. Next, we project the automaton to the universal part. The trace π is not accepted by the automaton $(\mathcal{P}^2 \otimes \mathcal{A}_\psi)^\forall_{1,C(1)}$. But since π is in $\mathcal{P}$ and feasible, it is identified as a counterexample.

7 Conclusions

We have extended HyperTSL with theories, resulting in HyperTSL(T), and provided the first infinite-state model checking algorithms for both TSL(T) and HyperTSL(T). As this is the first work to study (Hyper)TSL model checking, these are also the first algorithms for *finite-state* model checking for (Hyper)TSL. For TSL(T), we have adapted known software model checking algorithm for LTL to the setting of TSL(T). We then used the technique of self-composition to generalize this algorithm to the alternation-free fragment of HyperTSL(T).

We have furthermore described a sound but necessarily incomplete algorithm for finding counterexamples for $\forall^*\exists^*$-HyperTSL(T) formulas (and witnesses proving $\exists^*\forall^*$ formulas). Our algorithm makes it possible to find program executions violating properties like generalized noninterference, which is only expressible by using a combination of universal and existential quantifiers.

Finding model checking algorithms for other fragments of HyperTSL(T), and implementing our approach, remains as future work.

References

1. Aguirre, A., Barthe, G., Gaboardi, M., Garg, D., Strub, P.-Y.: A relational logic for higher-order programs. Proc. ACM Program. Lang. **1**(ICFP):21:1–21:29 (2017)
2. Alpern, B., Schneider, F.B.: Defining liveness. Inf. Process. Lett. **21**, 181–185 (1985)
3. Arora, S., Hansen, R.R., Larsen, K.G., Legay, A., Poulsen, D.B.: Statistical model checking for probabilistic hyperproperties of real-valued signals. In: Legunsen, O., Rosu, G. (eds.) SPIN 2022. LNCS, vol. 13255, pp. 61–78. Springer, Cham (2022). https://doi.org/10.1007/978-3-031-15077-7_4
4. Babiak, T., Křetínský, M., Řehák, V., Strejček, J.: LTL to Büchi automata translation: fast and more deterministic. In: Flanagan, C., König, B. (eds.) TACAS 2012. LNCS, vol. 7214, pp. 95–109. Springer, Heidelberg (2012). https://doi.org/10.1007/978-3-642-28756-5_8
5. Barthe, G., Crespo, J.M., Kunz, C.: Beyond 2-safety: asymmetric product programs for relational program verification. In: Artemov, S., Nerode, A. (eds.) LFCS 2013. LNCS, vol. 7734, pp. 29–43. Springer, Heidelberg (2013). https://doi.org/10.1007/978-3-642-35722-0_3
6. Barthe, G., D'Argenio, P.R., Rezk, T.: Secure information flow by self-composition. Math. Struct. Comput. Sci. **21**(6), 1207–1252 (2011)
7. Baumeister, J., Coenen, N., Bonakdarpour, B., Finkbeiner, B., Sánchez, C.: A temporal logic for asynchronous hyperproperties. In: Silva, A., Leino, K.R.M. (eds.) CAV 2021, Part I. LNCS, vol. 12759, pp. 694–717. Springer, Cham (2021). https://doi.org/10.1007/978-3-030-81685-8_33
8. Ben-Amram, A.M., Genaim, S.: On the linear ranking problem for integer linear-constraint loops. In: Giacobazzi, R., Cousot, R. (eds.) The 40th Annual ACM SIGPLAN-SIGACT Symposium on Principles of Programming Languages, POPL 2013, Rome, Italy, 23–25 January 2013, pp. 51–62. ACM (2013)
9. Benton, N.: Simple relational correctness proofs for static analyses and program transformations. In: Jones, N.D., Leroy, X. (eds.) Proceedings of the 31st ACM SIGPLAN-SIGACT Symposium on Principles of Programming Languages, POPL 2004, Venice, Italy, 14–16 January 2004, pp. 14–25. ACM (2004)
10. Beutner, R., Finkbeiner, B.: Software verification of hyperproperties beyond k-safety. In: Shoham, S., Vizel, Y. (eds.) CAV 2022, Part I. LNCS, vol. 13371, pp. 341–362. Springer, Cham (2022). https://doi.org/10.1007/978-3-031-13185-1_17
11. Bonakdarpour, B., Sanchez, C., Schneider, G.: Monitoring hyperproperties by combining static analysis and runtime verification. In: Margaria, T., Steffen, B. (eds.) ISoLA 2018, Part II. LNCS, vol. 11245, pp. 8–27. Springer, Cham (2018). https://doi.org/10.1007/978-3-030-03421-4_2
12. Bozzelli, L., Peron, A., Sánchez, C.: Expressiveness and decidability of temporal logics for asynchronous hyperproperties. In: Klin, B., Lasota, S., Muscholl, A. (eds.) 33rd International Conference on Concurrency Theory, CONCUR 2022, 12–16 September 2022, Warsaw, Poland. LIPIcs, vol. 243, pp. 27:1–27:16. Schloss Dagstuhl - Leibniz-Zentrum für Informatik (2022)
13. Bradley, A.R.: SAT-based model checking without unrolling. In: Jhala, R., Schmidt, D. (eds.) VMCAI 2011. LNCS, vol. 6538, pp. 70–87. Springer, Heidelberg (2011). https://doi.org/10.1007/978-3-642-18275-4_7

14. Bruttomesso, R., Pek, E., Sharygina, N., Tsitovich, A.: The OpenSMT solver. In: Esparza, J., Majumdar, R. (eds.) TACAS 2010. LNCS, vol. 6015, pp. 150–153. Springer, Heidelberg (2010). https://doi.org/10.1007/978-3-642-12002-2_12
15. Christ, J., Hoenicke, J., Nutz, A.: SMTInterpol: an interpolating SMT solver. In: Donaldson, A., Parker, D. (eds.) SPIN 2012. LNCS, vol. 7385, pp. 248–254. Springer, Heidelberg (2012). https://doi.org/10.1007/978-3-642-31759-0_19
16. Cimatti, A., Griggio, A.: Software model checking via IC3. In: Madhusudan, P., Seshia, S.A. (eds.) CAV 2012. LNCS, vol. 7358, pp. 277–293. Springer, Heidelberg (2012). https://doi.org/10.1007/978-3-642-31424-7_23
17. Cimatti, A., Griggio, A., Schaafsma, B.J., Sebastiani, R.: The MathSAT5 SMT solver. In: Piterman, N., Smolka, S.A. (eds.) TACAS 2013. LNCS, vol. 7795, pp. 93–107. Springer, Heidelberg (2013). https://doi.org/10.1007/978-3-642-36742-7_7
18. Clarke, E., Grumberg, O., Jha, S., Lu, Y., Veith, H.: Counterexample-guided abstraction refinement. In: Emerson, E.A., Sistla, A.P. (eds.) CAV 2000. LNCS, vol. 1855, pp. 154–169. Springer, Heidelberg (2000). https://doi.org/10.1007/10722167_15
19. Clarkson, M.R., Finkbeiner, B., Koleini, M., Micinski, K.K., Rabe, M.N., Sánchez, C.: Temporal logics for hyperproperties. In: Abadi, M., Kremer, S. (eds.) POST 2014. LNCS, vol. 8414, pp. 265–284. Springer, Heidelberg (2014). https://doi.org/10.1007/978-3-642-54792-8_15
20. Clarkson, M.R., Schneider, F.B.: Hyperproperties. J. Comput. Secur. **18**(6), 1157–1210 (2010)
21. Coenen, N., Finkbeiner, B., Hahn, C., Hofmann, J.: The hierarchy of hyperlogics. In: 34th Annual ACM/IEEE Symposium on Logic in Computer Science, LICS 2019, Vancouver, BC, Canada, 24–27 June 2019, pp. 1–13. IEEE (2019)
22. Coenen, N., Finkbeiner, B., Hofmann, J., Tillman, J.: Smart contract synthesis modulo hyperproperties. In: 36th IEEE Computer Security Foundations Symposium (CSF 2023) (2023, to appear)
23. Coenen, N., Finkbeiner, B., Sánchez, C., Tentrup, L.: Verifying hyperliveness. In: Dillig, I., Tasiran, S. (eds.) CAV 2019, Part I. LNCS, vol. 11561, pp. 121–139. Springer, Cham (2019). https://doi.org/10.1007/978-3-030-25540-4_7
24. Colón, M.A., Sipma, H.B.: Practical methods for proving program termination. In: Brinksma, E., Larsen, K.G. (eds.) CAV 2002. LNCS, vol. 2404, pp. 442–454. Springer, Heidelberg (2002). https://doi.org/10.1007/3-540-45657-0_36
25. Daniel, J., Cimatti, A., Griggio, A., Tonetta, S., Mover, S.: Infinite-state liveness-to-safety via implicit abstraction and well-founded relations. In: Chaudhuri, S., Farzan, A. (eds.) CAV 2016, Part I. LNCS, vol. 9779, pp. 271–291. Springer, Cham (2016). https://doi.org/10.1007/978-3-319-41528-4_15
26. de Moura, L., Bjørner, N.: Z3: an efficient SMT solver. In: Ramakrishnan, C.R., Rehof, J. (eds.) TACAS 2008. LNCS, vol. 4963, pp. 337–340. Springer, Heidelberg (2008). https://doi.org/10.1007/978-3-540-78800-3_24
27. Dietsch, D., Heizmann, M., Langenfeld, V., Podelski, A.: Fairness modulo theory: a new approach to LTL software model checking. In: Kroening, D., Păsăreanu, C.S. (eds.) CAV 2015, Part I. LNCS, vol. 9206, pp. 49–66. Springer, Cham (2015). https://doi.org/10.1007/978-3-319-21690-4_4
28. Dimitrova, R., Finkbeiner, B., Torfah, H.: Probabilistic hyperproperties of Markov decision processes. In: Hung, D.V., Sokolsky, O. (eds.) ATVA 2020. LNCS, vol. 12302, pp. 484–500. Springer, Cham (2020). https://doi.org/10.1007/978-3-030-59152-6_27

29. Dobe, O., Ábrahám, E., Bartocci, E., Bonakdarpour, B.: HyperProb: a model checker for probabilistic hyperproperties. In: Huisman, M., Păsăreanu, C., Zhan, N. (eds.) FM 2021. LNCS, vol. 13047, pp. 657–666. Springer, Cham (2021). https://doi.org/10.1007/978-3-030-90870-6_35
30. Eilers, M., Müller, P., Hitz, S.: Modular product programs. ACM Trans. Program. Lang. Syst. **42**(1), 3:1–3:37 (2020)
31. Finkbeiner, B.: Model checking algorithms for hyperproperties (invited paper). In: Henglein, F., Shoham, S., Vizel, Y. (eds.) VMCAI 2021. LNCS, vol. 12597, pp. 3–16. Springer, Cham (2021). https://doi.org/10.1007/978-3-030-67067-2_1
32. Finkbeiner, B., Frenkel, H., Hofmann, J., Lohse, J.: Automata-based software model checking of hyperproperties. CoRR, abs/2303.14796 (2023)
33. Finkbeiner, B., Heim, P., Passing, N.: Temporal stream logic modulo theories. In: FoSSaCS 2022. LNCS, vol. 13242, pp. 325–346. Springer, Cham (2022). https://doi.org/10.1007/978-3-030-99253-8_17
34. Finkbeiner, B., Hofmann, J., Kohn, F., Passing, N.: Reactive synthesis of smart contract control flows. CoRR, abs/2205.06039 (2022)
35. Finkbeiner, B., Klein, F., Piskac, R., Santolucito, M.: Temporal stream logic: synthesis beyond the bools. In: Dillig, I., Tasiran, S. (eds.) CAV 2019, Part I. LNCS, vol. 11561, pp. 609–629. Springer, Cham (2019). https://doi.org/10.1007/978-3-030-25540-4_35
36. Finkbeiner, B., Passing, N.: Synthesizing dominant strategies for liveness. In: Dawar, A., Guruswami, V. (eds.) 42nd IARCS Annual Conference on Foundations of Software Technology and Theoretical Computer Science, FSTTCS 2022, 18–20 December 2022, IIT Madras, Chennai, India, volume 250 of LIPIcs, pp. 37:1–37:19. Schloss Dagstuhl - Leibniz-Zentrum für Informatik (2022)
37. Finkbeiner, B., Rabe, M.N., Sánchez, C.: Algorithms for model checking HyperLTL and HyperCTL*. In: Kroening, D., Păsăreanu, C.S. (eds.) CAV 2015, Part I. LNCS, vol. 9206, pp. 30–48. Springer, Cham (2015). https://doi.org/10.1007/978-3-319-21690-4_3
38. Frenkel, H., Grumberg, O., Sheinvald, S.: An automata-theoretic approach to model-checking systems and specifications over infinite data domains. J. Autom. Reason. **63**(4), 1077–1101 (2019)
39. Geier, G., Heim, P., Klein, F., Finkbeiner, B.: Syntroids: synthesizing a game for FPGAs using temporal logic specifications. In: Barrett, C.W., Yang, J. (eds.) 2019 Formal Methods in Computer Aided Design, FMCAD 2019, San Jose, CA, USA, 22–25 October 2019, pp. 138–146. IEEE (2019)
40. Heizmann, M., Hoenicke, J., Leike, J., Podelski, A.: Linear ranking for linear lasso programs. In: Van Hung, D., Ogawa, M. (eds.) ATVA 2013. LNCS, vol. 8172, pp. 365–380. Springer, Cham (2013). https://doi.org/10.1007/978-3-319-02444-8_26
41. Heizmann, M., Hoenicke, J., Podelski, A.: Software model checking for people who love automata. In: Sharygina, N., Veith, H. (eds.) CAV 2013. LNCS, vol. 8044, pp. 36–52. Springer, Heidelberg (2013). https://doi.org/10.1007/978-3-642-39799-8_2
42. Heizmann, M., Hoenicke, J., Podelski, A.: Termination analysis by learning terminating programs. In: Biere, A., Bloem, R. (eds.) CAV 2014. LNCS, vol. 8559, pp. 797–813. Springer, Cham (2014). https://doi.org/10.1007/978-3-319-08867-9_53
43. Ho, H.-S., Zhou, R., Jones, T.M.: On verifying timed hyperproperties. In: Gamper, J., Pinchinat, S., Sciavicco, G. (eds.) 26th International Symposium on Temporal Representation and Reasoning, TIME 2019, October 16–19, 2019, Málaga, Spain, LIPIcs, vol. 147, pp. 20:1–20:18. Schloss Dagstuhl - Leibniz-Zentrum für Informatik (2019)

44. Johnson, D.B.: Finding all the elementary circuits of a directed graph. SIAM J. Comput. **4**(1), 77–84 (1975)
45. Lamport, L., Schneider, F.B.: Verifying hyperproperties with TLA. In: 34th IEEE Computer Security Foundations Symposium, CSF 2021, Dubrovnik, Croatia, 21–25 June 2021, pp. 1–16. IEEE (2021)
46. Maderbacher, B., Bloem, R.: Reactive synthesis modulo theories using abstraction refinement. CoRR, abs/2108.00090 (2021)
47. McCullough, D.: Noninterference and the composability of security properties. In: Proceedings of the 1988 IEEE Symposium on Security and Privacy, Oakland, California, USA, 18–21 April 1988, pp. 177–186. IEEE Computer Society (1988)
48. Mochizuki, S., Shimakawa, M., Hagihara, S., Yonezaki, N.: Fast translation from LTL to Büchi automata via non-transition-based automata. In: Merz, S., Pang, J. (eds.) ICFEM 2014. LNCS, vol. 8829, pp. 364–379. Springer, Cham (2014). https://doi.org/10.1007/978-3-319-11737-9_24
49. Nguyen, L.V., Kapinski, J., Jin, X., Deshmukh, J.V., Johnson, T.T.: Hyperproperties of real-valued signals. In: Talpin, J.-P., Derler, P., Schneider, K. (eds.) Proceedings of the 15th ACM-IEEE International Conference on Formal Methods and Models for System Design, MEMOCODE 2017, Vienna, Austria, 29 September –02 October 2017, pp. 104–113. ACM (2017)
50. Pnueli, A.: The temporal logic of programs. In: 18th Annual Symposium on Foundations of Computer Science, Providence, Rhode Island, USA, 31 October–1 November 1977, pp. 46–57. IEEE Computer Society (1977)
51. Tsay, Y.-K., Vardi, M.Y.: From linear temporal logics to Büchi automata: the early and simple principle. In: Olderog, E.-R., Steffen, B., Yi, W. (eds.) Model Checking, Synthesis, and Learning. LNCS, vol. 13030, pp. 8–40. Springer, Cham (2021). https://doi.org/10.1007/978-3-030-91384-7_2
52. Unno, H., Terauchi, T., Koskinen, E.: Constraint-based relational verification. In: Silva, A., Leino, K.R.M. (eds.) CAV 2021, Part I. LNCS, vol. 12759, pp. 742–766. Springer, Cham (2021). https://doi.org/10.1007/978-3-030-81685-8_35

Condition Synthesis Realizability via Constrained Horn Clauses

Bat-Chen Rothenberg, Orna Grumberg, Yakir Vizel(✉), and Eytan Singher

Technion - Israel Institute of Technology, Haifa, Israel
yvizel@cs.technion.ac.il

Abstract. *Condition synthesis* takes a program in which some of the conditions in conditional branches are missing, and a specification, and automatically infers conditions to fill-in the holes such that the program meets the specification.

In this paper, we propose CoSyn, an algorithm for determining the realizability of a condition synthesis problem, with an emphasis on proving unrealizability efficiently. We use the novel concept of a *doomed* initial state, which is an initial state that can reach an error state along *every* run of the program. For a doomed initial state σ, there is no way to make the program safe by forcing σ (via conditions) to follow one computation or another. CoSyn checks for the existence of a doomed initial state via a reduction to Constrained Horn Clauses (CHC).

We implemented CoSyn in SeaHorn using Spacer as the CHC solver and evaluated it on multiple examples. Our evaluation shows that CoSyn outperforms the state-of-the-art syntax-guided tool Cvc5 in proving both realizability and unrealizability. We also show that joining forces of CoSyn and Cvc5 outperforms Cvc5 alone, allowing to solve more instances, faster.

1 Introduction

The automated synthesis of imperative programs from specifications is a very fruitful research area [1,9,16,18,22,25–28]. Our paper focuses on the important sub-problem of condition synthesis. Condition synthesis receives as input a partial program, where conditions are missing in conditional branches (e.g., `if` statements), and a specification. A solution to this problem is a set of conditions to fill-in the holes such that the resulting program meets the specification. If such a solution exists, the problem is *realizable*, otherwise it is *unrealizable*.

The main motivation for condition synthesis is automated program repair. The problem naturally arises whenever the source of a bug is believed to be in a conditional branch, and the condition has to be replaced for the program to be correct. Studies on repair have shown that many real-life bugs indeed occur due to faulty conditions [29]. Several program repair methods focus on condition synthesis [6,19,29]. These algorithms, however, do not guarantee formal verification of the resultant program, but only that it passes a certain set of tests used as a specification.

In this work, we propose CoSyn, a novel algorithm for determining the realizability of a condition synthesis problem, with an emphasis on proving unrealizability efficiently. We use a formal safety specification and conduct a search guided by semantics rather than syntax. Importantly, CoSyn's (un)realizability results are accompanied by an *evidence* to explain them.

K. Y. Rozier and S. Chaudhuri (Eds.): NFM 2023, LNCS 13903, pp. 380–396, 2023.
https://doi.org/10.1007/978-3-031-33170-1_23

Our semantics-guided search is based on the novel concept of *doomed* initial states. An initial state is called *doomed* if it eventually reaches an error state along *every* run of the program. For a doomed initial state σ, there is no way to make the program safe by forcing σ (via conditions) to follow one computation or another. It will lead to a failure anyway. Thus, the existence of such a state constitutes a proof that conditions cannot be synthesized at all, regardless of syntax.

To check for the existence of a doomed initial state, CoSYN uses a reduction to Constrained Horn Clauses (CHC). CHC is a fragment of First-Order Logic, associated with effective solvers [4]. Our reduction constructs a set of CHCs that are satisfiable iff the condition synthesis problem is realizable, and utilizes a CHC solver to solve them.

When CoSYN finds a problem unrealizable, its answer is accompanied by a *witness*: an initial doomed state. When it finds a problem realizable, it returns a *realizability proof.* A realizability proof consists of two parts: a constraint defining a range of conditions *for each hole* in the program, and a correctness certificate. The range of conditions for a hole in location l is defined using two logical predicates, $\Psi^f(l)$ and $\Psi^t(l)$. Every predicate $\Psi(l)$ for which the implication $\Psi^f(l) \implies \Psi(l) \implies \Psi^t(l)$ holds (in particular $\Psi^f(l)$ and $\Psi^t(l)$), is a valid solution for the hole in location l. Moreover, the certificate is a proof for the safety of the program when using $\Psi(l)$ as a solution.

An important feature of CoSYN is that it can complement existing synthesis algorithms such as syntax-guided-synthesis (SYGUS) [1]. SYGUS limits the search-space to a user-defined grammar, hence ensuring that if a solution is found, it is of a user-desired shape. However, if a SYGUS algorithm determines the problem is unrealizable, it is with respect to the given grammar. Instead, one can use CoSYN to determine if the problem is realizable or not. In the case that the problem is realizable, the implication $\Psi^f(l) \implies \Psi(l) \implies \Psi^t(l)$, and a grammar can be given to a SYGUS algorithm, which then synthesizes a solution that conforms with the given grammar. Note that the input problem to the SYGUS algorithm is now much simpler (as evident in our experimental evaluation). This strategy can assist users as it can indicate if a solution exists at all, or if debugging of the specification is required (when unrealizable). Moreover, it can reduce the burden from an iterative synthesis process that searches for a solution in the presence of increasingly many examples or increasingly complex grammars. This is achieved by detecting unrealizability up-front.

We implemented CoSYN in an open-source tool on top of SEAHORN, a program verification tool for C programs. We created a collection of 125 condition synthesis problems by removing conditions from verification tasks in the TCAS and SVCOMP collections and by implementing several introductory programming assignments with missing conditions. We conducted an empirical evaluation of CoSYN against the state-of-the-art SYGUS engine implemented in CVC5 on our benchmark collection. Two different variants were compared. In the first, we compare CoSYN and CVC5 without a grammar. In the second, a grammar was supplied, and we compare the performance of CoSYN in conjunction with CVC5[1] against CVC5 alone. The experiments show that in both variations, with and without grammar, CoSYN solves more instances, both realizable and unrealizable. The advantage of CoSYN is most noticeable on the unrealizable

[1] Where CoSYN is executed, and CVC5 is then invoked on the given grammar and implication $\Psi^f(l) \implies \Psi(l) \implies \Psi^t(l)$.

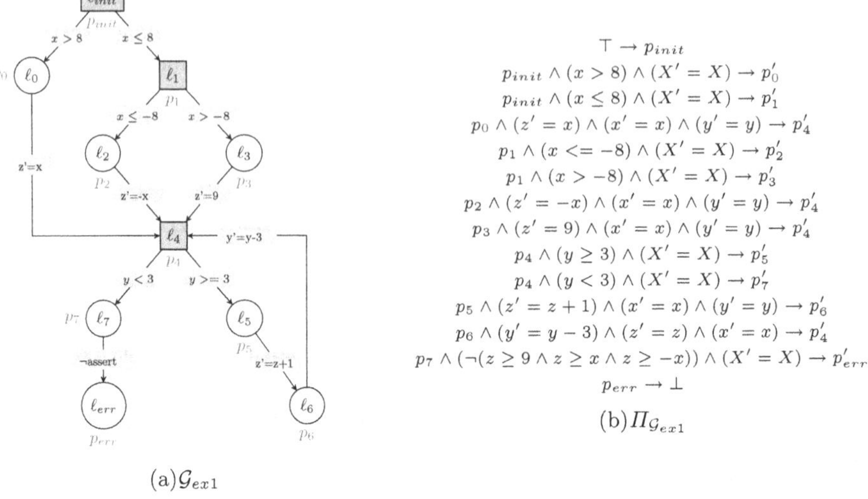

(a)$\mathcal{G}_{ex1}$
$\top \rightarrow p_{init}$
$p_{init} \wedge (x > 8) \wedge (X' = X) \rightarrow p'_0$
$p_{init} \wedge (x \leq 8) \wedge (X' = X) \rightarrow p'_1$
$p_0 \wedge (z' = x) \wedge (x' = x) \wedge (y' = y) \rightarrow p'_4$
$p_1 \wedge (x <= -8) \wedge (X' = X) \rightarrow p'_2$
$p_1 \wedge (x > -8) \wedge (X' = X) \rightarrow p'_3$
$p_2 \wedge (z' = -x) \wedge (x' = x) \wedge (y' = y) \rightarrow p'_4$
$p_3 \wedge (z' = 9) \wedge (x' = x) \wedge (y' = y) \rightarrow p'_4$
$p_4 \wedge (y \geq 3) \wedge (X' = X) \rightarrow p'_5$
$p_4 \wedge (y < 3) \wedge (X' = X) \rightarrow p'_7$
$p_5 \wedge (z' = z + 1) \wedge (x' = x) \wedge (y' = y) \rightarrow p'_6$
$p_6 \wedge (y' = y - 3) \wedge (z' = z) \wedge (x' = x) \rightarrow p'_4$
$p_7 \wedge (\neg(z \geq 9 \wedge z \geq x \wedge z \geq -x)) \wedge (X' = X) \rightarrow p'_{err}$
$p_{err} \rightarrow \bot$
(b)$\Pi_{\mathcal{G}_{ex1}}$

Fig. 1. The CFG $\mathcal{G}_{ex1}$ (left) and the set of CHCs $\Pi_{\mathcal{G}_{ex1}}$ (right).

problems. Further, CoSyn, in both variants, performs better w.r.t. runtime. This leads us to conclude that CoSyn can be an important addition to existing SyGuS tools.

To summarize, the main contributions of our work are:

- A novel algorithm, called CoSyn, for solving the (un)realizability problem of condition synthesis via a non-standard reduction to Constrained Horn Clauses (CHC). To the best of our knowledge, CoSyn is the first algorithm to determine that a condition synthesis problem is unrealizable w.r.t. any grammar.
- CoSyn's results are supported by an *evidence*: either a doomed initial state (for an unrealizable problem), or a realizability proof (for a realizable problem) that can be used by a synthesis tool to generate a solution w.r.t. a given grammar.

2 Preliminaries

2.1 Program Safety

To represent programs, we use control-flow-graphs with transitions encoded as logical formulas. We consider First Order Logic modulo a theory $\mathcal{T}$ and denote it by $FOL(\mathcal{T})$. $\mathcal{T}$ is defined over signature $\Sigma_\mathcal{T}$. We denote by X a set of variables representing program variables. A valuation σ of X is called a *program state*. We use the set $X^i = \{x^i \mid x \in X\}$ to represent variable values after i computation steps, where $i \geq 1$. For the special case of $i = 1$ (one computation step) we also use the set $X' = \{x' \mid x \in X\}$. A *state formula* is a (quantifier-free) formula in $FOL(\mathcal{T})$ defined over the signature $\Sigma_\mathcal{T} \cup X$. A *transition formula* is a (quantifier-free) formula in $FOL(\mathcal{T})$ defined over the signature $\Sigma_\mathcal{T} \cup X \cup X'$.

A *control-flow-graph (CFG)* is a tuple $\mathcal{G} = (\Lambda, \Delta, l_{init}, l_{err}, \Lambda_{cond})$, where Λ is a finite set of program locations, Δ is a set of transitions, $l_{init} \in \Lambda$ is the initial location and $l_{err} \in \Lambda$ is the error location. A *transition* τ is a triple $\langle l, \varphi, m\rangle$, where $l, m \in \Lambda$ are respectively the entry and exit locations of the transition, and φ is a transition formula. The set $\Lambda_{cond} \subset \Lambda$ is a set of locations, called *condition locations*, each of which having exactly two outgoing transitions in Δ, representing a condition and its negation. Formally, for every condition location $l_c \in \Lambda_{cond}$, there exist two distinct locations $l_c^f, l_c^t \in \Lambda$ and a state formula θ_c such that the only two outgoing transitions from l_c in Δ are $\langle l_c, \theta_c \wedge (X' = X), l_c^t\rangle$ and $\langle l_c, \neg\theta_c \wedge (X' = X), l_c^f\rangle$ (where the notation $X' = X$ is short for the conjunction of equalities between each variable and its primed version). A *path* π in the CFG is a sequence of transitions from Δ of the form

$$\pi = \langle l_0, \varphi_0, l_1\rangle\langle l_1, \varphi_1, l_2\rangle\langle l_2, \varphi_2, l_3\rangle \cdots$$

The path is an *error path* if it is finite and, in addition, $l_0 = l_{init}$ and $l_n = l_{err}$ for some $n \geq 0$. Let α_π be a sequence of formulas representing π. That is,

$$\alpha_\pi = \varphi_0(X^0, X^1), \varphi_1(X^1, X^2), \varphi_2(X^2, X^3) \cdots$$

A *run* along path π from state σ is a sequence of states $r = \sigma_0, \sigma_1, \sigma_2 \ldots$, where $\sigma = \sigma_0$ and for every $i \geq 0$, σ_i is a valuation of variables X^i, such that $(\sigma_i, \sigma_{i+1}) \models \varphi_i(X^i, X^{i+1})$. In that case, we say that r starts at l_0. Path π is *feasible* if there is a run along it. If a run $r = \sigma_0, \sigma_1, \sigma_2 \ldots$ along π starts at l_{init} (i.e., $l_0 = l_{init}$) then for every $i \geq 0$ we say that state σ_i is *reachable* at l_i.

A *safety verification problem* is to decide whether a CFG $\mathcal{G}$ is SAFE or UNSAFE. $\mathcal{G}$ is UNSAFE if there exists a feasible error path in $\mathcal{G}$. Otherwise, it is SAFE.

Example 1. The CFG $\mathcal{G}_{ex1}$ is presented in Fig. 1(a), where $\Lambda_{cond} = \{\ell_{init}, \ell_1\, \ell_4\}$. The Assertion at l_7 is $(z \geq 9 \wedge z \geq x \wedge z \geq -x)$. The path $\pi = \langle l_{init}, x \leq 8, l_1\rangle\langle l_1, x \leq -8, l_2\rangle\langle l_2, z' = -x, l_4\rangle\langle l_4, y < 3, l_7\rangle\langle l_7, \neg assert, l_{err}\rangle$ is a feasible error path in $\mathcal{G}_{ex1}$: there is a run along π from state σ, where $\sigma(x) = -8$ and $\sigma(y) = \sigma(z) = 0$. Consequently, the CFG $\mathcal{G}_{ex1}$ is UNSAFE.

2.2 Constrained Horn Clauses

Given the sets $\mathcal{F}$ of function symbols, $\mathcal{P}$ of uninterpreted predicate symbols, and $\mathcal{V}$ of variables, a *Constrained Horn Clause (CHC)* is a First Order Logic (FOL) formula of the form:

$$\forall \mathcal{V} \cdot (\phi \wedge p_1(X_1) \wedge \cdots \wedge p_k(X_k) \rightarrow h(X)), \text{ for } k \geq 1$$

where: ϕ is a constraint over $\mathcal{F}$ and $\mathcal{V}$ with respect to some background theory $\mathcal{T}$; $X_i, X \subseteq \mathcal{V}$ are (possibly empty) vectors of variables; $p_i(X_i)$ is an application $p(t_1, \ldots, t_n)$ of an n-ary predicate symbol $p \in \mathcal{P}$ for first-order terms t_i constructed from $\mathcal{F}$ and X_i; and $h(X)$ is either defined analogously to p_i or is $\mathcal{P}$-free (i.e., no $\mathcal{P}$ symbols occur in h). Here, h is called the *head* of the clause and $\phi \wedge p_1(X_1) \wedge \ldots \wedge p_k(X_k)$ is called the *body*. A clause is called a *query* if its head is $\mathcal{P}$-free, and otherwise, it is called a *rule*. A rule with body true is called a *fact*. We say a clause is *linear* if its body contains at most one predicate symbol, otherwise, it is called *non-linear*. For convenience, given a CHC C of the form $\phi \wedge p_1(X_1) \wedge \cdots \wedge p_k(X_k) \rightarrow h(X))$, we will use $head(C)$ to denote its head $h(X)$. We refrain from explicitly adding the universal quantifier when the set of variables is clear from the context.

A set Π of CHCs is *satisfiable* iff there exists an interpretation $\mathcal{I}$ such that all clauses in Π are valid under $\mathcal{I}$. For $p \in \mathcal{P}$ we denote by $\mathcal{I}[p]$ the interpretation of p in $\mathcal{I}$.

2.3 Program Safety as CHC Satisfiability

Given a CFG $\mathcal{G} = (\Lambda, \Delta, l_{init}, l_{err}, \Lambda_{cond})$, checking its safety can be reduced to checking the satisfiability of a set $\Pi_{\mathcal{G}}$ of CHCs [4], as described below. For each program location $l \in \Lambda$, define an uninterpreted predicate symbol p_l. $\Pi_{\mathcal{G}}$ is then defined as the set of the following CHCs:

1. $\top \rightarrow p_{init}(X)$
2. $p_l(X) \wedge \varphi \rightarrow p_m(X')$ for every $\langle l, \varphi, m \rangle \in \Delta$
3. $p_{err}(X) \rightarrow \bot$

Note that this formulation assumes there are no function calls in the CFG, and that all function calls in the original program are inlined. This also implies that the resulting CHCs are linear. When clear from the context, we omit X and X' from $p_l(X)$, $p_l(X')$ and $\varphi(X, X')$. Instead, we write p_l, p_l' and φ, respectively.

Example 2. Consider again the CFG $\mathcal{G}_{ex1}$, presented in Fig. 1(a), and its corresponding set of CHCs, $\Pi_{\mathcal{G}_{ex1}}$, given in Fig. 1(b). For brevity, we write p_i as short for $p_i(x, y)$ and p_i' as short for $p_i(x', y')$. As shown in Example 1, $\mathcal{G}_{ex1}$ is UNSAFE and therefore there is no satisfying interpretation for its predicate symbols.

Lemma 1. *Let p_i be the predicate symbol associated with location l_i in a CFG $\mathcal{G}$. Assume that $\Pi_{\mathcal{G}}$ is satisfiable by the interpretation $\mathcal{I}$. Then, the interpreted predicate $\mathcal{I}[p_i]$ has the property that for every state σ, if σ is reachable at l_i (from l_{init}), then $\sigma \models \mathcal{I}[p_i]$.*

3 From Realizability to CHC Satisfaibility

In this section we describe the synthesis problem we solve, named *condition synthesis*. We also show how realizability of this problem can be reduced to satisfiability of a set of CHCs. From this point on, we assume that all function calls in the original program are inlined. This implies that the set of CHCs representing the program's CFG contains only linear clauses.

3.1 Defining the Condition Synthesis Problem

Given a set of condition locations specified by the user, the goal of condition synthesis is to automatically find conditions to be placed in these locations so that the program becomes correct. We start by formally defining a program in which the conditions at some of the condition locations are missing. Intuitively, such a location imposes no constraint on the continuation of the program execution at that location. Hence, the resulting program behaves non-deterministically.

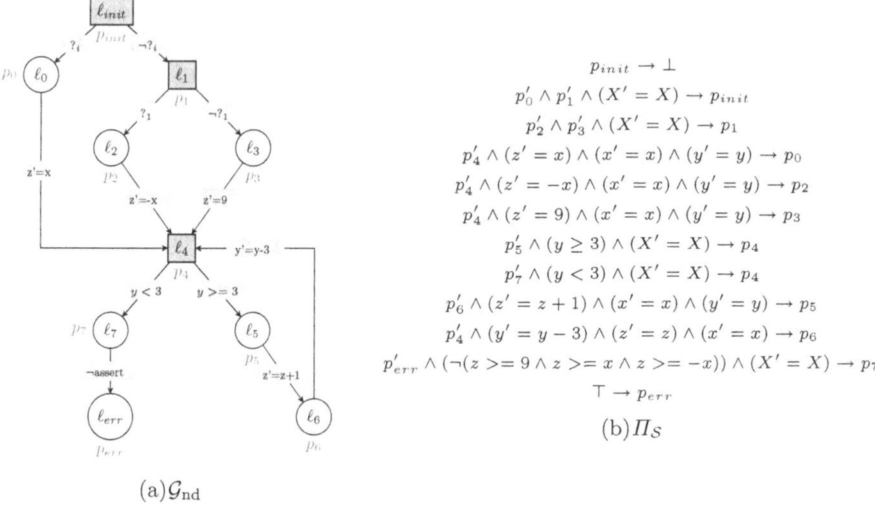

ℓ_{init}
$?_i$
$\neg ?_i$
ℓ_0
ℓ_1
$?_1$
$\neg ?_1$
ℓ_2
ℓ_3
z'=x
z'=-x
z'=9
ℓ_4
y'=y-3
$y < 3$
$y >= 3$
ℓ_7
ℓ_5
¬assert
z'=z+1
ℓ_{err}
ℓ_6
(a)$\mathcal{G}_{\text{nd}}$
$p_{init} \rightarrow \bot$
$p_0' \wedge p_1' \wedge (X' = X) \rightarrow p_{init}$
$p_2' \wedge p_3' \wedge (X' = X) \rightarrow p_1$
$p_4' \wedge (z' = x) \wedge (x' = x) \wedge (y' = y) \rightarrow p_0$
$p_4' \wedge (z' = -x) \wedge (x' = x) \wedge (y' = y) \rightarrow p_2$
$p_4' \wedge (z' = 9) \wedge (x' = x) \wedge (y' = y) \rightarrow p_3$
$p_5' \wedge (y \geq 3) \wedge (X' = X) \rightarrow p_4$
$p_7' \wedge (y < 3) \wedge (X' = X) \rightarrow p_4$
$p_6' \wedge (z' = z + 1) \wedge (x' = x) \wedge (y' = y) \rightarrow p_5$
$p_4' \wedge (y' = y - 3) \wedge (z' = z) \wedge (x' = x) \rightarrow p_6$
$p_{err}' \wedge (\neg(z >= 9 \wedge z >= x \wedge z >= -x)) \wedge (X' = X) \rightarrow p_7$
$\top \rightarrow p_{err}$
(b)Π_S

Fig. 2. The non-deterministic CFG $\mathcal{G}_{\text{nd}}$ with two non-deterministic nodes $\{l_{init}, l_1\}$ (left) and the set of CHCs Π_S (right).

Definition 1. *Let $\mathcal{G}$ be a CFG. A condition location $l_c \in \Lambda_{cond}$ is called* non-deterministic *if the two outgoing transitions from l_c have the following form: $\langle l_c, X' = X, l_c^t\rangle$ and $\langle l_c, X' = X, l_c^f\rangle$. If $\mathcal{G}$ has a non-deterministic condition location, we say that $\mathcal{G}$ is* non-deterministic.

Example 3. The left-hand-side of Fig. 2 presents the non-deterministic CFG $\mathcal{G}_{\text{nd}}$, which is identical to the CFG $\mathcal{G}_{ex1}$ of Fig. 1, except that locations $\{l_{init}, l_1\}$ are non-deterministic. The transitions leaving those locations are labeled with expressions of the form ? or ¬?, to indicate that no condition is associated with these locations.

A non-deterministic CFG $\mathcal{G}$ can be transformed into a deterministic CFG by replacing every non-deterministic control location with a deterministic condition[2]. More formally,

Definition 2. *Let $\mathcal{G} = (\Lambda, \Delta, l_{init}, l_{err}, \Lambda_{cond})$ be a non-deterministic CFG and $\Lambda_{cond}^? \subseteq \Lambda_{cond}$ be the set of non-deterministic control locations. Let $\Psi : \Lambda_{cond}^? \rightarrow \Gamma$ be a function where for every $l_s \in \Lambda_{cond}^?$, $\Psi(l_s) \in \Gamma$ is a predicate over the set of program variables. Ψ is called a resolving function. The resolved CFG $\mathcal{G}_\Psi = (\Lambda, \Delta_\Psi, l_{init}, l_{err}, \Lambda_{cond})$, is defined as follows.*

- *For $l \in (\Lambda \setminus \Lambda_{cond}^?)$ and for a formula φ and $m \in \Lambda$. If $\langle l, \varphi, m\rangle \in \Delta$, then $\langle l, \varphi, m\rangle \in \Delta_\Psi$*
- *For $l_s \in \Lambda_{cond}^?$, the only two transitions out of l_s in Δ_Ψ are $\langle l_s, \Psi(l_s) \wedge (X = X'), l_s^t\rangle$ and $\langle l_s, \neg\Psi(l_s) \wedge (X = X'), l_s^f\rangle$*

[2] We emphasize that a deterministic CFG can still contain non-deterministic assignments. In the context of CFG, non-determinisim only refers to the form/structure of the CFG.

We define the *synthesis problem* as $\mathcal{S} = (\mathcal{G}, \Lambda^?_{cond})$, where $\mathcal{G}$ is a non-deterministic CFG and $\Lambda^?_{cond}$ is the set of non-deterministic condition locations. A *solution* to $\mathcal{S}$ is a resolving function $\Psi : \Lambda^?_{cond} \to \Gamma$ such that $\mathcal{G}_\Psi$ is deterministic and SAFE.

3.2 Reducing Condition Synthesis Realizability to CHC Satisfiability

A realizability problem is to determine whether a given synthesis problem $\mathcal{S}$ has a solution or not. In this section we show how the problem of condition synthesis is reducible to the CHC satisfiability problem. In what follows we refer to realizability w.r.t. the condition synthesis problem given by $\mathcal{S} = (\mathcal{G}, \Lambda^?_{cond})$, where $\mathcal{G}$ is non-deterministic and $\Lambda^?_{cond}$ is the set of non-deterministic control locations.

Doomed States. To explain the reduction of realizability to CHC, we first introduce the notion of *doomed states*.

Definition 3. *A state σ is doomed at location l_i if every run from σ, starting at l_i, reaches the error location l_{err}.*

Note that, in particular, all runs from a state that is doomed at l_i are *finite*.

Intuitively, given a synthesis problem $\mathcal{S}$, if there exists a doomed state at location l_{init}, then $\mathcal{S}$ is *unrealizable*. Recall that $\mathcal{S} = (\mathcal{G}, \Lambda^?_{cond})$, and $\mathcal{G}$ is non-deterministic. Hence, if an initial state σ is doomed, then no matter which conditions are chosen for the non-deterministic control locations in $\mathcal{G}$, σ can reach the error location along every run. We exploit this observation to reduce the (un)realizability problem to identifying initial doomed states in a non-deterministic CFG, or proving their absence.

Example 4. Consider again the non-deterministic CFG $\mathcal{G}_{\text{nd}}$, presented in Fig. 2. The realizability problem in this case is to determine whether the synthesis problem $\mathcal{S} = (\mathcal{G}_{\text{nd}}, \{l_{init}, l_1\})$ has a solution or not.

Note that a state σ in which $\sigma(x) = 10$ and $\sigma(y) = 0$ is doomed at location l_1: All runs from this state starting at l_1 end up in l_{err}. In contrast, no state is doomed at the initial location l_{init}. That is, from any such state it is possible to find a run that does not proceed to l_{err}. As we will see later, this implies that the synthesis problem has a solution – we can assign conditions to l_{init} and l_1 s.t. the resulting program is SAFE.

Realizability to CHC. Finding the set of states that can reach l_{err} along some run from a given location $l \in \mathcal{G}$ can be achieved by iteratively computing the pre-image of bad states, starting from l_{err} up to the location l. Note that if there exists a condition location on paths from l to l_{err}, then the union of the pre-image along the "then" and "else" branches is computed.

In order to find doomed states, however, a non-deterministic condition location should be handled differently. Whenever the pre-image computation reaches a non-deterministic condition location l_s, the pre-image computed along the "then" and "else" branches need to be *intersected*. The result of this intersection is a set of states that reach l_{err} along *every* run that starts in l_s.

In what follows we describe how to construct a set of CHCs that captures doomed states. The construction is based on a transformation from the original set of CHCs $\Pi_{\mathcal{G}}$, and has two phases, described below. Due to lack of space, all proofs in the following sections are deferred to the full version.

Reversed CHC. Assume that for $\mathcal{S} = (\mathcal{G}, \Lambda^{?}_{cond})$, $\Pi_{\mathcal{G}}$ is a set of CHCs originating from $\mathcal{G}$ using the procedure presented in Sect. 2.3. As described above, computing doomed states requires computing the pre-image of states that can reach l_{err}. Hence, the first step of our reduction is to construct a new set of CHCs $\Pi^{R}_{\mathcal{G}}$, referred to as the *reverse* of $\Pi_{\mathcal{G}}$. As the name implies, $\Pi^{R}_{\mathcal{G}}$ is obtained by reversing the polarity of uninterpreted predicates in every clause. More precisely, a predicate that appears positively appears negatively in the reversed clause, and vice-versa. For example, if $p(X) \wedge \varphi(X, X') \rightarrow q(X')$ is a clause in $\Pi_{\mathcal{G}}$, then $q(X') \wedge \varphi(X, X') \rightarrow p(X)$, is a clause in $\Pi^{R}_{\mathcal{G}}$. Reversing a set of CHCs is performed using simple syntactic rules. We emphasize that this transformation is only applicable for linear CHCs. Reversing a non-linear CHC results in a clause that is not in Horn form.

Note that for a transition $\langle l, \varphi, m \rangle$, the clause $p_l(X) \wedge \varphi(X, X') \rightarrow p_m(X')$ captures the *image* operation. Namely, a given set of states in location l and their set of successors in location m satisfy the clause. Similarly, the reversed clause $p_m(X') \wedge \varphi(X, X') \rightarrow p_l(X)$ captures the *pre-image* operation. Meaning, a given set of states in location m and their predecessors at location l satisfy the reversed clause.

Theorem 1. *For every CFG $\mathcal{G}$, $\Pi_{\mathcal{G}}$ is satisfiable iff $\Pi^{R}_{\mathcal{G}}$ is satisfiable.*

Proof (sketch). Let $\mathcal{I}$ be an interpretation that satisfies $\Pi_{\mathcal{G}}$. Then, $\mathcal{I}^{R}[p_l] = \neg\mathcal{I}[p_l]$ for every location $l \in \Lambda$ is a satisfying interpretation for $\Pi^{R}_{\mathcal{G}}$. In the other direction, define $\mathcal{I}[p_l] = \neg\mathcal{I}^{R}[p_l]$, which satisfies $\Pi_{\mathcal{G}}$.

Lemma 2. *Let p_i be the predicate symbol associated with label l_i in the CFG $\mathcal{G}$. Assume that the reverse of $\Pi_{\mathcal{G}}$, $\Pi^{R}_{\mathcal{G}}$, is satisfiable by the interpretation $\mathcal{I}^{R}$. Then, for every state σ, if σ is a start of a run along a path from l_i to l_{err}, then $\sigma \models \mathcal{I}^{R}[p_i]$.*

Doomed States in Reversed CHCs. Reversing the set of CHCs allows us to capture the pre-image of l_{err}. This, as noted, is only the first step. Recall that in order to identify doomed states, whenever a non-deterministic condition location is reached, the pre-image of the "then" branch must be intersected with the pre-image of the "else" branch.

For a given non-deterministic condition location $l_s \in \Lambda^{?}_{cond}$, the reversed set of CHCs, $\Pi^{R}_{\mathcal{G}}$, contains the following two clauses:

$$p^{t}_{s}(X') \wedge (X = X') \rightarrow p_s(X) \quad \text{and} \quad p^{f}_{s}(X') \wedge (X = X') \rightarrow p_s(X),$$

where p^{t}_{s} and p^{f}_{s} represent the pre-image of the "then" branch and "else" branch, respectively. As described above, the intersection of the pre-image along the "then" and "else" branches represents the doomed states. In order to represent this intersection, the second phase of the transformation replaces every two such clauses with the clause:

$$p^{t}_{s}(X') \wedge p^{f}_{s}(X') \wedge (X = X') \rightarrow p_s(X).$$

We denote the resulting set of CHCs as $\Pi_{\mathcal{S}}$.

Example 5. Consider again the non-deterministic CFG $\mathcal{G}_{\rm nd}$, presented in Fig. 2. The right-hand-side of the figure presents the set $\Pi_{\mathcal{S}}$ of CHCs, which capture the doomed states in the control locations of $\mathcal{G}_{\rm nd}$. Assume $\mathcal{I}^{\mathcal{S}}$ is a satisfying interpretation for $\Pi_{\mathcal{S}}$. Since $\mathcal{I}^{\mathcal{S}}$ satisfies the clause $p_{init} \rightarrow \bot$ in $\Pi_{\mathcal{S}}$, then necessarily $\mathcal{I}^{\mathcal{S}}[p_{init}] = \bot$, which means that no initial state of $\mathcal{G}_{\rm nd}$ is doomed. As proved later, this guarantees that the synthesis problem $\mathcal{S} = (\mathcal{G}_{\rm nd}, \{l_{init}, l_1\})$ is realizable.

Lemma 3. *Let p_i be the predicate symbol associated with location l_i in the CFG $\mathcal{G}$. Let $\mathcal{I}^{\mathcal{S}}$ be an interpretation satisfying $\Pi_{\mathcal{S}}$ of $\mathcal{G}$. Then, for every state σ, if it is doomed at location l_i, then $\sigma \models \mathcal{I}^{\mathcal{S}}[p_i]$.*

The following theorem states that the satisfiability of $\Pi_{\mathcal{S}}$ determines the realizability of $\mathcal{S} = (\mathcal{G}, \Lambda^?_{cond})$. In fact, given a satisfying interpretation for $\Pi_{\mathcal{S}}$, it is possible to construct solutions to the synthesis problem $\mathcal{S} = (\mathcal{G}, \Lambda^?_{cond})$. Further, if $\Pi_{\mathcal{S}}$ is *not* satisfiable, then the synthesis problem is unrealizable.

Theorem 2. *$\mathcal{S} = (\mathcal{G}, \Lambda^?_{cond})$ is realizable iff $\Pi_{\mathcal{S}}$ is satisfiable.*

We partition the proof of the theorem into two. Below we present the first direction. In Sect. 4 we prove the second direction of the theorem.

Lemma 4. *If $\mathcal{S} = (\mathcal{G}, \Lambda^?_{cond})$ is realizable then $\Pi_{\mathcal{S}}$ is satisfiable.*

4 Realizability and the Satisfying Interpretation of $\Pi_{\mathcal{S}}$

In this section we first show that if $\Pi_{\mathcal{S}}$ is satisfiable, then *there exists* a solution to the realizability problem. Later in Sect. 4.2, we show how such a solution, i.e. a resolving function, can be constructed. By that, we also prove the other direction of Theorem 2.

Lemma 5. *If $\Pi_{\mathcal{S}}$ is satisfiable, then there exists a resolving function Ψ that solves $\mathcal{S} = (\mathcal{G}, \Lambda^?_{cond})$. That is, $\mathcal{G}_{\Psi}$ is SAFE.*

The above lemma implies that in the case where $\Pi_{\mathcal{S}}$ is satisfiable, then $\mathcal{S}$ is realizable. Before describing how the resolving function is constructed, we develop both the intuition and the needed technical material in the following section.

4.1 The Role of the Resolving Function

Let $\mathcal{S} = (\mathcal{G}, \Lambda^?_{cond})$ be a synthesis problem such that $\Pi_{\mathcal{S}}$ is satisfiable, and $\mathcal{I}^{\mathcal{S}}$ is its satisfying interpretation. We wish to find a solution Ψ of $\mathcal{S}$.

Recall that for a location $l_i \in \Lambda$ and its associated predicate $p_i \in \Pi_{\mathcal{S}}$, $\mathcal{I}^{\mathcal{S}}[p_i]$ is an over-approximation of states that are doomed at l_i (Lemma 3). Clearly, if a synthesized program has a reachable state that is also doomed, then the program is not SAFE. Hence, the goal is to synthesize a program where for every location $l_i \in \Lambda$, the set of states $\mathcal{I}^{\mathcal{S}}[p_i]$ is not reachable at location l_i.

The synthesis procedure can only affect non-deterministic locations, we therefore consider $l \in \Lambda^?_{cond}$ with its "else" and "then" branches, represented by l^f and l^t, respectively, and their associated predicates p, p^f and p^t[3].

Let Ψ be a resolving function for $\mathcal{S} = (\mathcal{G}, \Lambda^?_{cond})$ (by Lemma 5, Ψ exists). We can view $\Psi(l)$ as a router, directing program states that reach l to either the "then" branch (i.e., l^t) or the "else" branch (i.e., l^f). Intuitively, this router must ensure doomed states are unreachable at the "then" and "else" branches. As an example, if a state is doomed at l^f, $\Psi(l)$ "routes" it to the "then" branch (namely, to l^t) and hence it never reaches l^f.

To generalize this example, let us denote by D, D^f and D^t, the exact sets of doomed states (non-approximated) at locations l, l^f and l^t, respectively. Since Ψ is a resolving function, D, D^f and D^t *must* be unreachable at locations l, l^f and l^t, respectively.

First, let us consider the set D. Note that, $D = D^f \wedge D^t$, since a state is doomed at l iff it is doomed at both l^f and l^t. Since Ψ is a resolving function, we conclude that states in D must be unreachable at location l (otherwise, the synthesized program cannot be SAFE). This implies that $\Psi(l)$ can direct states that are in D to either the "then" or "else" branch.

Next, consider the set D^f. To ensure that this set is unreachable at l^f, all states in D^f that are reachable at l must be directed to the "then" branch (i.e. to l^t) by $\Psi(l)$. We emphasize that given the fact that D is unreachable, only states in $D^f \backslash D$ can be reachable in l. Symmetrically, all states in the set D^t that are reachable at l (namely, states in $D^t \backslash D$) must be directed to the "else" branch by $\Psi(l)$.

To summarize the above intuition, Fig. 3 presents guidelines for defining the function $\Psi(l)$. It illustrates the sets D^f and D^t inside the universe of all program states (i.e., all possible valuations of X) using a Venn diagram. There are four regions in the diagram, defining how $\Psi(l)$ behaves: states in $D^f \backslash D$ are directed to the "then" branch; states in $D^t \backslash D$ are directed to the "else" branch; and states in the Φ regions (states in D and in $(D^t \cup D^f)^c$) can be directed to either branch.

4.2 Defining a Resolving Function

As described in Sect. 3, for a location $l \in \Lambda$ with an associated predicate p, $\mathcal{I}^{\mathcal{S}}[p]$ is an over-approximation of states that are doomed at location l. We thus need to construct Ψ such that it directs states to the proper branch using the given over-approximations of doomed states, such that states in $\mathcal{I}^{\mathcal{S}}[p]$ are unreachable in $\mathcal{G}_\Psi$ at location l.

Based on the above we can use the satisfying interpretation $\mathcal{I}^{\mathcal{S}}$ in order to define the resolving function Ψ. We define two possible resolving functions: Ψ^f and Ψ^t. We prove that these two solutions are two extremes of a spectrum, hence defining a space

[3] For readability, in this section we omit s from l_s, l_s^f, l_s^t and their corresponding predicates.

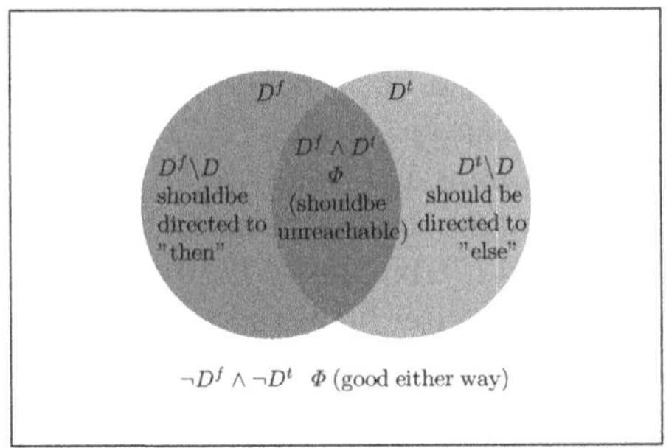

Fig. 3. Venn diagrams of the precise sets of doomed states, D^f and D^t

of possible solutions. Recall that a resolving function Ψ always defines the predicate for sending states to the "then" branch (i.e., a state is directed to the "then" branch iff it satisfies Ψ). Therefore, the resolving functions Ψ^f and Ψ^t are defined as follows:

$$\forall l_s \in \Lambda^?_{cond} : \Psi^f(l_s) \triangleq \mathcal{I}^S[p^f](X) \wedge \neg \mathcal{I}^S[p](X)$$

$$\forall l_s \in \Lambda^?_{cond} : \Psi^t(l_s) \triangleq \neg(\mathcal{I}^S[p^t](X) \wedge \neg \mathcal{I}^S[p](X)) \equiv \neg \mathcal{I}^S[p^t](X) \vee \mathcal{I}^S[p](X)$$

The following two lemmas prove that solution Ψ^f behaves as desired. That is, if it directs a state σ to the "then" branch, then σ is not doomed at l^t. Moreover, if it directs it to the "else" branch, then σ is either not doomed at l^f or unreachable at l, and therefore also unreachable at l^f. Similar lemmas can be proved for solution Ψ^t.

Lemma 6. *Let σ be a state such that $\sigma \models \Psi^f$. Then $\sigma \not\models D^t$.*

Lemma 7. *Assume that $\mathcal{I}^S[p]$ is unreachable at l. If σ is a state such that $\sigma \not\models \Psi^f$, then either $\sigma \not\models D^f$ or σ is unreachable.*

The Space of Possible Solutions. The functions Ψ^f and Ψ^t defined above are two extremes of a spectrum defining a space of solutions. More precisely, every function Ψ that satisfies $\Psi^f \to \Psi \to \Psi^t$ is a resolving function.

Next, we prove that a function Ψ, such that $\Psi^f \to \Psi \to \Psi^t$, is a solution for $\mathcal{S} = (\mathcal{G}, \Lambda^?_{cond})$. Recall that the goal of our approach is to synthesize a program where for every location $l_i \in \Lambda$, the set of states $\mathcal{I}^S[p_i]$ is not reachable at l_i. Moreover, the proof of the following lemma guarantees that $\mathcal{G}_\Psi$ is SAFE by showing that $\mathcal{I}^S$ is a satisfying interpretation of $\Pi^R_{\mathcal{G}_\Psi}$ (Theorem 1). Hence, we conclude that in the synthesized program $\mathcal{G}_\Psi$, for every location $l_i \in \Lambda$, the set of states $\mathcal{I}^S[p_i]$ (which is an over-approximation of states that reach l_{err} from l_i) is not reachable at l_i.

Lemma 8. *Let Ψ be a function s.t. for every $l \in \Lambda^?_{cond}$ the formula*

$$\Psi^f(l)(X) \to \Psi(l)(X) \to \Psi^t(l)(X)$$

is valid. Then, Ψ is a solution of $\mathcal{S}$.

Lemma 9. *There exists a function Ψ s.t. for every $l \in \Lambda^?_{cond}$ the following formula is valid: $\Psi^f(l)(X) \to \Psi(l)(X) \to \Psi^t(l)(X)$.*

Summary. Lemma 8 and Lemma 9 prove it is possible to synthesize a resolving function (in fact, a set of resolving functions) for $\mathcal{S}$ using the satisfying interpretation $\mathcal{I}^{\mathcal{S}}$ of $\Pi_{\mathcal{S}}$. This proves the correctness of the following Lemma:

Lemma 10. *If $\Pi_{\mathcal{S}}$ is satisfiable then $\mathcal{S} = (\mathcal{G}, \Lambda^?_{cond})$ is realizable.*

The correctness of Lemma 10 finalizes the proof of Theorem 2.

4.3 Synthesizing a Solution with a Grammar

While CoSyn does not require a grammar, in some cases where the problem is realizable, it may be desirable to synthesize a solution of a specific plausible shape. To achieve this, one can use CoSyn in conjunction with a synthesis framework such as the well-known Syntax Guided Synthesis (SyGuS) framework [1]. SyGuS is a prominent framework for program synthesis with respect to a formal specification. It limits the search-space to a user-defined grammar G. SyGuS algorithms have the advantage of ensuring that the solution found, if found, will be of a user-desired shape. However, they can only determine unrealizability w.r.t. to the given grammar.

In this setting, assume a grammar G is given, CoSyn is used in the following way:

(i) Execute CoSyn on the given condition synthesis problem. If the problem is unrealizable, stop and return "unrealizable".
(ii) If the problem is realizable, use the realizability proof to define a specification: for every $l \in \Lambda^?_{cond}$ the implication $\Psi^f(l)(X) \rightarrow$ [illegible]$(l)(X) \rightarrow \Psi^t(l)(X)$ must hold.
(iii) Execute a SyGuS tool on the above specification with the given grammar G (on a conjunction of all implications, or one by one[4]).
(iv) Return the synthesized result.

The above shows how CoSyn can be used to complement existing synthesis algorithms. In fact, the generated specification for the synthesis tool is much simpler as it does not need to capture the behavior of the program, only the constraints for each of the locations. This is evident in our experimental evaluation presented in Sect. 5.

5 Experimental Results

We implemented a prototype of CoSyn on top of the software verification tool SeaHorn [10], which uses Spacer [17] as the CHC solver. To evaluate CoSyn and demonstrate its applicability, we compared it against the SyGuS framework.

In order to compare against SyGuS, we implemented a procedure that translates a condition synthesis problem to SyGuS. We emphasize that since the (partial) program is given and the specification is program correctness, the translation results in a SyGuS problem that requires the solver to only synthesize the missing conditions and loop

[4] We emphasize that the implications in the different locations are independent, thus allowing synthesis of the conditions separately, one by one. Separate synthesis of conditions cannot be done trivially in regular SyGuS, due to the dependency between conditions in the synthesized program.

invariants. To solve SyGuS problems, we use Cvc5 as it is known to be efficient, as demonstrated in the SyGuS competition[5].

The experiments were executed on an AMD EPYC 7742 64-Core Processor with 504 GB of RAM, with a timeout of 60 min.

Benchmarks. The benchmark suite consists of three collections of C language programs: TCAS [7], SV-COMP [2], and Introductory.

The TCAS collection is part of the Siemens suite [7], and consists of 41 faulty versions of a program implementing a traffic collision avoidance system for aircraft. To make the benchmarks suitable for condition synthesis we removed one or more conditions from each of the faulty versions and required equivalence to the correct version as a specification.

The SV-COMP benchmarks are taken from the ReachSafety-ControlFlow category of the SV-COMP competition[6], where they are described as "programs for which the correctness depends mostly on the control-flow structure and integer variables". This collection includes three sub-categories: `nt-drivers-simplified`, `openssl-simplified`, and `locks`. For all SV-COMP benchmarks we selected a condition to remove at random.

For the Introductory collection we implemented a variety of common introductory programming tasks including sort algorithms, string and int manipulations, etc. Then, we removed one or more conditions in different critical points of each algorithm.

Results. Two different variants were tested and compared. In the first, no grammar is given to SyGuS, allowing it to synthesize any Boolean term as the solution[7]. This unrestricted mode is similar to how CoSyn is unrestricted by a grammar. The second variant executes SyGuS with a grammar $G1$. In this variant CoSyn executes as described in Sect. 4.3 using the same $G1$ grammar[8].

The table in Fig. 4 summarizes the results. For each tool, we count the number of benchmarks it was able to solve in each category, separated based on the realizability result. As can be seen from the table, in both variants, with and without a grammar, CoSyn solves the most problems, both realizable and unrealizable. The advantage of CoSyn is most noticeable on unrealizable instances.

Note that, in the second variant CoSyn and Cvc5 join forces, with the goal of achieving more syntactically appealing conditions. Note, however, that this effort sometimes leads to a timeout, as demonstrated in the table in Fig. 4, on lines 1 and 5, on the R (realizable) column. The "left" and "right" operands of the + sign that appears in the T column differentiate timeout results which are due to CoSyn and Cvc5, respectively. As expected, combining CoSyn and Cvc5 does not influence the unrealizability results (U column) when compared to CoSyn alone. That is, column U in CoSyn and CoSyn +Cvc5 are identical.

---

[5] Its predecessor, Cvc4, won the competition in most categories: https://sygus.org/comp/2019/results-slides.pdf.

[6] https://sv-comp.sosy-lab.org/2022/benchmarks.php.

[7] We used Cvc5's default configuration, except for the addition of `sygus-add-const-grammar` flag, following the advice of Cvc5's developers.

[8] $G1$ is a standard grammar allowing comparisons (e.g. $=$, $\leq$, etc.), using arrays, Integer and Boolean variables.

					Variant 1 No Grammar						Variant 2 Grammar G_1					
					Cosyn			CVC5			Cosyn+CVC5			CVC5		
category	p	c	l	LOC	R	U	T	R	U	T	R	U	T	R	U	T
introductory	35	59	54	1089	24	8	3	21	5	9	23	8	3+1	20	5	10
sv-comp/locks	13	15	13	909	11	2	0	11	2	0	11	2	0	11	2	0
sv-comp/ntdrivers-simplified	7	8	4	7831	5	2	0	4	2	1	5	2	0	4	1	2
sv-comp/openssl-simplified	23	51	23	12893	5	18	0	4	1	18	5	18	0	4	1	18
tcas	34	64	0	8059	21	13	0	5	0	29	2	13	0+19	2	0	32
total	112	197	94	30781	66	43	3	45	10	57	46	43	23	41	9	62

Fig. 4. Results summary. For each category, the columns p, c, l and LOC represent the total number of synthesis problems, conditions (after inlining), loops and lines-of-code, respectively. For each tool, columns R and U represent the number of realizable and unrealizable problems solved by the tool. T represents Timeout.

The graphs in Fig. 5 summarize runtime results on all examples. As evident by these graphs, it is not only that CoSyn solves more instances, it also performs better w.r.t. runtime. Moreover, using CoSyn in conjunction with Cvc5 (Fig. 5b), improves Cvc5's performance significantly, allowing it to solve more instances in less time. This shows that a SyGuS engine can greatly benefit from the addition of CoSyn.

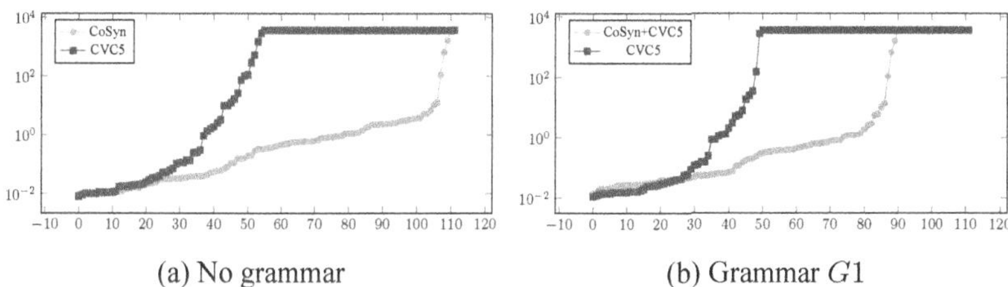

(a) No grammar

(b) Grammar $G1$

Fig. 5. Runtime (seconds) comparison. X/Y-axis represent the synthesis problems and runtime, respectively.

6 Related Work

As mentioned above, Syntax-guided synthesis (SyGuS) [1] is widely applicable and many state-of-the-art program synthesis algorithms use the SyGuS framework [3, 13, 14, 21, 23, 24]. Another significant framework is semantics-guided synthesis (SemGuS) [16], which in addition to the specification and grammar, supplies a set of inference rules to define the semantics of constructs in the grammar. This is implemented in the tool Messy.

Similar to our work, the realizability of a SemGuS problem is reduced in Messy to a CHC satisfiability problem and a solution is extracted from a satisfying interpretation, if one exists. However, the CHC satisfiability problem solved by Messy and by CoSyn are completely different. The query in Messy intuitively asks whether the initial symbol of the grammar can produce a term whose semantics coincide with the specification for a *particular, finite, set of inputs*. In contrast, our CHC satisfiability problem encodes the computation of doomed states for a given non-deterministic program. It does not encode any syntactic constraints, thus its unrealizability result is definite. Further, CoSyn ensures correctness for *all* inputs. However, CoSyn is specific to the problem of condition synthesis and cannot handle arbitrary synthesis problems.

Another synthesis approach is sketch-based synthesis [26], which allows to leave holes in place of code fragments, to be derived by a synthesizer. However, the code fragment that can be used to replace a hole in Sketch is always limited in both structure and size. Therefore, if Sketch finds the problem unrealizable, we can only conclude that there is no solution using the particular syntax. In contrast, our approach does not restrict the generated conditions syntactically at all. Further, [26] only performs bounded loop unwinding, while CoSyn guarantees correctness for unbounded computations. Another difference is that Sketch interprets integer variables as fixed-width bit-vectors while CoSyn relies on SeaHorn, which treats integer variables using integer semantics.

Finally, many synthesis and repair tools, including some mentioned above, use the counterexample guided inductive synthesis (CEGIS) framework [5,16,20,26]. They initially find a solution for only a finite set of inputs I. If verification fails for input $i \notin I$, then i is added to I and the process is repeated. However, the CEGIS process may diverge and may become very costly. CoSyn does not require the CEGIS framework since it directly solves the synthesis problem for all inputs.

Recently, several works focus mainly on unrealizability [8,11,12], while applying SyGuS or CEGIS. In [15] a logic for proving unrealizability has been proposed. However, these works do not solve condition synthesis problems or take advantage of the power of CHC solvers.

7 Conclusion

This work presents a novel approach to *(un)realizability of condition synthesis*, based on a reduction to Constrained Horn Clauses (CHC). Our algorithm, CoSyn, relies on a central notion called *doomed states*. We encode into CHC the question of whether the program includes an initial doomed state and exploit the encoding to determine (un)realizability of the synthesis problem. A doomed initial state is returned as evidence, if the problem is unrealizable. Otherwise, conditions are provided as evidence – based on these conditions the program can be proved SAFE.

Our approach can handle any number of missing conditions in the program. Our experiments show that CoSyn can solve both realizable and unrealizable examples efficiently, and can complement SyGuS tools.

References

1. Alur, R., et al.: Syntax-guided synthesis. In: Formal Methods in Computer-Aided Design, FMCAD 2013, Portland, OR, USA, 20–23 October 2013, pp. 1–8. IEEE (2013)
2. Beyer, D.: Competition on software verification. In: Flanagan, C., König, B. (eds.) TACAS 2012. LNCS, vol. 7214, pp. 504–524. Springer, Heidelberg (2012). https://doi.org/10.1007/978-3-642-28756-5_38
3. Bhatia, S., Padhi, S., Natarajan, N., Sharma, R., Jain, P.: OASIS: ILP-guided synthesis of loop invariants. CoRR (2019)
4. Bjørner, N., Gurfinkel, A., McMillan, K., Rybalchenko, A.: Horn clause solvers for program verification. In: Beklemishev, L.D., Blass, A., Dershowitz, N., Finkbeiner, B., Schulte, W. (eds.) Fields of Logic and Computation II. LNCS, vol. 9300, pp. 24–51. Springer, Cham (2015). https://doi.org/10.1007/978-3-319-23534-9_2
5. Bloem, R., et al.: FoREnSiC– an automatic debugging environment for C programs. In: Biere, A., Nahir, A., Vos, T. (eds.) HVC 2012. LNCS, vol. 7857, pp. 260–265. Springer, Heidelberg (2013). https://doi.org/10.1007/978-3-642-39611-3_24
6. DeMarco, F., Xuan, J., Le Berre, D., Monperrus, M.: Automatic repair of buggy if conditions and missing preconditions with SMT. In: Proceedings of the 6th International Workshop on Constraints in Software Testing, Verification, and Analysis, pp. 30–39. ACM (2014)
7. Do, H., Elbaum, S., Rothermel, G.: Supporting controlled experimentation with testing techniques: an infrastructure and its potential impact. Empir. Softw. Eng. **10**(4), 405–435 (2005)
8. Farzan, A., Lette, D., Nicolet, V.: Recursion synthesis with unrealizability witnesses. In: Jhala, R., Dillig, I. (eds.) PLDI 2022: 43rd ACM SIGPLAN International Conference on Programming Language Design and Implementation, San Diego, CA, USA, 13–17 June 2022, pp. 244–259. ACM (2022)
9. Fedyukovich, G., Gupta, A.: Functional synthesis with examples. In: Schiex, T., de Givry, S. (eds.) CP 2019. LNCS, vol. 11802, pp. 547–564. Springer, Cham (2019). https://doi.org/10.1007/978-3-030-30048-7_32
10. Gurfinkel, A., Kahsai, T., Komuravelli, A., Navas, J.A.: The SeaHorn verification framework. In: Kroening, D., Păsăreanu, C.S. (eds.) CAV 2015. LNCS, vol. 9206, pp. 343–361. Springer, Cham (2015). https://doi.org/10.1007/978-3-319-21690-4_20
11. Hu, Q., Breck, J., Cyphert, J., D'Antoni, L., Reps, T.W.: Proving unrealizability for syntaxguided synthesis. In: Dillig, I., Tasiran, S. (eds.) Computer Aided Verification - 31st International Conference, CAV 2019. LNCS, vol. 11561, pp. 335–352. Springer, Cham (2019). https://doi.org/10.1007/978-3-030-25540-4_18
12. Hu, Q., D'Antoni, L., Cyphert, J., Reps, T.: Exact and approximate unrealizability of syntax-guided synthesis problems. In: PLDI (2020)
13. Hu, Q., Evavold, I., Samanta, R., Singh, R., D'Antoni, L.: Program repair via direct state manipulation (2018)
14. Huang, K., Qiu, X., Shen, P., Wang, Y.: Reconciling enumerative and deductive program synthesis. In: PLDI, pp. 1159–1174 (2020)
15. Kim, J., D'Antoni, L., Reps, T.W.: Unrealizability logic. In: POPL 2023: Proceedings of the 50th Annual ACM SIGPLAN-SIGACT Symposium on Principles of Programming Languages. ACM (2023)
16. Kim, J., Hu, Q., D'Antoni, L., Reps, T.W.: Semantics guided synthesis. In: POPL (2020)
17. Komuravelli, A., Gurfinkel, A., Chaki, S.: SMT-based model checking for recursive programs. Formal Methods Syst. Des. **48**(3), 175–205 (2016)
18. Kuncak, V., Mayer, M., Piskac, R., Suter, P.: Complete functional synthesis. In: PLDI (2010)
19. Long, F., Rinard, M.: Staged program repair with condition synthesis. In: ESEC/FSE, pp. 166–178. ACM (2015)

20. Nguyen, T.-T., Ta, Q.-T., Chin, W.-N.: Automatic program repair using formal verification and expression templates. In: Enea, C., Piskac, R. (eds.) VMCAI 2019. LNCS, vol. 11388, pp. 70–91. Springer, Cham (2019). https://doi.org/10.1007/978-3-030-11245-5_4
21. Padhi, S., Sharma, R., Millstein, T.: LoopInvGen: a loop invariant generator based on precondition inference. arXiv (2017)
22. Polozov, O., Gulwani, S.: FlashMeta: a framework for inductive program synthesis. In: OOPSLA, vol. 25–30-Oct-, pp. 107–126 (2015)
23. Reynolds, A., Barbosa, H., Nötzli, A., Barrett, C., Tinelli, C.: CVC4SY: smart and fast term enumeration for syntax-guided synthesis. In: Dillig, I., Tasiran, S. (eds.) CAV 2019. LNCS, vol. 11562, pp. 74–83. Springer, Cham (2019). https://doi.org/10.1007/978-3-030-25543-5_5
24. Si, X., Lee, W., Zhang, R., Albarghouthi, A., Koutris, P., Naik, M.: Syntax-guided synthesis of datalog programs. In: ESEC/FSE, pp. 515–527 (2018)
25. So, S., Oh, H.: Synthesizing imperative programs from examples guided by static analysis. In: Ranzato, F. (ed.) SAS 2017. LNCS, vol. 10422, pp. 364–381. Springer, Cham (2017). https://doi.org/10.1007/978-3-319-66706-5_18
26. Solar-Lezama, A., Tancau, L., Bodik, R., Saraswat, V., Seshia, S., Saraswat, V.: Combinatorial sketching for finite programs. In: ACM Sigplan Notices, vol. 41, pp. 404–415. ACM (2006)
27. Srivastava, S., Gulwani, S., Foster, J.S.: From program verification to program synthesis. In: POPL (2010)
28. Wang, X., Dillig, I., Singh, R.: Program synthesis using abstraction refinement. arXiv, 2(January 2018) (2017)
29. Xiong, Y., et al.: Precise condition synthesis for program repair. In: ICSE (2017)

A Toolkit for Automated Testing of Dafny

Aleksandr Fedchin[1(✉)], Tyler Dean[3], Jeffrey S. Foster[1], Eric Mercer[3], Zvonimir Rakamarić[2], Giles Reger[2], Neha Rungta[2], Robin Salkeld[2], Lucas Wagner[2], and Cassidy Waldrip[3]

[1] Tufts University, Medford, USA
{aleksandr.fedchin,jeffrey.foster}@tufts.edu
[2] Amazon Web Services, Seattle, USA
{zvorak,reggiles,rungta,salkeldr,lgwagner}@amazon.com
[3] Brigham Young University, Provo, USA
egm@cs.byu.edu, {tyler_dean,cwaldrip}@byu.edu

Abstract. Dafny is a verification-ready programming language that is executed via compilation to C# and other mainstream languages. We introduce a toolkit for automated testing of Dafny programs, consisting of DUnit (unit testing framework), DMock (mocking framework), and DTest (automated test generation). The main component of the toolkit, DTest, repurposes the Dafny verifier to automatically generate DUnit test cases that achieve desired coverage. It supports verification-specific language features, such as pre- and postconditions, and leverages them for mocking with DMock. We evaluate the new toolkit in two ways. First, we use two open-source Dafny projects to demonstrate that DTest can generate unit tests with branch coverage that is comparable to the expectations developers set for manually written tests. Second, we show that a greedy approach to test generation often produces a number of tests close to the theoretical minimum for the given coverage criterion.

1 Introduction

Verification-ready languages and tools, such as Dafny [12,21,22] and Boogie [3], extend a core programming language with support for formal specifications such as preconditions, postconditions, and loop invariants. Developers verify programs against such specifications using built-in verifiers, thereby reducing the risk of hidden bugs. Verification-ready languages have been successfully used in scenarios ranging from low-level hypervisors [20] to entire program stacks [16].

It is common for a program written in a verification-ready language, such as Dafny, to first be compiled into a traditional programming language, such as C#, before being deployed to production. This way one can leverage the extensive compiler optimizations and libraries that have already been developed for popular programming languages. At the same time, one also needs to guarantee the correctness of the final deployed program. First, it is necessary to ensure that the Dafny compilers, such as the Dafny to C# compiler, do not introduce unexpected behavior [18]. One approach to ensure the correctness of a compiler

K. Y. Rozier and S. Chaudhuri (Eds.): NFM 2023, LNCS 13903, pp. 397–413, 2023.
https://doi.org/10.1007/978-3-031-33170-1_24

would be to verify it end-to-end. There have been such efforts in the past for other languages [23]. While successful, these efforts took years of manual human effort, and Dafny supports compilation to several different languages making verification of the entire toolchain very difficult. Second, many Dafny programs use external libraries, which are another potential source of bugs since they are not written in Dafny and hence are not verified to match their specifications. Incorrect specification of an external library may introduce bugs even if the library itself and the entire compilation pipeline are verified to be correct.

In this paper, we propose to increase assurance of the correctness of the compiled Dafny program by leveraging automated testing. More specifically, we introduce a toolkit for automated testing of Dafny programs, consisting of DUnit (unit testing framework), DMock (mocking framework), and DTest (automated test generation). The main purpose of the combined toolkit is to ensure that the guarantees provided by verified Dafny programs are preserved when those programs are executed via compilation to a different programming language, such as C#. The main component of the toolkit is DTest, a tool for automated generation of tests that achieve high coverage of Dafny programs. The tests themselves are written in Dafny and compiled to use testing frameworks in selected target languages, including C#. The tests assert that method postconditions verified in Dafny hold at runtime. Thus, we can use DTest to (i) generate tests to ensure a compiled program preserves the behavior verified in Dafny; (ii) increase confidence in specifications of external libraries that cannot be verified; and (iii) increase assurance that a Dafny program is functionally equivalent to an existing implementation that may be written in another language.

To compile tests to the target programming language, we introduce DUnit and DMock, unit testing and mocking frameworks for Dafny. DUnit extends Dafny with a method attribute :test, which signals the compiler to mark the corresponding method as a unit test in the testing framework of the target language. To support DUnit, DMock facilitates generation of complex heap structures as test inputs by adding mocking capabilities to Dafny. We introduce a new Dafny attribute (:synthesize) for tagging of mock methods, which have no body in Dafny but instead describe their return values with postconditions. Tests produced by DTest rely on mock methods to bypass the need to infer how to use existing constructors to create objects with specific field values. Instead, DMock automatically compiles mock methods to code (using the popular Moq mocking framework for C#) that returns objects that comply with the corresponding postconditions. Currently, DMock can produce mock implementations for a specific but broadly useful set of postconditions: one can supply concrete values for constant instance fields or redefine the behavior of instance functions.

Figure 1 shows the typical toolflow of the Dafny testing toolkit. DTest is implemented as an extension to Dafny and uses the existing Dafny verifier, which works by translating the Dafny program to the Boogie intermediate verification language [3,7]. Boogie, in turn, proves each assertion with Z3 [29,33]. DTest starts test generation by translating Dafny to Boogie (step 1 in the figure), including several changes to the existing translation pipeline (see Sect. 4.1).

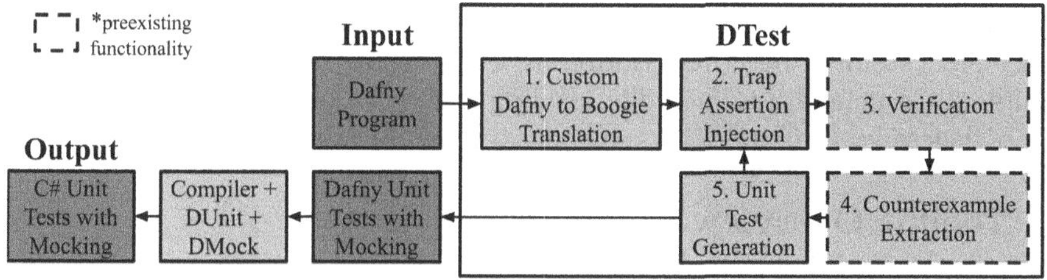

Fig. 1. Toolflow of the Dafny testing toolkit.

Next, DTest enters a loop where it systematically injects trivially failing *trap assertions* (meaning `assert false`) into the Boogie code and uses the Boogie verifier and counterexample extractor [8] to generate counterexamples that reach the assertions (steps 2–4). Then, DTest translates counterexamples into Dafny tests (step 5) using unit testing and mocking attributes understood by DUnit and DMock, and converts method postconditions into runtime oracles (see Sect. 4.3). We then compile the Dafny program and the generated tests to C# using the Dafny compiler augmented with the functionality that DUnit and DMock provide.

We evaluated our toolkit across two dimensions. First, we used DTest to generate unit tests for the Dafny utilities library (DUTIL) [24] and the portion of the AWS Encryption SDK (ESDK) that is implemented in Dafny [13]. We then compiled each library and its tests to C# and measured the coverage of the tests on the C# code: the tests produced by DTest achieved 79% (resp. 62%) statement and 84% (resp. 58%) branch coverage on DUTIL (resp. ESDK). This is promising since the ESDK developers target 80% statement and 35% branch coverage for their manually written unit tests as part of their wider testing strategy. Second, we compared the number of tests DTest generates to achieve full coverage to the number of tests generated by a brute-force algorithm that can optimally minimize the number of tests. We found that DTest often generates close-to-the-minimal number of tests, with the worst observed case (for some of the methods with the most complex control flow) being three times the optimal.

In summary, the main contributions of this work are as follows:

- We introduce DTest, a tool that uses the Dafny verifier to automatically generate unit tests for preexisting Dafny programs.
- We develop DUnit and DMock, unit testing and mocking frameworks for Dafny that support automated compilation of tests and construction of objects based on a formal description of their behavior.
- We evaluate the toolkit on a set of real-world Dafny programs and show that the generated tests achieve coverage expected by the developers.
- We released our toolkit with Dafny [12] and made the persistent artifact for the paper available at https://doi.org/10.5281/zenodo.7310719.

Overall, our results show that DUnit, DMock, and DTest are a promising toolkit for automatically generating high coverage tests for Dafny. More broadly, our work should be useful to researchers and practitioners working in verification-ready ecosystems other than Dafny, as we provide solutions for critical pain points in test generation, including dealing with pre- and postconditions, mocking in their presence, and leveraging the verifier for automatic test generation.

2 Toolkit Overview

Figure 2a gives the example Dafny method LexLeq (LexicographicByteSeqBelowAux originally) we extracted from the ESDK to illustrate how DUnit and DTest work. It takes byte sequences x and yand an index n as input, and returns a Boolean indicating whether x is equal to or precedes y in lexicographic order starting at position n. The core logic of the method (lines 5–7) is a disjunction of conditions that would make this true: either we have reached the end of x, or the byte at position n in x comes before y, or the two bytes are equal and x is before y lexicographically at position n+1. Otherwise, x is greater than y at n. Because the method is recursive, it is accompanied by a decreases clause (line 4), which allows Dafny to prove termination by stating that at each recursive call the value of $|x| - n$ decreases. The method also has a precondition (line 2) requiring that n is within a valid range for x and y, and a postcondition (line 3) ensuring that if the result is true then either we have reached the end of x or we have not reached the end of y. Note that the postcondition was not present in the original code, but we added it to more fully illustrate the features of DTest.

Dafny verifies programs by translating them to the Boogie intermediate verification language [3,7] and then verifying the Boogie code. For our example, DTest translates the Dafny code in Fig. 2a to the Boogie implementation in Fig. 2b. Note that this translation differs from one the regular Dafny to Boogie translator would produce—we discuss the differences in Sect. 4.1. The code in Fig. 2b takes three input parameters that directly map to the parameters in the Dafny code. The parameters x and y have type Seq Box, which is the type that the Dafny translator uses to encode sequences in Boogie. For clarity, we use Dafny notation in place of Boogie function calls for element access, a[i], and sequence length, |x|. On entry to the implementation, the Boogie program proceeds to either block A or B, each corresponding to one of the two possible values of the Boolean expression on line 5. Note that in Boogie, control flow is captured by non-deterministic branches to blocks guarded by assume statements. For example, here, block A is guarded by an assumption $n \neq |x|$ falsifying the condition on line 5 in Fig. 2a. Thus, the Boogie code has a block for each term of the Boolean expression in the original Dafny. Therefore, block coverage of the Boogie code essentially corresponds to branch coverage of the original Dafny code.

Recall that DTest finds inputs that reach target branches by iteratively inserting assert false in each block and then extracting a counterexample from the verifier. We call such assertions *trap assertions* because we do not expect the prover to successfully verify them. Here, DTest has added a trap assertion on line 19 in the Boogie code, with the goal of covering block L.

When we ask Boogie to verify the code in Fig. 2b, the verifier produces a counterexample. The counterexample itself is not human readable, but recent work [8]

```
function LexLeq (x: seq⟨uint8⟩, y: seq⟨uint8⟩, n: nat): (result: bool)
  requires n ≤ |x| ∧ n ≤ |y|
  ensures result ⇒ n ≡ |x| ∨ n ≠ |y|
  decreases |x| − n {
    n ≡ |x|
  ∨ (n ≠ |y| ∧ x[n] < y[n])
  ∨ (n ≠ |y| ∧ x[n] ≡ y[n] ∧ LexLeq(x, y, n + 1))}
```

(a) An example Dafny method from the ESDK.

```
implementation LexLeq (x: Seq Box, y: Seq Box, n: int)
  returns (result: bool) {
  var tmp: bool;
  Entry: goto A, B;
  A: assume n ≠ |x|;
     goto C, D;
  B: assume n ≡ |x|;
     goto E;
  // blocks C to K go here...
  L: assume n ≠ |y| ∧ x[n] ≡ y[n];
    call tmp := LexLeq(x, y, n + 1);
    assert false; // Added by DTest
    goto Return;
  Return:
    result := n ≡ |x| ∨ (n ≠ |y| ∧ x[n] < y[n])
                    ∨ (n ≠ |y| ∧ x[n] ≡ y[n] ∧ tmp);
    return;}
```

(b) (Simplified) Boogie translation with a trap assertion.

```
method {:test} test() {
  var d0: seq⟨int⟩ := [0, 133, 188];
  var d1: seq⟨int⟩ := [0, 133, 187];
  var r0 := LexLeq(d0, d1, 1);
  expect r0 ⇒ 1 ≡ |d0| ∨ 1 ≠ |d1|;}
```

(c) Generated Dafny unit test.

```
[Xunit.Fact]
public static void test() {
  var d0 = Sequence⟨int⟩
    .From(0, 133, 188);
  var d1 = Sequence⟨int⟩
    .From(0, 133, 187);
  bool r0 = LexLeq(d0, d1, 1);
  if (r0 ∧
     d0.Count ≠ 1 ∧
     d1.Count ≡ 1)
    throw new Dafny.Exception();}
```

(d) (Simplified) generated C# unit test.

Fig. 2. Unit test generation example.

allows us to infer counterexample arguments x = [0, 133, 188], y = [0, 133, 187], and n=1. DTest then uses these arguments to produce the unit test in Fig. 2c. Here the :test annotation signals to the compiler that this method should be compiled as a unit test in the target language of choice. The body of the test begins by constructing sequences d1 and d2 which, along with the literal 1, are the counterexample arguments. Next, the test case calls LexLeq with these arguments. The expect statement on line 29 is a runtime assertion. Here we check that the result satisfies the postcondition. Thus, the test not only covers block L, but also adds a level of assurance to the emitted code by introducing runtime checks.

Finally, Fig. 2d shows the C# unit test DUnit generates for the example Dafny unit test. Lines 32–35 correspond to lines 26–27 in Dafny and construct the counterexample arguments later used in the method call on line 36. The conditional on lines 37–40 throws an exception in case of a postcondition violation. Note that DUnit converts the :test annotation in Dafny to XUnit.Fact, which allows us to run the resulting test using .NET's XUnit framework [32].

3 Unit Testing and Mocking Frameworks

To support DTest, over the span of several years we developed DUnit and DMock, unit testing and mocking frameworks for Dafny. In this section, we describe the new unit testing and mocking constructs we introduced to the Dafny language as well as how we compile them into C#, the target compilation language used by most open-source Dafny projects.

As we discuss in Sect. 2 (see Fig. 2c), DUnit introduces the :test attribute for annotating unit tests. Within a unit test, we introduce expect statements to specify runtime assertion checks. In contrast to standard Dafny assert statements, the Dafny verifier does not prove expect statements but instead assumes they hold. Dafny compiles expect statements into runtime assertions in the target language, whereas assert statements are removed from compilation.

In addition to this basic unit testing support, we also introduce support for runtime *mocking*, which allows seamless creation of objects based on a description of their behavior. When compiling to C#, we translate Dafny mocks into code that uses the popular Moq library [28]. (Note that DMock also supports compilation to Java using the Mockito library [27], but we focus on C#.)

The key reason we developed DMock is to support the creation of heap-based structures (i.e., objects), which DTest heavily relies on. In particular, mocking solves the problem of having to synthesize a sequence of calls to constructors and other API methods to put a given object into the required state. In DMock, we introduce the :synthesize attribute for annotating mock methods, which is accompanied by postconditions describing the method's return value. We can use such postconditions to specify mocking behavior of constant instance fields and functions. DTest can infer from counterexamples the arguments with which to call mock methods, and we do not allow mocking of side-affecting properties, which ensures that the objects are consistent with preconditions and type invariants.

Figure 3a gives an example mock method that generates a new AwsKmsKeyring object and sets its instance fields to values given to the method call as arguments.

```
1 method {:synthesize} getKeyring
2   (client: ManagementServiceClient, key: String, arn: Identifier, tok: TokenList)
3   returns (o: AwsKmsKeyring)
4   ensures fresh(o)
5   ensures o.client≡client ∧ o.Key≡key ∧ o.Arn≡arn ∧ o.Tokens≡tok
```

(a) Dafny.

```
6 public static AwsKmsKeyring getKeyring
7   (ManagementServiceClient client, String key, Identifier arn, TokenList tok) {
8   var mock = new Mock⟨AwsKmsKeyring⟩();
9   mock.CallBase = true;
10  mock.SetupGet(x ⇒ x.client).Returns(client);
11  mock.SetupGet(x ⇒ x.Key).Returns(key);
12  mock.SetupGet(x ⇒ x.Arn).Returns(arn);
13  mock.SetupGet(x ⇒ x.Tokens).Returns(tok);
14  return mock.Object;}
```

(b) C#.

Fig. 3. An example use of the :synthesize attribute for mocking (simplified).

DTest automatically produced this method (simplified) and relevant arguments to call it with while generating tests for the ESDK. First, line 4 uses Dafny's fresh keyword to ensure the returned object is new and not aliased by an existing variable. The subsequent postconditions specify the values of each of the object's constant fields. DMock compiles this method into the code in Fig. 3b. On line 8, we use Moq to create a new class that extends AwsKmsKeyring. On the next line, we ensure that by default the mocked class behaves exactly as the original class it extends. Then, we override the field getter methods to return the values provided as arguments. Finally, we return a new instance of the mocked class that, by construction, behaves exactly as specified by the postconditions in Fig. 3a.

DMock also supports mocking of instance functions by redefining their behavior with arbitrary expressions. For example, we can add the following postcondition to the mock method in Fig. 3a to ensure that a call to the Identity instance function simply returns its argument: `ensures forall arg:int :: o.Identity(arg) ≡ arg` . DMock compiles this postcondition into the C# statement below (which would be added to Fig. 3b) to override the behavior of the Identity function:[1]

```
mock.Setup(x ⇒ x.Identity(It.IsAny⟨BigInteger⟩())).Returns((BigInteger arg) ⇒ arg);
```

This functionality is particularly useful for instantiating traits, which are Dafny types similar to interfaces in Java that also cannot be instantiated directly. A method annotated with :synthesize can both return an object extending a given trait and ensure the instance functions of that object behave as the postconditions dictate. Note that we can only mock instance functions, not methods, since method calls cannot appear inside postconditions, which are expressions.

[1] Dafny's int is compiled to C#'s BigInteger because in Dafny integers are unbounded.

However, Dafny programs are typically written in a functional style, and hence DTest can still handle most real-world uses of traits.

4 Automated Test Generation

In this section, we describe DTest's test generation approach (steps 1–5 in Fig. 1).

4.1 Custom Dafny to Boogie Translation

DTest customizes (step 1 in Fig. 1) Dafny's standard translation to Boogie with two key modifications to support automated test case generation.

Preprocessing to Support Inserting Trap Assertions. The Dafny code we have analyzed makes extensive use of functions. Function bodies are syntactically expressions and are translated as such into Boogie. However, an assertion is a statement, and cannot be inserted into the body of a Boogie function. To address this issue, DTest preprocesses the Dafny code to turn functions into function-by-methods, which are functions with an equivalent imperative definition provided as a method. In our case, we wrap the original expression in a return statement, which then prompts the translator to create an imperative Boogie implementation. Hence, for each input function-by-method, Dafny emits both a standard Boogie function—used for verification—and an imperative implementation, as in Fig. 2b. DTest can then insert trap assertions into implementations' bodies.

Inlining. If we are using DTest to generate unit tests of individual methods, no further translation steps are needed. However, an issue arises if we wish to generate system-level tests via calls to a `main` method entry point or similar. The challenge is that Boogie verifies methods one at a time, and any callee methods are represented by their specifications. Any trap assertions aside from those in a `main` method will essentially be "hidden" behind the specifications of the methods they are inside of.

Our solution to this problem is inlining: DTest can optionally inline the program into a user-specified `main` method before proceeding with test generation. Recursive methods can also be inlined (unrolled) up to a manually chosen bound. This way, DTest can provide coverage of the entire Dafny program. Boogie supports inlining, but to take advantage of this support, we have made several changes to the Boogie code emitted by Dafny. These changes allow translating functional-style code, such as conditional expressions, to their imperative equivalents, such as conditional statements, which makes the code more amenable to trap-assertion injection and inlining.

4.2 Trap Assertion Injection

DTest generates tests while iterating over the basic blocks of the Boogie representation. Iteration happens in reverse topological order of the control-flow graph in order to greedily reduce the number of tests by generating tests that are likely to cover multiple blocks at a time. For each block that has not yet been covered, DTest inserts a trap assertion (step 2 in Fig. 1) and queries the Boogie verifier for a counterexample (step 3). Alongside the counterexample, the verifier also reports the error trace, i.e., blocks leading up to the trap assertion that the counterexample also covers. We use the error trace to prune away already covered blocks. DTest then uses previous work [8] to extract the counterexample to a Dafny-like format and then concretizes the result (step 4 in Fig. 1).

One can construct more complex trap assertions that fail when a program takes a specific path through the control flow graph. We can, therefore, use DTest to generate test suites with path-coverage guarantees, although we do not fully explore this use case here and only apply this version of DTest to study the sizes of potential test suites (see Sect. 5.2.)

Note that a successfully verified trap assertion serves as proof that no input can cause a given block to be visited, i.e. it signifies the presence of dead code. This also allows us to uncover dead code using DTest, which is an option we implemented but have not experimented with extensively.

4.3 Unit Test Generation

The key challenge DTest faces when generating unit tests (step 5 in Fig. 1) involves selecting concrete values that are not constrained by the counterexample because they are irrelevant to a particular assertion failure. For example, consider the method in Fig. 2a. A counterexample returned by the solver may suggest that calling the method with $n = 1$ and x being a one-element sequence covers block B. To generate a unit test, DTest also has to emit a value for x's single element. DTest is free to choose any value assuming it satisfies the corresponding type constraint if any such constraint is present.

To generate such values, DTest relies on *witnesses*—user-supplied (using the `witness` keyword in Dafny) or sometimes automatically inferred values that Dafny uses to prove a given type is nonempty. We define such values for all primitive types and collections (e.g., `0` for integers), and user-defined witnesses are typically available for subset types, i.e., types that are constrained with arbitrary predicates. In the rare case that a user does not suggest a witness for a given subset type, DTest will emit a default value for the corresponding supertype, which may lead to a test that violates a type constraint. We call any such test that violates the specification of the target method or a type constraint *unreliable* and discuss all cases in which DTest might generate such tests in Sect. 4.4.

One way to exclude unreliable tests would be to verify them in Dafny. However, DTest might generate a correct test while at the same time failing to find the right value for a ghost variable—irrelevant at execution—to make the test verify. Moreover, some tests may be unreliable yet still explore the targeted branch when compiled to C#. Therefore, to allow more flexibility, we aim to filter unreliable tests at runtime with checks that preemptively terminate execution if a test violates a method precondition over non-ghost fields, violates a type constraint, or calls a trait instance method that is not explicitly mocked by DTest. For example, in Fig. 2c we add such a check after the last local variable initialization on line 27 as the runtime assertion expect $1 \leq |d0| \wedge 1 \leq |d1|$,"Unmet precondition". In our evaluation, such runtime checks terminate 94% of all unreliable tests that would otherwise have led to difficult-to-interpret failures.

To strengthen the assurance provided by the tests, DTest converts postconditions of methods under test into runtime assertions such as the one on line 29 in Fig. 2c. We support all specification constructs allowed by Dafny, provided they are not ghost. We leave compilation of ghost constructs such as unbounded quantifiers as future work. Whenever DTest encounters ghost specifications, which are infrequent in our evaluation, it does not create a corresponding runtime check; this, of course, does not affect coverage.

4.4 Limitations

DTest has several limitations that can either prevent it from being able to generate a test for every block in the Boogie representation of a given procedure or might cause DTest to occasionally produce unreliable tests (Sect. 4.3).

- **Solver Timeouts.** As is the case with any tool that relies on an SMT solver, timeouts may occur, in which case DTest might not cover some blocks. We currently set the timeout to 5 s, and our empirical evaluation shows that increasing the timeout does not make a significant difference.
- **Spurious Counterexamples.** Dafny might generate a spurious counterexample (i.e., one that does not in fact lead to a trap assertion violation) due to several reasons. First, specifications, such as post-conditions or loop invariants, might be over-approximations that under-constrain the program state. Second, the Dafny translation into Boogie might not provide a complete axiomatization of some features, such as set cardinality. Third, the back-end SMT solver itself is incomplete in the presence of quantified formulas, which Dafny always generates. This can lead to a counterexample that does not expose a trap assertion or may even violate method preconditions.
- **Information Elided in the Counterexample.** If the user does not provide a witness for a certain subset type (Sect. 4.3), DTest may not be able to generate a value that satisfies the corresponding type constraint.
- **Ghost Specifications.** DTest cannot compile ghost specifications into runtime checks, so there could be unreliable tests we fail to identify.
- **Unsupported Language Features.** DTest does not support tuples, arrays, infinite maps, infinite sets, or multisets. These Dafny types and collections are rarely used in practice (sequences are used instead of arrays; finite maps and sets are preferred to their infinite counterparts) and only appear in a handful of methods in our benchmarks. Moreover, DTest does not fully support traits and function types. For any argument of a function type, DTest synthesizes a lambda expression with a matching type signature. For example, for a function that maps an integer to an integer, DTest synthesizes a lambda expression that always returns `0`. Given that function types are rarely constrained, this approach works in the majority of cases. For a discussion of traits, see Sect. 3.

5 Empirical Evaluation

We perform two experiments to evaluate the testing toolkit. First, we evaluate DTest's running time and coverage achieved on two preexisting Dafny projects. Second, we compare the number of tests DTest generates to the minimal number of tests required for full coverage.

The subject programs for our evaluation are two real-world projects: the Dafny utilities library (DUTIL) [24] and the AWS Encryption SDK (ESDK) [13]. DUTIL spans 1382 lines of code and presents a collection of useful methods for non-linear arithmetic; manipulating Dafny maps, sequences, and sets; and performing miscellaneous operations. The ESDK comprises 4596 lines of code and implements a Dafny-verified encryption library, which provides an interface between encryption backends and consumer applications. The two projects are, to the best of our knowledge, the largest open-source Dafny programs, with the exception of Ironclad [16] which, despite manually updating it to the latest Dafny syntax, we were unable to get to verify (and hence use in our experiments). While our benchmarks are small by industry standards, they are representative of how Dafny is used in practice and showcase most of Dafny's features.

5.1 Unit Testing and Coverage

In our first experiment, we measure the statement and branch coverage on the binary obtained by compiling DUTIL and the ESDK to C#. To maximize DTest's performance, we augmented the ESDK with about two dozen *witnesses* (Sect. 4.3). Doing so took us less than an hour of manual work. We find that DTest can quickly generate tests that provide sufficient coverage to identify unexpected behavior in an external library.

Performance. DTest took 158 min to generate 918 tests for the 436 methods in the two benchmarks. This does not include methods that exist only to aid verification and are not compiled, methods that have no body in Dafny (external methods), and methods introduced by the Dafny compiler (e.g., ToString). Figure 4 shows that the runtime it takes DTest to process one method is close to linear in the number of blocks in the Boogie representation of that method (Pearson's coefficient ≈0.86, $p < 0.0005$). The outliers are methods for which DTest

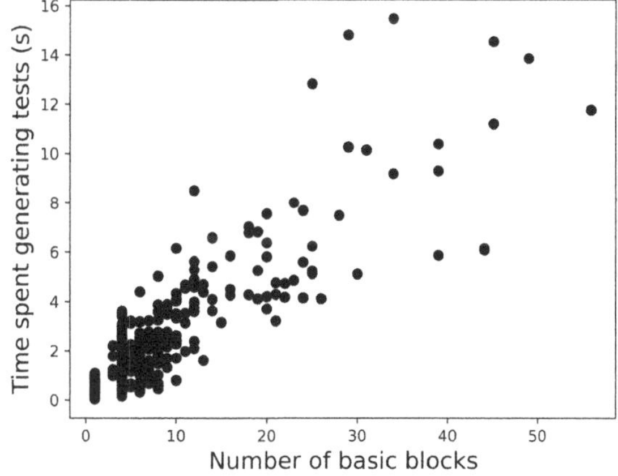

Fig. 4. Runtime of DTest on methods from ESDK and DUTIL.

can cover multiple blocks with one test, such as the methods we analyze in Sect. 5.2. Methods that cause solver timeouts are also a source of outliers.

Coverage. Table 1 shows the coverage that the tests achieve on the compiled C# code, as measured with the Coverlet framework [11]. We give the results for each source folder in DUTIL and ESDK, including the lines of code (LOC) count, target method count, and the number of generated tests for each entry. Each folder consolidates files with similar functionality. The table includes a *Block* column showing the fraction of Boogie basic blocks for which DTest reports that it successfully generated tests. We report the actual statement and branch coverage in the last two columns, with unreliable tests (Sect. 4.4) not contributing to the result. We took all methods compiled from Dafny to C#, even those for which DTest fails to generate tests, into account when measuring coverage. We achieve 62% statement and 58% branch coverage on the ESDK. The lower coverage of the SDK folder is due to extensive use of traits, which DTest only partially supports (Sect. 4.4). These results are comparable to the thresholds that the ESDK developers set as a minimum bar for manual tests as part of their overall testing and verification strategy, with DTest scoring above the 35% threshold for branch coverage but below the 80% threshold for statement coverage.

We observe in the table that the Boogie basic block coverage does not match the C# statement coverage, but is either an over- or under-approximation. The difference is due to two key factors. First, a C# test generated for one method might cover code in a method invoked by it, which at the Boogie level we cannot observe since we are doing intraprocedural test generation in the experiments (no inlining). This leads to the Boogie coverage being an under-approximation of the C# coverage. Second, some tests may be identified as unreliable at runtime, and so they contribute to the Boogie coverage but not to the C# coverage, leading to the former being an over-approximation of the latter.

Table 1. Overview of achieved coverage.

	Source Folder	LOC	Methods	# Tests	Boogie Block	C#	
						Statement	Branch
DUTIL	Maps	55	7	13	100%	98%	88%
	Sequences	1114	131	169	67%	76%	84%
	Sets	42	4	8	100%	83%	69%
	Nonlinear Arithmetic	78	7	11	72%	91%	88%
	Misc	93	16	22	90%	98%	88%
	Total	**1382**	**165**	**223**	**72%**	**79%**	**84%**
ESDK	Crypto Material Providers	1871	67	270	87%	62%	50%
	Crypto	153	13	25	90%	82%	70%
	Generated	61	4	8	83%	100%	100%
	SDK	1878	116	205	58%	51%	45%
	Standard Library	414	45	121	90%	93%	93%
	Util	219	26	66	74%	75%	91%
	Total	**4596**	**271**	**695**	**77%**	**62%**	**58%**

Overview of Tests. Of the 918 tests DTest generated for DUTIL and ESDK, 85 are unreliable. Of these, our runtime checks preemptively terminated 80 (see Sects. 4.3 and 4.4): 11 violate preconditions, 40 violate type constraints, and 29 call methods on traits that are not mocked. Five more tests fail because DTest does not fully support function types. As we describe above (Sect. 4.4), arguments of function types are generated from type signatures rather than counterexamples. Overall, half of the generated tests have no return value check due to absence of postconditions. However, even such tests check for runtime errors, which is valuable as shown by the success of black-box fuzzers (that do not check return values either) [26]. In our experiments, the outcomes of two tests are worth noting: one test causes an external method to throw an exception, which, however, is allowed by that method's signature. Another test causes the execution to continue for an indefinite amount of time (we killed the process after two hours). The developers identified this case to be from a particular internal test method (not part of code exposed to the user) for an external .NET RSA library. Thus, our test uncovered an external library behaving differently from the developers' expectations, and they fixed the test method accordingly.

5.2 Test Suite Size

In our second experiment, we evaluate the size of the test suite DTest generates by comparing it to a minimal number of tests required to achieve full coverage. Test suite size is an important factor for software development and has prompted significant research effort in recent years [15,17].

For the purpose of this comparison, we designed an algorithm to enumerate sets of control flow paths of a Boogie procedure in order of increasing set cardinality, terminating when we find a set of paths that guarantee full coverage, are all feasible, and that we can generate tests for. We determine the feasibility of a path via a query to the SMT solver, in which a trap assertion is added that fails only if all the blocks along the path are visited. We then generate a test for each path in the same way that DTest would generate a test for a given block. This approach is exponential in the number of SMT queries (running on all benchmarks as in Table 1 would take weeks), but we do allow the users of DTest to optionally use this costly method since reducing the number of tests is sometimes of utmost importance (e.g., if tests are being executed over and over again as a part of continuous integration).

To compare the default (greedy) and optimal approaches, we selected nine methods from DUTIL and ESDK with the most complex control flow as determined by the number of basic blocks in their Boogie representation. Such methods present high potential for test minimization, since one carefully chosen test could cover many blocks; we expect differences between the two approaches to be less pronounced when viewed in a broader context. We omit any methods for which DTest could not reach all blocks, or for which it generated unreliable tests.

Table 2 summarizes the results of this comparison. We give the number of basic blocks in the Boogie representation of each method in a separate column.

Table 2. Comparison of minimization strategies.

Method	# blocks	Running time (s)		# Tests	
		Default	Optimal	Default	Optimal
UTF8.Uses3Bytes	53	18	1860	13	12
UTF8.Uses4Bytes	53	19	422	13	12
UTF8.ValidUTF8Range	21	12	36	9	6
Base64.IsBase64Char	19	16	112	8	3
AwsKmsArnParsing.AwsArn.Valid	16	17	30	6	2
Base64.IndexToChar	16	14	19	5	5
Base64.Is1Padding	16	13	24	6	2
Base64.Is2Padding	16	14	25	6	2
Sorting.LexicographicByteSeqBelowAux	14	8	8	5	3

For each Dafny method and minimization technique, we report the time that the test generation process takes (mean of three runs), and the number of tests in the resulting suite. The default (greedy) algorithm appears to generate more tests whenever there are independent branching points in the control flow of the method, i.e., when the choice of the path at one branching point does not dictate the choice at the next one. Even so, the greedy algorithm is within two tests of minimal for four of the methods, and it never generates more than three times the minimal number of tests. It is also several times faster than the alternative.

6 Related Work

Testing of Verification-Ready Languages. Test generation has been explored in the context of Dafny by Delfy [9,31], a concolic test generation tool. Delfy has not been updated for nearly ten years and only supports a limited subset of Dafny, and hence a direct comparison was not possible. In contrast to Delfy, DTest fully supports the features commonly used by Dafny programmers, such as algebraic datatypes, sequences, sets, and maps. Unlike Delfy, which relies heavily on compilation to C# for both concrete and symbolic execution, DTest is independent of the target language since it generates tests (in Dafny) from counterexamples provided by the Dafny verifier itself.

Another tool for automated testing of Dafny is XDSmith [18], which randomly generates Dafny programs with known verification outcomes and uses these programs to test the Dafny verifier and compilers. XDSmith is complementary to DTest—the former focuses on testing the Dafny toolchain itself in isolation, while the latter helps to increase assurance that the compiled target programs are correct, particularly in their interaction with external libraries.

Concrete execution of verifier-produced counterexamples has been explored in the Why3 verification environment [4,14]. The goal of this work is to ascertain the validity of a counterexample by observing the runtime behavior it triggers under various assumptions. DTest, by contrast, relies on the correctness of counterexamples to generate tests. This technique and, more broadly, the use of a verifier to generate tests has been explored in the context of other languages, such as C [5] and B [1], but Dafny presents a particular challenge due to its verification-related features (e.g., rich type system, specifications).

To the best of our knowledge, neither Boogaloo [30], a nondeterministic interpreter for Boogie, nor Symbooglix [25], a symbolic execution engine, have been used to generate test suites for Boogie or Dafny programs although both tools can be used to explain a failing assertion. Symbolic-execution-based program exploration algorithms and the verifier have different trade-offs, especially in the presence of loops. We plan to develop, as future work, a portfolio-based approach, similar to CoVeriTest [6], with several backend reachability analyses.

Automated Software Testing. There is a large body of work on automated software testing, involving techniques such as fuzzing (see [26] for a survey), symbolic execution [2], and others. We might augment DTest with some of these techniques in the future since, for example, the approach used by QuickCheck [10] and the related family of fuzzers for generating values of function types offers more flexibility than DTest's current implementation. One of the challenges often accompanying automated testing is object initialization. Our approach to this problem is close to lazy symbolic initialization [19], a process whereby an object is initialized on an "as-needed" basis—we similarly override the value of an object's field only if it is constrained by the counterexample or a precondition.

Mocking. A number of mocking frameworks exist for various languages, of which Mockito [27] and Moq [28] are some of the most popular options for Java and C#, respectively. For our purposes, it is crucial that a mocked object behaves exactly like an instance of the corresponding type unless an instance field or function is specifically redefined by the user. DMock relies on both Mockito and Moq to support this functionality, which is sometimes also referred to as *spying*.

7 Conclusions

In this paper, we presented a toolkit for automated testing of Dafny programs: DUnit (unit testing framework), DMock (mocking framework), and DTest (automated test generation). The main component of the toolkit, DTest, works with the Boogie representation of a Dafny program to generate tests that (i) target branch coverage of the compiled code and (ii) contain runtime assertions extracted from method specifications in the Dafny code. We evaluated the coverage DTest achieves on several preexisting Dafny programs, showed that it can help identify unexpected behavior in external libraries, and compared it to an alternative more costly solution that optimally minimizes the number of tests. Overall, our results show that DUnit, DMock, and DTest are a promising toolkit for automatically generating high coverage tests for Dafny.

Acknowledgments. The authors would like to thank Aleks Chakarov, Cody Roux, William Schultz, and Serdar Tasiran for their invaluable feedback on the usability of the toolkit, Ryan Emery and Tony Knapp for facilitating the use of the ESDK as a benchmark dataset, Rustan Leino, Mikael Mayer, Aaron Tomb, and Remy Williams for their feedback on the source code, and the anonymous reviewers for helping improve this text. This work is partly supported by an Amazon post-internship graduate research fellowship.

References

1. de Azevedo Oliveira, D., Medeiros, V., Déharbe, D., Musicante, M.A.: *BTestBox*: a tool for testing b translators and coverage of B models. In: Beyer, D., Keller, C. (eds.) TAP 2019. LNCS, vol. 11823, pp. 83–92. Springer, Cham (2019). https://doi.org/10.1007/978-3-030-31157-5_6
2. Baldoni, R., Coppa, E., D'Elia, D.C., Demetrescu, C., Finocchi, I.: A survey of symbolic execution techniques. ACM Comput. Surv. **51**(3) (2018). https://doi.org/10.1145/3182657
3. Barnett, M., Chang, B.-Y.E., DeLine, R., Jacobs, B., Leino, K.R.M.: Boogie: a modular reusable verifier for object-oriented programs. In: de Boer, F.S., Bonsangue, M.M., Graf, S., de Roever, W.-P. (eds.) FMCO 2005. LNCS, vol. 4111, pp. 364–387. Springer, Heidelberg (2006). https://doi.org/10.1007/11804192_17
4. Becker, B.F.H., Lourenço, C.B., Marché, C.: Explaining counterexamples with giant-step assertion checking. In: Workshop on Formal Integrated Development Environment, pp. 82–88 (2021). https://doi.org/10.4204/EPTCS.338.10
5. Beyer, D., Chlipala, A., Henzinger, T., Jhala, R., Majumdar, R.: Generating tests from counterexamples. In: International Conference on Software Engineering, pp. 326–335 (2004). https://doi.org/10.1109/ICSE.2004.1317455
6. Beyer, D., Jakobs, M.C.: CoVeriTest: cooperative verifier-based testing. In: Fundamental Approaches to Software Engineering, pp. 389–408 (2019). https://doi.org/10.1007/978-3-030-16722-6_23
7. Boogie. https://github.com/boogie-org/boogie
8. Chakarov, A., Fedchin, A., Rakamarić, Z., Rungta, N.: Better counterexamples for Dafny. In: Fisman, D., Rosu, G. (eds.) TACAS 2022. LNCS, vol. 13243, pp. 404–411. Springer, Cham (2022). https://doi.org/10.1007/978-3-030-99524-9_23
9. Christakis, M., Leino, K.R.M., Müller, P., Wüstholz, V.: Integrated environment for diagnosing verification errors. In: Chechik, M., Raskin, J.-F. (eds.) TACAS 2016. LNCS, vol. 9636, pp. 424–441. Springer, Heidelberg (2016). https://doi.org/10.1007/978-3-662-49674-9_25
10. Claessen, K., Hughes, J.: QuickCheck: a lightweight tool for random testing of haskell programs. In: International Conference on Functional Programming, pp. 268–279 (2000). https://doi.org/10.1145/351240.351266
11. Coverlet. https://github.com/coverlet-coverage/coverlet
12. Dafny. https://github.com/dafny-lang/dafny
13. AWS Encryption SDK. https://github.com/aws/aws-encryption-sdk-dafny
14. Filliâtre, J.-C., Paskevich, A.: Why3—where programs meet provers. In: Felleisen, M., Gardner, P. (eds.) ESOP 2013. LNCS, vol. 7792, pp. 125–128. Springer, Heidelberg (2013). https://doi.org/10.1007/978-3-642-37036-6_8
15. Hao, D., Zhang, L., Wu, X., Mei, H., Rothermel, G.: On-demand test suite reduction. In: International Conference on Software Engineering, pp. 738–748 (2012). https://doi.org/10.1109/ICSE.2012.6227144
16. Hawblitzel, C., et al.: Ironclad apps: end-to-end security via automated full-system verification. In: Symposium on Operating Systems Design and Implementation, pp. 165–181 (2014)

17. Hsu, H.Y., Orso, A.: MINTS: a general framework and tool for supporting test-suite minimization. In: International Conference on Software Engineering, pp. 419–429 (2009). https://doi.org/10.1109/ICSE.2009.5070541
18. Irfan, A., Porncharoenwase, S., Rakamarić, Z., Rungta, N., Torlak, E.: Testing Dafny (experience paper). In: International Symposium on Software Testing and Analysis, pp. 556–567 (2022). https://doi.org/10.1145/3533767.3534382
19. Khurshid, S., PĂsĂreanu, C.S., Visser, W.: Generalized symbolic execution for model checking and testing. In: Garavel, H., Hatcliff, J. (eds.) TACAS 2003. LNCS, vol. 2619, pp. 553–568. Springer, Heidelberg (2003). https://doi.org/10.1007/3-540-36577-X_40
20. Leinenbach, D., Santen, T.: Verifying the microsoft hyper-V hypervisor with VCC. In: Cavalcanti, A., Dams, D.R. (eds.) FM 2009. LNCS, vol. 5850, pp. 806–809. Springer, Heidelberg (2009). https://doi.org/10.1007/978-3-642-05089-3_51
21. Leino, K.R.M.: Dafny: an automatic program verifier for functional correctness. In: Clarke, E.M., Voronkov, A. (eds.) LPAR 2010. LNCS (LNAI), vol. 6355, pp. 348–370. Springer, Heidelberg (2010). https://doi.org/10.1007/978-3-642-17511-4_20
22. Leino, K.R.M.: Accessible software verification with Dafny. IEEE Softw. **34**(6), 94–97 (2017). https://doi.org/10.1109/MS.2017.4121212
23. Leroy, X.: A formally verified compiler back-end. J. Autom. Reason. **43**(4), 363–446 (2009). https://doi.org/10.1007/s10817-009-9155-4
24. Dafny utilities library. https://github.com/dafny-lang/libraries
25. Liew, D., Cadar, C., Donaldson, A.F.: Symbooglix: a symbolic execution engine for boogie programs. In: International Conference on Software Testing, Verification and Validation, pp. 45–56 (2016). https://doi.org/10.1109/ICST.2016.11
26. Manès, V.J., et al.: The art, science, and engineering of fuzzing: a survey. IEEE Trans. Softw. Eng. **47**(11), 2312–2331 (2019). https://doi.org/10.1109/TSE.2019.2946563
27. Mockito. https://github.com/mockito/mockito
28. Moq. https://github.com/moq/moq
29. de Moura, L., Bjørner, N.: Z3: an efficient SMT solver. In: Ramakrishnan, C.R., Rehof, J. (eds.) TACAS 2008. LNCS, vol. 4963, pp. 337–340. Springer, Heidelberg (2008). https://doi.org/10.1007/978-3-540-78800-3_24
30. Polikarpova, N., Furia, C.A., West, S.: To run what no one has run before: executing an intermediate verification language. In: Legay, A., Bensalem, S. (eds.) RV 2013. LNCS, vol. 8174, pp. 251–268. Springer, Heidelberg (2013). https://doi.org/10.1007/978-3-642-40787-1_15
31. Spettel, P.: Delfy: dynamic test generation for Dafny. Master's thesis, Eidgenössische Technische Hochschule Zürich (2013). https://doi.org/10.3929/ethz-a-010056933
32. XUnit. https://github.com/xunit/xunit
33. Z3. https://github.com/Z3Prover/z3

Verified ALL(*) Parsing with Semantic Actions and Dynamic Input Validation

Sam Lasser[1(✉)], Chris Casinghino[2], Derek Egolf[3], Kathleen Fisher[4], and Cody Roux[5]

[1] Draper, Cambridge, USA
slasser@draper.com
[2] Jane Street, New York, USA
ccasinghino@janestreet.com
[3] Northeastern University, Boston, USA
egolf.d@northeastern.edu
[4] Tufts University, Medford, USA
kfisher@eecs.tufts.edu
[5] Amazon Web Services, Cambridge, USA
codyroux@amazon.com

Abstract. Formally verified parsers are powerful tools for preventing the kinds of errors that result from ad hoc parsing and validation of program input. However, verified parsers are often based on formalisms that are not expressive enough to capture the full definition of valid input for a given application. Specifications of many real-world data formats include both a syntactic component and one or more non-context-free semantic properties that a well-formed instance of the format must exhibit. A parser for context-free grammars (CFGs) cannot determine on its own whether an input is valid according to such a specification; it must be supplemented with additional validation checks.

In this work, we present CoStar++, a verified parser interpreter with semantic features that make it highly expressive in terms of both the language specifications it accepts and its output type. CoStar++ provides support for semantic predicates, enabling the user to write semantically rich grammars that include non-context-free properties. The interpreter also supports semantic actions that convert sequential inputs to structured outputs in a principled way. CoStar++ is implemented and verified with the Coq Proof Assistant, and it is based on the ALL(*) parsing algorithm. For all CFGs without left recursion, the interpreter is provably sound, complete, and terminating with respect to a semantic specification that takes predicates and actions into account. CoStar++ runs in linear time on benchmarks for four real-world data formats, three of which have non-context-free specifications.

Keywords: parsing · semantic actions · interactive theorem proving

1 Introduction

The term "shotgun parsing" refers to a programming anti-pattern in which code for parsing and validating input is interspersed with application code for pro-

K. Y. Rozier and S. Chaudhuri (Eds.): NFM 2023, LNCS 13903, pp. 414–429, 2023.
https://doi.org/10.1007/978-3-031-33170-1_25

cessing that input. Proponents of high-assurance software argue for the use of dedicated parsing tools as an antidote to this fundamentally insecure practice [12]. Such parsers enable the user to write a declarative specification (e.g., a grammar) that describes the structure of valid input, and they reject inputs that do not match the specification, ensuring that only valid inputs reach the downstream application code. Formally verified parsers offer even greater security to the applications that rely on them. Verification techniques can provide strong guarantees that a parser accepts all and only the inputs that are valid according to the user's specification.

However, dedicated parsing tools are not always expressive enough to capture the full definition of valid input. For many real applications, the input specification includes both a context-free *syntactic* component and non-context-free *semantic* properties; in such a case, a parser for context-free grammars (CFGs) provides limited value. For example, a CFG can represent the syntax of valid XML, but it cannot capture the requirement that names in corresponding start and end tags must match (assuming that the set of names is infinite). Similarly, the syntactic specification for JSON is context-free, but some applications impose the additional requirement that JSON objects (collections of key-value pairs) contain no duplicate keys. Data dependencies are another common type of non-context-free property; many packet formats have a "tag-length-value" structure in which a length field indicates the size of the packet's data field. In each of these cases, a CFG-based parser is an incomplete substitute for shotgun parsing because it cannot enforce the semantic component of the input specification.

In this work, we present CoStar++, a verified parser interpreter[1] with two features—semantic predicates and semantic actions—that enable it to capture semantically rich specifications like those described above. Predicates enable the user to write input specifications that include non-context-free semantic properties. The interpreter checks these properties at runtime, ensuring that its output is well-formed. Actions give the user fine-grained control over the interpreter's output type. Actions also play an important role in supporting predicates; the interpreter must produce values with an expressive type in order to check interesting properties of those values. CoStar++ builds on the CoStar parser interpreter [11]. Like its predecessor, CoStar++ is based on the ALL(*) parsing algorithm, and it is implemented and verified with the Coq Proof Assistant.

Extending CoStar with predicates and actions gives rise to several challenges. CoStar is guaranteed to detect syntactically ambiguous inputs (inputs with more than one parse tree). In a semantic setting, the definition of ambiguity is more complex; it can be syntactic (multiple parse trees for an input) or semantic (multiple semantic values). In addition, it is not always possible to infer one kind of ambiguity from the other, because two parse trees can correspond to (a) two semantic values, (b) a single semantic value when the semantic actions for the two derivations produce the same value, or (c) no semantic value at all

[1] We use the term "parser interpreter" instead of "parser generator" because CoStar++ does not generate source code from a grammar; it converts a grammar to an in-memory data structure that a generic driver interprets at parse time.

when predicates fail during the semantic derivations! Finally, detecting semantic ambiguity is undecidable in the general case where semantic values do not have decidable equality, and we choose not to require this property so that the interpreter can produce incomparable values such as functions. However, it is still possible to detect the *absence* of semantic ambiguity. In the current work, we modify the CoStar ambiguity detection mechanism so that CoStar++ detects uniquely correct semantic values, and it detects syntactic ambiguity in the cases where semantic ambiguity is undecidable.

A second challenge is that ALL(*) as originally described [14] and as implemented by CoStar is incomplete with respect to the CoStar++ semantic specification. ALL(*) is a predictive parsing algorithm; at decision points, it nondeterministically explores possible paths until it identifies a uniquely viable path. This prediction strategy does not speculatively execute semantic actions or evaluate semantic predicates over those actions, for both efficiency and correctness reasons (the actions could alter mutable state in ways that cannot be undone). While this choice is reasonable in the imperative setting for which ALL(*) was developed, it renders the algorithm incomplete relative to a predicate-aware specification, because a prediction can send the parser down a path that leads to a predicate failure when a different path would have produced a successful parse. CoStar++ solves this problem by using a modified version of the ALL(*) prediction algorithm that evaluates predicates and actions only when doing so is necessary to guarantee completeness. CoStar++ semantic actions are pure functions, so speculatively executing them during prediction is safe.

This paper makes the following contributions:

- We present CoStar++, an extension of the CoStar verified ALL(*) parser interpreter that adds support for semantic predicates and actions. These new semantic features increase the expressivity of both the language definitions that the interpreter can accept and its output type.
- We present a modified version of ALL(*) prediction that CoStar++ uses to ensure completeness in the presence of semantic predicates.
- We prove that for all CFGs without left recursion, CoStar++ is sound, complete, and terminating with respect to a semantics-aware specification that takes predicates and actions into account.
- We prove that CoStar++ identifies uniquely correct semantic values, and that it detects syntactic ambiguity when semantic ambiguity is undecidable.
- We use CoStar++ to write grammars for four real-world data formats, three of which have non-context-free semantic specifications, and we show that CoStar++ achieves linear-time performance on benchmarks for these formats. As part of the evaluation, we integrate the tool with the Verbatim verified lexer interpreter [6,7] to create a fully verified front end for lexing and parsing data formats.

CoStar++ consists of roughly 6,500 lines of specification and 7,000 lines of proof. The grammars used in the performance evaluation comprise another 700 lines of specification and 100 lines of proof. CoStar++ and its accompanying performance evaluation framework are open source and available online [9].

```
Inductive json_value : Type :=
| JObj  (kv_pairs : list (string * json_value))
| JArr  (vs : list json_value)
| JBool (b : bool)
| JNum  (i : Z)
| JStr  (s : string)
| JNull.
```

Fig. 1. Algebraic data type representation of JSON values, shown in the concrete syntax of Gallina, the functional programming language embedded in Coq.

```
Value  ::= Object            ⟦λ(ps,_).nodup ps⟧?  ⟦λ(ps,_).JObj ps⟧!
         | Array                                  ⟦λ(vs,_).JArr vs⟧!
         | ...
Object ::= '{' Pair Pairs '}'                     ⟦λ(_,p,ps,_,_).p :: ps⟧!
         | '{'            '}'                     ⟦λ_. []⟧!
...
```

Fig. 2. JSON grammar fragment annotated with semantic predicates and actions.

The paper is organized as follows. In Sect.2, we introduce CoStar++ by example. We present the tool's correctness properties in Sect.3. We then discuss the challenges of specifying the tool's behavior on ambiguous input (Sect.4) and ensuring completeness after adding predicates to the tool's correctness specification (Sect.5). In Sect.6, we evaluate the tool's performance and describe the semantic features of the grammars used in the evaluation. Finally, we survey related work in Sect.7.

2 CoStar++ by Example

In this section, we give an example of a simple grammar that includes a non-context-free semantic property, and we sketch the execution of the CoStar++ parser that this grammar specifies, with a focus on the parser's semantic features.

2.1 A Grammar for Parsing Duplicate-Free JSON

Suppose we want to use CoStar++ to define a JSON parser, and we only want the parser to accept JSON input in which objects contain no duplicate keys. The parser's output type might look like the algebraic data type (ADT) in Fig. 1. To obtain a parser that produces values of this type, and that enforces the "unique keys" invariant, we can provide CoStar++ with the grammar excerpted in Fig. 2. A CoStar++ grammar production has the form $X ::= \gamma \; [\![p]\!]? \; [\![f]\!]!$, where X is a nonterminal, γ is a sequence of terminals and nonterminals,[2] p is an optional semantic predicate, and f is a semantic action.

Semantic actions build the semantic values that the parser produces. An action is a function with a dependent type that is determined by the grammar symbols in the accompanying production. An action for production $X ::= \gamma$ has type $[\![\gamma]\!] \to [\![X]\!]$, where the semantic tuple type $[\![\gamma]\!]$ is computed as follows:

$$[\![\bullet]\!] = \mathbb{1}$$
$$[\![s\beta]\!] = [\![s]\!] \times [\![\beta]\!]$$

and $[\![s]\!]$ is a user-defined mapping from grammar symbols to semantic types. For the example grammar, $[\![\texttt{Value}]\!] = \texttt{json\_value}$ (i.e., the parser produces a `json_value` each time it processes a `Value` nonterminal), and $[\![\texttt{Object}]\!] = $ `list (string * json_value)`.

In addition, productions are optionally annotated with semantic predicates. A predicate for production $X ::= \gamma$ has type $[\![\gamma]\!] \to \mathbb{B}$. At parse time, CoStar++ applies predicates to the semantic values that the actions produce and rejects the input when a predicate fails.

A production like this one:

$$\texttt{Value} ::= \texttt{Object} \quad [\![\lambda\texttt{(prs,\_).nodupKeys prs}]\!]? \quad [\![\lambda\texttt{(prs,\_).JObj prs}]\!]!$$

can be read as follows: "To produce a result of type $[\![\texttt{Value}]\!]$, first produce a tuple of type $[\![\texttt{Object}]\!]$ and apply predicate $[\![\lambda\texttt{(prs,\_).nodupKeys prs}]\!]?$ to it (where the `nodupKeys` function checks whether the string keys in an association list are unique). If the check succeeds, apply action $[\![\lambda\texttt{(prs,\_).JObj prs}]\!]!$ to the tuple."

2.2 Parsing Valid and Invalid Input

In Fig. 3, we illustrate how CoStar++ realizes the example JSON grammar's semantics by applying CoStar++ to the grammar and tracing the resulting parser's execution on valid JSON input.

CoStar++ is implemented as a stack machine with a small-step semantics. At each point in its execution, the machine performs a single atomic update to its state based on its current configuration. Figure 3 shows the machine's stack at each point in the trace (other machine state components are omitted for ease of exposition). Each stack frame $[\alpha \;\&\; \bar{v}, \beta]$ holds a sequence of processed grammar symbols α, a semantic tuple $\bar{v} : [\![\alpha]\!]$ for the processed symbols, and a sequence of unprocessed symbols β. In the initial state σ_0, the stack consists of a single frame $[\bullet \;\&\; \texttt{tt}, \texttt{Value}]$ that holds an empty sequence of processed symbols $\bullet$, a semantic value of type $[\![\bullet]\!]$ (`tt`, the sole value of type `unit`), and a sequence of unprocessed symbols that contains only the start symbol `Value`.

[2] Throughout this paper, nonterminals begin with capital letters and terminals appear in single quotes. When it is necessary to distinguish between terminals and the literal values that they match, we write terminal names in angle brackets (e.g., `<int>` for a terminal that matches an integer).

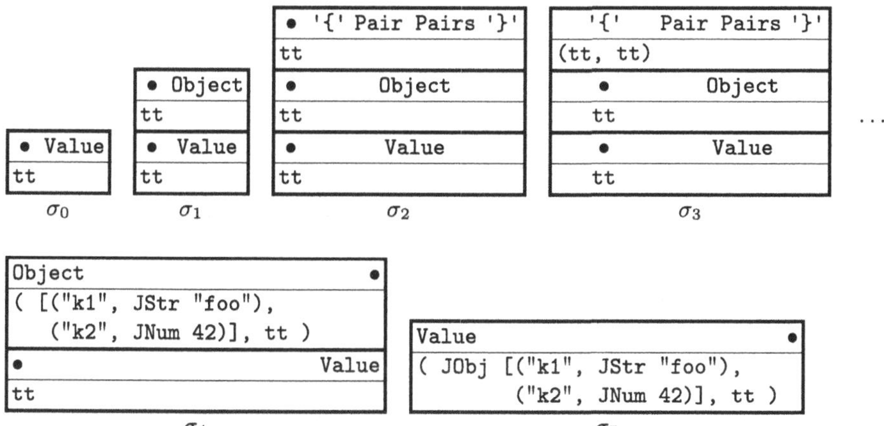

Fig. 3. Execution trace of a CoStar++ JSON parser applied to the valid string `{"k1": "foo", "k2": 42}`. A stack frame contains processed grammar symbols α (upper left portion of the frame), unprocessed grammar symbols β (upper right portion), and semantic tuple $\bar{v} : [\![\alpha]\!]$ (lower portion).

Each machine state also stores the sequence of remaining tokens. A token $(a \,\&\, v)$ is the dependent pair of a terminal symbol a and a literal value $v : [\![a]\!]$. (In our performance evaluation, we use a verified lexing tool that produces tokens of this type; see Sect. 6 for details.) In the Fig. 3 example, the input string before tokenization is:

`{"k1": "foo", "k2": 42}`

Thus, in initial state σ_0, the machine holds tokens for the full input string:

`('{' & tt), (<str> & "k1"), (':' & tt), (<str> & "foo") ...`

In the transition from σ_0 to σ_1, the machine performs a **push** operation. A push occurs when the top stack symbol (the next unprocessed symbol in the top stack frame) is a nonterminal—`Value`, in this case. During a push, the machine examines the remaining tokens to determine which grammar right-hand side to push onto the stack. The prediction subroutine that performs this task is what distinguishes ALL(*) from other parsing algorithms. Parr et al. [14] describe the prediction mechanism in detail; in brief, the parser launches a subparser for each candidate right-hand side and advances the subparsers only as far as necessary to identify a uniquely viable choice. In the example, the prediction mechanism identifies the right-hand side `Object` as the uniquely viable choice and pushes it onto the stack in a new frame.

The transition from σ_1 to σ_2 is another push operation, in which the prediction mechanism identifies `'{' Pair Pairs '}'` as the unique right-hand side for nonterminal `Object` that may produce a successful parse. To transition from σ_2 to σ_3, the machine performs a **consume** operation. A consume occurs when the top stack symbol is a terminal a. The machine matches a against terminal a'

from the head remaining token. In this case, the top stack terminal `'{'` matches the terminal in token (`'{'` & `tt`), so the machine pops the token and stores its semantic value `tt` in the current frame.

After several more operations, the machine reaches state σ_4. At this point, the machine has fully processed nonterminal `Object`, producing a semantic value of type $[\![$`Object`$]\!]$ = `list (string * json_value)`, there are no more symbols left to process in the top frame, and nonterminal `Value` in the frame below has not yet been fully processed (we call such a nonterminal "open", and the frame containing it the "caller" frame). In such a configuration, the machine performs a **return** operation, which involves the following steps:

1. The machine retrieves the predicate and action for the production being reduced. In the Fig. 3 example, the production is `Value` ::= `Object`, the predicate is $[\![\lambda$`(ps,_).nodup ps`$]\!]$? (where the `nodup` function checks whether string keys in an association list are unique), and the action is $[\![\lambda$`(ps,_).JObj ps`$]\!]$!.
2. The machine applies the predicate to the semantic tuple $\bar{v}$ in the top frame. In the example, the predicate evaluates to `true` because the list of key/value pairs contains no duplicate keys.
3. If the predicate succeeds (as it does in the example), the machine applies the action to $\bar{v}$, producing a new semantic value v'. It then pops the top frame, moves the open nonterminal in the caller frame to the list of processed symbols, and stores v' in the caller frame. In this case, the machine makes `Value` a processed symbol (the nonterminal has now been fully reduced), and it stores v' = `JObj [("k1", JStr "foo"), ("k2", JNum 42)]` in the caller frame.

In state σ_5, the machine is in a final configuration; there are no unprocessed symbols in the top frame, and no caller frame to return to. In such a configuration, the machine halts and returns the semantic value it has accumulated for the start symbol. It tags the value as `Unique` or `Ambig` based on the value of another machine state component: a boolean flag indicating whether the machine detected ambiguity during the parse. In our example, the input is unambiguous, so the result of the parse is `Unique (JObj [("k1", JStr "foo"), ("k2", JNum 42)])` .

We now describe how the example JSON parser's behavior differs on the string `{"k1": "foo", "k1": 42}` , which is syntactically well-formed but violates the "no duplicate keys" property. During the first several steps involved in processing this string, the machine stacks match those in Fig. 3. When the machine reaches a state that corresponds to state σ_4 in Fig. 3, it attempts to perform a return operation by applying the predicate for production `Value` ::= `Object` to the list of key/value pairs `[("k1", JStr "foo"), ("k1", JNum 42)]` . This time, the predicate fails because of the duplicate keys, so the machine halts and returns a `Reject` value along with a message describing the failure.

3 Interpreter Correctness

In this section, we describe the CoStar++ interpreter's correctness specification and then present the interpreter's high-level correctness properties.

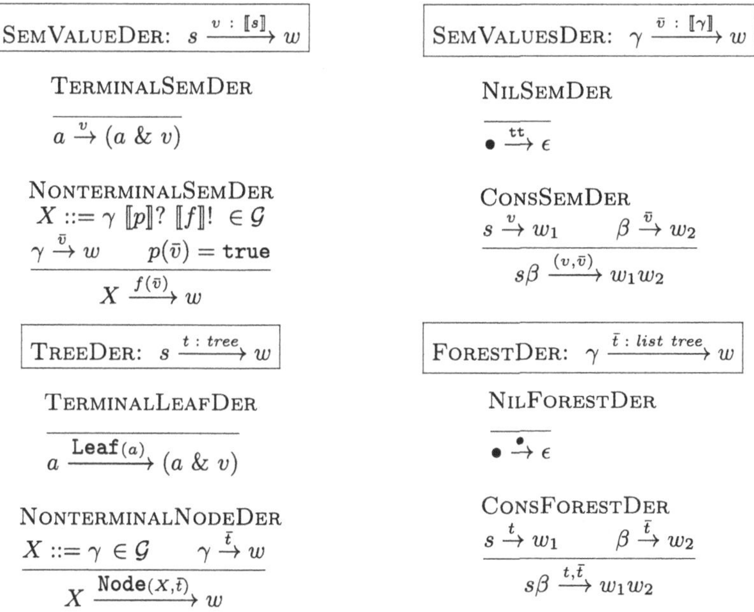

Fig. 4. Grammatical derivation relations for semantic values and parse trees.

3.1 Correctness Specification

CoStar++ is sound and complete relative to a grammatical derivation relation called SemValueDer with the judgment form $s \xrightarrow{v} w$, meaning that symbol s derives word w, producing semantic value v. Figure 4 shows this relation as well as a mutually inductive one, SemValuesDer, over sentential forms (grammar right-hand sides). This latter relation has the judgment form $\gamma \xrightarrow{\bar{v}} w$ (symbols γ derive word w, producing semantic tuple $\bar{v}$). In terms of predicates and actions, the key rule is NonterminalSemDer, which says that if (a) $X ::= \gamma\ [\![p]\!]?\ [\![f]\!]!$ is a grammar production; (b) the right-hand side γ derives word w, producing the semantic tuple $\bar{v}$; and (c) $\bar{v}$ satisfies predicate p, then applying action f to $\bar{v}$ produces a correct value for left-hand nonterminal X.

Portions of the correctness theorems refer to the existence of correct parse trees for the input. Parse tree correctness is defined in terms of a pair of mutually inductive relations, TreeDer and ForestDer (also in Fig. 4). These relations are isomorphic to SemValueDer and SemValuesDer, but they produce parse trees and parse tree lists (respectively), where a parse tree is an n-ary tree with terminal-labeled leaves and nonterminal-labeled internal nodes.

3.2 Parser Correctness Theorems

The main CoStar++ correctness theorems describe the behavior of the interpreter's top-level `parse` function, which has the type signature shown in Fig. 5a.

```
parse (g  : grammar)
      (Hw : grammar_wf g)
      (s  : nonterminal)
      (ts : list token) :
      parse_result s
```

(a) parse type signature

```
parse_result (x : nonterminal) :=
| Unique (v : ⟦x⟧)
| Ambig  (v : ⟦x⟧)
| Reject (s : string)
| Error  (e : parse_error)
```

(b) parse return type

Fig. 5. The type signature of the interpreter's top-level entry point (a), and the interpreter's return type (b).

The `parse` function takes a grammar `g`, a proof that `g` is well-formed,[3] a start nonterminal `s`, and a token sequence `ts`. The function produces a `parse_result s`, a dependent type indexed by `s`. As shown in Fig. 5b, a `parse_result x` is either a semantic value of type ⟦x⟧ tagged as `Unique` or `Ambig` (indicating whether the input is ambiguous), a `Reject` value with a message explaining why the input was rejected, or an `Error` value indicating that the stack machine reached an inconsistent state.

We list the CoStar++ high-level correctness theorems below, and we highlight several interesting aspects of their proofs in Sects. 4 and 5. Each theorem assumes a non-left-recursive grammar $\mathcal{G}$.

Theorem 1 (Soundness, unique derivations). If `parse` applied to $\mathcal{G}$, nonterminal S, and word w returns a semantic value `Unique`(v), then v is the sole correct semantic value for S and w.

Theorem 2 (Soundness, ambiguous derivations). If `parse` applied to $\mathcal{G}$, nonterminal S, and word w returns a semantic value `Ambig`(v), then v is a correct semantic value for S and w, and there exist two correct parse trees t and t' for S and w, where $t \neq t'$.

Theorem 3 (Error-free termination). The interpreter never returns an `Error` value.

Theorem 4 (Completeness). If v is a correct semantic value for nonterminal S and word w, then either (a) v is the sole correct semantic value for S and w and the interpreter returns `Unique`(v), or (b) multiple correct parse trees exist for S and w, and the interpreter returns a correct semantic value `Ambig`(v').

The theorems above have been mechanized in Coq. Each theorem has a proof based on (a) an invariant I over the machine state that implies the high-level theorem when it holds for the machine's final configuration; and (b) a preservation lemma showing that each machine operation (push, consume, and return) preserves I. Section 5.2 contains an example of such an invariant.

[3] Internally, a CoStar++ grammar is a finite map in which each base production $X ::= \gamma$ maps to an annotated production $X' ::= \gamma'$ $[\![p]\!]?$ $[\![f]\!]!$. The well-formedness property says that $X = X'$ and $\gamma = \gamma'$ for each key/value pair in the map. This property enables the interpreter to retrieve the predicate and action for key $X := \gamma$.

```
X ::= <int> Y            [[λ(i,(s,_),_).i - String.length s]]!
    | Z <bool>           [[λ((_,s),b,_).if b then String.length s else 0]]!
Y ::= <string> <bool>    [[λ(s,b,_).(s,b)]]!
Z ::= <int> <string>     [[λ(i,s,_).(i,s)]]!
```

Fig. 6. Grammar that recognizes an `<int><string><bool>` sequence. For some inputs, two different syntactic derivations produce the same semantic value.

4 Semantic Actions and Ambiguity

There is an apparent type mismatch between the "unique" and "ambiguous" soundness theorems in Sect. 3. According to Theorem 1, a `Unique`(v) parse result indicates that v is a uniquely correct *semantic value* for the input, while Theorem 2 says that an `Ambig`(v) result implies the existence of multiple correct *parse trees* for the input. The reason for this asymmetry is that syntactically ambiguous inputs may not be ambiguous at the semantic level; actions can map two distinct parse trees for an input to the same semantic value, and predicates can eliminate semantic ambiguity by rejecting semantic values as malformed. For these reasons, the problem of identifying semantic ambiguity is undecidable when semantic values lack decidable equality. When CoStar++ flags an ambiguous input, it is only able to guarantee that ambiguity exists at the syntactic level.

We illustrate this point with an example involving the somewhat contrived grammar in Fig. 6. Start symbol `X` matches an `<int><string><bool>` sequence in two possible ways—one involving the first right-hand side for `X`, and one involving the second right-hand side. These two right-hand sides can be used to derive two distinct parse trees for such a token sequence (we represent leaves as terminal symbols for readability):

(1a) `Node X [<int>, Node Y [<string>, <bool>]]`
(1b) `Node X [Node Z [<int>, <string>], <bool>]`

However, while any `<int><string><bool>` sequence is ambiguous at the syntactic level, only some inputs are semantically ambiguous. For example, on input

(`<int>` & `10`) (`<string>` & `"apple"`) (`<bool>` & `false`)

the actions attached to the two right-hand sides for `X` produce two distinct values:

(2a) `10 - String.length "apple" = 5`
(2b) `if false then String.length "apple" else 0 = 0`

However, replacing the literal value in the `<bool>` token with `true` makes the two derivations produce the same semantic value:

(3a) `10 - String.length "apple" = 5`
(3b) `if true then String.length "apple" else 0 = 5`

In theory, when CoStar++ identifies multiple semantic values for these examples, it could determine whether the input is semantically ambiguous by comparing the values, because integer equality is decidable. However, semantic types are user-defined, and we do not require them to have decidable equality; the user may want the interpreter to produce functions or other incomparable values. Therefore, in the general case, the interpreter can only certify that the input has two distinct parse trees—this guarantee is the one that Theorem 2 provides.

5 Semantic Predicates and Completeness

One of the main challenges of implementing and verifying CoStar++ was ensuring completeness in the presence of semantic predicates. ALL(*) is a predictive parsing algorithm; at decision points, it launches subparsers that speculatively explore alternative paths. ALL(*) as originally described [14] does not apply semantic actions or check CoStar++-style predicates at prediction time. However, a predicate-oblivious prediction algorithm results in an interpreter that is incomplete relative to the SemValueDer specification (Fig. 4). In other words, it can make a choice that eventually causes the interpreter to reject input as invalid due to a failed predicate, when a different choice would have led to a successful parse. In this section, we present a modification to the ALL(*) prediction mechanism and prove that it makes the interpreter complete with respect to its semantic specification.

5.1 A Semantics-Aware Prediction Mechanism

The semantics-aware version of CoStar++ uses a modified version of ALL(*) prediction that is guaranteed not to send the interpreter down a "bad path." In designing this modification, we faced a tradeoff between speed and expressiveness; checking predicates and building semantic values along all prediction paths is expensive, but it is sometimes necessary to ensure completeness.

Our solution leverages the fact that the original ALL(*) prediction mechanism addresses a similar problem; it is actually a combination of two prediction strategies that make different tradeoffs with respect to speed and expressiveness:

- **SLL prediction** is an optimized algorithm that ignores the initial parser stack at the start of prediction. As a result, subparser states are compact and recur frequently, which makes them amenable to caching. The tradeoff is that because of the missing context, SLL prediction must sometimes overapproximate the parser's behavior by simulating a return to *all* possible contexts.
- **LL prediction** is a slower but sound algorithm in which subparsers have access to the initial parser stack; the algorithm is thus a precise nondeterministic simulation of the parser's behavior. When the SLL algorithm detects an ambiguity, the prediction mechanism fails over to the LL strategy to determine whether the ambiguity is genuine or involves a spurious path introduced by the overapproximation; using the result of SLL prediction directly in such a case would render the parser incomplete.

Semantics-aware prediction works as follows:

- SLL prediction is unchanged; subparsers do not build semantic values or check semantic properties. SLL is thus still an overapproximation of the parser; not evaluating the predicates is equivalent to assuming that they succeed.
- LL prediction builds semantic values and checks semantic properties along all paths. It thus remains a precise nondeterministic simulation of the parser.

This approach assumes that most predictions are unambiguous without considering predicates, and the more expensive LL strategy is thus rarely required.

5.2 A Backward-Looking Completeness Invariant

Adding semantic features to LL prediction makes CoStar++ complete with respect to the SemValueDer specification. Theorem 4 (the interpreter completeness theorem) relies on the following lemma:

Lemma 1 (Completeness modulo ambiguity detection). If v is a correct semantic value for nonterminal S and word w, then there exists a semantic value v' such that the interpreter returns either `Unique`(v') or `Ambig`(v') for S and w.

In essence, this lemma says that the interpreter does not reject valid input. Its proof is based on an invariant over the machine state guaranteeing that no machine operation can result in a rejection.

In the absence of semantic predicates, a natural definition of this invariant says that the concatenated unprocessed stack symbols recognize the remaining token sequence. Such an invariant is purely forward-looking; it refers only to symbols and tokens that the interpreter has not processed yet. However, this invariant is too weak to prove that CoStar++ never rejects valid input, because a predicate can fail on semantic values that were produced by earlier machine steps. To rule out such cases, we need an invariant that is both backward- and forward-looking; i.e., one that refers to both the "past" and "future" of the parse.

The CoStar++ completeness invariant, StackAcceptsSuffix_I, appears in Fig. 7. It holds when the remaining tokens can be split into a prefix w_1 and suffix w_2 such that the unprocessed symbols β in the top stack frame produce a semantic tuple for w_1, and the auxiliary invariant FramesAcceptSuffix_I holds for the lower frames and w_2.

The FramesAcceptSuffix_I definition (also in Fig. 7) is parametric over symbols γ and semantic tuple $\bar{v} : [\![\gamma]\!]$. The $\bar{v}$ parameter represents the "incoming" tuple during the eventual return operation from the frame above the ones in scope. The base case of FramesAcceptSuffix_I says that if the list of remaining frames is empty, then the remaining token sequence must be empty as well. In the case of a non-empty list of frames, the following properties hold:

- The remaining tokens can be split into a prefix w_1 and suffix w_2 such that the unprocessed symbols in the head frame produce a semantic tuple for w_1. This property (which appears in StackAcceptsSuffix_I as well) is the forward-looking portion of the invariant.

$$\boxed{\textsc{FramesAcceptSuffix\_I} : (\bar{v} : [\![\gamma]\!]), \phi \vartriangleright w}$$

$$\textsc{FramesAcceptSuffix\_Nil} \quad \frac{}{\bar{v}, \bullet \vartriangleright \epsilon}$$

$$\textsc{FramesAcceptSuffix\_Cons} \quad \frac{\begin{array}{c}\bar{v}_\gamma : [\![\gamma]\!] \quad \bar{v}_\alpha : [\![\alpha]\!] \quad \bar{v}_\beta : [\![\beta]\!] \quad p : [\![\gamma]\!] \to \mathbb{B} \quad f : [\![\gamma]\!] \to [\![X]\!] \\ \beta \xrightarrow{\bar{v}_\beta} w_1 \quad X ::= \gamma \ [\![p]\!]? \ [\![f]\!]! \in \mathcal{G} \quad p(\bar{v}_\gamma) = \mathtt{true} \\ \mathtt{revTup}(\bar{v}_\alpha) \ [\![+\!\!+]\!] \ (f(\bar{v}_\gamma), \bar{v}_\beta), \phi \vartriangleright w_2\end{array}}{\bar{v}_\gamma, [\alpha \ \& \ \bar{v}_\alpha, X\beta]\phi \vartriangleright w_1 w_2}$$

$$\boxed{\textsc{StackAcceptsSuffix\_I} : \phi \blacktriangleright w}$$

$$\frac{\bar{v}_\alpha : [\![\alpha]\!] \quad \bar{v}_\beta : [\![\beta]\!] \quad \beta \xrightarrow{\bar{v}_\beta} w_1 \quad \mathtt{revTup}(\bar{v}_\alpha) \ [\![+\!\!+]\!] \ \bar{v}_\beta, \phi \vartriangleright w_2}{[\alpha \ \& \ \bar{v}_\alpha, \beta]\phi \blacktriangleright w_1 w_2}$$

Fig. 7. The StackAcceptsSuffix_I machine state invariant over stack ϕ and token sequence w. The invariant guarantees that the interpreter does not reject valid input. The $[\![+\!\!+]\!]$ function concatenates two semantic tuples, and the `revTup` function reverses a semantic tuple.

- There exists a grammar production $X ::= \gamma \ [\![p]\!]? \ [\![f]\!]!$, where X is the open nonterminal in the head frame and γ is the right-hand side from the frame above, such that semantic tuple $\bar{v}_\gamma$ from the frame above satisfies p. This condition is the backward-looking portion of the invariant.
- FramesAcceptSuffix_I holds for the remaining frames and w_2.

Lemma 2 (Completeness invariant prevents rejection). If StackAcceptsSuffix_I holds at machine state σ, then a machine transition out of σ never produces a `Reject` result.

Lemma 3 (Preservation of completeness invariant). If StackAcceptsSuffix_I holds at machine state σ and $\sigma \rightsquigarrow \sigma'$, then StackAcceptsSuffix_I holds at state σ'.

6 Performance Evaluation

We evaluate CoStar++'s parsing speed and asymptotic behavior by extracting the tool to OCaml source code and recording its execution time on benchmarks for four real-world data formats. In each experiment, we provide CoStar++ with a grammar for a data format to obtain a parser for that format, and we record the parser's execution time on valid inputs of varying size. The benchmarks are as follows:

- **JSON** is a popular format for storing and exchanging structured data. The actions in our JSON grammar build an ADT representation of a JSON value with a type similar to the one in Figure 1. The predicates ensure that JSON objects contain no duplicate keys. The JSON data set contains biographical information for US Members of Congress [1].
- **PPM** is a text-based image file format in which each pixel is represented by a triple of (red, green, blue) values. A PPM file includes a header with numeric values that specify the image's width and height, and the maximum value of any pixel component. The actions in our PPM grammar build a record that contains the header values and a list of pixels. The predicates validate the non-context-free dependencies between the image's header and pixels. We generated a PPM data set by using the ImageMagick command-line tool `convert` to convert a single PPM image to a range of different sizes.
- **Newick trees** are an ad hoc format for representing arbitrarily branching trees with labeled edges. They are used in the evolutionary biology community to represent phylogenetic relationships. The Newick grammar's actions convert an input to an ADT representation of an arbitrarily branching tree. Our Newick data set comes from the 10kTrees Website, Version 3 [2], a public database of phylogenetic trees for various mammalian orders.
- **XML** is a widely used format for storing and transmitting structured data. An XML document is a tree of elements; each element begins and ends with a string-labeled tag, and the labels in corresponding start and end tags must match—a non-context-free property in the general case where the set of valid labels is infinite. The actions in our XML grammar build an ADT representation of an XML document, and the predicates check that corresponding tags contain matching labels. Our XML data set is a portion of the Open American National Corpus [13], a collection of English texts with linguistic annotations.

CoStar++ requires tokenized input. We use the Verbatim verified lexer interpreter [6,7] to obtain lexers for all four formats. In the benchmarks, we use these lexers to pre-tokenize each input before parsing it.

We ran the CoStar++ benchmarks on a laptop with 4 2.5 GHz cores, 7 GB of RAM, and the Ubuntu 16.04 OS. We compiled the extracted CoStar++ code with OCaml compiler version 4.11.1+flambda at optimization level -O3.

The CoStar++ benchmark results appear in Fig. 8. Each scatter plot point represents the parse time for one input file, averaged over ten trials. While the worst-case time complexity of ALL(*) is $O(n^4)$ [14], and CoStar++ lacks an optimization based on the *graph-structured stack* data structure [16] that factors into this bound, the tool appears to perform linearly on the benchmarks. For each set of results, we compute a least-squares regression line and a Locally Weighted Scatterplot Smoothing (LOWESS) curve [3]. LOWESS is a non-parametric technique for fitting a smooth curve to a set of data points; i.e., it does not assume that the data fit a particular distribution, linear or otherwise. The LOWESS curve and regression line correspond closely for each set of results, suggesting that the relationship between input size and execution time is linear.

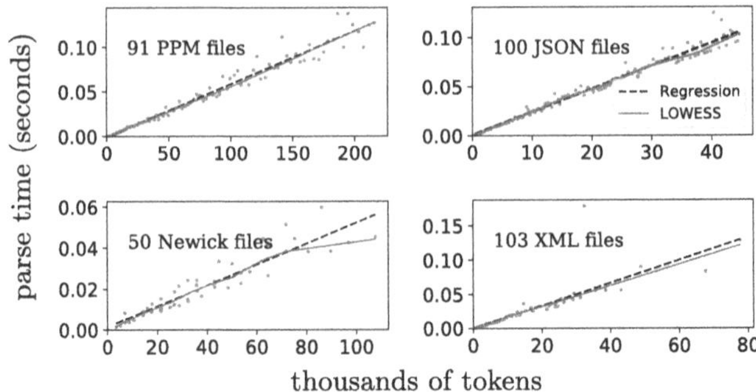

Fig. 8. Input size vs. CoStar++ average execution time on four benchmarks.

7 Related Work

CoStar++ builds on CoStar [11], another tool based on the ALL(*) algorithm and verified in Coq. CoStar produces parse trees that are generic across grammars modulo grammar symbol names. It is correct in terms of a specification in which a parse tree is the witness to a successful derivation. CoStar++ improves upon this work by supporting semantic actions and predicates.

ALL(*) was developed for the ANTLR parser generator [14]. While ALL(*) as originally described and as implemented in ANTLR supports a notion of semantic predicates, its prediction mechanism does not execute semantic actions, and thus cannot evaluate predicates over the results of those actions. The original algorithm is therefore incomplete with respect to our predicate-aware specification. These design choices are reasonable in terms of efficiency, and in terms of correctness in an imperative setting. It is potentially expensive to execute predicates and actions along a prediction path that the parser does not ultimately take. More importantly, doing so can produce counterintuitive behavior when the actions alter mutable state in ways that cannot be easily undone. These concerns do not apply to our setting, in which semantic actions are pure functions.

Several existing verified parsers for CFGs support some form of semantic actions. Jourdan et al. [8] and Lasser et al. [10] present verified parsing tools based on the LR(1) and LL(1) parsing algorithms, respectively. Both tools represent a semantic action as a function with a dependent type computed from the grammar symbols in its associated production. CoStar++ uses a similar representation of predicates and actions. Edelmann et al. [5] describe a parser combinator library and an accompanying type system that ensures that any well-typed parser built from the combinators is LL(1); such a parser therefore runs in linear time. Danielsson [4] and Ridge [15] present similar parser combinator libraries that can represent arbitrary CFGs but do not provide the linear runtime guarantees of LL(1) parsing.

Acknowledgments. Sam Lasser's research was supported by a Draper Scholarship.

References

1. Congress-legislators database (2022). https://github.com/unitedstates/congress-legislators
2. Arnold, C., Matthews, L.J., Nunn, C.L.: The 10kTrees website: a new online resource for primate phylogeny. Evol. Anthropol. Issues News Rev. **19**(3), 114–118 (2010)
3. Cleveland, W.S.: Robust locally weighted regression and smoothing scatterplots. J. Am. Stat. Assoc. **74**(368), 829–836 (1979)
4. Danielsson, N.A.: Total parser combinators. In: International Conference on Functional Programming (2010). https://doi.org/10.1145/1863543.1863585
5. Edelmann, R., Hamza, J., Kunčak, V.: Zippy LL(1) parsing with derivatives. In: Programming Language Design and Implementation (2020). https://doi.org/10.1145/3385412.3385992
6. Egolf, D., Lasser, S., Fisher, K.: Verbatim: a verified lexer generator. In: LangSec Workshop (2021). https://langsec.org/spw21/papers.html#verbatim
7. Egolf, D., Lasser, S., Fisher, K.: Verbatim++: verified, optimized, and semantically rich lexing with derivatives. In: Certified Programs and Proofs (2022). https://doi.org/10.1145/3497775.3503694
8. Jourdan, J.-H., Pottier, F., Leroy, X.: Validating *LR*(1) parsers. In: Seidl, H. (ed.) ESOP 2012. LNCS, vol. 7211, pp. 397–416. Springer, Heidelberg (2012). https://doi.org/10.1007/978-3-642-28869-2_20
9. Lasser, S., Casinghino, C., Egolf, D., Fisher, K., Roux, C.: GitHub repository for the CoStar++ development and performance evaluation framework (2022). https://github.com/slasser/CoStar
10. Lasser, S., Casinghino, C., Fisher, K., Roux, C.: A verified LL(1) parser generator. In: Interactive Theorem Proving (2019). https://doi.org/10.4230/LIPIcs.ITP.2019.24
11. Lasser, S., Casinghino, C., Fisher, K., Roux, C.: CoStar: a verified ALL(*) parser. In: Programming Language Design and Implementation (2021). https://doi.org/10.1145/3453483.3454053
12. Momot, F., Bratus, S., Hallberg, S.M., Patterson, M.L.: The seven turrets of babel: a taxonomy of LangSec errors and how to expunge them. In: IEEE Cybersecurity Development (2016). https://doi.org/10.1109/SecDev.2016.019
13. Open American National Corpus (2010). https://www.anc.org/data/oanc/download/
14. Parr, T., Harwell, S., Fisher, K.: Adaptive LL(*) parsing: the power of dynamic analysis. In: Object-Oriented Programming, Systems, Languages, and Applications (2014). https://doi.org/10.1145/2660193.2660202
15. Ridge, T.: Simple, functional, sound and complete parsing for all context-free grammars. In: Jouannaud, J.-P., Shao, Z. (eds.) CPP 2011. LNCS, vol. 7086, pp. 103–118. Springer, Heidelberg (2011). https://doi.org/10.1007/978-3-642-25379-9_10
16. Scott, E., Johnstone, A.: GLL parsing. Elect. Notes Theor. Comput. Sci. **253**(7), 177–189 (2010). https://doi.org/10.1016/j.entcs.2010.08.041

Subtropical Satisfiability for SMT Solving

Jasper Nalbach(✉) and Erika Ábrahám

RWTH Aachen University, Aachen, Germany
nalbach@cs.rwth-aachen.de

Abstract. A wide range of problems from aerospace engineering and other application areas can be encoded logically and solved using satisfiability modulo theories (SMT) tools, which themselves use dedicated decision procedures for the underlying theories.

Subtropical satisfiability is such a decision procedure for the theory of real arithmetic. Though incomplete, it is a very efficient algorithm and has a high potential for SMT solving. However, yet it has been seldomly used in this context. In this paper we elaborate on possibilities for the efficient usage of subtropical satisfiability in SMT solving.

Keywords: Satisfiability checking · real arithmetic · subtropical satisfiability

1 Introduction

Quantifier-free non-linear real arithmetic (QFNRA) is an expressive but still decidable first-order theory, whose formulas are Boolean combinations of constraints that compare polynomials to zero. Though the complexity of the satisfiability problem for QFNRA is known to be singly exponential, the only complete decision procedure—named the *cylindrical algebraic decomposition (CAD)* method [9]—that is applied in practice has a doubly exponential complexity.

The complexity can be reduced if we are ready to pay the price of giving up completeness. An incomplete but highly efficient method is the *subtropical real root finding* algorithm of Sturm [22] for checking the satisfiability of *one* multivariate *equation*. This method was later extended by Fontaine et al. [14] for the incomplete check of *conjunctions* of multivariate *in*equations for satisfiability.

Both [22] and [14] encode a sufficient condition for satisfying the original problem in *linear* real arithmetic, which can be solved in practice much more efficiently e.g. via a *satisfiability modulo theories (SMT)* solver. SMT solving [5,16] is a technology for checking the satisfiability of quantifier-free first-order logic formulas over different theories. Most SMT solvers are based on the CDCL(T) framework and combine a SAT solver [11,12,18] with one or more theory solver(s). The SAT solver checks whether the Boolean structure of a formula can be satisfied if a set of theory constraints can be assumed to be true, and consults the theory solver(s) to check the feasibility of these *sets (conjunctions)* of theory constraints.

Jasper Nalbach was supported by the DFG RTG 2236 *UnRAVeL*.

K. Y. Rozier and S. Chaudhuri (Eds.): NFM 2023, LNCS 13903, pp. 430–446, 2023.
https://doi.org/10.1007/978-3-031-33170-1_26

This paper is devoted to the usage of the above mentioned subtropical methods [14,22] in SMT solving. The subtropical methods either detect satisfiability or return unknown. However, the computations are typically very fast, such that solutions bring a huge benefit by avoiding the heavy CAD machinery, and otherwise we can still fall back to the CAD method with only little effort wasted. Surprisingly, we are aware of just two SMT solvers—veriT [7] and SMT-RAT [10]—that use the subtropical methods for theory solving.

Our contributions are the following:

1. It is known that any QFNRA formula can be transformed to a satisfiability-equivalent equation (see e.g. [17]), whose satisfiability can be (incompletely) checked by subtropical real-root finding [22]. For SMT solving, this approach could serve as preprocessing, which tries to solve an input QFNRA formula and supersede the actual SMT call. However, we are not aware of any implementation, thus the practical relevance is unclear. We provide an implementation, attach it as a preprocessor to different SMT solvers and evaluate their efficiency.
2. Our second contribution is another preprocessing technique that is based on the subtropical method [14] for sets of inequations. We suggest a simple but elegant extension to QFNRA formulas with an arbitrary Boolean structure. This method can also be employed as a preprocessing algorithm independently of the internals of the SMT solver which uses it, thus the embedding requires low effort. We provide an implementation and evaluate it again in combination with different SMT solvers.
3. To put the above results in context, we also employ subtropical satisfiability as a theory solver in our CDCL(T)-based SMT solver named SMT-RAT. This allows us to compare the usefulness of subtropical satisfiability as a theory module in CDCL(T) versus using it as a preprocessor.

Outline. After introducing some preliminaries in Sect. 2, we present our novel subtropical extension in Sect. 3. We report on experimental results in Sect. 4 and conclude the paper in Sect. 5.

2 Preliminaries

Let $\mathbb{N}$, $\mathbb{Z}$, $\mathbb{R}$ and $\mathbb{R}_{>0}$ denote the sets of natural (including 0), integer, real resp. positive real numbers. Assume $d \in \mathbb{N} \setminus \{0\}$ and let $x = (x_1, \dots, x_d)$ be variables. The transpose of a vector v is denoted by v^T.

Polynomials. A *monomial* m over x is a product $\prod_{i=1}^{d} x_i^{e_i}$ with $e_1, \dots, e_d \in \mathbb{N}$; we call $\sum_{i=1}^{d} e_i$ the *degree* of m. Note that the monomial of degree 0 is the constant 1. A *term* over x with coefficient domain $\mathbb{Z}$ is a product $c \cdot m$ with $c \in \mathbb{Z}$ and m a monomial over x. A *polynomial* over x with coefficient domain $\mathbb{Z}$ is a sum $\sum_{i=1}^{k} c_i \cdot m_i$ where $k \in \mathbb{N} \setminus \{0\}$ and $c_i \cdot m_i$ are terms over x with coefficient domain $\mathbb{Z}$, such that their monomials are pairwise different. We write $\mathbb{Z}[x]$ for the set of all polynomials over x with coefficient domain $\mathbb{Z}$. A polynomial is *linear* if its monomials are all of degree at most 1.

Constraints. A *(polynomial) constraint* over x with coefficient domain $\mathbb{Z}$ has the form $p \sim 0$ with *defining polynomial* $p \in \mathbb{Z}[x]$ and *relation* $\sim \in \{=, \neq, <, >, \leq, \geq\}$. *Equations* are constraints of the form $p = 0$; *disequations* are constraints shaped $p \neq 0$; *weak inequations* are constraints formed as $p \leq 0$ or $p \geq 0$, *strict inequations* are constraints built as $p < 0$ or $p > 0$; finally, *inequations* are either weak or strict inequations. We use $p(x)$ to explicitly refer to the variables in p, and for $v = (v_1, \ldots, v_d) \in \mathbb{R}^d$ we write $p(v)$ for the value to which p evaluates when we substitute v_i for x_i for $i = 1, \ldots, d$. A *solution* for $p \sim 0$ is any $v \in \mathbb{R}^d$ such that $p(v) \sim 0$ evaluates to true. The solution set of a linear equation (weak inequation) is called a *hyperplane* (*half-space*), whose *normal vector* $n = (n_1, \ldots, n_d)$ is the vector of the coefficients of $x = (x_1, \ldots, x_d)$ in the defining polynomial.

Formulas. Quantifier-free non-linear real arithmetic (QFNRA) formulas are Boolean combinations of constraints. A *quantifier-free linear real arithmetic (QFLRA)* formula is a QFNRA formula whose defining polynomials are all linear. Let φ and ψ be QFNRA formulas and a be a constraint in φ, then $\varphi[\psi/a]$ denotes the formula φ where each occurrence of a is substituted by ψ.

Polytopes. A set $P \subset \mathbb{R}^d$ is *convex* if $v_1 + \lambda(v_2 - v_1) \in P$ for all $v_1, v_2 \in P$ and all $\lambda \in [0, 1] \subseteq \mathbb{R}$. The *convex hull* of a set $V \subset \mathbb{R}^d$ is the smallest convex set $P \subseteq \mathbb{R}^d$ with $V \subseteq P$. *Polytopes* are convex hulls of finite subsets of $\mathbb{R}^d$. A point $v \in \mathbb{R}^d$ is a *vertex* of a polytope $P \subseteq \mathbb{R}^d$ if there exists a linear polynomial $p = c_0 + \sum_{i=1}^{d} c_i \cdot x_i \in \mathbb{Z}[x_1, \ldots, x_d]$ with $p(v) \geq 0$ and $p(u) < 0$ for all $u \in P \setminus \{v\}$; we call v the *vertex of P with respect to the normal vector* $(c_1, \ldots, c_d)$ and refer to $-c_0$ as the *bias*.

Frame and Newton Polytope. Let $p = \sum_{i=1}^{k} c_i \cdot \prod_{j=1}^{d} x_j^{e_{i,j}} \in \mathbb{Z}[x]$. We define

- the *frame of* p as $\mathit{frame}(p) = \{(e_{i,1}, \ldots, e_{i,d}) \mid i \in \{1, \ldots, k\} \wedge c_i \neq 0\}$;
- the *positive frame* of p as $\mathit{frame}_+(p) = \{(e_{i,1}, \ldots, e_{i,d}) \in \mathit{frame}(p) \mid c_i > 0\}$;
- the *negative frame* of p as $\mathit{frame}_-(p) = \{(e_{i,1}, \ldots, e_{i,d}) \in \mathit{frame}(p) \mid c_i < 0\}$;
- the *Newton polytope of* p as the convex hull of $\mathit{frame}(p)$.

2.1 SMT Solving

Satisfiability modulo theories (SMT) is a technique for checking the satisfiability of quantifier-free first-order logic formulas over different theories. Most SMT solvers implement the CDCL(T)-based framework [5], where a SAT solver [11, 12, 18] tries to satisfy the Boolean structure of the problem and consults theory solver(s) regarding the consistency of certain theory constraint *sets*.

For QFLRA, an adaptation of the *simplex* method named *general simplex* [13] can be employed as a theory solver. For QFNRA, the only complete decision procedure used in practice is the *cylindrical algebraic decomposition* method [9] and algorithms derived from it, such as the *cylindrical algebraic coverings* method [3] and *NLSAT* [15] in combination with the *single-cell construction* algorithm [8] (the latter is not based on CDCL(T)). Due to its doubly exponential complexity, it might be advantageous to supplement the CAD by methods that are incomplete but oftentimes faster, e.g. by *interval constraint propagation* [6] or the *virtual substitution* method [23].

2.2 Subtropical Satisfiability for a Single Inequation

The subtropical satisfiability method as introduced in [14,22] provides an incomplete but efficient method for finding solutions for a constraint $p > 0$ with $p \in \mathbb{Z}[x]$. Note that any solution to $p > 0$ is also a solution to $p \geq 0$, and that $p < 0$ and $p \leq 0$ are equivalent to $-p > 0$ respectively $-p \geq 0$, such that the method can be applied to all forms of inequations.

We first recall the sufficient condition from [14,22] for positive solutions.

Theorem 1. *[14, Lemma 2] Assume $k \in \mathbb{N} \setminus \{0\}$, $p = \sum_{i=1}^{k} c_i \cdot \prod_{j=1}^{d} x_j^{e_{i,j}} \in \mathbb{Z}[x] \setminus \{0\}$, and $i' \in \{1, \ldots, k\}$ such that $(e_{i',1}, \ldots, e_{i',d}) \in frame(p)$ is a vertex of the Newton polytope of p with respect to some $n = (n_1, \ldots, n_d) \in \mathbb{R}^d$. Then there exists $a_0 \in \mathbb{R}_{>0}$ such that for all $a \geq a_0$ it holds:*

1. $|c_{i'} \cdot \prod_{j=1}^{d} (a^{n_j})^{e_{i',j}}| > |\sum_{i \in \{1,\ldots,k\} \setminus \{i'\}} c_i \cdot \prod_{j=1}^{d} (a^{n_j})^{e_{i,j}}|$,
2. $sgn(p(a^{n_1}, \ldots, a^{n_d})) = sgn(c_{i'})$.

Assume a non-empty polytope $P \subseteq \mathbb{R}^d$ and a hyperplane with normal vector $(n_1, \ldots, n_d) \in \mathbb{R}^d$ that separates a vertex e of P from the rest of P (see the solid line hyperplane in Fig. 1). Now, assume any polynomial $p = \sum_{i=1}^{k} c_i m_i \in \mathbb{Z}[x]$ with Newton polytope P. Then p has a term, say $c_{i'} m_{i'}$, with the exponent vector e. If the coefficient $c_{i'}$ is positive (negative) then we can make $c_{i'} m_{i'}$ larger (smaller) than the sum of all the other terms of p by the point $(a^{n_1}, \ldots, a^{n_d})$ for a large enough value $a \in \mathbb{R}$.

More concretely, a positive solution for $p > 0$, $p = \sum_{i=1}^{k} c_i \cdot \prod_{j=1}^{d} x_j^{e_{i,j}} \in \mathbb{Z}[x]$ can be obtained by:

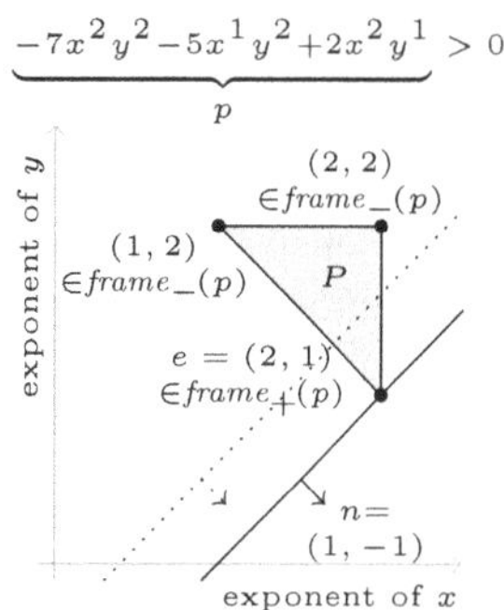

Fig. 1. Solving $p > 0$.

1. Check whether there exists $e \in frame_+(p)$ that is a vertex of the Newton polytope of p with respect to some $n = (n_1, \ldots, n_d) \in \mathbb{R}^d$.
2. If no then return unknown.
3. Otherwise let $a \in \mathbb{R}_{>0}$ and $c \in \mathbb{R}$ with $c > 1$.
4. If $p[a^{n_1}/x_1] \ldots [a^{n_d}/x_d] > 0$ then return $(a^{n_1}, \ldots, a^{n_d})$ as solution.
5. Otherwise update a to $c \cdot a$ and go to 4.

Note that Theorem 1 assures termination. Step 1 is executed by encoding the existence of the desired normal vector n as a QFLRA formula $\mathcal{ST}_{p>0}(n)$, which can then be solved by any QFLRA-solver. Most QFLRA solvers use adaptions of the simplex method, for which weak inequations are more advantageous. Therefore, the encoding uses another characterization for e being a vertex of a polytope P: Its definition requiring the *existence of a half-space that contains the whole polytope P but e is the only point from P that lies exactly on its hyperplane* is equivalent to requiring the *existence of a half-space that excludes e but contains all other vertices of a polytope P* (see the hyperplane with the dotted line in Fig. 1).

$$\mathcal{ST}_{p>0}(n) := \exists b. \bigvee_{e \in \mathit{frame}_+(p)} \left(n^T \cdot e > b \wedge \bigwedge_{u \in \mathit{frame}(p) \setminus \{e\}} n^T \cdot u \leq b \right) .$$

This property can be encoded even more efficiently as suggested in [14]:

$$\mathcal{ST}_{p>0}(n) := \exists b. \left(\bigvee_{e \in \mathit{frame}_+(p)} n^T \cdot e > b \right) \wedge \left(\bigwedge_{u \in \mathit{frame}_-(p)} n^T \cdot u \leq b \right) .$$

With the above encoding we can only find positive solutions from $\mathbb{R}^d_{>0}$. However, the encoding can be extended to the general case based on the observation that we could substitute in p any subset of the variables x_i by $-x_i$: If we find a positive solution for this modified problem, then we get a solution for the original problem by exchanging the positive values v_i for $-x_i$ by the negative values $-v_i$ for x_i. To encode all possible such *sign changes*, we introduce for every variable x_i, $i = 1, \ldots, d$ a Boolean variable neg_i which encodes whether we search for a negative ($\mathit{neg}_i = 1$) or a positive ($\mathit{neg}_i = 0$) value for x_i. The exponent vector of a term $c \cdot x_1^{e_1} \ldots x_d^{e_d}$ of p with $c \neq 0$ is in the positive frame iff ($c > 0 \leftrightarrow |\{x_i \mid \exists k \in \mathbb{N}.\ e_i = 2k + 1 \wedge \mathit{neg}_i = 1\}|$ is even). For details on the encoding, we refer to [14].

The encodings above for a constraint of the form $p > 0$ can be generalized to constraints of all types but equations. To do so, for any polynomial p we define

$$\begin{aligned}
\mathcal{ST}_{p\geq 0}(n, \mathit{neg}) &:= \mathcal{ST}_{p>0}(n, \mathit{neg}) \\
\mathcal{ST}_{p\leq 0}(n, \mathit{neg}) &:= \mathcal{ST}_{p<0}(n, \mathit{neg}) := \mathcal{ST}_{-p>0}(n, \mathit{neg}) \\
\mathcal{ST}_{p\neq 0}(n, \mathit{neg}) &:= (\mathcal{ST}_{p>0}(n, \mathit{neg}) \oplus \mathcal{ST}_{p<0}(n, \mathit{neg}))
\end{aligned}$$

where $\oplus$ denotes the exclusive-or operator. Given the fact that from each solution of $\mathcal{ST}_{p>0}(n, \mathit{neg})$ we can derive positive values for p, it is easy to see that the satisfiability of $\mathcal{ST}_c(n, \mathit{neg})$ implies the satisfiability of c.

Example 1. The encodings of $x_1 + x_1 \cdot x_2^3 < 0$ and $x_2 + x_1^3 > 0$ are

$$\begin{aligned}
\mathcal{ST}_{x_1+x_1\cdot x_2^3<0}(n, \mathit{neg}) =& \exists b_1. ((\neg \mathit{neg}_1 \wedge n_1 > b_1) \vee (\neg(\mathit{neg}_1 \oplus \mathit{neg}_2) \wedge n_1 + 3n_2 > b_1)) \\
& \wedge (\mathit{neg}_1 \rightarrow n_1 \leq b_1) \wedge ((\mathit{neg}_1 \oplus \mathit{neg}_2) \rightarrow n_1 + 3n_2 \leq b_1) \\
\mathcal{ST}_{x_2+x_1^3>0}(n, \mathit{neg}) =& \exists b_2. ((\neg \mathit{neg}_2 \wedge n_2 > b_2) \vee (\neg \mathit{neg}_1 \wedge 3n_1 > b_2)) \\
& \wedge (\mathit{neg}_2 \rightarrow n_2 \leq b_2) \wedge (\mathit{neg}_1 \rightarrow 3n_1 \leq b_2) .
\end{aligned}$$

The above approach strictly separates a positive frame point from all negative ones. However, there are cases where a weak separation suffices (i.e. the separated positive frame point may lie on the hyperplane). The work presented in [20] defines an encoding considering these cases, but this encoding seems to be larger and without much computational advantage.

2.3 Subtropical Satisfiability for a Single Equation

To find a solution for a single equation $p = 0$, $p \in \mathbb{Z}[x]$, the method from [14,22] tries to identify two points $v_-, v_+ \in \mathbb{R}^d$ such that $p(v_-) < 0$ and $p(v_+) > 0$ and use the intermediate value theorem to construct a $v_0 \in \mathbb{R}^d$ with $p(v_0) = 0$:

1. Choose $v_- = (1, \ldots, 1)$.
2. If $p(v_-) = 0$ then return v_- as a solution to $p = 0$.
3. If $p(v_-) > 0$ then we set p to $-p$. (Note that now $p(v_-) < 0$.)
4. Apply the method from Sect. 2.2 to find a $v_+ \in \mathbb{R}^d$ with $p(v_+) > 0$.
5. If unsuccessful then return unknown.
6. Let $p^* : [0,1] \to \mathbb{R}$, $t \mapsto p(v_- + t \cdot (v_+ - v_-))$. Since p^* is continuous, $p^*(0) < 0$ and $p^*(1) > 0$, we know that $p^*(t_0) = 0$ at some $t_0 \in (0,1) \subseteq \mathbb{R}$. We can use real root isolation techniques based on Descartes' rule of signs or Sturm sequences to find such a t_0, which yields $p(v_0) = 0$ for $v_0 = v_- + t_0(v_+ - v_-)$.

2.4 Subtropical Satisfiability for Conjunctions of Inequations

For finding solutions for a conjunction of inequations $\varphi = p_1 \sim_1 0 \wedge \ldots \wedge p_\ell \sim_\ell 0$ with $\sim_i \in \{<, >, \leq, \geq, \neq\}$ for $i = 1, \ldots, \ell$, Fontaine et al. [14] propose to apply the method from Sect. 2.2 to simultaneously separate a suitable frame point for each involved polynomial through hyperplanes but with the same normal vector and assure to agree on a common sign change, resulting in the encoding

$$\mathcal{ST}_\varphi(n, neg) := \mathcal{ST}_{p_1 \sim_1 0}(n, neg) \wedge \ldots \wedge \mathcal{ST}_{p_\ell \sim_\ell 0}(n, neg) .$$

We solve $\mathcal{ST}_\varphi(n, neg)$ with a linear arithmetic solver. If $\mathcal{ST}_\varphi(n, neg)$ is satisfiable then from each solution μ of $\mathcal{ST}_\varphi(n, neg)$ we can derive a solution for φ by multiplying the value of some $a \in \mathbb{R}_{>0}$ with a factor $c \in \mathbb{R}$, $c > 1$ until all inequations are satisfied by the values $(-1)^{\mu(neg_i)} \cdot a^{\mu(n_i)}$ for x_i, $i = 1, \ldots, d$.

2.5 Transformation of a QFNRA Formula into a Single Equation

Assume a QFNRA formula φ in negation normal form (i.e. only constraints are allowed to be negated). The transformation proposed in [21] introduces for every constraint c in φ a fresh (real-valued) variable y_c to generate an equisatisfiable formula $Tr(\varphi)$ as follows, using a transformer sub-function tr and the negation operator from Fig. 2 for $\sim \in \{<, >, \leq, \geq, =, \neq\}$:

$\sim$	$<$	$>$	$\leq$	$\geq$	$=$	$\neq$
$\not\sim$	$\geq$	$\leq$	$>$	$<$	$\neq$	$=$

Fig. 2. Predicate negation

$$\begin{aligned}
Tr(p = 0) &:= p = 0 & Tr(\textstyle\bigwedge_{i=1}^n \varphi_i) &:= tr(\textstyle\bigwedge_{i=1}^n Tr(\varphi_i)) \\
Tr(p \geq 0) &:= p - (y_{p\geq 0})^2 = 0 & Tr(\textstyle\bigvee_{i=1}^n \varphi_i) &:= tr(\textstyle\bigvee_{i=1}^n Tr(\varphi_i)) \\
Tr(p > 0) &:= (y_{p>0})^2 \cdot p - 1 = 0 & Tr(\neg(p \sim 0)) &:= Tr(p \not\sim 0) \\
Tr(p \leq 0) &:= p + (y_{p\leq 0})^2 = 0 & tr(\textstyle\bigvee_{i=1}^n p_i = 0) &:= \textstyle\prod_{i=1}^n p_i = 0 \\
Tr(p < 0) &:= (y_{p<0})^2 \cdot p + 1 = 0 & tr(\textstyle\bigwedge_{i=1}^n p_i = 0) &:= \textstyle\sum_{i=1}^n (p_i)^2 = 0 \\
Tr(p \neq 0) &:= y_{p\neq 0} \cdot p + 1 = 0 & &
\end{aligned}$$

In this paper, we build on the work done in the thesis [17] which considered this transformation for solving Boolean combinations of constraints using subtropical real root finding.

3 Subtropical Satisfiability for QFNRA Formulas

Subtropical satisfiability is restricted to finding solutions for either a single equation or a conjunction of inequations. This is already sufficient for its embedding within a CDCL(T)-based SMT solver as a fast but incomplete theory solver backend, applicable only to a single equation or a set of inequations, and possibly returning unknown even in those cases. Using it in an MCSAT-based SMT solver would be possible to derive consistent extensions of partial assignments, even though we are not aware of any solver exploiting this possibility. However, in both cases, a relatively difficult individual adaption of the SMT solver is required to implement and embed the subtropical method.

In the following, we aim to increase the scope of the subtropical method by making it *applicable to general QFNRA formulas.* In Sect. 3.1 we first revisit and slightly adapt the method from Sect. 2.5 to transform any QFNRA formula into a single equation, which can be solved with the subtropical root finding from [14,22]. Then in Sect. 3.2 we propose two slightly different novel subtropical encodings for general QFNRA formulas. Similarly to the original method, we define a transformation to QFLRA, whose formulas can be checked by a linear SMT solver. Our method aims to serve as an incomplete but efficient *preprocessing check* for satisfiability before the main solver is called; as such, our C++ implementation could be relatively easily adapted as a preprocessor for other solvers, as it has no interaction with the main SMT algorithm.

3.1 Transforming a QFNRA Formula into a Single Equation

With the method from Sect. 2.5, we can transform any QFNRA formula φ to a single equisatisfiable equation $Tr(\varphi)$ and then use the subtropical root finding algorithm as described in Sect. 2.3 for finding a solution for the equation $Tr(\varphi)$, which will also be a solution for φ. However, this transformation has one weakness: the transformation of a conjunction $\bigwedge_{i=1}^{n} p_i = 0$ results in a sum-of-square polynomial $\sum_{i=1}^{n}(p_i)^2 = 0$; a disjunction of conjunctions $\bigvee_{i=1}^{n} \bigwedge_{j=1}^{n_i} p_{i,j} = 0$ results in a product of sum-of-squares polynomials $\prod_{i=1}^{n} \sum_{i=1}^{n_i}(p_{i,j})^2 = 0$, which is itself a sum-of-squares. In both cases, the resulting sum-of-squares polynomials are non-negative at all points, thus the subtropical real root finding (which needs a positive as well as a negative value for a polynomial for finding a real root for it) will fail. We are not aware of any alternative for the transformation of conjunctions that makes the subtropical method applicable. To avoid computational effort in these cases, we alter the transformation by setting

$$Tr(\bigwedge_{i=1}^{n} \varphi_i) := \textit{false}.$$

3.2 Generalizing the Subtropical Encoding to QFNRA Formulas

In this work we propose an alternative approach, which generalizes the idea of Sect. 2.4 from conjunctions of in- and disequations to arbitrary Boolean combinations of constraints. The generalization is straight-forward and simple to implement, and still surprisingly efficient.

Remember that the method in Sect. 2.4 takes a conjunction of constraints $\varphi = p_1 \sim_1 0 \wedge \ldots \wedge p_\ell \sim_\ell 0$ with $\sim_i \in \{<, >, \leq, \geq, \neq\}$ as input and encodes by

$$\mathcal{ST}_\varphi(n, neg) := \mathcal{ST}_{p_1 \sim_1 0}(n, neg) \wedge \ldots \wedge \mathcal{ST}_{p_\ell \sim_\ell 0}(n, neg)$$

the existence of a separating hyperplane for each in-/disequation but requiring a shared normal vector n for all separating hyperplanes and a shared sign change vector neg. If the formula $\mathcal{ST}_\varphi(n, neg)$ is satisfiable, then we get values for n_i and neg_i from which we can construct a solution for φ by setting x_i to the value of $neg_i \cdot a^{n_i}$ for $i = 1, \ldots, d$ with a large enough value for a.

We generalize this idea to arbitrary QFNRA formulas φ. First we eliminate all negations in φ by bringing the formula to negation normal form and applying negation to the predicates as in Fig. 2. We assume in the following that φ contains *no negation*.

We use the same encoding $\mathcal{ST}_c(n, neg)$ as before for in- and disequations c, but apply the formula's Boolean structure to these encodings. As the formula might also contain equations, which we cannot handle in combination with other constraints, we extend the previous encoding $\mathcal{ST}$ to

$$\hat{\mathcal{ST}}_{p \sim 0}(n, neg) := \begin{cases} \mathcal{ST}_{p \sim 0}(n, neg) & \textit{if } \sim \in \{<, >, \leq, \geq, \neq\} \\ \textit{false} & \textit{otherwise} \end{cases}$$

Note that even though we neglect the possibility of satisfying the formula by fulfilling equations, the following encodings might still lead to a subtropical solution when a solution can be found by satisfying in- or disequations. Let in the following $c_1, \ldots, c_\ell$ be all the different constraints that occur in φ. We follow two approaches for the encoding.

1. Direct substitution of constraints. Our first approach generates an encoding $\mathcal{ST}_\varphi^{\text{direct}}(n, neg)$ by replacing each constraint c_i in the formula φ directly by $\hat{\mathcal{ST}}_{c_i}(n, neg)$. This way, we preserve the Boolean structure of the formula and assure that each satisfying solution of $\mathcal{ST}_\varphi^{\text{direct}}(n, neg)$ encodes separating hyperplanes with a common normal vector and a common sign change vector for a set of constraints, whose satisfaction implies the satisfaction of the Boolean structure of φ:

$$\mathcal{ST}_\varphi^{\text{direct}}(n, neg) := \varphi[\hat{\mathcal{ST}}_{c_1}(n, neg)/c_1] \ldots [\hat{\mathcal{ST}}_{c_\ell}(n, neg)/c_\ell].$$

2. Encoding via auxiliary variables. In our second approach we separately encode the Boolean structure by building φ's Boolean skeleton and combine this with the encodings of the sufficient conditions for the satisfaction of constraints. The motivation behind this variant is to enable the encoding of more knowledge about the relations between the formula's constraints.

In this encoding, we first fix some monomial ordering and normalize all constraints in φ such that the leading coefficients of their defining polynomials become 1 (through divisions by suitable constants), and replace each disequation $p \neq 0$ by $(p < 0 \vee p > 0)$. Note that these transformations might change the number of different constraints. Next we replace all occurrences of all constraints $c_1, \ldots, c_k$ in the formula, c_i having the form $p_i \sim_i 0$ with $\sim_i \in \{<, \leq, =, \geq, >\}$, by fresh Boolean variables $a = (a_1, \ldots, a_k)$. Remember that we assumed the input formula to contain no negation, such that after this transformation no proposition is negated. The encoding is defined as

$$\begin{aligned} \mathcal{ST}^{\mathrm{aux}}_{\varphi}(n, b, a) := \varphi[a_1/c_1] \ldots [a_k/c_k] \wedge & \bigwedge_{i \in \{1,\ldots,k\}} (a_i \rightarrow \hat{\mathcal{ST}}_{c_i}(n, neg)) \\ \wedge & \bigwedge_{\substack{i,j \in \{1,\ldots,k\} \\ i \neq j,\ p_i = p_j, \\ \sim_i \in \{<,\leq\},\ \sim_j \in \{>,\geq\}}} (\neg a_i \vee \neg a_j) \end{aligned}$$

While this encoding shares the subtropical encoding idea with the previous one, there are two main differences: 1) The first encoding would correspond to an iff "$\leftrightarrow$" for defining the meaning of the propositions a_i, which is weakened here to an implication. 2) The second row encodes additional knowledge about constraints with identical defining polynomials: each pair of constraints putting zero as a lower respectively upper bound on the same polynomial are considered to be conflicting. Note that, even though such a pair of weak bounds might be simultaneously satisfied if the polynomial evaluates to 0, since the subtropical method is unable to handle equations, we neglect this possibility in our sufficient condition.

Number of Auxiliary Variables. For the first encoding, we need d real variables $n = (n_1, \ldots, n_d)$ to encode the shared normal vector of the separating hyperplanes, d Boolean variables $neg = (neg_1, \ldots, neg_d)$ to encode the sign changes, and ℓ real variables $d = (d_1, \ldots, d_\ell)$ to encode the offsets of the hyperplanes for the constraints. Thus in total we introduce $2d+\ell$ variables for the whole formula.

For the second encoding, in addition we introduce at most 2ℓ Boolean variables for the abstraction of constraints and at most double the number of offset variables (note that the elimination of $\neq$ might double the number of constraints). This gives us in total $2d + 4\ell$ variables for the whole formula.

Example 2. The second encoding for $x_1 + x_1 \cdot x_2^3 < 0 \vee x_2 + x_1^3 > 0$ yields: $\exists a_1.\ \exists a_2.\ (a_1 \vee a_2) \wedge (a_1 \rightarrow \mathcal{ST}_{x_1+x_1 \cdot x_2^3<0}(n, neg)) \wedge (a_2 \rightarrow \mathcal{ST}_{x_2+x_1^3>0}(n, neg))$ where a_1 and a_2 are the abstraction literals of the two constraints, and the encodings of neg_1, neg_2, n_1, n_2, b_1, and b_2 are given in Example 1.

4 Experimental Results

In order to evaluate their practical usefulness, we implemented the previously presented algorithms in our `SMT-RAT` framework [10].

For the experiments, we employ the complete *QFNRA* [1] benchmark set from *SMT-LIB* [2]. This covers 12134 benchmarks (5209 known to be satisfiable, 5029 known to be unsatisfiable, remaining with unknown status). When comparing different approaches, we also consider a *virtual best (VB)* solver, which is computed by taking the best solver for each benchmark (i.e. for each benchmark we take the best solver for it: we prefer solved instances over unknowns over timeouts over memouts, and take the shortest running time). Furthermore, we apply standard preprocessing on all benchmarks.

For the execution we used an *Intel® Xeon® Platinum 8160 2.1GHz* processor with a memory limit of *4 GB* per run and a timeout of *two minutes*. For QFNRA, this timeout suffices to cover almost all benchmarks that can be solved (as indicated also in the results below); further, the relatively short timeout is justified as we aim to apply the subtropical methods for fast incomplete satisfiability checks to supplement a complete solver.

The implementation which generated the following results is available at https://doi.org/10.5281/zenodo.7509171.

4.1 Pure Subtropical Solvers

Solvers. We first use the presented ideas for solving a QFNRA formula φ four different ways:

- `Equation` We transform φ into a single equation as in Sect. 3.1 and solve the equation with subtropical root finding from Sect. 2.2. We use SMT-RAT for the involved QFLRA checks.
- `Formula` We generate the first encoding $\mathcal{ST}_{\varphi}^{\text{direct}}$ as in Sect. 3.2 and invoke SMT-RAT for solving the result.
- `FormulaAlt` We generate the second encoding $\mathcal{ST}_{\varphi}^{\text{aux}}$ as in Sect. 3.2 and invoke SMT-RAT for solving the result.
- `Incremental` We apply to φ SMT-RAT with CDCL(T) and the subtropical satisfiability method for conjunctions from Sect. 2.4 as the only theory solver. If the input contains an equation or a disequation then the theory solver returns *unknown*.

Benchmarks. We observed that both `Formula` and `FormulaAlt` could conclude unsatisfiability on 2614 benchmarks, either during the transformation of the formula to negation normal form or due to detecting unsatisfiability of the Boolean structure during preprocessing. Therefore, in this subsection we decided to omit trivial benchmarks from the benchmark set to make the differences between the approaches better visible. The omitted benchmarks are those which - after standard preprocessing is performed - can be solved either by calling a SAT solver on the Boolean abstraction, or with a CDCL(T)-based SMT solver with

Table 1. Results for the pure subtropical solvers on 3580 benchmarks with a timeout of 120 s. Each cell contains the number of benchmarks in the given category; where meaningful, mean running times in seconds are given in parentheses.

	`Equation`	`Formula`	`FormulaAlt`	`Incremental`	`VB`
solved/sat	16 (0.01)	1399(0.17)	1398(0.12)	1399(0.13)	1399(0.11)
unknown	2232 (1.84)	782(5.58)	793(5.83)	272(1.05)	852(4.89)
timeout	990	1057	1046	1566	995
memout	342	342	343	343	334

basic conflict detection (i.e. normalizing the input constraints and checking for contradictory relation symbols).

This reduces the benchmark set from 12134 to 3580 benchmarks (1735 of them are known to be satisfiable, 499 of them are known to be unsatisfiable, and for the remaining benchmarks the status is unknown).

Results. The results are listed in Table 1. The `Equation` transformation finds a solution only in a few cases. This was expected as it fails on conjunctions; in the benchmark set, conjunctions on the top-level are common.

`Formula` solves 1399 of the satisfiable benchmarks while `FormulaAlt` solves one large benchmark less. Furthermore, `Formula` returns unknown on 782 benchmarks, while `FormulaAlt` returns unknown on 11 benchmarks more (one of which is unsatisfiable and the others have unknown status and are thus rather big). However, `FormulaAlt` has fewer timeouts. Thus this encoding might pay off in the sense that if it does not find a solution then it terminates earlier.

`Formula` and `FormulaAlt` do timeout on unsolved benchmarks less often than `Incremental` but return *unknown* instead. As also indicated in Fig. 3, `Incremental` is slightly faster than `Formula` on about 15 benchmarks, but slower on one benchmark. However, due to the relatively low number of benchmarks, it is hard to draw a clear conclusion.

The mean running times in seconds, given in parentheses in Table 1, clearly show that finding solutions is very fast. Determining unknown, i.e. that the encoding is unsatisfiable, takes a bit more time, but at this point we note that SMT-RAT is tuned for QFNRA and is not very competitive on QFLRA. Table 3 on page 14 contains running times as for `Formula` but using Z3 (column `ForZ3`) resp. cvc5 (column `ForCvc5`) instead of SMT-RAT; there, both sat and unknown results are computed in 0.03–0.04 s (seconds) in average, with just a few timeouts and without any memouts.

4.2 Combining Subtropical Methods with a Complete Procedure

*Solvers.*Next we combine `Formula`, `FormulaAlt` and `Incremental` with the complete *cylindrical algebraic covering (CAlC)* algorithm as a theory solver to decide the satisfiability of sets of polynomial constraints. We consider `CAlC`, which is a CDCL(T)-based solver with the CAlC algorithm as a complete theory solver

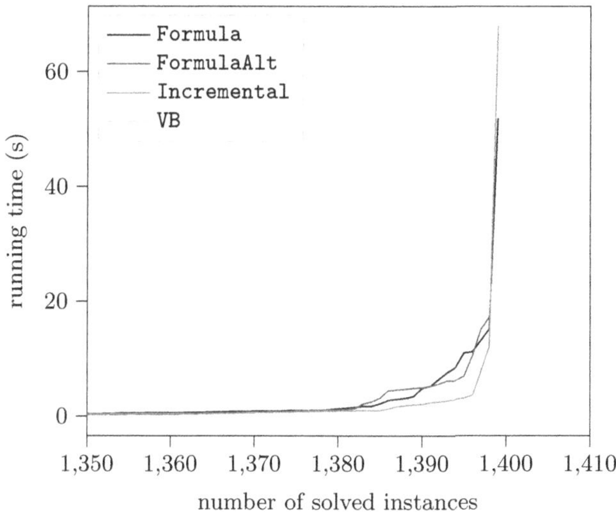

Fig. 3. Performance profile for the plain variants. A point on a line can be understood as follows: the horizontal axis denotes the number of benchmarks which can be solved (i.e. satisfiability can be concluded) if the timeout is set to the value on the vertical axis.

backend (implemented in SMT-RAT). The solvers `F+CAlC` and `FA+CAlC` run `Formula` respectively `FormulaAlt` and if the result is inconclusive then they invoke `CAlC`. `I+CAlC` is like `Incremental` but for each theory call, if the subtropical theory solver fails then the complete CAlC theory solver backend in invoked. Furthermore, we consider the combinations `F+I+CAlC` and `FA+I+CAlC`, running run `Formula` respectively `FormulaAlt` first and if they cannot solve the problem then invoking `I+CAlC`. In addition, we again list the virtual best (`VB`) results. All variants employ standard preprocessing.

Results for Satisfiable Benchmarks. Results for all 12134 SMT-LIB benchmarks are shown in Table 2. The subtropical methods do gain some slight improvements: the `I+CAlC` variant solves 16 satisfiable benchmarks more than `CAlC`, `F+CAlC` and `FA+CAlC` solve 19 respectively 18 satisfiable benchmarks more than `CAlC`. The combinations `F+I+CAlC` and `FA+I+CAlC` solve 21 and 20 satisfiable benchmarks more. Note that `I+CAlC` and `F+CAlC` do not solve the same set of benchmarks because `VB` solves the most satisfiable benchmarks.

Results for Unsatisfiable Benchmarks. The number of solved unsatisfiable benchmarks (and thus the total number of solved benchmarks) needs to be interpreted carefully: Some benchmarks are detected to be unsatisfiable by the transformation to negation normal form (as done in the implementations of `Formula` and `FormulaAlt`) and relatively simple conflict checks based on normalizing of the constraints and comparing for contradictory relation symbols (as implemented

Table 2. Results for the combination with the CAlC backend. Each cell contains the number of benchmarks in the given category; where meaningful, mean running times in seconds are given in parentheses.

	CAlC	I+CAlC	F+CAlC	FA+CAlC	F+I+CAlC	FA+I+CAlC	VB
sat	5055 (0.27)	5071 (0.27)	5074 (0.31)	5073 (0.29)	5076 (0.28)	5075 (0.26)	5076 (0.26)
unsat	4825 (1.40)	4837 (1.45)	4829 (1.51)	4830 (1.48)	4837 (1.44)	4841 (1.46)	4845 (1.48)
solved	9880 (0.82)	9908 (0.84)	9903 (0.90)	9903 (0.87)	9913 (0.85)	9916 (0.85)	9921 (0.85)
timeout	1854	1843	1843	1839	1837	1839	1840
memout	400	383	388	392	384	379	373

in Incremental); these implementation details lead to more solved unsatisfiable benchmarks in our experiments.

Subtropical as Preprocessing vs Subtropical as Incremental Theory Solver. In general, the differences in solved benchmarks between the different variants are not big enough to draw any reliable conclusion. Still, we find that the F+CAlC and FA+CAlC variants are comparable to the incremental I+CAlC variant - which supports our idea to use subtropical as an efficient preprocessing method to complement other solvers.

4.3 Z3 and Cvc5

As Formula and FormulaAlt can be employed as a preprocessing unit without any modification to an SMT solver, we can easily combine them with Z3 [19] and cvc5 [4]. In the following we focus on the Formula transformation. Out of the 12134 SMT-LIB benchmarks, Formula is applicable (i.e. the transformation does not directly simplify to false) to 4717 benchmarks (3170 satisfiable, 1439 unsatisfiable, and the others have unknown status) and not applicable to the remaining 7417.

We have run the solvers Z3 and cvc5 on the QFLRA transformation results of Formula (ForZ3 resp. ForCvc5) as well as on the original QFNRA benchmarks (Z3 resp. Cvc5), and combined the results into virtual solvers ForZ3+Z3 resp. ForCvc5+cvc5 by first applying ForZ3 resp. ForCvc5, and only if the result is inconclusive then calling Z3 resp. Cvc5 on the original formula. In Table 3 we set the timeout for the subtropical solver Formula to 10 seconds, leaving at least 110 seconds solving time for the SMT solver if a call is needed. In total, the combination of both solvers has a timeout of 120 s. We ignore the time required for the subtropical transformation here, claiming that this time is negligible.

Effectiveness of the Subtropical Method. The subtropical method solves a good portion of the satisfiable benchmarks: ForZ3 and ForCvc5 solve 1357 resp. 1352

Table 3. Results for Z3 and cvc5 without subtropical preprocessing (`Z3`, `cvc5`), only the subtropical preprocessing employing Z3 and cvc5 for solving the encodings (`ForZ3`, `ForCvc5`) and their sequential combination (`ForZ3+Z3`, `ForCvc5+cvc5`). The last row in the header specifies the respective timeouts. Each cell contains the number of benchmarks in the given category; where meaningful, mean running times in seconds are given in parentheses. Not applicable means that the transformation directly simplifies to false.

	`ForZ3` to = 120	`Z3` to = 10	`ForZ3` `+Z3` to = 120	`cvc5` to = 120	`ForCvc5` to = 10	`ForCvc5` `+cvc5` to = 120
sat	5515(0.64)	1357(0.04)	5524(0.62)	5370(1.51)	1352(0.04)	5395(1.49)
unsat	5336(1.20)	-	5336(1.21)	5728(2.13)	-	5728(2.14)
solved	10851(0.92)	1357(0.04)	10860(0.91)	11098(1.82)	1352(0.04)	11123(1.82)
unknown	3(15.36)	3333(0.03)+ 7417 not appl.	3(15.36)	0	3324(0.04)+ 7417 not appl.	0
timeout	1280	27	1271	1036	41	1011

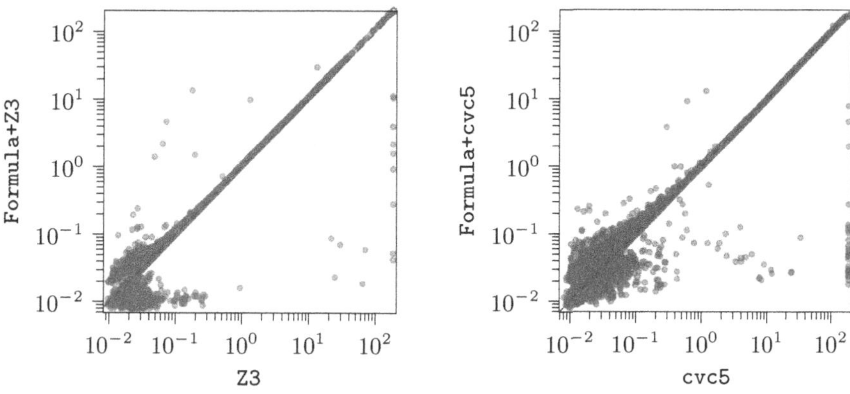

Fig. 4. Scatter plots for `Z3` and `cvc5`, without versus with subtropical preprocessor.

satisfiable benchmarks within 10 s timeout, with a mean running time of just 0.04 seconds. Both have relatively few timeouts. The unknown results are presented as a sum of (i) the applicable but not solvable and (ii) the not applicable cases.

Effectiveness of Subtropical as Preprocessing to Complete Solvers. The results shown in Table 3 are similar to the previous findings that some additional benchmarks can be solved. The supplementation with the subtropical method solves 9 benchmarks which cannot be solved by `Z3`; in the case of `cvc5` 25 new benchmarks are solved. Although these gains are small in number, the gained instances are hard for the considered SMT solvers. Furthermore, we remind that we cannot generalize these statements beyond the given benchmark set as the applicability of the subtropical method heavily depends on the structure of its input. If the method is applicable, it can be very efficient: Fig. 4 shows that the subtropical

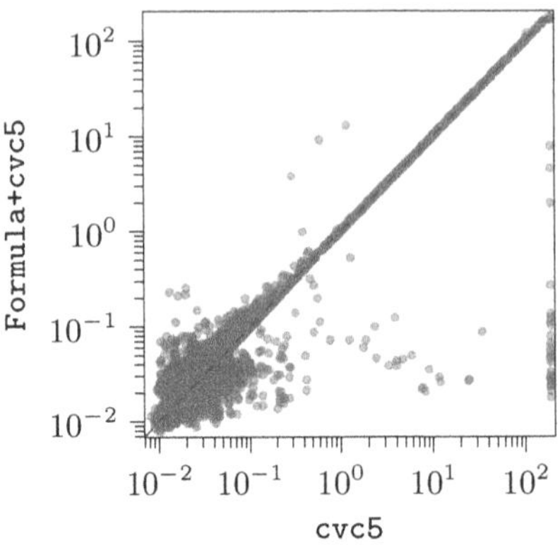

(a) Instances known to be satisfiable.

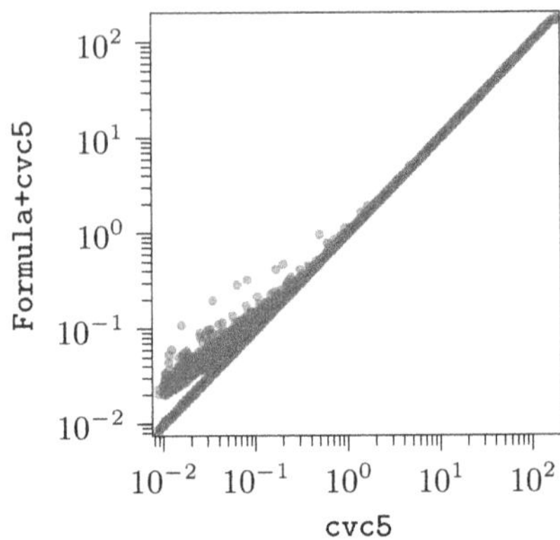

(b) Instances known to be unsatisfiable.

Fig. 5. Scatter plots for cvc5, without versus with subtropical preprocessor.

method solves some benchmarks on which the pure solvers fail even in the relatively short time of 10 s. Furthermore, Fig. 4 also illustrates nicely that even if it fails, the subtropical method has no remarkable negative effect on the running time. Figure 5 shows that subtropical fails relatively quickly on unsatisfiable instances, while it may fail later on satisfiable ones.

5 Conclusion

In this paper we introduced and evaluated different variants of the subtropical satisfiability method for checking the satisfiability of QFNRA formulas. While some of the approaches need to be integrated into an SMT solver, other methods are suitable as preprocessing algorithms that can be implemented outside of an existing solver and are thus more generally applicable. The results demonstrate that our new approach for such a preprocessing enabled the solvers to solve some more instances which could not be solved before.

Though the number of additionally solved instances is relatively small, these problems are hard for mature SMT solvers like Z3 or cvc5. Furthermore, we need to keep in mind that the variety of real-algebraic benchmarks in SMT-LIB is still limited; the evaluation in [14] discusses that the benchmarks do not contain inequations with high degrees on which the subtropical method should be efficient.

Acknowledgements. We thank Ömer Sali and Gereon Kremer for the implementation of the subtropical method as a CDCL(T) theory solver in SMT-RAT, and Giang Lai for discussions.

References

1. Satisfiability modulo theories library for QF_NRA. https://clc-gitlab.cs.uiowa.edu:2443/SMT-LIB-benchmarks/QF_NRA
2. The Satisfiability Modulo Theories Library (SMT-LIB). https://www.SMT-LIB.org
3. Ábrahám, E., Davenport, J., England, M., Kremer, G.: Deciding the consistency of non-linear real arithmetic constraints with a conflict driven search using cylindrical algebraic coverings. J. Logical Algebraic Methods Program. **119**, 100633 (2021). https://doi.org/10.1016/j.jlamp.2020.100633
4. Barbosa, H., et al.: cvc5: a versatile and industrial-strength SMT solver. In: Fisman, D., Rosu, G. (eds.) TACAS 2022. LNCS, vol. 13243, pp. 415–442. Springer, Cham (2022). https://doi.org/10.1007/978-3-030-99524-9_24
5. Barrett, C., Sebastiani, R., Seshia, S.A., Tinelli, C.: Satisfiability modulo theories. In: Handbook of Satisfiability, Frontiers in Artificial Intelligence and Applications, vol. 185, chap. 26, pp. 825–885. IOS Press (2009)
6. Benhamou, F., Granvilliers, L.: Continuous and interval constraints. Found. Artif. Intell. **2**, 571–603 (2006). https://doi.org/10.1016/S1574-6526(06)80020-9
7. Bouton, T., Caminha B. de Oliveira, D., Déharbe, D., Fontaine, P.: veriT: an open, trustable and efficient SMT-solver. In: Schmidt, R.A. (ed.) CADE 2009. LNCS (LNAI), vol. 5663, pp. 151–156. Springer, Heidelberg (2009). https://doi.org/10.1007/978-3-642-02959-2_12
8. Brown, C.W., Košta, M.: Constructing a single cell in cylindrical algebraic decomposition. J. Symb. Comput. **70**, 14–48 (2015). https://doi.org/10.1016/j.jsc.2014.09.024
9. Collins, G.E.: Quantifier elimination for real closed fields by cylindrical algebraic decompostion. In: Brakhage, H. (ed.) GI-Fachtagung 1975. LNCS, vol. 33, pp. 134–183. Springer, Heidelberg (1975). https://doi.org/10.1007/3-540-07407-4_17
10. Corzilius, F., Kremer, G., Junges, S., Schupp, S., Ábrahám, E.: SMT-RAT: an open source C++ toolbox for strategic and parallel SMT solving. In: Heule, M., Weaver, S. (eds.) SAT 2015. LNCS, vol. 9340, pp. 360–368. Springer, Cham (2015). https://doi.org/10.1007/978-3-319-24318-4_26
11. Davis, M., Logemann, G., Loveland, D.: A machine program for theorem-proving. Commun. ACM **5**(7), 394–397 (1962)
12. Davis, M., Putnam, H.: A computing procedure for quantification theory. J. ACM **7**(3), 201–215 (1960)
13. Dutertre, B., de Moura, L.: A fast linear-arithmetic solver for DPLL(T). In: Ball, T., Jones, R.B. (eds.) CAV 2006. LNCS, vol. 4144, pp. 81–94. Springer, Heidelberg (2006). https://doi.org/10.1007/11817963_11
14. Fontaine, P., Ogawa, M., Sturm, T., Vu, X.T.: Subtropical satisfiability. In: Dixon, C., Finger, M. (eds.) FroCoS 2017. LNCS (LNAI), vol. 10483, pp. 189–206. Springer, Cham (2017). https://doi.org/10.1007/978-3-319-66167-4_11
15. Jovanović, D., de Moura, L.: Solving non-linear arithmetic. In: Gramlich, B., Miller, D., Sattler, U. (eds.) IJCAR 2012. LNCS (LNAI), vol. 7364, pp. 339–354. Springer, Heidelberg (2012). https://doi.org/10.1007/978-3-642-31365-3_27
16. Kroening, D., Strichman, O.: Decision Procedures - An Algorithmic Point of View. Springer, Cham (2008)
17. Lai, G.: Subtropical satisfiability for polynomial constraint sets (2022). https://ths.rwth-aachen.de/wp-content/uploads/sites/4/lai_bachelor.pdf

18. Marques-silva, J.P., Sakallah, K.A.: **GRASP**: a search algorithm for propositional satisfiability. IEEE Trans. Comput. **48**, 506–521 (1999)
19. de Moura, L., Bjørner, N.: Z3: an efficient SMT solver. In: Ramakrishnan, C.R., Rehof, J. (eds.) TACAS 2008. LNCS, vol. 4963, pp. 337–340. Springer, Heidelberg (2008). https://doi.org/10.1007/978-3-540-78800-3_24
20. Sali, Ö.: Linearization techniques for nonlinear arithmetic problems in SMT. Master's thesis, RWTH Aachen University (2018). https://ths.rwth-aachen.de/wp-content/uploads/sites/4/teaching/theses/sali_master.pdf
21. Seidenberg, A.: A new decision method for elementary algebra. Ann. Math. **60**(2), 365–374 (1954). https://doi.org/10.2307/1969640
22. Sturm, T.: Subtropical real root finding. In: Proceedings of the 2015 ACM on International Symposium on Symbolic and Algebraic Computation (ISSAC 2015), pp. 347–354 (2015). https://doi.org/10.1145/2755996.2756677
23. Weispfenning, V.: Quantifier elimination for real algebra-the quadratic case and beyond. Appl. Algebra Eng. Commun. Comput. **8**(2), 85–101 (1997). https://doi.org/10.1007/s002000050055

A Linear Weight Transfer Rule for Local Search

Md Solimul Chowdhury(✉), Cayden R. Codel, and Marijn J.H. Heule

Carnegie Mellon University, Pittsburgh, Pennsylvania, United States
{mdsolimc,ccodel,mheule}@cs.cmu.edu

Abstract. The *Divide and Distribute Fixed Weights* algorithm (DDFW) is a dynamic local search SAT-solving algorithm that transfers weight from satisfied to falsified clauses in local minima. DDFW is remarkably effective on several hard combinatorial instances. Yet, despite its success, it has received little study since its debut in 2005. In this paper, we propose three modifications to the base algorithm: a linear weight transfer method that moves a dynamic amount of weight between clauses in local minima, an adjustment to how satisfied clauses are chosen in local minima to give weight, and a weighted-random method of selecting variables to flip. We implemented our modifications to DDFW on top of the solver **yalsat**. Our experiments show that our modifications boost the performance compared to the original DDFW algorithm on multiple benchmarks, including those from the past three years of SAT competitions. Moreover, our improved solver exclusively solves hard combinatorial instances that refute a conjecture on the lower bound of two Van der Waerden numbers set forth by Ahmed et al. (2014), and it performs well on a hard graph-coloring instance that has been open for over three decades.

1 Introduction

Satisfiability (SAT) solvers are powerful tools, able to efficiently solve problems from a broad range of applications such as verification [12], encryption [26], and planning [10,18]. The most successful solving paradigm is conflict-driven clause learning (CDCL) [20,25]. However, stochastic local search (SLS) outperforms CDCL on many classes of satisfiable formulas [7,19,23,24,28], and it can be used to guide CDCL search [8].

SLS algorithms solve SAT instances by incrementally changing a truth assignment until a solution is found or until timeout. At each step, the algorithm flips the truth value of a single boolean variable according to some heuristic. A common heuristic is flipping variables that reduce the number of falsified clauses in the formula. The algorithm reaches a *local minimum* when no variable can be flipped to improve its heuristic. At that point, the algorithm either adjusts its truth assignment or internal state to *escape* the local minimum, or it starts over. Refer to chapter 6 from the Handbook of Satisfiability [4] for a more detailed discussion of SLS algorithms.

The authors were supported by NSF grant CCF-2006363. Md Solimul Chowdhury was partially supported by a NSERC Postdoctoral Fellowship.

K. Y. Rozier and S. Chaudhuri (Eds.): NFM 2023, LNCS 13903, pp. 447–463, 2023.
https://doi.org/10.1007/978-3-031-33170-1_27

Dynamic local search (DLS) algorithms are SLS algorithms that assign a weight to each clause. They then flip variables to reduce the amount of weight held by the falsified clauses. DLS algorithms escape local minima by adjusting clause weights until they can once again flip variables to reduce the amount of falsified weight.

Several DLS algorithms have been studied. For example, the Pure Additive Weighting Scheme algorithm (PAWS) [27] and the Scaling and Probabilistic Smoothing algorithm (SAPS) [15] both increase the weight of falsified clauses in local minima. A drawback of this method of escaping local minima is that the clause weights must periodically be re-scaled to prevent overflow.

The Divide and Distribute Fixed Weights algorithm (DDFW) [16] introduces an alternative way of escaping local minima: increase the weight of falsified clauses by taking weight from satisfied clauses. In local minima, DDFW moves a fixed, constant amount of weight to each falsified clause from a satisfied clause it shares at least one literal with. The transfer method keeps the total amount of clause weight constant, eliminating the need for a re-scaling phase. Another consequence of this transfer method is that as more local minima are encountered, difficult-to-satisfy clauses gather more weight. Thus, DDFW dynamically identifies and prioritizes satisfying hard clauses.

Recent work using DDFW as a black box showed the effectiveness of the algorithm. For example, DDFW (as implemented in UBCSAT [29][1]) is remarkably effective on matrix multiplication and graph-coloring problems [13,14]. Yet despite its success, DDFW has received little research attention. In this paper, we revisit the DDFW algorithm to study why it works well and to improve its performance.

Our contributions are as follows. We propose three modifications to the DDFW algorithm. We first introduce a linear weight transfer rule to allow for a more dynamic transfer of weight in local minima. We then adjust a performance-critical parameter that randomizes which satisfied clause gives up weight in local minima. Our adjustment is supported by an empirical analysis. Finally, we propose a new randomized method for selecting which variable to flip. We implement each of our modifications on top of the state-of-the-art SLS solver `yalsat` to create a new implementation of DDFW that supports parallelization and restarts. We then evaluate our solver against a set of challenging benchmarks collected from combinatorial problem instances and the past three years of SAT competitions. Our results show that our modifications boost the performance of DDFW: Our best-performing version of DDFW solves 118 SAT Competition instances, a vast improvement over a baseline of 83 solves from the original algorithm. Our solver also exhibits a 16% improvement over the baseline on a set of combinatorial instances. Moreover, in parallel mode, our solver solves instances that refute a conjecture on the lower bound of two van der Waerden numbers [2], and it matches performance with the winning SLS solver from the

[1] To the best of our knowledge, there is no official implementation or binary of original DDFW [16] available.

2021 SAT competition on a graph-coloring instance that has been open for the past three decades.

2 Preliminaries

SAT solvers operate on propositional logic formulas in *conjunctive normal form* (CNF). A CNF formula $F = \bigwedge_i C_i$ is a conjunction of clauses, and each clause $C_i = \bigvee_j \ell_j$ is a disjunction of boolean literals. We write v and $\overline{v}$ as the positive and negative literals for the boolean variable v, respectively.

A truth assignment α maps boolean variables to either true or false. A literal v (resp. $\overline{v}$) is satisfied by α if $\alpha(v)$ is true ($\alpha(v)$ is false, respectively). A clause C is satisfied by α if α satisfies at least one of its literals. A formula F is satisfied by α exactly when all of its clauses are satisfied by α. Two clauses C and D are *neighbors* if there is a literal ℓ with $\ell \in C$ and $\ell \in D$. Let Neighbors(C) be the set of neighbors of C in F, excluding itself.

Many SLS algorithms assign a weight to each clause. Let $W : \mathcal{C} \rightarrow \mathbb{R}_{\geq 0}$ be the mapping that assigns weights to the clauses in $\mathcal{C}$. One can think of $W(C)$ as the cost to leave C falsified. We call the total amount of weight held by the falsified clauses, the *falsified weight*. A variable that, when flipped, reduces the falsified weight is called a *weight-reducing variable* (`wrv`). A variable that doesn't affect the falsified weight when flipped is a *sideways variable* (`sv`).

3 The DDFW Algorithm

Algorithm 1 shows the pseudocode for the DDFW algorithm. DDFW attempts to find a satisfying assignment for a given CNF formula F over MAXTRIES trials. The weight of each clause is set to w_0 at the start of the algorithm. Each trial starts with a random assignment. By following a greedy heuristic method, DDFW selects and then flips weight-reducing variables until none are left. At this point, it either flips a sideways variable, if one exists and if a weighted coin flip succeeds, or it enters the weight transfer phase, where each falsified clause receives a fixed amount of weight from a maximum-weight satisfied neighbor. Occasionally, DDFW transfers weight from a random satisfied clause instead, allowing weight to move more fluidly between neighborhoods. The amount of weight transferred depends on whether the selected clause has more than w_0 weight.

There are five parameters in the original DDFW algorithm: the initial weight w_0 given to each clause, the two weighted-coin thresholds `spt` and `cspt` for sideways flips and transfers from random satisfied clauses, and the amount of weight to transfer in local minima $\mathtt{c}_{>}$ and $\mathtt{c}_{=}$. In the original DDFW paper, these five values are fixed constants, with $w_0 = 8$, $\mathtt{spt} = 0.15$, $\mathtt{cspt} = 0.01$, $\mathtt{c}_{>} = 2$, and $\mathtt{c}_{=} = 1$.

DDFW is unique in how it transfers weight in local minima. Similar SLS algorithms increase the weight of falsified clauses (or decrease the weight of satisfied clauses) globally; weight is added and removed based solely on whether

Algorithm 1: The DDFW algorithm

Input: CNF Formula F, w_0, `spt`, `cspt`, $c_>$, $c_=$
Output: Satisfiability of F

1 $W(C) \leftarrow w_0$ for all $C \in F$
2 **for** $t = 1$ *to MAXTRIES* **do**
3   $\alpha \leftarrow$ random truth assignment on the variables in F
4   **for** $f = 1$ *to MAXFLIPS* **do**
5   **if** *α satisfies F* **then** return "SAT"
6   **else**
7   **if** *there is a wrv* **then**
8   Flip a `wrv` that most reduces the falsified weight
9   **else if** *there is a sv and rand $\leq$ spt* **then**
10   Flip a sideways variable
11   **else**
12   **foreach** *falsified clause C* **do**
13           $C_s \leftarrow$ maximum-weighted satisfied clause in Neighbors(C)
14   **if** $W(C_s) < w_0$ or *rand $\leq$ cspt* **then**
15             $C_s \leftarrow$ random satisfied clause with $W \geq w_0$
16   **if** $W(C_s) > w_0$ **then**
17   Transfer $c_>$ weight from C_s to C
18   **else**
19   Transfer $c_=$ weight from C_s to C
20 return "No SAT"

the clause is satisfied. DDFW instead moves weight among clause neighborhoods, with falsified clauses receiving weight from satisfied neighbors.

One reason why this weight transfer method may be effective is that satisfying a falsified clause C by flipping literal $\overline{\ell}$ to ℓ ($\in C$) increases the number of true literals in satisfied clauses that neighbor C on ℓ. Thus, C borrows weight from satisfied clauses that tend to remain satisfied when C itself becomes satisfied. As a result, DDFW satisfies falsified clauses while keeping satisfied neighbors satisfied.

The existence of *two* weight transfer parameters $c_>$ and $c_=$ deserves discussion. Let *heavy clauses* be those clauses C with $W(C) > w_0$. Lines 16-19 in Algorithm 1 allow for a different amount of weight to be taken from heavy clauses than from clauses with the initial weight. Because lines 14-15 ensure that the selected clause C_s will have at least w_0 weight, $c_=$ is used when $W(C_s) = w_0$ and $c_>$ is used when $W(C_s) > w_0$ (hence the notation). The original algorithm sets $c_> = 2$ and $c_= = 1$, which has the effect of taking more weight from heavy clauses.

4 Solvers, Benchmarks, and Hardware

The authors of the original DDFW algorithm never released their source code or any binaries. The closest thing we have to a reference implementation is the one in the SLS SAT-solving framework UBCSAT [28,29]. We call this implementation `ubc-ddfw`, and we use it as a baseline in our experiments.

Unfortunately, `ubc-ddfw` cannot be extended to implement our proposed modifications due to its particular architecture. Instead, we implemented DDFW on top of `yalsat` [5], which is currently one of the strongest local search SAT solvers. For example, it is the only local search solver in Mallob-mono [22], the clear winner of the cloud track in the SAT Competitions of 2020, 2021, and 2022. `yalsat` uses PROBSAT [3] as its underlying algorithm, which flips variables in falsified clauses drawn from an exponential probability distribution.

One benefit of implementing DDFW on top of `yalsat` is that is `yalsat` supports parallelization, which can be helpful when solving challenging formulas. In our experiments, we compare our implementation of DDFW to `ubc-ddfw` to verify that the two implementations behave similarly.

Our implementation of DDFW on top of `yalsat` was not straightforward. First, we switched the underlying SLS algorithm from PROBSAT to DDFW. Then we added additional data structures and optimizations to make our implementation efficient. For example, one potential performance bottleneck for DDFW is calculating the set of weight-reducing variables for each flip. Every flip and adjustment of clause weight can change the set, so the set must be re-computed often. A naive implementation that loops through all literals in all falsified clauses is too slow, since any literal may appear in several falsified clauses, leading to redundant computation. Instead, we maintain a list of variables `uvars` that appear in any falsified clause. After each flip, this list is updated. To compute the set of weight-reducing variables, we iterate over the variables in `uvars`, hitting each literal once. In this way, we reduce redundant computation.

Adding our proposed modifications to our implementation was simpler. We represent clause weights with floating-point numbers, and the linear weight transfer rule replaced the original one. We also made the variable selection and weight transfer methods modular, so our modifications slot in easily.[2]

We evaluated our implementations of DDFW against two benchmarks. The **Combinatorial (COMB)** set consists of 65 hard instances from the following eight benchmarks families collected by Heule:[3] (i) `26x26` (4 grid positioning instances), (ii) `asias` (2 almost square packing problems), (iii) `MM` (20 matrix multiplication instances), (iv) `mphf` (12 cryptographic hash instances), (v) `ptn` (2 Pythagorean triple instances), (vi) Steiner (3 Steiner triples cover instances [21]), (vii) `wap` (9 graph-coloring instances [17]), and (viii) `vdw` (13 van der Waerden number instances). These benchmarks are challenging for modern SAT solvers, including SLS solvers. The `wap` benchmark contains three instances that have been open for three decades, and `vdw` contains two instances that, if solved, refute conjectures on lower-bounds for two van der Waerden numbers [2].

The **SAT Competition (SATComp)** set consists of all 1,174 non-duplicate main-track benchmark instances from the 2019 SAT Race and the 2020 and

[2] Source code of our system are available at https://github.com/solimul/yal-lin
[3] https://github.com/marijnheule/benchmarks

2021 SAT Competitions. The competition suites contain medium-hard to very challenging benchmarks, most of which are contributed by the competitors.

Unless otherwise specified, we used a timeout of 18,000 and 5,000 seconds for the COMB and SATComp instances, respectively, in our experiments.

We used the StarExec cluster [1], where each node has an Intel CPU E5 CPU with a 2.40 GHz clock speed and a 10240 KB cache. For experiments in this cluster, we used at most 64 GB of RAM. To perform experiments on the 3 open `wap` and 2 `vdw` instances, we used a different cluster with the following specifications: we use the Bridges2 [6] cluster from the Pittsburgh Supercomputing Center with the following specifications: two AMD EPYC 7742 CPUs, each with 64 cores, 256MB of L3 cache, and 512GB total RAM memory.

5 Modifications to the DDFW Algorithm

We propose three modifications to DDFW. The first is a linear rule for transferring a dynamic amount of weight in local minima. The second is an adjustment of the `cspt` parameter. The third is the introduction of a weighted-random method for selecting which variable to flip.

5.1 The Linear Weight Transfer Rule

The reference implementation of DDFW, `ubc-ddfw`, represents its clause weights as integers and transfers fixed integer weights in local minima. While this design decision allows `ubc-ddfw` to have a fast implementation, it unnecessarily restricts the amount of weight transferred in local minima to be integer-valued. In addition, the choice to transfer a fixed, constant amount of weight prevents DDFW from adapting to situations where more weight must be transferred to escape a local minimum, thus requiring multiple weight transfer rounds. To address these concerns, we propose a dynamic linear weight transfer rule to operate on floating-point-valued clause weights.

Let C_S be the selected satisfied clause from which to take weight in a local minimum, as in line 13 in Algorithm 1. Our new rule transfers

$$\mathtt{a} * W(C_S) + \mathtt{c}$$

weight, where $0 \leq \mathtt{a} \leq 1$ is a multiplicative parameter and $\mathtt{c} \geq 0$ is an additive parameter.

It is not clear that the addition of a multiplicative parameter is helpful, nor what a good pair of $(\mathtt{a}, \mathtt{c})$ values would be. So, we performed a parameter search with our solver for $\mathtt{a} \in [0, 0.2]$ in steps of 0.05 and $\mathtt{c} \in [0, 2]$ in steps of 0.25 for both of our instance sets with a 900 second timeout per run. (A parameter search using all 1,174 instances in the SATComp set was not feasible. We instead did the search on the 168 instances from SATComp set that were solved by some setting in earlier experimentation. In Section 6, all instances are used.) The PAR-2 scores[4] for the SATComp and COMB benchmark sets for each pair of (a, c) values are shown in Figure 1.

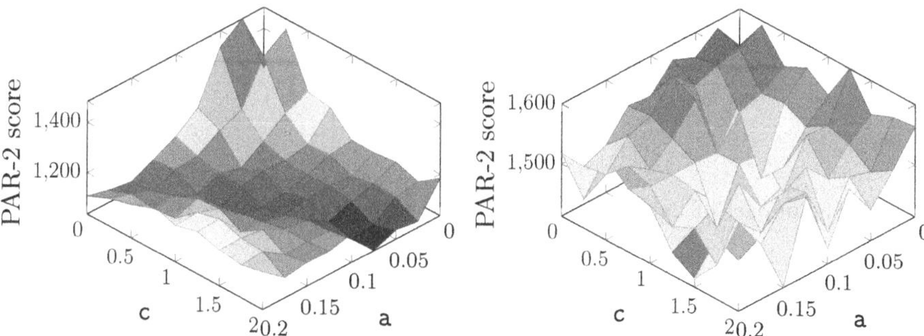

Fig. 1. Parameter searches for $\mathsf{a} \in [0, 0.2]$ in steps of 0.05 and $\mathsf{c} \in [0, 2]$ in steps of 0.25 on the SATComp (left plot) and COMB (right plot) instances. A lower PAR-2 score is better. There is not a datum for $(\mathsf{a}, \mathsf{c}) = (0, 0)$ since no weight would be transferred.

The plots in Figure 1 show that values of a and c close to 0 degrade performance, likely due to the need for many weight-transfer rounds to escape local minima. The beneficial effect of higher values of a and c is more pronounced in the parameter search on the SATComp instances (the left plot). Since the best-performing settings have nonzero a and c values, we infer that both parameters are needed for improved performance.

5.2 How Much Weight Should be Given Away Initially?

On lines 16-19 of Algorithm 1, DDFW takes $\mathsf{c}_{>}$ weight away from the selected clause C_s if C_s is heavy and $\mathsf{c}_{=}$ weight otherwise. The linear rule introduced above can similarly be extended to four parameters: $\mathsf{a}_{>}$, $\mathsf{a}_{=}$, $\mathsf{c}_{>}$, and $\mathsf{c}_{=}$.

In the original DDFW paper, $\mathsf{c}_{>}$ $(= 2)$ is greater than $\mathsf{c}_{=}$ $(= 1)$, meaning that heavy clauses give away more weight than clauses with the initial weight in local minima. The intuition behind this is simple: clauses with more weight should give away more weight. For the extended linear rule, one could adopt a similar strategy by setting $\mathsf{a}_{>}$ greater than $\mathsf{a}_{=}$ and $\mathsf{c}_{>}$ greater than $\mathsf{c}_{=}$.

However, one effect of our proposed linear rule is that once clauses give or receive weight, they almost never again have exactly w_0 weight. As a result, the parameters $\mathsf{a}_{=}$ and $\mathsf{c}_{=}$ control how much weight a clause gives away *initially*. Since the maximum-weight neighbors of falsified clauses tend to be heavy as the search proceeds, the effect of $\mathsf{a}_{=}$ and $\mathsf{c}_{=}$ diminishes over time, but they remain important at the start of the search and for determining how much

[4] The PAR-2 score is defined as the average solving time, while taking 2 * `timeout` as the time for unsolved instances. A lower score is better.

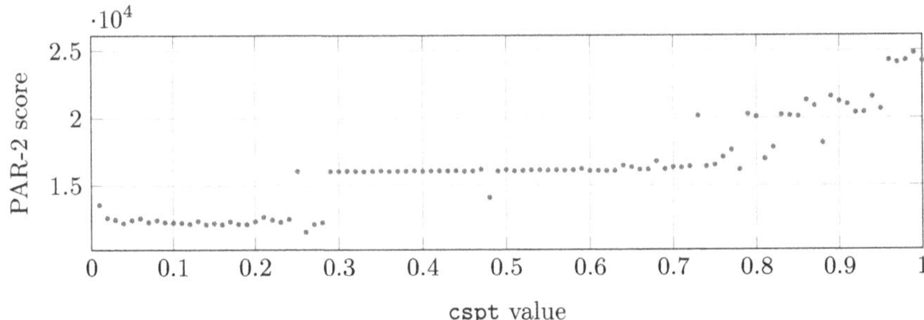

Fig. 2. The impact of `cspt` values on the performance of DDFW on the `wap` instances.

weight the algorithm has available to assign to harder-to-satisfy clauses. The findings in a workshop paper [9] by two co-authors of this paper indicate that DDFW achieves a better performance when clauses initially give more weight. These findings suggest setting $\texttt{c}_=$ greater than $\texttt{c}_>$ and $\texttt{a}_=$ greater than $\texttt{a}_>$. In Section 6, we evaluate DDFW on the extended linear rule and investigate whether clauses should initially give away more or less weight.

5.3 The `cspt` Parameter

On lines 14-15 of Algorithm 1, DDFW sometimes discards the maximum-weight satisfied neighboring clause C_s and instead selects a random satisfied clause. The `cspt` parameter controls how often the weighted coin flip on line 14 succeeds. Though these two lines may appear to be minor, a small-scale experiment revealed that the `cspt` parameter is performance-critical. We ran our implementation of the original DDFW algorithm on the COMB set with an 18,000 second timeout. When we set `cspt` to 0, meaning that falsified clauses received weight solely from satisfied neighbors, it solved a single instance; when we set `cspt` to 0.01 (the value in the original DDFW algorithm), it solved 21 instances.

Among the eight families in COMB, the `wap` family was the most sensitive to the change of `cspt` value from 0 (solved 0) to 0.01 (solved 6 out of 9). We isolated these nine instances and ran a parameter search on them for $\texttt{cspt} \in [0.01, 1]$ in steps of 0.01, for a total of 900 runs. We used an 18,000 second timeout per run. The PAR-2 scores are reported in Figure 2.

In Figure 2, we observe that `cspt` values near 0 and above 0.2 cause an increase in the PAR-2 score. These results indicate that DDFW is sensitive to the `cspt` value and that the `cspt` value should be set higher than its original value of 0.01, but not too high, which could potentially degrade the performance of the solver. We use these observations to readjust the `cspt` parameter in our empirical evaluation presented in Section 6.

5.4 A Weighted-random Variable Selection Method

On line 8 of Algorithm 1, DDFW flips a weight-reducing variable that most reduces the amount of falsified weight. Such a greedy approach may prevent DDFW from exploring other, potentially better areas of the search space. Inspired by PROBSAT, which makes greedy moves only some of the time, we introduce a new randomized method that flips a weight-reducing variable according to the following probability distribution:

$$\mathbb{P}(\text{Flipping } \texttt{wrv}\ v) = \frac{\Delta W(v)}{\sum_{v \in \texttt{wrv}} \Delta W(v)},$$

where $\Delta W(v)$ is the reduction in falsified weight if v is flipped.

6 Empirical Evaluation

In this section, we present our empirical findings. Since we evaluated several different solvers, we refer to the solvers by the following names: the UBCSAT version of DDFW is `ubc-ddfw`, the version of `yalsat` that implements PROBSAT is `yal-prob`, and our implementation of DDFW on top of `yalsat` is `yal-lin`. In all of our experiments, we use the default random seed[5] present in each solver, and we set the initial clause weight $w_0 = 8$, as in the original DDFW paper.

In our experiments with `yal-lin`, we varied the configuration of the solver according to our proposed modifications. We use the identifying string `W-cC-P` to refer to a configuration for `yal-lin`, where $\texttt{W} \in \{\texttt{fw}, \texttt{lw}\}$ is the weight transfer method (`fw` stands for "fixed weight," `lw` for "linear weight"), $\texttt{C} \in \{0.01, 0.1\}$ is the `cspt` value, and $\texttt{P} \in \{\texttt{grdy}, \texttt{wrnd}\}$ is the variable selection method (`grdy` stands for the original "greedy" method, and `wrnd` stands for our proposed "weighted random" method). For example, the string `fw-c.01-grdy` describes the original DDFW algorithm, with $\texttt{c}_> = 2$ and $\texttt{c}_= = 1$.

6.1 Evaluation Without Restarts

We evaluate how `yal-lin` performs without restarts, meaning that DDFW runs until timeout without starting from a fresh random assignment. To disable restarts, we set MAXTRIES to 1 and MAXFLIPS to an unlimited number of flips. For the COMB and SATComp benchmark sets, we set a timeout of 18,000 and 5,000 seconds, respectively.

We first checked that our solver `yal-lin` (with configuration `fw-c.01-grdy`) behaves similarly to the baseline implementation, `ubc-ddfw`. The solvers performed almost identically on the two benchmark sets: `ubc-ddfw` solved 22 of the COMB instances and 80 of the SATComp instances; `yal-lin` solved 21 and 83,

[5] Results for additional experiments with a different seed is available at: https://github.com/solimul/additional-experiments-nfm23/blob/master/additional_results_nfm2023.pdf

Table 1. Solve counts and PAR-2 scores for different configurations of `yal-lin`. The configurations vary the `cspt` value and the variable selection method, with the weight transfer method being `fw`. The best configuration for each benchmark is bolded.

	COMB				SATComp			
`cspt`	`grdy`		`wrnd`		`grdy`		`wrnd`	
value	#solved	PAR-2	#solved	PAR-2	#solved	PAR-2	#solved	PAR-2
0.01	21	25393	24	23871	83	9339	87	9312
0.1	24	23137	**25**	**22538**	98	9223	**103**	**9188**

respectively. We attribute the slight difference in solve counts to random noise. These results indicate that we implemented `yal-lin` correctly.

We next evaluate how `yal-lin` performs under changes in the `cspt` value and variable selection method. We run `yal-lin` with the fixed weight transfer method on both benchmarks with all four combinations of $\mathtt{C} \in \{0.01, 0.1\}$ and $\mathtt{P} \in \{\mathtt{grdy}, \mathtt{wrnd}\}$. The solve counts and PAR-2 scores are shown in Table 1.

Isolating just the change in variable selection method (scanning across rows in Table 1), we see that the weighted-random method outperforms the greedy method for each benchmark and `cspt` value. There is improvement both in the solve count (ranging from an additional 1 to 5 solves) and in the PAR-2 score. While the improvements may be random noise, the results indicate that injecting some randomness into how variables are flipped may lead to better performance.

Isolating the change in `cspt` value (scanning down columns in Table 1), we see that the higher `cspt` value of 0.1 outperforms the `cspt` value of 0.01. Improvements range from 1 additional solve to 16 additional solves. We note that the improvements when increasing the `cspt` value are more pronounced than when changing the variable selection method, which gives further evidence that the `cspt` value is performance-critical. In Section 7, we present a possible explanation for why the `cspt` parameter is so important.

The linear weight transfer rule. As we noted in Section 5.2, the linear weight transfer rule can be extended to include four parameters: two multiplicative and two additive. We tested `yal-lin` on three particular settings of these four parameters, which we call `lw-itl` (linear **w**eight **i**nitial **t**ransfer **l**ow), `lw-ith` (linear **w**eight **i**nitial **t**ransfer **h**igh), and `lw-ite` (linear **w**eight **i**nitial **t**ransfer **e**qual).

- `lw-itl` takes a low initial transfer from clauses in local minima by setting $\mathtt{a}_= < \mathtt{a}_>$ and $\mathtt{c}_= < \mathtt{c}_>$.
- `lw-ith` takes a high initial transfer from clauses in local minima by setting $\mathtt{a}_= > \mathtt{a}_>$ and $\mathtt{c}_= > \mathtt{c}_>$.
- `lw-ite` does not distinguish clauses by weight, and sets the two pairs of parameters equal.

In the left plot of Figure 1, $\mathtt{a}$ values for the top 10% of the settings (by PAR-2 scores) are in the range [0.05, 0.1]. Hence, we use 0.05 and 0.1 as the values for

$a_>$ and $a_=$ in `lw-itl` and `lw-ith`. We keep the values for $c_>$ and $c_=$ at 2 and 1, following the original DDFW algorithm. For `lw-ite`, we take values in between the pair of values, with $a_> = a_= = 0.075$ and $c_> = c_= = 1.75$. Table 2 shows the parameter values for the three configurations that we tested.

Table 2. Parameter values for three versions of `linearwt`

`linearwt` versions	$a_>$	$a_=$	$c_>$	$c_=$
`lw-itl`	0.1	0.05	2	1
`lw-ite`	0.075	0.075	1.75	1.75
`lw-ith`	0.05	0.1	1	2

We compare our three new configurations against the original one across the two variable selection methods. We set `cspt` = 0.1, as our prior experiment showed it to be better than 0.01. Table 3 summarizes the results.

Table 3. Solve counts and PAR-2 scores for different configurations of `yal-lin`. The configurations vary the linear weight transfer method while keeping the `cspt` value fixed at 0.1. The best configuration for each benchmark is bolded.

Weight	COMB				SATComp			
Transfer	`grdy`		`wrnd`		`grdy`		`wrnd`	
Method	#solved	PAR-2	#solved	PAR-2	#solved	PAR-2	#solved	PAR-2
`fixedwt`	24	23871	25	22538	98	9223	103	9188
`lw-itl`	26	22256	27	21769	98	9237	104	9189
`lw-ite`	**28**	**21233**	27	22228	111	9129	113	9114
`lw-ith`	26	22142	**28**	21338	115	9082	**118**	**9055**

Scanning down the columns of Table 3, we see that all three linear weight configurations perform at least as well as the fixed weight version, regardless of variable selection method. The improvements on the COMB benchmark are modest, with at most 4 additional solved instances. The improvements on the SATComp benchmark are more substantial, with a maximum of 17 additional solved instances.

Overall, the best-performing linear weight configuration was `lw-ith`, which transfers the more weight from clauses with the initial weight. These results support prior findings that more weight should be freed up to the falsified clauses in local minima. The best-performing variable selection method continues to be the weighted random method `wrnd`.

Analysis of solve count over runtime. In addition to solve counts and PAR-2 scores for the three linear weight configurations, we report solve counts as a function of solving time. The data for ten experimental settings of `yal-lin` on the two benchmarks are shown in Figure 3. Note that the original DDFW setting is represented by the setting `fw-c.01-grdy`, and is our baseline.

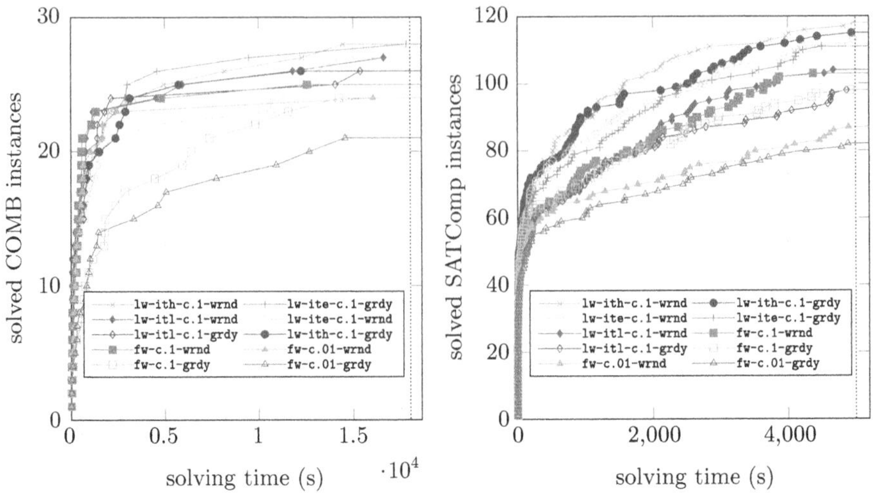

Fig. 3. Performance profiles of `yal-lin` (`fw-c.01-grdy`) and nine modifications for COMB (left) and SATComp (right).

For the COMB benchmark (Figure 3, left plot), all nine other settings (our modifications) outperform the baseline in terms of solving speed and number of solved instances. The best settings are `lw-ith-c.1-wrnd` and `lw-ite-c.1-grdy`, which perform on par with each other and solve 28 instances by timeout. For the SATComp benchmark (Figure 3, right plot), the success of the setting `lw-ith-c.1-wrnd` is more pronounced. For about the first 1,000 seconds, this setting performs similar to `lw-ith-c.1-grdy`. After that, however, it begins to perform the best of all the settings, and it ends up solving the most instances by timeout, at 118. The baseline setting `fw-c.01-grdy` ends up solving 83 instances at timeout, which is 35 less than `lw-ith-c.1-wrnd`.

These two plots clearly show that our modifications substantially improve the original DDFW algorithm.

6.2 Evaluation With Restarts

Many SLS algorithms restart their search with a random assignment after a fixed number of flips. By default, `yalsat` also performs restarts. However, at each restart, `yalsat` dynamically sets a new restart interval as $r = 100,000x$ for some integer $x \geq 1$, which is initialized to 1, and updated after each restart as follows: if x is power of 2, then x is set to 1, otherwise to $2 * x$. The way `yalsat` initializes its assignment at restart also differs from many SLS algorithms. On some restarts, `yalsat` uses the best cached assignment. For all others, it restarts with a fresh random assignment. In this way, it attempts to balance exploitation and exploration.

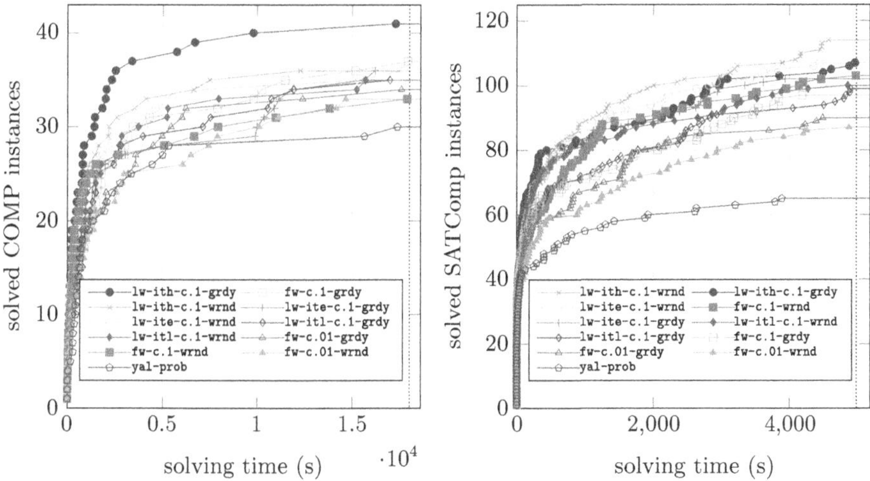

Fig. 4. Solve time comparisons between base `yal-prob`, and 10 `yal-lin` settings for COMB and SATComp, where restarts are enabled

Our experiments with `yal-lin` included runs with `yalsat`-style restarts. On a restart, the adjusted clause weights are kept. The hope is that the adjusted weights help the solver descend the search landscape faster.

We compare `yal-prob` against ten experimental settings of `yal-lin` with restarts enabled. The best solver in this evaluation is `yal-lin` with the setting `lw-ith-c.1-grdy` on the COMB benchmark and the setting `lw-ith-c.1-wrnd` on the SATComp benchmark, which solve 11 and 49 more instances than `yal-prob`, respectively. Figure 4 shows solve counts against solving time, and it confirms that all the `yal-lin` settings solve instances substantially faster than `yal-prob`.

6.3 Solving Hard Instances

Closing wap-07a-40. The `wap` family from the COMB benchmark contains three open instances: wap-07a-40, wap-03a-40 and wap-4a-40. We attempted to solve these three instances using the parallel version of `yal-lin` with the ten `yal-lin` settings (without restarts) used in Section 6.1 in the cluster node with 128 cores and 18,000 seconds of timeout. All of our settings except `fw-c.01-grdy` (the baseline) solve the wap-07a-40 instance. The best setting for this experiment was `lw-itl-c.1-wrnd`, which solves wap-07a-40 in just 1168.64 seconds. However, we note that lstech_maple (`LMpl`) [31], the winner of the SAT track of the SAT Competition 2021, also solves wap-07a-40, in 2,103.12 seconds, almost twice the time required by our best configuration `lw-itl-c.1-wrnd` for solving this instance. Thus, for solving this open instance, our best setting compares well with the state-of-the-art solver for solving satisfiable instances.

With restarts, the setting `lw-itl-c.1-wrnd`, the best setting for this experiment, were not able to solve any of these three instances.

New lower bounds for van der Waerden/Green numbers. The *van der Waerden theorem* [30] is a theorem about the existence of monochromatic arithmetic progressions among a set of numbers. It states the following: there exists a smallest number $n = W(k; t_1, \ldots, t_i, \ldots, t_k)$ such that any coloring of the integers $\{1, 2, \ldots, n\}$ with k colors contains a progression of length t_i of color i for some i. In recent work, Ben Green showed that these numbers grow much faster than conjectured and that their growth can be observed in experiments [11]. We therefore call the CNF formulas to determine these numbers Green instances.

Ahmed et al. studied 20 van der Waerden numbers $W(2; 3, t)$ for two colors, with the first color having arithmetic progression of length 3 and the second of length $19 \leq t \leq 39$, and conjectured that their values for $t \leq 30$ were optimal, including $W(2; 3, 29) = 868$ and $W(2, 3, 30) = 903$ [2]. By using `yal-lin`, we were able to refute these two conjectures by solving the formulas Green-29-868-SAT and Green-30-903-SAT in the COMB set. Solving these instances yields two new bounds: $W(2; 3, 29) \geq 869$ and $W(2; 3, 30) \geq 904$.

To solve these two instances, we ran our various `yal-lin` configurations (without restarts) using `yalsat`'s parallel mode, along with a number of other local search algorithms from UBCSAT, in the same cluster we used to solve wap-07a-40. Among these solvers, only our solver could solve the two instances. `lw-itl-c.1-wrnd` solved both Green-29-868-SAT and Green-30-903-SAT, in 942.60 and 6534.56 seconds, respectively. The settings `lw-ith-c.1-wrnd` and `lw-ite-c.1-wrnd` also solved Green-29-868-SAT in 1374.74 and 1260.16 seconds, respectively, but neither could solve Green-30-903-SAT within a timeout of 18,000 seconds. The CDCL solver `LMpl`, which solves wap-07a-40, could not solve any instances from the Green family within a timeout of 18,000 seconds.

With restarts `lw-itl-c.1-wrnd`, the best setting for this experiment only solves Green-29-868-SAT in 2782.81 seconds within a timeout of 18,000 seconds.

7 Discussion and Future Work

In this paper, we proposed three modifications to the DLS SAT-solving algorithm DDFW. We then implemented DDFW on top of the SLS solver `yalsat` to create the solver `yal-lin`, and we tested this solver on a pair of challenging benchmark sets. Our experimental results showed that our modifications led to substantial improvement over the baseline DDFW algorithm. The results show that future users of `yal-lin` should, by default, use the configuration `lw-ith-c.1-wrnd`.

While each modification led to improved performance, the improvements due to each modification were not equal. The performance boost due to switching to the weighted-random variable selection method was the weakest, as it resulted in the fewest additional solves. However, our results indicate that making occasional non-optimal flips may help DDFW explore its search space better.

The performance boost due to adjusting the `cspt` value was more substantial, supporting our initial findings in Section 5.3. One metric that could explain the importance of a higher `cspt` value is a clause's *degree of satisfaction* (DS),

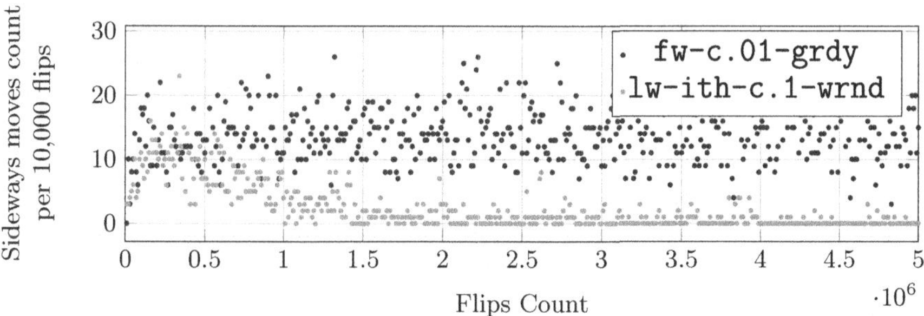

Fig. 5. Comparison of sideways move count per 10,000 flips with search progression for our baseline (fw-c.01-grdy) and best setting (lw-ith-c.1-wrnd) from yal-lin for an COMB instance sted2_0x0_n219-342.

which is the fraction of its literals that are satisfied by the current assignment. We noticed in experiments on the COMB benchmark with cspt = 0.01 that clauses neighboring a falsified clause had an average DS value of 0.33, while clauses without a neighboring falsified clause had an average DS value of 0.54. If this trend holds for general yal-lin runs, then it may be advantageous to take weight from the latter clauses more often, since flipping any literal in a falsified clause will not falsify any of the latter clauses. A higher cspt value accomplishes this. However, we did not investigate the relationship between DS and cspt further, and we leave this to future work. Performance also improved with the switch to a linear weight transfer method. The best method, lw-ith, supports the findings from the workshop paper that DDFW should transfer more weight from clauses with the initial weight. Future work can examine whether the heavy-clause distinction is valuable; a weight transfer rule that doesn't explicitly check if a clause is heavy would simplify the DDFW algorithm.

When restarts are enabled, all ten settings in yal-lin perform better for COMB than when restarts are disabled. This better performance with restarts comes from solving several MM instances, for which these settings without restarts solve none of them. However, for SATComp, yal-lin performs better when restarts are disabled. Since SATComp comprises larger number of heterogeneous benchmarks than COMB, these results suggest that the new system performs better when restarts are disabled.

Future work on weight transfer methods can take several other directions. Different transfer functions can be tested, such as those that are a function of the falsified clause's weight or those based on rational or exponential functions. Alternate definitions for neighboring clauses are also possible. For example, in formulas with large neighborhoods, it may be advantageous to consider clauses neighbors if they share $k > 1$ literals, rather than just 1.

Throughout this paper, we kept the spt parameter set to 0.15. Yet, when clause weights are floating point numbers, it is rare for our solver to make sideways moves. This evident in Figure 5, which compares count of sideways moves per 10,000 flips between our baseline setting (`fw-0.01-grdy`), and best setting (`lw-ith-c.1-wrand`) for a randomly chosen SATComp instance sted2_0x0_n219-342 up to 5 millions flips. With `fw-0.01-grdy`, `yal-lin` makes some sideways moves, albeit rarely. However, with floating weight transfer in `lw-ith-c.1-wrand`, the solver makes almost no sideways moves as search progresses. We further investigated the effect of sideways moves on solver performance. We tested the setting `lw-ith-c.1-wrnd` against a version that did not perform sideways moves on the SATComp benchmark. The version with sideways moves solved 118 instances, while the version without them solved 113. This suggests that sideways moves may add a slight-but-beneficial amount of random noise to the algorithm. Future work can more fully investigate the effect of sideways moves on DDFW. One goal is to eliminate the parameter entirely in order to simplify the algorithm. Alternatively, the algorithm could be modified to occasionally flip variables that *increase* the falsified weight to help DDFW explore the search space.

Overall, we find that the DDFW algorithm continues to show promise and deserves more research interest. Our solver closed several hard instances that eluded other state-of-the-art solvers, and the space of potential algorithmic improvements remains rich.

References

1. Aaron Stump, Geoff Sutcliffe, C.T.: StarExec. https://www.starexec.org/starexec/public/about.jsp (2013)
2. Ahmed, T., Kullmann, O., Snevily, H.S.: On the van der Waerden numbers w(2; 3, t). Discrete Applied Mathematics **174**, 27–51 (2014). https://doi.org/10.1016/j.dam.2014.05.007
3. Balint, A.: Engineering stochastic local search for the satisfiability problem. Ph.D. thesis, University of Ulm (2014)
4. Biere, A., Heule, M., van Maaren, H., Walsh, T.: Handbook of Satisfiability: Volume 185 Frontiers in Artificial Intelligence and Applications. IOS Press, Amsterdam, The Netherlands (2009)
5. Biere, A.: YalSAT Yet Another Local Search Solver. http://fmv.jku.at/yalsat/ (2010)
6. Brown, S., Buitrago, P., Hanna, E., Sanielevici, S., Scibek, R., Nystrom, N.: Bridges-2: A platform for rapidly-evolving and data intensive research. In: Association for Computing Machinery, New York, NY, USA. pp. 1–4 (2021)
7. Cai, S., Luo, C., Su, K.: CCAnr: A configuration checking based local search solver for non-random satisfiability. In: Heule, M., Weaver, S. (eds.) Theory and Applications of Satisfiability Testing - SAT 2015, pp. 1–8. Springer International Publishing, Cham (2015)
8. Cai, S., Zhang, X., Fleury, M., Biere, A.: Better Decision Heuristics in CDCL through Local Search and Target Phases. Journal of Artificial Intelligence Research **74**, 1515–1563 (2022)
9. Codel, C.R., Heule, M.J.: A Study of Divide and Distribute Fixed Weights and its Variants. In: Pragmatics of SAT 2021 (2021)
10. Feng, N., Bacchus, F.: Clause size reduction with all-UIP learning. In: Pulina, L., Seidl, M. (eds.) Proceedings of SAT-2020. pp. 28–45 (2020)

11. Green, B.: New lower bounds for van der Waerden numbers (2021). https://doi.org/10.48550/ARXIV.2102.01543
12. Gupta, A., Ganai, M.K., Wang, C.: SAT-based verification methods and applications in hardware verification. In: Proceedings of SFM 2006. pp. 108–143 (2006)
13. Heule, M.J.H., Karahalios, A., van Hoeve, W.: From cliques to colorings and back again. In: Proceedings of CP-2022. pp. 26:1–26:10 (2022)
14. Heule, M.J.H., Kauers, M., Seidl, M.: New ways to multiply 3x3-matrices. J. Symb. Comput. **104**, 899–916 (2019)
15. Hutter, F., Tompkins, D.A.D., Hoos, H.H.: Scaling and probabilistic smoothing: Efficient dynamic local search for SAT. In: Hentenryck, P.V. (ed.) Proceedings of CP 2002. pp. 233–248 (2002)
16. Ishtaiwi, A., Thornton, J., Sattar, A., Pham, D.N.: Neighbourhood clause weight redistribution in local search for SAT. In: Proceedings of CP-2005. pp. 772–776. Lecture Notes in Computer Science (2005)
17. Johnson, D.J., Trick, M.A.: Cliques, Coloring, and Satisfiability: Second DIMACS Implementation Challenge, Workshop, October 11–13, 1993. American Mathematical Society, USA (1996)
18. Kautz, H., Selman, B.: Planning as satisfiability. In: Proceedings of the 10th European Conference on Artificial Intelligence. p. 359–363. ECAI '92, John Wiley & Sons Inc, USA (1992)
19. Li, C.M., Li, Y.: Satisfying versus falsifying in local search for satisfiability. In: Cimatti, A., Sebastiani, R. (eds.) Theory and Applications of Satisfiability Testing – SAT 2012. pp. 477–478. Springer Berlin Heidelberg, Berlin, Heidelberg (2012)
20. Moskewicz, M.W., Madigan, C.F., Zhao, Y., Zhang, L., Malik, S.: Chaff: Engineering an efficient SAT solver. In: Proceedings of DAC 2001. pp. 530–535 (2001)
21. Ostrowski, J., Linderoth, J., Rossi, F., Smriglio, S.: Solving large steiner triple covering problems. Operations Research Letters **39**(2), 127–131 (2011)
22. Schreiber, D., Sanders, P.: Scalable SAT solving in the cloud. In: Li, C.M., Manyà, F. (eds.) Theory and Applications of Satisfiability Testing – SAT 2021. pp. 518–534. Springer International Publishing, Cham (2021)
23. Selman, B., Kautz, H.A., Cohen, B.: Local search strategies for satisfiability testing. In: Cliques, Coloring, and Satisfiability, Proceedings of a DIMACS Workshop 1993. pp. 521–532 (1993)
24. Selman, B., Levesque, H.J., Mitchell, D.G.: A new method for solving hard satisfiability problems. In: Proceedings of AAAI 1992. pp. 440–446 (1992)
25. Silva, J.P.M., Sakallah, K.A.: GRASP: A search algorithm for propositional satisfiability. IEEE Trans. Computers **48**(5), 506–521 (1999)
26. Soos, M., Nohl, K., Castelluccia, C.: Extending SAT solvers to cryptographic problems. In: Proceedings of SAT 2009. pp. 244–257 (2009)
27. Thornton, J., Pham, D.N., Bain, S., Jr., V.F.: Additive versus multiplicative clause weighting for SAT. In: McGuinness, D.L., Ferguson, G. (eds.) Proceedings of AAAI-2004. pp. 191–196 (2004)
28. Tompkins, D.: Dynamic Local Search for SAT: Design, Insights and Analysis. Ph.D. thesis, The University of British Columbia (2010)
29. Tompkins, D.: UBCSAT. http://ubcsat.dtompkins.com/home (2010)
30. van der Waerden, B.L.: Beweis einer baudet'schen vermutung. J. Symb. Comput. **15**, 212–216 (1927)
31. Xindi Zhang, Shaowei Cai, Z.C.: Improving CDCL via Local Search. In: SAT Competition-2021. pp. 42–43 (2021)

Adiar 1.1
Zero-Suppressed Decision Diagrams in External Memory

Steffan Christ Sølvsten(✉) and Jaco van de Pol

Aarhus University, Aarhus, Denmark
{soelvsten,jaco}@cs.au.dk

Abstract. We outline how support for Zero-suppressed Decision Diagrams (ZDDs) has been achieved for the external memory BDD package Adiar. This allows one to use ZDDs to solve various problems despite their size exceed the machine's limit of internal memory.

Keywords: Zero-suppressed Decision Diagrams · External Memory Algorithms

1 Introduction

Minato introduced Zero-suppressed Decision Diagrams (ZDDs) [15] as a variation on Bryant's Binary Decision Diagrams (BDDs) [5]. ZDDs provide a canonical description of a Boolean n-ary function f that is more compact than the corresponding BDD when f is a characteristic function for a family $F \subseteq \{0,1\}^n$ of sparse vectors over some universe of n variables. This makes ZDDs not only useful for solving combinatorial problems [15] but they can also surpass BDDs in the context of symbolic model checking [21] and they are the backbone of the PolyBoRi library [4] used in algebraic cryptoanalysis.

The Adiar BDD package [19] provides an implementation of BDDs in C++17 that is I/O-efficient [1]. This allows Adiar to manipulate BDDs that outgrow the size of the machine's internal memory, i.e., RAM, by efficiently exploiting how they are stored in external memory, i.e., on the disk. The source code for Adiar is publicly available at

github.com/ssoelvsten/adiar

All 1.x versions of Adiar have only been tested on Linux with GCC. But, with version 2.0, it is ensured that Adiar supports the GCC, Clang, and MSVC compilers on Linux, Mac, and Windows.

We have added in Adiar 1.1 support for the basic ZDD operations while also aiming for the following two criteria: the addition of ZDDs should (1) avoid any code duplication to keep the codebase maintainable and (2) not negatively impact the performance of existing functionality. Section 2 describes how this was achieved and Sect. 3 provides an evaluation.

Other mature BDD packages also support ZDDs, e.g., CUDD [20], BiDDy [13], Sylvan [8] and PJBDD [2], but unlike Adiar none of these support manipulation of ZDDs beyond main memory. The only other BDD package designed for out-of-memory BDD manipulation, CAL [16], does not support ZDDs.

K. Y. Rozier and S. Chaudhuri (Eds.): NFM 2023, LNCS 13903, pp. 464–471, 2023.
https://doi.org/10.1007/978-3-031-33170-1_28

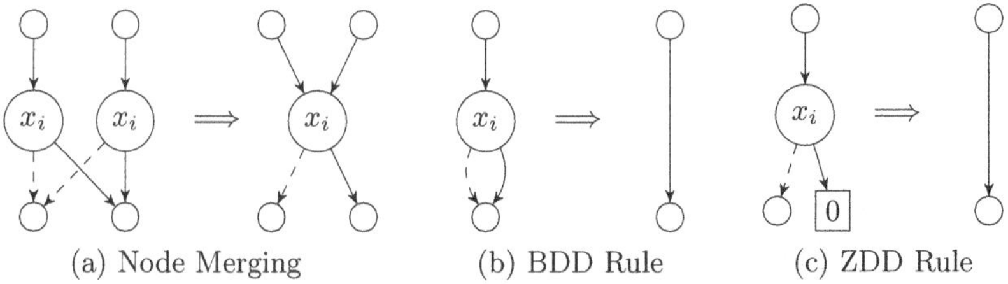

Fig. 1. Reduction Rules for BDDs and ZDDs.

2 Supporting both BDDs and ZDDs

The Boolean function $f : \{0,1\}^n \to \{0,1\}$ is the characteristic function for the set of bitvectors $F = \{\boldsymbol{x} \in \{0,1\}^n \mid f(\boldsymbol{x}) = 1\}$. Each bitvector $\boldsymbol{x}$ is equivalent to a conjunction of the indices set to 1 and hence F can quite naturally be described as a DNF formula, i.e., a set of set of variables.

A decision diagram is a rooted directed acyclic graph (DAG) with two sinks: a 0-leaf and a 1-leaf. Each internal node has two children and contains the label $i \in \mathbb{N}$ to encode the *if-then-else* of a variable x_i. The decision diagram is *ordered* by ensuring each label only occurs once and in sorted order on all paths from the root. The diagram is also *reduced* if duplicate nodes are merged as shown in Fig. 1a. Furthermore as shown respectively in Fig. 1b and 1c, BDDs and ZDDs also suppress a certain type of nodes as part of their reduction to further decrease the diagram's size. The suppression rule for ZDDs in Fig. 1c ensures each path in the diagram corresponds one-to-one to a term of the DNF it represents.

Both BDDs and ZDDs provide a succinct way to manipulate Boolean formulae by computing on their graph-representation instead. The difference in the type of node being suppressed in each type of decision diagram has an impact on the logic within these graph algorithms. For example, applying a binary operator, e.g., *and* for BDDs and *intersection* for ZDDs, is a product construction for both types of decision diagrams. But since the *and* operator is shortcutted by the 0-leaf, the computation depends on the shape of the suppressed nodes.

Hence, as shown in Fig. 2, we have generalized the relevant algorithms in Adiar with a *policy-based design*, i.e., a compile-time known *strategy pattern*, so the desired parts of the code can be varied internally. For example, most of the logic within the BDD product construction has been moved to the templated `product_construction` function. The code-snippets that distinguish the `bdd_apply` from the corresponding ZDD operation `zdd_binop` are encapsulated within the two *policy* classes: `apply_prod_policy` and `zdd_prod_policy`. This ensures that no code duplication is introduced. This added layer of abstraction has no negative impact on performance, since the function calls are known and inlined at compile-time. No part of this use of templates is exposed to the end-user, by ensuring that each templated algorithm is compiled into its final algorithms within Adiar's `.cpp` files.

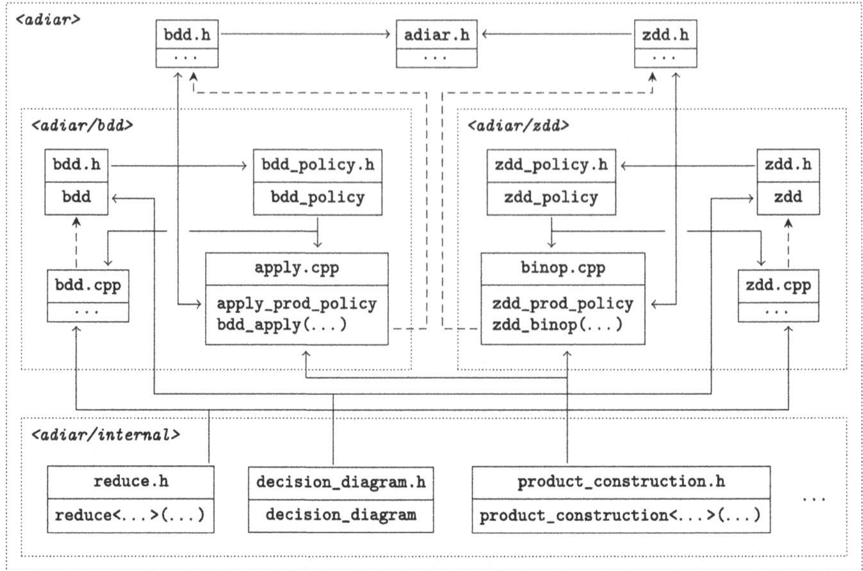

Fig. 2. Architecture of Adiar v1.1. Solid lines are direct inclusions of one file in another while dashed lines represent the implementation of a declared function.

Table 1. Supported ZDD operations in Adiar v1.1. The semantics views a ZDD as a set of sets of variables in *dom*.

Adiar ZDD function	Operation Semantics	Generalised BDD function
ZDD Manipulation		
`zdd_binop(`A`,`B`,`$\otimes$`)`	$\{x \mid x \in A \otimes x \in B\}$	`bdd_apply`
`zdd_change(`A`, vars)`	$\{(a \setminus vars) \cup (vars \setminus a) \mid a \in A\}$	
`zdd_complement(`A`, dom)`	$\mathcal{P}(dom) \setminus A$	
`zdd_expand(`A`, vars)`	$\bigcup_{a \in A} \{a \cup v \mid v \in \mathcal{P}(vars)\}$	
`zdd_offset(`A`, vars)`	$\{a \in A \mid vars \cap a = \emptyset\}$	`bdd_restrict`
`zdd_onset(`A`, vars)`	$\{a \in A \mid vars \subseteq a\}$	`bdd_restrict`
`zdd_project(`A`, vars)`	$proj_{vars}(A)$	`bdd_exists`
Counting		
`zdd_size(`A`)`	$\|A\|$	`bdd_pathcount`
`zdd_nodecount(`A`)`	N_A	`bdd_nodecount`
`zdd_varcount(`A`)`	L_A	`bdd_varcount`
Predicates		
`zdd_equal(`A`, `B`)`	$A = B$	`bdd_equal`
`zdd_unequal(`A`, `B`)`	$A \neq B$	`bdd_equal`
`zdd_subseteq(`A`, `B`)`	$A \subseteq B$	`bdd_equal`
`zdd_disjoint(`A`, `B`)`	$A \cap B = \emptyset$	`bdd_equal`
Set elements		
`zdd_contains(`A`, vars)`	$vars \in A$	`bdd_eval`
`zdd_minelem(`A`)`	$\min(A)$	`bdd_satmin`
`zdd_maxelem(`A`)`	$\max(A)$	`bdd_satmax`
Conversion		
`zdd_from(`f`, dom)`	$\{x \in \mathcal{P}(dom) \mid f(x) = \top\}$	
`bdd_from(`A`, dom)`	$x : \mathcal{P}(dom) \mapsto x \in A$	

For each type of decision diagram there is a class, e.g., `bdd`, and a separate policy, e.g., `bdd_policy`, that encapsulates the common logic for that type of decision diagram, e.g., the reduction rule in Fig. 1b and the `bdd` type. This policy is used within the `bdd` and `zdd` class to instantiate the specific variant of the Reduce algorithm that is applied after each operation. The algorithm policies, e.g., the two product construction policies above, also inherit information from this diagram-specific policy. This ensures the policies can provide the information needed by the algorithm templates.

Table 1 provides an overview of all ZDD operations provided in Adiar 1.1, including what BDD operations they are generalized from. All but five of these ZDD operations could be implemented by templating the current codebase. The remaining five operations required the addition of only a single new algorithm of similar shape to those in [19]; the differences among these five could be encapsulated within a policy for each operation.

3 Evaluation

3.1 Cost of Modularity

Table 2a shows the size of the code base, measured in lines of code (LOC), and Table 2b the number of unique operations in the public API with and without aliases. Due to the added modularity and features the entire code base grew by a factor $\frac{6305}{3961} = 1.59$. Yet, the size of the public API excluding aliases increased by a factor of $\frac{23+24}{22} = 2.14$; including aliases the public API grew by a factor of 1.98.

3.2 Experimental Evaluation

Impact on BDD Performance. Table 3 shows the performance of Adiar before and after implementing the architecture in Sect. 2. These two benchmarks, N-Queens and Tic-Tac-Toe, were used in [19] to evaluate the performance of its BDDs – specifically to evaluate its `bdd_apply` and `reduce` algorithms. The choice of N is based on limitations in Adiar v1.0 and v1.1 (which are resolved in Adiar v1.2). We ran these benchmarks on a consumer grade laptop with a 2.6 GHz Intel i7-4720HQ processor, 8 GiB of RAM (4 of which was given to Adiar) and 230 GiB SSD disk.

Table 2. Lines of Code compared to number of functions in Adiar's API.

Folder	v1.0	v1.1
`adiar`	3939	1643
`adiar/bdd`	–	1019
`adiar/zdd`	–	1052
`adiar/internal`	–	2568

(a) Lines of Code.

Adiar's API	v1.0	v1.1
BDD	22	23
(w/aliases)	+20	+22
ZDD	–	24
(w/aliases)	–	+14

(b) Size of the Public API.

Table 3. Minimum running time (s) before and after the changes in Sect. 2.

(a) Queens

N	Before (v1.0)	After (v1.1)
13	107.8	108.9
14	680.8	625.2

(b) Tic-Tac-Toe

N	Before (v1.0)	After (v1.1)
22	616.8	517.9
23	3202.9	2881.1

The 1% slowdown for the 13-Queens problem is well within the experimental error introduced by the machine's hardware and OS. Furthermore, the three other benchmarks show a performance increase of 9% or more. Hence, it is safe to conclude that the changes to Adiar have not negatively affected its performance.

ZDD Performance. We have compared Adiar 1.1's and CUDD 3.0's [20] performance manipulating ZDDs. Our benchmarks are, similar to Sect. 2, templated with *adapters* for each BDD package. Sylvan 1.7 [8] and BiDDy 2.2 [13] are not part of this evaluation since they have no C++ interface; to include them, we essentially would have to implement a free/protect mechanism for ZDDs for proper garbage collection.

Figure 3 shows the normalized minimal running time of solving three combinatorial problems: the N-Queens and the Tic-Tac-Toe benchmarks from earlier and the (open) Knight's Tour problem based on [6]. We focus on combinatorial problems due to what functionality is properly supported by Adiar at time of writing. These experiments were run on the server nodes of the *Centre for Scientific Computing, Aarhus.* Each node has two 3.0 GHz Intel Xeon Gold 6248R processors, 384 GiB of RAM (300 of which was given to the BDD package), 3.5 TiB of available SSD disk, runs CentOS Linux, and uses GCC 10.1.0.

Adiar is significantly slower than CUDD for small instances due to the overhead of initialising and using external memory data structures. Hence, Fig. 3 only shows the instances where the largest ZDD involved is 10 MiB or larger since these meaningfully compare the algorithms in Adiar with the ones in CUDD.

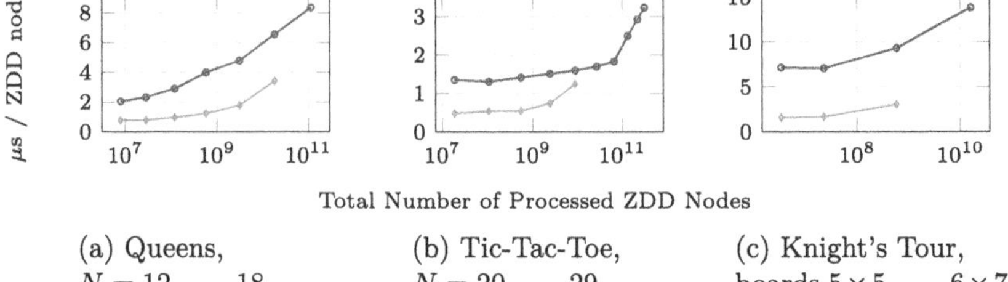

(a) Queens, $N = 12, \ldots, 18$

(b) Tic-Tac-Toe, $N = 20, \ldots, 29$

(c) Knight's Tour, boards $5 \times 5, \ldots, 6 \times 7$

Fig. 3. Normalised minimal running time of Adiar (blue) and CUDD (red). (Color figure online)

Similar to the results in [19], also for ZDDs the gap in running time between Adiar and CUDD shrinks as the instances grow. When solving the 15-Queens problem, Adiar is 3.22 times slower than CUDD whereas for the 17-Queens problem it is only 1.91 times slower. The largest Tic-Tac-Toe instance solved by CUDD was $N = 24$ where Adiar was only 1.22 times slower. In both benchmarks, Adiar handles more instances than CUDD: 18-Queens, resp. Tic-Tac-Toe for $N = 29$, results in a single ZDD of 512.8 GiB, resp. 838.9 GiB, in size.

The Knight's Tour benchmark stays quite benign up until a chess board of 6×6. From that point, the computation time and size of the ZDDs quickly explode. Adiar solved up to the 6×7 board in 2.5 days, where the largest ZDD was only 2 GiB in size. We could not solve this instance with CUDD within 15 days. For instances also solved by CUDD, Adiar was up to 4.43 times slower.

4 Conclusion and Future Work

While the lines of code for Adiar's BDDs has slightly increased, that does not necessarily imply an increase in the code's complexity. Notice that the architecture in Sect. 2 separates the recursive logic of BDD and ZDD manipulation from the logic used to make these operations I/O-efficient. In fact, this separation significantly improved the readability and maintainability of both halves. Furthermore, the C++ templates allow the compiler to output each variant of an algorithm as if it was written by hand. Hence, as Sect. 3 shows, the addition of ZDDs has not decreased Adiar's ability to handle BDDs efficiently.

Adiar can be further modularized by templating diagram nodes to vary their data and outdegree at compile-time. This opens the possibility to support Multi-terminal [9], List [8], Functional [11], and Quantum Multiple-valued [14] Decision Diagrams. If nodes support variadic out-degrees at run-time, then support for Multi-valued [10] and Clock Difference [12] Decision Diagrams is possible and it provides the basis for an I/O-efficient implementation of Annotated Terms [3].

This still leaves a vital open problem posed in [19] as future work: the current technique used to achieve I/O-efficiency does not provide a translation for operations that need to recurse multiple times for a single diagram node. Hence, I/O-efficient dynamic variable reordering is currently not supported. Similarly, `zdd_project` in Adiar v1.1 may be significantly slower than its counterparts in other BDD packages. This also hinders the implementation of other complex operations, such as the multiplication operations in [4,14,15], the generalisation of composition in [5] to multiple variables, and the Restrict operator in [7].

Acknowledgements. Thanks to Marijn Heule and Randal E. Bryant for requesting ZDDs are added to= Adiar. Thanks to the Centre for Scientific Computing, Aarhus, (phys.au.dk/forskning/cscaa/) for running our benchmarks.

Data Availibility Statement. The data presented in Sect. 3 is available at [18] while the code to obtain this data is provided at [17].

References

1. Aggarwal, A., Vitter, J.S.: The input/output complexity of sorting and related problems. Commun. ACM **31**(9), 1116–1127 (1988). https://doi.org/10.1145/48529.48535
2. Beyer, D., Friedberger, K., Holzner, S.: PJBDD: a BDD library for Java and multi-threading. In: Hou, Z., Ganesh, V. (eds.) ATVA 2021. LNCS, vol. 12971, pp. 144–149. Springer, Cham (2021). https://doi.org/10.1007/978-3-030-88885-5_10
3. BrandVan den Brand, M.G.J., Jongde Jong, H.A., Klint, P., Olivier, P.: Efficient annotated terms. Softw. Pract. Exp. **30**, 259–291 (2000)
4. Brickenstein, M., Dreyer, A.: PolyBoRi: a framework for Gröbner-basis computations with Boolean polynomials. J. Symb. Comput. **44**(9), 1326–1345 (2009). https://doi.org/10.1016/j.jsc.2008.02.017
5. Bryant, R.E.: Graph-based algorithms for Boolean function manipulation. IEEE Trans. Comput. **C-35**(8), 677–691 (1986)
6. Bryant, R.E.: `Cloud-BDD`: Distributed implementation of BDD package (2021). https://github.com/rebryant/Cloud-BDD
7. Coudert, O., Madre, J.C.: A unified framework for the formal verification of sequential circuits. In: 1990 IEEE International Conference on Computer-Aided Design. Digest of Technical Papers, pp. 126–129 (1990). https://doi.org/10.1109/ICCAD.1990.129859
8. Van Dijk, T., Van de Pol, J.: Sylvan: multi-core framework for decision diagrams. Int. J. Softw. Tools Technol. Transf. **19**, 675–696 (2016). https://doi.org/10.1007/s10009-016-0433-2
9. Fujita, M., McGeer, P., Yang, J.Y.: Multi-terminal binary decision diagrams: an efficient data structure for matrix representation. Formal Methods Syst. Des. **10**, 149–169 (1997). https://doi.org/10.1023/A:1008647823331
10. Kam, T., Villa, T., Brayton, R.K., Alberto, L.S.V.: Multi-valued decision diagrams: theory and applications. Multiple-Valued Log. **4**(1), 9–62 (1998)
11. Kebschull, U., Rosenstiel, W.: Efficient graph-based computation and manipulation of functional decision diagrams. In: European Conference on Design Automation with the European Event in ASIC Design, pp. 278–282 (1993). https://doi.org/10.1109/EDAC.1993.386463
12. Larsen, K.G., Weise, C., Yi, W., Pearson, J.: Clock difference diagrams. In: Nordic Workshop on Programming Theory, Turku, Finland. Aalborg Universitetsforlag (1998). https://doi.org/10.7146/brics.v5i46.19491
13. Meolic, R.: BiDDy - a multi-platform academic BDD package. J. Softw. **7**, 1358–1366 (2012). https://doi.org/10.4304/jsw.7.6.1358-1366
14. Miller, D., Thornton, M.: QMDD: a decision diagram structure for reversible and quantum circuits. In: 36th International Symposium on Multiple-Valued Logic, pp. 30–36 (2006). https://doi.org/10.1109/ISMVL.2006.35
15. Minato, S.I.: Zero-suppressed BDDs for set manipulation in combinatorial problems. In: Proceedings of the 30th International Design Automation Conference, pp. 272–277. DAC 1993, Association for Computing Machinery (1993). https://doi.org/10.1145/157485.164890
16. Sanghavi, J.V., Ranjan, R.K., Brayton, R.K., Sangiovanni-Vincentelli, A.: High performance BDD package by exploiting memory hierarchy. In: 33rd Design Automation Conference (DAC), pp. 635–640. Association for Computing Machinery (1996). https://doi.org/10.1145/240518.240638

17. Sølvsten, S.C., Jakobsen, A.B.: `SSoelvsten/bdd-benchmark`: NASA formal methods 2023. Zenodo, September 2022. https://doi.org/10.5281/zenodo.7040263
18. Sølvsten, S.C., van de Pol, J.: Adiar 1.1.0: experiment data. Zenodo, March 2023. https://doi.org/10.5281/zenodo.7709134
19. Sølvsten, S.C., de Pol, J., Jakobsen, A.B., Thomasen, M.W.B.: Adiar binary decision diagrams in external memory. In: TACAS 2022. LNCS, vol. 13244, pp. 295–313. Springer, Cham (2022). https://doi.org/10.1007/978-3-030-99527-0_16
20. Somenzi, F.: CUDD: CU decision diagram package, 3.0. Technical report, University of Colorado at Boulder (2015)
21. Yoneda, T., Hatori, H., Takahara, A., Minato, S.: BDDs vs. zero-suppressed BDDs: for CTL symbolic model checking of Petri nets. In: Srivas, M., Camilleri, A. (eds.) FMCAD 1996. LNCS, vol. 1166, pp. 435–449. Springer, Heidelberg (1996). https://doi.org/10.1007/BFb0031826

Satisfiability of Non-linear Transcendental Arithmetic as a Certificate Search Problem

Enrico Lipparini[1](✉) and Stefan Ratschan[2]

[1] DIBRIS, University of Genoa, Genoa, Italy
enrico.lipparini@edu.unige.it

[2] Institute of Computer Science of the Czech Academy of Sciences, Prague, Czechia

Abstract. For typical first-order logical theories, satisfying assignments have a straightforward finite representation that can directly serve as a certificate that a given assignment satisfies the given formula. For non-linear real arithmetic with transcendental functions, however, no general finite representation of satisfying assignments is available. Hence, in this paper, we introduce a different form of satisfiability certificate for this theory, formulate the satisfiability verification problem as the problem of searching for such a certificate, and show how to perform this search in a systematic fashion. This does not only ease the independent verification of results, but also allows the systematic design of new, efficient search techniques. Computational experiments document that the resulting method is able to prove satisfiability of a substantially higher number of benchmark problems than existing methods.

1 Introduction

SAT modulo theories (SMT) is the problem of checking whether a given quantifier-free first-order formula with both propositional and theory variables is satisfiable in a specific first-order theory. In this paper, we consider the case of SMT($\mathcal{NTA}$), non-linear real arithmetic augmented with trigonometric and exponential transcendental functions. This problem is particularly important in the verification of hybrid systems and in theorem proving. Unfortunately, $\mathcal{NTA}$ is a very challenging theory. Indeed, it is undecidable [26], and, moreover, there is no known finite representation of satisfying assignments that could act as a direct certificate of satisfiability. This does not only make it difficult for an SMT-solver to prove satisfiability, but also raises the question of how to verify the result given by an SMT-solver.

In this paper, we introduce the notion of a satisfiability certificate for $\mathcal{NTA}$. Such a certificate allows independent entities to verify the satisfiability of a given input formula without having to re-do a full check of its satisfiability. More specifically, based on such a certificate, the check of satisfiability is both easier in terms of computational effort and effort needed to implement the checker and to ensure its correctness. The certificate will be based on the notion of topological

K. Y. Rozier and S. Chaudhuri (Eds.): NFM 2023, LNCS 13903, pp. 472–488, 2023.
https://doi.org/10.1007/978-3-031-33170-1_29

degree [1,11,12], generalizing the idea that a sign change of a continuous function f implies satisfiability of $f = 0$. The basic tool for checking correctness of the certificate is interval arithmetic [24,25,28].

The idea to verify satisfiability of SMT($\mathcal{NTA}$) in such a way, is not new [21]. However, the formulation as the problem of searching for a certificate is. In addition to the possibility of independent verification, such a formulation makes the corresponding search problem explicit. This allows us to introduce new, efficient search heuristics that guide the algorithm toward finding a certificate and prevent the procedure from getting stuck in computation that later turns out to not to lead to success.

We have implemented our method in the tool UGOTNL [21] and present computational experiments with different heuristics configurations over a wide variety of $\mathcal{NTA}$ benchmarks. The experimental results show that this new version of UGOTNL outperforms the previous version, making it—to the best of our knowledge—the most effective solver for proving satisfiability of $\mathcal{NTA}$ problems.

It is possible to integrate the resulting method into a conflict-driven clause learning (CDCL) type SMT solver [21]. However, in order to keep the focus of the paper on the concern of certificate search, we ignore this possibility, here.

Content. The paper is organized as follows: In Sect. 2 we provide the necessary background. In Sect. 3 we give the formal definitions of *certifying SMT solver* and of *satisfiability certificate* in SMT($\mathcal{NTA}$). In Sect. 4 we outline our method for searching for a certificate, and in Sect. 5 we illustrate the heuristics that we introduce in detail. In Sect. 6 we experimentally evaluate our method. In Sect. 7 we discuss related work. Finally, in Sect. 8, we draw some conclusions.

2 Preliminaries

We work in the context of *Satisfiability Modulo Theories* (SMT). Our theory of interest is the quantifier-free theory of non-linear real arithmetic augmented with trigonometric and exponential transcendental functions, SMT($\mathcal{NTA}$). We assume that the reader is familiar with standard SMT terminology [5].

Notation. We denote SMT($\mathcal{NTA}$)-formulas by ϕ, ψ, clauses by C_1, C_2, literals by l_1, l_2, real-valued variables by $x_1, x_2, \ldots$, constants by a, b, intervals of real values by $I = [a, b]$, boxes by $B = I_1 \times \cdots \times I_n$, logical terms with addition, multiplication and transcendental function symbols by f, g, and multivariate real functions with F, G, H. For any formula ϕ, we denote by $vars_{\mathcal{R}}(\phi)$ the set of its real-valued variables. When there is no risk of ambiguity we write f, g to also denote the real-valued functions corresponding to the standard interpretation of the respective terms. We assume that formulas are in Conjunctive Normal Form (CNF) and that their atoms are in the form $f \bowtie 0$, with $\bowtie \in \{=, \leq, <\}$. We remove the negation symbol by rewriting every occurrence of $\neg(f = 0)$ as $(f < 0 \vee 0 < f)$ and distributing $\neg$ over inequalities.

Points and Boxes. Since we have an order on the real-valued variables $x_1, x_2, \ldots$, for any set of variables $V \subseteq \{x_1, x_2, \ldots\}$ we can view an assignment

$p : V \to \mathbb{R}$ equivalently as the $|V|$-dimensional point $p \in \mathbb{R}^{|V|}$, and an *interval assignment* $B : V \to \{[a, b] : a, b \in \mathbb{R}\}$ equivalently as the $|V|$-dimensional box $B \subseteq \mathbb{R}^{|V|}$. By abuse of notation, we will use both representations interchangeably, using the type $\mathcal{R}^V$ both for assignments in $V \to \mathbb{R}$ and points in $\mathbb{R}^{|V|}$, and the type $\mathcal{B}^V$ both for interval assignments in $V \to \{[a, b] : a, b \in \mathbb{R}\}$ and corresponding boxes. This will allow us to apply mathematical notions usually defined on points or boxes to such assignments, as well. Given a point $p \in \mathcal{R}^V$, and a subset $V' \subseteq V$, we denote by $proj_{V'}(p) \in \mathcal{R}^{V'}$ the projection of p to the variables in V', that is, for all $v \in V'$, $proj_{V'}(p)(v) := p(v)$.

Systems of Equations and Inequalities. We say that a formula ϕ that contains only conjunctions of atoms in the form $f = 0$ and $g \leq 0$ is a *system of equations and inequalities.* If ϕ contains only equations (inequalities) then we say it is a *system of equations* (*inequalities*). A system of equations $f_1 = 0 \wedge \cdots \wedge f_n = 0$, where the $f_1, \cdots, f_n$ are terms in the variables $x_1, \cdots, x_m$, can be seen in an equivalent way as the equation $F = 0$, where F is the real-valued function $F := f_1 \times \cdots \times f_n : \mathbb{R}^m \to \mathbb{R}^n$ and 0 is a compact way to denote the point $(0, \cdots, 0) \in \mathbb{R}^n$. Analogously, we can see a system of inequalities $g_1 \leq 0 \wedge \cdots \wedge g_k \leq 0$ as the inequality $G \leq 0$, where G is the real-valued function $G := g_1 \times \cdots \times g_k : \mathbb{R}^m \to \mathbb{R}^k$ and $\leq$ is defined element-wise. We will write $eq(\phi)$ for the function F defined by the equations in the formula ϕ and $ineq(\phi)$ for the function G defined by the inequalities in ϕ. The handling of strict inequalities would be an easy, but technical extension of our method, which we avoid to stream-line the presentation.

Dulmage-Mendelsohn Decomposition. Given a system of equations ϕ, it is possible to construct an associated bipartite graph $\mathcal{G}_\phi$ that represent important structural properties of the system of equations. This graph has one vertex per equation, one vertex per variable, and an edge between a variable x_i and an equation $f_j = 0$ iff x_i appears in f. The Dulmage-Mendelsohn decomposition [2, 10] is a canonical decomposition from the field of matching theory that partitions the system into three parts: an over-constrained subsystem (more equalities than variables), an under-constrained subsystem (less equalities than variables), and a well-constrained subsystem (as many equalities as variables, and contains no over-constrained subsystem, i.e. it satisfies the Hall property [17]).

Example 1. Let $\phi := x - tan(y) = 0 \wedge z^2 = 0 \wedge w = 0 \wedge sin(w) = 0$. Through the DM-decomposition we obtain an under-constrained sub-system $x - tan(y) = 0$ (two variables, one equation), a well-constrained sub-system $z^2 = 0$ (one variable, one equation), and an over-constrained sub-system $w = 0 \wedge sin(w) = 0$ (one variable, two equations).

Topological Degree. The notion of the degree of a continuous function (also called the topological degree) comes from differential topology [11]. For a continuous function $F : B \subseteq \mathbb{R}^n \to \mathbb{R}^n$, such that $0 \notin F(\partial B)$ (where ∂B is the topological boundary of B), the degree $deg(F, B, 0)$ is a computable [1,12] integer. This integer provides information about the roots of F in B, and can be seen as a generalization of the intermediate value theorem to higher-dimensional functions. In analogy to the fact that opposite signs of a continuous function on the endpoints of an interval imply the existence of a zero within the interval, $deg(F, B, 0) \neq 0$ implies that F has a root in B. The converse is not true, and the existence of a root does not imply nonzero degree in general. Still, if a box contains one isolated zero with non-singular Jacobian matrix, then the topological degree is non-zero [11]. For alternatives to the topological degree test see our discussion of related work.

Interval Arithmetic. The basic algorithmic tool that underlies our approach is floating point interval arithmetic ($\mathcal{IA}$) [24,25,28] which, given a box B and an $\mathcal{NTA}$-term representing a function H, is able to compute an interval $\mathcal{IA}_H(B)$ that over-approximates the range $\{H(x) \mid x \in B\}$ of H over B. Since this is based on floating point arithmetic, the time needed for computing $\mathcal{IA}_H(B)$ does not grow with the size of the involved numbers. Moreover conservative rounding guarantees correctness under the presence of round-off errors. In the paper, we will use interval arithmetic within topological degree computation [12], and as a tool to prove the validity of inequalities on boxes.

Robustness. We say that a formula ϕ is robust if there exists some $\epsilon > 0$ such that ϕ is satisfiable iff every ϵ-perturbation of ϕ is satisfiable (for the precise definition of ϵ-perturbation see [13]). If ϕ is both robust and (un)satisfiable, we say that it is robustly (un)sat.

Relation Between Robustness and System of Equations: An over-constrained system of equations is never robustly sat [13, Lemma 5]. It easily follows that a system of equations that contains an over-constrained sub-system (in the sense of the Dulmage-Mendelsohn decomposition) is never robustly sat as well.

Relation Between Robustness and Topological Degree: Even in the case of an isolated zero, the test for non-zero topological degree can fail if the system is non-robust. For example, the function $F(x) \equiv x^2$ has topological degree 0 in the interval $[-1, 1]$, although the equality $x^2 = 0$ has an isolated zero in this interval. However, the zero of $x^2 = 0$ is not robust: it can vanish under arbitrarily small changes of the function denoted by the left-hand side x^2. It can be shown that the topological degree test is able to prove satisfiability in all robust cases for a natural formalization of the notion of robustness [13]. We will not provide such a formalization, here, but use robustness as an intuitive measure for the potential success when searching for a certificate.

Logic-To-Optimization. While symbolic methods usually struggle dealing with $\mathcal{NTA}$, numerical methods, albeit inexact, can handle transcendental functions efficiently. For this reason, an SMT solver can benefit from leveraging numerical techniques. In the Logic-To-Optimization approach [15,21], an SMT($\mathcal{NTA}$)-formula ϕ in m variables is translated into a real-valued non-negative function $\mathcal{L2O}(\phi) \equiv H : \mathbb{R}^m \mapsto \mathbb{R}^{\geq 0}$ such that—up to a simple translation between Boolean and real values for Boolean variables—each model of ϕ is a zero of H (but not vice-versa). When solving a satisfiability problem, one can try to first numerically minimize this function, and then use the obtained numerical (approximate) solution to prove, through exact symbolic methods, that the logical formula has indeed a model. For the precise definition of the operator $\mathcal{L}2\mathcal{O}$ see [21, Section 3].

3 Goal

Consider an SMT solver that takes as input some formula ϕ and as output an element of $\{\texttt{sat}, \texttt{unknown}, \texttt{unsat}\}$. How can we gain trust in the correctness of the result of such an SMT solver? One approach would be to ensure that the algorithm itself is correct. Another option is to provide a second algorithm whose output we compare with the original one. Both approaches are, however, very costly, and moreover, the latter approach still may be quite unreliable.

Instead, roughly following McConnell et. al. [23] (see also Fig. 1), we require our solver to return—in addition to its result—some information that makes an independent check of this result easy:

Definition 1. *An SMT solver is* certifying *iff for an input formula ϕ, in addition to an element $r \in \{\texttt{sat}, \texttt{unknown}, \texttt{unsat}\}$, it returns an object w (a* certificate*) such that*

- *(ϕ, r, w) satisfies a property W where $W(\phi, r, w)$ implies that r is a correct result for ϕ, and*
- *there is an algorithm (a* certificate checker*) that*
  - *takes as input a triple (ϕ, r, w) and returns $\top$ iff $W(\phi, r, w)$, and that*
  - *is simpler than the SMT solver itself.*

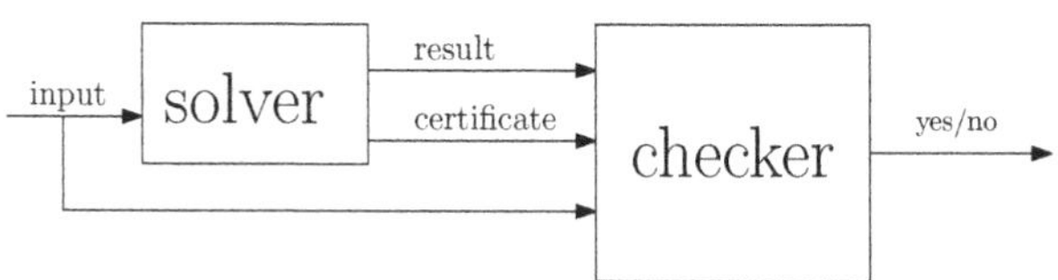

Fig. 1. Certifying SMT Solver

So, for a given formula ϕ, one can ensure correctness of the result (r, w) of a certifying SMT solver by using a certificate checker to check the property $W(\phi, r, w)$. Since the certificate checker is simpler than the SMT solver itself, the correctness check is simpler than the computation of the result itself.

The definition leaves it open, what precisely is meant by "simpler". In general, it could either refer to the run-time of the checker, or to the effort needed for implementing the certificate checker and ensuring its correctness. The former approach is taken in computational complexity theory, the latter in contexts where correctness is the main concern [23]. Indeed, we will later see that our approach succeeds in satisfying both requirements, although we will not use complexity-theoretic measures of run-time, but will measure run-time experimentally.

The use of such certificates is ongoing research in the unsatisfiable case [4]. In the satisfiable case, for most theories, one can simply use satisfying assignments (i.e., witnesses) as certificates. Here the property W simply is the property that the given assignment satisfies the formula, which can be checked easily.

For SMT($\mathcal{NTA}$), however, the situation is different: Here, no general finite representation of satisfying assignments is available. Hence one needs to use certificates of a different form. We introduce the following definition:

Definition 2. *Let ϕ be a formula in $\mathcal{NTA}$. A* (satisfiability) certificate *for ϕ is a triple (σ, ν, β) such that $W(\phi, \mathtt{sat}, (\sigma, \nu, \beta))$ iff*

- *σ is a function selecting a literal from every clause of ϕ*
- *ν is a variable assignment in $\mathcal{R}^V$ assigning floating point numbers to a subset $V \subseteq vars_{\mathcal{R}}(\sigma(\phi))$ (where $\sigma(\phi)$ is a compact way of writing $\bigwedge_{C \in \phi} \sigma(C)$), s.t. $\sigma(\phi)$ contains as many equations as real-valued variables not in V.*
- *β is a finite set of interval assignments in $\mathcal{B}^{vars_{\mathcal{R}}(\phi) \setminus V}$ such that their set-theoretic union as boxes is again a box B_β and, for the system of equations $F := eq(\nu(\sigma(\phi)))$ and the system of inequalities $G := ineq(\nu(\sigma(\phi)))$, it holds that:*
    - $0 \notin F(\partial B_\beta)$,
    - $deg(F, B_\beta, 0) \neq 0$, *and*
    - *for every* $B \in \beta$, $\mathcal{IA}_G(B) \leq 0$.

Example 2. Consider the formula

$$\phi := C_1 \wedge C_2 \wedge C_3 \wedge C_4$$

$$\begin{aligned} C_1 &\equiv cos(y) = 0 \ \vee \ sin(y) = e^x & \quad C_3 &\equiv x - y \leq cos(z) \\ C_2 &\equiv sin(y) = 0 \ \vee \ cos(y) = sin(8x^2 - z) & \quad C_4 &\equiv x + y \geq sin(z) \end{aligned}$$

The following (σ, ν, β) is a certificate:

- $\sigma := \{C_1 \mapsto sin(y) = e^x \ ; \ C_2 \mapsto cos(y) = sin(8x^2 - z) \ ;$
  $C_3 \mapsto C_3 \ ; \ C_4 \mapsto C_4\}$
- $\nu := \{z \mapsto 0.2\}$
- $\beta := \{B\}$, where $B := \{x \mapsto [-0.1, 0.05] \ ; \ y \mapsto [1.4, 1.9]\}$

As can be seen in Fig. 2, the solution sets of C_1 and C_2 cross at a unique point in B, which reflects the fact that the degree of the function $(x, y) \to (sin(y) - e^x, cos(y) - sin(8x^2 - 0.2))$ is non-zero. Moreover, the inequalities C_3 and C_4 hold on all elements of the box.

Due to the properties of the topological degree and of interval arithmetic discussed in the preliminaries, we have:

Property 1. $W(\phi, \mathtt{sat}, (\sigma, \nu, \beta))$ implies that ϕ is satisfiable.

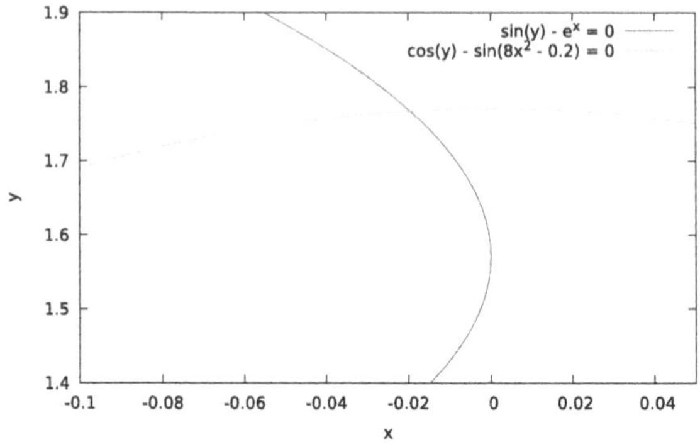

Fig. 2. Solution Sets of Equalities of Example Certificate

Moreover, the topological degree can be computed algorithmically [1,12], and one can easily write a certificate checker based on such an algorithm. Hence such a triple can be used as a certificate for satisfiability.

In this paper, we will show that in addition to the discussed benefits for correctness, formulating satisfiability checking as the problem of search for such certificates also is beneficial for efficiency of the SMT solver itself. Since we will concentrate on satisfiability, we will simply ignore the case when an SMT solver returns `unsat`, so the reader can simply assume that an SMT solver such as the one from Fig. 1 only returns an element from the set $\{\mathtt{sat}, \mathtt{unknown}\}$.

4 Method

Our goal is to find a triple (σ, ν, β) that is a certificate of satisfiability for a given formula ϕ. So we have a search problem. In order to make this search as efficient as possible, we want to guide the search toward a triple that indeed turns out to be a certificate, and for which the corresponding conditions are computationally easy to check.

Intuitively, we view the search for a certificate as a hierarchy of nested search problems, where the levels of this hierarchy correspond to the individual components of certificates. We formalize this using a search tree whose nodes on the i-th level are labeled with i-tuples containing the first i elements of the tuple searched for, starting with the root note that is labeled with the empty tuple (). The tree will be spanned by a function ch that assigns to each node $(c_1, \ldots, c_i)$ of the tree a sequence $\langle x_1, \ldots, x_n \rangle$ of possible choices for the next tuple component. Hence the children of $(c_1, \ldots, c_i)$ in the tree are $(c_1, \ldots, c_i, x_1), \ldots, (c_1, \ldots, c_i, x_n)$. We will do depth-first search in the resulting tree, searching for a leaf labeled by a certificate of satisfiability for the input formula ϕ.

Based on the observation that on each level of the tree one has the first i components of the tuple available for determining a good sequence of choices, we will add additional information as the first tuple component in the form of a variable assignment p that satisfies the formula ϕ approximately. Hence we search for a 4-tuple (p, σ, ν, β).

It is easy to see that it would be possible to generalize such a search tree to a more fine-grained one, where the individual levels are formed by parts of the choices described above, and where the order of those levels can be arbitrary. For example, it would be possible to first choose an interval for a variable (i.e., part of the box β), then select a literal from a certain clause (i.e., part of the selection function σ), and so on. However, in this paper, we keep these levels separated, as discussed above, in order to achieve a clear separation of concerns when exploring design choices at the individual levels.

5 Certificate Search

In this section, we will discuss possibilities for search strategies by defining for every search tree node labeled with tuple τ, the ordered sequence $ch(\tau)$ of choices for the next tuple element. Our framework allows for many more possibilities from which we choose strategies that both demonstrate the flexibility of the framework, and allow for efficient search, as will be demonstrated by the computational experiments in Sect. 6.

In order to be able to refer to different variants of the search strategy in the description of computational experiments, we will introduce keywords for those variants that we will write in teletype font.

5.1 Points

The points $ch() = \langle p_1, \ldots, p_k \rangle$ determining the first level of the search tree are generated by an optimization problem defined on the formula ϕ following the Logic-To-Optimization approach [21]. Here we translate the satisfiability problem into a numerical minimization problem, mapping the logic formula ϕ into the non-negative real-valued function $\mathcal{L}2\mathcal{O}(\phi) \equiv H : \mathbb{R}^n \to \mathbb{R}_{\geq 0}$ (called the *objective function*) such that for every satisfying assignment, this objective function is zero, and for assignments that do not satisfy the formula, the objective function is typically (but not always) non-zero. Then we find local minima of H through an unconstrained optimization algorithm such as basin hopping [30]. In our implementation, we compute $k = 100$ local minima, and process them in the order of their value.

5.2 Literals

Given a point p, we choose literal selector functions $ch(p) = \langle \sigma_1, \ldots, \sigma_k \rangle$ by restricting ourselves, for each clause C, to the literals l for which the objective function restricted to l and evaluated in the point p is below a certain threshold. That is, we determine the set of approximately satisfiable literals

$$L_C := \{l \in C \mid \mathcal{L}2\mathcal{O}(l)(p) \leq \epsilon\}.$$

Our literal selector functions will then correspond to the set of all approximately satisfiable combinations,

$$\{\sigma \mid \text{for all } C \in \phi, \sigma(C) \in L_C\},$$

that is, each σ selects exactly one approximately satisfiable literal from each clause. In order to maximize the chances of choosing a better literal combination, we can sort each L_C according to the value of the respective objective functions and then choose literal combinations using the corresponding lexicographic order (we will refer to this heuristic as (`sort-literals`)).

While the point p is usually a good candidate in terms of *distance from a zero*, it can sometimes lead to an inconsistent problem:

Example 3. Let $\phi := C_1 \wedge C_2$, where $C_1 \equiv (x + y = 0) \vee (x = e^{10^6 * y})$, and $C_2 \equiv (x+y \geq \epsilon_1) \vee (x = tan(y+\epsilon_1))$. The numerical optimizer will be tempted to first return a point p_1 such as $\{x \mapsto 1; y \mapsto -1\}$ that *almost* satisfies $(x+y = 0) \wedge (x + y \geq \epsilon_1)$, instead of a harder approximate solution involving transcendental functions and heavy approximations, such as $(x = e^{10^6 * y}) \wedge (x = tan(y + \epsilon_1))$, that is exactly satisfiable in a point p_2 near $(0, -\pi)$.

Such inconsistencies may occur in many combinations of literals. We use a strategy that detects them in situations where for certain clauses C, the set L_C contains only one literal l. We will call such a literal l a *forced literal*, since, for every literal selector function σ, $\sigma(\phi)$ will include l. Before starting to tackle every approximately satisfiable literal combination, we first analyze the set of forced literals. We do symbolic simplifications (such as rewriting and Gaussian elimination) to check whether the set has inconsistencies that can be found at a symbolic level (as in the previous example). If the symbolic simplifications detect that the forced literals are inconsistent then we set $ch(p)$ to the empty sequence $\langle\rangle$ which causes backtracking in depth-first search. We refer to the variant of the algorithm using this check as (`check-forced-literals`).

Filtering Out Over-Constrained Systems. Given a literal selector function σ, we analyze the structure of the system of equations formed by the equations selected by σ through the Dulmage-Mendelsohn decomposition, that uniquely decomposes the system into a well-constrained subsystem, an over-constrained subsystem and an under-constrained subsystem. We filter out every literal combination having a non-empty over-constrained subsystem, since this leads to a non-robust sub-problem, referring to this heuristic as (`filter-overconstr`).

5.3 Instantiations

We define the instantiations $ch(p, \sigma) = \langle \nu_1, \ldots, \nu_k \rangle$ based on a sequence of sets of variables $V_1, \ldots, V_k$ to instantiate, and define $\nu_i := proj_{V_i}(p)$. The uninstantiated part of p after projection to a set of variables V_i is then $proj_{vars_{\mathcal{R}}(\phi) \setminus V_i}(p)$, which we will denote by $p_{\neg V_i}$.

For searching for the variables to instantiate, we use the Dulmage-Mendelsohn decomposition constructed in the previous level of the hierarchy.

We do not want to instantiate variables appearing in the well-constrained subsystem, since doing so would make the resulting system after the instantiation over-constrained. Hence the variables to be instantiated should be chosen only from the variables occurring in the under-constrained subsystem. This substantially reduces the number of variable combinations that we can try. Denoting the variables satisfying this criterion by V_{under}, this restricts $V_i \subseteq V_{under}$, for all $i \in \{1, \ldots, k\}$. This does not yet guarantee that every chosen variable combination leads to a well-constrained system after the instantiation. For example, the under-determined system of equations $x + y = 0 \wedge z + w = 0$ has four variables and two equations, but becomes over-constrained after instantiating either the two variables x and y, or the variables z and w. So, for each V_i, we further check whether the system obtained after the instantiation is well-constrained (we refer to this heuristic as (`filter-overconstr-V`)).

The method described in the previous paragraph only uses information about which equations in the system contain which variables (i.e., it deals only with the *structure* of the system, not with its *content*). Indeed, it ignores the point p.

To extract more information, we use the fact that a non-singular Jacobian matrix of a function at one of its zeros implies a non-zero topological degree wrt. every box containing this single zero [11]. So we compute a floating point approximation of the Jacobian matrix at point p (note that, in general, this matrix is non-square). Our goal is to find a set of variables V to instantiate such that the Jacobian matrix corresponding to the resulting square system at the point $p_{\neg V}$ has full rank. This matrix is the square sub-matrix of the original Jacobian matrix that is the result of removing the instantiated columns.

A straight-forward way of applying the Jacobian criterion is, given random variable instantiations, to filter out instantiations whose corresponding Jacobian matrix is rank-deficient (`filter-rank-deficient`), similarly to what is done in the previous paragraph with the overconstrained filter. Note that, as the Jacobian matrix of non-well-constrained system of equations is always rank-deficient, this filter is stronger than the previous one. However, it may filter out variable instantations that result in a non-zero degree (e.g., the function x^3 has non-zero degree in $[-1, 1]$, but its Jacobian matrix at the origin is rank deficient since $f'(0) = 0$).

We can further use the information given by the Jacobian matrix not only to filter out bad variable instantiations, but also to maximize the chance of choosing good variable instantiations from the beginning. Indeed, not all variable instantiations will be equally promising, and it makes sense to head for an instantiation such that the resulting square matrix not only has full rank, but—in addition—is far from being rank-deficient (i.e., it is as robust as possible). We can do so by modifying Kearfott's method [19, Method 2] which fixes the coordinates most tangential to the orthogonal hyper-plane of F in p by first computing an approximate basis of the null space of the Jacobian matrix in the point, and then choosing the variables with maximal sum of absolute size. We use a modification of the method that uses a variable ordering w.r.t. this sum, and then extracts the sets of variables $V_1, V_2, \ldots$ in decreasing order w.r.t. the cumulative sum of the value of the variables in each set. We refer to this heuristic as `(Kearfott-ordering)`.

5.4 Box

We construct boxes around $p_{\neg V}$, where V is the set of variables ν instantiates, that is, $\nu \in \mathcal{R}^V$. So we define $ch(p, \sigma, \nu) := \langle \beta_1, \ldots, \beta_k \rangle$ s.t. for all $i \in \{1, \ldots, k\}$, for all $B \in \beta_i$, $B \in \mathcal{B}^{vars_{\mathcal{R}}(\phi)-V}$ and $p_{\neg V} \in \bigcup_{B \in \beta_i} B$.

We use two different methods, `(eps-inflation)` and `(box-gridding)`:

- Epsilon-inflation [22] is a method to construct incrementally larger boxes around a point. In this case, the $\beta_1, \ldots, \beta_k$ will each just contain one single box B_i defined as the box centered at $p_{\neg V}$ having side length $2^i\epsilon$, where, in our setting, $\epsilon = 10^{-20}$. We terminate the iteration if either $\mathcal{IA}_G(B_i) \leq 0$ and $deg(F, B_i, 0) \neq 0$, in which case we found a certificate, or we reach an iteration limit (in our setting when $2^i\epsilon > 1$).
- Box-gridding is a well-known technique from the field of interval arithmetic based on iteratively refining a starting box into smaller sub-boxes. Here we use a specific version, first proposed in [13] and then implemented with some changes in [21]. In the following we roughly outline the idea behind the algorithm, and refer to the other two papers for details. We start with a grid that initially contains a starting box. We then iteratively refine the grid by splitting the starting box into smaller sub-boxes. At each step, for each sub-box B we first check whether interval arithmetic can prove that the inequalities or the equations are unsatisfiable, and, if so, we remove B from the grid. We check also whether $deg(F, B, 0) \neq 0$ and interval arithmetic can prove the satisfiability of the inequalities, and, if so, then we terminate our search, finding a certificate with the singleton $\beta_i = \{B\}$. In some cases, in order to verify the satisfiability of the inequalities, we will have to further split the box B into sub-boxes, using the set of resulting sub-boxes instead of the singleton $\{B\}$. After each step, if there are sub-boxes left in the grid, we continue the refinement process. Otherwise, if the grid is empty, we conclude that there cannot be solutions in the starting box. If a certain limit to the grid size is exceeded, we also stop the box gridding procedure without success.

For both methods, if the method stops without success, we have arrived at the last element of the sequence of choices $\langle \beta_1, \ldots, \beta_k \rangle$ without finding a certificate, which results in backtracking of the depth-first search for a certificate.

Both mentioned methods have their advantages, and can be seen as complementary. Epsilon-inflation is quite fast, and performs particularly well if the solution is isolated and is near the center. However, if there are multiple solutions in a box, the topological degree test can potentially fail to detect them[1], and if the solution is far from the center then we need a bigger box to encompass it,

[1] For example, for $f(x) = x^2 - 1$, $deg(f, [-10, 10], 0) = 0$, while $deg(f, [-10, 0], 0) = -1$, and $deg(f, [0, 10], 0) = 1$.

which is less likely to be successful than a smaller box, as we require the inequalities to hold everywhere in the box, and, moreover, the chance of encompassing other solutions (thus incurring in the previous problem) grows.

The box-gridding procedure, on the other side, can be quite slow, as in the worst case the number of sub-boxes explodes exponentially. However, grid refinement leads to a very accurate box search, which allows us to avoid the issues faced with epsilon inflation (i.e. multiple solutions, or a solution far from the center). Moreover, if the problem is robust, we have the theoretical guarantee that the procedure will eventually converge to a solution [13], although this does not hold in practice due to the introduced stopping criterion.

Indeed, a third approach is to combine the two methods: first use epsilon inflation, that is often able to quickly find a successful box, and, if it fails, then use the more accurate box-gridding procedure.

6 Computational Experiments

Implementation. We implemented the different heuristics presented in the paper in a prototype tool called UGOTNL (firstly presented in [21]). In order to make the results comparable with the ones obtained earlier, in addition to the search method discussed in Sect. 5, we preserve the following heuristics used by UGOTNL: If the local minimizer cannot find any minimum of $\mathcal{L}2\mathcal{O}(\phi)$ for which for every clause $C \in \phi$, the set of approximately satisfiable literals L_C is non-empty, we restart the procedure on every conjunction resulting from the DNF of ϕ. The tool handles strict inequalities of the form $f < 0$ directly until the box construction phase, where they are replaced by $f \leq -\varepsilon$ (with $\varepsilon = 10^{-20}$). For computing the topological degree, we use TopDeg[2]. For the symbolic simplifications used in `(check-forced-literals)`, we use the *simplify* and the *solve-eqs* tactics provided by z3 [9][3]. For the computation of the rank used in `(filter-rank-deficient)`, we observe that the rank of a matrix is equal to the number of non-zero singular values, hence we consider a matrix far from rank-deficiency iff all its singular values are bigger than some threshold (to account for approximation errors). We use a threshold widely used by algorithms for determining the matrix rank, which is $\sigma_{\max} dim(A) \varepsilon$, where $\sigma_{\max}$ is the largest singular value of A, and ε is the machine epsilon.

Setup. We run the experiments[4] on a cluster of identical machines equipped with 2.6 GHz AMD Opteron 6238 processors. We set a time limit of 1000 s, and a memory limit of 2 Gb. We considered all SMT($\mathcal{NTA}$) benchmarks from the dReal distribution [16] and other SMT($\mathcal{NTA}$) benchmarks coming from the discretization of Bounded Model Checking of hybrid automata [3,27], totaling 1931

[2] Available at https://www.cs.cas.cz/~ratschan/topdeg/topdeg.html.

[3] For a description of the two tactics: https://microsoft.github.io/z3guide/docs/strategies/summary. The version of z3 used is 4.5.1.0.

[4] The results of the experiments are available at https://doi.org/10.5281/zenodo.7774117.

	Heuristics			(id.)
N. solved	Literals	Instantiations	Boxes	
323			(box-gridding)	(1.a.)
355			(eps-inflation)	(1.b.)
356			(eps-inflation) (box-gridding)	(1.c.)
362	(sort-literals)		(eps-inflation)	(2.b.)
361	(sort-literals)		(eps-inflation) (box-gridding)	(2.c.)
370	(sort-literals) (filter-overconstr)		(eps-inflation)	(3.b.)
367	(sort-literals) (filter-overconstr)		(eps-inflation) (box-gridding)	(3.c.)
406	(sort-literals) (filter-overconstr) (check-forced-literals)		(eps-inflation)	(4.b.)
410	(sort-literals) (filter-overconstr) (check-forced-literals)		(eps-inflation) (box-gridding)	(4.c.)
409	(sort-literals) (filter-overconstr) (check-forced-literals)	(Kearfott-ordering)	(eps-inflation)	(5.b.)
412	(sort-literals) (filter-overconstr) (check-forced-literals)	(Kearfott-ordering)	(eps-inflation) (box-gridding)	(5.c.)
424	(sort-literals) (filter-overconstr) (check-forced-literals)	(Kearfott-ordering) (filter-overconstr-V)	(eps-inflation)	(6.b.)
426	(sort-literals) (filter-overconstr) (check-forced-literals)	(Kearfott-ordering) (filter-overconstr-V)	(eps-inflation) (box-gridding)	(6.c.)
427	(sort-literals) (filter-overconstr) (check-forced-literals)	(Kearfott-ordering) (filter-overconstr-V) (filter-rank-deficient)	(eps-inflation)	(7.b.)
426	(sort-literals) (filter-overconstr) (check-forced-literals)	(Kearfott-ordering) (filter-overconstr-V) (filter-rank-deficient)	(eps-inflation) (box-gridding)	(7.c.)
441	Virtual best			

Fig. 3. Summary of the results for different heuristics configurations. Each row correspond to a configuration. The first column from the left contains the number of benchmarks solved; the central columns indicate the heuristics used, separated by search level; the last column contains an identifier of the configuration. The last row is for the virtual best of the different configurations.

benchmarks. All of these benchmarks come with "unknown" status. According to experiments performed on other solvers (cvc5, MathSAT, dReal), among these benchmarks 736 (respectively, 136) are claimed to be unsatisfiable (satisfiable) by at least one solver[5]. We tested our tool with different heuristics configurations (Fig. 3), and, for each configuration, we checked that our tool never contradict the other tools. We have arranged the heuristics into 3 columns (Literals, Instantiations, and Boxes) according to the search level they are used in. As the number of possible configurations is quite high, we proceed as follows: We start with the simpler configurations (just one method for finding a box that contains a solution), and then we add heuristics.

Results. In the first configurations we tested the 3 possible ways to search for a box. We note that `(box-gridding)` (1.a.) performs considerably worse than the other two, `(eps-inflation)` (1.b.) and `(eps-inflation)` +`(box-gridding)` (1.c.), which produce comparable results. Because of that, and for readability's sake, we did not use `(box-gridding)` alone with other heuristics in the next configurations, but only considered the other two options. We then added heuristics based on the following criteria: first heuristics for the "Literals" choice, then heuristics for the "Instantiations" choice, and first ordering heuristics (i.e. `(sort-literals)` and `(Kearfott-ordering)`), then filtering heuristics (all the others). At every new heuristic added, we see that the number of benchmarks solved grows regardless of the "Boxes" choice, with the best configuration reaching 427 benchmarks using 7 heuristics. If we consider the virtual best (i.e. run in parallel all the configurations and stop as soon as a certificate is found) we are able to solve 441 benchmarks. This is because in cases such as `(eps-inflation)` vs. `(eps-inflation)` +`(box-gridding)`, or such as `(filter-overconstr-V)` vs. `(filter-rank-deficient)`, there is no dominant choice, with each configuration solving benchmarks that the other does not solve and vice-versa.

Discussion. The first configuration (1.a.) essentially uses a method proposed earlier [21] and implemented in a tool called UGOTNL$_{\text{EAGER}}$ (of which the tool presented in this paper is an upgrade). Already in the previous paper, UGOTNL$_{\text{EAGER}}$ outperformed the other solvers able to prove satisfiability in SMT($\mathcal{NTA}$), solving more than three times the benchmarks than MATHSAT [8], CVC5 [20], and ISAT3 [14], and almost as twice as the benchmarks solved by the *lazy* version MATHSAT+UGOTNL (where UGOTNL had been integrated *lazily* inside MATHSAT). Here we show that the new heuristics introduced further improve the performances of our tool, that is now able to solve around 100 benchmarks more.

Run-Time of the Certificate Checker. In Sect. 3 we claimed that, with our approach, checking a certificate requires less run-time than the certificate search itself. Here we experimentally quantify this amount: for each benchmark solved by the best configuration (7.b.), we observe the run-time required to check the certificate (which amounts, essentially, to the computation of topological degree and interval arithmetic for the successful box). In terms of median (respectively, mean), checking the certificate requires 0.10% (1.07%) of the run-time used by the solver.

---

[5] For the results of such experiments, see [21].

7 Related Work

One strategy for proving satisfiability in SMT($\mathcal{NTA}$) is to prove a stricter requirement that implies satisfiability, but is easier to check. For example, one can prove that *all* elements of a set of variable assignments satisfy the given formula [14], or that a given variable assignment satisfies the formula for *all possible interpretations* of the involved transcendental functions within some bounds [7]. Such methods may be quite efficient in proving satisfiability of formulas with inequalities only, since those often have full-dimensional solution sets. However, such methods usually fail to prove satisfiability of equalities, except for special cases with straightforward rational solutions.

Computation of formally verified solutions of square systems of equations is a classical topic in the area of interval analysis [24,25,28]. Such methods usually reduce the problem either to fixpoint theorems such as Brouwer's fixpoint theorem or special cases of the topological degree, for example, Miranda's theorem. Such tests are easier to implement, but less powerful than the topological degree (the former fails to verify equalities with double roots, such as $x^3 = 0$, and the latter requires the solution sets of the individual equalities to roughly lie normal to the axes of the coordinate system).

In the area of rigorous global optimization, such techniques are applied [18,19] to conjunctions of equalities and inequalities in a similar way as in this paper, but with a slightly different goal: to compute rigorous upper bounds on the global minimum of an optimization problem. This minimum is often attained at the boundary of the solution set of the given inequalities, whereas satisfiability is typically easier to prove far away from this boundary.

We are only aware of two approaches that extend verification techniques for square systems of equations to proving satisfiability of quantifier-free non-linear arithmetic [21,29], one [29] being restricted to the polynomial case, and the other one also being able to handle transcendental function symbols. Neither approach is formulated in the form of certificate search. However, both could be interpreted as such, and both could be extended to return a certificate. The present paper actually does this for the second approach [21], and demonstrates that this does not only ease the independent verification of results, but also allows the systematic design of search techniques that result in significant efficiency improvements.

An alternative approach is to relax the notation of satisfiability, for example using the notion of δ-satisfiability [6,16], that does *not* guarantee that the given formula is satisfiable, but only that the formula is not too far away from a satisfiable one, for a suitable formalization of the notion of "not too far away". Another strategy is to return candidate solutions in the form of bounds that guarantee that certain efforts to prove unsatisfiability within those bounds fail [14].

8 Conclusions

We introduced a form of satisfiability certificate for SMT($\mathcal{NTA}$) and formulated the satisfiability verification problem as the problem of searching for such a certificate. We showed how to perform this search in a systematic fashion introducing new and efficient search techniques. Computational experiments document that the resulting method is able to prove satisfiability of a substantially higher number of benchmark problems than existing methods.

Acknowledgments. The authors thank Alessandro Cimatti, Alberto Griggio, and Roberto Sebastiani for helpful discussions on the topic of the paper. The work of Stefan Ratschan was supported by the project GA21-09458S of the Czech Science Foundation GA ČR and institutional support RVO:67985807.

References

1. Aberth, O.: Computation of topological degree using interval arithmetic, and applications. Math. Comput. **62**(205), 171–178 (1994)
2. Ait-Aoudia, S., Jégou, R., Michelucci, D.: Reduction of constraint systems. CoRR, abs/1405.6131 (2014)
3. Bak, S., Bogomolov, S., Johnson, T.T.: HYST: a source transformation and translation tool for hybrid automaton models. In: Proceedings of the 18th International Conference on Hybrid Systems: Computation and Control, HSCC 2015, New York, NY, USA, pp. 128–133. Association for Computing Machinery (2015)
4. Barbosa, H., et al.: Flexible proof production in an industrial-strength SMT solver. In: Automated Reasoning: Proceedings of 11th International Joint Conference, IJCAR 2022, Haifa, Israel, 8–10 August 2022, pp. 15–35. Springer (2022)
5. Barrett, C., Sebastiani, R., Seshia, S.A., Tinelli, C.: Satisfiability modulo theories. In: Handbook of Satisfiability. Frontiers in Artificial Intelligence and Applications, vol. 336, pp. 1267–1329 (2021). https://doi.org/10.3233/FAIA201017
6. Brauße, F., Korovin, K., Korovina, M.V., Müller, N.T.: The `ksmt` calculus Is a δ-complete decision procedure for non-linear constraints. In: Platzer, A., Sutcliffe, G. (eds.) CADE 2021. LNCS (LNAI), vol. 12699, pp. 113–130. Springer, Cham (2021). https://doi.org/10.1007/978-3-030-79876-5_7
7. Cimatti, A., Griggio, A., Irfan, A., Roveri, M., Sebastiani, R.: Incremental linearization for satisfiability and verification modulo nonlinear arithmetic and transcendental functions. ACM Trans. Comput. Logic **19**(3) (2018)
8. Cimatti, A., Griggio, A., Schaafsma, B.J., Sebastiani, R.: The MathSAT5 SMT solver. In: Piterman, N., Smolka, S.A. (eds.) TACAS 2013. LNCS, vol. 7795, pp. 93–107. Springer, Heidelberg (2013). https://doi.org/10.1007/978-3-642-36742-7_7
9. de Moura, L., Bjørner, N.: Z3: an efficient SMT solver. In: Ramakrishnan, C.R., Rehof, J. (eds.) TACAS 2008. LNCS, vol. 4963, pp. 337–340. Springer, Heidelberg (2008). https://doi.org/10.1007/978-3-540-78800-3_24
10. Dulmage, A.L., Mendelsohn, N.S.: Coverings of bipartite graphs. Can. J. Math. **10**, 517–534 (1958)
11. Fonseca, I., Gangbo, W.: Degree Theory in Analysis and Applications. Clarendon Press, Oxford (1995)
12. Franek, P., Ratschan, S.: Effective topological degree computation based on interval arithmetic. Math. Comput. **84**, 1265–1290 (2015)
13. Franek, P., Ratschan, S., Zgliczynski, P.: Quasi-decidability of a fragment of the first-order theory of real numbers. J. Autom. Reason. **57**(2), 157–185 (2016)
14. Fränzle, M., Herde, C., Teige, T., Ratschan, S., Schubert, T.: Efficient solving of large non-linear arithmetic constraint systems with complex Boolean structure. JSAT **1**, 209–236 (2007)

15. Fu, Z., Su, Z.: XSat: a fast floating-point satisfiability solver. In: Chaudhuri, S., Farzan, A. (eds.) CAV 2016. LNCS, vol. 9780, pp. 187–209. Springer, Cham (2016). https://doi.org/10.1007/978-3-319-41540-6_11
16. Gao, S., Kong, S., Clarke, E.M.: dReal: an SMT solver for nonlinear theories over the reals. In: Bonacina, M.P. (ed.) CADE 2013. LNCS (LNAI), vol. 7898, pp. 208–214. Springer, Heidelberg (2013). https://doi.org/10.1007/978-3-642-38574-2_14
17. Hall, P.: On representatives of subsets. J. London Math. Soc. **s1-10**(1), 26–30 (1935)
18. Hansen, E.: Global Optimization Using Interval Analysis. Marcel Dekker, New York (1992)
19. Kearfott, R.B.: On proving existence of feasible points in equality constrained optimization problems. Math. Program. **83**(1), 89–100 (1998)
20. Kremer, G., Reynolds, A., Barrett, C., Tinelli, C.: Cooperating techniques for solving nonlinear real arithmetic in the cvc5 SMT solver (system description). In: Blanchette, J., Kovács, L., Pattinson, D. (eds.) IJCAR 2022. LNCS, vol. 13385, pp. 95–105. Springer, Cham (2022)
21. Lipparini, E., Cimatti, A., Griggio, A., Sebastiani, R.: Handling polynomial and transcendental functions in SMT via unconstrained optimisation and topological degree test. In: Bouajjani, A., Holík, L., Wu, Z. (eds.) ATVA 2022. LNCS, vol. 13505, pp. 137–153. Springer, Cham (2022). https://doi.org/10.1007/978-3-031-19992-9_9
22. Mayer, G.: Epsilon-inflation in verification algorithms. J. Comput. Appl. Math. **60**, 147–169 (1994)
23. McConnell, R.M., Mehlhorn, K., Näher, S., Schweitzer, P.: Certifying algorithms. Comput. Sci. Rev. **5**(2), 119–161 (2011)
24. Moore, R.E., Kearfott, R.B., Cloud, M.J.: Introduction to Interval Analysis. SIAM (2009)
25. Neumaier, A.: Interval Methods for Systems of Equations. Cambridge University Press, Cambridge (1990)
26. Richardson, D.: Some undecidable problems involving elementary functions of a real variable. J. Symb. Log. **33**(4), 514–520 (1968)
27. Roohi, N., Prabhakar, P., Viswanathan, M.: HARE: a hybrid abstraction refinement engine for verifying non-linear hybrid automata. In: Legay, A., Margaria, T. (eds.) TACAS 2017. LNCS, vol. 10205, pp. 573–588. Springer, Heidelberg (2017). https://doi.org/10.1007/978-3-662-54577-5_33
28. Rump, S.M.: Verification methods: rigorous results using floating-point arithmetic. Acta Numer. 287–449 (2010)
29. Tung, V.X., Van Khanh, T., Ogawa, M.: raSAT: an SMT solver for polynomial constraints. Formal Methods Syst. Design **51**(3), 462–499 (2017). https://doi.org/10.1007/s10703-017-0284-9
30. Wales, D.J., Doye, J.P.K.: Global optimization by basin-hopping and the lowest energy structures of Lennard-Jones clusters containing up to 110 atoms. J. Phys. Chem. A **101**(28), 5111–5116 (1997)

Author Index

K. Y. Rozier and S. Chaudhuri (Eds.): NFM 2023, LNCS 13903, pp. 489–490, 2023.
https://doi.org/10.1007/978-3-031-33170-1

Printed in the United States
by Baker & Taylor Publisher Services